A Guide to the
Wildflowers of
South Carolina

A Guide to the
Wildflowers of
South Carolina

Richard D. Porcher *and* Douglas A. Rayner

UNIVERSITY OF SOUTH CAROLINA PRESS

© 2001 University of South Carolina

Published in Columbia, South Carolina, by the
University of South Carolina Press

Manufactured in the Korea

17 16 15 14 13 12 11 10 09 08   10 9 8 7 6 5 4 3 2

Library of Congress Cataloging-in-Publication Data

Porcher, Richard D. (Richard Dwight)
   A guide to the wildflowers of South Carolina / Richard D. Porcher and
Douglas A. Rayner.
      p.   cm.
   Includes bibliographical references (p.   ).
   ISBN 1-57003-437-0 (cloth) —
   ISBN 1-57003-438-9 (paper : alk. paper)
   1. Wild flowers—South Carolina—Identification. 2. Wild flowers—
South Carolina—Pictorial works. I. Rayner, Douglas A. II. Title.
   QK185 .P82   2001
   582.13'09757—dc21   2001001298

ISBN-13: 978-1-57003-438-1 (pbk)

Dedication

THE AUTHORS DEDICATE THIS BOOK to Dr. Wade Thomas Batson, distinguished professor emeritus in the Biological Sciences Department at the University of South Carolina. Dr. "B," as generations of students have affectionately called him, was the major professor of both authors when we were graduate students at the university. Both authors entered graduate school intending on careers in zoology but changed to field botany after coming under his influence. Field botany became our life's work and passion.

Undergraduate and graduate students were drawn to Dr. B's charisma and his love of field botany. He opened a world unknown to many. Those who spent a semester enrolled in his spring, fall, or summer flora course will never forget the experience. Dr. Batson's enthusiasm for and knowledge of the flora of South Carolina was contagious. The woods and fields no longer were a mass of indistinguishable brown and green; they became a garden of wood-lilies or windflowers. Long after leaving school, students recalled the scientific names of plants they learned in his course and practiced the environmental ethics he taught. He worked hard to make his courses stimulating and informative and was a friend to every student. Years after graduating, his former students still seek his advice on any number of subjects.

Whatever measure of success this book achieves, much of it is owed to Dr. Batson. We thank him for being our mentor and friend and for beginning our life's journey into the world of botany, and particularly our appreciation of wildflowers.

Contents

List of Figures

Preface

THE GENESIS OF THIS STATE WILDFLOWER BOOK was the publication of *Wildflowers of the Carolina Lowcountry and Lower Pee Dee* in 1995 by the first author. At one point the author and the University of South Carolina Press realized that a state wildflower book would be an obvious outgrowth of the *Carolina Lowcountry* book. Since a statewide book would be too demanding for one author, the decision was made to engage a second author, one with field experience and knowledge of the mountain and piedmont regions. The choice was obvious. The scientific editing of Dr. Douglas A. Rayner contributed greatly to the success of *Wildflowers of the Carolina Lowcountry and Lower Pee Dee*. When approached to assist with the state book, he accepted immediately. Thus the team was born. The first author was responsible for the photography and coverage of the coastal plain, Dr. Rayner was responsible for coverage of the mountains and piedmont, and the University of South Carolina Press, under the guidance of press director Catherine Fry, provided its marketing and publishing skills.

It has been a pleasure working on this book with the press and with Dr. Rayner. At times it was physically and emotionally demanding. Carrying photographic equipment up and down mountains and trekking miles through the Carolina sandhills in the summer certainly made me aware of my physical and emotional limitations. More than once, a trip had to be made to the upcountry to photograph a single plant. However, working on the book was often a pure pleasure. Having the opportunity to botanize with Dr. Rayner throughout the mountains and piedmont made me aware of the rich, natural beauty of an area of South Carolina with which I had had only a cursory knowledge beforehand.

We are proud of this final product. May it bring students of botany countless years of pleasure.

Richard Dwight Porcher

Acknowledgments

A BOOK OF THIS SCOPE is never the sole product of the authors. Rather, this book was built on the knowledge and data accumulated by many dedicated and talented botanists. Just as this book has made use of that knowledge, the authors hope that botanists will use the material added to field botany in *Wildflowers of South Carolina* when future botanical books on South Carolina are written.

We could have never completed this book without the support of our respective academic institutions. They arranged teaching schedules to allow us time for fieldwork and provided financial support. We gratefully acknowledge the assistance of our colleagues at The Citadel and Wofford College.

We gratefully acknowledge the valuable editorial assistance and suggestions of Angela W. Williams, director of The Citadel Writing Center, who spent many hours reviewing and editing the manuscript.

No book of this magnitude has a more important contribution than the critical review for technical, scientific accuracy. We are deeply grateful to Patrick D. McMillan and Dr. Victoria C. Hollowell for their review of the manuscript and helpful comments and appropriate questions throughout the project.

We also wish to thank Catherine Fry, Linda Fogle, Dr. Alex Moore, and the staff of the University of South Carolina Press for their work in bringing this volume to publication.

We are indebted to the following people and organizations for financial support: The Citadel Development Foundation; the Biology Department at The Citadel, and its chairman, Dr. Robert E. Baldwin; Wofford College; William Cain, Jr., M.D.; The Nature Conservancy of South Carolina; and the United States Fish and Wildlife Service.

Throughout the four years we worked on the book, numerous colleagues and friends provided suggestions on the manuscript, helped with field photography, and gave encouragement for the project. We are gratefully indebted to Jim Bates, Gwen Beavans, Paul B. Burris, Robin L. Roecker, and Perry D. Shatley of the United States Forest Service; Dale C. Soblo of The Nature Conservancy of South Carolina; Dr. Albert B. Pittman, Mary B. Strayer, Johnny Stowe, and James A. Sorrow of the South Carolina Department of Natural Resources; Richard P. Ingram of the Carolina Sandhills National Wildlife Refuge; Joseph S. Anderson and William R. Marrell of the South Carolina Department of Parks, Recreation and Tourism; Nora A. Murdock of the United States Fish and Wildlife Service; Dr. Jean B. Everett of the College of Charleston; Dr. Charles N. Horn of Newberry College; Dr. Terry A. Ferguson of Wofford College; Dr. John B. Nelson of the A. C. Moore Herbarium of the University of South Carolina; Dr. A. Joseph Pollard of Furman University; Albert E. Sanders of the Charleston Museum; John F. Townsend of Clemson University; Dr. L. L. Gaddy; and friends John A. Brubaker, Carolyn S. Burke, Thaddeus and Suzanne Ellett, Grayson and Bibs Hanahan, Roy Rooks, Grace and Allison Wilder, and Dr. Kathleen A. Kegley.

We gratefully acknowledge the use of two photographs: Abandoned Rice Fields along the Cooper River (figure 7) by Dr. B. Joseph Kelley, Jr., and Native American Shell Rings and Shell Mound (figure 9) by David S. Soliday.

Dr. Rayner especially thanks his wife, Ellen Tillett, and his children, Emma and Leland, for their patience and forbearance throughout the four years' work on this book.

As an acknowledgment of their passion for the profession, the authors donate all royalties to support future studies of field botany in South Carolina.

Introduction

PURPOSE AND SCOPE

People are so accustomed to the domesticated landscape of South Carolina that it is hard to imagine the primeval wilderness that once existed. Everywhere, the beauty of the state was obvious. From the mountains to the seashore, a wilderness stretched before the eyes of early settlers, shaped only by the forces of nature and Native Americans. Pine savannas, with their plethora of fire-adapted herbs, mountain coves with showy wildflowers, and maritime forests with majestic live oaks all gave evidence of a bountiful land. One only has to read the accounts of the early naturalists who lived in or passed through the state to understand the scope of our lost heritage. Agricultural conversion, urban spread, countless roads, and alien species have all contributed to today's mostly domesticated landscape. Still, unparalleled natural beauty is present still in the state. One just has to go farther afield than the early Carolinians to enjoy what they experienced every day. The authors hope *Wildflowers of South Carolina* captures glimpses from this earlier era so that readers can experience our predecessors' views of South Carolina, while at the same time appreciating present wildflower communities and the forces that have shaped and will continue to shape the distribution and diversity of South Carolina's natural communities and wildflowers.

Wildflowers of South Carolina includes color photographs of 711 wildflowers and natural communities and is intended primarily to help amateur botanists identify many native and naturalized wildflowers that grow in South Carolina, as well as in adjacent states. It provides basic information on botanical natural history that hopefully will stimulate interest, enjoyment, conservation, and management of wildflowers. At the same time, the reader will find technical information not readily available from other sources that will be useful to academicians and educators, as well as governmental and private organizations.

This book emphasizes a habitat approach to wildflower identification; therefore, one section takes the reader to sites that harbor the natural communities (habitats) where native wildflowers abound. Forty-eight sites in South Carolina, supporting a variety of natural communities, are included. The South Carolina Department of Natural Resources acquired many of these sites, establishing them as state heritage preserves to protect these natural communities and rare species. Once the reader identifies the natural community in which a particular wildflower grows and identifies the wildflower using the color photographs, a series of essays can take the reader to a higher level of understanding and appreciation of wildflowers and plants.

Wildflowers of South Carolina separates the weedy, nonnative species into a separate category, the ruderal communities. This provides the reader with a useful message: The balance between native and nonnative species has shifted greatly over the years. While some nonnative plants, such as chickweed from Europe, are quite common, some native plants, such as Oconee bells, are rare today. People contribute to this ruderal shift by intentionally or unwittingly introducing nonnative plants along roadsides and into gardens, where they escape and become established (that is, naturalized). Grouping the nonnative species into the ruderal communities emphasizes this situation.

Wildflowers contains eleven essays on the natural history of vascular plants. For example, the essay on carnivorous plants provides a convenient reference on the ecology of these "animal-eating" plants, which have long fascinated botany students. The essay on the reproductive strategies of vascular plants helps the reader to understand the unusual methods that ensure a plant's continued reproduction as well as the dispersal and establishment of its propagules. The essay on medicinal plants and folk remedies illustrates the myriad ways that plants benefit humans.

Further, this book incorporates a series of essays on ecology that explain how fire in native communities and agricultural practices have shaped today's landscape. The present abundance and distribution of wildflowers are inextricably tied with these and other edaphic factors. Modern conservation of South Carolina's wildflower heritage should be based on such knowledge.

Perhaps the most diverse and useful part of the book is the comments entry that follows each species description. The comments include interesting facts about each species, many of which are not widely known or readily available to readers. Some of the information includes: (1) whether a plant is a source for drugs; (2) whether a native plant would make a good cultivated plant; (3) whether a plant is poisonous; (4) the ecological parameters that are necessary for the survival of a plant; and (5) the origin of a species' common or scientific name.

Wildflowers of South Carolina will also be useful to persons living in other southeastern states, especially the adjacent states of Georgia and North Carolina, since many of the wildflowers found in South Carolina are found in these areas. Although several recent books cover the wildflowers of these states as well as the southeast (see "General References"), this book contains photographs of many plants not included in other books and thus serves as a valuable supplement.

Another goal of this book is to provide a text that can be used in academic courses; therefore, as much information as possible is included on the general botany of South Carolina. *Wildflowers of South Carolina* is also intended to complement *Wildflowers of the Carolina Lowcountry and Lower Pee Dee* (hereinafter abbreviated as *WCL*). The two books contain over 800 photographs of different wildflowers found in South Carolina.

The authors hope that stimulating interest in wildflowers will result in more eyes searching the state for rare plants and unique habitats, which can then be recorded with the South Carolina Department of Natural Resources' Heritage Trust Program. Somewhere along a river bluff is an undiscovered limestone outcrop with Wagner's spleenwort, or a mountain cove harboring an undiscovered population of Oconee bells, or a Native American shell mound with a unique assemblage of calcicoles (plants that thrive in calcium-rich soils). As botanists who have conducted fieldwork for thirty years, the authors still find unrecorded, unique natural areas and rare species. But the scientific community needs the public's help. Organizations such as The Nature Conservancy of South Carolina help preserve natural areas, but first they must know of their existence. Readers who find sites worth recording are encouraged to contact the South Carolina Heritage Trust Program.

Finally, wildflowers are part of nature's grand picture. Wildflowers in natural communities are part of a complex system where energy flow, nutrient recycling, and life histories of all organisms—from soil microbes to higher plants and animals—interact in a "web of life." To fully appreciate the role of wildflowers in the grand picture of nature, you must become a student of ecology. May this book start your journey!

PHYSIOGRAPHIC REGIONS OF SOUTH CAROLINA

For ease of organization, but mostly for ecological reasons, this book divides South Carolina into the three physiographic provinces that are accepted by most geographers and botanists: the Blue Ridge Province, the Piedmont Province, and the Coastal Plain Province (figure 1). The Coastal Plain Province is further divided into four regions: (1) fall-line sandhills; (2) inner coastal plain; (3) outer coastal plain; and (4) maritime strand.

Some of the state's natural communities occur in all three provinces, while others occur only in one physiographic province or in just one region.

FIGURE 1. Physiographic Regions of South Carolina.

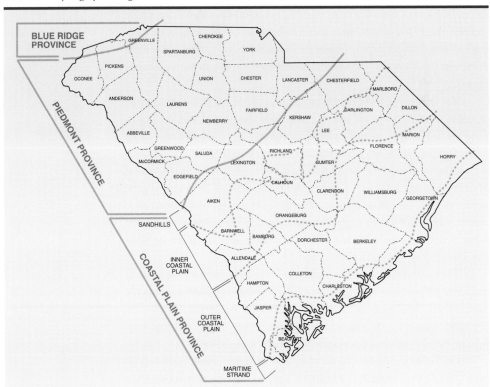

Although no natural communities occur only in the fall-line sandhills, some are best developed there. Most of the natural communities in the maritime strand (that portion of the coastal plain subject to the influence of wind-borne salt spray and/or water with significant salt concentration) are found only in that region.

The Blue Ridge Province, a belt of mountains at the front wall of the Appalachian Mountains, is the westernmost physiographic province in South Carolina. This is an area of generally high relief, although the mountains of the Blue Ridge are often described as "subdued" because they are old and relatively weathered. Once taller than the much younger Rocky Mountains, their elevation varies from 1000 feet to over 3100 feet. Rocks are mostly granites and gneisses. The boundary between the Blue Ridge Province and the Piedmont Province to the east is the Blue Ridge Escarpment, a narrow belt of especially abrupt and steep relief. In a horizontal distance of about 5 to 8 miles, the mountains can rise over 2000 feet vertically from the piedmont below. This escarpment is especially noticeable in Oconee and Pickens Counties. The Blue Ridge Province also includes a small part of upper Greenville County.

The Piedmont Province is a broad region of rolling hills that extends from the Blue Ridge Escarpment to the unconsolidated sediments of the coastal plain. The term "piedmont" literally means "foot of the mountain," with the term "foothills" sometimes used as a synonym. The rolling hills of the piedmont are dissected by numerous small streams; valleys are generally wider than in the mountains, in large part because piedmont rocks are generally less resistant to erosion than those of the Blue Ridge. Elevation begins at 300 to 400 feet in the east and extends to 1000 to 1200 feet in the west. Rocks are mostly gneisses, slates, and schists, with some quartzite and amphibolite. The piedmont is also characterized by occasional monadnocks (e.g., Glassy Mountain in Pickens County, figure 10), isolated hills of resistant rock that arise abruptly above the land.

The boundary between the piedmont and the coastal plain is often described as the "fall line" because of a noticeable change in elevation—that is, a vertical "fall" that is most frequently recognized as rapids or shoals along rivers. Fall-line rapids are most prevalent at the Georgia-South Carolina border, on the Savannah River at Augusta, and at the junction of the Broad and Saluda Rivers, which form the Congaree River at Columbia. Distinguishing the piedmont from the coastal plain is sometimes difficult, especially since some coastal plain sandhills are higher in elevation than the adjacent piedmont. When in doubt, examine the soil; if the soil is clayey, it is the piedmont; if the soil is sandy, it is the coastal plain.

The Coastal Plain Province is composed mostly of unconsolidated sands and clays, with some sedimentary rocks. The unconsolidated sediments of the coastal plain were washed off the piedmont and mountains. They were deposited in the sea or on land not far from the seashore. These sediments have been repeatedly shifted and sorted by the wandering tidal seas.

Geologists divide the coastal plain into an inner coastal plain and an outer coastal plain, using the Orangeburg Scarp as the boundary between the two. The Orangeburg Scarp is a reasonably well-defined terrace produced by an ancient seashore. Lands inland from this scarp are hillier, and lands seaward are relatively flat. Much of the inner coastal plain consists of sandhills that border the fall line. These fall-line sandhills form a discontinuous belt, 5 to 20 miles wide, across the middle of the state. Sandhills border most of the fall line, although there is a narrow band from Leesville in Lexington County west to the Savannah River where the sandhills are below the fall line. The fall-line sandhills consist of exposed Cretaceous-age sediments, mostly deep sands (some consolidated into sandstones), which support a distinctive flora. The only researchers that tried to map and define the fall-line sandhills were John Barry (1980) in *Natural Vegetation of South Carolina* and Charles Wharton (1978) in *The Natural Environments of Georgia*. The authors agree with these scientists that the deep sands of the fall-line sandhills have a significant influence on plant distribution and should be treated as a distinct region of the Coastal Plain Province.

There are other sandhills that are not associated with the fall line that lie in the coastal plain, including some that were produced by river-related events and others associated with Carolina bays. These sandhills produce similar xeric plant communities, but because of the lack of similar relief, they usually don't produce the extensive hillside pocosins, seepages, and Atlantic white-cedar communities that are present in the hilly, fall-line sandhills.

The outermost portion of the outer coastal plain is defined as the maritime strand. This area is comprised of vegetation that is significantly influenced by wind-borne salt spray and/or water with significant concentrations of salt. Although not usually distinguished by geographers or geologists, botanists and ecologists generally agree that this region is distinctive enough to warrant separation from the rest of the coastal plain.

NATURE OF THE FLORA

Although a small state compared to others in the southeast, South Carolina supports a rich and varied vascular plant flora, with some 3160 species of native and naturalized vascular plants. Georgia, a state almost twice the size of South Carolina, has 3600 species; and North Carolina, which is 50 percent larger, has 4100 taxa. Three reasons explain South Carolina's rich and diverse vascular flora: (1) South Carolina exhibits a wide range of physiographic provinces and regions; (2) South Carolina is the northern range limit for many Florida coastal plain species but the southern limit for many species of the distinctive North Carolina coastal plain flora, which harbors many endemics; and (3) South Carolina's southeast area is slightly influenced by the semitropical climate of Florida, yet its northeast section is influenced more by the mid-Atlantic coastal plain climate.

The 1968 publication of the *Manual of the Vascular Flora of the Carolinas* (Radford et al., 1968) was a landmark in our understanding of South Carolina's flora. For the first time, botanists had documented distribution maps of all the known species of vascular plants in the Carolinas. Since then, botanists (and knowledgeable laypersons) have added numerous records of state occurrence and other distribution records to the vascular flora recorded in the *Manual.*

With the formation of the South Carolina Heritage Trust Program, a central reservoir of records of significant collections was created, making it easier for botanists to determine collection gaps.

Today, Alan S. Weakley, with support from The Nature Conservancy, is updating distribution records of the flora of the Carolinas and Virginia. His *Flora of the Carolinas and Virginia* (latest working draft, 2001) incorporates much of the information from the *Manual of the Vascular Flora of Carolinas* and is augmented by an extensive review of the literature and collection records that were added to herbariums since 1968. His work gives botanists a valuable update of the state's flora. Many of the distribution records in this book are based on Weakley's updated *Flora*.

In 1999 *The Atlas of the Flora of South Carolina* was completed (Sorrow et al., 1999). The *Atlas* includes updated distribution records that were supplied by field botanists working throughout the state. It has greatly advanced our understanding of the state's vascular flora. The *Atlas* has recorded 3160 taxa of vascular plants, of which approximately 10% are naturalized. In addition, the *Atlas* contains a county-by-county listing of occurrences. Undoubtedly, future fieldwork will add to this floristic documentation, which will be updated in future editions of the *Atlas*.

No attempt is made to include a complete update on the vascular flora of the state. Updated records on sedges and grasses, for example, falls beyond the scope of this book. An effort is made, however, to include as many county, province, and state records of wildflowers that have been added to the flora since 1968, so the book may serve as a partial update for botanists studying the state flora. Species descriptions include notes that reference new species records.

WHAT ARE WILDFLOWERS?

What is meant by the term "wildflower"? Some authors use it to refer to any flowering plant growing without cultivation. Some restrict the term to native annual or perennial herbs with showy flowers, such as bloodroot and trillium. However, native trees, such as bull bay and tulip tree as well as shrubs such as sweet-shrub and pawpaw, have showy flowers and are more conspicuous than many of the herbaceous species. Many naturalized species such as Japanese honeysuckle are as showy as the native species and are included in most wildflower books. Native and naturalized species that have small flowers may be abundant and aggressive and are often designated as weeds. When viewed under magnification, their flowers are just as beautiful as the more showy species. Showy displays of the flowers of these species, like heliotrope along roadsides or common toadflax in fields, give color and character to the land. Some sedges, like blue sedge, and grasses, like seaside panicum, are as conspicuous as classic wildflowers. And what plants add more beauty to South Carolina than the native woody vines, such as cow-itch and coral honeysuckle? Some consider these plants as noxious weeds, but surely these are also colorful wildflowers.

Wildflowers in this book are defined in a broad sense to include the rich diversity of South Carolina's plant life. Showy native annual and perennial herbs are emphasized, but shrubs, vines, and trees with showy flowers, showy introduced species, and conspicuous grasses, rushes, and sedges are also considered as wildflowers. Eighteen species of pteridophytes (ferns and their allies) are included. These plants are a conspicuous and interesting aspect of the native flora. To exclude them would be derelict in representing the state's varied flora.

Many factors were considered in choosing the species to include in this book. The principal factor was the desire to interest the reader in and educate the reader about native wildflowers and the plant communities in which they grow. Showy herbaceous species that are the most obvious in communities are emphasized, and selected indicator species of each native community are included. For instance, turkey oak is featured because it is an indicator species of the xeric sandhills; pond cypress identifies the pond cypress savannas; and white oak is pictured because it is a dominant tree of the oak-hickory forests of the piedmont.

All native species of *Trillium* and *Rhododendron* and four species of *Hexastylis* are pictured because these genera have attracted exceptional interest from wildflower lovers. In addition, special keys to these three genera are included as an appendix.

Certain species were chosen because they represent interesting accounts about the botanical history of the state. Mexican-tea, a weedy introduction, is included because of its use as a folk remedy for "worms"; sweet grass is mentioned because of its past and present use in making sweet grass baskets; poison oak is noted because of its poisonous nature; wintergreen is a source of wintergreen oil; and mistletoe illustrates a fascinating group of plants, the parasitic vascular plants. Many federally listed endangered species such as swamp pink, smooth purple coneflower, and American chaff-seed are included because of the recent and growing interest in the protection of rare and endangered species.

Another criterion for selecting species was to include many of the species that are not included in the wildflower books that cover part or all of the southeastern U.S. Obviously, however, some overlap occurs.

One final consideration in the choice of plants was recognizing the special interests of students and wildflower enthusiasts. They have made it a pleasure to produce this book. Certain plants, for whatever reason, seem to attract their attention, whether it is a large-flowered herb or inconspicuous sedge. These species appear in appreciation of their love of wildflowers.

CONSERVATION OF NATIVE WILDFLOWERS

As natural habitats are altered, native species do not always compete successfully with the weedy introductions that quickly invade disturbed land. Year after year, more and more native habitats are lost. This escalating loss has prompted several efforts to conserve native wildflowers. But none of the multifaceted efforts can be totally successful alone. Successful wildflower conservation requires the mutual work of many individuals and groups.

Most successful conservation of native wildflowers protects them in their natural habitats. Only by placing large tracts of natural communities under protection will we insure that future generations receive the same pleasures we experience when viewing a bloodroot or pitcher-plant in its natural setting. Many South Carolina organizations are leading the way to conserve natural communities. The South Carolina Department of Natural Resources through its Heritage Trust Program has purchased almost 100,000 acres throughout the state, establishing numerous heritage preserves, many of which are described in this book. Numerous nonprofit organizations have augmented the state's system of protected lands. The Nature Conservancy has developed a sophisticated and successful system to locate and protect critical habitat for both plants and animals. Many of these protected habitats are described in the "Field guide to natural plant communities" section of the book. The conservancy also assists the state by negotiating deals with private landowners, then selling the land to the state for protection and management.

The South Carolina Native Plant Society has done much to bring wildflower heritage to the public's attention. Through seminars, workshops, lectures, and field trips, the society encourages native wildflower conservation and provides information on native wildflowers that was previously unavailable. The success of the parent chapter in Clemson has led to the establishment of local chapters throughout the state, making wildflower knowledge more available to the public.

Local land trusts have been formed as legal vehicles for the acceptance of conservation easements on private properties. Owners keep legal ownership, but for a tax break, they give up, in perpetuity, development rights to the property. Much of the protection success of the ACE Basin (Ashepoo, Combahee, and Edisto basin) in the lowcountry has been through this method.

Landscape designers have contributed to wildflower conservation by using native plants in their garden designs. If given adequate light, water, and soil conditions, some native wildflowers respond well to cultivation and are as beautiful and interesting as the more typical horticultural species. Although native wildflower gardens teach little of the habitat and natural history of the plants, gardening is often the first wildflower experience for some, and it can lead to a lifelong interest in native wildflowers and their habitats. Plant nurseries are propagating native wildflowers and providing stock and seed sources, making native wildflowers increasingly available to anyone.

The United States Forest Service has also been active in the conservation of unique natural areas in South Carolina. In the Francis Marion and Sumter National Forests, countless acres have been removed from timbering operations to preserve natural communities. Both authors have assisted the Forest Service in locating areas to be protected and drafting management plans for unique natural areas. Several of these natural areas are included in the "Field guide to natural plant communities" section.

Protection of wildflowers has also benefited from the compilation of rare species lists. Under the Endangered Species Act of 1973, the United States Fish and Wildlife Service is charged with protecting rare species. Species listed as threatened or endangered are given legal protection, and the designation "species of concern" alerts botanists and laypersons to the many species that need systematic study in order to determine if legal protection is needed. Whether a species is federally designated as threatened or endangered is part of the justification used by the South Carolina Department of Natural Resources for the purchase, or acceptance by donation, of sites that harbor these species. The Crosby *Oxypolis* Heritage Preserve in Colleton County, for example, was purchased to protect the endangered *Oxypolis canbyi* (plate 561). Establishment of preserves concomitantly protects numerous other rare wildflowers, as well as preserving their natural communities.

Conservation of many wildflowers requires a factor that the public is not generally aware of—*fire*. Coastal plain communities such as pocosins, pine flatwoods, and pine savannas as well as mountain pine-oak heaths, and piedmont xeric hardpan forests require periodic fire to maintain natural conditions. These communities evolved with fire as a dynamic natural component. Fire suppression can threaten the very existence of countless communities. In coastal plain pine savannas and flatwoods, fire suppression ultimately eliminates understory wildflowers because hardwood species invade these communities. One aim of this book, and of those organizations mentioned above, is to raise public awareness of the role of fire in natural communities. The essay "Fire in the South Carolina landscape" stresses the value of fire in the natural world. Perhaps in the future the public will be more tolerant of smoke generated from fires.

In spite of these numerous conservation programs and efforts, much still needs to be done. The areas already protected in South Carolina are not sufficient to insure the level necessary to conserve all native communities, much less all the species of rare, native South Carolina wildflowers and the threatened and endangered species. Several species are known from only a few sites, and catastrophic events such as Hurricane Hugo could thwart the best conservation efforts. A goal of this book is to make people aware of the rare natural wildflower communities in the hope that more people will join professional botanists and organizations in finding and protecting the sites that support these diverse native communities.

COLLECTING NATIVE WILDFLOWERS

The collection of native wildflowers from the wild has always been controversial. Some sources state that no native wildflower should be harvested from the wild, while other sources suggest a more liberal policy. The authors take a middle-ground approach. Some native plants are so common that they may be safely harvested without depleting the size of the population. Water-shield, an aquatic herb, is so common that collection from the wild could never significantly decrease its population size. Collecting common wildflowers to plant in a natural garden is endorsed because the appreciation gained for wildflowers through this experience may develop into a more permanent love for wildflowers. But remember: Collecting on heritage preserves, state parks, and on other protected sites that are listed in this book is *not* allowed. Even on private lands, permission must be obtained from the owner(s).

The sad news is that many sites that harbor wildflowers are slated for development. In the mid-1980s, a botany class rescued numerous herbs, including pitcher-plants, and moved them to the Bluff Plantation Wildlife Sanctuary on the Cooper River. They survive today and provide an educational resource for those visiting the sanctuary. Such "plant rescue missions" are certainly one valid method for preservation and take very little effort. In most cases, landowners eagerly give permission to groups wanting to remove plants that face obliteration.

On the other hand, the authors agree with most botanists and wild-flower lovers that any native plants considered rare or uncommon should not be removed (unless in rescue situations). Each of our species descriptions includes mention of a species' rarity. However, collecting seeds of rare species is acceptable, provided that sufficient seed is left for natural propagation and the plant is not otherwise harmed.

Specialized groups of plants such as the trilliums, gentians, orchids, carnivorous plants, and species of wild ginger present a different problem. Collecting by poachers for commercial resale and over-collecting by the public has severely reduced populations of these plant groups. True, some species are common, but each group contains rare species that are difficult to distinguish from the common species. For this reason, the public should not collect members of any of these groups. Besides, many of these species exist in such an intimate relationship to a variety of parameters in their environment that their successful establishment is almost impossible. The most common and easy-to-establish members of these groups, however, are now available from nurseries; one can easily enjoy them in gardens without resorting to collecting in the wild.

HOW TO USE THIS FIELD GUIDE

Routine, confident wildflower identifications are made by continually studying plants in the field. No one can expect to learn the flora of a state, or even the flora of a region, in a few sessions. Wildflower identification is a lifelong commitment. This book should be a companion on every field trip. As each new species is added to one's understanding of wildflowers, confidence in identification grows.

Wildflowers of South Carolina follows a natural habitat approach to native wildflower identification that was first developed in *Wildflowers of the Carolina Lowcountry and Lower Pee Dee.* When you select a plant for identification, first turn to the plant community photographs. Using the descriptions or photographs, choose the one that most resembles the plant's surroundings. Read the description of the community in "South Carolina's natural wildflower communities" to be certain you have made the best selection. Next, turn to the wild-flower photographs for that particular community and match the photograph to the plant you have found. If the plant cannot be found in the selected community, select the next best community that resembles the plant's surroundings. When you feel that the plant is successfully identified, turn next to the species descriptions and locate the description for the identified plant. The information in the description is used to confirm or reject the identification. Here is an invaluable suggestion: A small, 10x power hand lens will be a great asset in the field for examining flower and plant structures.

Caution: Not every species of wildflower that grows in South Carolina is included in this book. If you check all the photographs for the communities where the plant is most likely to be found, and you fail to find a match, it may be that the wildflower is not pictured.

The habitat approach may not always be the fastest identification method, especially for amateur botanists with little practical field training, but in the long run it will be the most rewarding. Not only will it yield the most frequent positive identification, but you will be also learning the native communities, something of inestimable value if you seriously journey into the world of native wildflowers.

Ruderal species (weedy species that inhabit disturbed areas) are included in a separate section. Almost everyone is aware of disturbed sites where these species grow, such as lawns, roadsides, and abandoned home sites. Match the plant in the field with a photograph in the book, then use the description to verify its identification.

This book is organized into four major sections that mirrors the habitat approach to wildflower identification: (1) essays on natural history and ecology; (2) descriptions of natural communities; (3) species descriptions and color plates; and (4) a field guide to sites of natural communities.

Essays

Topics were chosen to represent as wide a range of the botanical natural history of the state as possible. One suggestion is to read thoroughly, for example, the essay on carnivorous plants, then plan a trip to one of the sites described in the book where these occur. Preparation before going to the field will make the experience more meaningful, especially if you are able to locate some of these species.

Natural communities

The authors suggest becoming familiar with the natural communities that are included in the book through the descriptions and photographs. Then choose a heritage preserve or state park that harbors these natural communities so they can be recognized when they are encountered. Again, this is a continual learning process.

Species descriptions and color plates

The format for each species description contains the following elements. Note that not every species description includes all twelve elements. Elements 8–12 may not be applicable to some species.

1. Color plate number.
The color plate number is given in bold type and precedes the common name in each species description; the corresponding photo appears adjacent to its description.

2. Common name(s).
At least one common name is given for each species. Many species have numerous common names, which would be impracticable to enumerate. When two or more are given, the one thought to be most often used in South Carolina is listed first.

FORMAT OF SPECIES DESCRIPTIONS

1. Color Plate Number.
2. Common Name(s).
3. Scientific Name.
4. Pronunciation Guide.
5. Family Name.
6. Description.
7. Range-Habitat.
8. Similar Species.
9. Comments.
10. Taxonomy.
11. Synonymy.
12. Protection Status.

3. Scientific name.

The choice of the scientific names used in the book is explained in the essay "Origins of plant names."

4. Pronunciation guide.

A pronunciation guide for each species follows the scientific name. Instructions on how to use the guide are given in the essay "Pronunciation guide to scientific names."

5. Family name.

The technical family name (which ends in -*aceae*) for each species is included, as well as the common name of the family.

6. Description.

The plant description is an abbreviated version from standard taxonomic manuals. It should be used to confirm or reject an identification when photographic identification is uncertain. For instance, if the plant in question has opposite leaves with a solitary flower and these features do not agree with the description, identification is suspect. Additional examination is needed.

The simplest and most distinctive characteristics are used in the descriptions. The glossary and figure 11, "Illustrations of plant structures," contain supplementary information to assist with the descriptions.

Each description contains the flowering and/or fruiting times for the species. This information is also included with the color plates. Be aware, however, that flowering times vary from year to year and from region to region. Early and warm springs may result in a species flowering in February; the next year a late spring may postpone flowering of the same species to March or later. A plant that flowers in April in the coastal plain may not flower until May or even later in the mountains. Nevertheless, most wildflowers flower at a particular time in the year. These are the times that are listed in the descriptions.

7. Range-habitat.

The range of each species is given, both within and outside the state. The range outside the state is obtained primarily from manuals. The range provided for within the state is based on a combination of sources including manuals, records from the Heritage Trust Program, state herbariums, and the authors' own fieldwork. Field botany is an ongoing process, and distribution records within states are being continually updated. Terms denoting frequency used in this book (rare, occasional, common, locally abundant) are highly subjective and are especially difficult to apply to widespread species. A plant rare in the state may be common elsewhere, while a plant rare outside the state may be more abundant and even locally abundant in some sites in South Carolina. A plant common in the mountains, such as downy rattlesnake plantain, is rare and scattered in the coastal plain. The authors have tried to be consistent in the determinations of frequency and have based these determinations on literature and our own professional observations.

8. Similar species.

This section describes how to distinguish between species that look very similar.

9. Comments.

Included here is information on folklore, ecology, origins of common names, etc., which were taken from the literature as well as from the authors' observations. These comments are given to help "personalize" the plant.

10. Taxonomy.

The taxonomic status of several plants is unsettled and complex. For example, some sources list pond cypress (*Taxodium ascendens*) as a variety of bald cypress (*Taxodium distichum*), and use the taxon *Taxodium distichum* var. *nutans* for pond cypress. Others include both as separate species. All sources recognize that the two taxa are different but differ on their taxonomy. This section attempts to alert the reader about unsettled questions like this.

11. Synonymy.

The use of synonyms is given in the essay "Origins of plant names."

12. Protection status.

The definitions of the various federal and state protective statuses that are used in this section are given in the essay "Rarity of vascular plants." The protective status given in this book is based on information at the time of publication. As new information is discovered, the status of a particular plant may change. A plant considered endangered in the state in 2000 may shift to threatened as new populations are discovered. Both the United States Fish and Wildlife Service and the Heritage Trust Program continually update status designation of all species they monitor.

Field guide

The "Field guide to natural plant communities" includes 48 sites that harbor natural communities in South Carolina, excellent examples of places where the majority of South Carolina's wildflowers occur. Each site has been researched to locate and describe the trails that traverse the best examples of each natural community described in this book. Using this resource to locate and identify natural communities will allow the reader to learn quickly the wildflowers and native communities, providing more time to search out new sites.

The authors offer three additional tips on wildflower identification. First, visit regional herbariums. Much information can be gleaned from observing herbarium specimens. In particular, such specimens can be used to confirm a field identification. The appendix includes contacts and information on herbariums located in South Carolina. Second, take a course in field botany at a local college or university. Third, join local chapters of organizations such as the South Carolina Native Plant Society and the South Carolina Association of Naturalists. These organizations, and others, host field trips, which are valuable sources of information.

ORIGINS OF PLANT NAMES

Scientific names

Since this book is primarily for the layperson, the authors use the *Manual of the Vascular Flora of the Carolinas*, by Radford, Ahles, and Bell, (hereafter referred to as the *Manual*) as the main reference for scientific names. Published in 1968, the *Manual* remains a landmark scientific work. It updated and generally replaced Small's *Manual of the Southeastern Flora*, published in 1933, for the flora of the Carolinas. The *Manual* is by far the most widely used manual in the Carolinas, both for the layperson and the scientist.

When we are convinced that names of species in the *Manual* are technically incorrect or presently not in current use, the authors defer to Alan Weakley's 2001 draft of the *Flora of the Carolinas and Virginia*. For example, the *Manual* uses the scientific name *Chrysobalanus oblongifolius* Michaux for gopher-apple and places it in the rose family (Rosaceae). Weakley places this plant in the family Chrysobalanaceae and uses the name *Licania michauxii* Prance. The authors agree with Weakley's designation of this species. *Chrysobalanus oblongifolius* becomes a synonym for *L. michauxii* and listed as *Chrysobalanus oblongifolius* Michaux—RAB. RAB refers to Radford, Ahles, and Bell, the authors of the *Manual*.

For a species in Weakley's *Flora* that differs from the *Manual*, the authors list Weakley's scientific name as a synonym and follow it with —W (for Weakley). For example, Weakley uses the scientific name *Sideroxylon tenax* L. for tough bumelia; this book retains the name used in the *Manual*, *Bumelia tenax* (L.) Willdenow. Weakley's scientific name is listed as a synonym: *Sideroxylon tenax* L.—W.

Scientific names for plants, unlike their common names, are governed by a system of rules outlined in the International Code of Botanical Nomenclature (ICBN). These rules are reviewed and modified every six years. In this system, every plant no matter how widely distributed, has only one scientific name; furthermore, only one plant can have this scientific name. Also, a plant can have only one valid scientific name by which it may be identified at any one point in time. It may have picked up several scientific names, but any names besides the valid one are synonyms. Synonyms, then, are names that have become invalid or discarded by an author for whatever reason.

The scientific or binomial name always consists of two Latin or latinized words (the binomial system of nomenclature): a genus or generic name and a specific epithet for the species. The specific epithet is followed by the name of the person(s) who first described the plant according to the rules of the ICBN. For example, for the following scientific name:

Acer rubrum L. or <u>*Acer*</u> <u>*rubrum*</u> L.

The generic name is *Acer*, and its specific epithet is *rubrum*. The authority is the Swedish botanist Carl Linnaeus (1707–1778); he is honored by the use of the single letter "L." Linnaeus is the scientist who effectively created the modern system of nomenclature. No other botanist is honored with the use of a single letter abbreviation.

Scientific names should always be italicized when printed or underlined when typed or written by hand. The generic name is sometimes given as an abbreviation if the context makes its meaning clear: *A. rubrum* L., where *A.* stands for *Acer*.

In using scientific names in text, the genus is always capitalized while the letters of the specific epithet are all in lowercase. Formerly, some botanists used uppercase for the initial letter of the specific epithet if the epithet was honoring a person or serving some other commemorative purpose. For example, in *Gray's Manual of Botany*, the specific epithet *Gronovii* in *Hieracium Gronovii* honors Jan Frederick Gronovius. However, botanists now initiate *all* specific epithets with lowercase. This method is followed throughout the book, and *Hieracium Gronovii* is written as *Hieracium gronovii*.

Changes are made in botanical nomenclature as our biological understanding of a plant improves. For instance, when a species is better understood, it may be shifted from one genus to another. The name of the original author is then placed in parentheses and is followed by the name of the person making this change. The following example illustrates this:

Azalea calendulacea Michaux
changed to
Rhododendron calendulaceum (Michaux) Torrey

Michaux, who originally named and placed the plant in the genus *Azalea*, becomes the parenthetical authority. Torrey reassessed the plant's relationships and moved the species to the genus *Rhododendron,* and he becomes the current authority.

Botanists often recognize variations below the species level in plants that are different yet not sufficiently distinctive to be considered a separate species. These subdivisions are, in descending order of magnitude, subspecies, variety, and form. Some authors use the terms subspecies and variety interchangeably. Examples of the first two are given for instructive purposes:

Nuphar luteum subsp. *sagittifolium* (Walter) E. O. Beal
Eryngium aquaticum L. var. *aquaticum*

Common names

Common names are not dependable resources for several reasons: (1) the same plant may have many common names (e.g. 140 common names exist for woolly mullein); (2) the same common name may apply to several plants, either in the same geographical area or in different geographical areas; (3) common names may be misleading (for example, silver-leaved grass is not a grass, but a composite); and (4) they are not standardized.

In spite of the above problems, common names remain an important part of plant folklore. They often are appealing and tell us something about the plant. Recall the common name "heal-all" for *Prunella vulgaris* var. *lanceolata* in reference to its use in folk medicine as a cure-all, or "boneset" for *Eupatorium perfoliatum*, from a belief that it could be used to set broken bones. Common names are often the only means of communication for those unfamiliar with the scientific names. It may be easier to remember words such as "windflower" and "white oak." Sometimes common names are remarkably descriptive. For example, "blueberry" is a member of the heath family with (mostly) blue berries, and "swamp chestnut oak" refers to a swamp-loving oak with leaves similar to those of American chestnut.

With these considerations in mind, the authors include at least one common name for each plant. When more than one name is given, the one most frequently used in South Carolina is listed first.

NOTES ON WILDFLOWER PHOTOGRAPHY

The methods used to produce the wildflower photographs included in this book are available to anyone with photography experience who also has access to quality equipment and film. A standard 35 mm Nikon FE Single Lens Reflex camera was used. The following Nikkor lenses were used: 55 mm macro, 105 mm macro, and 70–180 mm zoom macro. Occasionally, a Nikon close-up (diopter) No. 5T lens was used on the 105 mm macro or 70–180 zoom lens for small flowers or plants.

One main production decision for photographs included in a book on wildflowers is the choice between natural light or artificial light. Natural light gives better results; the colors are warmer and closer to natural colors (see plates 37 and 139). However, using natural light in the field to produce photographs with enough depth of field to show the flower and associated structures in focus, requires the right combination of natural light and near windless conditions, especially in close-up frames. This combination rarely occurs. Producing 700 photographs when these conditions were available would have required too much time. Consequently, artificial light by flash was used for most photographs. Whenever conditions were optimal for photographing in natural light, photographs were made using both natural and artificial light. The natural-light photograph was used if it was superior to the one taken using artificial light.

Artificial light was provided by a Lumedyne #067x power pack attached to two #001E flash heads supplied with 800 ws standard flashtubes. Each flash head was attached to a Bogen light stand. The flash heads were set about 3 feet from the subject and at 45 degree angles. This allowed the light to fill in dark spots. Adequate depth of field was achieved becuase the shutter speed on the camera had to be set at 125th second to synchronize with the flash, resulting in an f-stop of around 11 producing the best exposures. The higher the f-stop, the greater is the depth of field.

Bracketing was used extensively (with both natural and artificial light). Bracketing of shots involves making exposures at different f-stops. This allowed for a choice of the best exposure to print. A flower, which is usually small, may appear washed-out when the darker parts are exposed correctly. In these situations, the photographer must judge which exposure to use. Most often the best exposure is one that slightly washes-out the flower but gives an adequate exposure of the darker parts (see wintergreen, plate 151). Bracketing, of course, uses considerably more film; however, the cost of having to make a return trip to make another photograph is far higher.

In the authors' opinion, the most important aspect of photographing wildflowers in a way that is useful in identifying the species is composition. Usually the flower was framed with surrounding leaves or other parts helpful to identification. This is especially important for yellow flowers of the aster family, which are difficult to identify by flower alone. The photograph of *Rudbeckia laciniata* (plate 50) includes a ternately dissected leaf. The leaf along with the flower is needed for a correct identification. The photograph of staggerbush (plate 341) includes as much of the plant as possible and shows the leaves, flowers, and arrangement of the flowers. Often it is the arrangement of flowers that is an important key to identification.

As often as was possible, the frame was filled with the subject to avoid a distracting background. Often this meant searching through an entire plant population to find the right combination of parts to fill the frame. When this was not possible, the natural fade-out of the flash was used to create a dark background that would not distract from the subject. When using natural light, the depth of field was reduced to cause the background material to appear out of focus.

At times, parts of plants were rearranged to enhance composition. In the photograph of *Rudbeckia laciniata* (plate 50), the flower is positioned closer to the leaf in order to show both in the photograph. Never, however, was an arrangement created that could not occur naturally.

This essay is not an extensive discourse on photography, cameras, technique, films, etc. A few procedures are mentioned that are not normally covered in standard courses or books on photographing wildflowers. The reader can refer to Adams and Casstevens (1996) and Shaw (1987) in the "General references" for detailed information on the art of wildflower photography.

RARITY OF VASCULAR PLANTS

A rare species is difficult to define since the concept involves two variables: (1) the overall species distribution and (2) the abundance of individuals within that distribution. Figure 2 (from Hardin, 1977) illustrates this relationship. One example of an extreme in rareness in South Carolina, Point A, is mountain sweet pitcher-plant (*Sarracenia jonesii*, plate 29), represented by a few individual plants restricted to an extremely limited geographic area (in this case, only a few sites in the mountains and piedmont). Point B is exemplified by cancer-root (*Orobanche uniflora*, plate 189), which is scattered throughout South Carolina but with only a few specimens at any one site. Point C is exemplified by pondspice (*Litsea aestivalis*, plate 514), which is locally abundant in Berkeley and Charleston Counties, often being the dominant shrub in pond cypress depressions. It is rare since the center of its distribution is limited to

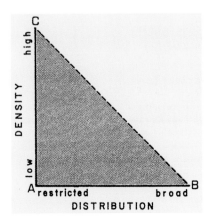

FIGURE 2. Relative Rareness of Plants as a Function of Distribution and Abundance.

these counties. Evaluation of rareness, then, is a function of distribution and abundance and includes all possible intermediates of the three extremes shown in figure 2.

In 1966 the Endangered Species Act first recognized the intrinsic value of species; it also recognized that some species were so rare that they were near extinction. Unfortunately the 1966 act only recognized animals. In 1973 the act was broadened to include plants. Since the passage of these acts, numerous organizations have come forward with programs that locate and provide protected habitat for rare species. More importantly these groups realized that preservation of our natural heritage depends on preservation of biological diversity. With this concept as its standard, various organizations have protected numerous sites in South Carolina. Many of these sites are listed in the "Field guide to natural plant communities" since they harbor examples of the natural communities described in this book. At both state and federal levels, programs have been established to document species distributions, to monitor population fluctuations, and to determine appropriate categories for rare species.

Three categories of plant rarity are recognized at the federal level, with the first two given legal status by the United States Department of Interior under the Endangered Species Act of 1973.

> *Federal Endangered Species:* a species that is in danger of becoming extinct in the near future. In South Carolina, thirteen vascular plants are listed as endangered.

> *Federal Threatened Species:* a species not now endangered but one that is heading in that direction. Six species in South Carolina are listed as threatened.

> *Federal Species of Concern:* a species that the Fish and Wildlife Service is monitoring to determine if it warrants federal listing, as either a threatened or an endangered species.

At the state level, the Heritage Trust Program keeps a database on all species of vascular plants considered rare in the state. Associated with the Heritage Trust Program is the Rare Plant Advisory Committee, comprised of professional botanists. The advisory committee continually updates the rare plant list, adding new species, or deleting species that are found to be more common than originally determined. The latest revision was completed in 2001.

Unlike state law that gives protection to rare animals, there is no state law that provides protection for rare plants. The categories of rare plants developed by the Rare Plant Advisory Committee are biological, not legal.

The committee developed the following categories of rare state plants, which are used in this book. If a plant is listed under any of the three federal categories, it is not given a state category.

> *State Endangered Species:* a species with 1 to 5 documented populations in South Carolina.

State Threatened Species: a species with 6 to 20 documented populations in South Carolina.

State Species of Concern: a species with 21 to 100 populations.

State Endangered Peripheral Species: a species with 1 to 5 documented populations in South Carolina, but which is significantly more abundant in an adjacent state(s).

Any species pictured in this book that fits any of the above federal or state categories is so indicated in the protective status section in the species description. The status of a plant, however, can change as new information becomes available. The authors expect that over the life of this book, many changes will occur. Interested individuals should obtain updated information from the South Carolina Heritage Trust Program.

PRONUNCIATION GUIDE TO SCIENTIFIC NAMES

Popular wildflower books or botanical field guides usually do not include pronunciation guides for scientific names. In fact, it is difficult to find any botanical guide with a pronunciation key. Many laypersons (and some scientists) are hesitant to use scientific names because of pronunciation difficulties. With proper guidance, however, the pronunciation of scientific names is easy. To assist the reader, the species descriptions include a pronunciation key for the scientific name of each plant pictured in this book.

Today, botanists and gardeners in English-speaking countries generally use traditional (or standard) English sounds for vowels and consonants, while following the rules of classical Latin for accenting syllables and syllabism. This book follows this plan and uses the system found in *Gray's Manual of Botany* (Fernald, 1950), where the grave accent (`) denotes a long vowel in the accented syllable and an acute accent (´) denotes a short vowel in the accented syllable. Each word is divided into syllables to make its pronunciation easier. For example:

Yúc-ca glo-ri-ò-sa

Following are the rules used in this book for pronunciation of scientific names. The material is modified from *Vascular Plant Systematics* (Radford et al., 1974) and *Botanical Latin* (Stearn, 1992).

Commemorative names

Rules of pronunciation cannot be satisfactorily applied to all generic names and specific epithets that commemorate an individual. A standard system of pronunciation of commemorative names does not exist because different languages use the same letters for different sounds and different letters for the same sounds. The English family name Jàmes becomes ja-mè-si-i in its latinized form, since in Latin every vowel must occur in a separate syllable. In this form the name is unrecognizable. The authors agree with those who believe it is preferable to pronounce the family name as close as possible to the way it sounds in English. Jàmes then becomes jàmes-i-i. In this form the name is recognizable. The English name Hàles in its latinized form would be ha-lè-si-a, which is how it now is most commonly pronounced. The authors, however, choose to pronounce it hàles-i-a to sound as close to the original name as possible. Likewise, the specific epithet *smallii* and the genus *Mitchella* (Latin for Small and Mitchell) are pronounced as smáll-i-i and mít-chell-a. Again, the Latin rules for accenting and syllabism are not followed (see below); however, in these forms the names more closely represent how they are pronounced in their original English.

Syllabism

Before a word can be accented, it must be divided into syllables, and every Latin word has as many syllables as it has separate vowels or diphthongs.

a. When a single consonant comes between two vowels, it is pronounced with the vowel that follows it: Cà-<u>r</u>ex; Mò-<u>r</u>us; Là-<u>mi</u>-um; Smì-<u>l</u>ax.

b. When two consonants come between two vowels, one is pronounced with the first vowel and the other with the second vowel: ál-<u>b</u>i-dum; Ver-nò-ni-a; Ver-bá<u>s</u>-<u>c</u>um; Se<u>s</u>-<u>b</u>à-ni-a.

c. When two consonants come between two vowels, and the first consonant is <u>b</u>, <u>c</u>, <u>d</u>, g, <u>k</u>, <u>p</u>, or <u>t</u>, and the second is either <u>l</u> or <u>r</u>, both consonants are pronounced with the second vowel: glà-<u>br</u>a; Pte-ro-<u>gl</u>os-sás-pis.

d. If two consonants that come between two vowels are <u>ch</u>, <u>ph</u>, or <u>th</u>, each pair is counted as one letter and is pronounced with the second vowel: Rá-<u>ph</u>a-nus; Oe-no-<u>th</u>è-ra.

e. When there are more than two consonants, all but the first are pronounced with the second vowel: a<u>m</u>-<u>br</u>o-si-oì-des; Ca<u>r</u>-<u>ph</u>é-pho-rus.

f. The letter <u>x</u> is always pronounced with the vowel preceding it: Ta<u>x</u>-ò-di-um.

Classic Latin rules of accenting

a. The last syllable of a word is never accented.

b. Two syllable words are always accented on the first syllable: Cà-rex; Ì-lex.

c. The next to last syllable is called the *penult;* the third syllable from the end is called the antepenult.

d. In a word of more than two syllables, the accent is on the penult, if the penult is long. The penult is long if it ends in a long vowel (cy-mò-sa), a diphthong (gen-ti-a-nòi-des), or a consonant (Pre-ná<u>n</u>-thes). In the latter, the vowel is short, but the syllable is accented.

e. If the penult is short, the accent is on the antepenult (gra-mi-ni-<u>fò</u>-li-a).

f. The accent never appears on a syllable coming before the antepenult.

Consonants

a. When one of the following pairs of consonants begins a word, the first letter is silent: <u>cn</u>, <u>ct</u>, <u>gn</u>, <u>mn</u>, <u>pn</u>, <u>ps</u>, <u>pt</u>, <u>tm</u>, or <u>ts</u>. For example: <u>C</u>nidoscolus

= ni-dós-co-lus; Ctenium = té-ni-um; Gnaphalium = na-phá-li-um; Psoralea = so-rà-le-a; Pterocaulon = te-ro-caú-lon; Tsù-ga = sù-ga.

b. When the consonants c and g are followed by e, i, y, ae, or oe, they have the soft sound of s and j, respectively. For example: cy-pe-rì-nus = si-pe-rì-nus; Gy-nán-dra = ji-nán-dra.

c. An initial x is pronounced as a z: Xán-thi-um = zán-thi-um.

d. When ci, si, and ti follow an accented syllable and are followed by another vowel, they often have the sound of sh or zh: Se-nè-ci-o = se-nè-sh-o; Ar-te-mí-si-a = ar-te-mí-zh-a.

e. Ch, ph, and th are each considered one letter. Ch has the sound of k, but is silent when it comes before th at the beginning of a word; ph is pronounced as f; and th is pronounced as it is in the word "thing." For example: Chas-màn-thi-um = kas-màn-thi-um; phél-los = fél-los.

Diphthongs

A diphthong consists of two vowels that are pronounced as a single vowel and are classified as a long vowel. The diphthongs are:

ae (pronounced like the long e in "me": laè-vis = leè-vis).

oe (pronounced like the long e in "me": a-moè-na = a-meè-na).

ei (pronounced like the long i in "kite": cu-nei-fò-li-a = cu-ni-fò-li-a).

eu (pronounced like the u in "neuter": mos-cheù-tos = mos-chù-tos).

au (pronounced like the aw in "awful": a-caù-lis = a-càw-lis).

oi (Some botanists treat oi as a diphthong, pronounced like the word "oil," and not as separate vowels, following Latin rules. For example, a-lo-pe-cu-ro-ì-des becomes a-lo-pe-cu-roì-des. In this book oi is treated as a diphthong.)

Vowels

All vowels in scientific names are pronounced, and every Latin word has as many syllables as it has separate vowels or diphthongs.

a. The vowel y is always sounded like an i: Ly-co-pó-di-um = li-co-pó-di-um.

b. Final vowels have a long sound (si-nén-se = si-nén-see), except when the final vowel is an a, which is pronounced ah: ca-ro-li-ni-à-na = ca-ro-li-ni-à-nah.

c. The es at the end of a word is pronounced ease: a-lo-pe-cu-roì-des = a-lo-pe-cu-roì-deez.

d. Two vowels that occur together and do not form a diphthong are always pronounced separately, with the first vowel having a short sound: quin-que-fò-li-us, where the i in li is short.

e. Note that the above rule does not hold for words transcribed from Greek. For example, the e in *Staphylea* and *Centaurea* is long because it is a contraction of the Greek diphthong ei. A diphthong is always treated as a long vowel, even if transcribed as a single letter. Since the penult is long, the genera are pronounced as Sta-phy-lè-a and Cen-tau-rè-a.

f. In some works, a diacritic mark (diaeresis) is placed over the second of two adjoining vowels when they represent two sounds, e.g., *Leucothoë* and *Isoëtes*. Here <u>oe</u> is not treated as a diphthong, and the names are pronounced Leu-cóth-o-ë and I-sò-ë-tes.

Family names

Family names end in <u>aceae</u>. Since <u>ae</u> is a diphthong and is therefore long, <u>ce</u> (the penult) is short and the accent is on the antepenult. Examples of family names and their pronunciations are: As-te-rà-ce-ae, Ro-sà-ce-ae, Li-li-à-ce-ae, Or-chi-dà-ce-ae, and I-ri-dà-ce-ae.

A Guide to the
Wildflowers of
South Carolina

Natural History of Selected Groups of Vascular Plants

CARNIVOROUS PLANTS

Carnivorous plants are unusual in the plant world because of their unique method of supplementing their nutrition. Their leaves have become modified through natural selection to trap insects and other small animals. Carnivorous plants inhabit acidic soil or water. In acid soils, many minerals, especially nitrogen, are strongly bound to soil particles, and they are unavailable for plants to absorb into their roots. In habitats like these, carnivory evolved as a supplementary means to obtain minerals. After a carnivorous plant traps an animal, usually a small insect, the digestion of animal protein results in the release of minerals that are then absorbed by the plant. As a result of selection pressure, plants that evolved carnivory were able to inhabit and flourish in acidic soils.

Carnivorous plants do not obtain food from their prey, only dissolved minerals. Like all green plants, photosynthesis occurs. To convert carbohydrates made during photosynthesis into other compounds (e.g., lipids, proteins, and nucleic acids), a mineral source, particularly nitrogen, is needed. For carnivorous plants, these minerals are supplied from trapped animals.

The leaves of carnivorous plants that have become modified to trap insects are so changed that they only remotely resemble what are normally recognized as leaves. However, their green color indicates that they still function in photosynthesis. There are two major types of traps: passive and active. Passive traps do not employ any type of movement to entrap prey, although ingenious methods have evolved to attract prey. Active traps not only attract prey but move to catch and hold the prey.

Among the many myths associated with carnivorous plants is that some species are large enough to eat people. The truth is that the largest animals that could be caught by any carnivorous plant, anywhere in the world, are small mammals and reptiles. Slack (1979) reports that species of *Nepenthes* in the Old World tropics do catch small mammals and reptiles, but such catches are probably fortuitous rather than intentional. Because animals other than insects are often caught as prey, the term carnivorous is preferred over insectivorous.

All carnivorous plants produce fertile flowers and viable seeds. In the case of some pitcher-plants, the flowers develop before the leaves, and one often does not equate the two structures as being from the same plant. Other species of pitcher-plants and the other four genera of carnivorous plants in South Carolina produce flowers and leaves (traps) at the same time.

Worldwide there are about 450 species of carnivorous plants, representing 15 genera. In South Carolina, there are five genera (*Sarracenia, Drosera, Utricularia, Pinguicula,* and *Dionaea*), represented by approximately 25 species. The reader can refer to the following sources, which are listed in the general reference section, for more information on carnivorous plants: Lloyd (1976); Pietropaola and Pietropaola (1986); Schnell (1976); and Slack (1979).

Sarracenia (pitcher-plants)

Pitcher-plants have perennial rosettes of leaves that are modified to trap insects. The pitchers represent passive traps and are tubular, like elongated funnels, and overtopped by hoods (plate 496). Usually this hood is supported by a narrow column, which may be reflexed over the pitcher and open, as exhibited in the hooded pitcher-plant (*Sarracenia minor,* plate 377), or vertical, as in frog's breeches (*S. purpurea* var. *venosa,* plate 331). Two mechanisms attract insects: the coloration of the pitchers and the secretions from a nectar gland. The nectar gland is at the rolled up margin of the hood along the lip opposite the column. In frog's breeches, once an insect lands on the brim of the tubular opening or on the underside of the hood, downward-pointing stiff hairs drive the insect into the pitcher. Often the insect loses its footing and falls into the pitcher. The upper portion of the pitcher is lined with a slippery, smooth wax that makes it difficult for the insect to crawl out. Ultimately, the insect falls into the watery mixture of enzymes at the base of the pitcher, where digestion takes place and absorption occurs through a wax-free zone.

The leaves of pitcher-plants arise from subterranean rhizomes in early spring. The subterranean rhizomes allow the plants to survive the periodic fires that remove the competing vegetation in the savannas and bogs where they grow. These rhizomes also function as a means of asexual reproduction.

Five species of pitcher-plants grow in the state: hooded pitcher-plant (*S. minor,* plate 377); yellow trumpet (*S. flava,* plate 496); sweet pitcher-plant (*S. rubra,* plate 484); frog's breeches (*S. purpurea* var. *venosa,* plate 331); and mountain sweet pitcher-plant (*S. jonesii,* plate 29). The first four occur in the coastal plain and sandhills regions; mountain sweet pitcher-plant occurs along mountain streams and bogs. The specific habitats of all five species are provided in the individual species descriptions.

Drosera (sundews)

Sundews are herbaceous plants, having a basal rosette of leaves (plate 334) that arise from a fibrous root system. In South Carolina, they are perennial. Leaves are produced continuously all year. A single fertile stalk, arising from between the leaves, supports from 1 to 25 white flowers in a raceme (plate 374). The lowest flower opens for about two days, closes, and the flower above it then opens. The flowering process ultimately moves to the top of the inflorescence. Flowering occurs throughout the spring and summer.

The leaves are an active trap to only a limited degree and are often referred to as a flypaper mechanism. The leaf blade is covered with stalked glands, some of which secrete mucilage (which holds the insect), while others secrete digestive enzymes. Small, crawling insects, either attracted to the plant by the leaf coloration and/or by the nectar from the glands or as a result of a chance wandering, become mired in the sticky secretions. As the insect struggles to get free, the motion causes signals to be sent through the leaf blade, by some yet unclear process, to the long-stalked marginal glands, which then bend to the center of the blade and further entangle the insect. In some species, the leaf blade may fold over the insect, which results in a greater leaf surface area contacting the insect, thus increasing the rate of mineral absorption. A leaf that has trapped an insect will subsequently die. A supply of new leaves ensures the trapping mechanism will continue through the growing season.

The common name of *Drosera,* sundew, comes from the sticky, dewlike tentacles that shine like dew, glittering in the early morning sun.

Four species of sundews occur in the state: round-leaf sundew (*Drosera rotundifolia,* plate 334, in the mountains and sandhills); and in the coastal plain and sandhills, dwarf sundew (*D. brevifolia,* plate 374), pink sundew (*D. fili-formis*), and water sundew (*D. intermedia,* plate 333).

Pinguicula (butterworts)

Butterworts are fibrous-rooted perennials that in summer form a flat rosette of blunt, oblong leaves. The older leaves lie prostrate against the ground, with the younger, nearly flat leaves lying on top of the older leaves (*P. caerulea,* plate 375). Butterworts retain their leaves over the winter and do not form winter resting buds.

Their leaf surfaces contain two kinds of glands: (1) stalked glands that are important in catching and holding prey, and (2) sessile glands that are active in digestion. The trapping mechanism is an active flypaper type. Evidently, the leaves do not have any method of attracting prey since no nectar glands have been identified. Crawling and flying insects probably come into contact with the leaves by chance. Prey become mired in the gland's secretions and are held until digestion and absorption gradually occur. The leaf margins curl over the prey, perhaps preventing the partially digested insect from being washed off by rain, but certainly bringing more leaf surface into contact with the prey and increasing absorption.

The rosette form of the butterworts' leaves resembles so many other plants that they are inconspicuous and often overlooked. However, in late spring and early summer their flowers make butterworts highly conspicuous.

Three species of butterworts occur in South Carolina, and all grow in the coastal plain. The species are violet butterwort (*P. caerulea,* plate 375), yellow butterwort (*P. lutea,* plate 321 in *WCL*), and small-flowered butterwort (*P. pumila*).

Utricularia (bladderworts)

The common name, bladderworts, originates from the modified leaves, or bladders, that function as traps. Species are either aquatic or terrestrial; the terrestrial species grow in moist soil.

The traps are activated when an aquatic insect touches one of the sensitive hairs that surround the bladder opening. Functioning like a hinged door, the bladder quickly opens, water rushes into the bladder, sweeping with it the insect, then it closes, trapping the prey inside. Digestion takes place inside the bladder. Because of the tiny size of the bladders, only small aquatic insects, such as mosquito larvae, are trapped. The most prolific bladder producers are the aquatic species; terrestrial species only produce bladders when they are growing in very moist soil.

One spectacular bladderwort is the floating bladderwort (*Utricularia inflata*, plate 548). This is a coastal plain species that forms a remarkable flotation device to support the flowering stalk. Six to ten floats (modified leaves) radiate from the middle of the stalk. Initial development of the stalk and bladders begins under water. As the floats grow, their buoyancy, which is caused by the presence of aerenchyma tissue, makes the entire plant rise to the surface. This fertile stalk then produces from 9 to 14 yellow flowers.

Twelve species of *Utricularia* occur in South Carolina; only the saline maritime strand has no representatives. Horned bladderwort (*U. cornuta*, plate 30) is included to represent terrestrial species in the state.

Dionaea (Venus' fly trap)

Venus' fly trap (*Dionaea muscipula*, plate 378) is a terrestrial carnivorous plant that is endemic to the coastal plain of the Carolinas. In South Carolina, it occurs only in Georgetown and Horry Counties. Viable populations occur in Lewis Ocean Bay Heritage Preserve and Cartwheel Bay Heritage Preserve. It favors damp, sandy soil with a small portion of peat (like that found around Carolina bays) and open, sunny conditions. It has particularly exacting habitat requirements. The seedling stage is the most sensitive life-history stage because the habitat requirements are very specific at this time. This species is not yet near extinction, but much of its special habitat has been so altered that it must be monitored to ensure its preservation. It is one of many savanna herbs that requires frequent fire to prevent invasion by shrubs and trees, which would cause its elimination.

The trapping mechanism, a modified leaf, is an active, springlike trap. The foliage is a rosette that grows from a perennial rhizome, with each leaf blade consisting of two lobes, and each lobe is attached to the blade's midrib. Pronglike teeth occur along the free margins of the lobes. On the inner surface of the lobes are two types of glands: nectar glands, near the margin to attract insects, and digestive glands on the surface. The latter turn red when exposed to the sun, giving the leaf a reddish coloration, which also attracts insect prey. On the upper surface of each leaf lobe are trigger hairs (generally three), which spring the trap when an insect touches them. The lobes close in about half a second, trapping the prey, and then digestion and absorption begin. Springing a trap requires two touches of a single hair or a touch of two separate hairs, occurring in about a 20 second interval. This prevents wind-blown objects from prematurely closing the trap and wasting the plant's energy. Usually, each trap can catch three insects before it dies or no longer responds when stimulated. The continual production of new leaves during the growing season compensates for this loss.

Venus' fly trap produces a stalk of white flowers in the early summer (plate 334 in *WCL*).

NATIVE ORCHIDS

The orchid family (Orchidaceae) is one of the most fascinating and diverse families of flowering plants in the world. It is a cosmopolitan family that attains its highest development in the mountains of the tropics and sub-tropics of both hemispheres. Orchids are found throughout the world at sites where at least some amount of moisture is present. They are absent only from deserts and from polar regions, where the ground is permanently frozen. There are at least 30,000 species of orchids recognized worldwide. Within the United States and Canada, botanists recognize 210 species and varieties. In South Carolina, 45 species and varieties and two hybrids have been identified.

From an aesthetic view, orchids are often accorded first place in nature. The beauty of their flowers has made the orchid family the center of a multi-million dollar floral industry in the United States and Europe, but the family is otherwise of little economic importance. The most important natural product that comes from an orchid is vanilla flavoring from the seedpods of *Vanilla planifolia,* a climbing orchid native to tropical America and cultivated in many tropical countries.

Despite its wide habitat range and large number of species, the orchid family is often overlooked by botanists and laypersons because the majority of our native orchids have small, inconspicuous flowers. Most people associate orchids with exotic tropical species or with the myriad of large-flowered forms sold for corsages. On close examination, however, our native orchids are just as alluring.

Orchids are specialized perennial herbs that are terrestrial, lithophytic (growing on rocks), or epiphytic (growing on another plant, usually a tree). Terrestrial orchids are common in temperate areas, such as South Carolina, while epiphytic orchids are more common in tropical areas. With the exception of the green-fly orchid (plate 451), all orchids in South Carolina are terrestrial. North of the sub-tropics, the epiphytic habitat is restricted because of cold temperatures and insufficient moisture. In cold temperatures, exposure to the atmosphere and a lack of insulation from soil kills the roots of epiphytes. Only along the coast of South Carolina, where the ocean moderates the temperatures (often a few degrees above the inland areas in the winter) and where moisture is high, is the epiphytic growth possible for orchids. More commonly, the green-fly orchid is found on the branches of tall bald cypress and tupelo gum trees in swamp forests or on live oaks in upland habitats.

Many orchids, after a normal period of flowering, do not produce aboveground vegetative parts for a year or more. In other words, they "disappear" for a time. Snowy orchid (*Platanthera nivea,* plate 381) may cover a coastal savanna one year, then be absent for years, only to return in great numbers another year. Some reports claim that during the hiatus the orchid is building up food supplies in the underground stem that will provide energy for the flowering process.

One of the most unusual of specialized orchid lifestyles is saprophytism. Saprophytes are plants that lack chlorophyll and are unable to manufacture food. They obtain food from decaying organic matter in the soil. Saprophytic orchids are terrestrial species that depend on a soil fungus to supply food. The fungus lives in the roots of the orchid and sends its mycelium out into the soil. This mass of mycelium (a large, entangled network of filaments that forms the body of a fungus) greatly increases the surface area that is available for the absorption of water, minerals, and food. The fungus secretes enzymes into the soil to digest organic material, absorbs the digested material and converts it to simpler compounds, and then transfers them to the orchid. Usually saprophytic orchids are confined to humus- and moisture-rich habitats that can support mycelial development.

Three species of saprophytic orchids occur in South Carolina: autumn coral-root (*Corallorhiza odontorhiza,* plate 135), spring coral-root (*C. wisteriana* Conrad), and crested coral-root (*Hexalectris spicata,* plate 436).

The orchid family is noteworthy among higher plants for three reasons: (1) the diversity of its highly specialized flowers, (2) the large number of extremely minute seeds that lack an endosperm, and (3) the wide diversity of habitats where they are found. The flower is unusual because the male and female parts (stamens and pistil) are fused into one structure called the column. At the apex of the column is the male anther; here pollen grains are aggregated into masses called pollinia. Below the anther is the stigma, the terminal receptive portion of the pistil. The surface of the stigma is sticky, thus allowing pollinia, which are brought from other flowers by insects, to adhere to its surface.

Insects primarily pollinate orchids, with each orchid species apparently having an association with its own insect pollinator. All orchid flowers have three sepals (outer floral whorl) and three petals (inner floral whorl). One of the petals, the central lip, is different from the two lateral ones, often being larger and more showy. Usually the flower grows so that the lip is lower than the lateral petals; however, in the genus *Calopogon* (plate 373), the lip is above the lateral petals.

The seed capsule of orchids requires about nine months to mature and may contain millions of dustlike seeds. The seeds contain no endosperm and are dependent on external aid for germination and seedling growth. A soil fungus penetrates the seed and establishes a symbiotic relationship with the embryo. The embryo grows by absorbing the externally produced digestion or secretion by-products of the fungus. The fungus will eventually penetrate the orchid's roots, where it remains in a symbiotic mycorrhizal relationship that is permanent and obligate. Thus, all orchids, at least as seedlings, are saprophytic. The balance of orchid, soil, and soil fungus is so delicate that transplanting orchids from their native habitat is difficult and it is not advised for wildflower gardens.

The diversity of habitats and growth forms attests to the remarkable adaptations of the orchid family. One can find pink lady's slipper (*Cypripedium acaule,* plate 146) in mountain bogs and pine-oak heaths, and showy orchis (*Orchis spectabilis,* plate 63) and lily-leaved twayblade (*Liparis lilifolia,* plate 71) in cove hardwoods. In the coastal plain, two species of *Spiranthes* have been found in abandoned farm fields and another species in freshwater pools behind coastal dunes. Five species of *Platanthera* occur in the longleaf pine savannas, while two species of *Platanthera* grow in swamp forests. In the freshwater tidal marshes along the coastal rivers, grow two species: water-spider orchid (*Habenaria repens,* plate 521) and fragrant ladies'-tresses (*Spiranthes odorata*). Furthermore, some orchids grow statewide, while others grow only in restricted habitats. For example, shadow-witch (*Ponthieva racemosa,* plate 437) is confined to the coastal plain, growing in calcium-rich sites, while the small green wood-orchid (*Platanthera clavellata,* plate 283) is found in bogs or swamps throughout the state.

Three excellent references on orchids are Correll (1978); and Luer (1972 and 1975).

POISONOUS PLANTS

Throughout history, human poisoning by plants has always been a serious health problem. In the United States thousands of people are poisoned annually. The majority of poisoning results from two situations: (1) small children grabbing and eating brightly colored plant parts, such as berries, and (2) wild food aficionados mistaking poisonous plants for edible ones. The best deterrent to accidental poisoning is to become familiar with the poisonous plants in your area. *Wildflowers of South Carolina* can be used as a guide to many of the poisonous plants in the state. Many species in this book are poisonous, and information on a species' poisonous designation is provided in the comments entry under the species description.

Two references on poisonous plants are Westbrooks and Preacher (1986) and Kingsbury (1964).

Considering the many species of plants that are known to be poisonous world wide, it is beyond most laypersons to be familiar with all the poisonous plants that they may come into contact with. Even experienced botanists are not fully aware of all the poisonous plants in their area. The following may serve as a precautionary guide:

1. Do not suck the nectar of flowers since many have poisonous nectar.
2. Never eat any part of an unknown plant.
3. Never chew or suck jewelry made from imported fruits or seeds.
4. Never use twigs as skewers for cooking over open fires because the poisonous product may diffuse into the food.
5. Avoid smoke from campfires since it may carry toxic substances from the burning wood.
6. Never make or drink a tea made from an unknown plant.

It would be easy if we could look at a plant and determine from its physical features whether or not it is poisonous. Unfortunately, this is not possible; clues to the poisonous nature of plants may not be obvious. Consider the following:

1. The ripe fruit of the may-apple is edible, while the unripe fruit is poisonous.
2. The pulp of the apple is edible, while the seeds are poisonous.

As a ready reference, the following is a list of the vascular plant genera
that are pictured or mentioned in this book that have poisonous species.

GENERA PRODUCING INTERNAL POISONS ONLY			GENERA CAUSING DERMATITIS	GENERA PRODUCING INTERNAL POISONS AND CAUSING DERMATITIS	
Aconitium	Ipomoea	Prunus	Acer	Apocynum	Iris
Allium	Juniperus	Pyrularia	Actaea	Asclepias	Ligustrum
Aquilegia	Kalmia	Rhododendron	Anemone	Campsis	Manfreda
Arisaema	Lathyrus	Rumex	Aralia	Caulophyllum	Orontium
Baccharis	Lachnanthes	Sambucus	Aster	Chenopodium	Phoradendron
Baptisia	Lobelia	Saponaria	Catalpa	Clematis	Podophyllum
Calycanthus	Lonicera	Sesbania	Cypripedium	Datura	Ranunculus
Cassia	Lupinus	Solanum	Daucus	Dicentra	Sanguinaria
Cicuta	Lyonia	Spigelia	Erythronium	Euphorbia	Sapium
Cnidoscolus	Malus	Tephrosia	Eupatorium	Gelsemium	Senecio
Corydalis	Melia	Thalictroides	Hypericum	Helenium	
Crotalaria	Menispermum	Trillium	Laportea		
Croton	Morus	Vicia	Rhus		
Erythrina	Oxypolis	Wisteria	Rosa		
Euonymus	Parthenocissus	Yucca	Sedum		
Glottidium	Peltandra	Zephyranthes.	Tradescantia		
Hydrangea	Phytolacca				
Ilex	Pontederia				

3. The rhizome of jack-in-the-pulpit is poisonous, but parching the rhizome removes the poison.
4. The same amount of poison that may cause illness in a child may have no effect in an adult.
5. Plants that are bitter to taste may be harmless, while plants that are pleasant to taste may be poisonous.
6. Plants that are harmless to animals, especially livestock, may be poisonous to people.
7. A substance may be relatively harmless if ingested after a heavy meal, since the stomach's contents will dilute it and decrease its absorption, yet on an empty stomach it could be poisonous.
8. The young leaves of some plants are harmless (and often eaten), while the older leaves may be poisonous (for example, pokeweed).
9. Not all plants with milky juice are poisonous. While the milky juice from the poinsettia causes dermatitis in some people, the basis of chewing gum is the milky juice of a tree native to Mexico.
10. Three members of the genus *Rhus,* poison ivy, poison oak and poison sumac, cause dermatitis, but another member, winged sumac, is harmless. In fact, its ripe berries are used to make a drink.

WOODY VINES

Woody vines represent a specialized evolutionary adaptation that allows their
leaves to grow above the leaves of a competing plant and receive more sun-

light. By definition, woody vines are vascular plants that remain rooted in the soil but keep their stems erect by using other objects for support. Supporting objects are either other plants or structures such as telephone poles, fence posts, and buildings. Woody vines are not parasitic since they obtain no food from the host, only support. Nevertheless, they can be harmful to supporting trees and shrubs in two ways: (1) by spreading their foliage over the host plant and blocking its source of sunlight, and (2) by twining and constricting the supporting hosts' trunk or stem such that downward translocation of food may be impaired, which in extreme cases can kill the supporting plant.

Woody vines have limited economic importance in the United States with the exception of the genus *Vitis* (grape) and horticultural genera such as *Clematis* and *Actinidia*. The native vines do provide, however, valuable forage, seeds, and fruits for wildlife.

Woody vines that occur in South Carolina can be classified into four categories based on their method of climbing.

Vines with thorns.

These vines have thorns or prickles that passively aid in climbing. Cherokee rose (*Rosa laevigata*, plate 625) is an example. Its clinging habit is undoubtedly aided by its large, curved prickles.

Vines that twine.

Twiners are woody vines in which the entire stem twines about the supporting structure. An unusual feature of twiners is that within a particular taxon, twining is either consistently clockwise or consistently counterclockwise.

Numerous species of twining vines occur in the state; for example, Japanese honeysuckle (plate 638), supplejack, coral honeysuckle (plate 227), yellow jessamine (plate 223), and yellow honeysuckle (plate 4).

Vines with tendrils.

Tendrils are specialized organs that facilitate climbing and may be modified parts of leaves, stipules, leaf stalks, or stems. The tendrils may either twine about the supporting structure or adhere to the surface of the support. Initially, tendrils are weak structures, but once they become attached to the supporting structure, their tissues harden to such a degree that they are capable of supporting the weight of the vine.

Numerous vines that climb by tendrils have showy flowers (or fruits) and are considered wildflowers. Representatives in the state that have conspicuous flowers or fruits include Virginia creeper, cross-vine (plate 470), cow-itch (plate 678), climbing hydrangea, coral greenbrier (plate 454), muscadine (plate 262), and ladies'-eardrops (plate 447).

Vines with flattened stems.

Climbing fetterbush (*Pieris phillyreifolia*, plate 513) is a coastal plain woody vine with an unusual climbing method. The vine grows under or in the crevices of a tree's outer bark. In South Carolina, pond cypress is the host tree, which is only found in the coastal plain. The plant originates as a shrub at the base of a pond cypress; in time its main branch may grow under or in a crevice of the outer bark. When this happens, the stem assumes a flattened form that enables it to grow under the bark. Considerably higher up the tree, the stem sends out lateral branches that produce white flowers in the spring.

A good reference to woody vines is *Woody Vines of the Southeastern United States* (Duncan, 1975).

EPIPHYTIC VASCULAR PLANTS

Epiphytes grow on other plants. The term is derived from *epi,* meaning "upon," and *phyte,* meaning "plant." The evolution of the epiphytic habit allows these plants to "raise" themselves above the competition of the forest floor into a habitat where there is less competition. Epiphytes depend on their host only for physical support, unlike parasites that depend on the host for water, minerals and/or food. Epiphytes include a variety of life forms, such as fungi, algae, mosses, liverworts, lichens, and vascular plants.

Of all the ecological groups of plants, epiphytes are the most dependent on rainwater; survival is dependent on their ability to endure drought. They have specialized structures that absorb moisture from the atmosphere. In Spanish moss the roots serve mainly for anchorage, while the stems and leaves act to absorb moisture. The leaves and stems are covered with gray, peltate scales that collect and absorb water by capillary action. During drought, because the plant shrinks in size, scales cover the uncutinized areas and prevent water loss. In the tropical orchids, layers of empty, whitish cells from the epidermis of the root, called the velamen, can take up water rapidly from the atmosphere even after a light rain. The living core of the root then absorbs the water from this storage tissue.

Vascular epiphytes are photosynthetic plants. Both carbon dioxide and water, which are necessary for photosynthesis, are obtained from the atmosphere. Minerals are derived from three sources: (1) decaying bark of the host tree; (2) rainwater that collects dissolved substances; and (3) wind-borne particles that collect in the crevices of the host tree's bark. Once basic carbohydrates are produced in photosynthesis, they can combine with available minerals to make other organic compounds.

Epiphytes and their hosts are well adapted to their relationship, and the epiphytes cause no appreciable damage to their hosts. Occasionally, however, the weight of the epiphyte may break a supporting branch and allow fungi and insects to infect the host. Or, massive growths of Spanish moss may block sunlight to the branches and reduce normal foliage production. Spanish moss has been reported to reduce the yield of pecan trees because they shade young pecan buds.

Vascular epiphytes are generally located in the fork of tree trunks and on horizontal branches; they are less common on vertical and smooth surfaces. Horizontal branches and trunk forks provide a place where organic matter can accumulate, creating conditions more conducive for establishing and maintaining propagules.

Three vascular epiphytes occur in the state: resurrection fern (*Polypodium polypodioides,* plate 594), which grows throughout the state; and two flowering plants, green-fly orchid (*Epidendrum conopseum,* plate 451) and Spanish moss (*Tillandsia usneoides,* plate 585). The latter two are primarily coastal plain and maritime species.

SAPROPHYTIC VASCULAR PLANTS AND MYCOTROPHY

Plants that live by using preformed organic material (food) are heterotrophic, which means they have no chlorophyll and do not photosynthesize. Their food comes from one of two sources: They are either parasitic and obtain their food from a living host, or they are saprophytic and obtain their food from decaying organic matter. In the living world the majority of saprophytes are the fungi and bacteria. These decomposers are essential for the breakdown of biological waste and dead organisms, returning the carbon from these wastes to the air as carbon dioxide and releasing minerals to the soil.

But saprophytism is not confined to the lower organisms. Two families of flowering plants, the Orchidaceae and the Ericaceae, have saprophytic representatives. Saprophytism in flowering plants probably originated from photosynthetic species that grew in forests. A mechanism first evolved to transfer supplementary food from the soil environment into the photosynthetic plant; then, when the ability to make chlorophyll was lost, food sources that are readily available in the forest allowed for the evolution of saprophytism. Flowering saprophytes are still confined to forests because a buildup of dead organic matter occurs in this habitat.

The mechanism that evolved to transfer food from the soil into the saprophyte is mycotrophy (Gr. *mykes* = fungus, *trophia* = nourishment). The roots of many photosynthetic vascular plants harbor a filamentous fungus, forming a fungus-root combination called a mycorrhizae. The role of the fungus for the photosynthetic plants is to absorb water and minerals from the soil and pass it to the host plant. Mycorrhizal absorption of water and minerals is often more efficient than plant root absorption because of the increased surface area provided by fungal hyphae. Some biologists believe that for many forest trees the additional water provided by the fungus is necessary under certain natural conditions to replace water lost by transpiration. The mycorrhizal fungus can also tap a mineral supply from its digestion of organic matter in the soil that is not readily available to the plant.

The mycorrhizal association in saprophytic flowering plants probably evolved from a mycorrhizal association of fungi and photosynthetic plants. With the loss of the ability to make chlorophyll, the fungus became the vehicle to pass not only water and minerals from the soil to the saprophyte but also food. The relationship is obligate, and the saprophyte will not survive without the fungus.

Six species of saprophytic flowering plants occur in South Carolina: three members of the Ericaceae family, Indian pipe (*Monotropa uniflora*, plate 251), pinesap (*M. hypopithys*, plate 247), and sweet pinesap (*Monotropsis odorata*, plate 139); and three members of the orchid family, crested coral-root (*Hexalectris spicata*, plate 436), autumn coral-root (*Corallorhiza odontorhiza*, plate 135), and spring coral-root (*Corallorhiza wisteriana*).

PARASITIC VASCULAR PLANTS

Parasitism is a symbiotic relationship between two organisms living in direct contact; nutrition passes from one organism, the host, to the other organism, the parasite. In this relationship, the host is adversely affected to varying degrees while the parasite benefits from the association. Parasitic relationships between animals are well known to laypersons and scientists. Just think of the tapeworms in animals, as well as humans, or the displeasure of removing a tick after a trek through Carolina fields and forests. Parasitism in plants is equally common.

Two major types of parasitic flowering plants are known: hemiparasites and holoparasites. Hemiparasites contain chlorophyll and only depend on their hosts for water and minerals. However, they do receive some organic material that is present in the xylem of the host. The following hemiparasites occur in South Carolina: mistletoe (*Phoradendron serotinum,* plate 455); five species of dodder (*Cuscuta gronovii,* plate 701, is a representative species); three species of the Santalaceae family (Nestronia, *Nestronia umbellula,* plate 237, buffalo-nut, *Pyrularia pubera,* plate 96, and bastard toadflax, *Comandra umbellata*); as well as several genera of the Scrophulariaceae (figwort family).

The most spectacular of the hemiparasitic flowering plants are members of the figwort family. Nine genera with brightly colored flowers are reported to occur in South Carolina; six of these genera are represented in this book: *Aureolaria, Agalinis, Pedicularis, Schwalbea, Seymeria,* and *Castilleja.* There is little precise information on the specific hosts of these parasitic figworts.

Holoparasites represent the most advanced parasitic condition; they lack chlorophyll and do not photosynthesize. They are completely dependent on their hosts for water, minerals, *and* food. Three holoparasites, all belonging to the broomrape family (Orobanchaeceae), occur in South Carolina: squaw-root (*Conopholis americana,* plate 225), beech-drops (*Epifagus virginiana,* plate 221), and cancer-root (*Orobanche uniflora,* plate 189).

The one structure unique to plant parasites is the haustorium, a bridge of xylem tissue (figure 3) between the host and parasite through which water, minerals, and limited amounts of food pass from the host to the parasite. The haustorium evolved from the undifferentiated xylem of the root of the parasite.

FIGURE 3. Generalized Plant-Parasite Haustorium.

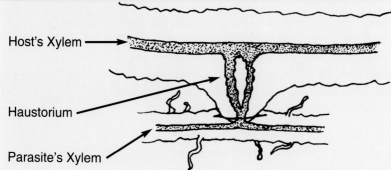

Reduction in seed size and leaf surface size evolved in the highly specialized holoparasite. Leaf surface became reduced because there was no selective pressure to maintain light-trapping structures. This reduction is clearly visible in squaw-root and beech-drops. In the holoparasites, which are parasitic of the roots of trees, seeds do not germinate until they get to the rhizosphere (the soil immediately surrounding the root system of a plant). Water carries the seeds down through the soil. Once in the rhizosphere, they germinate after being stimulated by a chemical exudate from the host's roots. The selective advantage of the small seeds is obvious: Small seeds are able to pass more readily through the soil pores, and their size makes it possible to produce large numbers per capsule. After germination, the embryonic root of the seed contacts the host root and adheres to it by a special tissue. An intrusive organ develops and penetrates the root. Then the bridge of xylem forms. This combination of adhesive tissue, intrusive organ, and xylem functions as the haustorium.

There is great variation in the effects of the parasite's interference in the host's physiology, ranging from spectacular malformations to no recognizable symptoms. A heavy mistletoe infestation on fruit trees may cause a significant decrease in the reproductive capacity of the host trees and result in a reduced fruit crop. The dodders are noxious weeds that infect crops such as clover and alfalfa. In a very short time, a crop can be covered by a thick web of intertwined and matted dodder stems that drain the host's minerals. On the other hand, squaw-root, beech-drops, and cancer-root have little obvious effect on their hosts (their mass is relatively small when compared to the trees they parasitize). The parasite does not usually kill the host plant because the life-support system of the parasite would also be eliminated, and parasitism would never have evolved.

MEDICINAL PLANTS AND FOLK REMEDIES

People have used plants in an attempt to cure diseases and relieve pain from the earliest times. These primitive medicinal attempts were often based on speculation and/or superstition, as people believed that diseases were due to evil spirits in the body and could only be expelled by ingestion of substances disagreeable to the spirits. Curative agents must have been discovered by trial and error, with knowledge accumulating slowly through the centuries and spreading by word of mouth from generation to generation.

Perhaps the first substantiated record of the use of plants as medicine comes from the Code of Hammurabi, a series of tablets from Babylon written in about 1770 B.C.E. It mentions such plants as henbane, licorice, and mint, all of which are still used in folk medicine. The Egyptians recorded their cures on temple walls and on the Ebers Papyrus (1550 B.C.E.), which contains over 700 medicinal formulas, including substances from species now documented to have therapeutic value, such as castor-bean, mandrake, and hemp.

The Golden Age of Greece was a time of great advancement in medicinal and biological knowledge by men such as Hippocrates, Aristotle, and Theophrastus. Hippocrates did not believe evil spirits caused sickness, and he prescribed plant products as cures. The most significant surviving Greek work is *De Materia Medica* written by Dioscorides in 77 B.C.E., which dealt with the properties of all the medicinal substances then known. Although poorly organized and often inaccurate, it became the prototype for future pharmacopoeias and was accepted without question by Europeans until the fifteenth century.

The Middle Ages were a period of relative stagnation in medicine. Some historians blame this stagnation on Dioscorides and his contemporaries, claiming that Europeans blindly followed their detailed but often incorrect ideas about diseases and cures. Others blame it on the dormancy of intellectualism in Europe. Some progress was made, however, during this period as botany and medicine became more closely linked.

In the fourteenth century, the Renaissance brought a new desire for knowledge. Studies of the human body were renewed, and surgical procedures improved. Medicine did suffer a slight setback when Paracelsus (1493–1541) denounced the works of the Greeks and proposed the Doctrine of Signatures. According to this superstitious doctrine, all plants possessed some sign given by the Creator that indicated the use for which they were intended. Thus a plant with heart-shaped leaves should be used for heart ailments. As absurd as it seems now, it received great acclaim when proposed. It was soon displaced by less subjective and more secular methods of determining a plant's medicinal properties.

By the seventeenth and eighteenth centuries, science advanced to the formulating of hypotheses using more modern scientific methodology, which led to an improved understanding of physiology and provided a framework for testing medicines. The first half of the twentieth century saw advancements in medicine as causes of diseases were discovered and new drugs were isolated and synthesized. Many of these drugs were products from traditional, plant-derived extracts such as morphine, digitalis, quinine, and ephedrine. Plants are still being investigated as possible sources of wonder drugs, especially as potential antitumor agents.

In the New World, long before the settlers arrived, Native Americans learned the medicinal uses of the plants growing around them. Indeed, the highly developed cultures of the Aztecs, Mayas, and Incas may have been attributed in part to their valuing plants as medicines. Aboriginal knowledge of the native flora can be demonstrated for all but a few indigenous vegetable drugs. In fact, many of the plants used by Native Americans are included in drug formulas and pharmaceuticals in the United States and elsewhere. Extracts of the roots of may-apple were used as purgatives and for skin disorders and tumorous growth; today, may-apple alkaloids are used to treat lymphoblastic leukemia and several other cancers. The bark of the willow tree was used to relieve headaches and ease sore muscles. The active compound in willow bark is salicin, a derivative of which, acetylsalicylic acid, is today's aspirin. New Jersey tea was a favorite tea substitute during the American Revolution among the settlers, who noted that Native Americans used it frequently. Current research shows that this plant reduces high blood pressure.

According to Cherokee Indian legend, animals were the source of diseases. These diseases were inflicted on man to lessen his numbers, which was necessary to reduce man's destruction of the animals' environment, his slaughter of animals for food and skins, or his carelessness. On the other hand, plants were seen as man's friend and as a source for remedies "to defeat their [animals'] evil designs." When the conjurer or shaman was doubtful which plant to use to treat an ailment, the spirit of the appropriate plant suggested the proper treatment. It was believed that different animals caused different diseases, so treatments sometimes involved plants with animals in their name. Native American therapeutics also involved elements similar to the Doctrine of Signatures. For example, when a patient vomited yellow bile, the treatment of choice was yellowroot (*Xanthorhiza simplicissima,* plate 44).

In the 1600s, settlers came from the Old World, settling first near seaports. Along the South Carolina coast, English and French Huguenots developed a plantation system, first based on rice, then briefly indigo, and finally cotton. African slaves, as well as the colonists, quickly acquired Native American knowledge on the use of plants as remedies. The settlers also had access to European medical books and herbals. By the mid-nineteenth century, the medicine of the colonists contained elements of Native American and European medicine. In addition, the African slaves, who came from a culture that employed plants for remedies, discovered plants that could be used medicinally.

The development of folk medicines by coastal plantation slaves was a necessity. Plantations in the 1700s and 1800s were large and located along rivers or on the sea islands, such as Edisto Island and James Island. Communication between all but the adjacent plantations was difficult; trips to cities were even more difficult. Planters who maintained satisfactory medical facilities for the treatment of diseases were the exception, and those who did attempt to care for the slaves were fairly ignorant of good health practices. Except in the most severe cases, masters and overseers made their own diagnoses and prescribed remedies without the aid of a doctor. In addition, the planters generally left the plantations in the summer and moved to pineland villages or ocean villages to escape the ravages of malaria, leaving the slaves' care to overseers. More often than not, the overseer was unable or chose not to administer adequate medical care. Under these conditions, the slaves maintained their own medical practices, especially to cure everyday illnesses.

The use of native folk remedies was not confined to the African slaves or planters along the coast. The development of port cities and Native American trails created an entrance to the state's interior. Indentured servants, after serving out their time, sought freedom and opportunity in a new area. Swiss immigrants settled Purrysburgh on the Savannah River in Jasper County in 1726; in 1735 an influx of Germans settled in Orangeburg; Amelia township, covering roughly Calhoun County, was established by English settlers in the 1730s. In 1735 German Swiss settled a township that consisted of present Lexington County, southwest of the Saluda and Congaree Rivers; English and Germans settled around 1737 in the fork of the Congaree and Wateree Rivers, which later became Richland County; and the Welsh settled in the Pee Dee around 1736. In the early 1740s a southward migration occurred from Virginia and Pennsylvania, and in 1752 there were 40 families between Stevens Creek and the present-day town of Ninety Six. This influx from the north continued to the 1770s, consolidating the midlands and pushing northwest above present-day Lancaster, Fairfield, Newberry, Saluda, and Edgefield Counties. Treaties, wars, and purchases from the Creeks and Cherokees later opened the rest of the piedmont and mountain areas of the state.

Many of these inland settlers came with only meager supplies. It is not too surprising that they relied on the land for subsistence. The rich native flora satisfied many of their needs, including their medical needs. The comments entry under the species descriptions indicates if early pioneers used a plant as a folk remedy or for medicines.

The most important work dealing with the use of plants as medicine in the South was *Resources of the Southern Fields and Forest,* written by Dr. Francis Peyre Porcher in 1863. During the Civil War, when the South was cut off from imported drugs because of a naval blockade, it turned to its native resources for drugs, food, etc. The Surgeon General of the Confederate Army commissioned Dr. Porcher of St. John's Parish, Berkeley County, South Carolina, to explore the use of native plants in order, as Dr. Porcher stated in *Resources,* that "the physician in his private practice, the planter on his estate, or . . . the regimental surgeon in the field may collect these substances within reach, which are frequently quite as valuable as others obtained abroad." Within a year's time, Dr. Porcher published his extraordinary book in which he listed over 600 species of plants that were of some value in the South. In 1991 Norman Publishing reprinted it.

The use of folk remedies has not ceased in modern, rural South Carolina. Dr. Julia Morton, in her 1974 book *Folk Remedies of the Low Country,* documented that rural people still used local plants for folk remedies. Some of the uses can be attributed to the recent homeopathic movement that emerged at that time. For others, however, it represents a continuation of lives that are dictated by a rural lifestyle, poor economic status, unavailable medical facilities, and superstitions.

In recent years, the United States has seen an enormous increased interest in the use of herbs to treat or prevent disease. Duke (1997) defines an herb as "any medicinal plant." This second "green revolution" (the first involved the phenomenal increase in crop productivity in less-developed countries) has long been raging in Europe and Asia. It is late in coming to the United States because of the strict burden-of-proof for the safety and efficacy of medicines, as imposed by the United States FDA (Food and Drug Administration), and the understandable unwillingness by drug companies to spend the $200 to $500 million and the 10 to 12 years sometimes needed for FDA drug approval. Since medicinal herbs (whole plant parts) can not be patented, there is no economic incentive to prove the efficacy or safety of herbal remedies.

Two well-known and well-respected proponents of this new "green pharmacy" are Varro E. Tyler and James A. Duke. Tyler is conservative in his recommendations of herbal products and Duke is liberal. Both are Ph.D. scientists and argue strongly that "herbs are good medicine" (Duke, 1997) and that "rational herbal medicine is conventional medicine" (Tyler, 1994). They also argue that herbal therapies are often more effective, cheaper, safer, and have fewer side effects than pharmaceuticals. Duke notes that ginger, for example, has been proven to be more effective than Dramamine in treating motion sickness.

Until the publication of Duke's *The Green Pharmacy,* rational use of herbal medicines was difficult because of bewildering, contradictory information, and the FDA prohibited makers of herbal products from specifying medicinal or therapeutic use of herbs or detailing possible harmful interactions with other drugs. Duke remedies this glut of misinformation and the FDA's regulatory miasma by providing a rational basis for the healing uses of medicinal herbs.

The comments entry under the species descriptions includes comments by Duke and other sources on the potential use of native and naturalized plants as herbal medicines. These uses are provided to encourage an appreciation of plants as medicines and the need to preserve plant (and animal) biodiversity, locally, regionally, and globally.

EDIBLE WILD PLANTS

South Carolina is a paradise for anyone who wishes to become independent of commercial sources of food or for anyone who simply wishes to sample wild plants in a limited manner. Numerous native and naturalized plants in the state are sources of beverages or food; many appear in this book.

Almost anyone with a limited exposure to the outdoors is familiar with some common edible plants such as plums, blackberries, hickory nuts, blueberries and grapes. Only the experienced outdoor person, however, knows the true variety of edible wild plants. Many people hesitate to seek wild foods because there are so many poisonous plants. A careful observer, who takes time to study poisonous plants, can easily identify them. The best recommendation for someone serious about learning the edible and poisonous plants is to take an introductory course in plant taxonomy or field botany. For those unable to do so, frequent field trips with persons who are knowledgeable of the local plants will suffice.

The following are various categories of edible wild plants. Note that some species have parts that are included in more than one category.

Flour. A large number of plants can be used as breadstuff or can be ground into flour. These include cat-tail, groundnut, serviceberry, kudzu, and soft-stem bulrush.

Teas. The forests and fields abound with plants that can be used as substitutes for Asian teas. Many of the plants used as teas have a history of medicinal use. Others, however, are used because they possess a pleasant flavor, having come into use during the American Revolution when Asian tea was under embargo. Whatever their origin, tea substitutes have grown in popularity in recent years and are now widely used. Native and naturalized plants used for teas include witch-hazel, dewberry, yaupon, New Jersey tea, winged sumac, sweet goldenrod, and wax myrtle.

Pickles. A variety of native plants have been used throughout America as pickles. The plant part is first soaked in alum-water, then in salted water, and finally preserved by boiling in spiced vinegar. Roots, tubers, leafy young plants, flower buds, and young fruits have all been pickled. Wildflowers that can be pickled include, young pokeweed leaves, elderberry flowers, glasswort, red-bud flowers, and young flower heads of cat-tail.

Fritters. Fritters are prepared by cutting flower blossoms at the peak of bloom, dipping then into an egg batter, and then dropping them into hot fat until they are fried to a light-brown color. The fritters may be sprinkled with a variety of seasonings. Wildflowers that have been commonly used as fritters include elderberry, cat-tail, day-lily, and common dandelion.

Jellies and Marmalades. The local flora abounds with plants whose fruits can be made into jellies and marmalades and includes may-apple, red choke-berry, swamp rose, crab-apple, chickasaw plum, muscadine, persimmon, elder-berry, blueberries, huckleberries, white mulberry, dewberries, blackberries, hog plum, and viburnums.

Condiments and Seasonings. Numerous wildflowers can be used as sub-stitutes for traditional condiments and seasonings including wax myrtle, sas-safras, swamp rose, day-lily, elderberry, wild ginger, and red bay.

Wines and Beers. Throughout history many plants have been made into beer or wine. While all plant parts have been used, those made from the flow-ers and fruits are the most suitable. Local plants used for wines include dew-berries, blackberries, black cherry, common dandelion, elderberry, muscadine, and chickasaw plum; for beer, honey locust, persimmon, and catbrier.

Starchy Soups. Starchy soups are made from substances that, when boiled, thicken and also add nutrients. Three plants used in this way are blue violets, sassafras, and day-lily.

Fresh Fruits. Wildflowers producing edible fruits include may-apple, chickasaw plum, muscadine grape, maypop, elderberry, wild strawberry, white mulberry, partridge berry, blackberries, dewberries, huckleberries, blueberries, ground-cherries, and hawthorns.

Nuts and Large Seeds. Mockernut hickory, black walnut, and American hazelnut produce edible nuts, while pickerelweed, hog peanut, and sacred bean produce edible, large seeds.

Coffee Substitutes. In the local flora there are three caffeine-free species used as substitutes for coffee: common dandelion roots, persimmon fruits, and acorns.

Cooked Green Vegetables. Numerous wildflowers can be cooked and served like familiar garden vegetables. These include cat-tail, young pods of *Asclepias* spp., common dandelion, day-lily, pokeweed, young shoots of *Smilax*, common chickweed, wild garlic, sea rocket, cabbage palmetto, early win-ter-cress, and redbud.

Cold Drinks. Acid fruits used to make cold drinks include blackberries, dewberries, black cherry, winged sumac, elderberry, muscadine, red maple, sassafras, and maypops.

Salads. The following plants contain tender parts that can be eaten with-out cooking, including ones that can be used in place of lettuce or eaten raw:

young shoots of *Smilax* spp., cat-tail, chickweed, common dandelion, day-lily, violets, redbud, pickerelweed, and prickly sow-thistle.

Masticatories. Masticatories are plants that are chewed to relieve thirst. Some of the lesser known masticatories are sourgrass, horse sugar, and muscadine.

NATURALIZED PLANTS

Naturalized plants are plants native to another area that are thoroughly established in a new area. They are able to reproduce naturally, become well established, and spread without cultivation. The majority of flowering plants in disturbed sites are nonnative species that have replaced or supplemented native wildflowers. A quick glance at the section on ruderal communities in this book reveals how many nonnatives followed the early settlers across the Atlantic from Europe, and to a lesser extent, from other parts of the world. The list of naturalized plants is long: henbit, crimson clover, sour clover, common dandelion, wild carrot, yarrow, and woolly mullein, to name but a few. These ruderal species, which easily adapt to newly created or disturbed sites, quickly found a home. Approximately 10% of South Carolina's present vascular flora are considered nonnative.

In general, the nonnative, weedy species are what ecologists refer to as an r-strategists, species that occupy disturbed habitats, have a short growth form, reproduce early in life, have high fecundity, and have well-dispersed seeds. In disturbed areas, these characteristics give them a competitive advantage over most native species, and they quickly dominate. This is not to say, however, that native species do not occupy disturbed areas. Many natives were originally edge species and quickly found a home in disturbed sites. Ruderal areas, then, are dominated by native and nonnative species, but it is the ruderal areas that most nonnatives claim as their home in the New World.

The coastal area is home to hundreds of nonnative plants. This is easily understood when you consider the first cities were seaports. Seaports were sites of entry for these nonnatives, often arriving as hitchhikers with overseas shipments. Once established around the port cities, their propagules were unwittingly carried into the interior. As native habitats became altered, the nonnatives gained additional footholds. Drainage ditches lowered water tables and changed sloughs and wetlands to drier land. Woods were cleared for fields and homesites, and railroads bridged rivers that might have represented a barrier, if only temporarily, for the spread of nonnatives. Hardwood and pine forests were often clear-cut of timber, creating additional disturbed ground. One hundred and fifty thousand acres of tidal freshwater swamp forests and marshes along the coastal rivers were banked in the 1700s and 1800s, then cleared of vegetation to grow rice. After the rice industry collapsed in the early 1900s, the rice fields were abandoned, creating ideal sites for nonnative, aquatic weeds. With the discovery of electricity, free-flowing rivers were converted into lakes to provide waterpower to generate electricity. These lakes are ideal sites for exotic, aquatic weeds such as water hyacinth, water primrose, and alligator-weed.

Not all the nonnative species entered accidentally. Numerous species were purposefully brought from overseas to adorn plantation and city gardens. André Michaux introduced mimosa, popcorn tree, and China-berry shortly after he established his botanical garden near Charleston in 1786; all three have become naturalized and today are common. Rattlebox (*Crotalaria spectabilis*, plate 700), brought from Japan, was cultivated as a soil-building, green manure. It escaped and is one of our most noxious weeds in agricultural fields in the piedmont and coastal plain. Princess tree (*Paulownia tomentosa*, plate 640), introduced into North America in 1834 as an ornamental tree due to its large, upright clusters of purple flowers, has spread quickly beyond its cultivation along roadsides and streambanks throughout the state because its tiny, winged seeds are blown for considerable distances. Its ability to invade native woodlands is a serious concern. Three species of clover from the Old World, rabbit foot clover (plate 647), crimson clover (plate 648), and red clover (plate 649), brought over for erosion control, fodder, or green manure, now line major roads in the state. Early colonists introduced white mulberry (*Morus alba*, plate 664) for a silk industry that never materialized. The tree, however, became naturalized and often dominates disturbed areas such as dredge soil disposal sites in the coastal area (for example, Drum Island in Charleston Harbor).

Some nonnative species have become legend because of their aggressive nature. A grass that is causing a serious problem in coastal marshes is common reed (*Phragmites australis*, plate 692). It reproduces rapidly by rhizomes and long, leafy stolons and can quickly dominate a marsh to the exclusion of all native species. It first appeared in the South Carolina coastal area in the mid-1970s, primarily in dredge soil disposal sites along the Intracoastal Waterway. Some scientists believe that it is spread when its rhizomes are embedded in mud of the dredges, which move from site to site along the waterway. Because it has little food value for wildlife, its replacement of the more useful native forage species is a serious problem for wildlife managers.

Kudzu (*Pueraria lobata*, plate 696) was introduced into southern states from Asia in the 1920s and 1930s to stabilize eroded areas and roadsides. This exceedingly aggressive vine can grow up to 50 to 60 feet in a year and forms a continuous blanket of foliage over trees. Kudzu can quickly dominate waste areas and kill off competing vegetation by blocking sunlight. Since it can climb to the tops of tall trees, entire forest areas can be destroyed. Fortunately, it does not invade natural areas as readily and does not produce viable seeds in our area. The leaves and younger stems are highly sensitive to frost; however, older stems tend to be resistant to the coldest southern winters and quickly produce new growth in the spring.

Another event that might further shift the balance between nonnative and native species is the current program of planting wildflower strips along major roadways and vacant lots in cities. This is an ambitious program, and the results are usually spectacular. The number of these species, if any, that will become naturalized and replace native wildflowers waits to be seen.

To emphasize the extent to which nonnative species have become established in the New World, particularly in South Carolina, this book includes a chapter on the ruderal communities, where the majority of nonnative plants thrive. The comments entry under the species descriptions indicates which species are nonnative and their source of origin, if known.

DUCKWEEDS

The members of the duckweed family, Lemnaceae, are the smallest flowering plants (figure 4). Members range in size from *Wolffia*, the smallest, which is barely discernable to the naked eye, to *Spirodela polyrhiza,* the largest of the duckweeds (fronds are about 0.02″ long or wide). Duckweeds are aquatic plants, free-floating on or below the water surface. Aquatic habitats include sluggish freshwater ponds, pools, lakes, swamps, streams, drainage ditches, canals, and sloughs. Acidic waters with high organic content seem to favor duckweeds, although they are also found in crystal clear spring water.

Structurally the plants consist of a frond, or thallus, and are not differentiated into stems or leaves. The frond acts as a leaf. Asexual reproduction occurs by budding from the parent plant, with the daughter plant then separating or remaining attached by a short stipe, thus producing connected colonies. Sexual reproduction by flowers occurs infrequently; flowers are produced in small pouches or pits at the edge of the frond or on its upper surface. The flowers are too small to be seen with the naked eye.

In a given body of water, a species of duckweed can be present in small numbers one day and then occur in great abundance at another time. Several species can be intermixed or only a single species can occur. Often only the edge of a pond is populated, followed by a bloom that lasts for a few weeks, ultimately covering the pond surface with a dense growth. Within another few weeks most of the growth disappears from the open water and only the edge is populated. When a body of water dries up, the plants are often stranded in

FIGURE 4. Genera of Duckweeds (Family Lemnaceae).

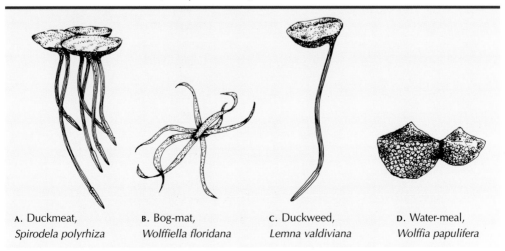

A. Duckmeat,
Spirodela polyrhiza

B. Bog-mat,
Wolffiella floridana

C. Duckweed,
Lemna valdiviana

D. Water-meal,
Wolffia papulifera

mats along the edge. As long as the substratum remains wet, the plants remain alive and can repopulate the system when it fills with water.

Duckweeds are used sparingly as food for a variety of waterfowl. Aquatic animals associated with the duckweeds probably contribute significantly to the food value of the diet.

Four genera of duckweeds occur in the South Carolina, all restricted to the sandhills, coastal plain, and maritime strand: *Spirodela* (duckmeat), *Lemna* (duckweed), *Wolffia* (water-meal), and *Wolffiella* (bog-mat). Plate 553 depicts a bloom of *Spirodela* and *Wolffiella* on a pond. The four genera are easily recognized with the naked eye or a hand lens. *Spirodela* has several roots per frond and is red beneath; *Lemna* has one root per frond and is green beneath; *Wolffia* consists of almost meal-like bodies without roots; and *Wolffiella* is made up of straplike bodies without roots. The preceding diagrams of the four genera will aid identification.

History of Field Botany in South Carolina

Initially, field botany in North America was primarily a process of exploring and describing new species. The unexplored American frontier contained a vast treasure of undescribed plants, providing fertile ground for early explorers. Often the objective of these explorations was to gather horticultural material for the gardens of western Europe. Sometimes field botanists did the exploring and wrote contributions based on their collections. More often, the explorer was simply the person who sent specimens back to a botanist at a herbarium, who then identified and described them. With the publication of Linnaeus' *Species Plantarum* in 1753, botanists had a workable system for naming plants. A burgeoning of field activity followed, and by the 1900s most taxa in North America had been formally described.

The role of the modern field botanist has changed. Today, field botanists study the geographic ranges of plants, the communities in which plants grow, and develop management plans for rare plants and their associated communities. New temperate species are still described but to a limited degree. New species generally are found in restricted habitats or are in plant groups that are taxonomically difficult.

South Carolina's contribution to the study of the flora of the southeastern United States is considerable. Not only did South Carolina provide native sons (Ravenel, Porcher, Elliott) for the advancement of botanical knowledge, but it also became home to noted naturalists and physicians (Michaux, Walter, Garden), who left their native Europe to come to the New World. These men settled in cities along the coast, mainly Charleston, and traveled extensively in the upcountry of South Carolina and the mountains of the Carolinas. During the colonial and antebellum periods, Charleston was the cultural and intellectual center in the South, and these early naturalists and physicians found fertile scientific ground for their studies. Early botany was centered in Charleston and along the coast. As the upcountry became settled, botanists like A. C. Moore of the University of South Carolina and Sumner A. Ives of Furman University continued the tradition of earlier field botanists. In the 1900s, major field botany studies in the state began to shift from Charleston to the major academic institutions such as the University of South Carolina, Clemson University, and Furman University.

This history is divided into five periods, beginning with the colonial period and ending with the retirement of botanist Wade T. Batson from the University of South Carolina in 1983. The divisions are somewhat arbitrary but aim to reflect the distinct periods that historians generally recognize. An individual's life that spans two periods is placed in the period in which the most significant contribution was made. Only a sketch is given on each, with a reference to their major contribution(s) to field botany. Through these brief biographies the authors present a historical summary of field botany in the state.

THE COLONIAL PERIOD: 1670–1785

John Lawson (?–1711)

John Lawson's sojourn in South Carolina was brief but productive. He was the first naturalist to record the natural history of the Carolinas. He was articulate and observant in his detailed account of his two-month journey from Charleston to the upper Catawba region in 1700. His *A New Voyage to Carolina* was published in London in 1709. Although *New Voyage* was primarily a natural history report, with much information on the monetary potential of the areas he visited, his report is laced with observations on the plant life he encountered and gives a glimpse of the richness of the early Carolina flora.

In the years following his journey, Lawson lived in North Carolina, working as a surveyor. During a later exploration, Tuscarora Indians put him to death.

Mark Catesby (1679–1749)

Catesby was a natural historian. England was his home, but during a trip to Virginia in 1712 (where he remained for seven years), he sent many plant specimens back to England and made plans to write a natural history of the southern colonies and the Bahamas.

He returned to the New World, arriving in Charleston in 1722, and spent four years traveling through South Carolina, Georgia, and Florida. The result of these travels was the first volume of *The Natural History of Carolina, Florida, and the Bahamas,* completed in 1731 after he returned to England. He wrote a second volume and an appendix in 1743 and 1748, respectively. These books are filled with fascinating illustrations of the fauna and flora he saw, with detailed and often quaint descriptions typical of the writings of early naturalists.

His publications contained a wealth of previously unknown descriptions on the natural history of the New World, including South Carolina. His portrayals of the plants that he discovered were brought to the attention of gardeners, including native trees and shrubs such as dahoon holly, cherry-laurel, fringe-tree, and catalpa. Indeed, these became incorporated into gardens in early Charleston.

Thomas Walter honored Mark Catesby's contributions to field botany and natural history by naming the beautiful pine lily in his honor: *Lilium catesbaei* Walter (plate 389). Other plants named to commemorate Catesby appear throughout this book.

Alexander Garden, M.D. (1730–1792)

The life and contributions to botany of Alexander Garden are well documented in Edmund and Dorothy Berkeley's book *Dr. Alexander Garden of Charles Town* (1969). Alexander Garden was born in Scotland in 1730, and after completing his medical training in 1752, came to Charles Town [Charleston] and established a medical practice. Here he remained until 1782. He remained loyal to the Crown during the Revolution, which led to his banishment to England after the war. During his tenure in Charleston, he became one of the most prominent physicians of colonial times and was an influential participant in the city's pre-Revolutionary intellectual and social life.

His contributions to science are well documented, going well beyond the mere collection of specimens. His intellectual curiosity led him to investigate a wide range of scientific problems, including plants and animals and new medical treatments, but also diverse subjects such as ocean currents, minerals, and meteorology.

Garden made no landmark discoveries in botany that would place him among the scientific great. His publications were few; however, he made discoveries that were valued by others of his own day and were useful in shaping the early history of botany. He sent numerous specimens to Linnaeus, accompanied with authentic information from the field, which greatly contributed to Linnaeus' classical work. Although he discovered and described a number of new genera and species (including *Halesia*), few were credited to him since he did not publish them himself.

Linnaeus commemorated Garden by naming the *Gardenia* after him, and Murray honored him with the specific epithet of *Fothergilla gardenii* (plate 480).

William Bartram (1739–1823)

William Bartram was born in Philadelphia, the son of the famous botanist and naturalist John Bartram. In his youth he shared his father's interests in natural history and accompanied him on an expedition to Florida from 1765 to 1766. He soon acquired a reputation as a botanist in his own right. He secured a commission from a British botanist, John Fothergill, to explore what is now the southeastern United States and to search for rare and useful productions of nature, chiefly in the vegetable kingdom. The record of his journey during a five-year odyssey (1773–1778), *Travels through North and South Carolina, Georgia, East & West Florida,* first published in 1791, was a scientific marvel and was translated into several languages. He wrote with reverence about his travels. Though he attempted to be as objective as possible, his imagination and emotion were so strong that some of his descriptions and narration have to be taken in context. Still, he provides a vivid description of the natural history of the Carolinas, Georgia, and west Florida (Bartram, 1791).

While traveling in the mountains, he states: "The Panax quinquefolium, or Ginseng, now appears plentifully on the North exposure of the hill, growing out of the rich mellow humid earth amongst the stones or fragments of rocks." His description of savannas and pine forests add support to ecologists' opinion that they were more common than today. His descriptions of the plant life of South Carolina still fascinate botanists.

Thomas Walter (circa 1740–1789)

Thomas Walter was born in Hampshire, England, and according to most accounts, immigrated to South Carolina sometime in the 1760s. Sometime thereafter he settled along the bank of the Santee River in Berkeley County. There appears to be no reason given in any account as to why he made this immigration to America, and in particular why he settled along the bank of the Santee River. But he did! Here in the solitude of the Santee wilderness, he led a productive life as scientist, family man, merchant, planter, politician, community leader, and patriot in the Revolution.

Walter's *Flora Caroliniana,* published in England in 1788, was a landmark scientific work. It was the first flora guide of a region in North America that used Linnaeus' system of classification. He worked, as he said in the preface to *Flora Caroliniana,* with "no help for him beyond that which Systema Naturae and Genera et Species Plantarum [provided]. . . . [He] investigated no botanical gardens. . . . [He gathered] more than a thousand types . . . from an area no greater than that of a line which can enclose fifty miles" (Rembert, 1980). Many considered *Flora Caroliniana* as the most complete work on American botany during the eighteenth century.

Most significant in the 1000 or so plants contained in *Flora Caroliniana* are 88 species from the Carolinas that Walter first named and described. The complete list appears in a history of Walter, *Thomas Walter, Carolina Botanist,* written by David H. Rembert (1980).

THE ANTEBELLUM PERIOD: 1785–1860

André Michaux (1746–1802)

The life and contributions of André Michaux are well documented by Henry and Elizabeth Savage in their 1986 book *André and François André Michaux.* In addition, an article by David H. Rembert (1979) outlining the plants Michaux named, first described, or that were named in his honor, fully brings to life this remarkable eighteenth-century botanist.

France's Louis XVI sent André Michaux to the American colonies to investigate plants that could possibly be introduced into France. He arrived in New York in 1785, collected plants, which he sent back home, then tried to set up a garden in New Jersey. He quickly realized that he needed a warmer climate, so he moved to Charleston in September, 1786. He purchased 111 acres outside Charleston (near the present Charleston International Airport) and established a garden and nursery, where he grew numerous native plants as well as introductions from other lands, and sent home plants and seeds.

He used Charleston as a base for his many expeditions around North America. He went to Florida in 1788; Oconee County, South Carolina, and Georgia in 1788. He visited North Carolina and then traveled from western Virginia to Philadelphia in 1789; New England and Canada in 1792; Kentucky and Tennessee in 1793 (on a diplomatic mission); the Carolina mountains in 1794; and on his last trip, the Mississippi River through North Carolina, Tennessee, and Kentucky, then into Ohio and Missouri.

During the eleven years Michaux spent in North America and in Charleston, he named 26 genera, 188 species, and 4 varieties (Rembert, 1979). He also named 95 species and varieties that botanists have since placed in other genera. The material Michaux gathered during his eleven years in North

America was the basis for *Flora Boreali-Americana*. His son, François André Michaux, arranged its publication in 1803, a year after Michaux's death. It was the first flora of North America based entirely on plants collected by the author.

Michaux lost the support of the French government for his work in North America in 1796, and with his funds depleted, he returned to France, never to return to Charleston or North America. He died in Madagascar of a fever in 1802. Prior to his death, the French government sold his garden in Charleston. No trace of the garden exists today, although a monument at the site of the garden honors Michaux.

Michaux's name is remembered in another way. He introduced into American horticulture many plants from overseas, including the common garden camellia, *Camellia japonica*, mimosa, crape myrtle, tea olive, china-berry, ginkgo, and *Azalea indica*. No one contributed more to the beauty of the gardens of Charleston than Michaux. Today, these species grace many gardens in and around the lowcountry.

One of South Carolina's most esteemed statesman, General Charles Cotesworth Pinckney, a signer of the Declaration of Independence, was honored by Michaux who named the fever tree, found in Jasper and Beaufort Counties, for Pinckney: *Pinckneya pubens* Michaux (plate 463). Michaux, in turn, was honored by other botanists for his contributions. Poiret named the beautiful Carolina lily (*Lilium michauxii* Poiret, plate 153) for him. Five other plants honor his name.

One of South Carolina's most beautiful mountain wildflowers, Oconee bells (plate 123), was first discovered by Michaux on the Keowee River. It was not included in his *Flora Boreali-Americana,* but Asa Gray found a specimen collected by Michaux in Paris and named it in honor of Dr. Wilkins Short. Although Gray twice searched for the plant, he never found it. It was finally located by an amateur botanist along the Catawba River, near Marion, North Carolina.

John Drayton (1766–1822)

John Drayton was born near Charleston, and after completing his legal education in England, returned to Charleston to practice law. He had a distinguished civic career and was elected to his first term as governor of South Carolina in 1800. After his political career, he served as an appointed judge of the district of South Carolina until his death.

His major contribution to botany in South Carolina was his book *A View of South Carolina,* published in 1802 (and reprinted in 1972). The book is a broad-based description of the state's natural history, geography, and agriculture. It contains the first attempt to catalogue the flora of the state, providing a twenty-four page list of native plants and a three-page list of introduced species.

Most interesting, however, is his description of the shell accumulations on Fort Johnson, which he attributes to Native Americans. Drayton describes ". . . a mound of oyster shells . . . of a circular form . . . measuring around two hundred and forty paces. [He] relates that it was an Indian Fort . . . as they were not possessed of proper tools for breaking the earth. . . . They could, however, carry on their heads these shells from neighboring shores; and by continual additions raise this curious structure."

Associated with two of the circular forms (referred to today as shell rings) along the coast are two shell mounds of questionable origin, one about 10 feet high and the other about 30 feet high. Surely if they could construct the circular structures by this method, they could have constructed the adjacent, higher shell mounds by the same method. Drayton's narration gives evidence that the mounds, indeed, like the circular structures, are of Native American origin.

From 1997 to 2000, botanists have been studying plants and communities associated with calcium-rich soils along the maritime strand. The shell mounds have been found to harbor numerous rare species. Native Americans, then, apparently created shell mounds that contributed to the establishment of rare species and communities that thrive in a calcium-rich environment.

John L. E. W. Shecut, M.D. (1770–1836)

John Shecut was prominent among the early botanists of South Carolina. Shecut was the son of French Huguenot immigrants, who after being driven from France, came to the New World and settled in Beaufort, South Carolina. Dr. Shecut was born in 1770 and received his M.D. in Philadelphia in 1791. He returned to Charleston and practiced medicine until his death.

Like most early physicians, the study of botany was a natural corollary to medicine. He was a versatile man with a number of interests that engaged his attention. Botany was a subject to which he devoted a great deal of time. His principal botanical work was *Flora Caroliniensis* published in 1806. In this work he claimed no other merit than the design of promoting a taste for the study of botany by simplifying the Linnaean system.

Stephen Elliott (1771–1830)

Stephen Elliott was born in Beaufort, South Carolina. He studied medicine at Yale College and graduated at age 20. After graduating in 1791, he returned to Beaufort County to become a southern planter. Elliott never practiced medicine.

In 1794 Elliott was elected to represent his district, St. Helena Parish, as a member of the South Carolina legislature. In 1800 he turned his attention to his private affairs. In 1808, however, he was elected to the state senate where he served until 1812. When the State Bank of South Carolina was established in 1812, he was appointed president. He resigned his seat in the senate and moved to Charleston, where he became active in civic, cultural, and scientific activities.

Between 1800 and 1808, Elliott lived in comparative retirement on one of his plantations in Beaufort County. It was during this period that he wrote his major work, *A Sketch of the Botany of South Carolina and Georgia*. It was published in a series of separate papers between 1816 and 1824 and finally bound into two large volumes. Although it was published more than 175 years ago, taxonomists working on the flora of the southeast today still consult his *Sketch*. In this major work, he described hundreds of plants new to science, many of them from his original collections, with minute details in both Latin and English. He made copious notes on collection sites, habitats, flowering and fruiting times, and personally drew the plates to illustrate the grasses. Many of the specimens that he used to first describe a new species (the type specimen) are in the Elliott Herbarium, which is housed in the Charleston Museum. Some of the plants featured in this book that bear Elliott as the authority are *Sabatia gentianoides* Elliott (plate 397), *Rudbeckia mollis* Elliott (plate 579), *Prunus umbellata* Elliott (plate 429), *Carex glaucescens* Elliott (plate 506), *Xyris fimbriata* Elliott (plate 509), and *Panicum amarum* Elliott (plate 579).

Elliott was certainly a man of many talents and interests. When the American Geological Society was founded in 1819, Elliott was one of the original vice presidents. His lifelong interest in education is well documented. He was a founding trustee of Beaufort College and served as a trustee of the South Carolina College [now the University of South Carolina] and the College of Charleston. He presented numerous papers on diverse topics before learned societies. He was a founder of the Literary and Philosophical Society of South Carolina and helped establish the Southern Review, a distinguished quarterly magazine to which he contributed many articles.

Elliott is honored by the name of one of the South's most beautiful shrubs. Elliott collected the shrub near Waynesboro, Georgia, around 1808. It was sent to Henry Muhlenberg, who named the genus in Elliott's honor. The plant, called Georgia plume, is technically *Elliottia racemosa* Muhlenberg ex Elliott. It occurs in about three dozen locations, all in Georgia. Although attributed to South Carolina, no extant populations are known to exist.

James MacBride, M.D. (1784–1817)

James MacBride was commemorated by Stephen Elliott when he named *Macbridea pulchra* Elliott in his honor. Today, it is called *Macbridea caroliniana* (Walter) Blake and is pictured in plate 452. MacBride was one of the four botanists of St. John's Parish, Berkeley County (along with F. P. Porcher, W. H. Ravenel, and Thomas Walter), who added much to our knowledge of the flora of the state and gives Berkeley County a unique position in botanical history.

Like many earlier botanists, MacBride was a physician. He was educated at Yale and practiced medicine first in Pineville in Berkeley County, and then in Charleston. He died at 33, depriving science of a brilliant mind that undoubtedly would have made major contributions to botany. Elliott said MacBride was "a gentleman, who uniting great sagacity and talent, to extensive and accurate botanical knowledge, [made] the medical properties of our plants a subject of careful investigation" (Taylor, 1998).

Evidently, his only scientific paper was a letter to Sir James E. Smith, president of the Linnaean Society, on the botany of pitcher-plants. "On the Power of *Sarracenia adunca* to Entrap Insects" was read before the Philosophical Transactions of the Royal Society in 1815. *Sarracenia adunca* is *Sarracenia minor* Walter (plate 377) of today's taxonomy. The complete text of this letter appears in *South Carolina Naturalists* (Taylor, 1998) and vividly demonstrates MacBride's keen intellect and scientific mind.

Reverand John Bachman (1790–1874)

John Bachman is best known for his association with John James Audubon. Audubon arrived in Charleston in 1831, and he and Bachman became close friends. Bachman lent valuable aid to Audubon during his work on *Birds of America* and *Ornithological Biography*. In 1840 Audubon and Bachman collaborated on their great contribution to American mammalogy, *The Viviparous Quadrupeds of North America;* Bachman wrote the text.

Bachman was minister of St. John's Lutheran Church in Charleston and between 1848 and 1853 served as professor of natural history at the College of Charleston. He was an avid naturalist, being proficient in ornithology and mammalogy, and he made valuable collections of birds and mammals for the Charleston Museum.

Bachman was also a credible field botanist. In the mid-1830s he published the *Catalogue of Phaenogamous Plants and Ferns, Native or Naturalized, Found Growing in the Vicinity of Charleston, South Carolina.* Undoubtedly his knowledge of plants helped in his works with Audubon. Although he did not make a major contribution to botany, his work contributes to the history of field botany.

Lewis R. Gibbes, M.D. (1810–1894)

Lewis Gibbes graduated from the South Carolina College in 1829 and taught mathematics at his alma mater. While in Columbia, he catalogued the plants of the Columbia area and in 1835 published *A Catalogue of the Phaenogamous Plants of Columbia, S.C., and Its Vicinity.* He moved to Charleston (his boyhood home) to complete his medical education, which he had started in Columbia. He remained in Charleston for the rest of his life. Gibbes was one of the founders of the Elliott Society of Natural History and served as its president in 1857.

Gibbes's *Botany of Edings' Bay* (1859), which appears in its entirety in *South Carolina Naturalists* (Taylor, 1998), gives a wonderful account of this barrier island along the South Carolina coast in Charleston County, north of Edisto Beach State Park and adjacent to Jeremy Inlet. The barrier island was the location of Edingsville, the summer home of Edisto Island planters who sought refuge from malaria in the summer months. The sea today has claimed Edings' Bay, along with the village. Only a narrow shrub thicket remains at the high tide line, and this is constantly moving landward as erosion continues.

Gibbes's essay on Edings' Bay is the earliest floristic account of a barrier island in the state. He gives detailed descriptions of the plant life on the island. Although he made several mistakes in his species identifications (he mentions *Ilex cassine,* cassena, which was undoubtedly yaupon, *Ilex vomitoria*), it is still a significant botanical work as a baseline for present-day studies of the maritime strand.

Henry William Ravenel (1814–1887)

Henry Ravenel was one of the South's leading botanists of the Civil War era. His life and contributions to botany are well documented in his published private journal (Childs, 1947) and in Haygood's biography (1987).

Ravenel was born in St. John's Parish, Berkeley County, on May 19, 1814. He was descended from a long line of prominent French Huguenots who made the South Carolina lowcountry their home after leaving France in 1685. He graduated from South Carolina College in 1832 and returned to St. John's Parish, where he settled on North Hampton Plantation and become a prosperous planter, scientist, family man, and civic leader. He remained there until 1853, when for health reasons, he moved his family to Aiken, where the air was less humid. There he remained until his death in 1887.

Ravenel was born in the same region (St. John's Parish) that produced Thomas Walter, Francis P. Porcher, and James MacBride. Sometime after he began life as a planter, he met Charles Olmstead who taught Ravenel how to make plant collections. From that time on, Ravenel turned much of his energy toward the study of botany, spending much of his time in the field, especially in and around St. John's Parish.

Ravenel critically studied the seed plants of South Carolina, but his main area of expertise was cryptogamic botany; the fungi were his specialty. He discovered and described a large number of new species of fungi and also a few new species of seed plants. The best known of his many works was *The Fungi Carolina Exsiccati,* published in five volumes from 1853 to 1860. This was the first published series of named specimens of American fungi. One genus and fifty new species of fungi were named after him. For a long time, he and his friend Dr. M. A. Curtis were the only Americans who specifically knew the fungi of the United States.

Ravenel gained international fame for his scientific studies and corresponded with Asa Gray, Edward Tuckerman, Moses Curtis, and Alvan W. Chapman, great scientists of the time. In 1849 he was elected as a correspondent of the Academy of Natural Sciences and was a correspondent for other world-renowned societies.

The Civil War left Ravenel financially wanting. To make a living, he turned to running his seed business, writing and editing for agricultural journals, and collecting and classifying plants for other botanists. During this time, he was also able to make significant contributions to field botany, as is evidenced by the list of his published works.

Although Ravenel was mostly honored by having fungi named in his honor, he is also honored by two vascular plants that occur in South Carolina: *Eriocaulon ravenelii* Chapman and *Eryngium aquaticum* var. *ravenelii* (Gray) Mathias & Constance. The Charleston Museum and Converse College have a herbarium of vascular plants collected by Ravenel.

Incidently, Ravenel is the great-great uncle of the first author.

THE CIVIL WAR AND THE POSTBELLUM PERIOD: 1860–1900

The years of the Civil War and Reconstruction were periods of botanical stagnation in South Carolina and throughout the South. Economic collapse and social upheaval left little time or energy for activities that were not related to economic survival. Only two persons, both physicians, were able to make any significant contributions to botany during these years: Francis P. Porcher and Joseph H. Mellichamp.

Francis Peyre Porcher, M.D. (1824–1895)

Francis Porcher was another product of St. John's Parish, Berkeley County, who made an inestimable contribution to the botany of the South. His boyhood home was Ophir Plantation in St. John's Parish. He was a linear descendent of Isaac Porcher, M.D., an early French Huguenot immigrant to Carolina. He was also a descendent of Thomas Walter on his maternal side.

Porcher obtained his A.B. from the South Carolina College [now the University of South Carolina] in 1844 and his medical degree from the Medical College of South Carolina in 1847. After graduation, he spent two years in Europe obtaining medical experience before returning to Charleston, where he spent the rest of his life practicing medicine and gaining international acclaim.

Like most early physicians, the study of botany was a practical corollary. He was the first honor graduate in medical college and wrote a thesis *A Medico-Botanical Catalogue of the Plants and Ferns of St. John's Parish, Berkeley, South Carolina.* This was followed by *A Sketch of the Medical Botany of South Carolina.* These two works were the foundation of his classic book, *Resources of the Southern Fields and Forests.*

Dr. Porcher became a surgeon in the Confederate Army and served first in the Holcombe Legion until 1862, then at the Naval Hospital in Norfolk, and finally at the South Carolina Hospital at Petersburg. While there, the Surgeon General detailed him to write a book documenting the native plants that could be used as substitutes for drugs that were unavailable to the army because of the Northern blockade. In a year's time, in the heat of the war, he produced the book, in which he said "the physician in his private practice, the planter on his estate, or . . . the regimental surgeon in the field may collect these substances within reach, which are frequently quite as valuable as others obtained abroad." *Resources* was published in 1863 and listed over 600 species of plants that were of value to the South. This book has been credited with maintaining the Southern war effort for many months. So complete was this book, revised and enlarged in 1869, that it is still referred to today. Norman Publishing republished it in 1991.

The book also offered many practical suggestions to the housekeeper and noted many substitutes that had potential industrial applications. The book was so encompassing that it prompted interest in the collection of plants, adding greatly to our knowledge of the distribution of plants in the state and in the South.

The first author, a cousin of Dr. Porcher, has a copy of Chapman's *Flora of the Southern United States* that Dr. Porcher once owned. Porcher made annotations throughout the book. One note is quite interesting: "My mother saw a plant in St. John's with red flowers—near the Barrows—F. P. P." The annotation is next to *Cornus florida*. Dr. Porcher was also an avid collector, and many of his specimens remain on deposit at the Charleston Museum Herbarium.

Joseph Hinson Mellichamp, M.D. (1829–1903)

Joseph Mellichamp, physician and botanist, was born in St. Luke's Parish in South Carolina, and graduated from the South Carolina College in 1849 and from the Medical College of South Carolina in 1852. He practiced medicine in Bluffton, in Beaufort County, and remained there, with the exception of the time when he was a surgeon in the Confederate Army and in his declining years.

Little is known about his botanical work. Like many physicians of his time, botany was a special interest to him. Although his medical practice made strong demands on his time, he found time for botanical research and collecting. His main contributions to field botany were the specimens he provided to other botanists working on various flora. He corresponded with major botanists, sending them specimens collected from around Bluffton, an area that harbored many of the rare species described by Walter, Michaux, and Elliott. He rediscovered *Pinus elliottii,* a pine Elliott considered a form of loblolly pine. The botanist George Englemann gave Mellichamp credit for its rediscovery and stated: "Without his diligent investigations, ample information and copious specimens, this paper could not have been written" (Gee, 1918). Also, Mellichamp's collection of a specimen of *Forestiera* in the Bluffton area was used by Loran C. Anderson when he described *Forestiera godfreyi* (plate 605) in 1985.

1900–1952: THE BEGINNING OF MODERN FIELD BOTANY

As the South and South Carolina were emerging from the shackles of Reconstruction, a rebirth was beginning in science and intellectual curiosity. One prominent individual that kept the flame of scientific curiosity alive during the Reconstruction and into the 1900s in South Carolina was Andrew C. Moore. With Moore's refusal to let ignorance prevail during the period during and after the Reconstruction, South Carolina once again became a fertile ground for scientific inquiry, and field botany was no exception. Botanists such as Small from the New York Botanical Garden, Wells, Coker, and Totten from the University of North Carolina, and Ives, Hunt, and Bragg, began studying the flora of the state. But at this time it was Moore that did more than anyone to keep scientific inquiry alive for a new generation of students in South Carolina.

Andrew Charles Moore (1866–1928)

Andrew Moore received a Bachelor of Arts from the South Carolina College [now the University of South Carolina] in 1887. After serving as a public school administrator in South Carolina and Alabama, he did graduate work at the University of Chicago (1888–1889). In 1900 he joined the faculty at the South Carolina College, and served as head of the Department of Biology from its inception (1905) until his death in 1928. Twice he served as acting president of the college.

Moore's greatest influence was speaking out on the poor state of scientific activity in South Carolina. He stated in an address to the South Carolina Academy of Science in 1925: "It is now recognized the world over that great educational institutions have two duties to perform—first to teach, that is to transmit the acquired treasurers of learning to the rising generations, and second to increase the treasure by original contributions through research" (Sanders and Anderson, 1999). He was also an outspoken opponent of the Fundamentalists' position of prohibiting the teaching of Darwinism, atheism, agnosticism, or evolution in schools.

Throughout his career Moore won high public acclaim for his outstanding service to the college and the state. He is little known, however, for his botany. He work on sporogenesis in *Pallavicinia* led him to coin the term meiosis six years prior to its broad historical recognition in the biological sciences. Although he was not primarily a field botanist, he did have a cursory interest in collecting, and started the herbarium in 1907. His collection of about 200 plants from the Columbia and Spartanburg areas was the initial collection for the herbarium. The herbarium was subsequently named in his honor and is called the A. C. Moore Herbarium. The University of South Carolina Arboretum on Blossom Street in Colombia was dedicated in his honor in 1938.

John Kunkel Small, Ph.D. (1869–1938)

John K. Small was renowned for his research on the flora of the southeastern United States. After receiving his Ph.D. from Columbia University, he became curator of the university's herbarium. In 1898 he became curator of the newly founded New York Botanical Garden, where he devoted his life's work. His writings on botanical subjects included more than 450 books and papers. His primary interest was the flora of Florida, where he did research for 36 years. Of particular significance are his photographs of Indian mounds and various views of natural hummocks before early development destroyed them. His collection of photographs is housed at the Florida State Archives.

In 1933 the University of North Carolina published his *Manual of the Southeastern Flora*, which remained the standard manual for the southeast until publication of the *Manual of the Vascular Flora of the Carolinas* (Radford et al., 1968). So complete was Small's manual that many of the distribution records cited in the *Manual* and Alan Weakley's *Flora of the Carolinas and Virginia* (1999) are based on Small's fieldwork.

Small did not conduct extensive field studies in South Carolina. Occasionally, however, on his trips to Florida, he made stops in South Carolina to document aspects of the flora. In 1916, at the request of Dr. Rose, he spent three days cactus hunting on the coast, mainly at the Isle of Palms. He documented this study in an article in the *Journal of the New York Botanical Garden* (1917).

William Chambers Coker, Ph.D. (1872–1953)

William Coker was born in Hartsville, South Carolina, the son of Major James Lide Coker, who helped to found Coker College for Women in Hartsville. Dr. Coker received his undergraduate education from the University of South

Carolina and his Ph.D. from Johns Hopkins University. In 1902 he became an associate professor at the University of North Carolina, and in 1908 he became chairman of the newly established Botany Department.

Coker's major interest was mycology (the study of fungi); however, he also had an interest in the woody flora of the southeast. In 1934 he teamed with his former student, Dr. Henry R. Totten (1892–1974), and published *Trees of the Southeastern States* (revised in 1937 and 1945). Their book was the first that dealt exclusively with the distribution and ecology of trees of the southeast. Not only did they rely on their fieldwork, but they also researched the work of previous botanists to make as complete a record of the tree flora of the southeast as possible. They also made extensive use of herbarium records to document distributions.

Throughout the book are notes on South Carolina trees. For example, on *Pinus glabra* Walter: "This is a beautiful tree of damp coastal woods in our area from the lower Santee River in South Carolina southward to central and western Florida. It is plentiful along much of the highway between Charleston and Beaufort, South Carolina." And on *Pinckneya pubens* Michaux: "Mrs. Wilder of Beaufort, S.C., says there are one large plant and several ones on the farm of Mr. Johnson near Bluffton, S.C."

The wealth of information on trees documented in this book is invaluable and will certainly be a major reference in a future book that updates the woody flora of South Carolina.

Laura M. Bragg (1881–1978)

Laura Bragg came to Charleston in 1909 as librarian to the Charleston Museum. From Northbridge, Massachusetts, she brought considerable talent to the museum. She had a background in natural sciences, with an interest in botany, and immediately began conducting field surveys. Apparently her main interest was ferns; she published an article on ferns of the coastal region. She also became interested in collecting in the upcountry and worked with A. B. Massey, a botanist at Clemson College. She made a good collection of plants from Oconee and Pickens Counties for the museum. Her collections are part of the museum's extensive herbarium.

Bragg became director of the Charleston Museum in 1920 and served in this position until 1930. The added administrative responsibilities and a growing interest in cultural and historical activities left little time for her botanical interests in later years. She is remembered as one of the first woman to take an active interest in the flora of South Carolina.

Sumner A. Ives, Ph.D. (1882–1944)

Sumner Ives was a native of Maine and spent most of his life as a biology teacher in liberal arts colleges of the South. He did his undergraduate work at Wake Forest College, and then went to the University of Chicago for his M.S. and Ph.D. He came to Furman University in 1926 and served on the faculty until 1944. During this time he introduced countless students to the wonders of the natural world, including field botany. Three of his students, Drs. Leland

Rodgers, Wade T. Batson, and Albert E. Radford, became outstanding field botanists.

Ives did extensive collecting in the 1930s and 1940s, greatly adding to the knowledge of the piedmont and mountain flora. Furman University's herbarium is today officially designated as the Sumner A. Ives Herbarium.

Kenneth W. Hunt, Ph.D. (1909–1995)

Kenneth Hunt was a professor at the College of Charleston from 1937 to 1946. He left for a position at Antioch College in 1946. Although his tenure in South Carolina was brief, he made significant contributions to the study of the flora of coastal South Carolina. His publication "The Charleston Woody Flora" (Hunt, 1947), was a well-researched and well-written article. Many of his records have been cited by botanists working on South Carolina's flora. One of the most interesting records is a collection of star-vine (*Schisandra glabra*) in beech woods along SC Highway 61 near Magnolia Gardens. Numerous searches have been made in this area, but no one has been able to relocate star-vine. It is not known from any site in the state today. Another of Hunt's articles, "Floating Mats on A Southeastern Coastal Plain Reservoir" (Hunt, 1943), is prophetic in that it outlined plant succession in aquatic habitats, which is occurring today in the abandoned rice fields of the Cooper River. His annotated fern checklist (Hunt, 1942) of the vicinity of Charleston added to the work of Laura Bragg and Velma D. Matthews. Hunt made many collections of plants in the coastal area; his specimens are on deposit in the Charleston Museum Herbarium.

1952–1983: THE WADE THOMAS BATSON ERA IN SOUTH CAROLINA

Two important events shaped field botany in South Carolina beginning in the early 1950s: The emergence of the University of North Carolina at Chapel Hill as a regional center of botany and the beginning of Wade T. Batson's tenure at the University of South Carolina in 1952.

Albert E. Radford, Ph.D. (1918–), Harry E. Ahles (1924–1981), and Clyde Ritchie Bell, Ph.D. (1921–)

In 1968 Radford, Ahles, and Bell, working out of the Botany Department at Chapel Hill, published their landmark *Manual of the Vascular Flora of the Carolinas*. In 1956 these botanists began an intensive, systematic, county by county survey of North and South Carolina to obtain representative material for distributional data. They collected more than 200,000 specimens that served as the primary reference material for the *Manual*. A summary of the flora of the Carolinas included in the *Manual* revealed a total of 4673 taxa of vascular plants.

With the publication of the *Manual*, botanists finally had a ready reference to see where plant distributional gaps occurred in the Carolinas. Field botanists in both states began filling in distributional gaps, reporting their findings in scientific papers and depositing voucher specimens in herbariums. In the 33 years since the publication of the *Manual*, much information on the flora of the Carolinas has been compiled. The *Manual*, in all its printings, will undoubtedly be a major floristic resource for years to come.

Wade Thomas Batson, Ph.D. (1912–)

Wade Batson (figure 5) was born in Marietta, Greenville County. He is one of the many outstanding botanists born in South Carolina who remained in his home state throughout his career. He received his B.S. degree from Furman University in 1934 and his Ph.D. from Duke University in 1952. At Duke he studied under H. L. Blomquist and obtained a sound background in taxonomy and field botany.

Dr. Batson came to the University of South Carolina in 1952 and retired in 1983. During this time, he was director of the A. C. Moore Herbarium, taught graduate and undergraduate courses, and published four books as well as numerous scientific papers on field botany. He received the Meritorious Teaching Award from the Association of Southeastern Biologists in 1968, served as president of the South Carolina Academy of Sciences in 1968. Upon his retirement in 1983, he was named Distinguished Professor Emeritus. In 1995 he was inducted into the South Carolina Hall of Science and Technology, and USC presented him with its Distinguished Teaching Award.

It was in the outdoor classroom, however, that Dr. Batson made his greatest contribution. No one who spent a semester enrolled in his spring, fall, or summer flora course will ever forget the experience. Dr. Batson's enthusiasm for and knowledge of the flora of South Carolina was contagious. The woods and fields no longer were a mass of brown and green, but became a field of wood-lilies or windflowers. Long after leaving school, students could still recall the scientific names of plants they learned in his courses. He worked hard to make his courses stimulating and informative and was a friend to every student he taught. Years after graduating, his former students still seek his advice on any number of subjects.

FIGURE 5.
Wade Thomas Batson.

No botanist in the history of South Carolina has been responsible for training more graduate students in field botany. The following graduate students of Dr. Batson became field botanists or pursued closely related fields and have made significant contributions to field botany in South Carolina: Cynthia Aulbach-Smith, John M. Barry, Leonard H. Buff, Caroline Crewz, W. Michael Dennis, Mark A. Dutton, Victoria C. Hollowell (Dr. Batson's last Ph.D. student and one of the scientific reviewers of this book), Hubert Hill, John F. Logue, Joseph N. Pinson, Albert B. Pittman, Richard D. Porcher, Douglas A. Rayner, Richard Stalter, Lawrence F. Swails, Jr., and Randy G. Westbrooks. Today, these students continue the lessons they learned under Dr. Batson, conducting research and introducing new students to the wonders of the natural world of plants.

The authors fondly and respectfully dedicated this book to Dr. Batson.

FIELD BOTANY TODAY IN SOUTH CAROLINA

The glory years of the Batson Era are gone, and the number of field botanists being trained today at the University of South Carolina and other academic institutions in the state are few. More alarmingly, is that throughout the nation, colleges and universities are abandoning field studies, especially botanical, for the more lucrative fields of molecular biology, genetics, and other fields that can attract sizable grant monies. No academic institution in the state has an active graduate program training Ph.D. students in field botany to keep up with the demand. When the present gang of field botanists in South Carolina retire, mostly trained by Dr. Batson, there will be a dearth of state-trained field botanists.

The authors' hope this essay and book will make readers aware of South Carolina's rich botanical heritage and will result in a renewed interest in field botany by its citizens and academic institutions. Although much is known about the botany of the state, much is still to be discovered. Future field studies will depend on a continuing supply of professional field botanists.

Selected Topics on Natural History and Ecology

SUCCESSION IN NATURAL COMMUNITIES

Vegetation on most sites is dynamic, not static. Return to an abandoned agricultural field after a number of years, and the field that was once goldenrods and asters has been replaced by a pine forest. Or, return to an abandoned rice field along a coastal river in the outer coastal plain, and what was once a tidal freshwater marsh is now a swamp forest. A process of ecological succession has occurred—an orderly sequence where one community replaces another over time. If given enough time and if no major disturbance occurs, succession eventually terminates in the climax community; the stable end community that is capable of self-perpetuation under prevailing environmental conditions. The entire sequence of communities that replace one another is called the sere, and each transitory community in the sere is called a seral stage.

Two general types of succession may occur. One type is primary succession, in which a community becomes established on a particular substrate for the first time—that is, no living organisms have previously colonized the substrate. Examples are newly formed coastal dunes or sandbars or spits along rivers. Secondary succession occurs where vegetation has occupied the substrate in the past. Some event such as fire, climatic changes, or human intervention has caused the original community to disappear. Examples of secondary succession are abandoned freshwater tidal rice fields and abandoned agricultural lands. In both cases, humans removed the original vegetation. After abandonment, these areas will undergo succession to swamp forests and hardwood forests, respectively.

An understanding of plant succession is critical if one is to fully appreciate the distribution of wildflowers and the composition of natural communities over time. The following two examples illustrate this process of succession.

Old-field succession in the piedmont: One example

The pioneer species in an abandoned agricultural field often is crabgrass. Crabgrass produces seeds profusely, and its seeds can remain dormant for years. When a field is under cultivation, crabgrass seeds are blown in or carried by birds; they remain dormant in the soil, germinating as soon as the field is abandoned. Crabgrass quickly covers the field. Toward the end of the first year and into the second, horseweed invades the crabgrass. Organic matter that is produced by horseweed inhibits its subsequent establishment and growth. Asters and ragweed quickly invade, and being taller than horseweed, shade out the surviving horseweed (and crabgrass) and assume dominance by the end of the third year. The previously established species have increased the soil's moisture content, which allows broomstraw to invade the field. Once present, broomstraw spreads rapidly and by the fifth year it dominates all other vege-

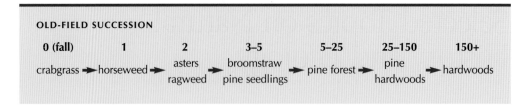

OLD-FIELD SUCCESSION

| 0 (fall) | 1 | 2 | 3–5 | 5–25 | 25–150 | 150+ |

crabgrass ➡ horseweed ➡ asters ragweed ➡ broomstraw pine seedlings ➡ pine forest ➡ pine hardwoods ➡ hardwoods

tation. Some shrubs may become established, but ultimately, around the second or third year after broomstraw becomes established, seeds of loblolly and/or shortleaf pine, blown in from a nearby seed source, germinate to produce a dense stand of pines.

When the pines get above the broomstraw, the reduced sunlight quickly eliminates this plant. The pines go on for years in complete charge of the former field. In time, however, the pines go the way of their predecessors. If a source is available, seeds of oaks, sweet gum, hickories, and maple are brought in by wind, birds, and other animals. Seedlings of these species are shade tolerant and quickly grow in the midst of the pine forest. First, the mature hardwoods shade and kill the lower pine branches. When the hardwoods grow to the height of the smaller pines, these trees die out in large numbers. This hardwood invasion occurs about 20 to 25 years after the pines are established. After about 150 years, the hardwood forest will replace the pine forest. Pine seedlings, which require high light intensities, cannot survive in the shaded forest floor. The pine trees that are large enough to survive the invasion of hardwoods will live out their lives in forest, about 125 to 150 years. When these die, a mixed hardwood forest results. The hardwood forest becomes the climax community since its broadleaf seedlings can trap sufficient sunlight to survive, even in a shaded forest floor. Unless disturbance again removes the hardwood forest, it will perpetuate itself indefinitely. The process of old-field succession is summarized above. The numbers refer to the years following abandonment.

Rice fields of the outer coastal plain

In abandoned tidal rice fields (see figure 7 in the essay, "Agriculture and forestry: effects on South Carolina's physical landscape"), hydrarch succession (succession that begins in water) starts with submerged, anchored hydrophytes such as waterweed (*Egeria*), fanwort (*Cabomba caroliniana*), pondweed (*Potamogeton*), and milfoil (*Myriophyllum*). These plants bind the loose soil matrix, trap sediment, and add to the accumulation of organic matter as they die. Next, floating-leaved, anchored hydrophytes such as water primrose (*Ludwigia uruguayensis*) and alligator-weed become established since their submerged stems can reach to the bottom. Some of the floating aquatics, such as the introduced water hyacinth, then become established in the open water of the fields. These plants trap more sediment and continue to add to soil accumulation as they die. When the leaves of the floating aquatics sufficiently block the source of sunlight for the submerged, anchored aquatics, they ultimately die. Finally, the soil level is raised close enough to the surface for emergent, anchored hydrophytes to establish themselves. These include persistent emergents such as cat-tails (*Typha* spp.), marsh bulrush (*Scirpus cyperinus*), rushes (*Juncus* spp.), giant beard grass (*Erianthus giganteus*), wild rice, southern wild rice (*Zizaniopsis miliacea*), and cordgrass (*Spartina cynosuroides*) and nonpersistent emergents such as swamp rose mallow, pickerelweed, water hemlock, obedient-plant (*Physostegia leptophylla*), water parsnip (*Sium suave*), and arrow arum (*Peltandra virginica*).

The emergent species ultimately replace the floating species. In turn, these emergent hydrophytes create the conditions for the next seral stage. They reduce soil moisture through transpiration, raise the soil level by trapping more sediment and decomposing, and create a more stable soil due to a mass of interlocking rhizomes. A marsh thicket can then develop as wind, water, and animals bring the seeds of woody plants. These include swamp rose, wax myrtle, button-bush (*Cephalanthus occidentalis*), and indigo-bush (*Amorpha fruticosa*). Finally, the soil is raised above the water table, and the wind-borne fruits of bald cypress, red maple, willows, loblolly pine, cottonwood, sweet gum, and swamp gum become established. This new swamp forest will be different in species composition from the original swamp forest because environmental parameters change over the years.

The swamp forests that develop on abandoned rice fields eventually become climax communities. There are enough examples of swamp forests reaching maturity in abandoned rice fields along the coastal rivers to conclude that they are in relative equilibrium with the environment and are self-perpetuating.

FIRE IN THE SOUTH CAROLINA LANDSCAPE

Archaeologists tell us that humans first entered North America between 12,000 and 15,000 years ago and that their presence in South Carolina is well documented for the past 12,000 years. Archaeologists also have good evidence that Native Americans changed the composition of forest communities by using wood for fuel and shelters, disturbing large areas of valley bottoms, altering the distribution of some species (e.g., bald cypress), and by using fire to increase the proportion of open lands (i.e., meadows, savannas, and savanna woodlands). Reports from early European explorers, such as Jean Ribault, and naturalists William Bartram, Mark Catesby, and John Lawson, suggest that both the coastal plain and piedmont of presettlement South Carolina consisted of vast stretches of open savanna or savanna-woodland interspersed with deep forest.

Archaeologists and historians believe that Native Americans regularly used fire for a variety of purposes, including clearing forests for planting crops and driving animals during fall and winter hunts. Early settlers apparently continued the practice of using fire to clear land for agriculture and to improve forage for their free-ranging cattle and pigs. Burning of forest undergrowth in the South has long been an accepted way of life. It was believed to be beneficial, and to this day intentionally set wildfires still occur in the coastal plain, especially in and near large tracts of publicly owned lands such as the Francis Marion National Forest and the Santee Coastal Preserve.

To what extent did fire alter the South Carolina landscape? How important were lightning-set fires compared to fires set by Native Americans and later by settlers? These questions have long been the purview of archaeologists and historians, and ecologists have recently provided new insights. The following observations are particularly pertinent to these questions: (1) the effects of fire differ depending on fire frequency, intensity, and burn season, with fire frequency being the most important; (2) fires seldom run down slopes that have a gradient that is greater than 15%; (3) the amount of acreage that can burn in a single ignition event varies with the variability of the topography; and (4) topographic variability increases from the coast to the inland.

Ecologists believe that nearly 95% of the uplands of the coastal plain, and even portions of the adjacent piedmont, were once dominated by longleaf pine, the only tree species in the South with seedlings resistant to fire. The flat outer coastal plain, with natural fire breaks dividing the uplands into fire compartments of 50 to 300 square miles, could easily burn annually, or at least every 1 to 3 years, with just a few ignitions. The more hilly inner coastal plain and sandhills had much smaller natural fire compartments and probably burned naturally every 5 to 15 years. There is convincing evidence that the uplands of the entire inner and outer coastal plain, excluding the maritime strand, were dominated by fire-adapted vegetation and that lightning alone was adequate for its development and maintenance. The use of fire by Native Americans, and later by settlers, probably did not contribute significantly to the openness of this landscape. Open meadows, savannas, and savanna-woodlands were the dominant plant communities prior to and during Native American occupation.

Numerous reports by early explorers from travels in the piedmont describe "wide prairies" and "woodlands without undergrowth," as well as "great forests." However, today the piedmont harbors few fire-maintained communities, so it is unlikely that large parts of the piedmont were once savannas or savanna-woodlands prior to Native American occupation. In an attempt to assist land managers who are interested in restoring the few parts of the piedmont that are fire-adapted to prairie-like condition, scientists have recently compiled detailed historical information on the prairie landscapes of the piedmont in the Carolinas. Examination of historical and meteorological evidence suggests that an open landscape was at least as extensive as early reports implied. For example, Barden (1997) has found maps published in 1676 and 1718 that designated much of the South Carolina piedmont as "Savannae" or "Grand Savannae." Some authors speculate that as much as 95% of the prairies and other open woodlands were the product of Native American burning and agricultural activities, but Barden points out that lightning fires are not uncommon in the piedmont and that they may have maintained the extensive grasslands. Only in the most extreme upland sites, best represented in parts of Chester and York Counties, where blackjack oak is presently a dominant tree, was the natural fire regime adequate to provide for the long-term maintenance of these sites. Brown (1953) cites a report from the time of the American Revolution that describes patriots traveling at night when they went to visit their families in Rock Hill in order to avoid being seen by Tories on the open "plain" during the day. Today, with natural fires long suppressed, nearly a dozen rare plants, usually found only in Midwestern prairies, cling to a perilous existence in canopy gaps, roadside margins, and power-line right-of-ways. Most of the prairie-loving plants in xeric hardpan forests and related communities apparently are part of the only fire-adapted community in the piedmont.

Ecologists are also concerned with this question: What have we lost in the process of altering the natural fire regime? Development has greatly reduced natural fire compartment size, and since about 1950 aggressive efforts have been made to protect forests from wildfires on both public and private lands. Fires still routinely occur in forests, mostly in the coastal plain, but these fires are almost all prescribed burns and mostly take place in the winter, which is not the natural fire season. Available data suggest that longleaf pine-dominated ecosystems in the southeast were once the most significant ecosystem east of the Mississippi River. This extraordinarily diverse ecosystem once occupied from 55 to 85 million acres. Today less than 3% remains in an undegraded condition. One concerned scientist compares this decline to the loss of the North American tall-grass prairie.

With loss of habitat comes a threat to species. An estimated 122 plant species that are associated with this ecosystem are threatened throughout their known range. Nearly 50 of these species occur in South Carolina. Loss of habitat was a significant contributor to the decline of these species, but one of the enduring mysteries in the natural history of the eastern United States, as one researcher put it, is "the spectacular failure of the primeval pine forest to reproduce itself after exploitation." No one knows for sure why this is true, but contributing factors probably include (1) the naturally low plant regeneration, even of the fire-adapted longleaf pine, under a heavy fire regime; (2) grazing pressure on pine seedlings by livestock, which until late in the nineteenth century were allowed to graze freely, while croplands were fenced to keep livestock out; and (3), the institution of state fire laws and fire suppression programs. According to the most recent inventory of South Carolina forest resources, longleaf pine continued its long-term decline from 1986 to 1993, declining from 396,000 to 369,000 acres. Longleaf pine now dominates only 6.7 % of the 5.5 million acres of pine-dominated forests in South Carolina.

CAROLINA BAYS OF THE COASTAL PLAIN

Carolina bays (figure 6) are geological formations of unknown origin that occur mainly on the South Atlantic Coastal Plain Province of North and South Carolina and Georgia. They are shallow depressions formed in the sandy coastal soil and vary in depth from a few feet to around twenty feet. They vary in length from a few hundred yards to several miles. The bays occur in three shapes: elliptical, oval, or asymmetrical, with their long axis oriented in a southeast direction. Often the bays overlap each other, as is seen by the outlines of smaller bays in the depressions of larger ones. Furthermore, their distribution is nonrandom. They occur in clusters, and within the clusters they are often aligned along an apparently undetermined physiographic gradient.

FIGURE 6. Aerial View of Woods Bay.

Although for years several workers made reference to "certain depressions" in the coastal plain, it was not until 1933 when two scientists, Melton and Schriever (1933), viewed aerial photographs of terrain near Myrtle Beach that the true abundance and distinctive characteristics of the bays became known. The photographs also revealed prominent sand ridges on the southeast side of the bays. Melton and Schriever then came to an astonishing conclusion: The depressions were formed by a shower of meteorites that came from the northwest at an angle of 35 to 55 degrees. The impact of the meteorite formed the depression and pushed up the sand ridge.

Some viewed their theory with skepticism while others accepted it as dogma. The scientific community has never accepted an extraterrestrial (or meteoritic) origin of the bays since so much convincing evidence against it has been gathered. At the same time, many laypersons will accept no other theory. As recently as 1982, Henry Savage, Jr., in his book *The Mysterious Carolina Bays*, argues for the meteorite theory of origin. His book, a must for students of the bays, is the first to present a complete review of the subject and includes an extensive bibliography.

Of all the theories postulated by scientists to explain the bay's origin, two general themes have been dominant: (1) the catastrophic, which envisioned the sudden shower of meteorites (extraterrestrial), or the sudden formation of artesian springs or sink holes (terrestrial); and (2) the uniformitarianist, which says the origin must be explained by the gradual effects of wind, soil solution, and wave-induced erosion.

With all the theories presented by the scientific community, why is there still such a controversy over the origin of the bays? Simply this: No theory adequately explains all the facts surrounding the bays. Until one does, their origin remains shrouded in uncertainty and mystery.

Whether or not the riddle of their origin is ever solved, the Carolina bays afford a wildflower paradise. Carolina bays act as basins, collecting rainwater from the surrounding uplands, which they hold perched above the normal water table. In the deeper bays, upland swamps develop. If cypress is a component of the swamps, it is always pond cypress (*Taxodium ascendens*), either in pure stands or mixed with swamp gum (*Nyssa biflora*). In more shallow bays, the beautiful pond cypress savannas (plate 495) may occur. For the most part, however, the Carolina bays harbor pocosins (plate 477). Here occur the three bay trees: loblolly bay, sweet bay, and swamp red bay. Did the Carolina bays get their name from the presence of the bay trees? Or, did the bay trees get their names because they occur in the bays? (Early on, the depressions were called bays.) The sand ridges are also an important component of the bays. Here the deep sands harbor xeric sandhill communities (plate 401), which contain many wildflowers pictured in this book: sandhills milkweed, sandhills baptisia, sandy-field beaksedge, and gerardia, to name a few.

Ecologically the bays are important for several reasons. First, they are wetland habitats, which are an oasis for numerous animals of the surrounding uplands. Two endangered animals, the black bear and pine barrens tree frog, make their homes in the pocosins. At least 36 plants that are considered rare in South Carolina grow in Carolina bays. Venus' fly trap (plate 378) and Carolina wicky (plate 481), two uncommon species, grow on the margins of the pocosins. Add to these the savanna gardens, with their floral display of orchids and carnivorous plants, and the xeric sandhills of the rims, and one can see why the Carolina bays are such important habitats.

Unfortunately, the majority of the Carolina bays are highly disturbed. In 1991, Steve H. Bennett and John B. Nelson conducted a study on the distribution and status of Carolina bays. They estimated that approximately 4000 bays of all size classes occur in South Carolina. Of these, only 400 to 500 remain relatively intact; the number of bays remaining in exemplary condition is considerably less. They concluded that there are far fewer bays than had been previously believed, and most bays have been significantly altered. Many have been drained for farmland or timber production; others have been converted to pastures; still others have been used as junk yards to dispose of household goods.

Saving Carolina bays has become a major goal of The Nature Conservancy of South Carolina and the South Carolina Heritage Trust Program. Through the work of these two organizations, plus the United States Forest Service, four areas in the coastal plain with Carolina bays have been protected for public use: Lewis Ocean Bay Heritage Preserve and Cartwheel Bay Heritage Preserve in Horry County, Santee Coastal Preserve in Charleston County, and the Francis Marion National Forest in Berkeley and Charleston Counties. Four sites that consist entirely of a Carolina bay have also been protected: Woods Bay State Park (figure 6), Savage Bay Heritage Preserve, Cathedral Bay Heritage Preserve, and Bennett's Bay. All these sites are described in the section "Field guide to natural plant communities."

REPRODUCTIVE STRATEGIES OF VASCULAR PLANTS

Native plants are well adapted to their habitat(s). If they weren't well adapted, they wouldn't survive the vagaries of their environment, including competition with other species. One of the real surprises is that plants may not grow best in the habitats where they are typically found. Given the freedom from competition afforded by the attentive gardener, many plants grow better in habitats that are more mesic (less dry or less wet) than where they are normally found. Good examples include bald cypress (plate 441) and black walnut (plate 438), species that typically are found in lowlands but under cultivation grow quite well in drier sites, and sandhills pyxie-moss (plate 310), which typically is found in xeric habitats but under cultivation grows well in mesic sites.

In reality, the situation is more complicated, and we do not include a lengthy discussion of plant adaptations. Instead, a logical life-history sequence is given, focusing on the four stages in the life history of any organism (reproduction, dispersal, establishment, and maintenance), with an emphasis on South Carolina plants. Keep in mind that if there is a weakness in any of these life-cycle stages, the distribution and abundance of the species will be affected accordingly. Many plants are rare because of a limitation in one of these stages.

Reproduction

For most plants cross-pollination is vital to reproductive health. As Charles Darwin put it over 100 years ago, "Cross-fertilization results in offspring which vanquish the offspring of self-fertilization in the struggle for existence." And, as Darwin detailed in an entire book devoted to the subject, no group of plants has evolved more contrivances to assure cross-pollination, and ultimately cross-fertilization, than the orchids. In lady's slippers (*Cypripedium* spp., plates 65 and 146), for example, the lip petal is modified into a pouch or slipper that has a small slit down the middle. The fruity fragrance inside the pouch attracts bees, but the slit restricts the size of the bees that can visit the flower. Exit from the pouch is directed by small windows of thin tissue, which direct the visiting bee past the overhanging stigma, where pollen that adhered to the bee's back during a visit to another flower is rubbed off. Once past the stigma the bee squeezes through a small opening and new pollen from an anther is attached to its back, which will be deposited on the flower of the next plant it visits.

It is a real challenge to observe insects pollinating a particular species and to determine if and how cross-pollination is maximized. Although self-sterility is always possible as the underlying mechanism to ensure cross-pollination, morphological and developmental mechanisms more often provide the answer. For example, in the ladies'-tresses orchids (e.g., *Spiranthes laciniata*, plate 502), flowers are in an elongated spike, with the oldest flowers at the base and the youngest flowers at the top. Bees work from bottom to top, and special mechanisms provide for the deposition of pollen from bees to the stigma of lower flowers and the attachment of pollen to bees visting upper flowers. Flowers are either able to release pollen or accept pollen but not both at the same time, thus preventing self-pollination and promoting cross-pollination.

Although cross-pollination is the ideal in theory, it is not always possible in practice. Breeding systems in plants actually vary from complete cross-fertilization (outcrossing) to complete self-fetilization (inbreeding or selfing), with most plants using some combination of the two. For example, some species hedge their bets by producing two kinds of flowers: small, inconspicuous, closed and self-pollinating (cleistogamous) flowers and showy cross-pollinating (chasmogamous) flowers. Cleistogamy is not uncommon, and although most frequent in the legume family, is also found in such well known genera as *Viola* (e.g., *Viola villosa,* plate 415) and *Polygala* (e.g., *Polygala lutea,* plate 376). One of the more unusual cleistogamous species is pool sprite (*Amphianthus pusillus,* plate 158), which grows in temporary pools on granitic rock outcrops. Its tiny, self-pollinating flowers are borne under water, while its solitary, larger cross-pollinating flower is borne between two leaves that float on the water. In hog peanut (*Amphicarpa bracteata,* plate 255), the underground, one-seeded fruits, which are the peanuts presumably loved by hogs, are produced from self-pollinating flowers, just as they are in regular peanuts. In a species that produces fruits from self-pollination and from cross-pollination, self-pollinated fruits generally produce many more seeds than fruits produced from cross-pollination. This suggests the likelihood that cleistogamy arose in these species because cross-pollination was not always effective.

Pollination, of course, requires some sort of pollinator. Major pollinators or vectors of pollen include wind, water, various kinds of insects (including bees, wasps, carrion and dung flies, moths, butterflies, bee-flies, and beetles), birds, bats, and even small mammals. Flowers are usually adapted for a single kind of carrier, which sometimes is a single species. Differences in flower size, shape, color, odor, as well as when the flower is receptive are all characters associated with pollination by different kinds of animal vectors. It is well known, for example, that hummingbirds are attracted to red (or red and yellow) flowers with long corolla tubes and abundant nectar, such as is seen in cardinal flower (*Lobelia cardinalis,* plate 533) and eastern columbine (*Aquilegia canadensis,* plate 2). It is less well known that hummingbirds have a poor sense of smell and that they usually pollinate odorless flowers. Similarly, bees are not attracted to solid red flowers. Since they can see using ultraviolet (UV) light, what bees see is not what we see. All bee-pollinated flowers have nectar guides, which are concentrations of UV-absorbing pigments in petals that are consolidated toward the center of the flower and direct the bees to the location of the nectar. There are few foul-smelling flowers in South Carolina, but perhaps the foulest occurs on red trillium (*Trillium erectum,* plate 130), sometimes called stinking benjamin, whose foul odor attracts carrion flies for pollination.

It is well known that different plants flower at different times of the year. What is less well known is that some species only open their flowers at specific times of the day or night. Ever wonder how morning-glorys (e.g., *Ipomoea macrorhiza,* plate 607) and evening-primroses (e.g., *Oenothera speciosa,* plate 665) got their names? The common dandelion opens its flowers in the morning after the sun is well up; its flowers close at night and during stormy weather. In many of the dayflowers (e.g., *Commelina virginica,* plate 465), the flowers open in the morning and close soon after noon, never to open again. These are but a few of the many possible examples. Linnaeus, the father of both plant and animal taxonomy, took an interesting advantage of this phenomenon. He produced a "flower clock," where flowers with sleep movement at different times of the day are planted in wedge-shaped sections in a circular garden. He determined the time of day by observing which plants were awake.

In terms of the amount of energy required, reproduction is costly, and for species that produce male and female plants, it is more costly to be a female than to be a male. Fruits, or "ripened" ovaries, are products of the female flower parts and require much more energy to produce than pollen grains, which are the products of male flower parts and deliver sperm to fertilize the eggs within the ovary. Individual plants of jack-in-the-pulpit (*Arisaema triphyllum,* plate 457) may be male, female, or both (perfect), and they can change sex depending on the availability of stored food resources. When food resources in an individual "jack" are in short supply, the plant typically produces only male, or staminate, flowers. When resources are in ready supply, the plant produces only female, or pistillate, flowers, or both staminate and pistillate flowers. Young plants are typically male; older plants are typically female. If stored resources decline substantially in an old plant, the plant will shift from female to male.

Dispersal

A seed is essentially an embryonic plant enclosed in a protective case—the seed coat. Seeds, or the fruits in which they are enclosed, must somehow get from the parent plant to places favorable for germination and establishment. Plants that occupy early stages of succession, like plants of ruderal environments, usually produce large numbers of small fruits that are dispersed great distances, usually by wind or animals. Familiar examples of wind-dispersed seeds include the plumed fruits of common dandelion and willows, the plumed seeds of milkweeds and dogbanes, and the winged fruits of maples (e.g., *Acer rubrum,* plate 27), ashes, and tree-of-heaven (plate 654). Fruits dispersed by animals include the fleshy fruits of cherries and junipers (*Juniperus silicicola,* plate 591), the spiny fruits of dune sandbur (plate 575), the hooked fruits of beggar tick (*Bidens* spp.), and the silky seeds of chickweeds.

Plants that occupy late stages of succession, such as oaks and hickories, usually produce few fruit that have large food reserves. These fruits usually are not dispersed great distances, and animals (or more rarely water) are their agents of dispersal. Seeds of touch-me-not (*Impatiens capensis,* plate 18) and witch-hazel (*Hamamelis virginiana*) are flung out of the ripe fruits when triggered by touch. Perhaps the most unusual animal vector of seed dispersal are seed-harvester ants. Ant-dispersed plants are common among the ephemeral spring wildflowers of rich woods throughout South Carolina. All the trilliums and heartleafs, showy species such as bloodroot, and species with inconspicuous flowers, such as some of the sedges (e.g., *Carex glaucescens,* plate 506), produce special oil bodies (elaisomes) on the seed or on the embryo that attract seed-gathering ants. Ants gather the seeds, return to their nests, and usually discard the seed once the elaisome has been eaten.

Establishment

Plants generally have little choice in where they are established. It has become clear, however, that species that produce fleshy fruits that are consumed whole by animals and then the seeds within are passed unharmed through the digestive tract can become coadapted to specific animals, just as plants can become coadapted to their pollinators. This is especially true in the tropics where fruits are available all year.

Plants with special soil requirements usually cannot become established unless specific conditions are met. Plants that have relatively high requirements for calcium are called calcicoles. Many of the herbaceous species in basic mesic forests and rich cove forests are calcicoles, including false rue anemone (plate 179), several species of trillium (southern nodding trillium, plate 177, and lanceleaf trillium, plate 176), and green violet (plate 192). Puck's orpine (plate 157) is a calcicole of xeric rock outcrops; it only grows under the partial shade of red cedar, which is also a calcicole and whose decaying leaves provide the required extra calcium.

Many members of the heath family (Ericaceae) require acid soils, but acid soils, especially boggy acid soils, tend to be low in available nitrogen. Ericads growing in such environments usually have special fungi associated with their roots that make the uptake of nitrogen easier. Special fungal-root associations, called mycorrhizae, are present in more than 85% of all vascular plants. The tiny, dustlike seeds of orchids have no stored food reserves and depend on associated mycorrhizae for food during early growth. Once the seedling produces its own food, it returns the favor, providing food produced by photosynthesis to the fungi in return for assistance in the uptake of water and certain minerals. Different orchids have different species of fungi associated with their roots. This explains in part why orchids are notoriously difficult to transplant.

Maintenance

Just because a plant species has become established in a habitat doesn't mean it will be able to maintain itself there. Early successional species as a whole, those with a high light requirement, high fruit/seed production, and a wide dispersal range, often are dispersed into openings within habitats that may be too dry, too wet, or subject to periodic fires, but which may be temporarily suitable for their establishment. Rock outcrops will always harbor some weedy species, as will streamsides and rocky shoals and most natural wildflower communities. Similarly, competition from species that are better adapted to a habitat often eliminates species from that habitat.

Obtaining adequate amounts of light under a dense canopy and subcanopy is a problem that spring ephemerals of rich woods have solved in an interesting fashion. They become photosynthetic in the early spring before the deciduous species of the canopy and subcanopy put on new leaves. Some species such as spring beauty (plate 284) and dimpled trout lily (plate 171) are often no longer visible to the observant visitor by the first of May. Other species such as bloodroot, may-apple, and many trilliums will linger until midsummer or fall; most of their food resources were obtained before the trees leafed out.

Miccosukee gooseberry (plate 173) occurs in a dense-canopied, basic-mesic forest community. It drops its leaves in late summer and puts on new growth of smaller leaves in December. It is not until late spring that the leaves resume normal adult size.

All but the wettest forested plant communities occasionally experience drought, and trees typically respond to drought conditions by dropping some leaves. Tulip tree (plate 212) and swamp gum (plate 517) are well known for this habit. Trees that best display this trick occupy the levee variant of bottomland hardwoods. This streamside habitat is so regularly wet and dry that its inhabitants are adapted to both. American sycamore (plate 475) and river birch (plate 476) are typical levee species that are so drought tolerant that they often are planted along the streets of subdivisions.

ECONOMIC AND CULTURAL NOTES

Many plants served Native Americans and early settlers as building materials, food, fiber for baskets, drugs, tools, ornamentals, etc. Just as important, is that many still serve us today. Indeed, the economic and cultural history of South Carolina is laced with plant uses. It is hard to comprehend how a settlement of the New World in the 1600s could be successful without a dependence on native plants. Later, as the New World became settled, naturalized species added an entire new dimension to plant uses. The following is a categorical summary of the uses of native and naturalized plants.

Fibers

South Carolina's rice industry, which helped shape the culture, economy, social structure, and ecology of the lowcountry, made use of coiled work-baskets that were constructed from needle rush (*Juncus roemerianus*, plate 60 in *WCL*) and bound with thin strips of white oak (*Quercus alba*, plate 265) or strips from the leaves of cabbage palmetto (*Sabal palmetto*, plate 593). One of the earliest work-baskets was the "fanner," which was used to winnow the rice (to throw threshed rice into the air allowing the wind to blow away the chaff). Coiled basketry was probably practiced along the entire range of the rice-growing region (from Cape Fear, North Carolina, to the St. Johns River in Florida). Descended from an ancient African folk art, Africans, who were brought to America to cultivate rice and other crops, introduced it into the Carolinas in the late seventeenth century.

Basket making survives today in the Charleston area, where sweet grass baskets are an art form. Four plants are used to make the baskets today: longleaf pine needles (leaves) (*Pinus palustris*, plate 309), stems of sweet grass (*Muhlenbergia filipes*, plate 580), needle rush stems, and strips of the leaves of cabbage palmetto. Collectable, native populations of sweet grass are becoming scarce or off limits to basket makers and threaten the industry. Local people are cultivating sweet grass to ensure a continued supply for this art.

Spanish moss (*Tillandsia usneoides*, plate 585) has done more than add beauty to the state. Early settlers used Spanish moss fiber as a binder in construction of mud and clay chimneys and for binding mud or clay in plastering houses. After the Civil War, it was used in overstuffed furniture, upholstery, and mattresses, and when the automobile was invented, this flowering "moss" was used for seat stuffing.

Cabbage palmetto yielded a valuable fiber known as "palmetto fiber." Fine fibers were obtained from the young leaf stalks still in the bud, while coarser fibers came from mature leaves or from the base of the old leaf stalks. The fiber was used to make various brushes. Cabbage palmetto first gained popularity when it was used to make forts in the Revolutionary War; the fibrous trunk absorbed the impact of cannon balls and did not shatter. Cabbage palmetto is now the state tree of South Carolina.

The wood of chestnut oak (*Quercus montana,* plate 97) has the special property of splitting into fine, tough ribbons of fibers. These fibers were woven into baskets that were used to haul cotton from the fields and to make chair bottoms. The inner bark of pawpaw (*Asimina triloba*) was woven into cloth by Louisiana Indians, and the pioneers used it to string fish. Indian-hemp (*Apocynum cannabinum,* plate 655), according to Porcher (1869), furnishes a fiber superior to true hemp (*Cannabis sativa*) fiber and was used by Native Americans for making cordage, fishing nets, and coarse cloth.

Ornamentals

Many home sites and gardens throughout the state are adorned with native shrubs and trees, which years ago were transplanted in the dead of winter. Sweet bay, fringe-tree, wild olive, American holly, dogwood, mountain laurel, common silverbell, redbud, bull bay, wax myrtle, American storax, loblolly bay, beauty-berry, plus many others can all be seen in gardens around homes in cities, towns, and villages throughout the state. Live oaks were planted along roads leading to plantation homes in the lowcountry. Today these trees are, in some cases, two hundred years old and form impressive avenues.

The native woodlands still provide many vines and herbs that are used to add color to gardens. Vines such as yellow jessamine, climbing hydrangea, cow-itch, cross-vine, and coral honeysuckle continue to be used as native landscape materials. Blended with these native plants are a wide variety of introduced species such as crape myrtle, camellia, azalea, and tea olive.

Not to be overlooked are the many native herbaceous plants, especially the spring ephemerals from all over the state, that find their way into home gardens: Joe-pye-weed, bloodroot, early black cohosh, blue cohosh, doll's-eyes, dwarf crested iris, pipevine, hepatica, trilliums, trailing arbutus, and partridge berry, to name a few.

Dyes

Natural dyes and stains that are derived from plants have been used by all peoples from the earliest times. The settlers learned from Native Americans which native plants provided dyes. The primary use of dyes was to color fabrics for home use and for the textile industry.

The bark of butternut (*Juglans cinerea*), which is found in the mountains, provided a dye for uniforms of the Confederate army. Black walnut (*Juglans nigra,* plate 438) was used in a similar manner. From the fruits of species of blueberry (*Vaccinium*) came blue or gray dyes. Red ink came from species of pokeweed (*Phytolacca*). Other plants from which blue dyes were obtained were fruits of elderberry (*Sambucus canadensis*), Chinese privet (*Ligustrum sinense,* plate 709), and red mulberry. From the bark of black oak (*Quercus velutina*) came the dye quercitron. This dye is an intense yellow color and was an important article for commerce. Native weavers in the Appalachian coves still use it. The leaves of horse sugar (*Symplocos tinctoria,* plate 142) were the source of a yellow dye that was used to dye wool. The dried leaves turn a vivid yellow on account of the dye within. The leaves of yellow false-indigo (*Baptisia tinctoria,* plate 343), yielded a blue dye.

Around the middle of the 1800s, natural dye products began to be supplemented by the synthetic dyes obtained from coal-tar products. Today native dyes are mostly used in the folk art industry.

Tannins

Tannins are organic compounds found in nearly all plants. They are commercially important because they react with proteins in animal hides to form a strong, flexible, resistant, insoluble substance that we know as leather. Animal hides not treated with tannins are brittle and almost useless. Although nearly all plants contain tannins, only a few have sufficient quantities to be commercially important.

The most important tannin source in the United States has been the bark of Canada hemlock (*Tsuga canadensis*), which grows in the mountains of South Carolina. In the 1930s, the plentiful supply of fallen American chestnut trees (*Castanea dentata,* plate 89) became a main source of tannins. In fact, it was because of the high tannin content of the wood that chestnut logs lay well preserved on the forest floor for years.

Other plants that supplied important sources of tannins in the South were species of oak, especially chestnut oak, and the leaves of three native sumacs: smooth sumac, winged sumac, and staghorn sumac (*Rhus typhina*).

Industrial uses

Numerous industries depended on the almost unlimited supply of native plants. The wood of dogwood is resistant to sudden shock and was used to make shuttles in the textile industry, which allowed cotton to become a major crop in the state. Longleaf pine provided tar and pitch, which formed the basis of the naval stores industry. Tar preserved a ship's rigging, and pitch was used to caulk wooden sailing vessels. Later, longleaf provided spirits of turpentine that were used in the paint and varnish industry, as well as resin, which had a variety of uses. Today, loblolly pine (*Pinus taeda*) is the species used almost exclusively in making kraft paper.

Tulip tree, the tallest hardwood in North America, was once among the most important lumber trees in the East. In the lowcountry, its wood was employed to a great extent by the noted furniture maker Thomas Elf, especially for bedsteads. Other native trees that were important in making fine furniture were bald cypress, oaks, and pines.

In pioneer days, candles and soap were made from the wax of wax myrtle berries, and the silk industry depended on the introduced white mulberry (*Morus alba,* plate 664) to nurture the silk worms. The livestock industry depended on a variety of native plants. Salthay (*Spartina patens*), which is a high-marsh plant of the maritime strand, was used in pioneer days as a natural pasture for livestock. Throughout the coastal area, early settlers used open range to allow cattle to graze. In the Hell Hole Swamp of Berkeley County, an area called "The Opening" was regularly burned to provide new green vegetation in the spring for cattle. Split-rail fences, made from a variety of durable woods, were used to fence livestock.

Essential oils

Essential oils are found in many different species of plants throughout the world. These oils evaporate or volatilize when they contact air and possess a pleasant taste and strong aromatic odor. They can be readily removed from plant tissues without any change in composition. All distinctly aromatic plants contain essential oils. Sixty families of flowering plants have species with essential oils. The following families are noteworthy because they have many representative species in the state: Asteraceae, Lamiaceae, Apiaceae, and Lauraceae. Although most essential oils today are derived from cultivated plants, there is still some backcountry production of essential oils from wild plants. Below are some of the native plants that have historically been important sources of essential oils.

Sassafras wood, because of the presence of essential oils that repel insects (such as bedbugs and fleas), was used to make bedsteads and flooring for cabins. At one time sassafras oil was considered a miraculous cure-all in Europe and was exported from the colonies. Today its oil is used to flavor tobacco, root beer, soaps, and perfumes. Cedar wood oil from eastern red cedar (*Juniperus virginiana*) is still used in perfumes, soaps, deodorants, and liniments. Cedar wood is especially popular for building cedar chests because the odor (essential oils) keeps away moths and other insects. Wintergreen (*Gaultheria procumbens,* plate 151), a mountain plant, is the source of wintergreen oil, which is used in medicine and in flavoring candy, gum, and soft drinks. Similar oil is obtained from sweet birch (*Betula lenta,* plate 51) and is used for the same purposes as wintergreen oil.

Witch-hazel (*Hamamelis virginiana*), found throughout the state, has long been and is still the source of witch-hazel extract, which is used to aromatize aftershave lotion and toilet water. Its value as an astringent and antiseptic is lost if the extract is prepared by steam distillation. It is still in demand today. Chenopodium oil is obtained from worm-seed (*Chenopodium ambrosioides,* plate 686), a naturalized plant from tropical America. The oil is used as a vermifuge to treat domestic stock for intestinal worms and to treat humans for hookworm.

The leaves of vanilla plant (*Carphephorus odoratissimus,* plate 353), which grow in the lowcountry pine flatwoods and savannas, are collected today from the wild and used for flavoring smoking tobacco. So aromatic is the plant that it can be detected from a distance. The leaves of red bay (*Persea borbonia*, plate 589) and swamp red bay (*P. palustris*) are used as a spice to flavor meats, soups, and other dishes.

Two excellent references for the economic and cultural use of plants are Hill (1952) and Simpson and Ogorzaly (1986).

LONGLEAF PINE AND THE NAVAL STORES INDUSTRY

One of the most important uses of the longleaf pine (and to a lesser degree, slash pine, *Pinus elliottii*) was for the turpentine and naval stores industries. Crude turpentine is found in the resin canals of the inner bark and sapwood of various coniferous trees like pine. Upon distillation, crude turpentine yields two components: resin (colloquially called rosin) and an essential oil called spirits of turpentine. Both products have many historic and present-day uses. Spirits of turpentine is important in the paint and varnish industry as a thinner, as a solvent for rubber, as well as in medicine. Resin, a brittle, faintly aromatic solid, is used in the manufacture of soap, varnish, linoleum, and drugs. It is also the chief sizing material for paper.

Crude turpentine was originally distilled over an open fire in cast-iron kettles, in which the turpentine, plus any chips, bark and pine needles were placed. This process produced low-grade resin. In 1834 steam distillation in copper stills replaced the open cast-iron kettles. These stills were centrally located, and the turpentine was brought from the surrounding area. Steam distillation fractionates the spirits of turpentine above water, and the resin remains as a heavy residue.

The original method of removing the crude turpentine was the box method, which required cutting a cavity a few inches wide and several inches deep into the base of the tree. The crude turpentine from the severed ducts flowed into the cavity (the box) where it was removed for distillation. Boxing continued until the early 1900s, when it was found that smaller diameter, second-growth trees did not suit the box method. At this time, the cup-and-gutter method replaced the box method. An incision was made into the trunk at a 20-degree angle, and a metal gutter was slipped into the cut. A container was placed below the gutter. A strip of bark about one-half inch in height was chipped above the gutter from which the crude turpentine flowed, via the gutter, into the container below. It was then collected from the container and taken to the distilling shed.

But it was tar and pitch, not the distillation products of crude turpentine, that were most important in the early development of the South because of their importance in the naval stores industry. Tar is the crude liquid that drips from the wood of conifers during slow combustion. Then, by boiling the tar, it converts into pitch, a partially carbonized and condensed product. The pitch was used to caulk wooden sailing vessels, and the tar was used to coat the ship's rope and rigging, protecting them from the elements. The use of tar and pitch reached its peak in 1908 and 1909. With the passing of the use of wooden sailing vessels, tar and pitch were no longer important commercial products, and the naval stores industry ceased.

The method used to remove tar from longleaf pine logs was called "tar-burning," which was practiced from colonial times until the end of the naval stores industry. The best description of the tar kiln was given by John K. Cross in an article in *Forests and People* in 1973.

> Tar burning was done in an earthen kiln. The kiln was a saucer-shaped excavation dug in the ground, about fifteen feet in diameter. The outer edge of the kiln was raised a few feet above the ground, and then it sloped toward the center. An outlet for the tar to drain from the bed was next constructed by digging a V-shaped gutter from the center of the bed along the radius to a point 5 or 6 feet beyond the edge of the bed. It ended in a pit about four feet in diameter and four feet deep.
>
> Pine logs were laid in the kiln, starting around the perimeter. The saucer-shaped depression caused the logs to slope toward the center. To seal the logs in an airtight enclosure, a layer of poles was laid in rail-like fashion around the kiln. Pine tops were stuffed into holes in the stacked wood. Then clay was placed between the stacked pine wood and the poles. Successively, layers and poles were added upward until the wall encircled the kiln. Across the top of the pine logs straw was laid, upon which clay was placed. At the top, around the perimeter, a small portion of the wood was left unexposed where the kiln would be lighted. The kiln was fired and allowed to burn slowly for the first 24 hours. Then the flames were choked off and the charring process began.
>
> The heat forced the tar from the logs and it flowed toward the center of the kiln. The outlet was blocked until the bed was full of tar, then opened to allow the tar to drain down the gutter into the tar hole. Here it was collected and used as tar or converted to pitch.

The production of naval stores and turpentine did not begin in the South, but in the North Atlantic colonies in the early 1600s. In this area pitch pine (*Pinus resinosa*) was used. As colonists began to arrive in North Carolina about 1665, it was soon discovered that the abundant longleaf pines were a better source of tar and turpentine. By 1700, the production of naval stores and turpentine were an important part of the economy of North Carolina and quickly spread to South Carolina, where it was equally important. In 1850 the Carolinas accounted for 95% of the total American production. As the supply of virgin pine forests was depleted, the center of production shifted southward and westward through the south Atlantic and Gulf Coast states into eastern Texas. Tar production ended between 1908 and 1909, and tree turpentining has declined steadily. Tree turpentining is practiced today in Georgia (using slash pine), but to a minor extent. Most future production of turpentine and related products today comes as a by-product of the kraft paper industry, which uses the abundant loblolly pine.

Tar burning is a forgotten art. Its legacy is the myriad of abandoned tar kilns scattered throughout the original longleaf pine belt as well as longleaf pine stumps used for kindling wood.

AGRICULTURE AND FORESTRY: EFFECTS ON SOUTH CAROLINA'S PHYSICAL LANDSCAPE

Rice

The growing of rice, from its introduction in 1685 until the end of its cultivation in the early 1900s, forever changed the diversity and structure of the flora (and fauna) of the outer coastal plain (and similar coastal areas in North Carolina and Georgia). Even today its ecological effects are evident. Plants introduced into plantation gardens have escaped and become naturalized; tidal river swamps and inland swamps that were cleared for rice fields and then later abandoned, today support a variety of secondary plant communities; upland woods that were cleared for provision fields and then abandoned, support flora and fauna different from the original woods. Rice culture, however, had the greatest influence on the vegetation of the inland and river swamps.

Rice was first planted in South Carolina prior to 1685 by Dr. Henry Woodward (Salley, 1919). This first rice flourished in the swamp lands of the lowcountry and became known as "Carolina Gold Rice" because of the hull's golden color. It became a major export crop of the state and, according to many sources, was the finest strain of rice grown anywhere in the world. Rice cultivation was subsequently introduced into North Carolina and Georgia.

Rice cultivation influenced every aspect of lowcountry life. A rich plantation system developed, and the planters, accumulating great wealth, sent their sons to Oxford and Cambridge. Fine homes were built on the river plantations and were landscaped with formal gardens. Many of the exotic plants that adorned the gardens escaped over time and have become naturalized. Summer homes were built in cities such as Georgetown and Charleston. Today these homes serve as tourist attractions, especially in Charleston. A slave trade developed as a labor source to work the fields; their descendants are an integral part of the social structure in the lowcountry today.

As malaria increased, the planters settled the inland pinelands and seacoast islands to pass the summer months (the malaria season). The pinelands were beyond the flight path of the *Anopheles* mosquitos (the vector of the malaria parasite) that bred in the freshwater swamps. Also, the sandy soils of the high pinelands did not accumulate water that could be used as mosquito breeding pools. Villages such as Plantersville, Pinopolis, and Cordesville sprang up throughout the lowcountry. Along the coastal islands, where the adjacent marshes breed the salt marsh mosquito, which does not carry the malaria-causing parasite, settlements developed as retreats for the planters. Pawleys Island in Georgetown County, for example, became the retreat for people of the Waccamaw area.

The industrial base of the lowcountry began as a result of the rice industry. With the introduction of the horizontal steam engine in the early 1800s, numerous foundries produced engines and accessory equipment to operate the mills that prepared the rice for market (Porcher, 1987). Many companies that serve the lowcountry today are descendants of these early foundries.

More pertinent to this book, however, is the effect of the rice industry on the natural history of the lowcountry. Rice growing can be separated into two distinct periods: the inland swamp system period and the tidal system period. The inland swamp system, the initial method of growing rice under a water-controlled regime, began around 1700 and lasted until the end of the Revolutionary War, when it was replaced by the tidal system. The inland swamp system depended on rainwater to fill reservoirs that were essential for growing rice. An earthen bank was built up across the upper part of an inland swamp, from highland to highland. In their upper reaches the inland swamps supported freshwater swamp forests, while in their lower reaches, where they drained into coastal streams or rivers, they supported fresh or brackish marshes. Farther down from the upper bank a second bank was constructed, similar to the upper one. The area between the two banks was then cleared of trees, ditched, and made ready for planting. Water from the reservoir, through a trunk-gate system, flooded the fields. Another trunk-gate system in the lower bank was then used to drain the water from the fields when the tide was low in the adjacent stream. With a system established for controlling the water source, rice growing became profitable.

The inland system had one main drawback: The reservoirs depended on rainwater. A drought, which often occurred, meant crop loss. It is understandable, then, that a more dependable water supply for rice growing was found: the tidal section of freshwater rivers that traverse the lowcountry.

This reliable supply of water from the tidal section allowed the tidal system of rice growing to emerge. The freshwater rivers were bordered by fringes of freshwater tidal marshes and wide expanses of low-lying, freshwater tidal swamps. Twice a day, as far as 30 miles inland, the tide ebbed and flowed, draining then flooding the marshes and swamps. Beginning around the middle 1700s, an ingenious system was devised to apply this "rhythm of nature" to rice growing, thus ensuring a consistent supply of fresh water. On every river in the lowcountry above the influence of salt water and on river sections where at least a three-foot difference in low and high tide occurred, an attempt was made to grow rice. A bank was constructed from the highland through the swamp to the river's edge, along the river's edge, then back through the swamp to the highland. This bank kept the river water out of the banked area during high tide. A series of lower "check-banks" were constructed within the large area, dividing it into smaller fields. Each field was fitted with a trunk-gate system so each could be flooded or drained independently. Next the task of clearing the swamp began. Slaves, using primitive hand tools and oxen, felled, piled and burned the trees. The largest trees were cut at ground level (their stumps can still be seen today in the abandoned fields). Fields were then made ready for planting. Using the trunk-gate system, each field could be flooded when the tide rose or drained at low tide. This dependable supply of fresh water made rice growing profitable. By the end of the Revolutionary War, the tidal system replaced the inland system as the principal method of growing commercial rice, and it remained the basic method of commercial rice culture until the end of the industry in the early 1900s.

Both systems of growing rice had major effects on the state's natural history. Acres of inland swamps were cleared for fields. When the inland system was abandoned, the fields reverted to swamp forests. No records of the species composition of these original inland swamps exist; thus, it is not known how similar the present swamp forests are to the original. But the most pronounced legacy of the inland system is the reservoirs. In many cases the upper bank is still intact, creating a permanently flooded swamp that provides valuable habitat, especially for wading birds. Washo Reserve on the Santee Coastal Preserve, the Reserve Swamp at the Bluff Plantation Wildlife Sanctuary, and the reservoir at Caw Caw County Park represent just three of the former inland reservoirs

The major legacy of the tidal system is approximately 150,000 acres of abandoned tidal fields. Many still have their banks intact and are managed for waterfowl. The ability to control the water in these banked fields allows for a management regime that selects plants that are preferred by waterfowl, such as redroot (*Lachnanthes caroliniana*) or widgeon grass (*Ruppia maritima*). The majority of the abandoned fields, however, have broken banks that allow free exchange with tidal water (figure 7). These fields are undergoing succession to secondary swamp forests. In fact, many of the fields have already reverted to

FIGURE 7. Abandoned Rice Fields along the East Branch of the Cooper River.

swamp forests. Whether the mature, secondary swamp forests will be similar to the original swamp forests is not known. It is in these abandoned tidal fields that one of the greatest displays of wildflowers occurs: those of the freshwater tidal marshes. One can paddle a small boat through the broken banks and follow a myriad of canals, each revealing a different combination of freshwater marsh plants in spring, summer, and fall.

Rice growing ended around 1910 to 1911, when two disastrous hurricanes struck two years in a row, breaking the banks, flooding the fields with salt water, and destroying the crops. These storms, the loss of slave labor after the Civil War, and the advent of mechanized rice growing in Arkansas, Texas, and Louisiana around 1880, made it impossible to grow rice profitably.

After the Civil War and the demise of the rice industry, many plantations were bought by wealthy northerners who used them as hunting preserves or business retreats. Even though there was resentment in the South at having had to lose their lands to "outsiders," it was fortuitous since many of these plantations were established as wildlife preserves. The northerners came to love the land so much, that rather than see these plantations developed to serve a select few, they preserved them for the people of South Carolina. A prime example: Tom Yawkey, who owned the Boston Red Sox, gave the state 20,000 acres on the North Santee River. Today it is managed by the SCDNR as the Tom Yawkey Wildlife Center. Other such gifts or purchases include the Bluff Plantation Wildlife Sanctuary, the Santee Coastal Preserve, and Hobcaw Barony.

Cotton

Cotton farming in South Carolina and the Deep South is a history of unbridled greed, slavery, human suffering, economic bondage to a single-crop agricultural system, and indifference to the ecological consequences of repeated long-term cultivation of agricultural land. Although the effects of the cotton industry on cultivated soils is our major interest here, a brief introduction to the associated social and economic aspects is necessary to understand why cotton was able to maintain its status as a principal money crop in South Carolina for nearly 150 years. In the process, it destroyed the agricultural viability of more than 40% of the piedmont.

The long-staple, black seed cotton that we now know as sea-island cotton was first grown successfully in South Carolina in about 1790. Sea-island cotton has the long staple needed to make fine cotton garments. Since it could only be grown in a small section of the coastal zone south of Charleston, supply seldom exceeded demand, and prices remained high and profitable. Its demise was brought on by the onslaught of the boll weevil between 1917 and 1922. Because of its long growing season, sea-island cotton was especially susceptible to boll weevil infestation. Much of the acreage devastated by boll weevil was replanted with less-susceptible, short-staple, upland cottons.

The rise of cotton to worldwide prominence, however, involved a number of short-staple, green seed cottons known collectively as upland cotton. Upland cotton could be grown just about anywhere in the South, except in the mountains. It soon came into high demand even though its short staple could only be made into relatively coarse cloth. The development of the cotton gin in 1793, at about the same time textile production became mechanized in England, was largely responsible for the rapid rise in the prominence of upland cotton. Robert Mills, in his *Statistics of South Carolina* published in 1826, reported that upland cotton was the major crop throughout the state, except where sea-island cotton and rice were grown. By 1860 cotton production was reported to involve 80% of the South's entire labor pool.

The plantation system, which originated with the cultivation of rice and indigo and involves large land holdings and abundant slave labor, spread from the coast to the lower piedmont with the spread of cotton farming. Since cotton production is labor intensive, the number of slaves increased rapidly with the increase in cotton cultivation. In fact, cotton has been vilified as the impetus for the eight-fold increase in the slave population in the South between 1784 and 1860. South Carolina was no exception. By 1850, more than 80% of South Carolina counties had slave populations in excess of 50% of the total population. The plantation system soon dominated cotton production, but many small farms were scattered among the plantations.

With the end of the Civil War, loss of slave labor, and nearly all of the best lands already in cultivation, one might have predicted a decline in cotton production. Instead there was an increase in cotton cultivation due to a new labor system: tenancy. By the 1880s, more than 50% of piedmont crops had liens on them. By 1920, 65% of the farms in South Carolina were run by tenants. This period of economic bondage lasted from the end of Reconstruction in 1876 until after World War II. Even the depredations of the boll weevil, beginning about 1917 and described by some as "a calamity somewhat comparable to the potato blight [in Ireland] of 1840," didn't stop the momentum of cotton farming. By reducing production, prices rose and provided encouragement for more planting, and scientific advancements made control of the boll weevil and subsequent crop recovery possible. The Agricultural Adjustment Act of 1933 paid farmers not to grow certain crops, including cotton. It ended overproduction and maintained high prices, but it also heralded the demise of the small-acreage cotton farmer.

In 1860, 77% of the cotton was produced in the lower piedmont and inner coastal plain, and these regions continued to dominate the state's production until about 1920. After 1920, cotton production shifted to the upper piedmont, and by 1940 one-third of South Carolina's production was from the upper piedmont. Evidence suggests that soil erosion and soil infertility in the lower piedmont and inner coastal plain were responsible for this shift.

Cultivation of upland cotton in South Carolina and the Deep South was typically a very wasteful process, and profits throughout the reign of cotton were based on a exploitation of the land, which has left a legacy of reduced soil fertility and a severely eroded landscape.

The usual practice of cotton cultivation during the plantation era was to clear the land, plant cotton, and when yields declined, plant corn, and eventually abandon the fields. Since land was cheap, and the major cost of production was labor, landowners were seemingly indifferent to the loss of soil fertility that resulted from continual cropping and from the severe erosion that often accompanied cotton cultivation and abandonment to agriculture, especially in hilly regions. This was in sharp contrast to the planters of sea-island cotton, for whom land was a limiting resource. Early on, these planters practiced many of the now-accepted soil conservation practices such as contour plowing, ditching, terracing, crop rotation, and allowing fields to lie fallow, as well as fertilizing with everything from manure and crushed oyster shells to what we now call compost.

As in any economy that is focused on production with no consideration to depletion of resources, many criticized the typical methods of growing upland cotton. Just as there were few who listened to critics of the wanton decimation of the passenger pigeon (now extinct) or the American bison (once reduced to a few thousand), there were few who listened to such critics as Robert Mills, who wrote: "We wish to see them [the farmers] giving back to the soil some portion of the nourishment which they take from it; otherwise the most deplorable results must follow: short crops, and barren fields, the disappearance of the forests, and a desolate country."

Post-Reconstruction cotton cultivation differed little from the wasteful practices of the plantation era. Often they were worse, since putting new lands in production generally involved clearing and planting marginal, easily eroded lands. Abandoned fields often were again cleared and planted after an extended fallow period of 20 years or so, and sometimes cattle were allowed to graze on the "resting" land. This went on until nearly all the piedmont had been cleared and cultivated and eventually abandoned at least once. Since the prosperity of landowners and merchants involved in the tenancy system depended on the poverty of their tenant farmers, perhaps it is not surprising that soil conservation practices were not typical of this era. Although some efforts were made to restore land depleted by years of constant cultivation, fertilization tended to be used much more than soil conservation practices. John Harrington, longtime geology professor at Wofford College and a careful student of the geology and landscape of the South Carolina piedmont, long wondered why piedmont cotton farmers so often plowed their furrows up and down (perpendicular to) the slope, which even the most casual observer should realize would increase soil erosion. While visiting Ireland, he believed he found an answer. There he observed farmers plowing their furrows perpendicular to the slope but with very little erosion occurring due to the hard-to-erode soils. Most of the farmers in the piedmont were of Scotch-Irish descent!

What is the legacy of 150 years of cotton growing? According to S. W. Trimble (1972), the southern portion of the piedmont is one of the most severely eroded agricultural areas in the United States, and the South Carolina piedmont is one of the worst. Based on existing soil profiles and comparisons with expected soil profiles, Trimble estimated that the average depth of erosion in South Carolina was just under 10 inches, and other sources suggest that more than 12 inches were removed from some large areas. Trimble estimated that 40% of the piedmont in South Carolina was so severely eroded and the topsoil so depleted that it was rendered useless for agriculture. Why so much erosion? First, the soils of the piedmont are highly erodible because they are easily weathered and friable (easily crumbled). Second, the piedmont receives abundant rainfall throughout the year, including times when soil is relatively unprotected. Heavy summer thunderstorms may have been particularly damaging. Lastly, cultivation year after year, with little effort at restoring the soil, and plowing up and down the slope rather than parallel to the slope promoted erosion.

The sediments that eroded off piedmont uplands were washed into streams and floodplains, particularly in the piedmont and inner coastal plain. These areas still carry a heavy burden of sediment. Clarity of all but the smallest streams declined substantially, and most streams turned brown with sediment following modest rain showers, a situation we still see today. Toward the end of the nineteenth century, streambeds in some piedmont stream valleys had risen as much as 9 to 18 feet, and some bridges were literally buried in sediments. Streambed erosion raises sediment loads downstream and increases the distance that separates the streambed from the adjacent floodplain, which in turn changes the frequency and duration with which the floodplains are flooded. As streambeds become farther and farther separated from their floodplains, floodplains flood less and eventually become so separated that they no longer act as functional floodplain wetlands that store and clean floodwaters and provide temporary fish-foraging habitat. The piedmont today contains few floodplains that are functional wetlands. Erosion has decreased substantially since the end of World War II, so streambeds are now lowering.

Another legacy of cotton growing is the dominance in the lower piedmont of plantation forestry. The deeply eroded, infertile soils are suitable for growing pines, especially shortleaf and loblolly, but are too poor for natural regeneration of the oak-hickory forest that once dominated the landscape. It is hard to predict when or if this will change.

The massive alteration of the landscape that is associated with cotton did leave one beneficial legacy: the present system of national forests in South Carolina. In 1933, with the Great Depression in full swing and an abundance of tax delinquent land, the National Forest Reservation Commission established the Enoree and Long Cane purchase units in the piedmont, with the express purpose of retiring some marginal farmland and returning it to productive forest. By 1936, nearly 97,000 acres had been purchased, mostly in units of less than 300 acres. The Francis Marion and Sumter National Forests were established by President Franklin Roosevelt in that same year. By 1938, 243,000 acres had been purchased for the Francis Marion National Forest in the coastal plain counties of Berkeley and Charleston, most of which had been cut-over and regularly burned. By 1941, 253,271 acres had been purchased for the Sumter National Forest, including the piedmont acreages purchased in 1933 and previously purchased mountain acreages. Purchase of the cut-over and eroding land of the mountain district, the Andrew Pickens District, began soon after the passage of the Weeks Law in 1911, which allowed for federal purchase of lands for watershed protection. The national forest system in South Carolina now totals about 605,000 acres and comprises some of the most heavily forested land and some of the most significant natural areas in the state.

Forestry

Although the impact of the forest products industry on the South Carolina landscape is readily visible today in the form of widespread pine plantations, wood yards, and pulp and paper mills, the vast majority of woodlands are not managed forests. In 1993 only 2.4 million acres (19.4%) of the 12.4 million acres of unreserved timberland in South Carolina were classified as forest industry timberland, and nearly 72% was classified as nonindustrial private forest. It is true that most of the woodlands in pine plantations are forest industry lands, but it is unfair to blame the forest products industry for the loss of natural, unmanaged forest. In reality, it is long history of human occupation that is the real culprit, and agriculture and uncontrolled development deserve share of the blame.

To the earliest settlers, trees were viewed either as a source of lumber for export markets (especially fine woods such as black walnut) or as an impediment to land they wished to plant. Few roads meant that trees cut for lumber were mostly those growing along large watercourses, where transport of logs by water was possible. Lumber remained a small but important export throughout colonial times, and most shipments went to the West Indies rather than to Europe. After 1729, the British marked trees reserved for the crown with the broad arrow (an inverted V). The tree most typically marked in South Carolina was the live oak, which was used for special items in shipbuilding. During the colonial period many trees were cut for domestic use. An amazing variety of trees were used for a bewildering array of uses. Most of the trees in colonial times, however, were cut because they were obstacles to agriculture, with rice and indigo being the most important export crops and corn being a major staple crop. In the early years, agriculture was essentially what we now know as slash-and-burn.

Naval stores included a variety of products, among them pitch, tar, and turpentine, all derived from the wood of pines (mostly longleaf pine) and so named because of their use in building wooden ships. They were especially important in the Carolinas after 1700 when the British supply of naval stores was threatened by wars in Europe. A dependable supply from the American colonies was encouraged by an act of Parliament in 1704, which provided a premium or bounty for naval stores produced there. Although North Carolina was the industry leader for many years, and production waxed and waned over the years, the naval stores industry continued until after the Revolutionary War, and South Carolina led the nation in production for a few years around 1880. The industry declined in the late nineteenth century and ended in the early twentieth century due to competition with the lumber industry for longleaf pine. One can still find, in the sandhills and outer coastal plain, evidence of the naval stores industry in the stumps of dead pines and occasionally on living trees in the form of a "faced" lower trunk (i.e., where the bark was peeled off and the trunk was cut to exude resin) and a pocket cut ("boxed"), which allowed for the collection of the resin. Unfortunately, using the nineteenth-century "boxing" technique, trees often remained in production for only about four years.

With the invention of an efficient cotton gin in 1793 and the almost simultaneous mechanization of the textile industry in England, demand for cotton burgeoned, beginning an onslaught of converting forests to farmland that would last nearly 150 years. The annual conversion of forests to farms was somewhat limited, but the impact was large because of the shifting agriculture that was practiced. As soils became infertile, new lands were cleared and planted. The forests of the piedmont and inner coastal plain were especially hard hit, and the only lands ultimately not put under the plow were lands unsuitable for growing crops.

Timber harvesting became increasingly important in the nineteenth century, but it was not until the national lumber industry had finished cutting much of the forest in the northeast that big-time, commercial logging came to South Carolina. Railroads were important to the exploitation of forests, most of which were far from rivers. The extension of railroad tracks into inaccessible pinelands, swamps, and mountain coves, along with the development of numerous portable sawmills, was the foundation that allowed for widespread logging in the pinelands of the outer coastal plain, deep swamps of the inner coastal, and hardwood forests of the mountains. Much of the harvesting of virgin forests took place between 1880 and 1920. Despite an awareness by the national forest industry of the desirability of treating forests as renewable resources, much of this logging took place under a policy commonly known as "cut out and get out." Similarly, significant acreage was high-graded (i.e., only the best trees were taken), leaving poor growing trees as seed trees.

In the 1930s and 1940s, the Soil Conservation Service planted pines in large portions of the piedmont, with assistance from the Civilian Conservation Corps. Most of these plantings have since been harvested and replanted. Natural regeneration has supplemented tree plantings, and in 1986 fully one-half of the forests in the piedmont were in pines.

Planting, growing, and treating trees as an agricultural crop began about 1940s in the Pacific Northwest. It spread rapidly, and by the late 1940s was in full swing nationwide. Large corporations in the forest industry had long been concerned with obtaining a dependable supply of raw materials, and scientific-based tree farming was the logical solution.

Today the major forest products industry in South Carolina is the pulp and paper mill. International Paper opened the first paper mill in Georgetown in the 1930s. Since then, seven additional plants have opened, the most recent in Marlboro County near Bennettsville. As competition has stiffened and prices for land and transportation increased in recent years, many forest products companies have begun consolidating their forest land holdings near their mills and all have begun paying more attention to every aspect of the planting, growing, and harvesting of trees. Some companies are now very high-tech. A few even use advanced biotechnology techniques, such as "gene guns," to incorporate desirable genetic traits in trees! The tree most often planted is loblolly pine, with some longleaf and slash pine planted in the coastal plain.

With an ever-increasing emphasis on productivity and the "bottom-line," it is not surprising that most commercial tree farms are not providing much habitat for wildlife or for wildflowers. However, as productivity increases, less land is needed to produce the same amount of fiber or lumber, leaving more land for other uses. Moreover, management of commercial forest lands is becoming more site-based. This means pines are grown on sites that best support pines, and hardwoods are grown on sites that are best for hardwoods. Lastly, many in the industry are recognizing the value of leasing timber lands for hunting and are managing their lands in ways more friendly to wildlife in general.

MARSHES, SWAMPS, PEATLANDS, BOGS, AND FENS

Marshes, swamps, peatlands, bogs, and fens are wetlands. No single, accepted term in the scientific community defines a wetland. In general terms, however, wetlands are lands where saturation with water is the dominant factor determining the nature of soil development and the types of plant and animal communities living in the soil and on its surface.

Marshes

Marshes are wetlands that are inhabited by herbaceous plants that have their roots in the substrate but with their photosynthetic and reproductive organs principally emerged. Marshes have predominantly mineral (nonorganic) soils, even though much organic material may be incorporated. The dominant species are grasses, rushes, and sedges along with numerous broadleaf flowering plants. Marshes in South Carolina can be classified as salt, brackish, or fresh water.

Salt marshes generally occur on a peaty substrate along tidal inlets, behind barrier islands, and on spits along the maritime strand. They are regularly flooded and drained by tidal action. The soil is saturated and has a high salt concentration and low oxygen levels. The most extensive salt marsh community in the coastal area is the *Spartina* marsh dominated by smooth cordgrass (*Spartina alterniflora*, plate 595). Vast stretches of this marsh system are readily visible as one drives from the mainland to the barrier islands, such as Kiawah, Folly, Hilton Head, and Pawleys.

Brackish marshes are transitional communities between the freshwater and saltwater marshes. They occur in the outer coastal plain where fresh water and salt water mix, so species of both systems occur here. The dominant species are emergent grasses, sedges, and rushes. The brackish marshes occur at varying distances up rivers from the coast. The more fresh water coming down the rivers, the closer the brackish zone occurs to the coast.

Freshwater marshes occur both inland and along the coastal rivers. Inland freshwater marshes occur throughout the state and are a diverse system fed by inflowing water, seepage, or precipitation. The variable water supply results in flooding during high rainfall and drawdown during dry periods, a feature that shapes the structure and composition of the marsh. Inland marshes occur along the edges of lakes and ponds, in canals and roadside ditches, and along the edge of inland swamps.

The dominant freshwater marshes of the state, however, are the tidal freshwater marshes (plate 520) of the outer coastal plain. These marshes occur along the edge of the brownwater and blackwater rivers and are close enough to be affected by daily freshwater tides but far enough to be unaffected by the intrusion of salt water. Vast expanses of these marshes occur in the abandoned rice fields along rivers. Narrow zones of freshwater marsh also occur where the tidal swamps border the rivers. The low marsh, with its deeper water, is characterized by broadleaf monocots such as arrow arum and pickerelweed and showy dicots such as bur-marigold. The high marsh is a mixture of low marsh species plus numerous grasses, rushes, and sedges.

Swamps

Woody plants dominate swamp wetlands. The substrate in swamps is flooded for one or more extended periods during each year. Sometimes the flooding is more or less permanent, but usually a swamp is without surface water for at least part of the year. Although much organic material may be incorporated in the soil, swamps have predominantly mineral (nonorganic) soils. South Carolina's swamps are extensive and varied and include the alluvial bottomland swamps (i.e., swamps associated with streams and rivers), tidal freshwater swamps, and nonalluvial swamps.

Bottomland swamps occur on the alluvial floodplains of the brownwater rivers of the lower piedmont and coastal plain, and on the blackwater rivers of the coastal plain. Brownwater rivers originate in the mountains and piedmont and have wide alluvial floodplains, while the blackwater rivers originate in the coastal plain and have narrower, less-developed alluvial floodplains. On the regions of the floodplain where the land is almost continually flooded, bald cypress-tupelo gum swamps (plate 441) occur. Here the trees exhibit typical hydromorphic features in response to growing in water: buttresses, knees (in bald cypress), and spongy roots. Hardwood bottoms (plate 456) occur in the coastal plain and piedmont on floodplains that are slightly elevated above the adjoining swamp forests. Here the land is often flooded, but it is dry through much of the year. The dominant vegetation is a mix of water-tolerant, deciduous hardwoods, with oaks predominating and an occasional cypress from the adjacent swamp forests also occurring.

Tidal freshwater swamps occur in the outer coastal plain, from the upper limit of tidal influence to the brackish water line downstream. Tidal freshwater swamps owe their nature to the river tides. Twice a day they are flooded and twice a day they are free of surface water. Both brownwater and blackwater rivers support tidal swamp forests. Tidal freshwater swamps today are mainly secondary swamps. The original tidal swamps were cleared to make rice fields. The fields were abandoned in the early 1900s, and today, secondary tidal swamps are gradually reclaiming the fields. The tidal swamps are similar in composition to the alluvial swamps.

A variety of nonalluvial swamps occur in the state. The main feature distinguishing these swamps is that they are not associated with moving river water. In other words, they are not alluvial or tidal systems. These swamps occur in two types of habitats: (1) upland, isolated sites such as lime sinks, Carolina bays, and irregular depressions, and (2) seepage slopes (see below) associated with river systems along the boundary of floodplains and uplands. The water supply for the bays, sinks, irregular depressions, and seepage slopes is predominately rainwater. One example of an upland, nonalluvial swamp that is covered in this book is the pond cypress swamp gum upland swamp (plate 512).

Peatlands

Peatlands are simply wetlands whose soils are peat, the partially decomposed remains of dead plants. The dominant peatlands in the state are the pocosins or evergreen shrub bogs. Pocosins (plate 477) are freshwater wetlands found extensively in the outer coastal plain of Virginia, North Carolina, South Carolina, and Georgia. They are fire-adapted systems dominated by a tangled mass of broadleaf evergreen or semievergreen shrubs and vines, with scattered pond pines and occasional bay trees (swamp red bay, sweet bay and loblolly bay). The most extensive pocosins are found on flat upland areas. Additionally, pocosins may be found in Carolina bays, wet seepage slopes, and in low areas of relict dune fields.

Another type of pocosin is the streamhead pocosin, which is found primarily in the sandhills. They occur along the headwaters of small streams, streamside flats, and extend up adjacent hillsides. This community is most common in the fall-line sandhills, but it does occur in the inner coastal plain.

Bogs

Bogs are ombrotrophic (mineral-poor) wetlands because they receive their water from rain, which contains few minerals. The only true bogs in South Carolina are the sphagnum openings in pocosins. Periodic fires create these openings in the shrub layer where sphagnum develops. If the openings are removed far enough from the boundary of the pocosin and adjacent upland so that they receive no seepage, only rainwater, they are true bogs.

Fens

Fens are wetlands that harbor an open, herb-dominated community, and receive water from rain and from seepage. Seepages are not plant communities per se. Seepage refers to a water source, which can allow wetland communities like a fen to develop. Seepage occurs when rainwater penetrates the soil to an impermeable layer (such as a clay hardpan). The water then moves laterally through the soil over this impermeable layer. Where the soil slopes so that the impermeable layer is exposed at the surface (outcrops), water seeps out of the soil and flows down the slope. The water picks up dissolved minerals from the soil, which contribute to the mineral supply of the seepage. Figure 8 (following page) illustrates a generalized seepage system.

If the seepage water feeding a fen is mineral-poor, it is a poor fen. Often, however, the water seeps through limestone or mafic rock and picks up minerals. These are rich fens because of the high mineral content.

In the section, "South Carolina's natural wildflower communities," two mountain communities are discussed, the montane bog and the cataract bog. These two communities are not bogs, as defined above, but fens. Their main source of water is seepage, not rainwater. However, the term bog has been used for so long for these communities that we retain this common usage and refer to them as bogs. The reader is now aware of their true nature—that is, they are fens.

FIGURE 8. Generalized Seepage System.

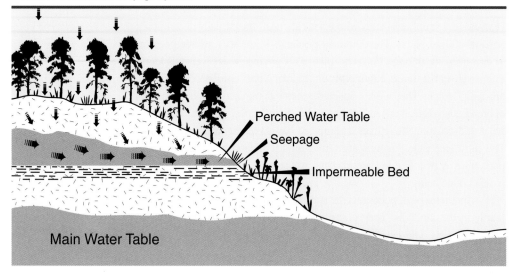

South Carolina's Natural Wildflower Communities

THE MOUNTAINS

The granitic dome community

Granitic domes

The typical granitic dome community (plate 1) is found mostly in the mountains but occasionally occurs on monadnocks (mountains of resistant rock) in the piedmont. It occurs on exposed upper slopes or ridges, usually as steep exposures, except for small gently sloping areas at the top. It is recognized by the smooth (exfoliating) surface of the exposed rock. Granitic domes are sometimes called exfoliation domes because they consist of layers of rock similar to the layers of an onion. These layers were produced during the formation of the rock as a means of relieving pressure. Soils generally are shallow, and trees and shrubs are restricted to the margins or to pockets of deeper soil, which tend to be rare because of the sparsity of fractures or crevices. Vegetation is zoned by soil depth. Only mosses and lichens occupy bare rock, but once a soil layer develops, a variety of vascular plants soon invade. Herbaceous species that are usually only found on domes include mountain dwarf-dandelion (*Krigia montana*), Allegheny live-for-ever (*Sedum telephoides,* plate 12), cliff saxifrage (*Saxifraga michauxii*), divided-leaf ragwort (*Senecio millefolium*), and spikemosses (*Selaginella tortipila* or *S. rupestris*). Herbaceous species that are also common to granitic domes include elf orpine (*Diamorpha smallii*), smallflower phacelia (*Phacelia dubia*), eggleaf rushfoil, several species of broomsedge, hairy and woolly lip-ferns (*Cheilanthes lanosa* and *C. tomentosa*), pineweed, and Small's ragwort. Woody species that occur at the edges of the dome or in mats that have deep soil include fringe-tree, wafer-ash (*Ptelea trifoliata*), winged sumac (*Rhus copallina*), eastern red cedar, Virginia pine, and, depending on the depth and richness of the soil, a variety of other xerophytic to mesophytic trees. Seepages at the upper edges may harbor interesting species such as round-leaf sundew (*Drosera rotundifolia*), horned bladderwort, flatrock pimpernel, and several species of meadow-beauty (*Rhexia mariana* and/or *R. virginica*). Higher elevation granitic domes may include such species as sand myrtle (*Leiophyllum buxifolium,* plate 292), prolific St. John's-wort (*Hypericum prolificum*), and Table Mountain pine (*Pinus pungens,* plate 155).

Granitic domes associated with calcium-producing rocks are sometimes described as a basic variant of granitic domes. These domes harbor such calcium-loving species as yellow honeysuckle (*Lonicera flava,* plate 4), southern thimbleweed (*Anemone berlanderi*), Canada columbine (*Aquilegia canadensis*), smooth indigo-bush (*Amorpha glabra*), Small's beardtongue (*Penstemon smallii,* plate 7), hairy mock-orange (*Philadelphus hirsutus*), and Seneca snakeroot

(*Polygala senega*). An abundant presence of red cedar along the outcrop margins is often a good indicator of this variant. The adjacent woodland often is quite rich, even on the shallow soils of the southern exposures.

A second variant of granitic domes is the acidic cliff. The community is characterized by sheer slopes, exposed rock, and a canopy cover that is less than 25%. The best sites have sheer exposures of fractured, acidic rock. This variant is common in the mountains and rare in the piedmont. In the driest, most open sites, many species of typical granitic domes or granitic flatrock outcrops are present, especially broomsedges, oat grasses, spikemosses, hawkweeds, and ragworts. On moister sites, granitic dome species such as mountain dwarf-dandelion and cliff saxifrage may occur. Because of the fractured rock, crevices are common and rock-loving ferns are present, including lipferns and mountain spleenwort (*Asplenium montanum*). Shrubs, trees, and other herbs are typical of the surrounding forest community; they may be mesic, xeric, or even boggy species depending on the nature of the adjacent forest community. Because of the open canopy, a variety of weedy species may occur, including fleabanes (*Erigeron* spp.), butterfly-weed (*Asclepias tuberosa* subsp. *tuberosa*), and Indian pink.

The spray cliffs community

Spray cliffs

The spray cliff (plate 15) is a distinctive community that has appeal for the naturalist because it is always associated with waterfalls. Since accessing some of these communities can be dangerous, care should be taken when exploring the spray cliff community.

Spray cliff communities occur on cliffs, ledges, and gently sloping rock faces that are frequently wetted by the spray or splash from adjacent waterfalls. Because constant spray and/or splash from the waterfall provide high humidity and moisture, mosses and liverworts are often abundant. Vascular plants are found in pockets of shallow soil that collect in tiny crevices and ledges of the rock face. Temperature is moderated in these communities by spray water and because it is sheltered from the sun and wind.

Although the spray cliff community is not high in species diversity, it does harbor a distinct assemblage of plants. The canopy from adjacent forest communities often provides some shade, but there are no trees in the spray cliff community, probably due to the combination of steepness, lack of soil, and wetness. A few dwarfed stems of Canada hemlock (*Tsuga canadensis*), northern wild raisin (*Viburnum cassinoides*), great laurel (*Rhododendron maximum*), or mountain laurel (*Kalmia latifolia*) are sometimes present. Herbs that are typically found here include Appalachian bluet (*Houstonia serpyllifolia,* plate 20), mountain meadow rue (*Thalictrum clavatum*), branch-lettuce (*Saxifraga micranthidifolia*), meadow spikemoss (*Selaginella apoda*), jewelweed (*Impatiens capensis*), common rockcap fern (*Polypodium virginianum*, plate 23), galax (*Galax urceolata*), and maidenhair spleenwort (*Asplenium trichomanes*). Rare species are only known from a few spray cliff communities and include American water-pennywort (*Hydrocotyle americana*, plate 22) and cave alumroot (*Heuchera parviflora*), which is found in either moist or dry overhanging rock ledges.

The seepage communities

Cataract bogs

Cataract bogs are one of the most distinctive and aesthetically pleasing wild-flower communities (plate 25). It is somewhat boggy and shares many of the species typical of bogs in the mountains and upper piedmont. The best examples of this community are along the margins of small streams that course over rather smooth rock surfaces (granitic dome). Since the water is sliding rather than falling vertically as in a typical waterfall, the term cataract is somewhat inaccurate. The community is primarily fed by seepage, although the stream margins sometimes are a significant water source. The community varies in elevation from about 1200 to 2400 feet and occurs on middle, upper, and occasionally lower slopes. Bog habitats are best developed where streams slide over a margin of rock outcrops that have a nearly level horizontal component and a slope of 5 to 20 degrees. These habitats are in many ways an ideal bog habitat because (1) light is abundant due to the adjacent rock outcrop, (2) moisture is abundant from seepage, and (3) plant succession is slowed because the bog is on shallow soil that overlays rock.

Cataract bogs form a narrow zone immediately adjacent to the associated stream and are shaded in part by trees and shrubs in the adjacent plant communities. Sometimes "bog" trees such as red maple (*Acer rubrum*) are present. Shrubs include tag alder (*Alnus serrulata*), red chokeberry (*Aronia arbutifolia*), yellowroot (*Xanthorhiza simplissima*), mountain laurel (*Kalmia latifolia*), great laurel (*Rhododendron maximum*), and smooth azalea (*R. arborescens*). Herbs tend to be more abundant than grasses and sedges. The distinctiveness of this community is derived from the presence of unusual herbs. Carnivorous plants are sometimes present in abundance, including mountain sweet pitcher-plant (*Sarracenia jonesii,* plate 29), frog's breeches (*Sarracenia purpurea* var. *venosa,* plate 331), a hybrid of *S. purpurea* and *S. jonesii,* horned bladderwort (*Utricularia cornuta,* plate 30), and round-leaf sundew (*Drosera rotundifolia,* plate 334). Other rare or unusual species include white fringeless orchid (*Platanthera integrilabia,* plate 31) and limeseep grass-of-Parnassus (*Parnassia grandifolia,* plate 34), and in drier margins, mountain witch-alder (*Fothergilla major*) and Indian paint brush (*Castilleja coccinea,* plate 28). The presence of *Parnassia* suggests a high calcium or magnesium content for at least some of the rocks in these areas. Additional orchids that occur in this community include small green wood-orchid (*Platanthera clavellata*), yellow-fringed orchid (*P. ciliaris*), rose pogonia (*Pogonia ophioglossoides*), fragrant ladies' -tresses (*Spiranthes cernua*), and common grass-pink (*Calopogon tuberosus*). Other species of interest include stiff cowbane (*Oxypolis rigidior*), Appalachian bluet (*Houstonia serpyllifolia*), several species of lobelia, and northern sundrops (*Oenothera tetragona*).

Montane bogs

Montane bogs, sometimes called sphagnum bogs, upland bogs, or Southern Appalachian bogs, are distinguished from other wetland or bottomland forests in the mountains by the presence of sphagnum-dominated openings. These open areas are depressions or seepage channels in streamside flats. In addition to being dominated by a variety of species of sphagnum mosses, they have poor drainage, acid pH, and many grasses, sedges, ferns, and broadleaf herbs. The best examples of this community have boggy openings of more than one acre, but the only good example in South Carolina has long linear openings along seepage channels.

The canopy of the forested portions of this community may be sparse or heavy, and the shrub layer, as the term "forested thicket" suggests, is dense and difficult to traverse. Bamboo-vine (*Smilax laurifolia*) is often abundant at the margins of the openings and in the adjacent shrub thickets, making movement difficult anywhere but in the openings.

Since there is only one montane bog in South Carolina, Mathews Creek Bog, refer to the description of this bog for an account of species that dominate the herb, shrub, and tree strata. Montane bogs are rare and harbor rare species. The most spectacular of the rarities are swamp pink (*Helonias bullata*, plate 37) and bog rose orchid (*Arethusa bulbosa*).

Bogs are rare in the mountains because of the scarcity of flat, wet sites and because they are successional plant communities that require some sort of disturbance to maintain the early successional status of the boggy openings. In the absence of disturbance, such as periodic fire, the boggy openings become filled in by shrubs and trees, and bog plants disappear.

Mathews Creek Bog was once a good example of a montane bog, but natural succession has degraded the site since 1979. The invasion of shrubs, mostly great laurel (*Rhododendron maximum*), has reduced the sphagnum-dominated areas by more than one-half. The population of swamp pink has declined and two rare orchids, Appalachian twayblade (*Listera smallii*) and bog rose orchid, have disappeared. Shrub diversity also appears to have declined, while species such as male-berry (*Lyonia ligustrina*) and clammy azalea (*Rhododendron viscosum*) seem to have increased. The herb layer also has decreased in diversity, while American climbing fern (*Lygodium palmatum*), northern long sedge (*Carex folliculata*), and galax (*Galax urceolata*) appear to have increased. Although the absence of fire is the likely culprit, the exact cause of this rapid natural succession is unknown. If appropriate active management is not initiated soon, this site may not be recoverable.

The rocky streamside community

Rocky streamsides

The rocky streamside community (plate 42) is in and adjacent to streams and rivers and consists of gravel bars or exposed bedrock and/or boulders with sandy/gravelly soil. It is common in the mountains and much less common in the piedmont. Plant composition is extremely variable from site to site because of differences in stream size, amount and degree of bedrock exposure, boulders, gravel, and extent and duration of flooding. Trees are usually not present in abundance because these habitats are too rocky, too wet, or too severely scoured by intermittent floods; however, black willow (*Salix nigra*) and sycamore (*Platanus occidentalis*) are usually present, at least as dwarfs in sites that have wide, rocky/gravelly streamsides. Shrub cover is generally sparse to moderate, with occasional dense thickets. A wide variety of shrub species may be present, with the best sites displaying tag alder (*Alnus serrulata*), Virginia willow (*Itea virginica*), bush-honeysuckle (*Diervilla sessilifolia*, plate 48), and several species of azaleas, including smooth azalea (*Rhododendron arborescens,* plate 46) and clammy azalea (*R. viscosum*). Herbs include mosses and liverworts, as well as grasses, sedges, and rushes. A great diversity of broadleaf herbs also may be present. Sites with variable microtopography may have a mix of dry, mesic, and wet-loving species as well as many weedy species. Herbs that occur in this community include brookfoam (*Boykinia anconitifolia*), Carolina tassel-rue (*Trautvetteria caroliniensis,* plate 49), common bluet (*Houstonia caerulea*), hollow-stem Joe-pye weed (*Eupatorium fistulosum*), and coneflower (*Rudbeckia laciniata*). Appalachian bluet (*H. serpylifolia*) and mountain meadow rue (*Thalictrum clavatum*), species that are more typical of seepages, are often present. Ash-leaf golden-banner (*Thermopsis fraxinifolia,* plate 148), a rare species that is more typical of dry ridges, is sometimes present. Mountain dwarf-dandelion (*Krigia montana*) may be more abundant here in dry rock crevices that are above the flood zone than it is in its granitic dome habitat. A variety of composites also are present, including goldenrods, asters, and coreopsis.

Because this is a wildflower community occurring in nearly full sun, species bloom all year, but a visit in early July allows one to see most of the characteristic species in bloom. The associated clear water stream makes this a pleasant plant community to visit any time of the year. The best examples of this plant community are along the Chattooga and Chauga Rivers in Oconee County.

The deciduous forest communities

Cove forests

Cove forests are the best known of the mountain communities and are appreciated by botanists and nature lovers for their diversity of plants in all strata, especially the herb layer. It is a mesic community, so it is always found in sheltered locations on the lower slopes of broad ravines or on broad flats adjacent to streams. It occasionally occupies midslope locations on north-facing slopes, especially where the soil is rich. The dictionary definition that fits the historical use of the term cove by early mountain residents is a "level area sheltered by hills or mountains." Soils on these sites are typically deep and rich, and in South Carolina at least some are almost always associated with amphibolite, a metamorphic rock with a high content of the calcium-rich mineral hornblende. The pH of the soil in rich cove forests is always above 6.0. Cove forests do occur in the piedmont, but they are rare.

The dense canopy includes a variety of mesophytic trees. Typical trees include Appalachian basswood (*Tilia heterophylla*), yellow buckeye (*Aesculus octandra*), sweet birch (*Betula lenta*), and northern red oak (*Quercus rubra*). Other trees include tulip tree (*Liriodendron tulipifera*), American ash (*Fraxinus americana*), beech (*Fagus grandifolia*), and Canada hemlock (*Tsuga canadensis*). Few oak species are present other than northern red oak.

The understory is usually sparse and includes such species as flowering dogwood (*Cornus florida*), hop hornbeam (*Ostrya virginiana*), ironwood (*Carpinus caroliniana*), common silverbell (*Halesia tetraptera*), and Fraser magnolia (*Magnolia fraseri,* plate 66).

The shrub layer is sparse but may be dense on acidic sites. Typical shrub species include sweet-shrub (*Calycanthus floridus* var. *laevigatus,* plate 45), wild allspice (*Lindera benzoin*), American hazelnut (*Corylus americana,* plate 220), pagoda dogwood (*Cornus alternifolia*), snowy hydrangea (*Hydrangea radiata),* and on acidic sites, great laurel (*Rhododendron maximum*) and mountain doghobble (*Leucothoë fontanesiana*).

The dense and diverse herb layer is characteristic of cove forests in the mountains, just as it is for basic-mesic forests in the piedmont. A great diversity of herbs may be present, but the species that are rare and distinctive to cove forests include blue cohosh, ginseng, walking fern, Canada enchanters'-nightshade, and yellow lady's slipper. Species that are found here and also in other communities include sharp-lobed liverleaf, bloodroot, maidenhair fern, common black cohosh, common white snakeroot, common foamflower, Christmas fern, wood-nettle, dwarf crested iris, lily-leaved twayblade, thimbleweed (*Anemone quinquefolia*), common blue wood aster, speckled woodlily, eastern goat's-beard, showy orchis, and other herbs typical of mesic forests in the mountains and piedmont. Additional rarities that are found in only one or in a few sites include sweet white trillium, pale yellow trillium, large-flowered trillium, miterwort (*Mitella diphylla*), fancy fern (*Dryopteris intermedia*), goldie's wood fern, fernleaf phacelia, mapleleaf waterleaf, Allegheny spurge, and Fraser's loosestrife.

Some botanists define a separate community, the acidic cove forest, for forests that have some of the mesophytic trees of the cove forests but whose shrub and herb layer is similar to those of the Canada hemlock forests. The observant naturalist will note that there are often transitional communities where two distinct communities meet. The transition zone between cove forests and adjacent forests seems to be especially wide.

Unlike many of the communities of the dry ridges and upper slopes in the mountains and piedmont, cove forests are not fire dependant. For the maintenance of diversity, they apparently do require disturbance in the form of canopy gaps, particularly in the tree and herb layers. High winds that topple tall trees are the main source for the creation of canopy gaps.

Chestnut oak forests

Chestnut oak may dominate forests in the inner coastal plain, the entire piedmont, and the mountains, but we restrict our definition of chestnut oak forests (plate 89) to the definition accepted by most ecologists: low to moderate elevation communities of the mountains and upper piedmont, where American chestnut (*Castanea dentata*) once dominated. Other chestnut oak dominated communities, including those associated with monadnocks and rock outcroppings, are included with the broadly defined oak-hickory forest. Chestnut oak forests in the mountains are found on low ridge tops and the upper slopes on any exposure, although they are more common on east- and west-facing slopes. In the upper piedmont, this forest type is rare and is only found at relatively high elevations, often on upper, north-facing slopes.

This community was the preferred community for American chestnut, which was once the most valuable tree in eastern North America. Fallen chestnut logs (plate 89) and old stumps are still abundant. Following devastation by chestnut blight in the early 1900s, American chestnut has been replaced by chestnut oak (*Quercus montana,* plate 97) and scarlet oak (*Q. coccinea*), which now dominate the closed canopy of this sub-xeric community. Chestnut oak, in particular, is fire-tolerant, and the number of trees probably increases following fire and timber harvest. Additional canopy species include many of the dry to dry-mesic oaks and hickories, especially white oak (*Q. alba*) and mockernut hickory (*Carya tomentosa*) as well as black gum (*Nyssa sylvatica*), various pines, and occasionally, where chestnut oak forests border rocky ledges, Carolina hemlock (*Tsuga caroliniana,* plate 154). Sprouts of American chestnut may dominate the subcanopy. Destruction by chestnut blight fungus at or just after the first flowering precludes this species ascension to canopy dominance. Additional understory trees include sourwood (*Oxydendron arboreum*), sassafras (*Sassafras albidum*), red maple (*Acer rubrum*), and downy serviceberry (*Amelanchier arborea*).

The shrub layer may be dominated by tall heaths such as mountain laurel (*Kalmia latifolia*) and great laurel (*Rhododendron maximum*) or low heaths such as bear huckleberry (*Gaylussacia ursina*) and southern deerberry (*Vaccinium stamineum* var. *melanocarpum*) or by a mix of tall and low heaths. Occasionally the shrub layer is poorly developed, in which case herbaceous plant diversity increases. Gorge rhododendron (*Rhododendron minus,* plate 92) and flame azalea (*R. calendulaceum,* plate 94) sometimes produce spectacular displays. The rare mountain witch-alder (*Fothergilla major*) is sometimes found here. This community is not known for its spring wildflower diversity, and although herb cover is sparse, some interesting species are present, including galax (*Galax urceolata*), trailing arbutus (*Epigaea repens*), veiny hawkweed (*Hieracium venosum*), Solomon's seal (*Polygonatum biflorum*), and Indian cucumber-root (*Medeola virginica*). Knowledgeable naturalists can let their nose lead them to a colony of the seldom-seen sweet pinesap (*Monotropsis odorata,* plate 139), whose cinnamon-scented flowers make the task of discovery at least possible, if not easy.

Because earlier logging operations took only quality hardwoods, leaving behind the poor quality trees, and because chestnut oak seldom grows straight and true as is desired by lumberman, most of the existing stands of chestnut oak forests are dominated by large, inferior chestnut oaks. Restoring these stands to their original high quality will be a challenge.

Woodland margins

Woodland margin communities include herbs with high light requirements that are not typical of ruderal environments. Designating such a community would not be necessary if fire had not been suppressed for so long. Several very rare species are largely restricted to this community, including smooth purple coneflower (*Echinacea laevigata,* plate 104), Blue Ridge bindweed (*Calystegia sericata*), and Fraser's loosestrife (*Lysimachia fraseri,* plate 109). These rare species are nearly confined to the woodland margins along roads, usually old logging roads. All respond well to fire. If natural pine-oak woodlands were subjected to periodic fire, these species probably would occur there. In fact, at Pine Mountain in the Andrew Pickens District of the Sumter National Forest, where fire is now being employed as a management tool, populations of both Blue Ridge bindweed and smooth purple coneflower have increased dramatically. Efforts to use fire to restore the pine-oak heath community at the Buzzards Roost Heritage Preserve also have increased the abundance and flowering frequency of Blue Ridge bindweed.

Other dry woodland species, such as hairy angelica and Indian-tobacco, are most abundant in openings or in woodland margins along roads. Species such as Robin's-plantain and fire pink are most obvious in the moist to dry woodland margins.

Montane oak-hickory forests

Montane oak-hickory forests are a high elevation variant of the oak-hickory forests that are common in the piedmont and mountains. These forests are generally found at elevations above 2500 feet, either on ridge tops or on upper slopes that slope gently and are exposed but not rocky. This community occurs in high-calcium soils. The canopy is dominated by oaks and hickories, with white oak (*Quercus alba,* plate 265), northern red oak (*Q. rubra*), chestnut oak (*Q. montana*), pignut hickory (*Carya glabra*), and shagbark hickory (*C. ovata*) most common. Tulip tree is usually present, and it may be abundant in sites subjected to past large-scale disturbance. Logs and sprouts of American chestnut are abundant. Shrub cover is generally moderate, with mountain laurel, witch-hazel, and flame azalea usually present. Common silverbell and cucumber magnolia (*Magnolia acuminata*) are usually present, either as understory trees or tall shrubs. The diverse herbaceous layer alerts the observant hiker to this somewhat unusual high-elevation community. Rare herbs (for South Carolina) may include Dutchman's pipe (*Aristolochia macrophylla,* plate 73), common blue monkshood (*Aconitum uncinatum,* plate 83), Appalachian mountain-mint (*Pycnanthemum montanum,* plate 76), Walter's crownbeard (*Verbesina walteri*), broadleaf coreopsis (*Coreopsis latifolia,* plate 116), and several species of trillium and violet. This community merges downslope with the chestnut oak forest or pine-oak heath community; elements of those communities may be present also.

The evergreen forest communities

Canada hemlock forests

This is one of the most abundant and easily recognized mesic communities in the mountains. It is found in only a few sites in the piedmont. This community (plate 121) is always on highly acidic soils and borders nearly every narrow ravine in the mountains that has a small stream running through it. It is also found on broad streamside flats, on north-facing slopes, and in bands of varying width above cove forests. The forest is characteristically dense with a high dominance of Canada hemlock (*Tsuga canadensis*). Other important trees include white pine (*Pinus strobus*) and sweet birch (*Betula lenta*). Great laurel (*Rhododendron maximum,* plate 133) usually forms a dense undergrowth, often mixed with mountain laurel. Mountain doghobble (*Leucothoë fontanesiana,* plate 129) sometimes forms a dense low shrub layer. In places where the understory is not dense, a variety of shrubs may be present, including buffalo-nut (*Pyrularia pubera*), witch-hazel (*Hamamelis virginiana*), strawberry-bush (*Euonymus americana*), mountain white-alder (*Clethra acuminata,* plate 134), and the rare mountain camellia (*Stewartia ovata*). Herbaceous plant diversity is low, and typical species include partridge berry, Indian cucumber-root, common foamflower (*Tiarella cordifolia* var. *collina*), sessile-leaf bellwort, black cohosh, round-leaf yellow violet, and sweet white violet. Ferns sometimes form a dense ground cover. The most common are New York fern (*Thelypteris novaboracensis*), hay-scented fern (*Dennstaedtia punctilobula*), and Christmas fern (*Polystichum acrostichoides*). At high elevations, painted trillium (*Trillium undulatum,* plate 128), long-spur violet (*V. rostrata*), French broad heartleaf (*Hexastylis rhombiformis,* plate 122), and Appalachian twayblade (*Listera smallii*) can occasionally be found. Where this community occurs on broad streamside flats, the understory is usually quite sparse and three-birds orchid (*Triphora trianthophora*) and persistent trillium (*Trillium persistens,* plate 125) are uncommon but delightful finds.

Since this community is often bounded by more diverse communities (i.e., cove forests or oak-hickory forest communities), some of the species typical of these communities may be present.

Pine-oak heaths

Pine-oak heaths (plate 137) are reminiscent of the pine barrens of New England and New Jersey. This community occurs on poor, highly acidic soils of narrow ridges, steep south slopes, and the entire tops of small mountains in the upper piedmont and mountains. A variety of pines and dry-site oaks dominate the often stunted canopy. Pitch pine (*Pinus rigida*) and Virginia pine (*P. virginiana*) are the most common pines, while Table Mountain Pine occurs on very dry soils in high-elevation sites, white pine (*P. strobus*) may dominate on more mesic high-elevation sites (especially sites that were previously cleared by man), and shortleaf pine (*P. echinata*) may be present on low-elevation sites, especially in the piedmont. Oaks in this community typically include scarlet oak (*Q. coccinea*), black oak (*Q. velutina*), chestnut oak (*Q. montana*), and less commonly white oak (*Q. alba*) or blackjack oak (*Q. marilandica*). Understory species include black gum, sourwood, sassafras, the stump sprouts of American chestnut, and occasionally Carolina hemlock (*Tsuga caroliniana,* plate 154). The shrub layer is usually dense, consisting of evergreen and deciduous ericads, and may be either "tall" or "low." Tall ericads include scattered to dense mountain laurel and/or gorge rhododendron (*Rhododendron minus*), interspersed with a dense cover of bear and black huckleberries (*Gaylussacia ursina* and *G. baccata* respectively) and mountain doghobble (*Leucothoë fontanesiana,* plate 129). Horse sugar is one of the few nonericad shrubs typically found here. Low heaths are dominated by a moderate to dense cover of the low-growing dryland blueberry (*V. vacillans*).

Herbaceous plant diversity is low, and typical species include trailing arbutus, pale yellow bellwort (*Uvularia puberula*), goat's rue (*Tephrosia virginiana*), galax, and spotted wintergreen. Bracken fern (*Pteridium aquilinum*) may form large stands or is widely scattered. Species that are characteristic of this community, but are rarely seen, include turkeybeard (*Xerophyllum asphodeloides,* plate 149), wintergreen (*Gaultheria procumbens,* plate 151), ash-leaf golden-banner (*Thermopsis fraxinifolia,* plate 148), gaywings (*Polygala paucifolia,* plate 90), sweet fern (*Comptonia peregrina,* plate 147), sweet pinesap (*Monotropsis odorata,* plate 139), and mountain witch-alder (*Fothergilla major*).

The attractive, small, spreading pogonia (*Cleistes bifaria*) is a common component of this community, but it is seldom seen because it blooms in the heat of June and July.

Like the pine barrens of New Jersey, this community probably depends on periodic fires for its maintenance. Lightening-ignited fires probably were important in the past. Today, most managers of these communities on state or federal lands seem reluctant to provide prescribed fires.

THE PIEDMONT

The granitic flatrocks community

Granitic flatrocks

Granitic flatrocks (plate 156) may be the most spectacular ecosystem in the piedmont. They are restricted to the piedmont and are best developed in Georgia and South Carolina. They consist of small to expansive exposures of granite or gneissic rocks that have a smooth (exfoliating) surface. Flatrock outcrops are level or slope gently and are distinguished from granitic domes and cliffs by the small elevation change from the top to the base of the outcrop.

Granitic flatrocks harbor a mosaic of nonforested plant communities, each occupying a habitat with a well-defined soil depth and a duration of soil moisture. Habitats include exposed rock surfaces, natural depressions with soil, rock crevices, and outcrop margins. Exposed rock surfaces do not provide habitat for any species of vascular plants, but they do consist of a distinctive assemblage of mosses and lichens, including the distinctive fruticose lichen *Cladonia caroliniana* (Carolina reindeer lichen).

Natural depressions are the most distinctive outcrop habitats and harbor many of the most unusual flatrock species. These depressions are most abundant at or near the crest of the flatrock and are sometimes called "solution" pools because they were formed as water dissolved the rock. Natural depressions may have intact rims or an eroded downslope rim, but regardless of the rim condition, the soil depth and the length of time that standing water remains in the depression determine the plant species.

In South Carolina, depressions with one or more eroded rims usually have shallow soil and are typically occupied by elf orpine (*Diamorpha smallii,* plate 159), piedmont sandwort (*Minuartia uniflora,* plate 162), and various species of *Cladonia* (reindeer lichen). Large mats of the elf orpine, with its succulent red leaves and its bright white flowers, make this a striking outcrop habitat.

Natural depressions with intact rims, shallow soils, and water one to three inches deep for weeks at a time in the early spring are sometime called vernal pools. This is the habitat for several rare aquatic plants that are endemic to flatrock outcrops, including pool sprite (*Amphianthus pusillus,* plate 158) and several species of quillwort (*Isoëtes melanospora, Isoëtes piedmontana,* and their hybrids).

The annual-perennial herb community is the most diverse of the natural depression communities. A zone of haircap moss (*Polytrichum* spp.) usually delineates this community from the annual-dominated shallow soil community. Visually dominant species in the spring include woolly ragwort (*Senecio tomentosus,* plate 161), Small's ragwort (*Senecio smallii,* plate 675), and (rarely in South Carolina) sunnybell (*Schoenolirion croceum*). This is also a community where a variety of weedy species occur, like common toadflax (*Nuttallanthus canadensis*), sourgrass (*Rumex hastatulus*), pineweed (*Hypericum gentianoides*), and outcrop rushfoil (*Crotonopsis elliptica,* plate 164).

The margins of flatrock outcrops provide habitat for a number of endemic or near endemic flatrock species. Shallow soils that lay beneath red cedar provide habitat for Puck's orpine (*Sedum pusillum,* plate 157). It is only found under red cedar, presumably, because of the high calcium content of fallen cedar leaves. A rare rockcress (*Arabis missouriensis*) is found in the deeper soils of some flatrock margins, and the diminutive rock-loving draba (*Draba aprica*) is sometime found on open, gravelly flatrock margins.

Seepages at outcrop margins may contain wetland species such as quillwort (*Isoëtes piedmontana*), flatrock pimpernel (*Lindernia monticola*), and bladderworts (*Utricularia juncea* or *U. cornuta*).

The rocky shoals community

Rocky shoals

Rocky shoals (plate 167) are restricted to the upper and middle piedmont. The community is characterized by the abundance of small boulders or bedrock near the surface (shoals) during periods of low water flow. The shoals are mostly submerged during periods of high water flow. Rocky shoals are most extensive near the fall line that separates the piedmont from the coastal plain on major rivers such as the Saluda, Savannah, Broad, and Congaree.

The rocky islands that are mostly submerged during high water are occupied by emergent aquatic or semiaquatic plants. Three species characterize this habitat: rocky-shoals spiderlily (*Hymenocallis coronaria,* plate 167), American waterwillow (*Justicia americana,* plate 169), and riverweed (*Podostemon ceratophyllum*). Riverweed, with its tiny dissected leaves and fleshy discs, which are used to attach the plant to submerged rocks, resembles an alga more than a vascular plant. Its flowers have no showy parts, and the plant must be viewed with a magnifying lens to fully appreciate its unusual nature.

Rocky-shoals spiderlily, often present in great abundance, with its five-foot stalks and large whitish flowers, is spectacular. In June of 1773, William Bartram, while at the shoals on the Savannah River at Augusta, stated, "nothing in vegetable nature was more pleasing that the odoriferous Pancratium fluitans [*Hymenocallis coronaria* of today's taxonomy], which almost alone possess the little rocky islets which just appear above the water." The greatest display of spiderlily today is at the rocky shoals of the Catawba River at Landsford Canal State Park.

A wide variety of rooted and emergent aquatics, species typical of marshy habitats or weeds typical of wet disturbed habitats, may be associated with the rocky shoals. These include mermaid-weed (*Myriophyllum* spp.), Brazilian elodea (*Egeria densa*), pickerelweed, water hemlock, broadleaf arrowhead (*Sagittaria latifolia*), cardinal flower, red tooth-cup (*Ammania coccinea*), winged monkey-flower (*Mimulus alatus*), and a variety of rushes, sedges, spikerushes, and bulrushes.

The deciduous forest communities

Basic-mesic forests

Basic-mesic forests (plate 170) are one of the rarest and most spectacular wildflower communities in South Carolina. They rival the richest cove forests of the mountains and the longleaf pine savannas of the coastal plain in terms of plant diversity, especially herbaceous plant diversity. In fact, it is the extremely high density and diversity of herbaceous plants that makes this community easily recognizable. As described in this book, basic-mesic forests are restricted to the piedmont. Coastal plain sites with basic and mesic soils are included in the beech forest community. Mountain sites, if any exist, are included in the cove forest community.

The adjectives used in the name of this community (i.e., basic and mesic) aptly describe the conditions necessary for its development. Technically, a basic soil is one that has a pH above 7.0. A pH of 7.0 is neutral; a pH of below 7.0 is acidic; and a pH of above 7.0 is basic. As used here, and in many non-techincal works in plant ecology, the term basic refers to soils that are high in bases, including minerals (especially calcium) that increase soil pH. Since there are no forest soils in South Carolina that have a pH greater than 7.0, the "basic" soils here are more technically described as circumneutral, i.e., approximating 7.0 in pH. The highest pH recorded in forests is about 6.8, and all basic-mesic forests have a pH above 6.3.

Basic-mesic forests are mesic in terms of soil moisture availability—that is, they have good soil moisture for most of the growing season. This requirement restricts basic-mesic forests to "sheltered" topographic positions that reduce total sunlight and minimize loss of soil moisture. Typical locations for this community type are north-facing slopes and lower slopes of small, deep ravines.

Although variable among sites, the canopy is distinctive. Trees that are typical of mesic sites in the piedmont may be present, but beech, the tree common in most mesic piedmont sites, is never dominant, although it is often present. Also, trees typical of adjacent bottomlands often move upslope into this community type. In a study of the basic-mesic forests at the Stevens Creek Heritage Preserve, which is the most outstanding example of this community in the entire piedmont, Dr. Al Radford (1959) recorded the following canopy dominants in order of their importance: bitternut hickory (*Carya cordiformis*), southern sugar maple (*Acer barbatum*), swamp chestnut oak (*Quercus michauxii*), northern red oak (*Q. rubra*), slippery elm (*Ulmus rubra*), hackberry (*Celtis laevigata*), shagbark hickory (*C. ovata*), black walnut (*Juglans nigra*), tulip tree (*Liriodendron tulipifera*), and white oak (*Q. alba*). Swamp chestnut oak, sugarberry, and walnut are all bottomland species, and slippery elm is well known as a calcium-loving tree. Less mesic sites tend to be dominated by white oak, with southern sugar maple and bottomland species as important associates. American beech is usually present but not an important contributor to the canopy.

The understory in basic-mesic forests always includes such trees as dogwood, sourwood, red maple, and American holly, but the abundance of ironwood (*Carpinus caroliniana*), a species more typical of bottomlands, and hop hornbeam (*Ostrya virginiana*) distinctively characterize this community. Yellowwood (*Cladrastis kentukea*) is a rare mountain disjunct found in some basic-mesic forests, and cucumber-tree (*Magnolia acuminata*) is a spectacular flowering tree.

Shrub diversity is high, and typical species include wild allspice (*Lindera benzoin*), bladdernut (*Staphylea trifolia*), painted buckeye (*Aesculus sylvatica*), mock-oranges (*Philadelphus inodorus* and *P. hirsutus*), pawpaw (*Asimina triloba*), and a host of additional shrubs typical of beech forests and oak-hickory forests in the piedmont. At least one of the following rare shrubs are present: bottlebrush buckeye (*Aesculus parviflora*, plate 194), upland swamp privet (*Forestiera ligustrina*), and wahoo (*Euonymus atropurpureus*), but seldom do more than two of these rarities occur at any one site. The presence of wahoo on upland sites is usually a good indicator of this community type. The Stevens Creek Heritage Preserve harbors one of only three populations in the world of Miccosukee gooseberry (*Ribes echinellum*, plate 173).

The herbaceous layer is a distinctive characteristic of basic-mesic forests. Some herbaceous plants are disjunct from the mountains, some are typical of rich bottomlands, and some are found only in this community. Rare mountain disjuncts include doll's-eyes (*Actaea pachypoda*, plate 59), Dutchman's breeches (*Dicentra cucularia*, plate 178), ginseng (*Panax quinquefolius*, plate 196), spreading bladder fern (*Cystopteris protrusa*), cancer-root (*Orobanche uniflora*, plate 189), blue cohosh (*Caulophyllum thalictroides*, plate 57), yellow lady's-slipper (*Cypripedium calceolus* var. *pubescens*, plate 65), and perfoliate tinker's-weed (*Triosteum perfoliatum*). Species that are distinctive to basic-mesic forests include shooting star (*Dodecatheon meadia*, plate 172), green violet (*Hybanthus concolor*, plate 192), and southern stoneseed (*Lithospermum tuberosum*, plate 180). Species that are more typical of rich bottomlands include wild ginger (*Asarum canadense*), yellow fumewort (*Corydalis flavula*), and moonseed (*Menispermum canadense*). Additional rare herbaceous species, often restricted to just a few sites, include lanceleaf trillium (*Trillium lancifolium*, plate 176), pale yellow trillium (*T. discolor*, plate 175), relict trillium (*T. reliquum*, plate 174), roundleaf ragwort (*Senecio obovatus*, plate 186), and spring coral-root (*Corallorhiza wisteriana*). Additional interesting species include hairy spiderwort (*Tradescantia hirsuticaulis*, plate 187), lopseed (*Phryma leptostachya*), spring beauty (*Claytonia virginica*), and dimpled trout lily (*Erythronium umbilicatum* subsp. *umbilicatum*, plate 171).

In order to see all the unusual plants in bloom, the visitor to a basic-mesic forest site should plan on visiting a site several times between mid-March and late-June.

Beech forests

Beech forests (plate 197), also known as mesic mixed hardwood forests, are restricted to the Piedmont Province and Coastal Plain Province. Steep, north-facing river bluffs and sheltered ravines are the locations were most beech forest communities occur. But they are also found in the coastal plain on the upland flats or on islands surrounded by swamp. Associated rocks and soils in the piedmont are acidic. In the coastal plain, they may be either acidic or circumneutral (i.e., calcium-rich). This wildflower community is easily recognized by the abundance of beech (*Fagus grandifolia,* plate 222). Canopy dominants also include tulip tree, red maple, shagbark hickory (*Carya ovata*), and northern red oak (*Quercus rubra*). The general paucity of other oak species is one of the defining characteristics of this community. Southern sugar maple (*Acer barbatum*) and sweet gum, and sometimes bull bay (*Magnolia grandiflora*), may also be important canopy trees in the coastal plain. Many of the same understory trees that are present in beech forests also occur in oak-hickory forests, including dogwood, sourwood, and American holly, but in the piedmont, hop hornbeam often is abundant. Swamp red bay (*Persea palustris*) is often present in beech forests in the coastal plain.

Common shrubs include strawberry-bush (*Euonymus americanus,* plate 219) and species of blueberry (*Vaccinium* spp.). Small amounts of mountain laurel are present in the piedmont, and witch-hazel (*Hamamelis virginiana*) and horse sugar are usually present in the coastal plain. The herbaceous layer is sparse to moderate in density and diversity. In the piedmont, herb density and diversity in beech forests are intermediate between basic-mesic forests and oak-hickory forests. In the coastal plain, beech forests are the richest upland community. Abundant and attractive species include bloodroot (*Sanguinaria canadensis,* plate 206), may-apple (*Podophyllum peltatum,* plate 205), bellwort (*Uvularia perfoliata*), various trilliums (mottled trillium, *Trillium maculatum,* in the coastal plain and Catesby's trillium, *T. catesbaei,* in the piedmont), wild geranium (*Geranium maculatum*), and green-and-gold (*Chrysogonum virginianum* var. *australe,* plate 202). Green adder's mouth (*Malaxis unifolia*) and southern twayblade (*Listera australis*) are rarities that are commonly found in beech forests in the coastal plain.

Oak-hickory forests

This is a complex community that is found in the lower mountains, piedmont, and coastal plain. It is difficult to characterize, with much variation among sites. Oak-hickory forests may be dominated by a surprising variety of canopy species, especially oaks. Considerable variation also exists in the understory, shrub, and especially in the herbaceous layer. Despite the site-to-site variation between physiographic provinces, there are unifying characteristics.

Oak-hickory forests are always associated with acid soils and are neither the most mesic nor the driest community in any region. Depending on elevation, aspect, and topography, an oak-hickory forest may occur on ridge tops, upper slopes, or midslopes. Occasionally, it occurs on upland flats. Although canopy dominants can vary considerably, white oak is found on most sites and is either dominant or codominant. Mockernut hickory (*Carya tomentosa*) or pignut hickory (*C. glabra*) is common. Southern red oak is found on drier sites, and tulip tree is usually present on mesic sites. Sourwood, black gum (*Nyssa sylvatica*), dogwood, and red maple are present in the subcanopy, with the former two species more abundant on drier sites and the latter two more abundant on more mesic sites. American holly and redbud (*Cercis canadensis*) also are abundant subcanopy trees on more mesic sites. On all but the driest sites, red maple becomes more abundant when there has been site disturbance.

Shrubs common throughout this community include various species of blueberry, including dryland blueberry (*Vaccinium vacillans*) and common deerberry (*V. stamineum* var. *stamineum*). Vines include muscadine (*Vitis rotundifolia*), coral honeysuckle (*Lonicera sempervirens,* plate 227), and poison ivy (*Rhus radicans*). In drier sites, New Jersey tea (*Ceanothus americanus*), Carolina jessamine (*Gelsemium sempervirens*), and sparkleberry (*Vaccinium arboreum*) are common. In more mesic sites, strawberry-bush (*Euonymus americanus*) and various buckeyes are abundant, including red buckeye (*Aesculus pavia*) in the coastal plain and painted buckeye (*A. sylvatica*) in the piedmont and mountains.

Herbaceous plant cover and diversity is generally sparse. Herbaceous species common throughout this community include flowering spurge (*Euphorbia corollata*), ruellia (*Ruellia caroliniensis*), hairy skullcap (*Scutellaria elliptica*), veiny hawkweed (*Hieracium venosum*), spotted wintergreen (*Chimaphila maculata*), arrowleaf (*Hexastylis arifolia,* plate 203), and Appalachian oak-leach (*Aureolaria laevigata,* plate 263). Drier sites usually harbor Indian pink (*Spigelia marilandica,* plate 245), goat's rue (*Tephrosia virginiana*), and whorled-leaf coreopsis (*Coreopsis major*). More mesic sites inevitably harbor Solomon's-seal (*Polygonatum biflorum,* plate 238), Catesby's trillium (*Trillium catesbaei,* plate 114), and pale Indian-plantain (*Arnoglossum atriplicifolium,* plate 253).

Oak-hickory forests were once the most abundant upland community in the piedmont. They were much less abundant in the coastal plain (because of the abundance of periodic fire) and the mountains (because of the abundance of more mesic and more xeric communities). Although still an abundant community, much of the original forests have been lost. Large, undisturbed stands are rare. Although small stands on steep slopes that show minimal disturbance remain common in the piedmont, stands that show no signs of past disturbance are rare. In the coastal plain, most oak-hickory forests have been disturbed, resulting in a dense subcanopy and shrub layer that makes ingress difficult, especially during the summer and fall. Oak-hickory forests are not hard to find in the low mountains since large acreages are in public ownership; however, sites with no disturbance are rare.

Piedmont xeric hardpan forests

This community (plate 268) has an impenetrable clay hardpan near the surface that inhibits infiltration of water and plant roots. This hardpan may also result from rock near the surface, but regardless of its origin, a very dry habitat is produced in the upland flats and gentle slopes of the piedmont, where it is typically found. The rock associated with this community type often is present as boulders that are usually gabbro, which is high in calcium-rich feldspars and weathers to produce a soil with a circumneutral pH.

Stunted trees and a relatively open canopy are characteristic of this community. In undisturbed, old-growth sites, post oak (*Quercus stellata*) and blackjack oak (*Q. marilandica*) dominate the canopy, and eastern red cedar and redbud dominate the understory. On many sites it is often difficult to distinguish the canopy from the understory or subcanopy. Virginia pine (*Pinus virginiana*) and shortleaf pine may be important components of disturbed sites. Additional canopy species include white oak (*Q. alba*), American ash (*Fraxinus americana*), a variety of other oaks, pignut hickory (*Carya glabra*), and the rare Carolina shagbark hickory (*C. carolinae-septentrionalis*). Additional understory trees include winged elm (*Ulmus alata*), fringe-tree (*Chionanthus virginicus*), and persimmon (*Diospyros virginiana*). Shrubs are not abundant, but sparkleberry (*Vaccinium arboreum*), black haw (*Viburnum prunifolium*), Carolina buckthorn (*Rhamnus caroliniana*), New Jersey tea (*Ceanothus americanus*), aromatic sumac (*Rhus aromatica*), and one or more hawthorns (*Crataegus* spp.) are present.

The stunted and spaced trees of the canopy provide no hint of the wonderful diversity of unusual plants in the herbaceous layer. Many of the herbs have affinities with Midwestern prairies, which gives credence to Lawson's (1709) descriptions of extensive prairies and grassy woodlands in the piedmont of South Carolina. Grasses such as northern oat grass (*Danthonia spicata*) and various species of broomsedge dominate the herbaceous layer, which is sparse except in canopy openings where herbs can be abundant and diverse. Unusual species include prairie dock (*Silphium terebinthinaceum*, plate 273), curlyheads (*Clematis ochroleuca*, plate 269), Schweinitz's sunflower (*Helianthus schweinitzii*, plate 275), deceptive spinypod (*Matelea decipiens*, plate 270), and Culver's root (*Veronicastrum virginicum*). Other herbs include a variety of mostly weedy herbs typical of dry woodland margins, including wild quinine (*Parthenium integrifolium* var. *integrifolium*), lanceleaf coreopsis (*Coreopsis lanceolata*), goat's rue (*Tephrosia virginiana*), St. Andrew's-cross (*Hypericum hypericoides*), nettle-leaf sage (*Salvia urticifolia*), whorled-leaf coreopsis (*Coreopsis major*), and Small's ragwort (*Senecio smallii*). Some herbs that are typical of more mesic woodlands also are present, including Solomon's-seal (*Polygonatum biflorum*), perfoliate bellwort (*Uvularia perfoliata*), and three-parted meadow-parsnip (*Thaspium trifoliatum*). Climbing dogbane (*Trachelospermum difforme*), an unusual vine that closely resembles Carolina jessamine except it has milky juice, is inevitably present.

The role of fire in the maintenance of this community is unclear, but undoubtedly periodic fires are required. Historical accounts by early naturalists suggest that prairie-like habitats and grassy woodlands were once much more abundant than they are today in the piedmont, probably as a result of the routine use of fire by Native Americans.

Good quality examples of this forest type are rare. Only one site, Rock Hill Blackjacks Heritage Preserve, has been partially protected to date.

The piedmont springhead seepage forest community

Piedmont springhead seepage forests

Well-developed examples of springhead seepage forests (plate 277) are restricted to the upper piedmont. The best sites are all in the vicinity of Traveler's Rest in Greenville County. Springhead forests begin at seepages at the base of slopes and may extend downslope for just a few feet or for hundreds or thousands of feet. They are characterized by the presence of seepage channels that have year-round, slow-moving, cool groundwater. Seepage channels often divide downslope from the seephead and may become so braided that water eventually does not flow continuously, which usually determines the lower extent of the springhead forest. All known springhead forests in South Carolina are bounded by pacolet sandy loam soils, which are apparently ideally suited to the uptake and storage of rainwater and its slow release as seepage.

Good examples of this community typically have a closed canopy composed of red maple, swamp gum, and tulip tree. Shrubs are sparse to dense, with dense shrub cover confined to canopy openings. A diversity of shrubs that are typical of boggy habitats may be present, especially tag alder (*Alnus serrulata*), wild raisin (*Viburnum nudum*), and red chokeberry (*Aronia arbutifolia*). Additional shrubs present in this community include American storax (*Styrax americana*), Virginia willow (*Itea virginica*), male-berry (*Lyonia ligustrina*), common winterberry (*Ilex verticillata*), and poison sumac (*Rhus vernix*). Important vines include climbing hydrangea (*Decumaria barbara*) and bamboo-vine (*Smilax laurifolia*), with the latter species sometimes forming impenetrable tangles.

The herbaceous layer varies from sparse to dense, and grasses and sedges are only abundant in canopy openings. Sphagnum moss is generally not abundant. Important herbs include cinnamon fern (*Osmunda cinamomea*), royal fern (*O. regalis* var. *spectabilis*), stiff cowbane (*Oxypolis rigidior*, plate 33), netted chain-fern (*Woodwardia areolata*), and partridge berry on drier hummocks. The edges of the seepages have at least some plants of the small green wood-orchid (*Platanthera clavellata*, plate 283), while the seepages typically harbor a hedge-hyssop (*Gratiola virginiana*), and in the best sites, the federally endangered bunched arrowhead (*Sagittaria fasciculata*, plate 279). Some seepages are being taken over by the nonnative weed *Murdannia keisak* (plate 281). Hummocks between the seepages may harbor the rare dwarf-flower heartleaf (*Hexastylis naniflora*, plate 278). Additional rare species that are found only at a few sites include littleleaf sneezeweed (*Helenium brevifolium*), mountain sweet pitcher-plant (*Sarracenia jonesii*), and Bailey's sedge (*Carex baileyi*).

In the best sites, seepage channels are over solid sands, and the forest is not especially boggy. As silt buildup occurs, which is accelerated by upslope disturbance, this community becomes more boggy. The seepage channels change from being clear and constantly flowing to being stagnant and filled with a reddish scum that is indicative of the activity of anaerobic fungi. It is unclear what management is needed to maintain this community long term.

The bottomland forest communities

Bottomland forests

Three bottomland forest communities occur in the piedmont: the bald cypress-tupelo gum swamp forests, the hardwood bottoms, and the levee forests. These three communities also occur in the coastal plain. In the piedmont, however, the floodplains have a shorter flooding duration and a lower flooding depth, and the acreage in the piedmont is considerably less than in the coastal plain. In the piedmont, these communities are a minor component of the vegetation, whereas in the coastal plain they are a dominant component. The detailed description of the bottomland forest communities is given under the coastal plain section.

The following are wildflowers that are found only in the piedmont bottomland forests: shrubs include painted buckeye (*Aesculus sylvatica*), bladdernut (*Staphylea trifolia,* plate 288), and silky dogwood (*Cornus amomum*); herbs include golden ragwort (*Senecio aureus*), little sweet Betsy (*Trillium cuneatum*), virgin's bower (*Clematis virginiana*), yellow fumewort (*Corydalis flavula*), and honewort (*Cryptotaenia canadensis*).

THE FALL-LINE SANDHILLS

The xeric communities

Longleaf pine-scrub oak sandhills
The name of this community (plate 290) references three of its most important components. It is dominated by an open canopy of longleaf pine, and a variety of scrub oaks dominate the open to dense subcanopy. It differs from the longleaf pine-turkey oak community in being less xeric and more fertile, which is probably a result of a shallower sand layer and more organic matter in the soil. This community harbors a greater diversity of species. It is found on middle and lower slopes in the sandhills but can be found on sand deposits throughout the coastal plain. Some authors suggest that this community has a clay layer near the surface, which is true of sites with an abundance of sand myrtle (*Leiophyllum buxifolium,* plate 292). It is bounded by longleaf pine-turkey oak upslope and dry oak-hickory forests or streamhead pocosins downslope. Fire suppression has significantly affected this community.

The longleaf pines that form the open canopy become flat-topped with age, creating a distinct and aesthetically pleasing appearance from a distance. The subcanopy is dominated by blackjack oak (*Quercus marilandica*), with lesser amounts of turkey oak, bluejack oak (*Q. incana*), and sand post oak (*Q. margaretta*). Sassafras and persimmon usually are present, and occasionally flowering dogwood (*Cornus florida*). The shrub layer is dominated by ericads, especially sparkleberry (*Vaccinium arboreum*), southern blueberry (*Vaccinium tenellum),* and southern dwarf huckleberry (*Gaylussacia dumosa* var. *dumosa*), poison oak, several species of hawthorn (especially southern haw, *Crataegus flava,* plate 293, and dwarf-thorn, *C. uniflora*), and Carolina jessamine. Rare to uncommon shrubs include dwarf bristly locust (*Robinia nana*) and nestronia (*Nestronia umbellula,* plate 237).

The herbaceous layer is well developed and dominated by wiregrass (*Aristida stricta* in the north and *Aristida beyrichiana* in the south) and creeping little bluestem (*Andropogon scoparium* var. *stoloniferum*). A variety of broadleaf herbs may be present, including senna seymeria (*Seymeria cassioides,* plate

306), puccoon (*Lithospermum caroliniense,* plate 294), jointweed (*Polygonella americana,* plate 301), narrowleaf dawnflower (*Stylisma patens* var. *angustifolia*), eastern green-eyes (*Berlandiera pumila,* plate 298), and sandhills thistle (*Cirsium repandum*).

Species that are more typical of dry oak-hickory forests or dry pine-oak woodlands and are found here include devil's shoestring and sweet goldenrod. Species that are more typical of the longleaf pine-turkey oak community include tread-softly (*Cnidosculus stimulosus*), Carolina ipecac (*Euphorbia ipecacuanhae,* plate 291), and sandhills St. John's-wort (*Hypericum lloydii,* plate 322). Many additional species characteristic of dry and/or dry and disturbed areas may be present, so don't be surprised if you can't identify everything.

Longleaf pine-turkey oak sandhills

The longleaf pine-turkey oak sandhills community is the most xeric and least fertile of all the pineland communities in South Carolina. It occurs on deep, coarse sands, most typically wind-blown sands on ridge tops of the fall-line sandhills. This community also is found on fluvial sand ridges (deposited by high waters) that parallel and are east of the major coastal plain rivers and on rims of Carolina bays. In the maritime strand, they are even found on old beach dunes. All of these systems are characterized by an open canopy of longleaf pine (*Pinus palustris,* plate 309), and all have the subcanopy dominated or codominated by turkey oak (*Quercus laevis,* plate 307). These systems also are characterized today by large patches of open sands and an abundance of ground lichens, commonly called British soldiers (*Cladonia* spp.).

The longleaf pine-turkey oak sandhills community is distinguished from longleaf pine-scrub oak sandhills by its abundance of turkey oak and bluejack oak (*Q. incana*) and the general lack of other scrub oaks, other than the occasional sand post oak (*Quercus margaretta*). Wiregrass is present in both communities but more abundant in the latter. The longleaf pine-turkey oak community grades downslope into a longleaf pine-scrub oak sandhills or streamside pocosin community.

No one who has ever stood in a xeric sandhills in the middle of a sunny July day has any doubt that this is a harsh habitat, but a number of species have adapted. Shrubs are as abundant as herbs, and both may be sparse to moderately dense. Characteristic shrubs include southern dwarf huckleberry (*Gaylussacia dumosa* var. *dumosa,* plate 312), rosemary (*Ceratiola ericoides,* plate 327), poison oak (*Rhus toxicodendron*), and the very attractive low shrub sandhills St. John's-wort (*Hypericum lloydii,* plate 322). Herbs include sandhills milkweed (*Asclepias humistrata*), wire-plant (*Stipulicida setacea,* plate 320), Carolina sandwort (*Arenaria caroliniana,* plate 313), hairy false foxglove (*Aureolaria pectinata*), sandhill wild-buckwheat (*Eriogonum tomentosum,* plate 326), tread-softly (*Cnidosculus stimulosus*), Carolina ipecac (*Euphorbia ipecacauanhae*), and roseling (*Tradescantia rosea* var. *graminea*). Unusual plants found at only a few sites include Pickering's dawnflower (*Stylisma pickeringii* var. *pickeringii,* plate 323), northern golden-heather (*Hudsonia ericoides,* plate 319), sandhills pyxie-moss (*Pyxidanthera barbulata* var. *brevifolia,* plate 310), and woolly-white (*Hymenopappus scabiosaeus,* plate 315). The "Field guide to natural plant communities" directs you to sites where all these species can be seen.

The sandhill seepage communities

Streamhead pocosins

Streamhead pocosins are found along the headwaters of small streams, stream-side flats, and extending up hillsides adjacent to streams. This community is most common in the fall-line sandhills, but it does occur in the inner coastal plain. Its presence is dependent on flowing water or seepage from the adjacent uplands. Although these communities tend to be long and narrow, fire seldom burns through the entire community because it tends to be wet. Fire often does burn into its upland margins, and it is in these frequently burned ecotones that most of the unusual species are found.

As in pocosins in general, the canopy of this community is dominated by pond pine (*Pinus serotina*, plate 494). However, hardwood species such as tulip tree, swamp gum, red maple, and even sweet gum may be abundant because of the overall rarity of fire. Sweet bay and swamp red bay sometime form a distinct subcanopy layer, and occasionally a dense tall shrub layer of mountain laurel is present. An alternative name for pocosin is "evergreen shrub bog," so it is not surprising that a dense layer of evergreen shrubs is present. Species especially abundant at the upland ecotone are deciduous species, including titi, sweet pepperbush (*Clethra alnifolia*), and huckleberry (*Gaylussacia frondosa*). Unusual shrubs, generally restricted to the frequently burned ecotones, include white wicky (*Kalmia cuneata,* plate 329), coastal witch-alder (*Fothergilla gardenii*), and pocosin loosestrife (*Lysimachia asperulaefolia*). Herbs are sparse, except in rare boggy openings. The dominant herb is probably cinnamon fern (*Osmunda cinnamomea*), with a variety of pitcher plants, the rare tawny cottongrass (*Eriophorum virginicum*), and a variety of grasses, sedges and rushes in boggy areas with an open canopy.

Ecotones maintained by regular fires are delightful places to botanize. However, an unburned ecotone and the wetter portions of the community are almost impenetrable because of the dense shrubs and the tangle of bamboo-vine (*Smilax laurifolia*).

Herbaceous seepages

The sandhills herbaceous seepage community (plate 330) develops where streamheads occur in frequently burned areas. Frequent fires remove the woody vegetation and allow herbaceous species to dominate. This community has been drastically reduced in the sandhills because of fire suppression. With the absence of fire, shrubs and trees move into the community and it is transformed into a streamhead pocosin. The best examples of this community occur on Fort Jackson and the Carolina Sandhills National Wildlife Refuge. One site that is readily available to the public occurs along the edges and within open areas of the Atlantic white-cedar community at Shealy's Pond Heritage Preserve.

This community harbors some of the showiest wildflowers in the sandhills. Look for three species of pitcher-plants and their hybrids: sweet pitcher-plant (*Sarracenia rubra*, plate 484), frog's breeches (*S. purpurea* var. *venosa*, plate 331), and yellow trumpet pitcher-plant (*S. flava*, plate 496). There are also several species of sundews, three orchids (small green wood-orchid [*Platanthera clavellata*, plate 283], rose pogonia [*Pogonia ophioglossoides*], and spreading pogonia [*Cleistes divaricata*]), several species of bladderworts (*Utricularia* spp.), Collins' sedge (*Carex collinsii*), and yellow hatpins (*Syngonanthus flavidulus*). Several species endemic to this community can be seen, which is a testimony to its natural and historical occurrence in the sandhills and include scabrous-leaved xyris (*Xyris scabrifolia*), Chapman's xyris (*Xyris chapmanii*), and Texas pipewort (*Eriocaulon texense*). Also present are several species that are disjunct between the mountains and coastal plain, including round-leaf sundew (*Drosera rotundifolia*, plate 334).

Atlantic white-cedar forests

The Atlantic white-cedar forests (plate 330) share many of the same species as pocosin and streamhead pocosin communities, but the thick canopy dominated by Atlantic white-cedar (*Chamaecyparis thyoides*, plate 336) easily distinguishes it from these closely related communities. Atlantic white-cedar forests may occur in Carolina bays or other depressions in the coastal plain, but they are best developed in the fall-line sandhills at sites with an abundance of flowing water or seepage. If a site has enough seepage and moist soils to retard the regular invasion of fires that originate in the adjacent sandhills and if a source of Atlantic white-cedar seeds is readily available, then an Atlantic white-cedar forest forms. A high water table, peaty, acid soils, abundant sphagnum moss, and long fire cycles (50–150 years) are additional distinguishing characteristics of the community.

The canopy of this natural community is typically dense and dominated by Atlantic white-cedar, with pond pine (*Pinus serotina*), red maple, swamp gum, and tulip tree present. Hardwoods become more abundant as the community ages. The presence of tulip tree helps distinguish it from closely related pocosin communities. The three species of bays, sweet bay, swamp red bay, and loblolly bay, dominate the subcanopy layer. The shrub layer is dense and dominated by evergreen species typical of pocosins, especially fetterbush (*Lyonia lucida*), titi (*Cyrilla racemiflora*), two species of *Myrica* (*M. cerifera* var. *cerifera* and *M. heterophylla*), and two species of holly (inkberry, *Ilex glabra,* and *Ilex coriacea*). Rare shrubs to look for include Moser's huckleberry (*Gaylussacia moseri*), bog spicebush (*Lindera subcoriacea*), and Rayner's blueberry (*Vaccinium sempervirens*, plate 335). Poison sumac (*Rhus vernix*) is usually present.

THE COASTAL PLAIN

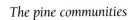

The pine communities

Longleaf pine flatwoods

The typical pine flatwoods (plate 337) are dominated by a canopy of tall, longleaf pines. The terrain is flat to gently rolling with a sandy soil and high water table. Although longleaf pine characterizes the community, loblolly and slash pine may occur.

In flatwoods where fire is infrequent, a well-developed shrub layer and understory may develop. Under high fire frequency, the shrubs and understory species are kept in check. Because of the site-to-site variation in the understory and shrub layers, pine flatwoods are difficult to characterize. Common understory trees include sweet gum, blackjack oak (*Quercus marilandica*), and black gum (*Nyssa sylvatica*). Common shrubs include wax myrtle (*Myrica cerifera* var. *pumila*), inkberry (*Ilex glabra*), huckleberry (*Gaylussacia frondosa*), running oak (*Quercus pumila,* plate 358), sweet pepperbush (*Clethra alnifolia*), and scrubby post oak (*Quercus margaretta*).

The herbs of frequently burned pine flatwoods include grasses, heaths, legumes, and composites but few of the showy species of the savannas. Grasses include broomstraws (*Andropogon* spp.), while the legumes include zornia (*Zornia bracteata*), beggar's lice (*Desmodium* spp.), *Lespedeza* spp., lead plant (*Amorpha herbacea*), and goat's rue (*Tephrosia virginiana*). The composites include black-root (*Pterocaulon pycnostachyum*), asters (*Aster squarrosus, A. tortifolius, A. reticulatus, A. linariifolius* and *A. concolor*), and goldenrods (*Solidago* spp., including fragrant goldenrod, *S. odora*). The ubiquitous bracken fern (*Pteridium aquilinum*) becomes the dominant herb in the spring after annual winter fires. The rare American chaff-seed (*Schwalbea americana,* plate 347) occurs in openings of the herb layer.

The pine flatwoods grade into the longleaf pine savanna community, and distinguishing between the two can be difficult. Slight depressions that have a high clay hardpan occur within the pine flatwoods and harbor the typical species that characterize the savannas. At other sites, savannas cover extensive areas that are easily distinguishable from the adjacent pine flatwoods. Two species can be used to identify the two habitats: hooded pitcher-plant (*Sarracenia minor,* plate 377) and toothache grass (*Ctenium aromaticum,* plate 386). Both species require more open and moist conditions than is normally found in the pine flatwoods; their presence indicates pine savannas. Pocosins, cypress savannas, and upland swamps also occur scattered within pine flatwoods. The pine flatwoods are a fire subclimax; prolonged absence of fire will lead to hardwood forests.

Pine/saw palmetto flatwoods

The pine/saw palmetto flatwood community (plate 359) is found only in Jasper and Beaufort Counties, its northern limit. It is more extensive in Florida and Georgia. The canopy consists of longleaf pine on the ridges and slash pine (*P. elliottii*) and/or pond pine (*Pinus serotina*) in depressions. A subcanopy of oaks is usually sparse. Saw palmetto (*Serenoa repens,* plate 362) dominates the shrub layer. Other shrubs include hairy wicky (*Kalmia hirsuta,* plate 365), rusty lyonia (*Lyonia ferruginea,* plate 361), and southern evergreen blueberry (*Vaccinium myrsinites,* plate 363). The latter two are confined to this community, occurring only in Beaufort and Jasper Counties. Typical pocosin and pine flatwood species such as sweet bay, swamp red bay, inkberry, sweet gallberry, fetterbush, sweet pepperbush, and honey-cups are also part of the shrub layer. The sparse herbaceous layer is a mixture of pine flatwood species and includes galactia (*Galactia elliottii,* plate 367), vanilla plant (*Carphephorus odoratissimus,* plate 353), and Walter's milkweed (*Asclepias cinerea,* plate 364). Periodic fires promote herbs and saw palmettos. An absence of fires leads to more of a dominance of shrubs.

The best example of this community available to the public is Victoria Bluff Heritage Preserve in Beaufort County.

Longleaf pine savannas

For showy wildflowers no natural community equals the longleaf pine savannas (plate 369). From early spring through late fall, a progression of herbaceous wildflowers graces the coastal plain with a mix of colors that the earliest settlers loved. Orchids, carnivorous plants, lilies, showy composites, plus many other groups all find a home in the sunny, pine savannas. This book contains photographs of 31 plants that grow in the longleaf savannas.

It is a paradox that fire is responsible for maintenance of the savannas. Native Americans burned the savannas to drive game and to clear the ground around settlements. Natural fires, started by lightning, swept through the pinelands, mostly during July and August. Trees and shrubs, with their growing tips at fire level, were killed. Herbaceous species, with their stems (rhizomes) underground, were protected. Shortly after a fire, these herbaceous species put up new growth, and what first appeared as a scene of utter desolation quickly becomes a wildflower garden again.

On the other hand, savannas, protected from fire, quickly succeed to a shrub community, then to a tree-dominated forest. Under a forest canopy, the savanna herbs, which require high light intensity, cannot survive.

One tree that is able to survive the frequent burning of the savannas is sweet bay (*Magnolia virginiana,* plate 483). It does so because its stem is buried in the soil. After a fire, it puts up a cluster of new shoots, giving the appearance of a shrub. If the root-stem system is dug up, one finds a single, enlarged rootstock, which is a testimony that the "tree" may be many years old even though its aboveground stems represent one or two years of growth.

Two general types of longleaf pine savannas can be recognized: one dominated by toothache grass (plate 386) and hooded pitcher-plant (*Sarracenia minor,* plate 377) and the other by wiregrass (*Aristida stricta* in the northeast, and *A. beyrichiana* in the southeast). Both types of savannas develop where the combination of fairly level topography and nondraining subsoil causes a high (or perched) water table in the rainy season. Loblolly pine, slash pine, and pond pine may occur with the longleaf. During droughts, the soil above the clay hardpan may become excessively dry. Only wiregrass and the bog species can tolerate these extreme changes. Wiregrass, however, favors coarse soil where there is some slope to allow lateral drainage, resulting in slightly drier conditions. Toothache grass and the showy herb species prefer wetter conditions. The greatest display of showy herbs occurs in the toothache grass longleaf savannas.

Most savannas today occur in national forests or on large plantations as a result of prescribed burning. Small, privately owned savannas are threatened since natural wildfires are quickly put out or do not spread because of barriers, such as roads. Pine savannas are threatened due to the construction of houses or commercial properties and drainage canals. These canals lower the water table, allowing for the invasion of less moisture-tolerant species. Recent data suggests that more than 95% of longleaf savannas have been lost. Unless protective measures are taken, by the next century this community may be insignificant.

Longleaf pine-turkey oak xeric ridges

The xeric longleaf pine-turkey oak communities of the coastal plain occur on sandy ridges. The ridges have three different origins. Although they share many common species, their distinguishing floristic composition is based on the origin of the sand. All three types of ridges have longleaf pine and turkey oak as the dominant trees (plate 401). Some of the classic wildflowers occurring on all three types of xeric ridges in the coastal plain include sandhills gerardia (*Agalinis setacea*), sandhills milkweed (*Asclepias humistrata*), sandhills thistle (*Cirsium repandum*), tread-softly (*Cnidoscolus stimulosus*), and wire-plant (*Stipulicida setacea* var. *setacea*).

Brownwater sand ridges.   Sand ridges along brownwater rivers, such as the Savannah River, which originates in the mountains, are fluvial (water deposited) in nature and come from erosion in the piedmont and mountains. They are nutrient-rich, unlike the Carolina bay ridges and blackwater ridges, and harbor several species not found on the bay and blackwater ridges. These species include rose dicerandra (*Dicerandra odoratissima,* plate 441), gopher-apple (*Licania michauxii,* plate 413), soft-haired coneflower (*Rudbeckia mollis,* plate 408), and warea (*Warea cuneifolia,* plate 409).

Tillman Sand Ridge Heritage Preserve in Jasper County, along the Savannah River, is a good example of a brownwater sand ridge.

Blackwater sand ridges.   The sands of the blackwater sand ridges are marine in origin since they come from the coastal plain. They develop along the blackwater, coastal plain rivers such as the Little Pee Dee and Edisto, and are deposited by wind and water. They are ancient in origin, deposited as the last glaciers retreated from the fall line. Their soils are less fertile than the brownwater sand ridges. Two good sites to see blackwater sand ridges are Little Pee Dee State Park in Dillon County and Little Pee Dee River Heritage Preserve (Vaughn Tract) in Horry County.

Four wildflowers that are characteristic of the blackwater sand ridges and bay ridges, but are usually absent from the brownwater ridges, are rosemary (*Ceratiola ericoides,* plate 327), sandy-field beaksedge (*Rhynchospora megalocarpa,* plate 406), Carolina ipecac (*Euphorbia ipecacuanhae,* plate 291), and southern bog buttons (*Lachnocaulon beyrichianum,* plate 405).

Bay ridges.   Bay ridges (often called bay rims) occur along the southeastern side of Carolina bays. Bay ridges, blackwater sand ridges, and brownwater sand ridges all harbor the longleaf pine–turkey oak ridge community. The ridges were deposited by winds blowing during the period when the bays originated. Excellent examples of Carolina bay ridges that support typical xeric species occur in Horry County in Cartwheel Bay Heritage Preserve and Lewis Ocean Bay Heritage Preserve, as well as Woods Bay State Park in Sumter County.

The wildflowers and vegetation of the bay ridges are similar to the blackwater ridges. No Carolina bays are associated with brownwater rivers.

The sandy, dry, open woodlands community

Sandy, dry, open woodlands

The sandy, dry, open wooland community (plate 414) is probably a successional community that develops on sand ridges following agricultural abandonment or after disturbance of a dry oak-hickory forests or dry pinelands.

Canopy trees are scattered and consist of "dry" oaks and hickories with occasional loblolly pines. Shrubs are sparse. The herbaceous plant layer is open and best defines the community. Invariably some of the following herbaceous wildflowers occur in the community: blazing star (*Liatris elegans,* plate 431), horse mint (*Monarda punctata*), blue star (*Amsonia ciliata*), three species of lupine (*Lupinus perennis,* plate 419, *L. villosus,* and *L. diffusus,* plate 416), wild pink (*Silene caroliniana* var. *caroliniana*), piriqueta (*Piriqueta caroliniana*), queen's-delight (*Stillingia sylvatica*), southern dawnflower (*Stylisma humistrata*), vase-vine (*Clematis reticulata*), and Canada frostweed (*Helianthemum canadense*). Several of the above herbs also occur in the xeric communities.

The calcareous forest communities

The calcareous forest communities do not occupy significant acreage in the coastal plain; however, they do contribute considerable diversity to the flora of the coastal plain as numerous rare and uncommon species are found there. Most of the undisturbed sites of this community are found on private lands that are not publicly available.

The calcareous forests occur on bluffs, slopes, or moist flats that overlay calcareous substrates. The substrate is either marl or limestone that was laid down as marine deposit when the ocean covered the coastal plain. The calcium from the underlying substrate is a major factor shaping the diversity and composition of the vegetation. Certain species of plants, referred to as calcicoles, thrive in a basic to circumneutral soil that results from the presence of calcium ions. These species generally are mixed with the flora of the surrounding community to form a diverse community. Classification of the various calcareous communities is not well developed; however, we do recognize two well-developed types.

Calcareous bluff forests

Calcareous bluff forests occur on mesic sites that overlay shallowly buried or exposed marl or limestone formations. These forests occur along rivers and creeks where erosion has exposed or brought the marl or limestone formation close to the surface.

Trees that characterize the calcareous bluff forests include yellow chestnut oak (*Quercus muhlenbergii*), hop hornbeam (*Ostrya virginiana*), white basswood (*Tilia heterophylla*), slippery elm (*Ulmus rubra*), Carolina buckthorn (*Rhamnus caroliniana*), black walnut (*Juglans nigra*), and southern sugar maple (*Acer barbatum,* plate 435). Elements of the other deciduous forest communities occur and include redbud, flowering dogwood, and eastern red cedar. Herbaceous species are common and include many that are found in other deciduous communities of the piedmont and coastal plain. Several species, however, are either confined to or are more common in this community. They include crested coral-root (*Hexalectris spicata,* plate 436), shadow-witch (*Pon-*

thieva racemosa, plate 437), mottled trillium (*Trillium maculatum,* plate 432), and thimbleweed (*Anemone virginiana*).

Often, where the calcareous substrate has been exposed, it hardens. Rainwater then erodes the substrate, forming recesses in which two rare ferns are able to become established by spore dispersal: blackstem spleenwort (*Asplenium resiliens,* plate 175 in *WCL*) and Wagner's spleenwort (*Asplenium heteroresiliens,* plate 440).

Three sites that harbor this community are Old Santee Canal Park and Wadboo Creek in Berkeley County and Santee State Park in Orangeburg County.

Wet, flat, calcareous forests

This calcareous community occupies low, wet flats adjacent to river systems. The underlying marl formation is not exposed, but it is close enough to the surface to influence plant composition. It is not a common community in the coastal plain. It fact, it has been studied only along the western side of the Cooper River in Berkeley County and in several sites in and around Huger Creek in the Francis Marion National Forest (FMNF). It is not known to what extent it occurs throughout the coastal plain.

Recent studies on Mulberry and Lewisfield Plantations reveal the distinct flora of the community. The calcicoles that are present include mottled trillium, crested coral-root, shadow-witch, and American alumroot. These species also occur in the calcareous bluff forests. Two rare woody species are nutmeg hickory (*Carya myristicaeformis*) and prickly-ash (*Zanthoxylum americana,* plate 433).

The bottomland forest communities

Bottomland forests occupy the floodplains above the upper limit of the tidal influence that flanks the coastal plain river systems. These forests and their associated fauna comprise remarkably productive riverine communities that are adapted to fluctuating water levels. In the face of intensive land use of the adjacent uplands, the bottomland forests today serve as refuges for floodplain species and upland wildlife species.

Two major types of rivers traverse the lowcountry: brownwater and blackwater. Brownwater rivers originate in the mountain and piedmont areas and have broad and fertile floodplains due to the great quantity of nutrient-rich alluvium that is deposited when the rivers overflow their banks. The brown color of the water comes from the silt and clay that erode from the piedmont and mountains and are suspended in the water. Most brownwater rivers, such as the Santee and Savannah Rivers, have periods of sustained high flow that result from the cumulative effects of many tributaries and distant rainfall.

Blackwater rivers and tributary streams originate in the coastal plain and receive most of their water from local rain. They have narrower, less well-developed floodplains than the brownwater rivers since little alluvium is deposited. Unlike the brownwater rivers, the blackwater rivers may have dry periods when discharge is low. The term blackwater comes from the relatively sediment-free, but highly colored water that results from the presence of organic acids derived from decaying leaves. Examples of blackwater rivers are the Cooper, Ashley, Combahee, Ashepoo, New, Four Holes, Waccamaw, and Black.

Three major bottomland communities occur on brownwater and black-water river floodplains above the zone of tidal influence: bald cypress-tupelo gum swamp forests, levee forests, and bottomland hardwoods.

Bald cypress-tupelo gum swamp forests

The bottomland bald cypress-tupelo gum swamps (plate 441) represent the forested community least disturbed in the coastal plain. Still, only a few original growth stands remain.

In swamps where the land is flooded almost continuously, bald cypress (*Taxodium distichum*, plate 441) and tupelo gum (*Nyssa aquatica*, plate 160 in *WCL*) may coexist, or each may occur separately in pure stands. Pure tupelo stands, however, often become established following the clear-cutting of cypress-tupelo stands. Knee formations of cypress, reaching 6 feet or more, and buttress formations of cypress and tupelo gum are more pronounced in deep sloughs. Shrubs and herbs are sparse because of the flooded conditions and dense canopy. Herbs growing on floating logs and stumps are a distinct swamp microhabitat. Species characteristic of this microhabitat are skullcap (*Scutellaria lateriflora*), St. John's-wort (*Hypericum walterii*), false nettle (*Boehmeria cylindrica*, plate 464), and clearweed (*Pilea pumila*).

The epiphytes green-fly orchid, Spanish moss, and resurrection fern grow on branches of trees. Vines such as cross-vine (*Bignonia capreolata*), coral greenbrier (*Smilax walterii*), supplejack (*Berchemia scandens*), and poison ivy exhibit pronounced growth, especially at the margin of the swamps. Ladies'-eardrops (*Brunnichia ovata*, plate 447), a rare semiwoody vine, can be found on the margin of the swamp forests near lakes or ponds. Often the swamps have lakes within them (remnants of old streams) where members of the freshwater aquatic and tidal freshwater marsh communities occur.

As the depth and duration of flooding decreases, mesic trees such as red maple, water ash, swamp gum, and cottonwood form a subcanopy. As the wet soil becomes more exposed, shrubs become common, including Virginia willow (*Itea virginica*), swamp dogwood (*Cornus stricta*), and leucothoe (*Leucothoë racemosa*). Southern rein-orchid (*Habenaria flava*) occurs on the edges of muddy sloughs. Where favorable conditions exist, lizard's tail (*Saururus cernuus*), blue flag iris (*Iris virginica*), butterweed (*Senecio glabellus*), and golden-club (*Orontium aquaticum*) flourish, adding color to the swamp.

A great diversity of species occurs from swamp to swamp. Age of the forest, past timbering activities, degree of flooding, soil composition, and freedom from disturbance all contribute to the composition of today's swamps. Only Beidler Forest in Four Holes Swamp, a blackwater system, harbors a significant stand of original growth forest.

Hardwood bottom forests

Hardwood bottom forests (plate 456) occur on floodplains that are somewhat elevated above the adjoining cypress-gum swamp forest community. Although flooded for a considerable period, the surface is dry through much of the year. Hardwood bottoms exhibit extreme floral diversity, and the floral composition is variable from one site to another. The vegetation of the hardwood bottoms is dense, and in the more undisturbed sites, trees grow over 3 feet in diameter. Small trees and shrubs are frequent and woody vines luxuriant. In the drier sites a rich, herbaceous flora flourishes. In areas that have been logged, trees are smaller but still dense. Often hardwood bottom forests are narrow strips with adjacent uplands on one side and the swamp forests on the other. At other times, the forests may be a broad expanse.

Many trees characterize this community, including sweet gum, loblolly pine (*Pinus taeda*), overcup oak (*Quercus lyrata*), water oak (*Q. nigra*), willow oak (*Q. phellos*), swamp chestnut oak (*Q. michauxii*), laurel oak (*Q. laurifolia*), cherry-bark oak (*Q. pagoda*), ash (*Fraxinus* spp.), sycamore (*Platanus occidentalis*), American holly, American elm (*Ulmus americana*), and hackberry (*Celtis laevigata*), among others.

A subcanopy of young canopy species is present, including ironwood (*Carpinus caroliniana*). Among the numerous shrubs that characterize the community are swamp dogwood (*Cornus stricta*), arrowwood (*Viburnum dentatum*), wild azalea (*Rhododendron canescens*), elderberry (*Sambucus canadensis*), and possum-haw (*Ilex decidua,* plate 467). These species also may occur in the adjacent swamp forests.

Woody vines are especially prominent and include cow-itch (*Campsis radicans*), poison ivy, supplejack (*Berchemia scandens*), climbing hydrangea (*Decumaria barbara*), and muscadine (*Vitis rotundifolia*).

Grasses, rushes, sedges, and wildflowers form a rich herbaceous layer in drier sites. Grasses and sedges often form a dense ground layer and separate the hardwood bottoms from the adjacent swamp forests. Many wildflowers from the swamp forests also grace the hardwood bottoms, but several additional species occur, including Easter lily (*Zephyranthes atamasco,* plate 460), Carolina least trillium (*Trillium pusillum* var. *pusillum,* plate 459), jack-in-the-pulpit (*Arisaema triphyllum,* plate 457), and Virginia dayflower (*Commelina virginica,* plate 465).

An interesting microhabitat in the hardwood bottoms is the "windthrow" community. The bottomland trees have shallow but broad root systems. When these trees are blown down, the uplifted soil clings to the roots, which is now in a sunlit area because the fallen tree created a gap in the canopy. This allows for the establishment of numerous weedy herbs.

Levee forests

Natural levees or "fronts" occur along the river edge. Levees are created as vegetation along the river's edge slow floodwaters and allow for the deposit of silt. These levees are slightly higher than the adjacent floodplain, which harbor the hardwood bottom and cypress-gum communities. The soil is very fertile, especially along alluvial rivers. Blackwater rivers have less-developed levees due to lower amounts of alluvium

The levees are occupied by pioneers species, with sycamore, river birch (*Betula nigra*), laurel oak (*Quercus laurifolia*), and willow (*Salix* spp.) being the major trees. Other trees include ash (*Fraxinus* spp.), tulip tree (*Liriodendron tulipifera*), silver maple (*Acer saccharinum*), American holly, and sweet gum.

Three common shrubs are pawpaw (*Asimina triloba*), wild allspice (*Lindera benzoin*), and switch-cane (*Arundinaria gigantea,* plate 471). "Cane bottoms" or "cane brakes" in South Carolina, both in the piedmont and coastal plain, are associated with large levees. In the coastal plain, these extensive areas of cane are now gone. Isolated patches are still found in the piedmont.

Herbs vary from site to site but generally include river oats (*Chasmanthium latifolium*, plate 472), butterweed, and false nettle.

The peatland community

Peatlands are wetlands where the soils are peat. Peat is the partially decomposed remains of dead plants and, to a lesser extent, animals. Peatlands develop where there is a net gain in organic matter over time; therefore, decomposition cannot exceed production if peatlands are to form. Water slows decomposition in the coastal plain. In water, dead plants and animals decompose at a much slower rate than when they are exposed to both air and moisture. Most bacteria and fungi that decompose organic matter need oxygen for respiration. In saturated conditions, no atmospheric oxygen is available. The accumulation of peat is also helped if the water moves slowly since slow-moving water does not carry away organic matter. Acids that build up as by-products of respiration further inhibit decomposition in bogs because bacteria and fungi do not work as effectively under acidic conditions. Bog waters develop a dark color from the acids that are not washed away by moving water.

Pocosins

The dominant peatland community in the coastal plain are the pocosins (or evergreen shrub bogs). Pocosins (plate 477) are found on the southeastern coastal plains of the United States and are botanical treasures. Pocosins grow on waterlogged, acid, nutrient-poor, sandy or peaty soils that are located on broad, flat topographic plateaus or in Carolina bays. They are usually removed from large streams and are subject to periodic burning. Natural drainage is poor. Pocosins are dominated by a dense mix of evergreen shrubs, vines, and scattered trees. In some pocosins, the vegetation is so thick and laced with bamboo-vine (*Smilax laurifolia*) that traversing in this community is difficult. One has to go down "on all fours" to get below the dense tangle of vegetation. Each step in the soft peat is uncertain. The reward is a pocosin community full of wildflowers.

The vegetation of pocosins is a dense growth of shrubs that are associated with scattered trees. Diversity is not great since few species can adapt to the mineral-poor, acid soils and long hydroperiods. The dominant trees are pond pine (*Pinus serotina*, plate 494) and loblolly bay (*Gordonia lasianthus*), with swamp red bay (*Persea palustris*) and sweet bay occurring as associates. The most frequently found shrubs are the evergreens fetterbush (*Lyonia lucida*), inkberry (*Ilex glabra*), sweet gallberry (*Ilex coriacea*), coastal plain serviceberry (*Amelanchier obovalis*), and the deciduous shrubs, titi (*Cyrilla racemiflora*) and honey-cups (*Zenobia pulverulenta*). All these species grow with bamboo-vine. Because of the evergreen shrubs, some people call the pocosins "evergreen shrub bogs." The shrubs in some sites are short (2–3 feet tall) with scattered pond pine and are called low pocosins. In other sites, both shrubs and trees are taller and the sites are called high pocosins. In some pocosins, tall zones exist around the margin with the low pocosin growth in the center. Poison sumac often grows along the margins of pocosins. Two rare evergreen ericads, leather-leaf (*Cassandra calyculata,* plate 478) and Carolina wicky (*Kalmia carolina,* plate 481), are found along the edges of pocosins.

Fires increase the habitat diversity of pocosins by unevenly burning the peat, creating boggy depressions below the water table. These depressions fill with sphagnum and herbaceous species such as yellow trumpet pitcher-plant (*Sarracenia flava*) and white arum (*Peltandra sagittaefolia,* plate 493).

For thousands of years, peat has been building up in these pocosins to a depth of 10 feet or more. During droughts, peat is susceptible to fires, and most pocosins burn about every 10 to 30 years. Pocosin plants have adapted to this fire cycle. After a fire, they vigorously sprout new growth from their rootstocks, which were protected from fire because they are buried in the deeper, wet zone of the peat. Pocosins are also mineral-poor since they receive water mostly from rainfall or drainage through coarse sands.

Pocosins today are being studied intensely as natural reservoirs for water and as habitat for plants and animals. During drought, lower layers of peat hold water that is available to animals or that can be slowly released into the surrounding areas. The dense vegetation also provides habitat for animals that avoid people, such as the endangered black bear and pine barrens treefrog. Pocosins have had a long history of human use; timbering, drainage for agricultural use and timber plantations, peat mining, and urban development all have greatly reduced pocosin habitat. Fortunately, concerned organizations are taking steps to preserve pocosins, especially in Carolina bays.

The pond cypress communities

Pond cypress savannas

Pond cypress savannas (plate 495) occupy flat, acidic, poorly drained lands within the longleaf pine forests. They have a slightly longer hydroperiod than that associated with pine flatwoods and pine savannas and are dominated by pond cypress, which can tolerate a longer hydroperiod than pines. The cypress canopy is open. Red maple and swamp gum may also be present. Pond cypress savannas occur scattered throughout the coastal plain with many of the best examples occurring within Carolina bays. Draining and ditching, along with absence of fire, have reduced the number of pond cypress savannas. Numerous excellent sites still occur in the Francis Marion National Forest.

Few shrubs occur except for some woody hypericums (*Hypericum fasciculatum,* plate 503), myrtle-leaved holly (*Ilex myrtifolia,* plate 519), and buttonbush. The herbaceous flora, blooming through the spring, summer, and fall, is rich. Some of the showy herbaceous species of the adjacent pine savannas, including many of the carnivorous plants, can be found. Certain herbs, however, appear to be more common or confined to the pond cypress savannas. These include sneezeweed (*Helenium pinnatifidum,* plate 497), bay blue-flag iris (*Iris tridentata,* plate 504), tall milkwort (*Polygala cymosa,* plate 501), awned meadow-beauty (*Rhexia aristosa,* plate 558), gerardia (*Agalinis linifolia,* plate 508), Boykin's lobelia (*Lobelia boykinii,* plate 555), and the federally endangered Canby's dropwort (*Oxypolis canbyi,* plate 561). Other wildflowers of note in the pond cypress savannas include blue sedge (*Carex glaucescens,* plate 506), pool coreopsis (*Coreopsis falcata,* plate 498), giant white-topped sedge (*Dichromena latifolia*), pipewort (*Eriocaulon decangulare*), tall hydrolea (*Hydrolea corymbosa*), savanna obedient plant (*Physostegia purpurea*), giant yellow-eyed grass (*Xyris fimbriata,* plate 509), lace-lip ladies'-tresses (*Spiranthes laciniata,* plate 502), and Carolina grass-of-Parnassus (*Parnassia caroliniana,* plate 510).

Pond cypress-swamp gum upland swamps
Pond cypress-swamp gum upland swamp forests (plate 512) are dominated by pond cypress or pond cypress and swamp gum, with pond pine (*Pinus serotina*) often present as an associate. These swamps occur in upland depressions where some water is on the surface for at least three months. The water is acidic because there is no drainage to remove accumulated acids. The depressions may be limestone sinks, irregular depressions, or Carolina bays. Generally the interior is open water, with shrubs confined more to the margin.

The herbaceous flora of this swamp is sparse compared to the riverine and other upland swamps. One rare herb is violet burmannia (*Burmannia biflora,* plate 515), which occurs in the drawdown zone. Numerous shrubs occur along the margins of the depressions. In the FMNF, several populations of pondberry (*Lindera melissifolia,* plate 516), a federally endangered species, occur in sink holes in the Honey Hill and Cainhoy areas. Another member of the laurel family, pondspice (*Litsea aestivalis*), which is rare throughout its range, is common in many of these swamp forests in the FMNF and elsewhere in the coastal plain. Other shrubs in this upland swamp forest include titi, button-bush, cassena (*Ilex cassine,* plate 518), and myrtle-leaved holly (*Ilex myrtifolia,* plate 519). The rare climbing fetterbush (*Pieris phillyreifolia,* plate 513) is known in South Carolina only from these pond cypress-swamp gum swamps in the FMNF. The open water is also habitat for the freshwater aquatics. Floating bladderwort is especially common.

The freshwater marsh communities

Marshes are wetlands that are inhabited by herbaceous plants that have their roots in the substrate but with their photosynthetic and reproductive organs principally emersed. Freshwater marshes are more or less permanently flooded. The dominant species are grasses, rushes, and sedges along with numerous broadleaf flowering plants. Freshwater marshes occur along tidal rivers and inland along pond and lake margins, in beaver ponds, in canals and ditches, and in managed impoundments. Of the two types of freshwater marshes, the inland and tidal, the latter covers by far the greater area in the coastal plain. Although both inland and tidal freshwater marshes have essentially the same flora, the tidal marshes do have some species that do not occur farther inland. For examples, wild rice (*Zizania aquatica,* plate 527), southern wild rice (*Zizaniopsis miliacea,* plate 58 in WCL), and saw-grass (*Cladium jamaicense,* plate 64 in WCL) generally tend to be absent from the inland marshes.

Tidal freshwater marshes
Tidal freshwater marshes (plate 520) are much more diverse ecologically and floristically than either salt marshes or brackish marshes. Indeed, they are among the most diverse wetland plant communities in the continental United States. In the freshwater tidal marshes along the Cooper River in Berkeley County, over

100 species of vascular plants have been identified. A similar diversity occurs in the marshes of the other rivers in the coastal area. The floristic composition varies from site to site within a river as well as between rivers. Zonation may exist within a site, but it is not repeated consistently from site to site.

In the pre-settlement rivers of the coastal plain, tidal freshwater marshes occurred as fringes along the rivers where tidal freshwater swamps bordered the rivers. Today, however, the majority of tidal freshwater marshes occur in abandoned rice fields (figure 7). The rice fields, in turn, were originally tidal cypress-gum freshwater swamps that occurred along every tidal river along the Carolina coast. Where there was a swamp that had at least a three-foot difference in tidal amplitude, the swamp was ultimately converted into rice fields. When rice growing ended in the early 1900s, the fields followed two fates: (1) either the banks around the fields were maintained and water control structures were used to select a water regime that encouraged the growth of plant species that attracted waterfowl, which were usually hunted, or (2) the fields were abandoned, allowing nature to take its course. It is these abandoned rice fields that today support the greatest acreage of tidal freshwater marshes.

The species that characterize this marsh community are those with their leaf-bearing stems or leaves extended above the water. They include various rushes, sedges, cat-tails, and broadleaf flowering species. These flowering species, most of which do not occur in brackish or salt marshes, make this one of the greatest wildflower communities. Although the flowering species do not dominate the system, they are sufficiently common to add a distinctive beauty and color to the marsh-scape. The best way to view this community is by boat.

Some of the more conspicuous wildflowers of the tidal marshes are cardinal flower, spiderlily (*Hymenocallis floridana,* plate 525), eryngo (*Eryngium aquaticum* var. *aquaticum,* plate 531), swamp rose, groundnut (*Apios americana*), water hemlock (*Cicuta maculata,* plate 524), swamp rose mallow (*Hibiscus moscheutos* subsp. *moscheutos,* plate 529), seashore mallow (*Kosteletskya virginica,* plate 532), pickerelweed (*Pontederia cordata,* plate 522), water-spider orchid (*Habenaria repens*), and tear-thumb (*Polygonum arifolium,* plate 534)

Inland freshwater marshes

Inland freshwater marshes occur in a variety of natural and human-made habitats: ditches and canals, lake and pond margins, beaver ponds, and managed impoundments. These marshes contain a wide mix of wetland species. Many of the species of the tidal marshes occur in the inland marshes. Some species that appear to be more common in these inland marshes include showy plants like Carolina water-hyssop (*Bacopa caroliniana*), golden canna (*Canna flaccida,* plate 539), creeping burhead (*Echinodorus cordifolius,* plate 542), long beach seedbox (*Ludwigia brevipes*), winged monkey-flower (*Mimulus alatus,* plate 544), and arrowhead (*Sagittaria graminea* var. *graminea,* plate 540).

The freshwater floating aquatics community

Freshwater floating aquatics

Hydrophytes include aquatic plants that normally grow in water or inhabit soils that contain more water than is optimal for the average plant. One of the outstanding structural features shared by most hydrophytes is aerenchyma tissue. This tissue is formed by the disintegration of groups of tissue cells or the separation of cells, which creates enlarged, intercellular cavities (lacunae) that become filled with gases. These air-filled cavities allow hydrophytes to float.

One group of hydrophytes is the freshwater floating aquatics, the true aquatic plants. They consist of three types: (1) the submerged, anchored; (2) the floating-leaf, anchored; and (3) the floating (no soil contact). These aquatics are greatly developed in lakes, ponds, freshwater sounds, canals, abandoned rice fields, and sluggish streams. They generally occur in the sandhills, coastal plain, and maritime strand. Today, much of the habitat for the aquatics is human-created. Reservoirs, such as Lake Moultrie and Lake Murray, harbor along their shores a rich, aquatic growth. Inland swamps that were dammed to create water reservoirs for growing rice now support aquatic populations, and many multipurpose canals that were dug for various reasons provide habitat for the aquatics. As was previously mentioned, the abandoned tidal rice fields support aquatics on the fringe of the marsh vegetation. The aquatics are also found in deepwater pockets in inland swamp forests where dams maintain the water level year-round and in ox-bow lakes that form along the major rivers.

A number of submerged, anchored aquatics occur in waterways throughout the state. Often their flowers project above the water's surface. Two species with conspicuous flowers are fanwort (*Cabomba caroliniana*) and Brazilian elodea (*Egeria densa*). The floating aquatics are represented by water hyacinth (*Eichhornia crassipes*) and four genera of the duckweed family (Lemnaceae): duckmeat (*Spirodela*), duckweed (*Lemna*), water-meal (*Wolffia*), and bog-mat (*Wolffiella*). The floating mosquito fern (*Azolla caroliniana*) is also common.

The most spectacular of the aquatics are the floating-leaf, anchored species, with their showy flowers borne above or on the water's surface. Most prominent of these is fragrant water-lily (*Nymphaea odorata*, plate 552). Other species are cow-lily (*Nuphar sagittifolia*, plate 546), frog's-bit (*Limnobium spongea*, plate 550), water-shield (*Brasenia schreberi*, plate 549), big floating-heart (*Nymphoides aquatica*, plate 547), and floating bladderwort (*Utricularia inflata*, plate 548).

The depression meadow community

Depression meadows

Depression meadows (plate 554) are temporally flooded herbaceous communities that have saturated soil. Since they are isolated wetlands, these meadows generally do not have a source of water other than rainwater. During times of drought, fires often occur, preventing a woody flora from becoming established. Depression meadows differ from freshwater marshes in that the latter are more or less permanently flooded. The lack of fire in marshes allows woody species to become established and sometimes to ultimately dominant the community.

Classification of depression meadows is unclear, and much fieldwork needs to be done to fully understand these communities. One type of depression meadow being studied occurs in clay-based Carolina bays. These seem to share a basic floristic similarity, with numerous species in common, especially rare ones. The clay soil prevents water from percolating down into the soil, and during times of rain, the bay is flooded. Since the bays are different depths, water level varies. The deeper bays often have open water that supports species of the floating aquatic community such as fragrant water-lily and water-shield. The more shallow bays are dominated by sedges, rushes, and grasses.

Some of the wildflower species of note are Boykin's lobelia (*Lobelia boykinii*, plate 555), shrubby seedbox (*Ludwigia suffruticosa*, plate 557), awned meadow-beauty (*Rhexia aristosa*, plate 558), Tracy's beaksedge (*Rhynchospora tracyi*, plate 559), sclerolepis (*Sclerolepis uniflora*, plate 556), and the endangered Canby's dropwort (*Oxypolis canbyi*, plate 561).

There are no depression meadows in the coastal plain that have been protected by South Carolina's Heritage Trust Program. Two Carolina bays that harbor depression meadows that are available to the public are Red Bluff Creek Carolina Bay in the FMNF and Craig Pond in Barnwell County. Both are described in the "Field guide to natural plant communities."

THE MARITIME STRAND

The maritime communities

Coastal beaches

Along the South Carolina coast, beaches (plate 562) form where ocean currents and waves deposit sand that was picked up by the waters from offshore coastal sites or brought down the rivers from inland areas. No vascular plants grow along the beach below the high-tide line because it is a dynamic zone, constantly changing because of the action of the wind and tides. Above the high-tide zone, a zone of detritus (driftline) develops, which is deposited by the tides. The dominant component of the detritus is the remains of smooth cordgrass from the nearby salt marshes, which washed down the tidal creeks. Seeds of two hardy species, sea rocket (*Cakile harperi*, plate 563) and Carolina saltwort (*Salsola caroliniana*, plate 564), are generally the first species to become established in this harsh environment. A rare beach plant is the federally endangered seabeach amaranth (*Amaranthus pumilus*, plate 565), which occurs from upper Charleston County to North Carolina.

Coastal dunes

Landward from the driftline is the berm, a zone of fairly level, loose sand that is subject to heavy salt spray and is located above all but the highest spring tides. The coastal dunes form here (plate 562). Dunes are mounds of unconsolidated sand formed in the berm area by winds blowing across the beach. Whenever a plant (or object) reduces the force of the wind, wind-borne sand is deposited and ultimately forms a dune. The plant most associated with building coastal dunes in the southeast is sea oats (*Uniola paniculata*, plate 573). Young seedlings act as windbreaks, slowing the wind. As the wind slows, the sand it carries accumulates behind and against the leaves. As the sand is added, the plant grows, keeping its leaves above the rising sand. In a few years a dune builds many feet high.

Coastal dunes front the barrier beaches and barrier islands of the Carolina coast. They are interrupted where inlets and sounds allow the ocean to surge through, with the ocean's energy being dissipated inward to the tidal flats and marshes. Dunes are also the first line of defense against oceanic forces, especially hurricanes and winter storms. Just as winds can build dunes, they can destroy what they have created. Where the vegetation is killed, the wind erodes dunes. Preservation-minded coastal residents have long fought to protect dunes from excess disturbance, such as trails made by people or dune buggies. The South Carolina law against disturbing sea oats on public property has done much to protect coastal dunes.

Other grasses that help build the dunes are seaside panicum (*Panicum amarum*) and dune sandbur (*Cenchrus tribuloides*). Once the dunes become fairly stable, various forbs become established to help further stabilize the dunes, including beach pea, horseweed, beach evening-primrose, dunes evening-primrose, camphorweed, seaside pennywort, and two species of cactus, prickly-pear (*Opuntia compressa*) and dune devil-joint (*O. pusilla*, plate 571).

Swales develop between the dunes. These are low-lying areas that are protected from the salt-laden winds and where a fresh to brackish system may develop because rainwater collects and floats atop the heavier salt water. In this microhabitat, common marsh-pink (*Sabatia stellaris*, plate 574) is abundant.

The dune communities may be replaced by maritime shrub thickets on barrier islands or on barrier beaches where accretion is occurring and the dunes are building seaward, which protects the inner dunes from the salt-laden winds, or where the shoreline has been stabilized for years. Maritime forests may in turn replace the maritime shrub thickets.

Maritime forests

Maritime forests (plate 582) occupy the barrier islands and barrier shores of the coast. The characteristic species are a variety of salt-tolerant, evergreen trees and shrubs. There is little herbaceous plant cover except in exposed sites, due to natural breaks in the canopy, and in disturbed areas.

On the ocean side, maritime forests are shaped (literally) by the effects of salt spray. The wind blowing from the sea carries salt, depositing it on the windward branches and leaves. These leaves and branches die from the salt, while those on the leeward side, protected from the salt spray, continue growing. The result is a "shearing effect" of the trees and shrubs. Inland, away from the effects of salt spray, the trees assume a typical appearance.

The characteristic evergreen trees of maritime forests are live oak, bull bay, loblolly pine, and laurel oak. The subcanopy includes the evergreen trees cabbage palmetto (*Sabal palmetto*, plate 593), American holly, red bay (*Persea borbonia*, plate 589), Hercules'-club (*Zanthoxylum clava-herculis*, plate 584), and in more open sites, wax myrtle, yaupon (*Ilex vomitoria*), wild olive, and southern red cedar (*Juniperus silicicola*). Herbaceous wildflowers are sparse because of the dense canopy, but two species can be found in more open sites, prickly-pear cactus and trailing bluet (*Houstonia procumbens*).

The maritime forests along the Atlantic Coast have been extensively timbered since colonial times. No original growth stands exist along the South Carolina coast, with the possible exception of the interior of St. Phillips Island in Beaufort County, where low swales prevented timbering. Islands such as Capers Island in Charleston County and Daufuskie Island in Beaufort County have had extensive agricultural fields in the interior, and the present forests are secondary growth.

Timbering began in the maritime forests in the 1700s, mainly for live oak to build wooden sailing vessels. After the War of 1812, "live oak mania" began. Expeditions were sent from the northern shipyards to the Atlantic and Gulf coasts to harvest live oak. After the invention of iron and steel ships, live oak was given a reprieve. Timber companies then began to harvest the pines of the maritime forests. Maritime forests of the lowcountry today are secondary forests. The existing large live oaks are either ones that were left, for whatever reasons, or that came from seedlings. Live oak is a fast-growing tree on good sites and can reach an impressive size in 50 years. The large live oaks that line plantation avenues were planted starting in the 1700s (note their large size today).

Salt marshes

Salt marshes (plate 595) occur on regularly flooded, peaty substrates along tidal inlets and behind barrier islands and spits. This community is species-poor, often supporting pure stands of smooth cordgrass (*Spartina alterniflora*, plate 595); however, it is one of the most productive in the world. It is the dominant wetland in the coastal zone of South Carolina, comprising approximately 150,000 acres. As cordgrass dies, it is washed into the inlets and the ocean, where it forms the basis of the estuarine food chain.

Three forms of smooth cordgrass occur: tall, medium and short. The tall *Spartina* grows next to the tidal creeks in relatively deep water, where it receives an energy subsidy from the tidewater. Away from the creek the tall cordgrass grades into the medium. The medium then grades into the short. Short cordgrass occurs at the highest elevation where it is flooded daily, but only to a depth of a few inches to one foot.

In the short zone, two species that also occur in the adjacent salt shrub thickets intermix with the short *Spartina*: sea lavender (*Limonium carolinianum*, plate 599) and saltmarsh aster (*Aster tenuifolius*, plate 598), adding a touch of color to the otherwise drab salt marshes.

Salt flats

Salt flats (plate 601) are formed where tidal waters drain incompletely and the soil becomes very salty. As the water evaporates, is leaves behind the salt, which often forms a white crust on the soil. Even the most salt-tolerant species cannot survive in these hypersaline areas, and the center of flats is often barren. However, as salinity decreases toward the margins, a variety of fleshy halophytes, salt-loving grasses, and other herbs appear. Closest to the center are perennial glasswort (*Salicornia virginica*, plate 602) and saltwort (*Batis maritima*, plate 603), which are obligate halophytes that tolerate high salinity. Salt flats grade into either salt marshes or salt shrub thickets. Intermixed with saltwort and glasswort are diminutive forms of species associated with the salt marshes and salt shrub thickets: sea ox-eye, marsh-elder, smooth cordgrass, sea lavender, saltmarsh aster, and seaside goldenrod.

Maritime shell forests

Natural and Native American shell deposits are scattered along the coast in salt marshes and on the tips of landmasses within estuaries. The natural shell deposits are not unique floristically. They generally support species of the adjacent maritime communities. The Native American deposits, however, are floristically unique and have only recently been studied along the Carolina coast. The key environmental parameter determining the floristic composition of the Native American shell deposits is the presence of calcium from the shells. Several calcium-loving species, called calcicoles, occur and are mixed with species of the adjacent maritime forests and salt shrub thickets

Native American shell deposits are of three types: shell rings, shell

FIGURE 9. Native American Shell Ring and Shell Mound.

Shell Mound

Shell Ring

mounds, and shell hummocks, which occur on marsh islands or on the mainland. Figure 9 shows a shell ring with an associated shell mound. The shell ring is a circular deposit of shells that rises several feet above the marsh. The shell mound is a mass of shells that are raised considerably higher than the shell ring (from 10 to 30 feet high). Shell hummocks are shells that were deposited in piles or in sinuous formations, probably as part of a campsite, on the mainland or on marsh islands. Considerable debate exists about the origin of these Native American shell deposits.

Shell rings are either isolated in the marsh or attached to a landmass. The isolated shell rings harbor few calcicoles, with only tough bumelia (*Bumelia tenax*) and shell-mound buckthorn (*Sageretia minutiflora*) being common. The shell rings attached to an adjacent landmass, however, harbor many of the rare calcicoles that are found on the high shell mounds and shell hummocks.

The shell mounds and shell hummocks harbor a maritime shell forest (plate 604). This is a rare forest community along the coast and, at the date of the printing of this book, has not been formally classified. There is no doubt, however, that the maritime shell forest is unique.

Maritime shell forests harbor a variety of woody trees, shrubs, and herbs that thrive in high-calcium soils. Trees and shrubs include tough bumelia (*Bumelia tenax*), basswood (*Tilia heterophylla*), red buckeye (*Aesculus pavia*), hackberry (*Celtis laevigata*), Carolina buckthorn (*Rhamnus caroliniana*), shell-mound buckthorn (*Sageretia minutiflora*), rough-leaved dogwood (*Cornus asperifolia*), the rare southern sugar maple (*Acer barbatum,* plate 435) and Godfrey's forestiera (*Forestiera godfreyi,* plate 605). Rare herbs include mottled trillium (*Trillium maculatum,* plate 432), *Cynanchum scoparium,* Indian-midden morning-glory (*Ipomoea macrorhiza,* plate 607), and crested coral-root (*Hexalectris spicata*)

Sites with southern sugar maple are the most spectacular. In the fall, their leaves turn a distinctive red, and the community can be spotted from the air. Maritime shell forests share many species in common with the inland calcareous forests since both are influenced by calcium in the soil.

Species Descriptions and Color Plates

THE MOUNTAINS

1. Granitic domes

2. Canada columbine; eastern Columbine

Aquilegia canadensis L.
  Aq-ui-lè-gi-a ca-na-dén-sis
  Ranunculaceae (Buttercup Family)

DESCRIPTION: Perennial herb from a thickened rootstock; stem to 3′ tall; leaves both basal and on the stem, compound, in units of 3; flowers red outside and yellow within, very conspicuous and distinctive; flowers March–May.

RANGE-HABITAT: Widespread in eastern North America; in SC occasional in the mountains and n. piedmont; rare in the coastal plain; in a variety of moist to dry habitats, usually rocky and often on high calcium soils; interestingly, it has been found on shell banks along a salt marsh on Hawkins Island in Onslow County, NC.

COMMENTS: Columbine is adapted for pollination by hummingbirds. The whole plant is poisonous.

3. Appalachian sandwort

Minuartia glabra (Michaux) Mattfeld
  Mi-nu-ár-ti-a glà-bra
  Caryophyllaceae (Pink Family)

DESCRIPTION: Tufted annual; stems smooth, erect, 3–10″ tall; basal rosette of leaves absent at flowering; larger stem leaves 0.4–1.2″ long; 1–50 flowered plant; flowers April–May.

RANGE-HABITAT: From ME and NH, south to GA and AL; in SC restricted to granitic domes and other rock outcrops in the mountains and piedmont; common in the mountains, occasional in the piedmont.

SIMILAR SPECIES: It is not difficult to distinguish between this species and *M. uniflora* (single-flowered sandwort, plate 162). *M. glabra* is a more vigorous plant and grows in tufts.

COMMENTS: Appalachian sandwort can be seen at Flat Creek Heritage Preserve.

SYNONYM: *Arenaria groenlandica* var. *glabra* (Michaux) Fernald—RAB

4. Yellow honeysuckle

Lonicera flava Sims
    Lo-níc-er-a flà-va
Caprifoliaceae (Honeysuckle Family)

DESCRIPTION: Twining vine to 15′ long; stem without hairs; leaves opposite; on flowering stems, the terminal 2 (3) pairs of leaves fused at the base; leaves gray beneath; flowers yellow or yellow-orange, in opposite terminal clusters of 3 flowers; flowers April–May.

RANGE-HABITAT: KY and MO, south to GA and AK; in SC restricted to granitic domes in the mountains.

COMMENTS: Probably the best indicator of calcareous granitic domes. The genus honors Adam Lonitzer, latinized Lonicerus, a sixteenth-century German herbalist.

5. Rattlesnake-master; eastern false-aloe

Manfreda virginica (L.) Salisbury ex Rose
    Mán-fred-a vir-gí-ni-ca
Amaryllidaceae (Amaryllis Family)

DESCRIPTION: Perennial herb with fleshy basal leaves 6–15″ long, often mottled with purple; flowering stem to 6′ tall, the upper ¼ bearing greenish to purplish flowers; flowers late May–mid-July.

RANGE-HABITAT: OH and MO, south to FL and TX; throughout SC; common; granitic outcrops and dry diabase or gabbro outcrops in the piedmont, around granitic domes in the upper piedmont and mountains, and in dry flatwoods in the coastal plain.

COMMENTS: The root produces a milky juice that can be very irritating to the skin. Western species of *Manfreda* produce precursors used in steroid synthesis. Named for Manfred, an ancient Italian writer.

SYNONYM: *Agave virginica* L.—RAB

6. Mountain dwarf-dandelion; mountain Cynthia

Krigia montana (Michaux) Nuttall
    Kríg-i-a mon-tà-na
Asteraceae (Aster or Sunflower Family)

DESCRIPTION: Perennial herb with milky juice, from a nontuberous rootstalk; leaves in a basal rosette and on a branched stem; heads of ray flowers only, 3–5, a single head on a long stalk from each leaf axil; flowers May–September.

RANGE-HABITAT: TN, NC, GA, and SC; restricted to the mountains in moist crevices in rocks and boulders of cliffs, granitic domes, and rocky streamsides.

COMMENTS: Often forms clusters of many stems, which, along with its perennial habit and nontuberous rootstalk, helps distinguish it from weedy relatives. The genus honors David Krig, a German physician, who was among the first to collect plants in MD.

7. Small's beard-tongue

Penstemon smallii Heller
Pen-stè-mon smáll-i-i
Scrophulariaceae (Figwort Family)

DESCRIPTION: Perennial herb with an obvious minty scent; stems to 30″ tall; internodes of the middle stem without hairs; flowers rose-purple, two-lipped, with an open, inflated throat and a heavily bearded (yellow-haired) sterile stamen (tongue); flowers in a terminal, panicle-like cluster, lower bracts leaflike; flowers May–June.

RANGE-HABITAT: TN, NC, SC, and GA; restricted to the mountains; rocky streamsides and moist woods margins as well as calcareous cliffs and granitic domes.

COMMENTS: This is the largest-flowered, most attractive beard-tongue in SC. The specific epithet honors John K. Small, 1869–1938, distinguished American botanist.

8. Cliff saxifrage

Saxifraga michauxii Britton
Sax-íf-ra-ga mi-chaùx-i-i
Saxifragaceae (Saxifrage Family)

DESCRIPTION: Perennial herb; leaves basal; flowers in an open panicle; corolla irregular; petals 5, white, the upper 3 each with 2 yellow spots; anthers orange; flowers June–August.

RANGE-HABITAT: Endemic to the southern Appalachians; in SC known only from the mountains; rock crevices on exposed granitic domes, in dry to moist conditions.

COMMENTS: This species is unmistakable in bloom because of its irregular flowers, the three upper petals each with two yellow spots.

9. Hop-tree; wafer-ash

Ptelea trifoliata L.
Ptè-le-a tri-fo-li-à-ta
Rutaceae (Rue Family)

DESCRIPTION: Deciduous shrub or small tree to 20′ tall; leaves with 3, stalkless leaflets, variable in size, usually less than 5″ long; flowers small, greenish white, in terminal flat-topped clusters; fruits flat, broadly winged; flowers April–June; fruits mature June–August.

RANGE-HABITAT: New England to WI, and south to FL, MS, and TX; occasional throughout SC; found on rocky bluffs, stream terraces, granitic domes, and calcareous outcrops.

COMMENTS: The plant is generally aromatic, and the flowers are foul smelling. It is common around calcareous outcrops in the coastal plain and mountains. Hop-tree was once thought to be a good substitute for hops in making beer.

10. Tall bellflower

Campanulastrum americanum (L.) Small
Cam-pa-nu-lás-trum a-me-ri-cà-num
Campanulaceae (Bellwort Family)

DESCRIPTION: Annual or perennial herb, 1.5–4′ tall, erect and usually unbranched; leaves alternate with blades tapering at both ends; flowers pale blue or white, petals 5, lobes forming a flat, round outline about 0.8–1.0″ broad; flowers solitary or in clusters in the axils of lower leaves and upper bracts; flowers late June–September.

RANGE-HABITAT: Widespread in eastern North America; rare in the piedmont and mountains; in SC in calcareous variant of granitic domes, rich coves in the mountains, and basic-mesic forests of the piedmont.

COMMENTS: Radford et al. (1968) include this species in the genus *Campanula,* but recent evidence suggests Small (1933) was correct in separating it into the genus *Campanulastrum.* Species of *Campanula* have corollas that are bell- or funnel-shaped.

SYNONYM: *Campanula americana* L.—RAB

PROTECTION STATUS: State Endangered

11. Mountain blazing star

Liatris spicata (L.) Willdenow var. *spicata*
Li-à-tris spi-cà-ta var. spi-cà-ta
Asteraceae (Aster or Sunflower Family)

DESCRIPTION: Perennial herb from a swollen, knotty rootstalk; stems 3–6′ tall, unbranched, often with fibrous remains of old leaf stalks at the base; largest leaves up to 0.8″ wide; heads of disc flowers only, with fewer than 14 flowers per head; corolla lavender, smooth within; flowers late July–early September.

RANGE-HABITAT: NY, MI, and MO, south to FL and LA; common in moist soils around granitic domes and in bogs in the mountains and upper piedmont.

TAXONOMY: A second variety of this species (*L. spicata* var. *resinosa,* plate 364 in *WCL*) occurs in moist longleaf pine savannas of the coastal plain.

12. Allegheny live-for-ever

Sedum telephioides Michaux
Sè-dum te-le-phi-oì-des
Crassulaceae (Stonecrop Family)

DESCRIPTION: Perennial herb; stems to 16″ tall; leaves bluish green, fleshy, elliptic, alternate, to 2″ long, reduced in size upwards; flowers white to pale pink; flowers July–September.
RANGE-HABITAT: PA and IN, south to NC and SC; in SC rare in the mountains; usually on granitic domes, which are very rare in SC.
COMMENTS: This is South Carolina's only native species of *Sedum* with large, flat, alternate leaves. "Live-for-ever" is in reference to the plant's ability to propagate itself from fragments of stem or leaves.

13. Purple cliff-brake

Pellaea atropurpurea (L.) Link
Pel-laè-a at-ro-pur-pù-re-a
Pteridaceae (Maidenhair Fern Family)

DESCRIPTION: Perennial, evergreen, rock-dwelling fern from a short creeping or ascending rhizome; leaves stiff, leathery; leaf stalks purplish black and sparsely hairy; blades 2x pinnately compound, ultimate segments remote, oblong, sometimes whitened below, but never shiny; fertile and sterile leaves separate.
RANGE-HABITAT: Widespread in eastern North America; in SC chiefly in the mountains, rare; very rare in the piedmont; marble or other calcareous rocks in dry habitats; a Pickens County population is on a granitic dome (calcareous variant), and a population in Oconee County is on marble boulders in a dry oak-hickory forest.
PROTECTION STATUS: State Endangered

14. Twisted-hair spikemoss; kinky-hair spikemoss

Selaginella tortipila A. Braun
Se-la-gi-nél-la tor-tí-pi-la
Selaginellaceae (Spikemoss Family)

DESCRIPTION: Rock-dwelling, mosslike, primitive vascular plant, forming large, compact, gray-green mounds 3–6″ tall; leaves linear, in spirals, apical bristle contorted (twisted), sometimes absent; fertile leaves forming a 4-angled cone only about 0.2″ long.
RANGE-HABITAT: Endemic to TN, NC, SC, and GA; common in the mountains, occasional in the upper piedmont and absent from the lower piedmont; found on granitic domes, cliffs, and ledges.

15. *Spray cliffs*

16. Golden saxifrage

Chrysosplenium americanum Schweinitz
Chry-so-splè-ni-um a-me-ri-cà-num
Saxifragaceae (Saxifrage Family)

DESCRIPTION: Tiny, low, creeping annual or perennial that forms matlike masses; leaves opposite, to 0.6″ long, widely spaced on a stem that forks often; flowers inconspicuous, with sepals only; flowers March–June.

RANGE-HABITAT: Quebec west to Saskatchewan, south to e. VA, w. NC, n. GA, TN, and IN; the only SC population is in the upper piedmont in a shady, boggy seepage; typically found in high elevation seepages, springheads, and along small rocky streams.

COMMENTS: *Chrysosplenium* is Greek and translates as "gold spleen," presumably in reference to its use in herbal medicine.

PROTECTION STATUS: State Endangered

17. Branch-lettuce

Saxifraga micranthidifolia (Haworth) Steudel
Sax-íf-ra-ga mi-cran-thi-di-fò-li-a
Saxifragaceae (Saxifrage Family)

DESCRIPTION: Perennial herb with leaves clustered at the base; basal leaves to 1′ long; flowering stem leafless, to 30″ tall; flowers May–June.

RANGE-HABITAT: PA and WV, south to SC and GA; in SC common in the mountains on exposed seepages, brook margins, and spray cliffs.

COMMENTS: As the common name suggests, the basal leaves are used as a substitute for lettuce in salads.

18. Jewelweed; spotted touch-me-not

Impatiens capensis Meerburgh
Im-pà-ti-ens ca-pén-sis
Balsaminaceae (Touch-me-not Family)

DESCRIPTION: Fleshy annual to 6' tall with hollow stems; leaves alternate; one sepal forms a prominent sac at the base of flower that ends in a curled spur; flowers May–frost.
RANGE-HABITAT: Newfoundland west to Saskatchewan and AK, south to FL panhandle, AL, and TX; common throughout SC; tidal freshwater marshes, streamsides, moist forests, and alluvial swamps.
COMMENTS: The first common name refers to the water-repelling nature of the leaves and stems. On horizontal surfaces, water often rolls into beads, giving the appearance of jewels reflected in the light. The second common name refers to the fruits, which, when mature, elastically coil into five sections and, when touched, explode, expelling the seeds.

The stem juice has fungicidal properties and has been used to treat athlete's foot. The stem juice is also a well-known treatment for poison ivy and stinging nettle; Duke (1997) recommends it as a remedy for hives.

19. Northern sundrops

Oenothera tetragona Roth
Oe-no-thè-ra te-tra-gò-na
Onagraceae (Evening-primrose Family)

DESCRIPTION: Perennial herb to 3' tall; stem branched above; leaves alternate, more than 0.25" wide; petals yellow, to 1" long; capsule angled, widest at the middle, smooth or with mostly glandular hairs; flowers May–August.
RANGE-HABITAT: Widespread in eastern North America; scattered throughout SC, but mostly in the mountains; primarily dry meadows and roadsides, but also in and around spray cliffs and seepages.
COMMENTS: The large yellow flowers and spreading glandular hairs on the ovary and capsule are distinctive.
SYNONYM: *Oenothera fruticosa* L. subsp. *glauca* (Michaux) Straley—W

20. Appalachian bluet; thyme-leaved bluet

Houstonia serpyllifolia Michaux
Hous-tòn-i-a ser-pyl-li-fò-li-a
Rubiaceae (Madder Family)

DESCRIPTION: Perennial herb with creeping, much branched stems; leaves opposite, tiny; flowers deep blue with a yellow or white center (eye), terminal and single or paired, on long stalks; flowers May–June.
RANGE-HABITAT: PA south to SC and GA; common in the mountains on spray cliffs, rocky streamsides, seepages, moist woods, and moist road banks.
COMMENTS: The genus honors Dr. William Houston, 1695–1733, an English botanist.

21. Umbrella leaf; pixie-parasol

Diphylleia cymosa Michaux
Di-phyl-leì-a cy-mò-sa
Berberidaceae (Barberry Family)

DESCRIPTION: Perennial herb from a thick rhizome; leaves to 15″ wide; one leaf on nonflowering plants and two alternate leaves on flowering plants; leaves with the stout leaf stalk attached at the middle, below the cleft that divides the leaf into 2 parts, each part with many toothed lobes; flowers white, in a cluster terminating a long stalk; flowers May–June.

RANGE-HABITAT: Endemic to the southern Appalachian Mountains of VA, TN, NC, SC, and GA; rare at moderately high elevations in the mountains; one of the two SC populations is in a rich cove forest, the other is in a seepage at the base of a spray cliff; it is apparently more common in seepages and along small brooks in NC and TN.

PROTECTION STATUS: State Threatened

22. American water-pennywort

Hydrocotyle americana L.
Hy-dro-có-ty-le a-me-ri-cà-na
Apiaceae (Parsley Family)

DESCRIPTION: Delicate perennial herb; stems semi-erect; leaves round, peltate; flowers white, on stalks less than 0.1″ long, much shorter than the leaf stalks; flowers June–September.

RANGE-HABITAT: Widespread in eastern North America; in SC restricted to the mountains on spray cliffs and gravelly seepages in partial sun; rare.

COMMENTS: This is the only species of water-pennywort in the mountains and the only mountain species with a leaf stalk attached at a sinus extending to the middle of the leaf.

PROTECTION STATUS: State Endangered

23. Common rockcap fern; rock polypody

Polypodium virginianum L.
Po-ly-pò-di-um vir-gi-ni-à-num
Polypodiaceae (Polypody Family)

DESCRIPTION: Evergreen, rock-dwelling fern from a creeping rhizome; leaf blades widest near the middle; sporangia in round clusters, in two rows adjacent to the midveins of the leaf segments.

RANGE-HABITAT: Widespread in eastern North America; also in a few western states; in SC uncommon on calcium-rich rocks of spray cliffs or cove forests in the mountains, very rare on calcium-rich rocks in the piedmont and coastal plain.

COMMENTS: Appears at a glance to be a large version of the resurrection fern (*Polypodium polypodioides,* plate 594); rock polypody is without the circular scales that densely cover the lower leaf surface of resurrection fern.

24. Maidenhair spleenwort

Asplenium trichomanes L. subsp.
   trichomanes
   As-plè-ni-um tri-chó-ma-nes
   subsp. tri-chó-ma-nes
Aspleniaceae (Spleenwort Family)

DESCRIPTION: Perennial, evergreen, rock-dwelling fern from a short rhizome; leaf blades 1-pinnate, oblong, to 10″ long but generally much shorter, in spreading clusters; leaflets opposite, with rounded apex and teeth; sporangia in distinct, linear clusters.

RANGE-HABITAT: Widespread in eastern North America and in some western states; in SC uncommon in the mountains, rare in the piedmont; moist outcrops of rocks high in calcium or magnesium.

SIMILAR SPECIES: *A. trichomanes* is similar to *A. platyneuron* (L.) Oakes (ebony spleenwort), which has alternate leaflets.

25. *Cataract bogs*

26. Tag alder; hazel alder

Alnus serrulata (Aiton) Willdenow
   Ál-nus ser-ru-là-ta
Betulaceae (Birch Family)

DESCRIPTION: Deciduous shrub to 30′ tall; usually growing in clumps; leaves alternate; flowers in elongate conelike spikes; male spikes conspicuous in the spring before leaves appear; female "cones" persist through the winter after shedding seeds; flowers February–March.

RANGE-HABITAT: Nova Scotia west to s. Quebec, MO, and OK, south to n. FL and TX; common throughout SC; rocky stream-sides, riverbanks, bogs, freshwater marshes, and in wet places in forests.

COMMENTS: Historically, tag alder had many folk uses. Native Americans used bark tea for diarrhea, childbirth pain, coughs, toothaches, and as a "blood purifier"; also a wash for hives, piles, and poison ivy rash.

27. Red maple

Acer rubrum L.
À-cer rù-brum
Aceraceae (Maple Family)

DESCRIPTION: Medium to large, deciduous tree; leaves opposite, usually 3–5-lobed; flowers perfect, or often male and female in separate clusters on the same or different trees; fruit a samara, matures March–May.

RANGE-HABITAT: Common throughout eastern North America; common throughout SC; alluvial and nonalluvial swamp forests, beech and oak-hickory forests, pine-mixed hardwood forests, thickets, and along fence rows.

COMMENTS: The flowers bloom sometimes as early as January, long before the leaves appear. Flowers are followed by the conspicuous winged fruits (samaras), bright red to yellow, creating a prominent display of color against the spring sky. Red maple is one of the pioneer trees in abandoned rice fields and can establish itself in cleared, upland sites.

Red maple is often planted as a shade tree; the wood is used for a variety of products and maple syrup can be made from the sap, although the sap contains less sugar than the sugar maple.

28. Indian paint brush

Castilleja coccinea (L.) Sprengel
Cas-til-lè-ja coc-cí-ne-a
Scrophulariaceae (Figwort Family)

DESCRIPTION: Erect, hairy, hemiparasitic annual or biennial herb; to 28″ tall, with 1 unbranched stem from a basal cluster of leaves; flowers variable, yellow to greenish yellow, and the leaflike bracts, subtending the flowers, vary from scarlet to yellow; flowers April–May.

RANGE-HABITAT: Widespread in eastern North America; woodlands, rock outcrops, meadows, wet pastures, grassy openings, usually over mafic rocks; in SC primarily a mountain and piedmont species; rare; several disjunct populations have been found in the coastal plain in Berkeley and Williamsburg Counties, where it is very rare in longleaf pine savannas.

COMMENTS: The beauty of this plant comes not from the small flowers but from the brightly tipped bracts. The common name comes from an Indian legend that tells of a brave's discarded brushes being used to paint a brilliant sunset which then grew into flowers. Native Americans used the roots, mixed with iron minerals, to dye deerskins black.

PROTECTION STATUS: State Threatened

29. Mountain sweet pitcher-plant

Sarracenia jonesii Wherry
Sar-ra-cèn-i-a jònes-i-i
Sarraceniaceae (Pitcher-plant Family)

DESCRIPTION: Herbaceous perennial, forming colonies from underground stems; leaves 15–30″ tall, modified into hollow tubes (pitchers) that are effective as passive insect traps; petals maroon; flowers May.

RANGE-HABITAT: NC and SC; in SC very rare and restricted to the upper piedmont and mountains; cataract bogs and piedmont seepage forests.

COMMENTS: The opening into the hollow leaves is exposed and considerably larger than the similar sweet pitcher-plant (*S. rubra*, plate 484) of the coastal plain, making it more effective at trapping insects. It grows at the cataract bog at the Eva Russell Chandler Heritage Preserve. The genus honors Dr. Michel Sarrasin de l'Étang, 1659–1734, a physician at the court of Quebec, who sent South Carolina's northern species to Europe. The specific epithet honors Dr. F. M. Jones who studied the insect associates of pitcher plants.

PROTECTION STATUS: Federal Endangered

30. Horned bladderwort

Utricularia cornuta Michaux
U-tri-cu-là-ri-a cor-nù-ta
Lentibulariaceae (Bladderwort Family)

DESCRIPTION: Terrestrial herb; subterranean leaves dissected, with small insect-trapping bladders; surface leaves, when present, linear and flat; flowering stalk to 12″ tall, leafless, but with small scales and bracts; flowers 2–6, yellow, at least 0.6″ long, with a spur 0.3–0.5″ long; flowers May–September.

RANGE-HABITAT: Widespread in eastern North America; also Cuba and the Bahamas; in SC rare in cataract bogs and seepages on granitic domes in the mountains, granitic flatrocks in the piedmont, and margins of limesink ponds in the coastal plain.

COMMENTS: Distinguished from the similar *U. juncea* Vahl (southern bladderwort) by the large flower and smaller number of flowers, which are in a crowded terminal raceme. Utricularias get their name from their distinctive, insect-trapping bladders (utriculus = small bladder).

31. White fringeless orchid; monkey face orchid

Platanthera integrilabia (Correll) Luer
Pla-tán-the-ra in-teg-ri-là-bi-a
Orchidaceae (Orchid Family)

DESCRIPTION: Perennial herb with simple
stems and alternate leaves; flowers showy
white, with a long spur and a fringeless,
unlobed lip; flowers late July–September.

RANGE-HABITAT: Endemic to KY, TN, VA, NC,
nw. SC, n. GA, AL, and MS; very rare and
restricted in SC to cataract bogs in the mountains.

COMMENTS: The SC sites are very fragile and
dangerous to visit.

SYNONYM: *Habenaria blephariglottis* var. *integrilabia* Correll—RAB.

PROTECTION STATUS: Federal Species of Concern

32. White turtlehead

Chelone glabra L
Che-lò-ne glà-bra
Scrophulariaceae (Figwort Family)

DESCRIPTION: Perennial herb with an erect or
spreading stem to 3′ long (usually much less);
leaves widest near the middle; leaf stalks less
than 0.6″ long; flowers white or tinged with
pink or purple toward the tip, sterile stamen
green; flowers August–October.

RANGE-HABITAT: Widespread in eastern North
America; widely scattered localities throughout SC, but chiefly the mountains; cataract
bogs, streamsides, swamps, and other low
woodlands.

COMMENTS: Bitter-tasting compounds in the leaves have been used for a variety
of ailments, both internal (laxative, worms, fever) and external (piles, ulcers,
herpes). Seven varieties have been described for this species.

33. Stiff cowbane

Oxypolis rigidior (L.) Rafinesque
Ox-ý-po-lis ri-gí-di-or
Apiaceae (Parsley Family)

DESCRIPTION: Perennial herb to 4.5′ tall, from a cluster of tuberous roots; stems smooth, stout, erect or slender, and arching;
leaves with about 7–11, flattened, linear, pinnately arranged
leaflets, with few scattered teeth; flowers tiny, white, in a flat-
topped cluster of 20 or more umbels; flowers August–October.

RANGE-HABITAT: NY and MN, south to FL and TX; occasional in
the mountains in cataract bogs and streamside wetlands; rare in
the piedmont in swamp forests and wet pastures; occasional in
the coastal plain in swamp forest, wet savannas, and seepages.

34. Limeseep grass-of-Parnassus

Parnassia grandifolia Augustin de Candolle
    Par-nás-si-a gran-di-fò-li-a
Parnassiaceae (Grass-of-Parnassus Family)

DESCRIPTION: Perennial herb from a rhizome; leaves on long stalks, in dense basal clusters, heart-shaped at the base and only slightly longer than broad; flowers white, solitary, on long stalks that bear a single clasping leaf below the middle; petals not stalked, main veins of each petal 5–9; ovary greenish; flowers late September–October.

RANGE-HABITAT: VA, WV, and MO, south to FL, AR and TX; in SC rare in seepages associated with cataract bogs and other seepages in the mountains.

COMMENTS: Cataract bogs are only in Greenville County in SC, and always harbor this grass-of-Parnassus rather than the more acid-loving, kidney-leaved grass-of-Parnassus (*P. asarifolia* Ventenat).

PROTECTION STATUS: State Threatened

35. Common sneezeweed

Helenium autumnale L.
    He-lén-i-um au-tum-nà-le
Asteraceae (Aster or Sunflower Family)

DESCRIPTION: Perennial clump-forming herb to 5′ tall; leaves alternate, basal, and on the stem, not much reduced upward, narrowed to a base that extends onto the stem as a wing; flower heads large, 6–many, comprised of both ray and disk flowers; both ray and disk flowers yellow; ray flowers 3-lobed at the apex; flowers September–October.

RANGE-HABITAT: Widespread in eastern North America; in SC common in the mountains and piedmont, less common in the coastal plain; variety of habitats, all fitting under the title of "moist low ground," including disturbed and undisturbed plant communities.

COMMENTS: Like bitterweed (*H. amarum,* plate 661), this species is distasteful to cattle and horses and therefore increases in abundance in wet pastures used for grazing. It is poisonous to insects, fish, and worms. It may cause dermatitis in humans. In National Cancer Institute studies, Helenalin in this and other species has shown significant antitumor activity. Linnaeus is said to have named the genus *Helenium* after Helena (Helen of Troy).

Montane bogs

36. American climbing fern

Lygodium palmatum Swartz
Ly-gò-di-um pal-mà-tum
Lygodiaceae (Climbing Fern Family)

DESCRIPTION: Perennial from a long creeping rhizome; frond (leaf) vinelike, coiling, and climbing; pinnae (leaflets) deeply and palmately 4–8-lobed.

RANGE-HABITAT: Widespread in eastern North America; rare throughout SC; most abundant in the mountains; in strongly acid soil of montane bogs, moist forests, and roadsides.

COMMENTS: The climbing habit is distinctive to *Lygodium* in SC. The only species easily confused with it is the exotic Japanese climbing fern, *L. japonicum* (Thunberg) Swartz, which has leaflets pinnately divided into saw-toothed segments.

37. Swamp pink

Helonias bullata L.
He-lò-ni-as bul-là-ta
Liliaceae (Lily Family)

DESCRIPTION: Perennial evergreen herb, to 3′ tall, sometimes forming dense clumps; leaves flat and glossy, in a dense basal rosette, pointed at the tips and widest toward the tips, to 12″ long; flowers in a dense cluster terminating a leafless stalk, pink with blue stamens; flowers April–early May.

RANGE-HABITAT: Swamp pink ranges from s. NY and NJ to e. VA on the coastal plain and from w. VA through w. NC to nw. SC and ne. GA in the Blue Ridge Mountains; sphagnum moss-dominated openings in montane bogs in SC and known only from a single population in the mountains in Mathews Creek Bog.

COMMENTS: The population in Mathews Creek Bog has declined significantly in the last 15 years, due in part to an untimely freeze and natural invasion of its boggy habitat by trees and shrubs.

PROTECTION STATUS: Federal Threatened

THE MOUNTAINS

38. Green fringed orchid

Platanthera lacera (Michaux) D. Don
  Pla-tán-the-ra lá-ce-ra
Orchidaceae (Orchid Family)

DESCRIPTION: Perennial herb 8–20″ tall, with tuberlike roots; leaves stiffly erect, to 5″ long; flowers whitish green or yellowish green, lip petal deeply fringed; flowers June–August.
RANGE-HABITAT: Widespread in northeastern North America and south to SC, GA, AL, AR, and OK; in SC scattered throughout (absent in the maritime strand) and rare; bogs, openings in wet swamps, longleaf pine savannas in the coastal plain, and in wet meadows.
COMMENTS: No one habitat predictably harbors this species.
SYNONYM: *Habenaria lacera* (Michaux) Loddiges—RAB

39. Hairy lobelia

Lobelia puberula Michaux
  Lo-bèl-i-a pu-bé-ru-la
Campanulaceae (Bellwort Family)

DESCRIPTION: Perennial herb to 4′ tall, from basal offshoots; stem usually unbranched, softly fine hairy throughout, including the portion bearing flowers; flowers blue or violet, more than 0.7″ long; flowers late July–October.
RANGE-HABITAT: NJ and OH, south to FL and TX; common throughout SC; most abundant in montane bogs and piedmont seepage forests; also common in wet meadows and woodland margins, habitats that are sometimes rather dry.
COMMENTS: The hairy stem separates this species from other lobelias that share its habitat. The genus honors Matthias de l'O-bel, 1538–1616, a Flemish herbalist.

40. Hardhack; steeplebush

Spiraea tomentosa L.
  Spi-raè-a to-men-tò-sa
Rosaceae (Rose Family)

DESCRIPTION: Shrub to 6′ tall, sparsely branched; leaves alternate, irregularly toothed, lower surface with a dense covering of white to rusty hairs; flowers pink, reddish or sometimes white; flowers July–September.
RANGE-HABITAT: From Nova Scotia west to MN, south to TN, SC, and AR; throughout SC; montane bogs, wet meadows, piedmont seepage forests, and swamp margins; common in the mountains and upper piedmont; occasional in the eastern coastal plain.
COMMENTS: The name steeplebush comes from the terminal, dense-flowered panicles that are steeplelike in outline.

41. Hollow-stem Joe-pye-weed

Eupatorium fistulosum Barratt
  Eu-pa-tò-ri-um fis-tu-lò-sum
Asteraceae (Aster or Sunflower Family)

DESCRIPTION: Perennial herb; stem to 10′ tall, hollow, whitish, and purple spotted throughout; leaves in whorls of 3–7; flowers pink-purple, 4–7 per head; flowers July–October.

RANGE-HABITAT: Widespread in eastern and central US; common throughout SC; marshes, wet ditches, moist forests, streamside forests, and montane bogs.

SIMILAR SPECIES: *Eupatorium maculatum* L., Joe-pye-weed, is very similar to *E. fistulosum,* but it has solid stems; it is rare in the mountains of SC.

COMMENTS: Both species attract butterflies.

42. *Rocky streamsides*

43. Tall scouring rush

Equisetum hyemale subsp. *affine* (Englemann) Calder &
  R. L. Taylor
  Eq-ui-sè-tum hye-mà-le subsp. af-fì-ne
Equisetaceae (Horsetail Family)

DESCRIPTION: Evergreen, perennial, nonflowering vascular plant from a creeping underground stem; aerial stems stiffly erect, unbranched, with ribbed internodes; leaves scalelike, in whorls that are fused at the base into a sheath; sporangia clustered into a terminal conelike structure.

RANGE-HABITAT: Scattered throughout North America and in Mexico and Guatemala; in SC chiefly in the mountains and piedmont; occasional; scattered and rare in the coastal plain; rocky streamsides, railroad banks, and roadsides.

COMMENTS: Silicon dioxide (sand) in the cell walls gives the stems a rough texture. The stems were once used to scour pots and to give wood a fine finish. It is poisonous to livestock and alters vitamin (thiamine) metabolism. The Commission E in Germany approved and Duke (1997) recommends its use as an herbal remedy for gallstones and kidney stones.

44. Yellowroot

Xanthorhiza simplicissima Marshall
Xan-tho-rhì-za sim-pli-cís-si-ma
Ranunculaceae (Buttercup Family)

DESCRIPTION: Deciduous shrub to 3' tall; stem unbranched; leaves clustered at the tip, with 3–5 leaflets, margins toothed and cleft; flowers brownish purple, on long stalks and in terminal drooping clusters; flowers March–May.

RANGE-HABITAT: NY and PA south to FL and AL; in SC common in the mountains and piedmont, rare in the sandhills and inner coastal plain; acid soils of shady rocky streamsides.

COMMENTS: The inner bark and wood of both stems and roots contains a bright yellow, bitter-tasting alkaloid that has been used for a dye and medicine. It contains berberine, which is known to have many useful properties, including the stimulation of bile and bilirubin. It may be useful in lowering tyramine for cirrhosis of the liver but is potentially toxic in large amounts. Duke (1997) recommends yellowroot as a herbal remedy for athlete's foot and ulcers.

45. Sweet-shrub

Calycanthus floridus var. *laevigatus*
(Willdenow) Torrey & Gray
Ca-ly-cán-thus fló-ri-dus
var. lae-vi-gà-tus
Calycanthaceae (Sweet-shrub Family)

DESCRIPTION: Deciduous shrub 3–6' tall; older branches purplish, enlarged and flattened at the nodes, with distinct dichotomous arrangement; leaves opposite, with smooth margins; flowers solitary and terminating axillary branches, purplish brown or greenish purple; plant essentially hairless (laevigate); all parts aromatic (like allspice?); flowers March–June.

RANGE-HABITAT: PA and OH, south to FL and MS; in SC chiefly in the mountains and upper piedmont; mixed deciduous forests and rocky streamsides.

TAXONOMY: A second variety of sweet-shrub in SC is *C. floridus* L. var. *floridus*. It is separated from var. *laevigatus* by its hairy leaves, twigs, and leaf stalks. It is chiefly in the piedmont and coastal plain.

COMMENTS: Sweet-shrub is planted as an ornamental because of the spicy fragrance of its flowers.

SYNONYM: *Calycanthus floridus* var. *glaucus* (Willdenow) Torrey & Gray—W

46. Sweet azalea; smooth azalea

Rhododendron arborescens (Pursh) Torrey
Rho-do-dén-dron ar-bo-rés-cens
Ericaceae (Heath Family)

DESCRIPTION: Nonclonal deciduous shrub or small tree to 20′ tall; young stems and leaves without hairs and with a whitish cast (lower leaf surface); flowers white or pink; flowers late May–early July.

RANGE-HABITAT: From PA and KY, south to GA and AL, mostly in the Appalachian Mountains; in SC very rare in the coastal plain and the piedmont; common in the mountains where it occurs on rocky streamsides and in bogs along streams.

COMMENTS: This is the only SC azalea with white-pink flowers and hairless stems and leaves. Both common names highlight its distinctive features.

47. Brookfoam; brook saxifrage

Boykinia aconitifolia Nuttall
Boy-kín-i-a a-co-ni-ti-fò-li-a
Saxifragaceae (Saxifrage Family)

DESCRIPTION: Perennial herb to 20″ tall, but usually much shorter; basal (few) and stem leaves deeply 5–7-lobed and toothed, wider than long, to 4″ wide; flowers June–mid-July.

RANGE-HABITAT: VA and WV, south to GA and AL; mountains of SC; occasional, except common along the Chattooga and Chauga Rivers in Oconee County; in SC nearly restricted to rocky streamsides.

COMMENTS: Leaves superficially resemble thimbleweed (*Anemone virginiana*, plate 213) or Carolina tassel-rue (*Trautvetteria caroliniensis*, plate 49) but are much smaller. The epithet *aconitifolia* translates literally as "with leaves of *Aconitum*," but brookfoam's leaves are much less similar to common blue monkshood (*Aconitum uncinatum* L., plate 83) than they are to thimbleweed or tassel-rue. The glandular hairs on the stems of the flower cluster separate this species from any of the above. The genus honors Samuel Boykin, 1786–1848, an early active GA botanist.

48. Bush-honeysuckle

Diervilla sessilifolia Buckley
Di-er-víll-a ses-si-li-fò-li-a
Caprifoliaceae (Honeysuckle Family)

DESCRIPTION: Deciduous shrub to 6′ tall; leaf stalks short; plants without hairs except for twig angles; flowers in clusters at branch tips or in leaf axils; flowers June–August.

RANGE-HABITAT: TN and NC, south to GA and AL; mountains of SC; occasional; around exposed outcrops of rocks and ridges at moderate to high elevations; rocky streamsides and shore communities along the Chattooga River in Oconee County.

COMMENTS: Flowers resemble those of honeysuckle but are only 0.8″ long, light yellow with a darker center and turn red with age. This is the only species of bush-honeysuckle in SC. The genus honors Dr. N. Dièrville, a French surgeon.

49. Carolina tassel-rue

Trautvetteria caroliniensis (Walter) Vail
Traut-vet-tèr-i-a ca-ro-li-ni-én-sis
Ranunculaceae (Buttercup Family)

DESCRIPTION: Perennial herb to 4′ tall; with basal (few) and stem leaves, to 12″ wide, reduced upward on the stem, palmately 3–11-lobed; flowers without petals, the numerous whitish filaments are the showy part of the flowers; flowers June–early July.

RANGE-HABITAT: PA and KY, south to GA; in SC very rare in the coastal plain and lower piedmont, occasional in the mountains; streamsides, cataract bogs, and seepages along mountain streams.

COMMENTS: Tassel-rue is distinctive when in fruit; sterile plants when not full sized resemble thimbleweed (*Anemone virginiana*) or brookfoam (*Boykinia aconitifolia,* plate 47). It is found on calcium-rich sites in the midwest and a few coastal plains locations. The genus honors Ernst Rudolph von Trautvetter, 1809–1889, a distinguished Russian botanist.

50. Coneflower; greenhead coneflower

Rudbeckia laciniata L.
Rud-béck-i-a la-ci-ni-à-ta
Asteraceae (Aster or Sunflower Family)

DESCRIPTION: Perennial herb; stem smooth, 3–8′ tall, well-branched; leaves alternate, long-stalked, reduced in size and in number of divisions from base upward; lower leaves pinnately dissected, with segments coarsely toothed; flowers July–October.

RANGE-HABITAT: Widespread in eastern North America; common throughout SC in moist soils of levee forests, bottomland hardwoods, rocky streamsides, and moist meadows.

COMMENTS: *Rudbeckia* species in general are reported to contain compounds that stimulate the immune system and may be useful in treating HIV. Several varieties of this variable taxon have been named. The genus name honors professors Rudbeck (Olaf, 1630–1702, and Olaf, 1660–1740, his son) predecessors of Linnaeus at Uppsala.

Cove forests

51. Sweet birch; cherry birch

Betula lenta L.
Bé-tu-la lén-ta
Betulaceae (Birch Family)

DESCRIPTION: Deciduous tree to 90' tall and 34" in diameter; inner bark with odor and taste of wintergreen; outer bark resembles black cherry (*Prunus serotina*); leaves alternate, to 4" long and 2.4" wide, sharply pointed and toothed; fruit a samara, winged apically, in headlike clusters (catkins); flowers March–April; fruits June–July.

RANGE-HABITAT: ME and OH, south to GA and AL; in SC common in the mountains; cove forests and Canada hemlock forests, at low to moderate elevations.

COMMENTS: The bark of young stems is distinctive (reddish brown with horizontally elongate lenticels), as is the wintergreen taste and odor. It was once the major source of oil of wintergreen used in medicines and confections. The lumber is valuable for cabinetwork and veneers. Wildlife use the twigs, leaves, buds, flowers, and fruits. In early spring, the stems can be tapped for sugar water. Duke (1997) recommends species of *Betula* as a useful remedy for warts.

52. Sharp-lobed liverleaf

Hepatica acutiloba Augustin de Candolle
He-pá-ti-ca a-cu-tí-lo-ba
Ranunculaceae (Buttercup Family)

DESCRIPTION: Herbaceous evergreen perennial from a short underground stem; leaves basal, deeply cleft into 3 acute lobes; flowers solitary on elongate, hairy stalks; petals absent; sepals petal-like and whitish; flowers March–April.

RANGE-HABITAT: Widespread in eastern North America; restricted to the mountains of SC; occasional; mesic forests, often associated with calcium-rich soils.

COMMENTS: Sometimes it is reported to hybridize with the more common round-lobed liverleaf. In SC, the blooming periods of these closely related species do not overlap. Old leaves are present at early flowering; new leaves develop well after flowering.

53. Windflower; rue-anemone

Thalictrum thalictroides (L.) Boivin
Tha-líc-trum tha-lic-troì-des
Ranunculaceae (Buttercup Family)

DESCRIPTION: Perennial herb with tuberous roots; stem to 10″ tall; leaves compound, with leaflets in 3s and 3-lobed at the apex; flowers in a single, terminal umbel subtended by opposite leaves; sepals 5, white; petals not present; flowers March–May.

RANGE-HABITAT: Widespread in eastern North America; in SC common in cove forests in the mountains and beech forests in the piedmont; rare in beech forests in the coastal plain.

COMMENTS: Some authors report that the tuberous roots are edible, but according to recent reports, they are potentially toxic.

SYNONYM: *Anemonella thalictroides* (L.) Spach—W

54. Sweet white trillium; confusing trillium

Trillium simile Gleason
Tríl-li-um sí-mi-le
Liliaceae (Lily Family)

DESCRIPTION: Perennial herb from a thick rhizome; stem erect, usually 10–14″ tall in SC; leaves uniformly green, wider than long; flower stalk long and held nearly erect; petals white, broadly ovate, overlapping at the base and producing a funnel-shaped flower; sepals boatlike at the tip; anther sacs yellow; ovary dark purple, strongly angled; flowers late March–early July.

RANGE-HABITAT: NC, SC, TN, and GA; in SC restricted to the mountains, rich cove forests, or other forests with calcium-rich soils.

COMMENTS: The epithet *simile,* meaning similar, is appropriate since it resembles forms of the *T. erectum* group. Its wide petals and boatlike sepals resemble *T. vaseyi* (plate 56), but the flowers are held erect on long stalks. It tends to form large colonies, which along with its large flowers, make for spectacular displays.

55. Large-flowered trillium

Trillium grandiflorum (Michaux) Salisbury
Tríl-li-um gran-di-flò-rum
Liliaceae (Lily Family)

DESCRIPTION: Herbaceous perennial from a short, thick rhizome; stem erect, to 12″ tall; leaves uniform green, sometimes with a reddish tinge in pink-flowered forms, without a leaf stalk; flower borne slightly below the vertical, on a long stalk (to 3″); petals white, rarely light or dark pink, overlapping at the base to form a strongly funnel-shaped flower, flared at the tip, usually obovate; anthers white or greenish white between the anther sacs; flowers April–May.

RANGE-HABITAT: WI and New England, south to AL, GA, and SC; rare in the piedmont and mountains of SC; only in rich cove forests and basic-mesic forests, sites with calcium-rich soil.

COMMENTS: Four-leaved forms occasionally occur; forms with double, 2, or 4 petals are not uncommon. Infection with mycoplasmas may result in unusual forms without petals or with green or green-and-white petals, or "knots" for sepals.

PROTECTION STATUS: State Endangered

56. Vasey's trillium; sweet Beth

Trillium vaseyi Harbison
Tríl-li-um và-sey-i
Liliaceae (Lily Family)

DESCRIPTION: Perennial herb from a short, thick rhizome; stem erect, to 20″ tall; leaves uniformly green, usually wider than long; flowers on a long stalk, horizontal or declined below the leaves; petals maroon or white, margins not wavy, bent backward between the sepals; stamens extending well beyond the pistil; filaments partly maroon; anthers yellow to maroon; ovary small and dark purple; flowers April–May.

RANGE-HABITAT: TN, NC, SC, GA, and AL; restricted to the mountains in SC; uncommon; restricted to rich cove forests.

COMMENTS: The specific epithet honors George R. Vasey, curator of botany at the Smithsonian Institution in 1872 and an expert on the grass family.

57. Blue cohosh

Caulophyllum thalictroides (L.) Michaux
Cau-lo-phýl-lum tha-lic-troì-des
Berberidaceae (Barberry Family)

DESCRIPTION: Smooth, erect perennial herb to 3′ tall, from a knotty rootstalk; all parts with a whitish cast; the stem bears a single leaf with 3 long stalks, each bearing many leaflets that are 2–5-lobed above the middle; leaf appearing to be 3 leaves because of the obscure common stalk; 1–3 clusters of yellowish green or greenish purple flowers terminate the stem; flowers to 0.4″ in diameter; flowers April–May; fruits July–August.

RANGE-HABITAT: Widespread in eastern North America; rich cove forests and basic-mesic forests, on soils high in calcium; in SC occasional in the mountains, rare in the piedmont.

COMMENTS: The developing seeds rupture the ovary soon after fertilization, so the dark blue seeds, which resemble drupes, ripen fully exposed. Native Americans used a root extract to induce labor and reduce menstrual cramps. Duke (1997) recommends it as an herbal remedy for inducing labor.

PROTECTION STATUS: State Species of Concern

58. Canada violet

Viola canadensis L.
Vĭ-o-la ca-na-dén-sis
Violaceae (Violet Family)

DESCRIPTION: Perennial herb from a rhizome; erect stem bears both leaves and flowers; leaves to 4″ long, gradually narrowed to a sharp apex, base heart-shaped; stipules long-triangular, with a sharp tip and smooth margins; petals white with a yellow center; spur shorter than 0.4″ long; flowers April–July.
RANGE-HABITAT: Widespread in eastern and central North America; in SC common in cove forests in the mountains; sometimes found in other rich woods.
COMMENTS: In SC this is one of the most characteristic cove forest species, seldom not present and seldom occurring elsewhere.

59. Doll's-eyes; white cohosh

Actaea pachypoda Elliott
Ac-taè-a pa-chý-po-da
Ranunculaceae (Buttercup Family)

DESCRIPTION: Erect perennial herb to 24″ tall; leaves large, 2–3-times ternately compound; petals white, 3–7, looking like modified stamens; fruit a berry, white and capped by a broad, red stigma; flowers April–mid-May; fruits August–October.
RANGE-HABITAT: Widespread in eastern North America; in SC occasional in the mountains in rich cove forests; rare in the piedmont in rich woods that overlay calcium-rich soils.
COMMENTS: Doll's-eyes refers to the mature fruit. The leaves are distinctive and readily distinguishable by swellings at the tips of the leaflets.

60. Dwarf crested iris

Iris cristata Aiton
Ì-ris cris-tà-ta
Iridaceae (Iris Famly)

DESCRIPTION: Perennial herb usually less than 15″ tall in flower, forming colonies from elongate rhizomes that are alternately tapered and widened; leaves broadly linear, 4–16″ long and 1″ wide; flowers with showy sepals, bluish to violet, with 2 crested ridges in the middle of a white or yellow central band; flowers April–May.
RANGE-HABITAT: MD and OK, south to GA; in SC common in the mountains, less common in the piedmont; cove forests and other rich forests.
COMMENTS: Readily distinguished from the similar dwarf iris (*I. verna* var. *verna*, plate 226) by habitat, the crested sepals, and wider leaves.

61. False solomon's-seal

Smilacina racemosa (L.) Desfontaines
Smi-la-cì-na ra-ce-mò-sa
Liliaceae (Lily Family)

DESCRIPTION: Perennial herb from a long rhizome; stem arching, unbranched, to 2′ long; leaves alternate, 2-ranked, to 6″ long and 2″ wide, somewhat leathery, with raised veins above and with fine hairs below; flowers in a terminal panicle; sepals and petals white to green; flowers mid-April–June.

RANGE-HABITAT: Widespread North American species absent only from the far west; in SC common in the mountains, piedmont, and inner coastal plain; rare in the outer coastal plain; moist deciduous forests.

COMMENTS: Vegetatively similar to true Solomon's-seal (*Polygonatum biflorum*, plate 238) from which it is easily separated by its whitish, lower leaf surface. Native Americans used the root smoke as a treatment for insanity and to quiet a sobbing child.

SYNONYM: *Maianthemum racemosum* L. (Uvulariaceae)—W

62. Fernleaf phacelia

Phacelia bipinnatifida Michaux
Pha-cè-li-a bi-pin-na-tí-fi-da
Hydrophyllaceae (Waterleaf Family)

DESCRIPTION: Biennial to 18″ tall from a taproot; stem and leaf stalks with glandular hairs; stem and basal leaves present; stem leaves pinnately dissected and incised, appearing compound; flowers April–May.

RANGE-HABITAT: WV, IL, and MO, south to AL and AR; in the mountains of SC; rare; cove forests and other rich forests.

PROTECTION STATUS: State Endangered

63. Showy orchis

Orchis spectabilis L.
Ór-chis spec-tá-bi-lis
Orchidaceae (Orchid Family)

DESCRIPTION: Perennial herb to 12″ tall from a fleshy, tuber-like rootstalk; leaves basal, to 4″ long and rounded at the apex; bracts subtending each flower leaflike to 3″ long; the lip petal has a prominent spur and forms the uppermost flower segment; flowers April–June (July?).

RANGE-HABITAT: Widespread in eastern North America; mountains of SC; uncommon; usually in cove forests and near streams.

COMMENTS: The spurred lip has nectar at its base; its length and position assure cross-pollination.

SYNONYM: *Galearis spectabilis* (L.) Rafinesque—W

64. Yellow mandarin; yellow fairybells

Disporum lanuginosum (Michaux)
Nicholson
Dís-po-rum la-nu-gi-nò-sum
Liliaceae (Lily Family)

DESCRIPTION: Perennial herb from a knotty
rootstalk; stem to 3′ tall, much branched,
lower portion brown and wiry; leaves alternate, to 4″ long and 2″ wide, soft hairy
below; flowers terminating the branches and
opposite the last leaf, greenish and without
spots, nodding; flowers April–May.

RANGE-HABITAT: Ontario and NY, south to GA
and AL; in SC restricted to the mountains; common; rich forests, especially rich
cove forests.

COMMENTS: The many-branched stem produces an overall look that is dissimilar
to other plants in SC.

SYNONYM: *Prosartes lanuginosa* (Michaux) D. Don (Uvulariaceae)—W

65. Yellow lady's slipper

Cypripedium calceolus var. *pubescens*
(Willdenow) Correll
Cy-pri-pè-di-um cal-cè-o-lus
var. pu-bés-cens
Orchidaceae (Orchid Family)

DESCRIPTION: Showy perennial herb to 28″
tall; leaves 3–5, alternate, to 8″ long and 4″
wide, with glandular hairs and parallel, raised
veins; flowers 1 or 2, terminal, the 2 lateral
petals twisted, green streaked with purple; the
"slipper" petal golden yellow and streaked or
spotted with purple on the inside; flowers
April–June.

RANGE-HABITAT: Widespread in eastern North America; in SC occasional in the
mountains and rare in the central piedmont; rich, moist forests (rich cove forests
in the mountains and basic-mesic forests in the piedmont).

COMMENTS: This showy species is becoming less abundant, primarily due to collection by thoughtless nature "lovers." Just "snatching the top" has long-term
consequences because it significantly reduces energy capture by photosynthesis.
Cypripedium comes from the Latin *Cypris* for Venus and *pedilon* for shoe, so
lady's slipper could be called "Venus' slipper." It was heavily collected in the
nineteenth century for its root, which has sedative properties.

SYNONYM: *C. parviflorum* Salisbury var. *pubescens* (Willdenow) Correll—W

PROTECTION STATUS: State Threatened

66. Fraser magnolia; umbrella tree

Magnolia fraseri Walter
    Mag-nòl-i-a frà-ser-i
Magnoliaceae (Magnolia Family)

DESCRIPTION: Tree to 100′ tall and 36″ in diameter; leaves deciduous, obovate, to 16–29″ long, base with ear-shaped lobes; flowers very large, to 8″ across; petals light yellow or white; flowers April–May.

RANGE-HABITAT: Endemic to the southern Appalachian Mountains; in SC common in the mountains, rare in the upper piedmont; cove forests, Canada hemlock forests, and other moist forests.

COMMENTS: The genus name honors Pierre Magnol, 1638–1715, a professor of botany at Montpellier. Thomas Walter honored his publisher John Fraser, 1750–1811, by naming this species for him. The SC state record was recorded in 1981 at 86′ tall and 24″ in diameter.

67. Sweet white violet

Viola blanda Willdenow
    Vî-o-la blán-da
Violaceae (Violet Family)

DESCRIPTION: Perennial herb without leafy stem; leaves nearly round, with a heart-shaped base, hairy, at least on the upper surface of the basal lobes, which often overlap; flowers white; flower stalk tinged with red; flowers April–early June.

RANGE-HABITAT: Widespread in eastern North America; in SC found only in the mountains in rich cove forests and Canada hemlock forests.

COMMENTS: Easily confused with wild white violet, *V. macloskeyi* var. *pallens* (Banks ex de Candolle) C. L. Hitchcock, which occurs in a different habitat (acidic seepages and banks of small streams) and which always has completely hairless leaf blades.

68. Puttyroot; Adam-and-Eve

Aplectrum hyemale (Muhlenberg ex Willdenow) Torrey
   A-pléc-trum hye-mà-le
Orchidaceae (Orchid Family)

DESCRIPTION: Perennial herb from a beadlike horizontal rootstalk; solitary basal leaf elliptic, with a purplish lower surface, and distinctly pleated with raised whitish veins; leaf produced in the fall and withering, but not disappearing before the appearance of the leafless flowering stem in spring; flowering stem 12–16″ tall; flowers on distinct stalks, greenish, yellowish or whitish and marked with purple or violet; flowers May–June.

RANGE-HABITAT: Widespread in the northeast; in SC occasional in the mountains and piedmont; in a variety of moist forests, including cove forests, moist oak-hickory forests, and upper margins of floodplains.

COMMENTS: Puttyroot is seldom found in colonies of more than a few plants and is probably more common than records indicate. It is easily distinguished from cranefly orchid (*Tipularia discolor,* plate 257), which has a similar habit, by the spurred flower and a leaf without prominent raised whitish veins. It is called puttyroot for the puttylike substance obtained from its roots. A thin connector attaches this year's leaf and its swollen underground stem (Eve) to last year's leaf and corm (Adam).

69. Common black cohosh; early black cohosh

Cimicifuga racemosa (L.) Nuttall
   Ci-mi-cí-fu-ga ra-ce-mò-sa
Ranunculaceae (Buttercup Family)

DESCRIPTION: Perennial herb to 5′ tall, from a thick, knotted rootstalk; leaves large, 2–3-times ternately compound; flowers without petals, in long terminal racemes; showy parts are modified stamens (staminodia); fruits 1 per flower, on a very short stalk; flowers May–July.

RANGE-HABITAT: Fairly widespread in eastern North America; common in the piedmont and mountains of SC; rich woods of cove forests and other mesic forests.

COMMENTS: One of several unrelated species of cove forests wildflowers with 2–3-times ternately compound leaves. The vascular bundles of the rootstalk are arranged in a 3-, 4-, or 5-parted star. Native Americans used cohosh for a variety of "female complaints"; research has confirmed sedative, estrogenic, anti-inflammatory, and hypoglycemic activity. Duke (1997) recommends it as a herbal remedy for menopause.

70. Eastern goat's-beard

Aruncus dioicus (Walter) Fernald
A-rún-cus di-oì-cus
Rosaceae (Rose Family)

DESCRIPTION: Perennial herb to 5′ tall with several stems from the same rootstalk; leaves 6–8 per stem, large, 2–3-times ternately compound; leaflets large, terminal usually unlobed; male and female flowers on separate plants, in a large pyramidal, terminal cluster; petals white in female flowers, greenish white on male flowers; fruit 3–4 follicles; flowers May–June.

RANGE-HABITAT: PA and IN, south to GA and AL; common in the mountains of SC; rich forests and seepage slopes.

SIMILAR SPECIES: Goat's-beard superficially resembles *Astilbe biternata* (Ventenat) Britton (Appalachian false goat's-beard), which has glandular hairs on the lower leaf surface, trilobed terminal leaflets, a 2-locular fruit, and does not have separate male and female plants.

COMMENTS: The epithet *dioicus* refers to the presence of separate male and female plants (dioecious). Goat's-beard refers to the dried cluster of male flowers.

71. Lily-leaved twayblade; large twayblade

Liparis lilifolia (L.) L. C. Richard
Lí-pa-ris li-li-fò-li-a
Orchidaceae (Orchid Family)

DESCRIPTION: Perennial herb from a small bulblike rootstalk; leaves 2, basal, sheathing the base of the flower stalk, keel-like on the lower surface; flowers in a leafless raceme to 12″ tall; petals dark purple, the lip lowermost, widest at the truncate apex; flowers May–July.

RANGE-HABITAT: ME to MN, south to AL and GA; in SC occasional in the mountains, rare in the piedmont; rich forests, cove forests, and mesic streamsides.

PROTECTION STATUS: State Endangered

72. Mapleleaf waterleaf

Hydrophyllum canadense L.
Hy-dro-phýl-lum ca-na-dén-se
Hydrophyllaceae (Waterleaf Family)

DESCRIPTION: Perennial herb from a fibrous rootstalk; basal leaves pinnately lobed, often variegated with 2–3 shades of green; stem leaves alternate and palmately lobed, broader than long, about 6″ wide; flowers in coiled clusters, appearing as racemes in fruit; flowers May–June.

RANGE-HABITAT: VT and Ontario, south to AL, AR, and MO; rare in the mountains of SC; restricted to cove forests and other calcium-rich forests.

COMMENTS: This is the only waterleaf in SC. The size and shape of the stem leaves are distinctive. Waterleaf comes from the variegated (water-stained) appearance of the leaves.

PROTECTION STATUS: State Threatened

73. Dutchman's pipe; pipevine

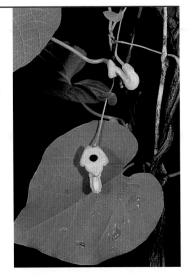

Aristolochia macrophylla Lamarck
A-ris-to-lò-chi-a mac-ro-phýl-la
Aristolochiaceae (Birthwort Family)

DESCRIPTION: Large woody vine that may climb high into trees; leaves large (to 12″ wide) and heart-shaped; flowers borne singly, dull brown-purple and shaped like some tobacco pipes; flowers May–June.

RANGE-HABITAT: Southcentral Appalachian endemic (PA to GA); restricted to cove forests in the mountains.

COMMENTS: This species requires high light and may be found in canopy gaps in communities upslope or downslope from cove forests. Aristolochic acid is known to have antitumor properties.

74. Speckled wood-lily

Clintonia umbellulata (Michaux) Morong
Clin-tòn-i-a um-bel-lu-là-ta
Liliaceae (Lily Family)

DESCRIPTION: Perennial herb; leaves 2–4, clustered on the lower stem, appearing basal, to 12″ long and 3.5″ wide, with obvious hairs the margins; flowers in a terminal umbel, white and tipped or speckled with purple; fruit a black berry; flowers mid-May–mid-June; fruits August.

RANGE-HABITAT: NY and OH, south to GA; in SC restricted to the mountains; occasional; cove forests and mesic or dry ridges and slopes.

COMMENTS: Named after DeWitt Clinton, governor of NY. The naming is said to have annoyed Henry David Thoreau, writer and self-proclaimed naturalist, who was never so honored.

75. Spikenard

Aralia racemosa L.
A-rà-li-a ra-ce-mò-sa
Araliaceae (Ginseng Family)

DESCRIPTION: Perennial herb 3–5′ tall, from a large aromatic rootstalk; the leaves few, the larger with 3 main divisions, each with 3–7 leaflets; flowers small, white, unisexual and bisexual on the same plant; in large terminal clusters of many umbels; flowers May–July.

RANGE-HABITAT: Widespread in eastern and central North America; in SC in rich cove forests and Canada hemlock forests in the mountains; common.

COMMENTS: Well known in the northeast for its large, aromatic roots. A close relative from the Himalayas was the source of the expensive ointment that Mary poured on Jesus' head.

76. Appalachian mountain-mint

Pycnanthemum montanum Michaux
Pyc-nán-the-mum mon-tà-num
Lamiaceae (Mint Family)

DESCRIPTION: Herbaceous perennial with long rhizomes; stems to 3′ tall; leaves opposite, lanceolate, to 5″ long and 1″ wide; flowers in headlike clusters terminating the stem and in the axils of the upper 2 pairs of leaves; bracts subtending flowers have long hairs on the margins; corolla with purple spots on a white-to-yellowish background; calyx lobes with long, spaced hairs; flowers June–August.

RANGE-HABITAT: VA and WV south through w. NC and e. TN, to ne. SC and n. GA; mountains of SC; occasional; cove forests, montane oak-hickory forests, and dry-moist woodland margins, especially at higher elevations.

77. Canada enchanters'-nightshade

Circaea canadensis (L.) Hill
Cir-caè-a ca-na-dén-sis
Onagraceae (Evening-primrose Family)

DESCRIPTION: Erect perennial to 18″ tall (to 3′ in some parts of its range), with rhizomes; flowers with parts in 2s, in racemes from the axils of reduced upper leaves; fruits with curved, bristly hairs; flowers June–August.

RANGE-HABITAT: Nova Scotia and New Brunswick, west to Manitoba and ND, south to e. NC, c. SC, s. GA, LA, OK, and NE; in SC very rare in the piedmont, rare in the mountains; most common in rich cove forests, but also found in rich woods of floodplains and streamsides.

COMMENTS: Although not spectacular, this is a distinctive wildflower that is not easily confused with other species.

SYNONYM: *Circaea lutetiana* subsp. *canadensis* (L.) Ascherson & Magnus—RAB

PROTECTION STATUS: State Species of Concern

78. Tall milkweed; poke milkweed

Asclepias exaltata L.
As-clè-pi-as ex-al-tà-ta
Asclepiadaceae (Milkweed Family)

DESCRIPTION: Perennial herb with milky sap; stems single, to 3′ tall; leaves opposite, to 8″ long and 4″ wide, stalked and pointed at both ends; flowers white, in umbels from the upper leaf axils; fruit a smooth follicle, to 9″ long; flowers June–July.

RANGE-HABITAT: Widespread in eastern North America; in SC restricted to the mountains; uncommon; rich forests and forest margins.

COMMENTS: South Carolina's only milkweed with stalked, broad, smooth leaves, and smooth, erect follicles. The epithet *exaltata* is literally translated as "very tall." The plant is often much taller in the northern portion of its range. Duke (1997) recommends tall milkweed as an effective herbal remedy for warts.

79. Wood-nettle

Laportea canadensis (L.) Weddell
La-pórt-e-a ca-na-dén-sis
Urticaceae (Nettle Family)

DESCRIPTION: Perennial herb to 3–4′ tall, with stinging hairs throughout; stems and leaf stalks nearly transparent; leaves coarsely toothed, to 6″ long, long-stalked; flowers in terminal and axillary panicles, inconspicuous, the upper female, the lower male; no corolla present; flowers late June–August.

RANGE-HABITAT: Nova Scotia and Manitoba south to FL and OK; in SC common in the mountains in cove forests, especially near seepages; common in the piedmont on floodplains; rare in the coastal plain in alluvial woods.

COMMENTS: The closely related *Urtica dioica* L. has been shown to be an effective remedy for arthritis, and Duke (1997) recommends wood-nettle for the same use. The genus honors François L. de Laporte, a nineteenth-century entomologist.

80. Commom white snakeroot

Eupatorium rugosum Houttuyn
Eu-pa-tò-ri-um ru-gò-sum
Asteraceae (Aster or Sunflower Family)

DESCRIPTION: Perennial herb usually 3–4′ tall, often forming dense colonies; leaves opposite; leaf stalks to 2″ long; blade coarsely toothed, distinctly longer than the leaf stalk, not resinous, usually more than 2.5″ long; flower heads in flat-topped clusters from the tip and upper leaf axils; flowers late July–August.

RANGE-HABITAT: Widespread in eastern North America; in SC common in the mountains and piedmont in cove forests and moist oak-hickory forests; uncommon in the coastal plain in oak-hickory forests and woodland borders.

COMMENTS: This species caused the notorious "milk sickness" of earlier times; the plant produces a poison that is transmissible in cow's milk.

SYNONYM: *Ageratina altissima* King & H. E. Robinson var. *altissima*—W

81. Mountain turtlehead

Chelone lyonii Pursh
Che-lò-ne ly-òn-i-i
Scrophulariaceae (Figwort Family)

DESCRIPTION: Perennial herb with erect stems 12–40″ tall; leaves ovate with round bases, on distinct leaf stalks 0.5–1″ long; corolla crimson, with yellow hairs, the "beard"; sterile stamen white, or with a rose tip; flowers July–September.

RANGE-HABITAT: Chiefly mountains of NC, SC, and TN; cultivated in New England and naturalizing there, perhaps elsewhere; open streamsides, rich forests, and coniferous forests at high elevations.

COMMENTS: The flower of turtlehead simulates the head of a turtle to a remarkable degree; the two lips (a half-open mouth) terminate a large open corolla.

PROTECTION STATUS: State Threatened

82. Horsebalm; Canada stoneroot

Collinsonia canadensis L.
Col-lin-sòn-i-a ca-na-dén-sis
Lamiaceae (Mint Family)

DESCRIPTION: Perennial herb from a thick and elongate woody rhizome; stem to 3′ tall, with several pairs of large (10–20″ long), toothed leaves scattered on the stem; flowers yellow, two-lipped, the middle lobe of the lower lip cut into narrow segments; flowers in an open terminal cluster (panicle); flowers late July–September.

RANGE-HABITAT: Widespread in eastern North America; in SC common in a wide variety of rich forests in the mountains, especially rich cove forests; common in basic-mesic forests and mesic oak-hickory forests in the piedmont; rare in beech forests and other rich forests in the coastal plain.

COMMENTS: Horsebalm is a coarse (= horse) plant similar to balm (*Melissa*). It is sometimes called stoneroot because of its very hard roots, which were once used to treat kidney stones. The roots contain rosmarinic acid, an antioxidant (preservative). The genus honors Peter Collinson, 1694–1768, an English botanist.

83. Common blue monkshood; Appalachian blue monkshood

Aconitum uncinatum L.
   A-co-nì-tum un-ci-nà-tum
   Ranunculaceae (Buttercup Family)

DESCRIPTION: Weak-stemmed perennial to 3′ tall; leaves alternate, deeply divided into 3–5 segments; flowers blue, irregular, the uppermost petal helmetlike; flowers August–September.

RANGE-HABITAT: MD, PA, and IN, south to GA and SC; mountains of SC; rare; spray cliff seepages and rich cove forests.

COMMENTS: Some authors subdivide into two subspecies. It is a highly poisonous relative of the European wolfsbane (*A. napellus* L.), which is the source of the drug aconite, famous in European legend for its use in poisoning wolves.

PROTECTION STATUS: State Threatened

84. Curtis' goldenrod

Solidago curtisii Torrey & Gray
   So-li-dà-go cur-tís-i-i
   Asteraceae (Aster or Sunflower Family)

DESCRIPTION: Perennial herb from a stout rootstalk and slender, long rhizomes; stem usually 3–5′ tall, green, angled and grooved; leaves numerous, larger to 6″ long, 3–10x as long as wide, sharply toothed, tapered to a fine tip and a broader base; flowers yellow, 5–10 per head; heads in clusters of 3–15 from the axils of the upper leaves; flowers August–October.

RANGE-HABITAT: Southern Appalachian endemic known from VA and WV, south to GA and AL; in SC common in rich forests in the mountains, especially rich oak-hickory forests and cove forests.

COMMENTS: Goldenrods are difficult to identify, but this is the only species with grooved and angled green stems, numerous, large stem leaves, and heads in short clusters in the axils of upper leaves. The specific epithet honors its discoverer, Moses Ashley Curtis, 1808–1872.

85. Common blue wood aster

Aster cordifolius L.
   Ás-ter cor-di-fò-li-us
   Asteraceae (Aster or Sunflower Family)

DESCRIPTION: One of South Carolina's 3 common species of woodland asters with heart-shaped leaves, well-developed leaf stalks, heads with blue to lavender ray flowers and yellow to red disk flowers; distinguished by its elongate (rather than flat-topped) clusters of flower heads and unwinged leaf stalks; flowers September–October.

RANGE-HABITAT: Nova Scotia and MN, s. to GA and AL; throughout SC; rich woods, cove forests, and wooded road banks; common in the mountains, scattered in the piedmont, and occasional in the coastal plain in calcareous bluff forests.

86. Maidenhair fern

Adiantum pedatum L.
    A-di-án-tum pe-dà-tum
    Pteridaceae (Maidenhair Fern Family)

DESCRIPTION: Fronds horseshoe-shaped; stalk black and shiny, about as long as the frond blade; blade with two equal divisions, each bearing pinnae on just one side.

RANGE-HABITAT: Widespread in eastern North America; in SC rare in the piedmont and common in the mountains; moist soils of rich cove forests or in seepages associated with cliffs.

COMMENTS: The shape and composition of the leaf is distinctive. The common name is derived from the reported use of the leaf as a hair rinse by Native Americans.

87. Walking fern

Asplenium rhizophyllum L.
    As-plè-ni-um rhi-zo-phýl-lum
    Aspleniaceae (Spleenwort Family)

DESCRIPTION: Evergreen from a short, erect rhizome; fronds in small clusters, 2–12″ long, simple and without lobes, the apex very long-pointed and usually producing a small plant at the tip.

RANGE-HABITAT: From s. Quebec, Ontario and MN, south to n. GA, AL, MS, AR, and OK; in SC known only from the mountains; restricted to calcium-rich rocks in rich cove forests.

COMMENTS: This distinctive little fern "walks" as it produces plantlets from successive leaf tips.

88. Goldie's wood fern

Dryopteris goldiana (Hooker ex Goldie)
    Gray
    Dry-óp-te-ris gol-di-à-na
    Dryopteridaceae (Wood Fern Family)

DESCRIPTION: Deciduous fern with an erect rhizome and frond stalks with red-brown scales; often producing a vaselike cluster of fronds up to 3′ tall; leaves 2-pinnatifid; fertile pinnae (leaflets) and segments not differentiated from the sterile; clusters of sporangia (sori) borne in two rows near the midribs of the ultimate segments and protected by kidney-shaped indusia.

RANGE-HABITAT: Eastern Canada to MN, south to SC and GA; very rare in the mountains of SC; the only SC population is in a cove forest among boulders at the base of a talus slope.

COMMENTS: Wood ferns are notorious for hybridizing. If two species of wood fern grow in a single habitat, hybrids usually will be present and will have characteristics intermediate between the parents. The specific epithet honors its discoverer, John Goldie, 1793–1886.

89. Chestnut oak forests

89. American chestnut

Castanea dentata (Marshall) Borkhausen
  Cas-tà-ne-a den-tà-ta
Fagaceae (Beech Family)

DESCRIPTION: Medium to tall tree, reaching 115′; leaves alternate, deciduous, 6–11″ long, tapering to a short or long-pointed tip, with numerous coarse, sharp-pointed teeth along the margin; fruits large spiny burs enclosing 1 to 3 nuts; fruits mature September–October.

RANGE-HABITAT: Eastern North America, where it reached its greatest size in the southern Appalachian Mountains; in SC in the mountains and piedmont; mesic and xeric forests.

COMMENTS: Today chestnut exists as stump sprouts or small trees. A blight, introduced from Asia to NY in 1904, swept through the entire range of the chestnut, killing nearly every standing tree. When a stump sprout reaches the size of first fruit production, the blight, which persists in the forests on oaks, reinfects the tree. Only rarely does a stump sprout grow large enough to produce fruits. One can still see vast numbers of fallen chestnut trees in the forests of the mountains and piedmont of SC (plate 89). Interestingly, populations of chestnut in NC are persisting as small flowering trees on amphibolite outcrops. People and animals prized the chestnut's large, sweet nuts. The reddish brown wood was lightweight, soft, easy to split, and resistant to decay. Split-rail fences of chestnut were popular and still can be seen along roads throughout the northeast and the Appalachian Mountains. Both the bark and wood were rich in tannins, which were used to tan animal hides to make leather.

90. Gaywings; fringed polygala

Polygala paucifolia Willdenow
  Po-lý-ga-la pau-ci-fò-li-a
Polygalaceae (Milkwort Family)

DESCRIPTION: Perennial herb, forming colonies from rhizomes; stem 3–6″ tall; scalelike leaves below, and 3–6 well-formed leaves clustered above; flowers 1–4 in a terminal raceme, pink to purple (rarely white), wings large, to 0.6–.8″ long; stamens 6; flowers April–June.

RANGE-HABITAT: Widespread in eastern North America; rare in the SC mountains; chestnut oak forests at moderate to high elevations.

COMMENTS: The unusual flower structure of all *Polygalas* makes identification using keys difficult. This is South Carolina's largest-flowered species, and the few large flowers above the sparsely clustered leaves are distinctive. Self-pollinating flowers are hidden under leaf litter.

PROTECTION STATUS: State Threatened

THE MOUNTAINS

91. Downy serviceberry; shadbush

Amelanchier arborea Michaux f.
A-me-lán-chi-er ar-bò-re-a
Rosaceae (Rose Family)

DESCRIPTION: Deciduous shrub or rarely a tree to 40′ tall and 30″ in diameter; leaves alternate, margins with 6–16 teeth per 0.5″, apex pointed or gradually tapering, downy below but becoming smooth with age; flowers white or infused with pink, in semierect clusters terminating new growth, appearing with or before the leaves; flowers March–early May.
RANGE-HABITAT: From New Brunswick to e. MN, south to e. TX and FL; in SC common in the mountains, piedmont, and inner coastal plain; rare in the outer coastal plain; dry to moist habitats including chestnut oak forests, moist oak-hickory forests, and margins of bottomland hardwood forests.
COMMENTS: The "service" referred to in the common name is Easter. The species usually blooms at Easter. The "shad" referred to in the other common name is a small fish that usually has its mating runs up major rivers about the time this species is in bloom. It contains antioxidants that retard spoilage. Blackfoot Indians used serviceberries with animal fat to make a type of pemmigan (sausage). The juicy fruits can be used in pies and muffins.

92. Gorge rhododendron; punctatum

Rhododendron minus Michaux
Rho-do-dén-dron mì-nus
Ericaceae (Heath Family)

DESCRIPTION: Evergreen shrub to 10′ tall; leaves leathery, to 4″ long, 2″ wide, lower surface dotted with circular brown scales; petals white to pink, the largest lobes spotted with green; fruit a 5-parted capsule; flowers late April–June, depending mostly on elevation.
RANGE-HABITAT: NC to GA and AL; mountains (common), piedmont (occasional), and sandhills (rare); in the mountains in rocky woods of acid bluffs from streamside to ridge top, depending on slope and aspect; acid bluffs along streams in the piedmont and coastal plain.
COMMENTS: This species is especially abundant in the escarpment gorges of Oconee and Pickens Counties. Some authors segregate a high-elevation variant as a separate species, Carolina rhododendron (*R. carolinianum* Rehder).

93. Galax

Galax urceolata (Poiret) Brummitt
    Gà-lax ur-ce-o-là-ta
Diapensiaceae (Diapensia Family)

DESCRIPTION: Evergreen perennial herb with long-stalked, round, and sharply toothed leaves clustered on a short stem; flowers May–July.

RANGE-HABITAT: MD, WV and VA, south to GA and AL; in SC common in the mountains and upper piedmont, rare elsewhere; dry to moist woods with mountain laurel (*Kalmia latifolia*).

COMMENTS: Plants in the mountains of SC have four complements of chromosomes; those elsewhere have two. A fungus associated with the roots produces the distinctive musty smell of many mountain locations. Vigorously brush the leaves with your hand, and then smell the leaves.

SYNONYM: *Galax aphylla* L.—RAB

94. Flame azalea

Rhododendron calendulaceum (Michaux)
    Torrey
    Rho-do-dén-dron ca-len-du-là-ce-um
Ericaceae (Heath Family)

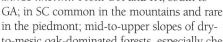

DESCRIPTION: Deciduous shrub to 12′ tall; leaves with gray hairs, at least along the midrib, to 3.5″ long; petals bright orange, yellow, or red; corolla tube with glandular hairs outside; flowers May–June.

RANGE-HABITAT: From OH and PA, south to GA; in SC common in the mountains and rare in the piedmont; mid-to-upper slopes of dry-to-mesic oak-dominated forests, especially chestnut oak forests.

COMMENTS: Red-flowered forms are very similar to Oconee azalea (*R. flammeum*, plate 232); their ranges do not overlap.

95. Downy rattlesnake plantain

Goodyera pubescens (Willdenow) R. Brown
    Good-yèr-a pu-bés-cens
Orchidaceae (Orchid Family)

DESCRIPTION: Perennial herb covered with short hairs, from a creeping rhizome; recognized by its distinctive basal leaves, which are blue-green and variegated with a network of white on the veins; flowers June–August.

RANGE-HABITAT: New Brunswick to Ontario and MN, and south to FL, MS, and AK; in SC common in the upper piedmont and mountains, rare in the coastal plain; wide variety of moist to dry coniferous or hardwood forests.

COMMENTS: The common name refers to the belief of superstitious country people that the mottled snake-striped leaves, when chewed and applied to a rattlesnake bite, would act as an antidote. After the rosette produces the flowering stalk, it withers and dies. From the rhizome, however, numerous plantlets sprout, creating a colony that ensures survival. Pollination must be effective since virtually every capsule produces a myriad of ripe seeds in the fall. The genus honors John Goodyer, 1592–1664, an English botanist.

96. Buffalo-nut; oil-nut

Pyrularia pubera Michaux
Py-ru-là-ri-a pù-be-ra
Santalaceae (Sandalwood Family)

DESCRIPTION: Deciduous shrub to 12′ tall; stem highly branched, arching; leaves alternate, thin, veins on lower surface raised; fruit pear-shaped, about 1″ long; flowers April–May; fruits July–October.

RANGE-HABITAT: PA and WV, south to GA; common in the mountains and upper piedmont in a variety of dry to moist forests.

COMMENTS: The oil is very poisonous. The source of the primary common name requires little imagination. Like all members of the sandalwood family in SC, the species gets some of its nutrition by parasitizing the roots of hardwoods.

97. Chestnut oak; basket oak

Quercus montana Willdenow
Quér-cus mon-tà-na
Fagaceae (Beech Family)

DESCRIPTION: Deciduous tree to 100′+ tall and 6′ in diameter; bark dark gray and deeply furrowed; leaves with 9–16, evenly spaced, rounded teeth on each side; lower leaf surface with star-like clusters of 2–5 hairs; acorns mature in September–November of the same year as flowering.

RANGE-HABITAT: ME to IL and IN, and south to AL and MS; in SC common in the mountains and piedmont and rare in the sandhills; variety of dry habitats and mostly on ridges and mid-to-upper slopes; often the dominant tree in chestnut oak forests but also common in pine-oak heaths and dry oak-hickory forests; also monadnocks in the piedmont.

COMMENTS: Chestnut oak does not grow well in shade. It has replaced much of the American chestnut that was lost to the blight. It is also called basket oak because the wood is easily split into long, tough ribbons that are used in making baskets and barrel staves. The wood was once prized for railroad cross ties. The SC state record was measured in 1987 at 130′ tall and 4.2′ in diameter.

Woodland margins

98. Wild strawberry

Fragaria virginiana Duchesne
    Fra-gà-ri-a vir-gi-ni-à-na
Rosaceae (Rose Family)

DESCRIPTION: Stemless herb with short rhizomes and long stolons; leaves basal with 3 leaflets; flower stalk 3–6″ tall; achenes imbedded in the fleshy receptacle (the strawberry); flowers March–June.

RANGE-HABITAT: Labrador and Newfoundland to Alberta, and south to GA, AL, and OK; in SC throughout the mountains and piedmont, occasional in the coastal plain; old fields and woodland borders.

COMMENTS: The generic name refers to the fragrance of the fruit. Wild strawberry was one of the parents that produced the cultivated table strawberry; the other parent is from South America (*F. chiloensis* var. *ananassa* Bailey). The fruit is the sweetest of the wild strawberries.

99. Robin's-plantain; fleabane

Erigeron pulchellus Michaux
    E-rí-ge-ron pul-chél-lus
Asteraceae (Aster or Sunflower Family)

DESCRIPTION: Perennial herb 15–20″ tall, forming clusters from long stolons, with spreading hairs throughout; leaves of basal rosette usually obovate, large and obvious; stem leaves smaller and reduced upward; flower heads with 50–100 ray flowers, white or lavender; disk flowers yellow; flowers April–early June.

RANGE-HABITAT: ME west to MN, south to GA and TX; in SC common in the mountains, less common in the piedmont, sandhills, and coastal plain; in a variety of mesic habitats but best developed in woodland margins and roadsides.

COMMENTS: Fleabane was used as a stuffing for mattresses in an unsuccessful attempt to reduce bites from fleas (and bed bugs?).

100. Wild vetch

Vicia caroliniana Walter
Ví-ci-a ca-ro-li-ni-à-na
Fabaceae (Pea or Bean Family)

DESCRIPTION: Perennial herb, sprawling to climbing; leaves with simple or branched tendrils; leaves compound with 10–18 leaflets; leaflets elliptic to oblong; flowers in loose racemes, mostly white, often with some blue or purple on the keel petal; flowers April–June.

RANGE-HABITAT: NY to MN, south to FL and TX; in SC common in the mountains and piedmont, occasional in the sandhills and coastal plain; woodland margins, open deciduous woods, and along streamsides.

SIMILAR SPECIES: Wild vetch is similar to *V. hugeri* Small, which grows in the upper piedmont. The leaflets of *V. caroliniana* are elliptic to oblong, while the leaflets of *V. hugeri* are linear.

101. Snowy hydrangea; silverleaf

Hydrangea radiata Walter
Hy-drán-ge-a ra-di-à-ta
Hydrangeaceae (Hydrangea Family)

DESCRIPTION: Shrub to 6′ tall; leaves deciduous, opposite, ovate and densely covered with white hairs below; flowers in head-shaped terminal clusters; flowers April–June.

RANGE-HABITAT: Southern Appalachian endemic of the mountains and piedmont, from NC and TN, south to GA; in SC in the mountains and nw. piedmont; common; in a variety of moist woodlands, often rocky; most conspicuous on woodland margins along roads.

COMMENTS: This is South Carolina's most common hydrangea in the mountains and piedmont. The root and bark were once used medicinally for both external and internal ailments; shown recently to produce cyanide-like poisoning, as well as bloody diarrhea and painful inflammation of the lining of the intestines and stomach.

SYNONYM: *Hydrangea arborescens* subsp. *radiata* (Walter) McClintock—RAB

102. Fire pink; catch-fly

Silene virginica L.
Si-lè-ne vir-gí-ni-ca
Caryophyllaceae (Pink Family)

DESCRIPTION: Perennial herb to 30″ tall; flowers April–July.

RANGE-HABITAT: NY, Ontario, and MI, south to GA and OK; common in the mountains and upper piedmont, rare elsewhere in SC; moist to dry habitats, usually with ample light, especially woodland margins and roadsides, often on rock outcrops.

COMMENTS: The sticky hairs on the calyx serve to reduce theft of pollen and nectar by nonpollinating flower visitors, especially ants (and flies?). The brilliant crimson flowers with cleft petals cannot be confused with any other plants in SC.

103. New Jersey tea

Ceanothus americanus L.
Ce-a-nò-thus a-me-ri-cà-nus
Rhamnaceae (Buckthorn Family)

DESCRIPTION: Low shrub to 3′ tall; roots dark red, large; leaves simple, alternate, deciduous, strongly 3-nerved beneath; flowers May–June.

RANGE-HABITAT: ME west to s. Manitoba, south to FL and TX; common throughout SC; oak-hickory forests, longleaf pine flatwoods, gladelike openings, dry pine or oak ridge forests in the mountains, and along roadsides.

COMMENTS: The dried leaves were used during the Revolutionary War as a substitute for oriental tea, but it contains no caffeine and does not provide the lift of oriental tea. The root is reported to be a stimulant, a sedative, and a means of loosening phlegm. The root is also strongly astringent because of its high tannin content. Nodules on the roots harbor bacteria that fix atmospheric nitrogen.

104. Smooth purple coneflower

Echinacea laevigata (C. L. Boynton
  & Beadle) Blake
  E-chi-nà-ce-a lae-vi-gà-ta
  Asteraceae (Aster or Sunflower Family)

DESCRIPTION: Perennial herb from a fibrous rootstalk; stem 24–48″ tall, unbranched, often in clumps; basal leaves with few, spaced teeth, smooth, or rough above and smooth below, to 6″ long and 3″ wide; stem leaves similar but smaller; flower heads solitary and terminal; ray flowers pale purple or violet, drooping; disc flowers purple; flowers late May–early July.

RANGE-HABITAT: From se. PA south to sw. SC and ne. GA; rare in the mountains, upper piedmont, and sandhills of SC; found in dry open woodlands on calcium-rich soil that overlay mafic or calcareous rocks.

COMMENTS: This plant and other *Echinacea* species are widely used as an herbal remedy for preventing and treating coughs and colds. Duke (1997) recommends it as an herbal remedy for viral infections, flu, and yeast infections. Some botanists believe the sandhills populations may have been introduced.

PROTECTION STATUS: Federal Endangered

105. Appalachian milkwort

Polygala curtissii Gray
  Po-lý-ga-la cur-tíss-i-i
  Polygalaceae (Milkwort Family)

DESCRIPTION: Smooth annual herb; stem solitary but often highly branched; leaves alternate, broader than linear; flowers small, pink, white, green, or a combination of these, subtended by persistent bracts, in headlike clusters about 0.4″ in diameter; flowers June–October.

RANGE-HABITAT: DE west to OH, south to SC and MS; common in the mountains, piedmont, and sandhills of SC; openings with dry rocky or sandy soils.

COMMENTS: Named for its discoverer, Allen Hiram Curtiss, 1845–1907.

106. Blue Ridge bindweed

Calystegia sericata (House) Bell
  Ca-lys-tè-gi-a se-ri-cà-ta
  Convolvulaceae (Morning-glory Family)

DESCRIPTION: Perennial trailing vine, stem often less than 3′ long, with silky hairs; leaves tapered to a sharp point, base heart-shaped and hastate, with a dense, silky white covering of hairs on the lower surface; flowers white, funnel-shaped, to 2″ long, borne in the axils of middle and upper leaves; flowers June–July.

RANGE-HABITAT: NC, SC, and GA; in SC in the mountains; rare; open woodlands or woodland margins, usually over calcareous soils; more common in rich cove forests, at least in N.C.

COMMENTS: Blue Ridge bindweed can be confused with low bindweed, *C. spithamaea* (L.) R. Brown, in the southern portion of its range that includes SC; low bindweed may sometimes be trailing rather than erect and have leaves similar in shape and pubescence, but has flowers from the lower leaf axils only.

107. Hairy angelica

Angelica venenosa (Greenway) Fernald
An-gé-li-ca ve-ne-nò-sa
Apiaceae (Parsley Family)

DESCRIPTION: Perennial herb from a taproot; stems to 3′ tall, covered with dense, fine hairs; leaves with long leaf stalks and blades 2x pinnately compound, at base and on stem, becoming smaller upward; flowers June–August.

RANGE-HABITAT: MA west to MN, south to FL panhandle, and west to MS and AR; in SC common throughout the mountains and piedmont, rare in the sandhills and coastal plain; sunny dry forests, woodland margins, dry, rocky streamside margins, and longleaf pine sandhills.

COMMENTS: The European angelica is reportedly useful for a variety of ailments, including heartburn, colic, and psoriasis. Duke (1997) recommends all species of *Angelica* as herbal remedies for these aliments.

108. White mountain-mint

Pycnanthemum incanum (L.) Michaux
Pyc-nán-the-mum in-cà-num
Lamiaceae (Mint Family)

DESCRIPTION: Perennial herb with clusters of bristles at the tips of the calyx lobes; easily recognized in its typical form with leaves whitened near the 2–3 headlike clusters of whitish to yellowish flowers that are heavily spotted with purple; flowers June–August.

RANGE-HABITAT: VT west to s. IL, south to FL, GA, and AL; essentially throughout SC; dry forests and woodland margins, habitats with an open canopy.

COMMENTS: The plants, when crushed, have a strong spearmint odor. A leaf tea was once used for fevers, colds, and coughs.

109. Fraser's loosestrife

Lysimachia fraseri Duby
Ly-si-má-chi-a frà-ser-i
Primulaceae (Primrose Family)

DESCRIPTION: Perennial herb to 4′ tall or more, forming colonies from underground stems; leaves in whorls of 3–6; translucent red band outlines leaf margins; flowers June–July.

RANGE-HABITAT: From w. NC and TN, south to n. SC, n. GA, and AL; rare in SC; Anderson County in the upper piedmont and the mountains of Oconee and Pickens Counties; dense herb cover of meadows along small streams, woodland borders, along roadsides, and sunny rocky slopes.

COMMENTS: The translucent red marginal band on the leaves and the distinctive knob-tipped hairs on the upper stems, stalks of flower clusters, and sepals are probably the best field characters. This plant has a high light requirement and probably was much more abundant in precolonial times when Native Americans routinely used fire as a tool to maintain open, grassy habitats. It generally flowers when exposed to extra sunlight created by a canopy opening.

PROTECTION STATUS: Federal Species of Concern

110. Indian-tobacco; pukeweed

Lobelia inflata L.
Lo-bèl-i-a in-flà-ta
Campanulaceae (Bellwort Family)

DESCRIPTION: Branched annual to 3′ tall; mid-stem leaves greater than 0.3″ wide, gradually reduced upward; flowers blue to lavender or sometimes white; most distinctive when the fruit swells (inflates) to become subglobose at maturity; flowers July–frost.

RANGE-HABITAT: ME to MN, and south to GA and MS; in SC common in the mountains, rare in the piedmont; open, dry-to-moist forests and woodland margins.

COMMENTS: Historically, Indian-tobacco is a plant of many uses. Native Americans smoked the leaves to relieve asthma, sore throats, and coughs. Traditionally it was used to induce vomiting and sweating. Lobeline (an alkaloid) is used in commercial "quit-smoking" preparations. Lobeline is similar to nicotine and binds to the same nerve receptors.

111. Virgin's-bower

Clematis virginiana L.
    Clé-ma-tis vir-gi-ni-à-na
Ranunculaceae (Buttercup Family)

DESCRIPTION: Scrambling, climbing herbaceous vine, by twisted stems or leaf stalks that wrap around other plants; leaves opposite, compound, with long stalks and 3 nearly symmetrical leaflets; flowers in many-flowered clusters from the leaf axils, white with petal-like sepals; flowers July–September.
RANGE-HABITAT: Widespread in eastern North America; in SC common in the mountains in moist woodland margins; uncommon in the piedmont and rare in the coastal plain on streamsides and moist forests.
COMMENTS: The sepals, not the petals, are the showy part of these flowers. All parts are reported to be highly irritating to the skin and mucous membranes.

112. Beauty-berry; French-mulberry

Callicarpa americana L.
    Cal-li-cár-pa a-me-ri-cà-na
Verbenaceae (Vervain Family)

DESCRIPTION: Deciduous shrub up to 8′ tall; stems arching, with star-shaped hairs; leaves opposite, simple; flowers June–July, but seldom noticed; fruits mature August–October.
RANGE-HABITAT: Primarily southeastern US; common throughout SC; maritime forests, fencerows, woodland borders, barnyards, pine-mixed hardwood and oak-hickory forests, and sandy or rocky woodlands.
COMMENTS: Some references indicate that the berries are edible but not very wholesome, and although sweet at first, they are pungent and astringent afterwards. Birds eat the berries, and it makes an attractive ornamental.

113. Southern grapefern

Botrychium biternatum (Savigny) Underwood
    Bo-trý-chi-um bi-ter-nà-tum
Ophioglossaceae (Adder's-tongue Family)

DESCRIPTION: Plant evergreen, producing spores in summer; stipe forking into an inclined, sterile blade and an erect, fertile segment, tipped by clustered globular sporangia.
RANGE-HABITAT: Widespread in the southeastern US; throughout and common in SC; moist forests, clearings, old fields, pinelands, and swamps.
COMMENTS: This fern has proved difficult to cultivate, even in damp woods resembling its native habitat. The common name comes from the grapelike clusters of sporangia.

Montane oak-hickory forests

114. Catesby's trillium; rosey wake-robin

Trillium catesbaei Elliott
Tríl-li-um càtes-bae-i
Liliaceae (Lily Family)

DESCRIPTION: Herbaceous perennial from a short, thick rhizome; stem erect, to 16″ tall; leaves uniformly green, with purplish tinge in sunny habitats; leaf stalk to 0.5″ long; flower stalk bent downward below leaves; petals white, pink, or rose; sepals sickle-shaped; anthers twisted outward; pollen sacs dark yellow; flowers late March–early May.

RANGE-HABITAT: NC to AL and TN; in SC common in the mountains, occasional in the piedmont; acid soils of mesic woods on slopes and floodplains in the piedmont, on drier, more exposed slopes in the mountains, usually oak-hickory forests merging into pine-oak heaths.

COMMENTS: Rare, erect-flowered forms are reported near Caesar's Head. This is one of many specific epithets honoring Mark Catesby, 1679–1749.

115. Bowman's root; mountain Indian physic

Gillenia trifoliata (L.) Moench
Gil-lèn-i-a tri-fo-li-à-ta
Rosaceae (Rose Family)

DESCRIPTION: Perennial herb from a woody rootstalk; stems 5 or more from the base, to 3′ tall; leaves alternate, comprised of 3 toothed leaflets on a very short leaf stalk; stipules persistent, about 0.25″ long; petals 5 and unequal in length; flowers April–June.

RANGE-HABITAT: Ontario and New England to MO and GA; common in the mountains, rare in the piedmont; rich forests, oak-hickory forests, and mesic roadsides.

COMMENTS: The five unequal white petals and 3-parted leaves together are distinctive. Native Americans used the powdered, dried root as a laxative and emetic—hence, the common names. The genus is dedicated to the seventeenth-century German botanist and physician, Arnold Gillen.

SYNONYM: *Porteranthus trifoliatus* (L.) Britton—W

116. Broadleaf coreopsis

Coreopsis latifolia Michaux
Co-re-óp-sis la-ti-fò-li-a
Asteraceae (Aster or Sunflower Family)

DESCRIPTION: Glabrous perennial with long rhizomes; stems erect, 28–60″ tall; leaves simple, opposite, coarsely serrate, 1.5–4.5 wide, lance-ovate to lance-elliptic; flowers August–September.

RANGE-HABITAT: Broadleaf coreopsis is a southern Appalachian endemic, ranging from sw. NC and se. TN south into nw. SC and ne. GA; known only from Pickens and Greenville Counties in SC; rare; moist cove forests and slopes at medium elevations.

COMMENTS: Broadleaf coreopsis often occurs with whiteleaf sunflower (*Helianthus glaucophyllus,* plate 117). Flowering appears to be initiated by canopy tree-fall light gaps.

PROTECTION STATUS: State Threatened

117. Whiteleaf sunflower

Helianthus glaucophyllus D.M. Smith
He-li-án-thus glau-co-phýl-lus
Asteraceae (Aster or Sunflower Family)

DESCRIPTION: Perennial herb 3–7′ tall with long rhizomes; stem leaves opposite, 4–10″ long and 1–3″ wide, rough above, smooth with a whitened bloom below; flowers July–September.

RANGE-HABITAT: Generally a narrow southern Appalachian endemic; w. NC, ne. TN, and SC; in SC in the mountains of Greenville and Pickens Counties, and McCormick County in the piedmont in basic-mesic forests; rare; calcium-rich montane oak-hickory forests, woodland borders, and moist forests.

COMMENTS: Whiteleaf sunflower was initially considered a mountain species found at medium elevations; however, Hill and Horne (1997) reported its occurrence along Stevens Creek in McCormick County, expanding its range into the piedmont. The leaves whitened below separate this species of *Helianthus* from other sunflowers in the same habitats.

PROTECTION STATUS: State Threatened

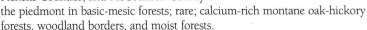

118. Mountain holly; mountain winterberry

Ilex montana Torrey and Gray
Ì-lex mon-tà-na
Aquifoliaceae (Holly Family)

DESCRIPTION: Deciduous shrub or small tree to 35′ tall; leaves 2.5–6.0″ long, margins sharply fine toothed; flowers on short stalks, white; sepals ciliate; male and female flowers on different plants; drupes red, spherical, with 4 seeds, each seed surrounded by a pit (pyrene); flowers April–June; fruits mature August–September.

RANGE-HABITAT: Appalachian Mountains and adjacent piedmont from MA to AL; common (occasional in piedmont); in a variety of mesic forests, including oak-hickory forests, cove forests, Canada hemlock forests, and montane oak-hickory forests; sometimes found in drier upland forests and sometimes in and adjacent to montane bogs.

COMMENTS: This is the only deciduous holly in mesic forests in the mountains of SC.

SYNONYM: *Ilex ambigua* var. *montana* (Torrey & Gray) Ahles—RAB

119. Gall-of-the-earth

Prenanthes trifoliolata (Cassini) Fernald
Pre-nán-thes tri-fo-li-o-là-ta
Asteraceae (Aster or Sunflower Family)

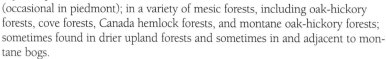

DESCRIPTION: Perennial herb with milky juice, from a thickened rootstock; stems to 5′ tall but often much less in shaded habitats; leaves very variable in shape and size, lobed or dissected below, much reduced upward, becoming less cut or lobed and with shorter leaf stalks upward; flowers cream to yellowish, not white, more than 8 per head; heads droop and are arranged in an open terminal cluster; flowers August–frost.

RANGE-HABITAT: Widespread in eastern North America; in SC common in the mountains; rare in the coastal plain; moist oak-hickory forests at relatively high elevations.

COMMENTS: *Prenanthes* comes from root words that in Greek mean "drooping blossom." The drooping heads make identification as a *Prenanthes* easy; identification to species requires technical examination of the bracts and pappus.

120. Appalachian gentian

Gentiana decora Pollard
  Gen-ti-à-na de-cò-ra
  Gentianaceae (Gentian Family)

DESCRIPTION: Perennial herb 10–20″ tall; stems densely covered with short hairs, unbranched, 1–8 from a root crown; flowers blue, white or violet, striped with blue or violet; corolla with unevenly 2-lobed plaits (appendages) between the 5, short corolla lobes; flowers September–October.

RANGE-HABITAT: WV and TN, south to SC and GA; common in the mountains, rare in the piedmont; wide variety of upland, mostly mesic, forest types, especially oak-hickory forests and montane oak-hickory forests.

COMMENTS: The other gentians present in the same habitats in the mountains are *G. quinquefolia* L. (ague-weed), which has no plaits between the corolla lobes, and *G. villosa* L. (striped gentian), which has a greenish white corolla sometimes tinged with purple.

121. *Canada hemlock forests*

122. French broad heartleaf

Hexastylis rhombiformis Gaddy
  Hex-ás-ty-lis rhom-bi-fór-mis
  Aristolochiaceae (Birthwort Family)

DESCRIPTION: Low evergreen, perennial herb, forming clumps with many leaves; leaves without mottling, 1.5–2.5″ wide and long; flowers solitary in leaf axils; calyx tube rhombic-ovate (widest in the middle), inner surface of calyx tube with a close network of reticulate ridges of high relief; flowers late March–June.

RANGE-HABITAT: Restricted to the mountains of Greenville County, SC, and four adjacent counties in NC; Canada hemlock forests or acidic cove forests, or in deciduous forests on sandy river bluffs.

COMMENTS: South Carolina botanist L. L. Gaddy described this species of heartleaf in 1986 (Gaddy, 1986).

PROTECTION STATUS: Federal Species of Concern

123. Oconee bells; shortia

Shortia galacifolia Torrey & Gray
Shórt-i-a ga-la-ci-fò-li-a
Diapensiaceae (Diapensia Family)

DESCRIPTION: Low evergreen plant forming dense colonies; leaves in basal clusters, shiny, circular, with the tip squared across or slightly indented; the white or pinkish flowers resemble nodding bells; flowers March–mid-April.

RANGE-HABITAT: A narrow endemic of the southern Blue Ridge Mountains and adjacent piedmont; known in SC only from Oconee and Pickens Counties; Canada hemlock forests and acid cove forests along mountain streams in gorges of the Blue Ridge Escarpment, usually under great laurel (*Rhododendron maximum*) or mountain laurel (*Kalmia latifolia*).

COMMENTS: Oconee bells was first collected in fruit in 1788 in Oconee County, SC, by the French botanist and early explorer of eastern North America, André Michaux. Harvard botanist Asa Gray discovered Michaux's collection in Paris in 1839 and named it for Charles W. Short, a prominent botanist and physician of Louisville, KY. Gray and others made many excursions to the "high mountains of Carolina," as the location of Michaux's original collection was described, with no success, not surprisingly, since the plant occurs at elevations from 600–2100′. In 1877, 17-year-old George Hyams "rediscovered" it on the banks of the Catawba River, near Marion, NC. The construction and filling of Lake Jocassee in SC destroyed the heart of the species' range.

PROTECTION STATUS: Federal Species of Concern

124. Sessile-leaf bellwort

Uvularia sessilifolia L.
U-vu-là-ri-a ses-si-li-fò-li-a
Liliaceae (Lily Family)

DESCRIPTION: Perennial herb forming colonies from underground stolons; stems to 18″ tall, 1-branched when flowering, upper portion without hairs; leaves usually whitish below; flowers usually 1 per stem, light yellow and nodding, bell-like; flowers late March–early May.

RANGE-HABITAT: Widespread in eastern North America; in SC common in the mountains and piedmont, rare in the coastal plain; moist forests, especially in Canada hemlock forests, in the mountains, beech forests and hardwood bottoms in the piedmont, and hardwood bottoms in the coastal plain.

SIMILAR SPECIES: Similar to pale yellow bellwort (*U. puberula* Michaux, plate 145), but distinct in terms of habitat and by having stolons, smooth upper stems, and whitish leaves.

COMMENTS: Sometimes called "wild oats" due to the clasping and upward-pointing leaves of the young stems.

125. Persistent trillium

Trillium persistens Duncan, Garst &
Neece
Trĭl-li-um per-sís-tens
Liliaceae (Lily Family)

DESCRIPTION: Low perennial herb from an
underground stem; a single whorl of 3 leaves,
solid green and narrowed to a pointed apex;
the single terminal flower is on a stalk that
droops slightly; the white petals turn pink
with age; the stamens are light yellow and
straight; flowers early March–mid-April.

RANGE-HABITAT: Restricted to the Tallulah-
Tugaloo River system and known only from Rabun and Habersham Counties in
GA and Oconee County in SC; acidic cove forests of deep ravines or gorges,
often under or near great laurel (*Rhododendron maximum*) or gorge rhododendron (*R. minus*).

COMMENTS: As with most of SC trilliums, this species is ant dispersed, with a
protein body on the seed (an elaiosome) that attracts ants. The small, narrow
petals, lance-shaped leaves, and pale yellow and straight anthers are characters
that separate this species from others.

PROTECTION STATUS: Federal Endangered

126. Round-leaf yellow violet; early yellow violet

Viola rotundifolia Michaux
Vĭ-o-la ro-tun-di-fò-li-a
Violaceae (Violet Family)

DESCRIPTION: Herbaceous perennial; leaves
basal only, nearly round, with a heart-shaped
base, hairy and fleshy; flowers yellow, on
stalks at least as long as the leaves; flowers
March–early April.

RANGE-HABITAT: ME and Ontario, south to
OH, GA and SC; in SC only in the mountains;
Canada hemlock forests and cove forests.

COMMENTS: This is the only yellow violet with
flowers on a leafless stalk; its flowers appear
when its leaves are only partly developed.

127. Common foamflower; false miterwort

Tiarella cordifolia var. *collina* Wherry
Ti-a-rél-la cor-di-fò-li-a var. col-lì-na
Saxifragaceae (Saxifrage Family)

DESCRIPTION: Perennial herb, 4–20″ tall; basal
leaves with a heart-shaped base and long leaf
stalk; flowering stalk leafless; petals white and
stalked; fruit a two-parted capsule; flowers
April–June.

RANGE-HABITAT: From KY and VA, south to AL
and MS; restricted to the piedmont and
mountains in SC; Canada hemlock forests,
beech forests, and cove forests.

COMMENTS: Foamflower is easily confused with miterwort (*Mitella diphylla* L.)

when not in fruit or flower; miterwort usually has just two basal leaves, oppositely arranged, whereas foamflower has many basal leaves. *Tiarella* means "little tiara," apparently in reference to the appearance of the fruit.

TAXONOMY: Mountain foamflower (*Tiarella cordifolia* L. var. *cordifolia*) is colonial, with plants connected by stolons (as in strawberry). It is found only in the mountains of SC in moist forests, cove forests, and margins of rock outcrops.

128. Painted trillium

Trillium undulatum Willdenow
   Tríl-li-um un-du-là-tum
   Liliaceae (Lily Family)

DESCRIPTION: Herbaceous perennial from a thick rhizome; stem erect, to 8″ tall; leaves uniformly dark green; flower stalk erect, 1–2″ long; petals white, with an inverted red V at the base, margins strongly wavy; anthers lavender to white, opening to the outside of the flower; flowers late April–May.

RANGE-HABITAT: Eastern Canada to GA, KY, and TN; in SC rare in the mountains in relatively high elevation Canada hemlock forests, which are rare in SC.

COMMENTS: This is South Carolina's rarest trillium; the inverted V at the base of the petals is distinctive.

PROTECTION STATUS: State Threatened

129. Mountain doghobble

Leucothoë fontanesiana (Steudel) Sleumer
   Leu-cóth-o-ë fon-ta-ne-si-à-na
   Ericaceae (Heath Family)

DESCRIPTION: Evergreen shrub 2–5′ tall, forming dense colonies; branches arching; leaves alternate, shiny, and leathery, long tapering at the tip and toothed on the margins; flowers white, urn-shaped, in dense racemes to 4″ long; flowers April–May.

RANGE-HABITAT: Endemic to the southern Appalachians, from TN and VA, south to GA and SC; in SC common in the mountains and upper piedmont, rare in the lower piedmont; moist acid soils, usually along streams; most common in Canada hemlock forests in the mountains and acidic bluffs in the piedmont.

COMMENTS: One of the most easily recognizable plants of ravines in the mountains and upper piedmont. Dense thickets of these plants apparently "hobble" the progress of hunting dogs. The genus is from Leucothoë, daughter of Orchamus, King of Babylon.

SYNONYM: *Leucothoë axillaris* var. *editorum* (Fernald and Schubert) Ahles—RAB

130. Red trillium; stinking benjamin

Trillium erectum L.
   Tríl-li-um e-réc-tum
Lialaceae (Lily Family)

DESCRIPTION: Perennial herb from a short, thick rhizome; stem erect, to 18″ tall; leaves uniformly green, about as wide as long and stalkless; flower stalk stiff, often very long (to 4″), usually positioning the flower below the vertical, sometimes just below the leaves; petals dark purple, pale yellow, or white; sepals weakly boat-shaped at the tip; flowers April–May.

RANGE-HABITAT: Widespread in eastern North America; in SC rare in the mountains on acid soils of Carolina hemlock forests and adjacent oak-hickory forests.

COMMENTS: The fragrance of the flower is like that of a wet dog and may be the easiest way to identify the species. Flowers are pollinated by one of the carrion flies, the green flesh fly.

131. Basil bergamont

Monarda clinopodia L.
   Mo-nár-da cli-no-pò-di-a
Lamiaceae (Mint Family)

DESCRIPTION: Perennial herb to 3′ tall; leaves ovate, usually 2x as long as wide; flowers in a terminal headlike cluster, subtended by green-ish or whitish leaflike bracts; flowers pink or greenish white, lower lip spotted with purple, upper lip without hairs; flowers late May–September.

RANGE-HABITAT: NY, NJ, and IL, south to GA and AL; common in the mountains, rare in the piedmont; mesic forests, and most abundant in Canada hemlock forests and cove forests.

COMMENTS: Recognizable as a *Monarda* by the terminal, headlike cluster of flowers subtended by leaflike colored bracts; recognizable as basil bergamot by the single flower cluster, the leaves about 2x as wide as long, and the hairless upper lip of the corolla. True bergamot is a species of orange (*Citrus bergamia* Risso); its rind is the source of an oil used in perfumery.

132. Large-flower heartleaf

Hexastylis shuttleworthii (Britten &
      Baker) Small
   Hex-ás-ty-lis shut-tle-wórth-i-i
Aristolochiaceae (Birthwort Family)

DESCRIPTION: Low evergreen, perennial herb; leaves mottled or not, rounded and heart-shaped, to 4″ long and 3.5″ wide, from terminal portion of rootstalk only; flowers solitary from the axils of leaves; calyx tube urn- or bell-shaped, to 1.6″ long and 1″ wide; flowers May–July.

RANGE-HABITAT: VA and TN, south to GA and AL; in SC common in the mountains; usually found in acid soils, along creeks

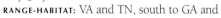

and under great laurel (*Rhododendron maximum*) in Canada hemlock forests.
COMMENTS: The very large flowers of this species make it readily identifiable.
The specific epithet honors Robert J. Shuttleworth, 1810–1874, an English plant
collector who designated it as new.

133. Great laurel; white rosebay

Rhododendron maximum L.
Rho-do-dén-dron máx-i-mum
Ericaceae (Heath Family)

DESCRIPTION: Evergreen shrub or small tree;
leaves leathery, to 10″ long, usually 3–5x as
long as wide, base wedge-shaped, apex acute;
petals pale pink to white, the longest lobe
spotted with green; flowers June–August.
RANGE-HABITAT: New England and Ontario,
south to GA and AL; in SC common in the
mountains in a variety of habitats, especially
Canada hemlock forests; rare in the piedmont
on north slopes.

COMMENTS: The angle of the leaves below the horizontal correlates highly with
temperature: the lower the temperature, the greater the angle of drooping. Great
laurel is an excellent ornamental planted along streams at higher elevations and
latitudes.

134. Mountain white-alder; sweet pepperbush

Clethra acuminata Michaux
Clè-thra a-cu-mi-nà-ta
Clethraceae (Clethra Family)

DESCRIPTION: Deciduous shrub to 15′ tall;
leaves to 7–8″ long, 3″ wide, toothed and
long tapered at the tip; flowers in terminal
racemes or narrow panicles; flowers small,
white; sepals and flower stalks densely covered with star-shaped hairs; flowers
July–August.
RANGE-HABITAT: Endemic to the Appalachian
Mountains, from PA and WV, south to GA;
common in SC in the mountains; moist forests, especially Canada hemlock
forests, and margins of rock outcrops.

COMMENTS: The shreddy, reddish bark is distinctive (cinnamon-like) and therefore very useful in identification. The flowers have been described as "deli-
ciously fragrant."

135. Autumn coral-root

Corallorhiza odontorhiza (Willdenow) Nuttall
    Co-ral-lo-rhì-za o-don-to-rhì-za
Orchidaceae (Orchid Family)

DESCRIPTION: Perennial herb without photosynthetic tissues, from a cluster of branched, coral-like roots; without leaves, but with a few sheathing scales toward the base; flowers small, with partly fused sepals and petals, purplish or purplish green, except for the lip petal which is white, spotted with purple and bearing 2 ridges near the base; flowers August–October.

RANGE-HABITAT: Widespread in eastern US (and south Ontario); throughout SC; occasional; habitat variously described as dry woodlands, forests, open woods, and coniferous forests.

COMMENTS: Autumn coral-root depends on saprophytic fungi associated with its roots for all of its nutritional needs. Its small size distinguishes it from other saprophytic orchids, except for the spring coral-root (*C. wisteriana* Conrad), which blooms in the spring and is found in richer habitats. There are two forms of this species: one has flowers that remain closed and are self-pollinating, the other has flowers that are open and are at least potentially cross-pollinating. The one in SC is the self-pollinating form.

136. Indian cucumber-root

Medeola virginiana L.
    Me-dè-o-la vir-gi-ni-à-na
Liliaceae (Lily Family)

DESCRIPTION: Perennial herb from a white, swollen rhizome; stems 0.8–2.5′ tall; leaves usually in two whorls, the upper whorl generally of 3 leaves, the lower of 6–10 leaves; flowers borne on recurved stalks beneath the top whorl of leaves; flowers April–June; in fruit, the stalks are ascending or erect; fruits mature September–October.

RANGE-HABITAT: Quebec and Ontario, west to MN, south to GA, FL panhandle, and LA; in SC in the mountains, generally absent from the piedmont and sandhills, present in the coastal plain; common; generally found in moist forests, usually with acidic soils.

COMMENTS: Native Americans used the rhizomes for food; they are crisp and starchy, with a taste similar to cucumber. One should not dig them because of their limited numbers. When the fruits are mature, the upper leaves become scarlet, possibly attracting animals that aid in seed dispersal.

137. Pine-oak heaths

138. Trailing arbutus; Mayflower

Epigaea repens L.
E-pi-gaè-a rè-pens
Ericaceae (Heath Family)

DESCRIPTION: Creeping shrub; stem 8–16″ long, branching, with spreading hairs; leaves evergreen, leathery, elliptic, to 2.5″ long; flowers fragrant, in tight terminal and axillary spikes, white to pink and conspicuous; flowers late February–early May.

RANGE-HABITAT: Widespread in eastern North America; common in the mountains, piedmont, sandhills, and inner coastal plain; rare in the outer coastal plain; in a wide variety of dry to somewhat moist habitats, with acidic soils, and usually sandy and/or rocky.

COMMENTS: This is another of South Carolina's many ant-dispersed species, the ant attractant in this case being the placental tissue around the seeds. This is the Mayflower of the Pilgrims, described as a messenger of hope in Whittier's poem *The Mayflower.* Finding this plant in the early spring at Plymouth Rock was a hopeful sign that the cold and apparently barren land of the New World was actually bountiful. Natural populations have been greatly depleted because the sweet-scented blossoms were picked for bouquets; now it is protected by law in many states.

139. Sweet pinesap

Monotropsis odorata Schweinitz ex Elliott
Mo-no-tróp-sis o-do-rà-ta
Ericaceae (Heath Family)

DESCRIPTION: Inconspicuous perennial, saprophytic herb; stems, leaves and flowers brownish, purplish, or pinkish; stems only to 2.5″ tall, nodding in early flower and erect at maturity; leaves reduced to scales that are spirally arranged and overlapping; flowers very fragrant; flowers February–March and September–November.

RANGE-HABITAT: MD and KY, south to GA and SC; in SC rare in the mountains, very rare in the piedmont; usually in pine-dominated uplands, especially pine-oak heaths.

COMMENTS: Leaf litter often partially covers Pineseap, and it blooms at times when few botanists are in the woods. This probably explains its reported rarity range wide. The flowers are fragrant, smelling like cinnamon, nutmeg, or even cloves. Forest Service biologists at the Andrew Pickens District of the Sumter National Forest recently have had success "smelling" for the species in mid-March in pine-oak heath communities.

PROTECTION STATUS: Federal Species of Concern

140. Hairy yellow stargrass

Hypoxis hirsuta (L.) Coville var. *hirsuta*
Hy-póx-is hir-sù-ta var. hir-sù-ta
Iridaceae (Iris Family)

DESCRIPTION: Herbaceous perennial from a swollen underground stem; leaves basal only, grasslike, ascending to nearly erect; flowers March–June.

RANGE-HABITAT: From MA to Manitoba, south to FL and TX; in SC common throughout except the outer coastal plain; open woodlands, meadows, road banks, and pine-oak heaths in the mountains.

COMMENTS: This is the only species of yellow stargrass in the mountains and piedmont of SC. According to Radford et al. (1968), "Our species in this genus are very poorly defined and perhaps all belong to one polymorphic species."

141. Plantain pussytoes

Antennaria plantaginifolia (L.) Richardson
An-ten-nà-ri-a plan-ta-gi-ni-fò-li-a
Asteraceae (Aster or Sunflower Family)

DESCRIPTION: Perennial, white, woolly herb with long, ascending stolons; leaves in a basal rosette, alternate, reduced on the stem, white-woolly above; flowers white to purplish and tiny; heads of disk flowers only, with several heads terminating the stem; flowers late March–early May.

RANGE-HABITAT: Widespread in eastern North America; common throughout SC except in the outer coastal plain, where it is rare; dry woods, including pine-oak heaths, oak-hickory forests, and chestnut oak forests.

COMMENTS: Soft, downy flower heads are crowded together into a cluster resembling a cat's paw—hence, the common name.

142. Horse sugar; sweetleaf; yellow-wood

Symplocos tinctoria (L.) L'Heritier de
  Brutelle
  Sým-plo-cos tinc-tò-ri-a
Symplocaceae (Sweetleaf Family)

DESCRIPTION: Shrub or small tree; leaves simple, alternate, deciduous, or sometimes tardily deciduous; flowers fragrant, in dense clusters on naked branches (or almost naked if leaves persist); flowers March–May.

RANGE-HABITAT: Horse sugar is widespread in the southeastern US, from DE south to n. FL, and west to e. TX and se. OK; in SC primarily a mountain and coastal plain species, but interestingly, present in the piedmont mainly near the borders of the adjacent provinces and in scattered sites in the central piedmont; oak-hickory and beech forests, longleaf pine flatwoods, maritime forests, thickets, ridge top forests, and streamsides.

COMMENTS: The bark and leaves yield a bold yellow dye. Dying with yellow-wood, a practice several centuries old in the South, is still practiced. Cattle and horses greedily consume the leaves, and whitetail deer browse on them. Older leaves often show signs of insect damage. The leaves can be chewed as a refreshing trail tidbit. The wood has no commercial value. Where protected from fire, it can grow quite tall. The SC state record was measured in 1984 at 46′ tall.

143. Mountain laurel

Kalmia latifolia L.
  Kálm-i-a la-ti-fò-li-a
Ericaceae (Heath Family)

DESCRIPTION: Shrub or small tree, usually 6–12′ tall, often forming dense thickets; leaves leathery and evergreen, with stalked glandular hairs on lower surface, which darken and fall with age; flowers white or pink, usually with purple around the 10 pockets in which the anthers are fitted; flowers April–June.

RANGE-HABITAT: Widespread in eastern North America; found throughout SC and common in the mountains, piedmont, sandhills, and inner coastal plain; acidic forests, bluffs, bogs, and a wide range of other habitats.

COMMENTS: The anthers forcefully spray pollen at maturity after a touch releases the tension. The hard root was once used to make pipe bowls. Mountain laurel is now being produced in nurseries by tissue culture; it makes a beautiful shrub on rocky hillsides that are not suitable for other shrubs. The genus honors Pehr Kalm, 1716–1779, a pupil of Linnaeus, who traveled and collected in America.

144. Mountain rosebay; purple laurel

Rhododendron catawbiensis Michaux
    Rho-do-dén-dron ca-taw-bi-én-sis
Ericaceae (Heath Family)

DESCRIPTION: Evergreen shrub or small tree; leaves leathery, to 6″ long and 2.5″ wide, base rounded, apex obtuse; petals purple to deep pink; sepals very short; flowers April–early June.

RANGE-HABITAT: KY and VA, south to GA and AL; very rare in the mountains and upper piedmont of SC; ridge tops and rocky woods at high elevations on acid soils in the mountains, and on north slopes in the piedmont.

COMMENTS: High elevations are rare in SC, and so is this species. This species is much showier than its close relative, great laurel, and is readily distinguished in leaf and flower. This is the dominant shrub of the heath balds of the southern Appalachian Mountains.

145. Pale yellow bellwort

Uvularia puberula Michaux
    U-vu-là-ri-a pu-bé-ru-la
Liliaceae (Lily Family)

DESCRIPTION: Perennial herb; stems 1–several from a crown, usually with 1–2 branches; stems to 16″ tall; flowers in upper leaf axils, 1–3 per stem, yellow and nodding, bell-like; flowers early April–early May.

RANGE-HABITAT: PA to GA, mostly in the mountains; in SC common in the mountains, less common in the piedmont; dry to moist forests on acid soils, usually in openings, especially in pine-oak heaths in the mountains and xeric oak-hickory forests in the piedmont.

COMMENTS: Readily distinguished from other bellworts by its habitat and its noncolonial growth.

SYNONYM: *U. pudica* (Walter) Fernald (in part)—RAB

146. Pink lady's slipper; moccasin-flower

Cypripedium acaule Aiton
Cy-pri-pè-di-um a-caù-le
Orchidaceae (Orchid Family)

DESCRIPTION: A showy perennial herb to 18″ tall; basal leaves 2, to 9.5″ long and 5.5″ wide, glandular-hairy, with riblike parallel veins; flower solitary and terminating at a leafless stalk; 3 sepals and 2 lateral petals are green and often tinged with purple; the "slipper" or "moccasin" petal is pink or rarely white; flowers April–June.

RANGE-HABITAT: Widespread in eastern North America; in SC common in the mountains, occasional in the upper piedmont, and rare in the sandhills; dry acid woodlands under pine, rare in bogs or under thickets of great laurel (*Rhododendron maximum*).

COMMENTS: Thoughtless nature enthusiasts often collect lady's slipper and bring it into the home garden, where it seldom survives. As with all wild orchids, its roots (and seeds) require the presence of highly specific soil fungi (mychorrhizae) for proper development and maintenance. Lady's slipper was widely used in the nineteenth century as a sedative for nervous headaches, hysteria, insomnia, and "female" diseases.

147. Sweet-fern

Comptonia peregrina (L.) Coulter
Comp-tòn-i-a pe-re-grì-na
Myricaceae (Bayberry Family)

DESCRIPTION: Deciduous shrub to 3′ tall, sometimes forming large colonies; leafy branches look very much like fern fronds; flowers without sepals or petals; male and female flowers on same plant; male flower clusters cylindrical and about 1.25″ long; female clusters burrlike and below the male; flowers April.

RANGE-HABITAT: Manitoba and Nova Scotia, south to SC and GA; mountains of SC; occasional; dry, open ridges and roadsides, and in fire-maintained pine-oak heath communities on very poor soils.

COMMENTS: The sweet-smelling foliage can sometimes be smelled from a distance. Native Americans made a leaf tea that was used to treat poison ivy rash. The genus honors Henry Compton, 1632–1713, a bishop of London and a patron of botany.

PROTECTION STATUS: State Endangered

148. Ash-leaf golden-banner

Thermopsis fraxinifolia (Nuttall ex
Torrey and Gray) M. A. Curtis
Ther-móp-sis frax-i-ni-fò-li-a
Fabaceae (Pea or Bean Family)

DESCRIPTION: Perennial herb to 3′ tall, from a
woody rootstalk; leaves with 3 leaflets, to 2.5″
long, and with obvious, persistent stipules;
flowers in arching terminal or axillary racemes;
legumes spreading, or at least not strictly erect,
on a short stalk, flattened; flowers May–July.
RANGE-HABITAT: NC, TN, SC, and GA; rare in
the mountains of SC; usually in pine-oak heaths
on dry ridges, but also in dry sandy/rocky margins of large mountain streams.
TAXONOMY: Considered a variety of *T. mollis* by some authors; Weakley (2001)
argues that the significant difference in peak blooming periods provides support
for the recognition of *T. fraxinifolia* and *T. mollis* as separate species.
SYNONYM: *Thermopsis mollis var. fraxinifolia* (Nutall ex Torrey & Gray) Isley

149. Turkeybeard; beargrass

Xerophyllum asphodeloides (L.) Nuttall
Xe-ro-phýl-lum as-pho-de-loì-des
Liliaceae (Lily Family)

DESCRIPTION: Perennial herb with a thick cluster of basal leaves;
basal leaves grasslike, stiff, to 20″ long, with fine saw-teeth on the
margin; stem leaves similar but greatly reduced upward; flowers
May–June.
RANGE-HABITAT: Two ranges: (1) coastal plain of s. NJ and DE; and
(2) mountains of w. VA south to e. TN, w. NC, nw. SC, and ne.
GA; rare in the mountains of SC; pine-oak heaths and dry pine-
oak-hickory forests.
COMMENTS: The basal leaves of turkeybeard greatly resemble the
"grass-stage" of the longleaf pine and apparently serve the same
function, protecting the apical meristem from the effects of fire.
The rarity of this species is probably due to fire suppression in its
fire-prone habitat. In the mountains of VA and NC and SC, it is
usually associated with pitch pine (*P. rigida* Miller) or Table Mountain pine (*P. pungens,* plate 155); in GA it is usually associated with
shortleaf pine (*P. echinata* Miller) or Virginia pine (*P. virginiana* Miller).
PROTECTION STATUS: State Threatened

150. Dryland blueberry; hillside blueberry

Vaccinium vacillans Kalm ex Torrey
Vac-cí-ni-um va-cíl-lans
Ericaceae (Heath Family)

DESCRIPTION: Shrub 12–24″ tall, forming
extensive colonies from rhizomes; leaves
deciduous, whitened below; flowers white or
greenish with a pink tinge, in a few short
racemes from the previous year's wood;
corolla urn-shaped; fruit blue with a thin covering of whitish wax that is easily rubbed off;
flowers March–April; fruits June–July.

RANGE-HABITAT: Widespread in eastern US; throughout SC; common in the mountains and piedmont, occasional in the sandhills and coastal plain; in a variety of forested slopes, that are usually rather xeric.

COMMENTS: The berries are sweet and edible and are an important food for wildlife. Duke (1997) recommends species of *Vaccinium* as herbal remedies for multiple sclerosis and bladder infections.

SYNONYM: *Vaccinium pallidum* Aiton—W

151. Wintergreen; teaberry

Gaultheria procumbens L.
　　Gaul-thèr-i-a pro-cúm-bens
　　Ericaceae (Heath Family)

DESCRIPTION: Semiwoody perennial, forming colonies from a horizontal rhizome; stem usually 5–6″ tall, with a few leaves crowded toward the tip; leaves evergreen, to 2.5″ long; flowers white or pale pink; flowers June–August.

RANGE-HABITAT: Widespread in northeast North America, extending south in the Appalachian Mountains to GA and AL; in SC known only from a few populations in the mountains; in openings in pine-oak heaths and under great laurel or mountain laurel.

COMMENTS: Leaves contain oil of wintergreen (methyl salicylate), which is used topically to treat muscle pain. Because of the potential for salicylate toxicity, the oil apparently should not be applied after heavy exercise or in hot humid weather. Duke (1997) states wintergreen is a useful herbal remedy for sore throats, backache, and sciatica. The genus honors Jean-François Gaultier, 1708–1756, a naturalist and court physician in Quebec.

152. Bear huckleberry

Gaylussacia ursina (M. A. Curtis) Torrey
　　& Gray ex Gray
　　Gay-lus-sàc-i-a ur-sì-na
　　Ericaceae (Heath Family)

DESCRIPTION: Erect shrub, usually 3′ tall; leaves deciduous, with a blunt projection at the tip of the tapering apex, with golden, sessile glands only on the lower surface; flowers white, on old wood, in racemes in the axil of leaves; fruits July–August.

RANGE-HABITAT: Restricted to the mountains of TN, NC, SC, and GA; upper slopes and ridge tops, most commonly in pine-oak heaths, but extending downslope into chestnut oak forests and oak-hickory forests.

COMMENTS: Often forming dense, clonal stands; similar to *G. baccata* (Wangenheim) K. Koch (black huckleberry), which has golden glands on both leaf surfaces, and to dangleberry (*G. frondosa,* plate 352), which has leaves that are somewhat whitened on the lower surface. Huckleberry tea once was widely used to treat rheumatism and arthritis. The genus honors Louis Joseph Gay-Lussac, 1778–1850, an eminent French chemist.

153. Carolina lily; turk's-cap lily

Lilium michauxii Poiret
Lí-li-um mi-chaùx-i-i
Liliaceae (Lily Family)

DESCRIPTION: Perennial herb from a scaly bulb; stem stout, strictly erect, to 3.5″ tall; leaves deciduous, whorled below, alternate above; flowers in terminal umbels of 1–2, rarely 3–4 or more, nodding; flower segments strongly recurved, orange-red and purple-spotted in the lower half; flowers July–August.
RANGE-HABITAT: VA and TN, south to FL, and west to MS and LA; in SC occasional in the mountains and rare in the piedmont and coastal plain; most common in pine-oak heaths or calcareous outcrops on ridges and upper slopes in the mountains.
COMMENTS: This is an attractive and hardy lily that should be stocked by nurseries. The specific epithet honors André Michaux, 1746–1802, a French botanist.

154. Carolina hemlock

Tsuga caroliniana Engelmann
Tsù-ga ca-ro-li-ni-à-na
Pinaceae (Pine Family)

DESCRIPTION: Evergreen tree to 90′ tall and 2′ in diameter; leaves flat, linear, 0.4–.0.75″ long, smooth on the margins and notched at the tip, with 2 white lines of pores (stomata) below; leaves extending in all directions from the twig; cones about 1.2″ long; cones shed seeds August–October.
RANGE-HABITAT: A southern Appalachian Mountains endemic, from TN south to GA; in SC common in the mountains, rare in the upper piedmont; open forests on ridge tops, rocky bluffs, or gorge walls.
COMMENTS: Easily distinguished from Canada hemlock by the leaf arrangement (a flat spray in Canada hemlock). Carolina hemlock is prized as an ornamental and as a Christmas tree. Today, it is threatened by the onslaught of the hemlock woolly adelgid.

155. Table Mountain pine; burr pine

Pinus pungens Lambert
Pì-nus pún-gens
Pinaceae (Pine Family)

DESCRIPTION: Tree to 72′ tall, usually much less; needles in 2s, stout, usually less than 2.5″ long, twisted; cones sessile, ovate, 2–3.5″ long, with stout, sharp upward-curved prickles; cones mature September–October.
RANGE-HABITAT: A central and southern Appalachian endemic; in SC common in the mountains, very rare in the piedmont; high elevations on dry ridges and cliffs that are often rocky.
COMMENTS: This species apparently needs fire for maintenance, and one of its known locations, Buzzard's Roost Heritage Preserve, underwent a prescribed fire in 1998. The unopened cones are reported to remain on the tree for as long as 20 years. The wood has little commercial value.

THE PIEDMONT

156. *Granitic flatrocks*

157. Puck's orpine; granite stonecrop

Sedum pusillum Michaux
Sè-dum pu-síl-lum
Crassulaceae (Stonecrop Family)

DESCRIPTION: Diminutive annual herb; stems to 3″ tall, few-branched; leaves fleshy, alternate, in spirals, cylindrical, to 0.5″ long, blue-green or sometimes reddish in full sun; flowers white, in flat-topped clusters; flowers March–April.

RANGE-HABITAT: NC, SC, GA, and AL; in SC rare, and restricted to the piedmont; found on granitic flatrocks, in shallow soil in partial shade, almost always under red cedar.

COMMENTS: Sometimes confused with elf orpine (*Diamorpha smallii,* plate 159), especially plants with reddish leaves growing in full sun. Puck's orpine blooms two weeks earlier, and the fruit opens by a lengthwise slit on the upper surface; the fruit of *D. smallii* opens by a small flap on the underside.

PROTECTION STATUS: Federal Species of Concern

158. Pool sprite; little amphianthus

Amphianthus pusillus Torrey
Am-phi-án-thus pu-síl-lus
Scrophulariaceae (Figwort Family)

DESCRIPTION: Diminutive annual herb; leaves both floating and submerged; submerged leaves less than 0.4″ long and in a rosette at the tip of a short stem; floating leaves in single pairs at the tips of threadlike stems, ovate, and less than 0.3″ long; flowers tiny, in clusters in the axils of both floating and submerged leaves, white to pale violet; flowers March–April.

RANGE-HABITAT: Endemic to granitic flatrocks in the piedmont of AL, GA, and SC; very rare in SC; granitic flatrocks in shallow soil of rock-rimmed depressions that hold water after a rain; only three populations known from SC, one of which is at Flat Creek Heritage Preserve.

COMMENTS: The presence of both exposed and submerged flowers provides for both cross- and self-pollination. Based on the extremely low amount of genetic diversity found both within and between populations, self-pollination has apparently been the primary mode of sexual reproduction.

PROTECTION STATUS: Federal Threatened

159. Elf orpine

Diamorpha smallii Britton ex Small
Di-a-mór-pha smáll-i-i
Crassulaceae (Stonecrop Family)

DESCRIPTION: Annual herb to 4″ tall; leaves fleshy, cylindrical, to 0.25″ long, reddish; fruit opening by a small flap on the undersides of each follicle; flowers April–May.

RANGE-HABITAT: From sc. VA to ec. AL, and locally north into se. TN; in SC common on granitic flatrocks in the piedmont, rare on sandstone outcrops in the coastal plain, and rare on granitic domes in the mountains.

COMMENTS: This species is uncommon because of its restricted habitat. It occurs on isolated flatrocks that are as small as 0.02 acres. Its habitat is shallow soils of rock-rimmed depressions that hold water following a rain and on sunny outcrop margins.

SYNONYM: *Sedum smallii* (Britton ex Small) Ahles—RAB

160. Flatrock phacelia

Phacelia maculata Wood
Pha-cè-li-a ma-cu-là-ta
Hydrophyllaceae (Waterleaf Family)

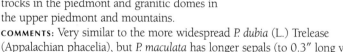

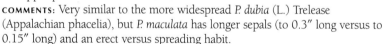

DESCRIPTION: Erect or sometimes sprawling annual herb, 4–16″ tall; stems hairy; leaves pinnately divided; flowers pale blue to white, spotted with purple; inflorescence a coiled terminal flower cluster that straightens and elongates as the flowers reach maturity; flowers April.

RANGE-HABITAT: NC to GA, and west to LA; in SC uncommon on and around granitic flatrocks in the piedmont and granitic domes in the upper piedmont and mountains.

COMMENTS: Very similar to the more widespread *P. dubia* (L.) Trelease (Appalachian phacelia), but *P. maculata* has longer sepals (to 0.3″ long versus to 0.15″ long) and an erect versus spreading habit.

161. Woolly ragwort

Senecio tomentosus Michaux
Se-né-ci-o to-men-tò-sus
Asteraceae (Aster or Sunflower Family)

DESCRIPTION: Perennial herb; stems 8–30″ tall with dense, white hairs; leaves toothed, basal, and on stem; heads of ray and disc flowers, both yellow, in open, terminal, flat-topped clusters; flowers April–early June.

RANGE-HABITAT: NJ to FL, and west to TX; in SC uncommon; moist, open habitats on or around granitic flatrocks in the piedmont; rare on moist sands in the coastal plain.

COMMENTS: Many ragworts contain highly poisonous alkaloids.

SYNONYM: *Packera tomentosa* (Michaux) A & D. Löve—W

162. Piedmont sandwort

Minuartia uniflora (Walter) Mattfeld
Mi-nu-ár-ti-a u-ni-flò-ra
Caryophyllaceae (Pink Family)

DESCRIPTION: Small, smooth annual with basal rosette and taproot, to 5″ tall; leaves narrow, to 0.20″ long; flowers April–May.

RANGE-HABITAT: From NC south to GA, west to AL; generally in the piedmont, but extending into the coastal plain of GA and AL; in SC on granitic flatrocks of the lower piedmont; common.

COMMENTS: Piedmont sandwort can be seen at Flat Creek Heritage Preserve.

SYNONYM: *Arenaria uniflora* (Walter) Muhlenburg—RAB

163. Appalachian fameflower

Talinum teretifolium Pursh
Ta-lì-num te-re-ti-fò-li-um
Portulacaceae (Purslane Family)

DESCRIPTION: Smooth, fleshy, perennial herb, 4–14″ tall; leaves cylindrical, arranged low on the stem; flowering stem long, with few, pink flowers in an open terminal cluster; flowers June–September.

RANGE-HABITAT: PA and WV, south to GA and AL; in SC common in the piedmont and mountains in shallow soils on granitic flatrocks and granitic domes.

COMMENTS: The flowers only open between 3–7 P.M. eastern standard time.

164. Outcrop rushfoil

Crotonopsis elliptica Willdenow
Cro-to-nóp-sis el-líp-ti-ca
Euphorbiaceae (Spurge Family)

DESCRIPTION: Annual herb to 14″ tall, with dichotomous or trichotomous branching; entire plant, except leaves, with red spots and starlike hairs; leaves alternate; male and female flowers on separate plants; flowers June–October.

RANGE-HABITAT: From CT, PA, IL, and se. KS, south to FL and TX; in SC chiefly in the piedmont; common; granitic flatrocks, thin soils around other outcrops, and sandy disturbed soil; on and around granitic domes in the upper piedmont and mountains.

SYNONYM: *Croton willdenowii* Webster—W

165. Pineweed; orange-grass

Hypericum gentianoides (L.) Britton, Sterns, & Poggenberg
Hy-pé-ri-cum gen-ti-a-noì-des
Hypericaceae (St. John's-wort Family)

DESCRIPTION: Annual herb with wing-angled stems to 15″ tall, and numerous filiform branches toward the tip; leaves appressed, scalelike, and less than 0.04″ wide; flowers July–October.

RANGE-HABITAT: Widespread in eastern US; common throughout SC in and around granitic flatrocks, granitic domes, and in sandy fields and roadsides.

COMMENTS: The bruised stems emit a fragrance that is like citrus orange.

166. Woolly lip-fern

Cheilanthes tomentosa Link
Chei-lán-thes to-men-tò-sa
Pteridaceae (Maidenhair Fern Family)

DESCRIPTION: Creeping or ascending evergreen fern; blades 3-pinnate; frond stalks and blades densely hairy.

RANGE-HABITAT: Primarily Appalachian, from PA south to KY, GA, and LA, and scattered localities west; in SC a mountain and piedmont fern; occasional; shale, granite, sandstone, and other rock outcrops.

167. Rocky shoals

167. Rocky-shoals spiderlily

Hymenocallis coronaria (Leconte) Kunth
Hy-me-no-cál-lis co-ro-nà-ri-a
Amaryllidaceae (Amaryllis Family)

DESCRIPTION: Perennial herb from a large bulb; bulb usually wedged in rock crevices; leaves basal, to 1.6″ wide and 32″ long; flowering stalk 1–3 per plant, to more than 40″ tall, each with an umbel of 6–9 flowers; flowers about 6″ across; flowers mid-May–mid-June.

RANGE-HABITAT: NC (?), SC, GA, and AL; rare in the piedmont; found in rocky shoals of major rivers and streams, which are rare.

COMMENTS: The taxonomy of *Hymenocallis* is controversial. Rocky-shoals spiderlily is more robust than any of the other species in SC, and its habitat is distinctive.

PROTECTION STATUS: Federal Species of Concern

168. Black willow

Salix nigra Marshall
   Sà-lix nì-gra
Salicaceae (Willow Family)

DESCRIPTION: Fast-growing, short-lived deciduous tree to 60′+ tall; leaves lanceolate, green beneath; male and female flowers in catkins, on separate plants; catkins produced before or during leaf expansion; capsules with many tiny, silky-haired seeds that readily disperse by wind; flowers March–April.

RANGE-HABITAT: Throughout eastern North America; common throughout SC; riverbanks, rocky streamsides, sandbars, and other open, moist areas.

SIMILAR SPECIES: Black willow is similar to swamp willow (*S. caroliniana* Michaux); the leaves of black willow are greenish beneath, while the leaves of swamp willow are whitish beneath. Swamp willow is common throughout the coastal plain in similar habitats.

COMMENTS: The dense root systems make black willow an ideal tree for soil stabilization. The light, springy wood is excellent for wickerwork baskets and furniture. The bark and roots contain a bitter (astringent) agent that once made a backcountry spring tonic. The genus *Salix* is a source of salicylic acid, a precursor of aspirin. Native Americans chewed the twigs of willow to relieve headaches. Duke (1997) recommends black willow as a remedy for warts, as well as all the uses for which aspirin is taken.

169. American waterwillow

Justicia americana (L.) Vahl
   Jus-tíc-i-a a-me-ri-cà-na
Acanthaceae (Acanthus Family)

DESCRIPTION: Perennial herb 9–30″ tall; leaves opposite, narrow; flowers purple to white, with purple at the base of the lower lip, and in headlike clusters at the tip of long stalks from the upper leaf axils; flowers June–October.

RANGE-HABITAT: Quebec to WI and MI, south to GA, TX, and KS; in SC common in rocky shoals in the piedmont, occasional along rocky streamsides in the mountains and along sandy streambeds in the sandhills.

COMMENTS: The unusual shape of the flowers is distinctive. The genus honors James Justice, an eighteenth-century Scottish horticulturist and botanist.

170. Basic-mesic forests

171. Dimpled trout lily

Erythronium umbilicatum Parks &
   Hardin subsp. *umbilicatum*
   E-ry-thrò-ni-um um-bi-li-cà-tum
   subsp. um-bi-li-cà-tum
   Liliaceae (Lily Family)

DESCRIPTION: Perennial herb from a bulb; the paired mottled leaves and the single, nodding, yellow flower flecked with purple are distinctive characteristics of the trout lilies; this species is distinguished by the absence of an auricle at the base of the petals, the slight flecking with purple, and the presence of an indentation at the apex of the fruit; flowers February–May.

RANGE-HABITAT: WV, VA, and TN, south to AL and GA; in SC common in the mountains and piedmont, rare in the sandhills and coastal plain, and absent in the maritime strand; bottomlands and dry to mesic upland forests.

COMMENTS: Vegetative development and flowering in late winter and early spring allow this species to take advantage of the sunlight that filters through leafless trees.

172. Shooting star

Dodecatheon meadia L.
   Do-de-cá-the-on meàd-i-a
   Primulaceae (Primrose Family)

DESCRIPTION: Smooth, perennial herb; leaves basal; flowering stalk leafless, terminated by a cluster of nodding flowers; flowers white or pink, the reflexed sepals and petals and erect stamens give the flower a very distinctive appearance; flowers late March–early June.

RANGE-HABITAT: WI and PA south to GA; in SC restricted to the high-calcium soils of basic-mesic forests in the piedmont (occasional) and similar forests in the coastal plain (rare).

COMMENTS: *Dodecatheon* in Greek means "twelve gods," which apparently are not easily seen by anyone other than Linnaeus, the person who described the species. The specific epithet honors Dr. Richard Mead, 1673–1754, an English physician and patron of Mark Catesby.

173. Miccosukee gooseberry; spiny gooseberry

Ribes echinellum (Coville) Rehder
Rì-bes e-chi-nél-lum
Saxifragaceae (Saxifrage Family)

DESCRIPTION: Low shrub with palmately lobed and veined leaves borne alternately on new wood and in clusters on short lateral branches; stiff spines at the nodes; ovary and fruit are densely covered in long, gland-tipped bristles; flowers March–April.

RANGE-HABITAT: Known only from Jefferson County, FL (near Lake Miccosukee), and McCormick County, SC; very rare but locally abundant in basic-mesic forests.

COMMENTS: In SC, this species drops its leaves in August or September and puts on new, small leaves in December, apparently as an adaptation to obtain food from photosynthesis at a time when the generally closed canopy is leafless.

PROTECTION STATUS: Federal Threatened

174. Relict trillium

Trillium reliquum Freeman
Tríl-li-um re-lí-qu-um
Liliaceae (Lily Family)

DESCRIPTION: Low perennial herb; stem 2–8″ long, curved, often positioning the whorled leaves just above the ground; leaves stalkless, elliptic and heavily mottled with blue-green, with a silvery streak down the middle; flowers with a foul odor; flowers March–April.

RANGE-HABITAT: Known only from widely separated populations in GA and SC; locally abundant in a narrow band along the Savannah River at the fall line; calcium-rich soils in hardwood forests of ravines and adjacent bottomlands.

COMMENTS: The curved stem, silver streak down the middle, and anthers prolonged into a distinct beak are characters found in no other trillium in SC.

PROTECTION STATUS: Federal Endangered

175. Pale yellow trillium

Trillium discolor Wray ex Hooker
Tríl-li-um dís-co-lor
Liliaceae (Lily Family)

DESCRIPTION: Herbaceous perennial from a short, thick rhizome; stem erect, to 9″ tall; leaves stalkless, mottled with 2–3 shades of green, sometimes almost circular in outline; petals spoon-shaped, incurved, pale yellow with a greenish or purplish stalklike base; at least one petal terminated by a distinct point; ovary distinctly 6-angled; flowers late March–early May.

RANGE-HABITAT: Restricted to the mountains and piedmont of the Savannah River drainage; rare; basic-mesic forests and cove forests.

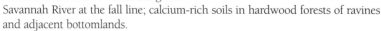

176. Lanceleaf trillium

Trillium lancifolium Rafinesque
Tríl-li-um lan-ci-fò-li-um
Liliaceae (Lily Family)

DESCRIPTION: Low perennial herb from a short horizontal root-stalk; leaves in 1 whorl of 3, sessile, and mottled with an irregular streak of silvery green through the middle; the single sessile flower is terminal and erect, with green, reflexed sepals and maroon, lanceolate petals that point straight up; flowers late March–April.

RANGE-HABITAT: TN south to FL panhandle; in SC known from only a few populations in the lower piedmont and inner coastal plain within the drainage of the Savannah River; rare; basic-mesic forests or bottomland hardwoods on calcium-rich soils.

COMMENTS: This plant has a unique symmetry; the leaves are parallel to the ground, the sepals point straight downward, and the petals point straight up.

177. Southern nodding trillium

Trillium rugelii Rendle
Tríl-li-um ru-gél-i-i
Liliaceae (Lily Family)

DESCRIPTION: Perennial herb from a thick rhizome; stem to 18″ tall, but usually less than 12″ in SC; leaves uniformly bright green, broader than long; flower stalk strongly recurved, positioning the flower beneath the leaves; petals broadly ovate, thick in texture, white or maroon, margins straight; stamens at most 1.5x longer than the pistil; filaments shorter than the ovary; anther sacs purple; flowers April–early May.

RANGE-HABITAT: TN, NC, SC, GA, and AL; in the mountains found in calcium-rich soils of rich cove forests; in the piedmont found on slopes and floodplains of basic-mesic forests.

COMMENTS: Nodding trillium is included under *T. cernuum* L. in Radford et al. (1968). *T. cernuum* is now considered to be restricted to the northeastern US, and *T. rugelii* is restricted to the southeast. The specific epithet honors Ferdinand Rugel, 1806–1878.

178. Dutchman's breeches

Dicentra cucullaria (L.) Bernhardi
Di-cén-tra cu-cul-là-ri-a
Fumariaceae (Fumitory Family)

DESCRIPTION: Perennial herb from a bulblet-bearing rootstalk; leaves basal, with long leaf stalks and deeply dissected blades; flowers March–April.

RANGE-HABITAT: Widespread, from Nova Scotia to GA and AR, and in a few western states; rare in SC and restricted to basic-mesic forests in the piedmont and rich cove forests in the mountains.

COMMENTS: The resemblance of the flowers to a "Dutchman's breeches" led believers in the Doctrine of Signatures to think this plant was useful in the treatment of syphilis.

PROTECTION STATUS: State Endangered

179. False rue-anemone

Isopyrum biternatum (Rafinesque) Torrey & Gray
I-so-pỳ-rum bi-ter-nà-tum
Ranunculaceae (Buttercup Family)

DESCRIPTION: Herbaceous perennial that withers and disappears by mid-May; 4–16" tall; basal leaves on long stalks, 2–3x ternately compound, with 3-lobed leaflets; stem leaves smaller and with only 3 leaflets; flowers less than 0.75" in diameter, with 5, white, petal-like sepals; flowers solitary, terminal, and in few-flowered clusters in the axils of upper leaves; flowers March–April; fruit a cluster of 4 podlike follicles.

RANGE-HABITAT: Ontario, NY, and MN, south to AR and FL; in SC known only from the lower piedmont; rare; basic-mesic forests.

COMMENTS: False rue-anemone is similar in appearance to windflower (*Thalictrum thalictroides,* plate 53), which has a terminal umbel of white flowers and a fruit that is a cluster of achenes. Vegetatively these two look-alikes can be distinguished by the single tier of leaves in windflower versus the multitiered leaves of false rue-anemone.

SYNONYM: *Enemion biternatum* Rafinesque—W

180. Southern stoneseed

Lithospermum tuberosum Rugel ex
Augustin de Candolle
Li-tho-spér-mum tu-be-rò-sum
Boraginaceae (Borage Family)

DESCRIPTION: Rough perennial 8–28" tall; stems slender, branched above; basal leaves clustered or in a rosette; stem leaves smaller, remote; inflorescence a spiraled cyme; flowers March–June.

RANGE-HABITAT: KY and TN, south to FL and LA: in SC rare and reported from the piedmont counties of McCormick and Abbeville; basic-mesic forests and other nutrient-rich forests.

COMMENTS: South Carolina represents the northern range of stoneseed. It grows at Stevens Creek Heritage Preserve.

PROTECTION STATUS: State Endangered

181. Early saxifrage

Saxifraga virginiensis Michaux
Sax-íf-ra-ga vir-gi-ni-én-sis
Saxifragaceae (Saxifraga Family)

DESCRIPTION: Perennial herb with basal leaves only; plant 4–20″ tall; hairy flower stalk has branched clusters of fragrant, white flowers; flowers March–May.

RANGE-HABITAT: New Brunswick west to Manitoba, south to GA, LA, and AR; common throughout the piedmont of SC; basic-mesic forests, rock outcrops, and moist alluvial forests and slopes.

COMMENTS: Early saxifrage does well in shaded rock gardens.

182. Lanceleaf anemone

Anemone lancifolia Pursh
A-ne-mò-ne lan-ci-fò-li-a
Ranunculaceae (Buttercup Family)

DESCRIPTION: Herbaceous perennial, to 16″ tall; with stem and basal leaves; stem leaves whorled, dissected into 3 segments, the outer segments not deeply cut; flowers single on erect stalks; petals absent; sepals white; flowers March–May.

RANGE-HABITAT: From s. PA south to GA, and west to AL; in SC common throughout the piedmont, occasional in the mountains; basic-mesic forests, cove forests, and hardwood bottoms.

SIMILAR SPECIES: Lanceleaf anemone is similar to *A. quinquefolia* L. Lanceleaf anemone has leaves with 3 segments, the lateral segments not deeply cut; *A. quinquefolia* has leaves dissected into 5 segments, or 3 segments and the lateral segments deeply cut. *A. quinquefolia* is a mountain plant.

183. Eastern slender toothwort

Cardamine angustata O. E. Schulz var. *angustata*
Car-dá-mi-ne an-gus-tà-ta var. an-gus-tà-ta
Brassicaceae (Mustard Family)

DESCRIPTION: Perennial herb with segmented, white rhizome; rhizome segments 0.75–1.5″ long; stems 8–16″ tall; basal leaves usually present; stem leaves usually 2, subopposite, palmately divided; flowers March–April.

RANGE-HABITAT: NJ and IN south to n. GA, c. TN, and ne. MS; in SC scattered in the piedmont, rare in the coastal plain; basic-mesic forests and alluvial forests.

COMMENTS: This species grows in basic-mesic forests at Flat Creek Heritage Preserve.

184. Wild ginger

Asarum canadense L.
Á-sa-rum ca-na-dén-se
Aristolochiaceae (Birthwort Family)

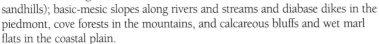

DESCRIPTION: Rhizome-producing, perennial herb, growing at ground level; leaves opposite, in pairs on a stem; flower solitary, arising between the 2 leaf stalks; flowers often inconspicuous, hidden by the forest litter; flowers April–May.

RANGE-HABITAT: Quebec to Manitoba and south to NC, SC, GA, AL, AR, and KS; uncommon throughout SC (absent in the sandhills); basic-mesic slopes along rivers and streams and diabase dikes in the piedmont, cove forests in the mountains, and calcareous bluffs and wet marl flats in the coastal plain.

COMMENTS: Wild ginger is a plant of many uses. The rhizomes have a strong odor similar to true ginger and can be used as a substitute. Native Americans made candy of the rhizomes by boiling until tender, then dipping in syrup. Numerous sources suggest, however, that consumption of excessive amounts of *Asarum* should be avoided because it may have cancer-causing properties.

TAXONOMY: Several varieties have been recognized, differing in the shape and position of the sepals; some botanists consider them distinct species.

185. Whorled horsebalm

Collinsonia verticillata Baldwin
Col-lin-sòn-i-a ver-ti-cil-là-ta
Lamiaceae (Mint Family)

DESCRIPTION: Perennial herb from a thick, tuberous rootstalk; stem 8–30″ tall and unbranched; leaves obovate, margins coarsely toothed, well-developed leaves in 2 (1, 3) pairs, appearing whorled; flowers in a narrow, terminal, panicle-like cluster; petals lavender to purplish, or rarely yellow, the middle lobe of the lower lip long and fringed; flowers late April–June.

RANGE-HABITAT: TN, OH, VA, NC, SC, GA, and MS; in SC known only from the upper piedmont, where it is rare and restricted to basic-mesic forests.

COMMENTS: The two pairs of opposite leaves, appearing whorled, is distinctive to this species.

186. Roundleaf ragwort

Senecio obovatus Muhlenberg ex Willdenow
Se-né-ci-o o-bo-và-tus
Asteraceae (Aster or Sunflower Family)

DESCRIPTION: Perennial with aboveground stolons; the basal cluster of obovate-shaped leaves is distinctive to this species of *Senecio* in SC; flowers April–June.

RANGE-HABITAT: Widespread in the eastern US; uncommon in the mountains and piedmont of SC and restricted to calcium-rich soils of basic-mesic forests and rich cove forests.

COMMENTS: An easy-to-recognize species whose presence suggests the presence of other interesting species.

SYNONYM: *Packera obovata* (Muhlenberg ex Willdenow) W. A. Weber & A. Love—W

187. Hairy spiderwort

Tradescantia hirsuticaulis Small
Tra-des-cánt-i-a hir-su-ti-caù-lis
Commelinaceae (Spiderwort Family)

DESCRIPTION: Perennial herb to 15″ tall; stem densely hairy, 1–several from a root crown; leaves densely hairy, the opened leaf sheath as wide as or wider than the leaf; flowers blue to rose, with a mix of glandular and nonglandular hairs; flowers April–June.

RANGE-HABITAT: NC, SC, GA, AL, AR, and OK; occasional in the piedmont and rare in the mountains; dry woods adjacent to rock outcrops, especially on calcium-rich soils upslope from basic-mesic forests, and around granitic outcrops or domes.

COMMENTS: The dense hairiness of this spiderwort appears to be distinctive, but some researchers apparently question the validity of this species. The genus honors John, the elder Tradescant, ?-1637, gardener to Charles the First of England.

188. Appalachian mock-orange

Philadelphus inodorus L.
Phi-la-dél-phus i-no-dò-rus
Saxifragaceae (Saxifrage Family)

DESCRIPTION: Shrub usually 4–8′ tall; stems reddish brown; leaves opposite, smooth below; flowers white, petals 4, styles separate above; sepals erect in fruit; flowers April–May.

RANGE-HABITAT: VA and TN, south to GA and AL; in SC common in the mountains and piedmont, rare in the coastal plain; rich woods and rocky bluffs, especially over calcium-rich soils.

SIMILAR SPECIES: The rare, hairy mock-orange (*P. hirsutus* Nuttall) occupies similar habitats and is distinguished by its dense, soft hairs on the lower leaf surface; united styles; and nonerect sepals in fruit.

189. Cancer-root

Orobanche uniflora L.
O-ro-bán-che u-ni-flò-ra
Orobanchaceae (Broomrape Family)

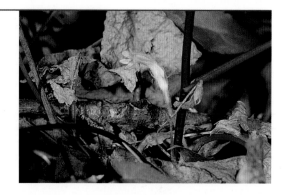

DESCRIPTION: Root parasite lacking chlorophyll; stems often clustered, mostly underground, 0.5–2″ long, with bract-like leaves; flowers white to violet, terminal and solitary on a flower stalk 2–5″ long; flowers April–May.

RANGE-HABITAT: Widespread in the US; throughout but occasional in SC; basic-mesic forests, levee forests, cove forests, and on streamsides.

190. Painted buckeye

Aesculus sylvatica Bartram
Aès-cu-lus syl-vá-ti-ca
Hippocastanaceae (Buckeye Family)

DESCRIPTION: Shrub or small tree, seldom over 20–25′ tall; leaves deciduous, palmately compound with 5 leaflets; flowers yellow-green to cream, tinged with red; stamens included or barely longer than the petals; flowers April–mid-May; capsule leathery, with 1–3 large, dark brown, shiny seeds; matures July–August.

RANGE-HABITAT: Southeastern U.S., from sc. VA south through c. NC, c. SC, and nc. GA to nc. AL; common in the low mountains and piedmont, uncommon in the inner coastal plain; cove forests, basic-mesic forests, alluvial swamp forests, and riverbanks.

COMMENTS: Painted buckeye is an excellent ornamental in shady, mesic forest sites along slopes and bluffs. Wildlife use this tree little if at all because the leaves and seeds are poisonous. The crushed fruits were once used to stupefy fish for easy harvest.

191. Virginia marbleseed

Onosmodium virginianum (L.)
Alphonse de Candolle
O-nos-mò-di-um vir-gi-ni-à-num
Boraginaceae (Borage Family)

DESCRIPTION: Harsh, strigose, perennial herb 8–32″ tall; stems slender, branched above; corolla light yellow to orange; flowers in a coiled, terminal arrangement that straightens as the flowers mature; flowers April–September.

RANGE-HABITAT: LA to FL, north to NY and MA; occasional throughout SC; barrens, glades, or woodlands over calcareous rocks in the mountains, basic-mesic forests in the piedmont, woodlands in the sandhills, and shell deposits and sandy woodlands in the coastal plain.

COMMENTS: Weakley (2001) states that the unifying factor determining its distribution may be open woodland conditions maintained by fire and that it generally occurs in small populations.

192. Green violet

Hybanthus concolor (Forster) Sprengel
   Hy-bán-thus cón-co-lor
Violaceae (Violet Family)

DESCRIPTION: Perennial herb; stems erect, 1.2–3′ tall, 1–several from the base; flowers green, irregular, nodding; flowers that never open are tiny and solitary in the axils of the uppermost leaves; flowers that open are produced in clusters in the axils of lower leaves; flowers late May–June.

RANGE-HABITAT: Widespread in the eastern US; occasional in SC; restricted to the piedmont and mountains; basic-mesic forests and rich cove forests.

COMMENTS: Although not appearing violetlike, it shares many technical features with the genus *Viola*, including the production of some flowers that open and are cross-pollinated and other flowers that never open and are self-pollinated.

193. Columbo

Frasera caroliniensis Walter
   Frà-ser-a ca-ro-li-ni-én-sis
Gentianaceae (Gentian Family)

DESCRIPTION: Robust biennial or triennial herb, 3–8′ tall; leaves 4–12″ long, in whorls of 3–9; flowers form an ample inflorescence at the summit; each of the 4 greenish yellow corolla lobes bears a gland surrounded by a fringe of hairs; flowers late May–June.

RANGE-HABITAT: From w. NY and s. Ontario, west to IL, MI, MO, and e. OK, south to w. SC, n. GA, and LA; in SC rare and known from only Fairfield, Newberry, Abbeville, Laurens, and Greenwood Counties; wooded slopes adjacent to streams or within the stream floodplain.

COMMENTS: Columbo was a drug erroneously believed to have come from Colombo in Ceylon, and *Frasera* provided a substitute. A root tea was used for a variety of folk remedies, including treatment for colic, cramps, dysentery, and diarrhea; also used as a general tonic. Thomas Walter honored his publisher, John Fraser, 1750–1811, by naming this genus in his honor.

SYNONYM: *Swertia caroliniensis* (Walter) Kuntze—RAB

PROTECTION STATUS: State Threatened

194. Bottlebrush buckeye

Aesculus parviflora Walter
Aès-cu-lus par-vi-flò-ra
Hippocastanaceae (Buckeye Family)

DESCRIPTION: Shrub or occasionally trees to 16′ tall; leaves deciduous, opposite, palmately compound with 5–7 leaflets; inflorescence narrow; flowers white with stamens 3–4x the length of the petals; flowers June–July; fruits with 1–2 seeds, mature October–November.

RANGE-HABITAT: From Aiken County SC southwest to AL; a southeastern endemic known only from Aiken County in SC; deciduous forests on fall-line river bluffs over calcium-rich soils.

SIMILAR SPECIES: Bottlebrush buckeye is easily separated in flower from *Aesculus sylvatica* (plate 190) by its long-protruding stamens; in the latter, the stamens are included or are slightly longer than the petals.

COMMENTS: Bottlebrush buckeye is found in the Savannah River Bluffs Heritage Preserve in Aiken County. Although not often used, this buckeye makes an excellent ornamental. "Bottlebrush" refers to the distinctive cluster of flowers with long stamens.

PROTECTION STATUS: State Endangered

195. Moonseed

Menispermum canadense L.
Me-ni-spér-mum ca-na-dén-se
Menispermaceae (Moonseed Family)

DESCRIPTION: Twining, woody vine, 8–12′
long; root bright yellow within; leaves peltate,
ovate, 5–7-lobed or angled, whitish beneath;
flowers June–August; drupes blue or bluish
black when mature in late summer.

RANGE-HABITAT: Quebec west to Manitoba,
south to GA and OK; scattered throughout SC
in moist nutrient-rich forests, especially on
floodplains, and lower slopes of basic-mesic
forests.

COMMENTS: The fruits, sometimes mistaken for grapes, are poisonous if eaten in
large quantities. Foster and Duke (1990) and Krochmal and Krochmal (1973)
report a myriad of folk uses of this plant, especially by Native Americans.

196. American ginseng

Panax quinquefolius L.
Pà-nax quin-que-fò-li-us
Araliaceae (Ginseng Family)

DESCRIPTION: Smooth, hairless perennial herb
with a fusiform root and single stem, 8–24″
tall; leaves palmately compound with 3–5
leaflets; flowers in terminal, solitary umbels;
flowers May–June; drupes mature
August–October.

RANGE-HABITAT: Quebec west to MN and SD,
south to e. VA, NC, SC, GA, c. AL, LA, and
OK; in SC rare and scattered in the mountains

and piedmont; basic-mesic forests, cove forests, and mesic deciduous forests. **COMMENTS:** The Chinese highly prize ginseng root as an aphrodisiac and heart stimulant. In our country it is in demand as a tonic. With America's rediscovery of the healing power of plants, more pressure is being put on native populations of ginseng and other plants. Formally abundant and occurring in large populations, ginseng has been reduced in most of its range to small, scattered populations. Today's method of collection has not helped. Rural people in past days would remove the fruits from the plant and plant them, ensuring future populations. Much of the collections today is done in haste, often before the plants produce mature fruits, and the seeds are not planted. Today in SC, it is hard to find good populations. Duke (1997) recommends ginseng as an herbal remedy for loss of libido and memory loss associated with aging.

197. *Beech forests*

198. Round-lobed liverleaf

Hepatica americana (Augustin de
    Candolle) Ker-Gawler
He-pá-ti-ca a-me-ri-cà-na
Ranunculaceae (Buttercup Family)

DESCRIPTION: Herbaceous perennial from a short rhizome; leaves basal, purplish beneath, 3-lobed, the lobes rounded; petals absent; sepals bluish, rarely white or pink; flowers February–April.

RANGE-HABITAT: Widespread in eastern North America; in SC common in the piedmont, rare in the mountains and coastal plain; moist, rich, deciduous forests.

COMMENTS: The genus name refers to the 3-lobed leaf that supposedly resembles the 3-lobed human liver, which early herbalists assumed to be effective in treating liver aliments. A "liver tonic" boom resulted in the consumption of 450,000 pounds of the dried leaves in 1883 alone. No medical evidence exists that indicates liverleaf has any medical benefit in treating liver diseases. Liverleaf often grows at the base of trees, prompting someone to call this plant "squirrel-cups."

199. Devil's-bit

Chamaelirium luteum (L.) Gray
Cha-mae-lí-ri-um lù-te-um
Liliaceae (Lily Family)

DESCRIPTION: Perennial herb with separate male and female plants; female plants to more than 3′ tall, male plants much shorter and less showy; flowers white, turning yellow on drying; flowers March–May.

RANGE-HABITAT: MA and Ontario, south to FL, AR, and LA; common in the mountains and piedmont; rare in the coastal plain; wide variety of upland and lowland habitats, including beech forests, oak-hickory forests, cove forests, hardwood bottoms, pocosin edges, and wet pine savannas.

COMMENTS: The pale green basal leaves are distinctive, as are the wandlike terminal clusters of flowers.

200. Halberd-leaved violet; spearleaf violet

Viola hastata Michaux
Vi-o-la has-tà-ta
Violaceae (Violet Family)

DESCRIPTION: Herbaceous perennial with yellow flowers on leafy stems; leaves distinctively spearpoint-shaped, usually mottled with silvery gray areas, and clustered near the tip; flowers late March–May.

RANGE-HABITAT: PA and OH, south to FL and AL; common in the mountains and upper piedmont in moist deciduous forests, especially beech forests, cove forests, and moist oak-hickory forests.

201. Common silverbell

Halesia tetraptera Ellis
Hàles-i-a te-tráp-te-ra
Styracaceae (Storax Family)

DESCRIPTION: Deciduous shrub or tree to 50′ tall; young stems with a distinctive pattern of dark and light stripes; flowers white, bell-shaped, 0.6–0.8″ long, on long stalks and drooping in clusters from the twigs of the previous year; style included or slightly exserted; fruit broadly 4-winged and 1.2–2″ long, broadest near the middle; flowers March–May; fruits mature August–September.

RANGE-HABITAT: From w. VA, WV, s. OH, and s. IL, south to FL and e. TX; throughout SC (but absent in the maritime strand); common in the mountains and upper piedmont, occasional in the lower piedmont and coastal plain; moist slopes, creek banks, river bottoms, beech woods, and cove forests.

COMMENTS: Silverbells are excellent native shrubs and small trees for planting in gardens, especially along streambanks, either in shade or full sun. The snow-white flowers are spectacular in the spring. They can either be planted in groups or as single plants. Nurseries in the southeast are beginning to carry stock of silverbells due to the increased demand. Veneer from its wood, when the log is turned against the rotary, has a beautiful bird's-eye figure. The genus honors Stephen Hales, 1677–1761, the author of *Vegetable Statics*.

TAXONOMY: Taxonomists now recognize *H. tetraptera* (= *H. carolina* L. in the *Manual*) as the common silverbell, and *H. carolina* (= *H. parviflora* Michaux in most manuals, including the *Manual*) as Carolina silverbell, which is rare in the piedmont and has corollas 0.3–0.5″ long, styles strongly protruding, fruit broadest towards the tip, and narrowly winged.

202. Green-and-gold

Chrysogonum virginianum var. *australe*
   (Alexander ex Small) Ahles
   Chry-só-go-num vir-gi-ni-à-num
   var. aus-trà-le
Asteraceae (Aster or Sunflower Family)

DESCRIPTION: Fibrous-rooted, herbaceous perennial, flowering early when very small; at first stemless or short-stemmed, but later flowering stems elongating to 4″ tall; leaves opposite; flowers late March–early June.

RANGE-HABITAT: From se. SC, nw. NC, and e. TN, south to FL, and ec. AL; piedmont, sandhills, and coastal plain; common; moist to fairly dry forests and woodlands.

TAXONOMY: Some authors recognize two varieties: *C. virginianum* var. *australe* and *C. virginianum* L. var. *virginianum*. Variety *australe* forms mats by stolons and has flowering stems mostly 4″ tall; var. *virginianum* is cespitose, without stolons or mat forming, with flowering stems 6–12″ tall. Variety *virginianum* occurs in the southeast piedmont of SC, while var. *australe* occurs in the south coastal plain and piedmont.

203. Arrowleaf; heartleaf

Hexastylis arifolia (Michaux) Small
   Hex-ás-ty-lis a-ri-fò-li-a
Aristolochiaceae (Birthwort Family)

DESCRIPTION: Rhizomatous, perennial herb with no aboveground stem; leaves arrowhead-shaped, aromatic, evergreen, often in clusters; flowers without petals; calyx flask-shaped; flowers often hidden under leaf litter; flowers March–May.

RANGE-HABITAT: From se. VA west to sw. VA, south to n. FL and s. MS; common throughout SC in dry to moist deciduous forests.

COMMENTS: This is the common heartleaf in SC and is the only heartleaf with arrowhead-shaped leaves.

204. Pennywort

Obolaria virginica L.
O-bo-là-ri-a vir-gí-ni-ca
Gentianaceae (Gentian Family)

DESCRIPTION: Fleshy perennial, 3–6″ tall; roots brittle; leaves opposite; flowers usually in groups of three in the axils of purplish, bract-like leaves; flowers March–April.

RANGE-HABITAT: NJ to IL, and south to FL and TX; in SC common throughout the mountains and piedmont; rare in the coastal plain; moist, nutrient-rich forests.

COMMENTS: Pennywort is often overlooked because of its small size, especially during early growth. Obolaria is a monotypic genus. The genus name comes from obolos, a Greek coin, similar to a penny, in reference to its round leaves.

205. May-apple; mandrake

Podophyllum peltatum L.
Po-do-phýl-lum pel-tà-tum
Berberidaceae (Barberry Family)

DESCRIPTION: Smooth, rhizomatous, perennial herb 12–18″ tall; solitary, nodding flower from the base of a pair of large, deeply lobed leaves; leaves deciduous; leaf stalk attached in the center on the underside of the leaf; flowers March–April; berry yellow or red when ripe in May–June.

RANGE-HABITAT: Widespread throughout most of eastern North America; common throughout SC in rich forests, bottomlands, meadows, pastures, and along moist road banks.

COMMENTS: Today, alkaloids from the rhizomes are being used as the basis of a drug to treat lymphocytic leukemia and testicular cancer. The plant has long been known to contain antitumor alkaloids. Native Americans used extracts of the rhizomes as purgatives and for skin disorders and tumorous growths. The leaves, rhizomes, and seeds are poisonous if eaten in large quantities. Ripe fruits can be made into marmalade. Only two-leaf plants bear flowers; the single-leaf plants never develop flowers.

206. Bloodroot

Sanguinaria canadensis L.
San-gui-ná-ri-a ca-na-dén-sis
Papaveraceae (Poppy Family)

DESCRIPTION: Perennial herb, 4–16″ tall, with no leafy stem; rhizome with bright orange-red juice; flower single on a leafless stem, opening in the day, closing at night and lasting only a short time; the single leaf continues to enlarge after the petals drop; flowers early March–April.

RANGE-HABITAT: Bloodroot ranges from Nova Scotia west to MN and Manitoba, south to FL and OK; in SC it grows chiefly in the mountains and piedmont, common; scattered in the coastal plain; in a variety of moist, nutrient-rich forests.

COMMENTS: Native Americans used the red juice from the roots to dye baskets and clothing and to make war paint. They used the sap as an insect repellent and used the dried root to cure rattlesnake bites. Appalachian crafters today still use the red juice to dye baskets and cloth. When it became known that the Native American's use of the root was somewhat successful in treating tumors, interest in the plant increased. Duke (1997) recommends bloodroot as an herbal remedy for gingivitis and tooth decay. Viadent toothpaste contains bloodroot extracts.

207. Allegheny spurge

Pachysandra procumbens Michaux
    Pa-chy-sán-dra pro-cúm-bens
    Buxaceae (Boxwood Family)

DESCRIPTION: Perennial herb from a woody base; annual stem only 6–9″ long, with the lower portion on the ground and the upper portion erect; the few, alternate leaves are mottled with lighter green and located near the tip of the erect stem; ill-scented flowers consist of 4–5 sepals produced on 1–several elongated stalks that originate from the lower portion of the stem; flowers March–April.

RANGE-HABITAT: KY south to FL panhandle; known only from Pickens County (upper piedmont) in SC; rare; basic-mesic forests; populations can be found along the Eastatoe River in Pickens County.

COMMENTS: In NC this species is restricted to the piedmont of Polk County, where it also occurs only in basic-mesic forests. The major distribution of this species is west of the Blue Ridge Mountains.

PROTECTION STATUS: State Threatened

208. Piedmont barren strawberry

Waldsteinia lobata (Baldwin) Torrey &
    Gray
    Wald-steìn-i-a lo-bà-ta
    Rosaceae (Rose Family)

DESCRIPTION: Evergreen perennial herb forming strawberry-like clumps via short subsurface runners; leaves in basal rosettes, rounded, with a heart-shaped base and 3–5 shallow lobes, each with irregular teeth; flowers March–May; fruits June–July.

RANGE-HABITAT: NC, SC, and GA; known in SC only from the upper piedmont of Oconee County; stream terraces and adjacent slopes in beech forests or oak-hickory forests.

COMMENTS: The leaves turn an attractive burgundy red in the fall, but are retained until replaced by new leaves in the spring. The leaves are quite distinctive, and close attention to their appearance should prevent possible misidentifications. The fruit is brown and dry and "barren" in that it is inedible. The genus honors Francis Adam, 1759–1823, a German botanist and Count of Waldstein-Wartenburg.

PROTECTION STATUS: Federal Species of Concern

209. Giant chickweed; star chickweed

Stellaria pubera Michaux
  Stel-là-ri-a pù-be-ra
Caryophyllaceae (Pink Family)

DESCRIPTION: Perennial herb; stems erect or ascending, 5–12″ tall with hairs in lines or dispersed; flowers white, the 5 petals so deeply incised as to appear to be 10; fruits split to the base to expose seeds; flowers April–June.

RANGE-HABITAT: NJ to IN, and south to FL and AL; common in the mountains and upper piedmont; rare in the sandhills and coastal plain; moist uplands and extending into adjacent hardwood bottoms.

COMMENTS: The common chickweed (*S. media,* plate 611), a weedy species of disturbed habitats, is smaller in all parts and has weak stems. Like common chickweed, giant chickweed may contain compounds that make the plant useful as an herbal medicine.

210. Wild geranium

Geranium maculatum L.
  Ge-rà-ni-um ma-cu-là-tum
Geraniaceae (Geranium Family)

DESCRIPTION: Herbaceous perennial from a thick rhizome; stems 8–24′ tall; basal leaves with long stalks; fruit with a long beak; flowers April–June.

RANGE-HABITAT: MA to Manitoba, south to GA, TN, AR, and SD; in SC chiefly in the mountains and piedmont and common; scattered and rare in the coastal plain; cove forests, bottomland forests, and other mesic, calcium-rich forests.

COMMENTS: Native Americans made a powder from the dried rhizome and used it as a styptic and astringent to slow bleeding from cuts. The method of seed dispersal is unusual. At the base of the fruit are five small cups, facing outward and attached to springy bands that are connected to the top of the fruit. As the bands dry, they come under tension. When touched, they break loose, and the cups are flung outward, throwing the seeds several feet from the plant.

211. American alumroot

Heuchera americana L.
    Heù-cher-a a-me-ri-cà-na
Saxifragaceae (Saxifrage Family)

DESCRIPTION: Rhizomatous perennial with long leaf stalks and rounded blades; 2–3′ tall; stamens with orange anthers that protrude from the flowers; flowers April–June.

RANGE-HABITAT: Throughout eastern North America; in SC primarily a mountain and piedmont species; common; rich woods and basic rock outcrops, particularly where soils are subacidic to circumneutral; rare in the coastal plain, generally on limestone bluffs, and wet, marl flats.

COMMENTS: The genus honors Johann Heinrich Heucher, 1677–1747, a German botanist.

212. Tulip tree; yellow-poplar

Liriodendron tulipifera L.
    Li-ri-o-dén-dron tu-li-pí-fe-ra
Magnoliaceae (Magnolia Family)

DESCRIPTION: Large, straight-trunk tree, 98–165′ tall; deciduous; winter buds flattened and enclosed by two nonoverlapping scales; flowers April–June.

RANGE-HABITAT: Widespread in eastern North America; common throughout SC; most common and typical in moist, rich soils such as cove forests or beech forests; easily moves into drier sites such as abandoned fields and timbered uplands; in the coastal plain, besides growing in rich soils, it grows in fire-maintained, acid soils such as streamhead pocosins, growing with *Pinus serotina, Nyssa biflora,* and *Acer rubrum.*

COMMENTS: Tulip trees of the original forest grew to 165′ tall. The SC state champion tree measured 135′ tall in 1984. Trees grown in forest conditions were 80–100′ tall before producing branches, a feature that made it a superior lumber tree. Tulip tree wood was sawed into lumber more than any other trees, except for pines. Today, its wood has a myriad of uses: interior finishes, furniture, general construction, and plywood. The Charleston furniture maker Thomas Elf (1719–1775) employed it in his works. It is planted as a shade tree. The seeds are an important food for wildlife. The common name comes from the leaves, flowers, and fruits, all resembling cultivated tulips.

213. Thimbleweed

Anemone virginiana L.
A-ne-mò-ne vir-gi-ni-à-na
Ranunculaceae (Buttercup Family)

DESCRIPTION: Herbaceous, hairy perennial, from a short, thick rootstock or rhizome; often growing in colonies; to 3' tall; petals absent and the sepals are showy-white; receptacle in the center of the flower is tall and becomes taller when the pistils mature; flowers May–July.

RANGE-HABITAT: Widespread in eastern North America; in SC primarily a mountain and piedmont species; rich forests and woodlands; rare in the coastal plain in calcareous wooded communities such as limestone bluffs.

COMMENTS: The thimble-shaped cluster of pistils is the distinctive feature of this species and accounts for the common name.

214. Spotted wintergreen; pipsissewa

Chimaphila maculata (L.) Pursh
Chi-má-phi-la ma-cu-là-ta
Ericaceae (Heath Family)

DESCRIPTION: Small rhizomatous herb to 8" tall; leaves evergreen, whorled, and variegated, with white on the midrib and larger veins; flowers nodding, fragrant; flowers May–June.

RANGE-HABITAT: Widespread in eastern North America; common throughout SC; beech, oak-hickory, pine-mixed hardwood forests, and coniferous forests.

COMMENTS: Pipsissewa has had a variety of medicinal uses. Native Americans used the plant to treat kidney stones. They used a poultice from the leaves to heal blisters or to reduce swelling in legs or feet. Early settlers used the leaves to make tea that served as a febrifuge to break the fever associated with typhus. A popular refreshing hot tea was made by pouring boiling water over chopped leaves. Until recently, it was used to flavor commercial root beer.

215. Summer bluet

Houstonia purpurea L.
Hous-tòn-i-a pur-pù-re-a
Rubiaceae (Madder Family)

DESCRIPTION: Perennial herb with several stems from the base; stems often branching near the tip; leaves widest toward the base; flowers in terminal clusters, dark lavender to almost white; flowers May–July.

RANGE-HABITAT: MD to OH and MO, south to GA and TX; common except in the outer coastal plain; found along road banks, around rock outcrops, and in a variety of moist to dry upland forests.

216. Partridge berry; twin-flower

Mitchella repens L.
    Mít-chell-a rè-pens
    Rubiaceae (Madder Family)

DESCRIPTION: Trailing, creeping, evergreen perennial; leaves opposite; flowers in pairs; a single berry forms from the fusion of the ripened ovaries of two flowers, leaving two scars on the mature fruit; flowers May–June; fruits mature in June–July but persist throughout the winter.

RANGE-HABITAT: From Nova Scotia west to MN, south to peninsular FL and TX; common throughout SC; deciduous and coniferous forests, streamsides, and maritime forests.

COMMENTS: The berries are edible although bland and seedy. It makes an excellent groundcover for home gardens, especially under acid-loving shrubs. Native American women made a tea from the leaves as an aid in childbirth. The genus honors Dr. John Mitchell, 1676–1768, an early correspondent of Linnaeus and a VA botanist.

217. Common anglepod

Gonolobus gonocarpus (Walter) Perry
    Go-nó-lo-bus go-no-cár-pus
    Asclepiadaceae (Milkweed Family)

DESCRIPTION: Perennial, twining herb; leaves opposite, widely ovate-elliptic to elliptic-oblong; corolla yellow to greenish brown, smooth within, with petals linear-lanceolate, 3x as long as the sepals; flowers June–July; follicles (fruit) smooth, sharply angled.

RANGE-HABITAT: From VA south to FL, west to TX, and north to KY, MO, and IL; in SC primarily in the piedmont; occasional; beech forests and thickets.

SYNONYM: *Matelea gonocarpa* (Walter) Shinners—RAB

218. Hop hornbeam

Ostrya virginiana (Miller) K. Koch
    Ós-try-a vir-gi-ni-à-na
    Betulaceae (Birch Family)

DESCRIPTION: Small, deciduous tree with brown, shredding bark; occasionally reaching 35–50' tall; male and female catkins produced in April–May; mature female catkin consists of nutlets, each enclosed by membranous inflated sacs, arranged in a spike; fruits mature August–October.

RANGE-HABITAT: Widespread in s. Canada, e., mw, and se. US, and into northern Mexico; in SC chiefly piedmont and mountains; common; mesic to dry forests, especially on calcium-rich soils, reaching high elevations; rare in the coastal plain on lime-stone bluffs and wet, marl flats.

COMMENTS: Hop hornbeam is usually an understory species and not large enough to be of commercial importance. The wood is extremely hard and used to make tool handles. The common name comes from the resemblance of the catkins to commercial hops. "Witches brooms," broomlike clusters of short branches, are common on this species.

219. Strawberry-bush; heart's-a-bustin

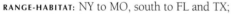

Euonymus americanus L.
Eu-ó-ny-mus a-me-ri-cà-nus
Celastraceae (Bittersweet Family)

DESCRIPTION: Straggling or erect deciduous shrub to 6' tall; stems distinctively dark green; leaves opposite and bright green, on short leaf stalks; flowers greenish, on long stalks from axils of the uppermost leaves; the fruits are distinctive with their warty, red exterior that splits to expose the seeds; flowers May–June; fruits September–October.

RANGE-HABITAT: NY to MO, south to FL and TX; common throughout SC in a variety of upland and lowland forests, including beech forests, oak-hickory forests, cove forests, Canada hemlock forests, hard-wood bottoms, and levee forests.

COMMENTS: The seeds are a strong laxative, and the fruits are toxic, causing coma if consumed in sufficient quantity.

220. American hazelnut

Corylus americana Walter
Có-ry-lus a-me-ri-cà-na
Betulaceae (Birch Family)

DESCRIPTION: Shrub 4–5' tall, forming small colonies; leaves broadly ovate, to 5" long, margins finely doubly serrate; leaf stalk glandular-hairy; fruit a nut enclosed in bracts, widest at apex and lobed into teethlike projections; nut matures September–October.

RANGE-HABITAT: Widespread in eastern North America; in SC rare in the coastal plain and lower piedmont, common in the upper piedmont and mountains; most common in beech forests and other mesic woods, but also found in rocky woodlands and roadside thickets.

COMMENTS: The nuts of this species are every bit as tasty as the commercial hazelnut. Native Americans used twig hairs to expel intestinal worms.

221. Beech-drops

Epifagus virginiana (L.) Barton
E-pi-fà-gus vir-gi-ni-à-na
Orobanchaceae (Broomrape Family)

DESCRIPTION: Holoparasite on the roots of beech trees; annual; plant 4–18″ tall, branched; dried stalks persisting throughout the winter; upper flowers sterile, lower flowers not opening and self-pollinated, producing abundant seeds; leaves reduced to scales; flowers September–November.
RANGE-HABITAT: Nova Scotia west to WI, and south to FL and LA; common throughout SC, wherever beech trees occur.
COMMENTS: The dustlike seeds are carried down through the soil by percolating water where they germinate only in the rhizosphere of beech roots.

222. Beech

Fagus grandifolia Ehrhart
Fà-gus gran-di-fò-li-a
Fagaceae (Beech Family)

DESCRIPTION: Large tree with smooth, gray bark; leaves deciduous, but often remaining throughout the winter; terminal buds long and slender, about 1″ long before just breaking open; flowers in March–April; male and female flowers in separate clusters on the same tree; large fruit production occurs every 2–3 years; fruits mature September–October.
RANGE-HABITAT: Common forest tree of lower

elevations (mostly below 3500′) over most of eastern North America; throughout SC; grows best in rich, moist, loam soils with a high humus content.
COMMENTS: Beech is a beautiful, long-lived tree relatively free from disease and ideal for cultivation. The oily seeds are an important wildlife food. Beech-nut oil has never been important in America, but in Europe beech oil (from *Fagus sylvatica* L.) is an important commercial product. The nut is one of the sweetest in North America. At one time, New England country groceries sold it. The wood has never been an important commercial product. It did gain short-lived fame when it was made into clothespins because of its elastic nature.

Oak-hickory forests

223. Yellow jessamine; Carolina jessamine

Gelsemium sempervirens (L.) Aiton f.
Gel-sè-mi-um sem-pér-vi-rens
Loganiaceae (Logania Family)

DESCRIPTION: Twining (left to right), woody
vine with opposite, pointed, evergreen leaves;
trailing or high-climbing; blades smooth,
entire; flowers fragrant; flowers (February)
March–early May; fruit a capsule, mature September–November, persistent into spring.
RANGE-HABITAT: VA to FL, west to e. TX and
AR; common throughout the piedmont, sandhills, coastal plain, and maritime strand;
longleaf pine flatwoods and savannas, oak-hickory, beech, pine-mixed hardwood and maritime forests, lowland woods where water stands only for short
periods, fencerows, thickets, and along roadsides.
COMMENTS: This is the state flower of SC and a harbinger of spring. All parts are
poisonous. According to Foster and Duke (1990), it can cause contact dermatitis. Children have been poisoned by sucking nectar from the flowers, probably
mistaking them for honeysuckle. F. P. Porcher (1869) and Foster and Duke
(1990) list many historical medicinal uses of this plant; however, no current
uses of the plant appear in the literature.

Yellow jessamine is often cultivated and when grown in full sunlight
becomes denser and more attractive than when growing naturally. It can be used
on trellises and as a groundcover.

224. Eastern redbud; Judas-tree

Cercis canadensis L.
Cér-cis ca-na-dén-sis
Fabaceae (Pea or Bean Family)

DESCRIPTION: Small, short-lived tree with
alternate, simple, deciduous, heart-shaped
leaves; flowers borne on old wood, appearing
in spring before the leaves; flowers
March–May.
RANGE-HABITAT: From s. Ontario to TX and
FL; common throughout SC; most often on
rich, moist sites; oak-hickory, beech, and
pine-mixed hardwood forests, river bottoms
and streamsides, forests over calcareous soil or
mafic rocks, and maritime shell hummocks.
COMMENTS: Redbud is one of the most popular native trees in cultivation. It is
an understory tree whose trunk is too small to be commercially important. The
flowers have an acidlike flavor and are put into salads. Also, the flower buds can
be pickled. The buds, flowers, and young pods are good when fried in butter or
made into fritters.

The common name, Judas-tree, is sometimes transferred to the eastern redbud from the related species of the Mediterranean (*Cercis siliquastrum* L.), the
tree on which Judas hanged himself. Legend states that the flowers were white
but turned to red either with shame or from the drops of blood shed by Jesus.

225. Squaw-root

Conopholis americana (L.) Wallroth
Co-nó-pho-lis a-me-ri-cà-na
Orobanchaceae (Broomrape Family)

DESCRIPTION: Herbaceous holoparasite on roots of the red oak group; 3–10″ tall; leaves reduced to brown scales; entire plant pale brown or yellow brown; flowers March–June.
RANGE-HABITAT: Nova Scotia west to WI, south to peninsular FL, AL, and TN; common throughout SC; under species of red oak in rich, moist forests, and oak-hickory forests.
COMMENTS: This plant starts its life cycle as an underground gall-like mass (combination of host and parasite tissue) on small oak roots. It takes about 5 years for the underground structure to mature, after which it produces aboveground flowering stems for many years. The stems die back in June, but the dried remains can be seen for months.

226. Dwarf iris

Iris verna L. var. *verna*
Ì-ris vér-na var. vér-na
Iridaceae (Iris Family)

DESCRIPTION: Erect, perennial herb from densely scaly rhizomes; stems (in SC) to 6″ tall, unbranched, hidden by sheathing bracts; leaves essentially straight, narrow; flowers very fragrant; flowers late March–early April.
RANGE-HABITAT: PA and OH, south to nw. FL, and west to MS; in SC primarily in the piedmont and coastal plain; occasional; sandy or rocky woods, dry pinelands, swamp edges, and edges of pocosins.
COMMENTS: Accordingly to Kingsbury (1964), "Various iris have been found to contain an irritant principle in the leaves or particularly in the rootstocks which produce gastroenteritis if ingested in sufficiently, relatively large amounts."
TAXONOMY: Radford et al. (1968) recognizes two varieties: *I. verna* var. *verna* with long and slender rhizomes, 2–6″ long between offshoots, and *I. verna* var. *smalliana* Fernald, with short and stocky rhizomes, 0.5–1.3″ long between offshoots. Variety *smalliana* is uncommon in SC and found in the mountains.

227. Coral honeysuckle; woodbine

Lonicera sempervirens L.
Lo-níc-er-a sem-pér-vi-rens
Caprifoliaceae (Honeysuckle Family)

DESCRIPTION: Trailing or high-climbing, woody vine with simple, opposite leaves; partially evergreen; twining is from left to right; last 1 or 2 pair of leaves below the inflorescence joined at their bases; flowers March–July; berries red, maturing July–September.
RANGE-HABITAT: ME to NB, south to FL and TX; in SC common in the piedmont,

sandhills, coastal plain, and maritime strand; thin oak-hickory and pine-hardwood forests, thickets, and fencerows.

COMMENTS: Woodbine does well under cultivation. It is quite vigorous and flowers abundantly in full sun.

228. Sassafras

Sassafras albidum (Nuttall) Nees
Sás-sa-fras ál-bi-dum
Lauraceae (Laurel Family)

DESCRIPTION: Small to medium-size, fast-growing tree, often forming thickets from lateral root sprouts; male and female flowers on separate plants, appearing in the spring before the leaves; leaves deciduous, alternate and polymorphic (either entire, with a 1-sided lobe, or 3-lobed); twigs and leaves spicy aromatic; flowers March–April.

RANGE-HABITAT: Throughout the eastern US from sea level to 4430′ in elevation; common throughout SC; wide variety of forests, along fencerows, abandoned fields, pine-mixed hardwood forests, and woodland borders.

COMMENTS: Sassafras is an early successional tree and, because it is shade intolerant, it is seldom found as an understory tree in a closed canopy. It is one of the first trees to invade abandoned fields, often appearing as small groves spreading from lateral root offshoots. Fruit production is sparse but does provide an important food for wildlife. Oil of sassafras is distilled from the bark of the roots and once was a flavoring material of considerable importance. The oil is used to flavor tobacco, root beer and other beverages, soaps, perfumes, and gums. A tea made from boiling the bark was once used as a spring tonic to "thin the blood" before the advent of summer; proven ineffective, it quickly fell into disrepute. Young leaves are ground into a fine powder to produce the mucilaginous gumbo of Creole cooking. The US Food and Drug Administration has banned the use of safrole, found in oil of sassafras, because it may be carcinogenic.

229. Pineland phlox

Phlox nivalis Loddiges ex Sweet var. *nivalis*
Phlóx ni-và-lis var. ni-và-lis
Polemoniaceae (Phlox Family)

DESCRIPTION: Prostrate, evergreen, semiwoody perennial; flowering shoots erect, 1–4″ tall, deciduous; leaves subulate to linear, opposite; flowers March–April.

RANGE-HABITAT: From nc. NC south to FL panhandle; in SC chiefly piedmont, sandhills, and inner coastal plain; common; sandhills, pinelands, dry deciduous woods and forests, and along road banks.

TAXONOMY: Two varieties are recognized: var. *nivalis* described above, and *P. nivalis* var. *hentzii* (Nuttall) Wherry. Variety *hentzii* has flowering shoots 6″ or more tall and occurs in dry deciduous woods, in SC primarily in the northeast piedmont.

230. Little sweet Betsy; purple toadshade

Trillium cuneatum Rafinesque
Tríl-li-um cu-ne-à-tum
Liliaceae (Lily Family)

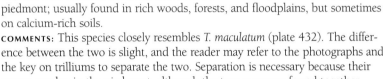

DESCRIPTION: Perennial herb from a short rhizome; stem erect, to 15″ tall; leaves sometimes so broad that the margins of the 3 whorled leaves overlap; petals purple, green, or yellow, usually less than 4x as long as wide; the two whorls of stamens are alike; flowers mid-March–April.

RANGE-HABITAT: NC to GA, and west to AL, KY, and TN; common in the mountains and piedmont; usually found in rich woods, forests, and floodplains, but sometimes on calcium-rich soils.

COMMENTS: This species closely resembles *T. maculatum* (plate 432). The difference between the two is slight, and the reader may refer to the photographs and the key on trilliums to separate the two. Separation is necessary because their ranges overlap in the piedmont, although the two are never found together.

231. Pinxterflower; common wild azalea

Rhododendron periclymenoides
(Michaux) Shinners
Rho-do-dén-dron pe-ri-cly-me-noì-des
Ericaceae (Heath Family)

DESCRIPTION: Deciduous shrub to 10′ tall; leaves not present or not fully expanded at flowering, with hairs on the margins and stiff hairs on the main veins below; flowers pink to white; sepals less than 0.04″ long, without stalked glands; flowers late March–May.

RANGE-HABITAT: MA, NY, and OH, south to GA and AL; in SC in the mountains, piedmont, and inner coastal plain; South Carolina's most common azalea, except in the coastal plain where it is rare; streambanks, beech forests, and a variety of moist to dry oak-hickory forests.

COMMENTS: This is the common azalea of upland woods throughout SC. In streamside habitats, the other azaleas that might be present are sweet azalea (*R. arborescens*), which blooms late May–July and has sepals to 0.2″ long and stems to 20′ tall, and clammy azalea (*R. viscosum*), which has glandular-hairy flower stalks and flowers that appear after the leaves.

SYNONYM: *Rhododendron nudiflorum* (L.) Torrey—RAB

232. Oconee azalea

Rhododendron flammeum (Michaux)
    Sargent
    Rho-do-dén-dron flàm-me-um
    Ericaceae (Heath Family)

DESCRIPTION: Deciduous shrub to 15′ tall;
petals brilliant red; corolla tube with short
hairs on the outside; scales of flower buds
with marginal hairs; flowers April.

RANGE-HABITAT: Restricted to the Savannah
River drainage in GA and SC; rare in the
sandhills and piedmont; dry-mesic oak-hickory forests on slopes.

COMMENTS: Can be confused with flame azalea,
but they have very different blooming periods (April versus May–June), as well
as technical floral characters, that should easily separate the two. Oconee azalea
is noted for its range of flower color; under cultivation it will tolerate drier soils
than any other native rhododendron.

233. Fringe-tree; old man's beard

Chionanthus virginicus L.
    Chi-o-nán-thus vir-gí-ni-cus
    Oleaceae (Olive Family)

DESCRIPTION: Fast-growing, short-lived shrub or small tree, occasionally reaching 30′ tall; leaves simple, opposite, deciduous and
entire; each flower has a 4-parted calyx and 4 white petals; flowers April–May; drupes blue, mature July–September.

RANGE-HABITAT: NJ south to FL, and west to MO, OK, and TX;
common throughout SC; wide variety of habitats, including dry,
mesic, or wet forests, granitic flatrocks and domes, glades and
barrens over various rocks, and swamp forests and pocosins in
the coastal plain.

COMMENTS: Fringe-tree is a widely cultivated native tree in SC; its
attraction is the airy clusters of fragrant, white flowers. A wide
variety of wildlife eat the drupes.

234. Crab-apple

Malus angustifolia (Aiton) Michaux
    Mà-lus an-gus-ti-fò-li-a
    Rosaceae (Rose Family)

DESCRIPTION: Small tree or thicket-forming
shrub from root sprouts; petals white or light-
pink; leaves deciduous, simple, alternate, with
margins of some leaves scalloped, toothed, or
nearly entire; flowers April–May; fruit a pome,
yellowish green, very sour, ripe in
August–September.

RANGE-HABITAT: Southeastern species, from
MD to FL, west to TX and AR; throughout
SC, but more common in the coastal plain; moist soil in oak-hickory forests,
woodland borders, thickets along riverbanks, and fencerows.

COMMENTS: Crab-apple is often used as an ornamental because of its showy and
fragrant flowers. The fruit is used to make jelly, preserves, and cider. It is an

important wildlife food, being consumed by deer, foxes, raccoons, quail, and turkeys. The wood is not commercially important.

235. Lousewort; wood betony

Pedicularis canadensis L.
Pe-di-cu-là-ris ca-na-dén-sis
Scrophulariaceae (Figwort Family)

DESCRIPTION: Perennial, hairy herb from thickened, fibrous roots; hemiparasite?; plant 6–12″ tall; lower leaves in a basal cluster; stem leaves alternate, reduced; all leaves deeply divided into toothed segments; corolla in various color combinations of yellow, red, and purplish; flowers April–May.

RANGE-HABITAT: Widespread and common in eastern North America; in SC chiefly in the mountains and piedmont; scattered and rare in the coastal plain; moist to dry forests, woodlands, and meadows; pine savannas and flatwoods in the coastal plain.

COMMENTS: The generic name comes from the Latin *pediculus*, "a louse," from an early European belief that cattle feeding where these plants abounded became infected with lice. This is one of the species of figworts believed to be a hemiparasite; however, no studies have indicated what the host plant(s) is (are).

236. Black cherry

Prunus serotina Ehrhart
Prù-nus se-rò-ti-na
Rosaceae (Rose Family)

DESCRIPTION: Large tree reaching 80–90′ tall; bark of small trees with horizontal lenticles, becoming fissured and scaly with age; leaves and inner bark contain the almond-flavored hydrocyanic acid that can readily be detected by breaking a twig and smelling the broken end; leaves alternate, simple, deciduous; flowers April–May; fruit a drupe, black when mature in July–August.

RANGE-HABITAT: Nova Scotia to MN, south to c. TX, and east to FL; also native from s. NM and w. AZ to Guatemala; common throughout SC; in a variety of natural and disturbed habitats such as cove forests, oak-hickory and pine-mixed hardwood forests, fencerows, thickets, pastures, longleaf pine flatwoods, and bottomland forests.

COMMENTS: Black cherry is one of South Carolina's most versatile native trees. Its reddish brown, close-grained wood takes a beautiful polish and is widely used to make furniture, veneers, and small wooden wares. Its use as a lumber tree is reduced because of the lack of large trees; today it is used mainly as a specialty wood.

As an astringent, the bark is used to make cough medicines and expectorants in the treatment of sore throats. Duke (1997) recommends black cherry as an herbal remedy in treating flu. Pioneers in the Appalachians used the ripe fruits to make a drink called cherry bounce. The juice was pressed from the fruits and infused in brandy or rum to give it the bitter taste desired. Even today the fruit is used to flavor liqueurs.

All parts of the plant are poisonous (except the pulp of the ripe fruit) because of hydrocyanic acid. Children have been poisoned by sucking the twigs. A wide variety of wildlife eat the fruits. The hydrocyanic acid in the wilted leaves may be harmful to deer and cattle, but whitetail deer can apparently eat the fresh leaves without ill effects.

237. Nestronia

Nestronia umbellula Rafinesque
Nes-trò-ni-a um-bél-lu-la
Santalaceae (Sandalwood Family)

DESCRIPTION: A colony-forming shrub 1.5–4.5′ tall; leaves opposite, entire, and 0.75–2″ long; male and female flowers are produced on different plants; the small greenish flowers consist of 4–5 petal-like sepals; the female flowers are borne singly in the axils of leaves, the male flowers are in umbels; the fruit is a greenish drupe, to 0.5″ in diameter; flowers April–May; fruits mature July.

RANGE-HABITAT: VA south to AL; also in KY; in SC rare in the piedmont, sandhills, and inner coastal plain; dry forests with a somewhat open canopy, usually upslope from Pacolet soils.

COMMENTS: Not a showy species, it is easily overlooked. Many populations consist of all male or all female plants, making reproduction from seeds impossible and a prime cause of the species' rarity. In recent years, a fungus that causes the early dropping of leaves has attacked plants in many populations.

PROTECTION STATUS: Federal Species of Concern

238. Solomon's-seal

Polygonatum biflorum (Walter) Elliott
Po-ly-gó-na-tum bi-flò-rum
Liliaceae (Lily Family)

DESCRIPTION: Perennial herb from elongate, white rhizomes; stem unbranched, arching, to 2′ long; leaves whitish below; flowers in all but the uppermost leaf axils, usually in pairs from a common stalk, but sometimes up to 9 may be present; flowers April–June.

RANGE-HABITAT: MO and IN, south to FL and MS; common in the mountains and piedmont; rare and scattered in the coastal plain and sandhills; in a variety of dry-moist forests.

COMMENTS: This species extends into drier habitats than its vegetative look-alike, false Solomon's-seal. Plants may be 4′ tall in deep loam soils and abundant light. The rhizome is jointed, and where a leaf breaks off, it leaves a distinct scar said to resemble the seal of King Solomon. Native Americans and colonists used the starchy rhizomes as food.

239. Carolina spinypod

Matelea caroliniensis (Jacquin) Woodson
Ma-tè-le-a ca-ro-li-nén-sis
Asclepiadaceae (Milkweed Family)

DESCRIPTION: Perennial, twining, herbaceous vine; leaves opposite, ovate; corolla maroon, 2–2.5x as long as wide, with lobes ovate-rounded; flowers April–June.

RANGE-HABITAT: DE, MD, KY, and s. MO, south to FL and MS; in SC chiefly in the piedmont and common, but scattered in the outer coastal plain; moist nutrient-rich forests, especially along streams.

SIMILAR SPECIES: Five species of *Matelea* occur in SC, and it is difficult to distinguish between the five. The best way to distinguish *M. caroliniensis* is its corolla lobes; the lobes are ovate-rounded, 2–2.5x as long as wide, and maroon.

240. Maple-leaved arrowwood

Viburnum acerifolium L.
Vi-búr-num a-ce-ri-fò-li-um
Caprifoliaceae (Honeysuckle Family)

DESCRIPTION: Low deciduous shrub, 3–6′ tall, rarely taller, usually colonial; leaves opposite, simple, 3-lobed (like a maple leaf); flowering stems with 1 pair of leaves; flowers late April–early June; drupes black, mature August–October.

RANGE-HABITAT: Quebec to MN, south to GA and TN; in SC common in the mountains and piedmont, occasional in the inner coastal plain and sandhills; deciduous forests communities.

COMMENTS: Arrowwood makes a good shade-tolerant ornamental since the foliage is especially colorful in the fall; allow it to develop into large, loose colonies.

241. Sparkleberry

Vaccinium arboreum Marshall
Vac-cì-ni-um ar-bò-re-um
Ericaceae (Heath Family)

DESCRIPTION: Erect shrub or small tree to 30′ tall; branches crooked, forming an irregular crown; leaves simple, alternate, shiny above, evergreen to tardily deciduous; flowers late April–June; berries black at maturity, September–October.

RANGE-HABITAT: Widely distributed in southeast US; common throughout SC; sandy or rocky woodlands, bluffs, and cliffs, usually xeric and fire maintained.

COMMENTS: The berries, often lasting through winter, are eaten by a wide variety of wildlife. The pulp is scanty but pleasant tasting and can be made into jelly or jam. The wood has little commercial value but is hard and used locally for tool handles and craft items. The roots, bark, and leaves were once used to treat diarrhea and dysentery.

242. Southern Deerberry

Vaccinium stamineum var. *melanocarpum*
Mohr
Vac-cí-ni-um sta-mí-ne-um
var. me-la-no-cár-pum
Ericaceae (Heath Family)

DESCRIPTION: Shrub to 5′ tall; branches, leaves, and fruit hairy; flowers mature April–June; berries mature August–October.
RANGE-HABITAT: From WV, KY, and TN, south to FL and west to MS; in SC in the mountains and piedmont along the Savannah River into Aiken County; rare; rocky and xeric woodlands, and oak-hickory forests.
TAXONOMY: The taxonomy of the genus *Vaccinium* is complex and, recently, under much revision. The *Vaccinium stamineum* complex illustrates this point. Radford et al (1968) list two varieties of *V. stamineum*: var. *melanocarpum* and *V. stamineum* L. var. *stamineum*. The branches, leaves, and fruits of var. *stamineum* are smooth or sparsely hairy, while they are hairy in var. *melanocarpum*. Variety *stamineum* is common throughout SC. Weakley (2001) lists five varieties for species *stamineum*. The authors prefer the conservative treatment.
SYNONYM: *Vaccinium stamineum* var. *sericeum* (Mohr) Ward—W

243. White milkweed

Asclepias variegata L.
As-clè-pi-as va-ri-e-gà-ta
Asclepiadaceae (Milkweed Family)

DESCRIPTION: Perennial herb with milky juice; stem simple, solitary, 1–3′ tall; leaves broad, in 2–5 pairs; corolla bright white; flowers May–June; follicles mature July–September.
RANGE-HABITAT: FL to TX, north to CT and MO; throughout SC, but primarily in the mountains and piedmont, where it is common; occasional elsewhere; dry oak-hickory forests, sandy, dry, open woods, and upland woodland margins.
COMMENTS: The following account applies to white milkweed and most other species. When almost mature but still solid, cooked seedpods make a palatable vegetable that is comparable to okra. The shoots and young leaves are used like spinach, after washing with water has removed the bitter taste from the milky juice. The raw shoots of any milkweed may be poisonous.

244. Samson's snakeroot

Psoralea psoralioides var. *eglandulosa* (Elliott) Freeman
Pso-rà-le-a pso-ra-li-oì-des var. e-glan-du-lò-sa
Fabaceae (Pea or Bean Family)

DESCRIPTION: Perennial herb, 1–3′ tall, arising from a cigar-shaped taproot; leaves trifoliolate; leaflet surfaces, bracts, calyces, and pods without glands or very sparsely glandular (hence, the specific epithet *eglandulosa*); racemes almost spikelike; flowers May–July; legume matures July–September.

RANGE-HABITAT: Primarily a western plant, but occurs scattered in and east of the Blue Ridge; in SC in the mountains and upper piedmont; xeric hardpan forests, open woodlands, fields, and clearings; rare.

COMMENTS: One of many plants that was believed to act against snake venom.

TAXONOMY: Radford et al. (1968) recognizes two varieties of snakeroot: the variety above and depicted in this book and *P. psoralioides* (Walter) Cory var. *psoralioides,* depicted in plate 339 in *WCL.* Variety *psoralioides* has leaflet surfaces, bracts, calyces, and pods conspicuously glandular and occurs in the lower piedmont, sandhills, and coastal plain of SC, where it is common.

SYNONYM: *Orbexilum pedunculatum* (P. Miller) Rydberg var. *pedunculatum*—W

245. Indian pink; worm-grass

Spigelia marilandica L.
Spi-gèl-i-a ma-ri-lán-di-ca
Loganiaceae (Logania Family)

DESCRIPTION: Erect perennial herb to 28″ tall; stems with 4–7 pairs of opposite, stalkless leaves; flower scarlet on outside, yellow-green on inside; flowers May–June.

RANGE-HABITAT: SC west to s. IN and OK, south to FL and TX; common and scattered throughout SC; upland forests and woodlands, usually on circumneutral soils, in the mountains and piedmont; in the sandhills, coastal plain, and maritime strand particularly abundant on calcareous sites.

COMMENTS: In the early 1800s the demand for Indian pink for use as a vermifuge almost lead to its extinction; however, severe side effects accompanied its use so that by the early 1900s its use was discontinued, and the plant is again common. The genus honors Adrian Spiegel, 1578–1625, who was perhaps the first to give directions for preparing an herbarium.

246. Whorled loosestrife

Lysimachia quadrifolia L.
Ly-si-má-chi-a qua-dri-fò-li-a
Primulaceae (Primrose Family)

DESCRIPTION: Perennial herb 1–3' tall; stems erect, hairy, rarely branched; leaves in whorls of 3–6; flowers solitary from the axil of each leaf in the upper 2–6 whorls; corolla streaked with black, marked with red around the center; flowers May–July.

RANGE-HABITAT: ME west to WI and MN, south to SC, AL, and TN; in SC common in the mountains and piedmont, occasional in the sandhills and coastal plain; in a wide variety of moist to very dry forests and openings, including longleaf pine savannas in the coastal plain, usually in full sun.

247. Pinesap

Monotropa hypopithys L.
Mo-nó-tro-pa hy-pó-pi-thys
Ericaceae (Heath Family)

DESCRIPTION: Saprophytic herbaceous perennial herb without chlorophyll; 4–16" tall; leaves reduced to scales; early season flowering plants are usually yellow or tawny, while the fall flowering plants are mostly pink to red, often marked with yellow; flowers May–October.

RANGE-HABITAT: Circumboreal, south nearly throughout North America; in SC occasional in forests and upland woods in the mountains and piedmont; rare in the coastal plain in upland woods and xeric ridges.

COMMENTS: Pinesap obtains its nourishment from a fungus associated with its roots that in turn feeds on decaying organic matter, then transfers nourishment to pinesap. An early yellow-flowered colony will not flower in the fall, and pink to red plants will not flower in the spring. Evidently these are not seasonal phases but genetic forms.

248. Starry rosin-weed

Silphium dentatum Elliott
Síl-phi-um den-tà-tum
Asteraceae (Aster or Sunflower Family)

DESCRIPTION: Coarse, erect, perennial herb, 2–10' tall; stems smooth, rough, or densely spreading and hairy; lower stem leaves well developed, opposite; upper stem leaves alternate; basal leaves usually absent; bracts on receptacle with small, stalked glands on the back near the tip; flowers May–August.

RANGE-HABITAT: NC and KY, south to FL to MS; common throughout SC; dry oak-hickory forests, old fields, and dry thin woodlands.

249. Wild Quinine

Parthenium integrifolium L.
    var. *integrifolium*
    Par-thè-ni-um in-teg-ri-fò-li-um
    var. in-teg-ri-fò-li-um
    Asteraceae (Aster or Sunflower Family)

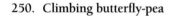

DESCRIPTION: Perennial herb with tuberous roots, 2–5′ tall; leaves large, oval, lanceolate, to 1′ long, rough, blunt-toothed; basal leaves with long leaf stalks; stem leaves reduced upward, the upper often sessile and clasping; flowers late May–August.

RANGE-HABITAT: VA west to MN, south to SC, GA, MS, and AR; in SC occasional in the mountains, common throughout the piedmont and north inner coastal plain; dry open woods and forests, old fields, and along roadsides.

COMMENTS: The flowering tops were once used for "intermittent fevers" like malaria—hence, the common name. Wild quinine may cause dermatitis or allergies.

TAXONOMY: Weakley (2001) recognizes three varieties of *P. integrifolium*.

250. Climbing butterfly-pea

Centrosema virginianum (L.) Bentham
    Cen-tro-sè-ma vir-gi-ni-à-num
    Fabaceae (Pea or Bean Family)

DESCRIPTION: Twining or trailing perennial, herbaceous vine from a tough, elongate root; leaves with 3 leaflets; flowers June–October.

RANGE-HABITAT: From s. NJ south to FL, and west to KY, AR, and TX; common throughout SC; oak-hickory forests, longleaf pine flatwoods, sandy, dry open woods, woodland openings, maritime forests, and coastal dunes.

251. Indian pipe

Monotropa uniflora L.
    Mo-nó-tro-pa u-ni-flò-ra
    Ericaceae (Heath Family)

DESCRIPTION: Saprophytic herb without chlorophyll; stem 2–8″ tall; leaves reduced to scales; specimens vary from white, pink, red, pale-yellow to lavender or a combination of two of these; flowers solitary at end of stem, drooping; flowers June–October; capsules become erect as they mature in August–November.

RANGE-HABITAT: Widespread in North America; also in South America and east Asia; common throughout SC; upland forests in the mountains and piedmont, and in sandy forests and pocosin borders in the sandhills and coastal plain.

COMMENTS: See essay "Saprophytic vascular plants and mycotrophy" for a more detailed coverage of Indian pipe. Foster and Duke (1990) give numerous medicinal uses of the plant.

252. Carolina moonseed; coralbeads

Cocculus carolinus (L.) Augustin de
    Candolle
    Cóc-cu-lus ca-ro-lì-nus
    Menispermaceae (Moonseed Family)

DESCRIPTION: Perennial, twining woody vine;
sometimes only woody basally, or woody
stems long, reaching high into trees; leaves
deciduous, entire to 3-lobed; male and female
flowers on separate plants; fruit a drupe,
mature June–August.

RANGE-HABITAT: VA south to FL, west to TX,
and north to the interior to s. IN and MO;
common throughout SC (but rare in the mountains); thickets, sandy woods,
oak-hickory forests, fields, and along roadsides.

COMMENTS: The common name "moonseed" alludes to the shape of the stone
within the fruit. Moonseed is ideal for cultivation on fences, arbors, and trellises.
In full sun it produces numerous, red drupes and grows in a variety of soils.

253. Pale Indian-plantain

Arnoglossum atriplicifolia (L.) H. E. Robinson
    Ar-no-glós-sum a-tri-pli-ci-fò-li-a
    Asteraceae (Aster or Sunflower Family)

DESCRIPTION: Large perennial herb, 4–9′ tall; stems smooth, with
a whitened bloom; leaves large, basal, triangular kidney-shaped;
flowers June–October.

RANGE-HABITAT: Widespread in eastern North America; in SC
throughout the mountains and piedmont, scattered in the coastal
plain and sandhills; woodland margins, mesic deciduous forests,
and clearings.

COMMENTS: Native Americans used the leaves as a poultice for
cancers, cuts, and bruises, and to draw out blood or poisonous
materials.

SYNONYM: *Cacalia atriplicifolia* L.—RAB

254. Sourwood

Oxydendrum arboreum (L.) Augustin
de Candolle
Ox-y-dén-drum ar-bò-re-um
Eriaceae (Heath Family)

DESCRIPTION: Medium-size tree with sour-tasting sap and leaves; leaves deciduous, alternate, smooth, lanceolate to elliptic-lanceolate; flowers erect, in a terminal raceme, white; flowers June–July.

RANGE-HABITAT: PA west to IN, south to FL and LA; in SC common throughout, except rare or absent in the outer coastal plain; streamsides, mesic to xeric deciduous forests, especially dry-mesic to xeric oak-hickory and oak-pine forests; in the fall-line sandhills in ecotones between sandhills and pocosins.

COMMENTS: The genus is monotypic with no close relatives in the family. The wood is not important commercially, but the flowers yield the prized sourwood honey. Sourwood has considerable ornamental value because of its drooping racemes of white flowers and early fall color (brilliant red). It is especially valuable along roadsides, where it can grow on the poor soils of road cuts. Native Americans chewed the bark for mouth ulcers and used a leaf tea for asthma, diarrhea, and indigestion.

255. Hog peanut; groundnut

Amphicarpa bracteata (L.) Fernald
Am-phi-cár-pa brac-te-à-ta
Fabaceae (Pea or Bean Family)

DESCRIPTION: Twining, climbing, annual vine; leaves trifoliolate; flowers of two types: those on upper branches open for pollination (chasmogamous) with petals pale purple or lilac to white; those on creeping, lower branches never open (cleistogamous), inconspicuous, without petals; fruit (legume) from cleistogamous flowers fleshy, often subterranean, 1-seeded; flowers July–October; legumes ripe August–October.

RANGE-HABITAT: Quebec and Nova Scotia south to FL, west to TX and NB, and north to MT and Manitoba; common throughout SC; dry to moist forests and thickets.

COMMENTS: Native Americans boiled the subterranean fruits. The seeds from the fruit, when seasoned with salt and pepper, are not unlike garden beans. Boiling easily removes the shell. The subterranean fruits retain their vitality throughout the winter, so they may be dug in the spring. The seeds of the aerial fruits are inedible. Birds feed on the seeds of both fruit types, and hogs consume the subterranean fruits.

256. Bear's-foot

Polymnia uvedalia L.
Po-lým-ni-a u-ve-dàl-i-a
Asteraceae (Aster or Sunflower Family)

DESCRIPTION: Perennial herb with thick, fleshy roots; stems erect, hollow, 3–10′ tall; glandular or with spreading hairs beneath the stems; leaves opposite, palmately lobed or cut, 4–12″ long, their shape suggesting the common name bear's-foot; flowers July–October.

RANGE-HABITAT: NY and IL, south to FL and TX; throughout SC, but less common in the coastal plain and maritime strand; moist forests and disturbed sites such as woodland borders and pastures; mostly on shell deposits or other calcareous sites in the maritime strand.

COMMENTS: The specific epithet honors Robert Uvedale, 1642–1722, who had the plant in his English garden.

257. Cranefly orchid

Tipularia discolor (Pursh) Nuttall
Ti-pu-là-ri-a dís-co-lor
Orchidaceae (Orchid Family)

DESCRIPTION: Perennial from a swollen underground stem bearing only a few spongy roots; single leaf produced in autumn, with a purplish lower surface, withering and disappearing at flowering time; flowers July–September.

RANGE-HABITAT: Widespread in eastern North America and Central America; common throughout SC in a variety of moist to dry habitats, usually on acid soils.

COMMENTS: The flower resembles a cranefly—hence, the common name. *Tipula* is a genus of cranefly. Both cranefly orchid and puttyroot orchid (*Aplectrum*) have single basal leaves that are purplish on the lower surface. Leaves of puttyroot are plicate, as in an incompletely unfolded fan, and the veins are distinctly raised and whitened.

258. Georgia savory; Georgia calamint

Satureja georgiana (Harper) Ahles
Sa-tu-rè-ja geor-gi-à-na
Lamiaceae (Mint Family)

DESCRIPTION: Loosely sprawling, freely branched, semi-evergreen shrub to 18″ tall; leaves opposite; corolla pink to lavender; flowers July–September.

RANGE-HABITAT: From s. NC south to FL, and west to LA; in SC primarily in the piedmont (occasional) and rare in the sandhills and coastal plain; dry, sandy, or rocky woods and forests.

COMMENTS: Georgia savory is a good landscape plant for problem areas with dry, thin soil in full sunlight.

SYNONYM: *Calamintha georgiana* (Harper) Shinners—W

259. Sweet goldenrod

Solidago odora Aiton
So-li-dà-go o-dò-ra
Asteraceae (Aster or Sunflower Family)

DESCRIPTION: Perennial erect herb 2–3' tall; plant essentially smooth; leaves alternate, smooth, narrow, stalkless, with small translucent dots; flower heads on one side of slightly arching branches; flowers July–October.

RANGE-HABITAT: New England south to FL, west to TX, and north to OH; common throughout SC; dry forests and woodlands, xeric sandhills, xeric hardpan forests, and longleaf flatwoods and savannas.

COMMENTS: The crushed leaves give off a licorice odor that readily identifies this goldenrod from similar species. A pleasant tea can be made from the leaves. The leaves were formally used as a digestive stimulant and for a variety of other uses.

260. Bitter-bloom

Sabatia angularis (L.) Pursh
Sa-bà-ti-a an-gu-là-ris
Gentianaceae (Gentian Family)

DESCRIPTION: Annual herb 12–20" tall; stems quadrangular, usually winged; bushy plant with leaves that "clasp" the stem between their basal lobes; leaves opposite, entire; inflorescence branches paired; flowers rose-pink with a greenish center, occasionally white; flowers July–August.

RANGE-HABITAT: NY west to s. MI, IL, and e. KS, south to FL panhandle and e. TX; throughout SC; deciduous forests and woodlands, freshwater marshes, along roadsides, granite outcrops, and fields; common.

COMMENTS: The genus is dedicated to Liberato Sabbati, an Italian botanist.

261. Whorled-leaf coreopsis; wood tickseed

Coreopsis major Walter
Co-re-óp-sis mà-jor
Asteraceae (Aster or Sunflower Family)

DESCRIPTION: Perennial herb, 20–40" tall; rhizomatous, but with stems commonly tufted; upper and middle nodes with opposite leaves; leaves deeply palmately divided into three segments, giving the appearance of 6 leaves in a whorl; middle leaflet of median leaves 0.2–1.2" wide; flowers July–August.

RANGE-HABITAT: From PA and OH, south to FL, and west to MS; common throughout SC; sandy streamsides, dry woodland margins, dry oak-hickory forests, longleaf pine flatwoods, sandy, dry, open woods, and along roadsides.

SIMILAR SPECIES: A similar species is *C. verticillata* L.; its leaf divisions are under 0.2″ wide, and it is restricted to the nc. piedmont of SC.

TAXONOMY: Various authors have described several varieties of *C. major.*

262. Muscadine; scuppernong

Vitis rotundifolia Michaux
Vī-tis ro-tun-di-fò-li-a
Vitaceae (Grape Family)

DESCRIPTION: High-climbing (100′ in trees) or trailing woody vine, climbing by simple tendrils; bark adherent (except on large stems), with prominent lenticles; drooping aerial roots originate from the stem; leaves round or widely ovate; berry (grape) black when ripe, August–October.

RANGE-HABITAT: From DE west to KY and MO, south to FL and TX; common throughout SC, except in the mountains where it is occasional; wide variety of habitats, such as coastal dunes, forests, swamps, low woods, and in thickets and along roadsides.

COMMENTS: Two types of domestic grapes originated from this species. Plants with amber-green fruits are called scuppernongs, and those with purple fruits are called muscadines (as are the wild, black-fruited plants). Few fruits have been used for so long and for so many uses as *V. rotundifolia.* The fruits can be eaten plain or made into wine, jelly, juice, preserves, used in pies, or sun dried for future use. Muscadine leaves can be stuffed or rolled with a wide assortment of foods, then boiled. Muscadines are rich in vitamins B and C and iron. A wide variety of wildlife eat muscadines, and they are excellent plants to cultivate for wildlife.

263. Appalachian oak-leach

Aureolaria laevigata (Rafinesque)
Rafinesque
Au-re-o-lá-ri-a lae-vi-gà-ta
Scrophulariaceae (Figwort Family)

DESCRIPTION: Hemiparasite on members of the white oak group; perennial herb to 3′ tall or more; plant essentially smooth; stem leaves opposite; lower leaves entire to serrate; flowers August–September.

RANGE-HABITAT: PA west to s. OH, and south to SC and GA; primarily a central and southern Appalachian endemic, but extending into adjacent provinces; in SC common in the mountains, occasional in the piedmont, rare in the coastal plain; deciduous upland forests and woodlands.

SIMILAR SPECIES: The following separates Appalachian oak-leach from two similar species: *A. flava* (L.) Farwell (plate 238 in *WCL*) has lower leaves pinnately lobed and is scattered throughout SC; *A. virginica* (L.) Pennell is hairy, flowers in May–July, and occurs throughout SC.

COMMENTS: The common name oak-leach refers to its role as a parasite on members of the white oak group.

264. Southern crownbeard

Verbesina occidentalis (L.) Walter
Ver-be-sì-na oc-ci-den-tà-lis
Asteraceae (Aster or Sunflower Family)

DESCRIPTION: Single-stemmed perennial herb
6–9′ tall; stems smooth or minutely hairy;
leaves opposite, with leaf stalks decurrent on
stem as a wide wing; rays unevenly spaced
around the head; flowers late August–October.
RANGE-HABITAT: MD west to OH and MO,
south to FL panhandle and MS; common
throughout SC; forests, woodlands, pastures,
along roadsides, and especially abundant in
alluvial areas or calcium-rich soils.

265. White oak; stave oak

Quercus alba L.
Quér-cus ál-ba
Fagaceae (Beech Family)

DESCRIPTION: Medium to tall deciduous tree to 115′ tall; leaves
alternate, divided into 7–10 shallow-to-deep rounded lobes;
acorns mature September–November.
RANGE-HABITAT: Widespread in eastern North America; essentially
throughout SC; mesic to xeric forests and woodlands, but best
growth in rich, well-drained loamy soils.
COMMENTS: Historically, white oak was one of the most valuable
lumber trees in eastern North America. Its wood is hard, tough,
strong, and close-grained, and although used in many ways, it is
best suited for support timbers, furniture, flooring, and interior
finishing. White oak was the mainstay in North American ships
prior to the use of steel. It is often referred to as "stave oak"
because the wood is used for whiskey and wine barrels. It is an
attractive, long-lived, shade tree, and its acorns are important to
wildlife. The inner bark is astringent, and a tea from the bark was
once used for diarrhea, dysentery, bleeding, and a gargle for sore throats.

266. Persimmon

Diospyros virginiana L.
Di-os-pỳ-ros vir-gi-ni-à-na
Ebenaceae (Ebony Family)

DESCRIPTION: Large shrub, or small to medium size tree reaching 70–80′ tall; leaves deciduous, simple, alternate, blades ovate or elliptic, upper surface dark green, often with black blemishes (evident in photograph), lower light green; male and female flowers on separate trees; fruits orange-yellow when mature in September–October.

RANGE-HABITAT: Widespread in eastern North America, but primarily a southern species; does not occur along the main range of the Appalachian Mountains; common throughout SC; dry deciduous forests, floodplains, pinelands, xeric sandhills, mesic forests, fencerows, and old fields.

COMMENTS: Persimmon wood is extremely hard but is not used as commercial lumber since it yields an inferior grade. Its main use is (was) for golf club heads. The sweet fruit is edible when fully ripe and can be eaten raw or made into a variety of dishes, including bread and pudding. When green, the fruit is strongly astringent. In folk usage, an astringent tea from the inner bark was used as a gargle for sore throat and thrush. Numerous wildlife feed on the fruits. The SC state record was measured in 1995 at 132′ tall.

267. Common running-pine

Lycopodium flabelliforme (Fernald) Blanchard
Ly-co-pó-di-um fla-bel-li-fór-me
Lycopodiaceae (Clubmoss Family)

DESCRIPTION: Evergreen, perennial, nonflowering vascular plant; horizontal stems creeping; erect stems producing several groups of sterile branchlets organized into fan-shaped units; branchlets dark green, flattened, not whitened, to only 0.16″ wide including the leaves; leaves scalelike, 4-ranked, with upper larger than lower; sporangia in cones to 2″ long, in groups of 3–4 from a 1–4″ long common stalk.

RANGE-HABITAT: Widespread in eastern North America; in SC chiefly mountains and piedmont; common; in a variety of dry to moist habitats, most commonly in successional pine-oak forests.

COMMENTS: The fine, dry spores were used as a flash powder in early photography. This species often occurs with pink lady's slipper in disturbed pine-oak forests.

268. Piedmont xeric hardpan forests

269. Curlyheads

Clematis ochroleuca Aiton
Clé-ma-tis o-chro-leù-ca
Ranunculaceae (Buttercup Family)

DESCRIPTION: Perennial herb with erect, unbranched stems to 2′ tall; leaves densely covered with soft hair below; flowers solitary and terminal; petals absent; sepals petal-like, bluish; flowers April–June.

RANGE-HABITAT: NY to GA; in SC mostly in the piedmont, rare in the coastal plain and sandhills, and unknown from the mountains; restricted to dry upland forests in calcium-rich soils associated with gabbro or diabase rocks.

COMMENTS: The common name derives from the fruit with its headlike clusters of achenes, each with a long, curling and feathery style. Rock Hill Blackjacks Heritage Preserve harbors a large population of curlyheads.

270. Deceptive spinypod

Matelea decipiens (Alexander) Woodsen
Ma-tè-le-a de-cí-pi-ens
Asclepiadaceae (Milkweed Family)

DESCRIPTION: Perennial, twining herb with opposite leaves; 10 or more flowers per inflorescence; corolla lobes 3–4x as long as wide; flower buds conical to cylindrical; flowers April–June; follicles mature August–October.

RANGE-HABITAT: From sc. VA south to GA, AL, and e. TX, north to s. IL and MO; scattered localities in the piedmont and coastal plain of SC; rare; forests, woodlands, and thickets, generally over mafic rock in the piedmont (xeric hardpan forests) and calcareous rocks in the coastal plain.

SIMILAR SPECIES: Members of the genus *Matelea* are easily separated from the similar genus *Gonolobus* (plate 217). *Matelea* has corolla lobes glandular-hairy on the outer surface, and *Gonolobus* has corolla lobes hairless on the outer surface. *M. decipens* is easily separated from the similar *M. caroliniensis* (plate 239) since *M. decipens* has conical flower buds and corolla lobes 3–4x as long as wide, and *M. caroliniensis* has ovoid flower buds and corolla lobes 2–2.5x as long as wide.

271. Diabase woodmint

Blephilia ciliata (L.) Bentham
Ble-phí-li-a ci-li-à-ta
Lamiaceae (Mint Family)

DESCRIPTION: Perennial herb with erect to ascending stems covered with short hairs; leaves on short leaf stalks; flowers pale blue with purple spots, in 1–5 terminal clusters, the lowermost subtended by leaflike bracts; flowers May–early June.

RANGE-HABITAT: MA and WI, south to GA and AR; occasional in SC; cove forests and Canada hemlock forests in the mountains and xeric hardpan forests in the piedmont.

COMMENTS: *Blephila* is from the Greek for "eyelash," in reference to the fringe of long hairs on the edges of the bracts.

272. Carolina Rose

Rosa carolina L.
Rò-sa ca-ro-lì-na
Rosaceae (Rose Family)

DESCRIPTION: Low, semi-upright shrub to 3′ tall; stems armed with straight prickles; leaves compound, with 5, rarely 7, coarsely serrate leaflets; flowers May–June and sporadically later; hips (fruits) mature August–October.

RANGE-HABITAT: Nova Scotia to MN, south to FL and TX; throughout SC (except the maritime strand); common; xeric hardpan forests, upland pastures, woodland borders, and pinelands.

SIMILAR SPECIES: Carolina rose is easily distinguished from swamp rose (*Rosa palustris,* plate 523); the former has straight prickles, the latter has prickles curved downward.

COMMENTS: Carolina rose is suitable for cultivation and requires full sun and well-drained soil. It does especially well on rocky places unsuitable for most plants.

273. Prairie dock

Silphium terebinthinaceum Jacquin
Síl-phi-um te-re-bin-thi-nà-ce-um
Asteraceae (Aster or Sunflower Family)

DESCRIPTION: Perennial herb from a taproot; leaves mostly basal, leaf stalks long, blades heart-shaped at base, very large (mostly 12–16″ long); flowering stems often 7–10′ tall; heads numerous, large, with yellow ray and disk flowers; flowers July–September.

RANGE-HABITAT: Ontario and MN, south to MS and AL; restricted in the Carolinas to the piedmont; rare; glades in xeric hardpan forests.

COMMENTS: One of many SC plants with prairie affinities, becoming more uncommon because fire is no longer part of the piedmont landscape.

PROTECTION STATUS: State Threatened

274. Southern obedient-plant

Physostegia virginiana subsp. *praemorsa* (Shinners)
Cantino
Phy-sos-té-gi-a vir-gi-ni-à-na subsp. prae-mór-sa
Lamiaceae (Mint Family)

DESCRIPTION: Perennial herb to about 4′ tall, with numerous long, slender rhizomes; stems 4-angled; leaves opposite, with stalks or sessile, the largest sharply serrate; flowers July–October.

RANGE-HABITAT: From OH west to IL, south to c. NC, n. FL, TX, and NM; local throughout the mountains and piedmont; rare in the sandhills and coastal plain; woodlands, glades, and seepages, especially over calcium-rich soils.

COMMENTS: The common name, obedient-plant, comes from the fact that the flowers tend to stay in a new position for a while after they are twisted to one side.

SYNONYM: *Dracocephalum virginianum* L.—RAB

275. Schweinitz's Sunflower

Helianthus schweinitzii Torrey & Gray
He-li-án-thus schwein-ítz-i-i
Asteraceae (Aster or Sunflower Family)

DESCRIPTION: Perennial herb from a tuberous rootstalk; stems to 4.5′ tall; leaves 6–10x as long as wide, covered with dense, short hairs below; heads small (the disk 0.2–0.6″ across), ray and disk flowers yellow; flowers late August–October.

RANGE-HABITAT: Restricted to the piedmont of NC and SC; glades in xeric hardpan forests with diabase or gabbro rocks, mowed power lines, roadsides, and field margins

COMMENTS: A fire-adapted species now found typically in mowed areas under power lines, roadsides, and field margins, as fires are no longer a part of the piedmont landscape. Its rarity is probably due to its inability to persist as its habitat becomes shaded during intervals between disturbances. The specific epithet honors Lewis David von Schweinitz, 1780–1834, a North American botanist whose work on fungi established him as the "patron saint of North American mycology."

PROTECTION STATUS: Federal Endangered

276. Grass-leaved blazing star

Liatris graminifolia Willdenow
Li-à-tris gra-mi-ni-fò-li-a
Asteraceae (Aster or Sunflower Family)

DESCRIPTION: Perennial herb to 5′ tall; basal rosette of leaves absent; leaves alternate, numerous, reduced in size upward, all linear or nearly so, 2–8″ long; flower heads longer than broad, sessile or on short stalks; flowers September–October.

RANGE-HABITAT: FL to se. MS, and north to NJ and PA; throughout the sandhills, piedmont, and coastal plain; common; old fields, thinly wooded habitats, and glades, especially among pines.

COMMENTS: The numerous species of *Liatris* in SC are difficult to distinguish.

277. Piedmont springhead seepage forests

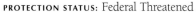

278. Dwarf-flower heartleaf

Hexastylis naniflora Blomquist
Hex-ás-ty-lis na-ni-flò-ra
Aristolochiaceae (Birthwort Family)

DESCRIPTION: Perennial herb from a short, underground stem; leaves rounded, heart-shaped at the base, 1.5–2.5″ long and wide, dark green with lighter mottlings; flowers solitary on short stalks, usually under leaf litter; calyx tube cylindrical, opening less than 0.2″ across; flowers March–June.

RANGE-HABITAT: Endemic to the upper piedmont of SC and NC; found in acidic soils (usually Pacolet sandy loam) on bluffs and in ravines, or on hummocks in piedmont seepage forests (where Pacolet soils occupy the adjacent upland).

Photo by Ed Pivorun

COMMENTS: *Hexastylis* is a difficult genus taxonomically. Proper identification requires fresh flowering material. However, the habitats of this and many other species are usually distinctive and aid in identification.

PROTECTION STATUS: Federal Threatened

279. Bunched arrowhead

Sagittaria fasciculata E. O. Beal
Sa-git-tà-ri-a fas-ci-cu-là-ta
Alismataceae (Water-plantain Family)

DESCRIPTION: Perennial herb with leafless flowering stems and basal leaves; emersed rosette of leaves spoon-shaped, usually 4–8″ long; submerged, winter rosette of leaves dark green and oblong; flowers white, in whorls of 3 at 2–4 nodes; lower flowers are female, the upper male; flowers mid-May–July.

RANGE-HABITAT: Restricted to the upper piedmont of Greenville County, SC, and the mountains of Henderson and Buncombe Counties in NC; springhead seepage forests; rare.

COMMENTS: Its rarity is due to the dearth of seepages with a year-round, nearly constant, slow flow of cool water. Ducks foraging on the tubers are a threat to those few populations that have expanded into seepages at pond margins.

PROTECTION STATUS: Federal Endangered

THE PIEDMONT

280. Poison sumac

Rhus vernix L.
Rhùs vér-nix
Anacardiaceae (Cashew Family)

DESCRIPTION: Smooth, tall shrub or small tree, 20–30′ tall; leaves deciduous, produced simultaneously with flowers; leaves alternate, odd-number leaves pinnately compound, with 7–13 leaflets, the leaf stalks and young twigs nearly always reddish; flowers May–early June.

RANGE-HABITAT: Common and widespread in eastern North America; throughout SC, but rare in the piedmont and mountains; montane bogs, seepage forests in the piedmont, streamhead pocosins, sandhill seepage bogs, and pocosins (more commonly on the edge) and adjacent, acidic swamps in the coastal plain.

COMMENTS: The oils in all parts of the plant can cause severe dermatitis in susceptible individuals, similar to poison oak and poison ivy. Smoke from burning leaves or twigs can carry the volatile oil. The whitish, waxy fruits ripen in early fall but may persist throughout the winter, when they are fed upon by numerous birds.

SYNONYM: *Toxicodendron vernix* (L.) Kuntze—W

281. Murdannia

Murdannia keisak (Hasskarl)
Handel-Mazzetti
Mur-dán-ni-a keì-sak
Commelinaceae (Spiderwort Family)

DESCRIPTION: Prostrate annual herb, usually rooting at the nodes; leaves alternate, linear to lanceolate; flowers solitary, or in 2–4-flowered racemes borne in the upper leaf axils; flowers May–October.

RANGE-HABITAT: Widespread in the southeastern US; throughout SC; rare in the mountains, occasional in the piedmont, and common in the sandhills and coastal plain; seepage areas, ditches, streamsides, marshes, swamp forests, and wet disturbed places.

SIMILAR SPECIES: *Murdannia nudiflora* (L.) Brenan differs from *M. keisak* in that it has fruits (capsules) on stalks about as long as the fruit, whereas *M. keisak* has fruits on stalks much longer than its fruits. This species was also introduced from Asia, and although it is a coastal plain plant found in similar habitats to *M. keisak,* it is less common.

COMMENTS: Murdannia is naturalized from Asia and has invaded a wide variety of wetland habitats.

SYNONYM: *Aneilema keisak* Hasskarl—RAB

282. Silky dogwood

Cornus amomum Miller
   Cór-nus a-mò-mum
Cornaceae (Dogwood Family)

DESCRIPTION: Shrub 4–10′ tall; older plants usually with several erect, arching, or leaning stems from the base; young branches green to dark red, pith brown; leaves opposite, blades mostly ovate; flowers and fruits in open cymes; flowers May–June; drupes blue with areas of cream color, mature August–September.

RANGE-HABITAT: Southern MA to IL, south to FL, west to ne. MS; in SC chiefly in the mountains and piedmont; common; scattered in the outer coastal plain; seepage forests, river and streamsides, wet thickets and clearings, borders of alluvial swamps, and marshes.

283. Small green wood-orchid; club-spur orchid

Platanthera clavellata (Michaux) Luer
   Pla-tán-the-ra cla-vel-là-ta
Orchidaceae (Orchid Family)

DESCRIPTION: Perennial herb to 16″ tall, from a cluster of thickened fibrous roots; 1 (2) foliage leaves on the lower half of the stem; flowers in a terminal, open cluster, dull white or tinged with green or yellow; lip petal neither fringed nor lobed, twisted so that the 0.4–0.6″ long spur is lateral; flowers June–September.

RANGE-HABITAT: Widespread in eastern North America; common but scattered throughout SC; montane bogs, swamps, seepages, and other wet places; especially common in montane bogs and piedmont seepage swamps.

COMMENTS: In the northern part of its range this species is pollinated by mosquitoes.

SYNONYM: *Habenaria clavellata* (Michaux) Sprengel—RAB

Bottomland forests

284. Spring beauty

Claytonia virginica L.
    Clay-tòn-i-a vir-gí-ni-ca
Portulacaceae (Purslane Family)

DESCRIPTION: Perennial herb usually less than 8″ tall, from a swollen underground stem (corm); a few leaves in a basal tuft, and one pair, usually opposite, on the stem; leaves with linear blades, not distinct from the leaf stalk, together 3–8″ long and to 0.4″ wide; flowers white to pink; flowers February–April.
RANGE-HABITAT: Nova Scotia west to MN, south to GA and TX; in SC rare in the coastal plain, common in the piedmont and mountains; rich forests, often on floodplains in the piedmont and coastal plain and in basic-mesic forests or rich cove forests in the piedmont and mountains.
COMMENTS: Some authors now separate this species into two varieties, but as Weakley (2001) suggests, this seems unwarranted without more information on distribution and habitat. Sometimes called "fairy spuds" because of its edible (when boiled) corms. The genus honors John Clayton, ?–1773, one of the earliest North American botanists, who contributed to Gronovius the materials for his *Flora Virginica.*

285. Bulbous bittercress

Cardamine bulbosa (Schreiber ex Muhlenberg) BSP.
    Car-dá-mi-ne bul-bò-sa
Brassicaceae (Mustard Family)

DESCRIPTION: Showy, perennial herb from 1–several tubers; stem smooth, strictly erect, to 20″ tall; leaves basal and on the stem, unlobed, lower often round-shaped; flowers white to rarely pink; flowers March–May.
RANGE-HABITAT: Widespread in eastern North America; in SC in the mountains, piedmont, and coastal plain; rare; hardwood bottoms, swamp forests, and bogs, primarily over calcium-rich soils.
COMMENTS: The roots reportedly can be ground and used as a substitute for horseradish.

286. Pawpaw

Asimina triloba (L.) Dunal
A-sí-mi-na trí-lo-ba
Annonaceae (Pawpaw Family)

DESCRIPTION: Large shrub or small tree, 16–33′ tall; twigs covered with fine, rust-colored hairs; leaves deciduous, alternate, simple, malodorous when crushed; flowers borne on the wood produced the previous year; winter buds flattened, covered with rust-colored hairs; flowers March–April; fruits mature in fall.

RANGE-HABITAT: NJ west to NY and Ontario, west to MN and NE, and south to FL panhandle, LA and ne. TX; throughout SC (except the maritime strand); common in the piedmont and mountains; occasional in the coastal plain; rich hardwood forests, alluvial forests, and other moist, nutrient-rich forests.

COMMENTS: The ripe fruit of pawpaw is sweet; it can be eaten raw, baked as pie filling or made into a variety of other foods. The fruits are collected when green (often from the ground) and kept until ripe. Early settlers made a yellow dye from the ripe pulp. Wildlife readily eat the fruits.

287. Wild hyacinth

Camassia scilloides Rafinesque
Ca-más-si-a scil-loì-des
Liliaceae (Lily Family)

DESCRIPTION: Perennial herb from a bulb, up to 2′ tall; leaves basal only, to 20″ long and 0.8″ wide; racemes to 0.5″ long; flowers pale blue to whitish, terminating a leafless stalk; flowers April–May.

RANGE-HABITAT: WI and PA, south to GA and AL; a typical prairie species of the Midwest; in SC a rare piedmont species in upland swamps.

COMMENTS: This common species of Midwestern prairies is one of many SC species with prairie affinities. It grows on calcium-rich soils, usually Elbert loam; known from only York and Chester Counties.

PROTECTION STATUS: State Threatened

288. Bladdernut

Staphylea trifolia L.
    Sta-phy-lè-a tri-fò-li-a
Staphyleaceae (Bladdernut Family)

DESCRIPTION: Shrub or small tree to 25′ tall;
flowers white or greenish white, in drooping
clusters from the leaf axils; fruit inflated and
podlike; flowers April.

RANGE-HABITAT: Widespread in the eastern US;
in SC rare in the mountains and coastal plain,
occasional in the piedmont; rich deciduous
woods, including hardwood bottoms, basic-
mesic forests, and cove forests.

COMMENTS: The opposite, compound leaves with 3, fine-toothed leaflets are distinctive.

289. Wild allspice; northern spicebush

Lindera benzoin (L.) Bloom
    Lín-der-a ben-zò-in
Lauraceae (Laurel Family)

DESCRIPTION: Deciduous, aromatic shrub,
much branched and usually 5–9′ tall; leaves
thin with a nearly clear leaf stalk; flowers yellow, in dense axillary umbels, before the
leaves appear; flowers March–April; drupes
mature August–September.

RANGE-HABITAT: Widespread in eastern North
America; common throughout SC (except
absent in the maritime strand); cove forests in
the mountains, rich hardwood bottoms,
swamp forests, basic-mesic forests in the piedmont, and beech forests in the coastal plain.

COMMENTS: The presence of this species on slopes is a good indicator of calcium-rich soils. All parts are aromatic, like sassafras or allspice. Pioneers used
wild allspice as a substitute for allspice. The genus name honors Johann Linder,
1676–1723, an early Swedish botanist.

THE FALL-LINE SANDHILLS

290. Longleaf pine-scrub oak sandhills

291. Carolina ipecac

Euphorbia ipecacuanhae L.
Eu-phòr-bi-a i-pe-ca-cu-àn-hae
Euphorbiaceae (Spurge Family)

DESCRIPTION: Perennial herb with milky sap from a deep taproot many feet long, branched near the top into many stems with only the tips above ground; aboveground stems smooth, dichotomously branched, forming low, dark green tufts or small mats; leaves variable, from linear to round; flowers March–May.

RANGE-HABITAT: From Long Island, NY, and NJ, south to GA; in SC common in the sandhills and inner coastal plain; deep sands of sand ridges, Carolina bay rims, longleaf pine-scrub oak sandhills, and longleaf pine-turkey oak sandhills.

COMMENTS: F. P. Porcher (1869) reported that this plant was "tolerably certain emetic; but liable sometimes to produce excessive nausea by accumulation." It is an extremely strong laxative, and the juice from the fresh plant may cause blistering.

292. Sand myrtle

Leiophyllum buxifolium (Bergius) Elliott
   Lei-o-phýl-lum bux-i-fò-li-um
   Ericaceae (Heath Family)

DESCRIPTION: Low, upright, widely branching evergreen shrub with crowded, leathery leaves; to around 3' tall; flowers white or pinkish; flowers late March–April.

RANGE-HABITAT: In the pine barrens of NJ, NC, SC, ne. GA, e. TN, and se. KY; in SC common in the fall-line sandhills in longleaf pine scrub-oak sandhills; also in the mountains (see comments below) in rocky woods and bluffs and granitic domes.

COMMENTS: Some manuals recognize a variety, *L. buxifolium* var. *prostratum* (Loudon) Gray, which occurs in the high mountains; however, Weakley (2001) and others now consider the variety a form, and the genus is therefore monotypic. Good populations of sand myrtle occur in Peachtree Rock Nature Preserve in Lexington County. Sand myrtle is hard if not impossible to transplant into cultivation and, because of its restricted range, should not be collected from the wild.

293. Southern haw: yellow hawthorn

Crataegus flava Aiton
   Cra-taè-gus flà-va
   Rosaceae (Rose Family)

DESCRIPTION: Shrub or small tree to 16' tall; branches armed with spines; leaves obovate, often shallowly lobed toward the tip, with serrate margins and teeth tipped with tiny black glands; flowers produced in 2–3-flowered clusters; flowers late March–May; fruit red at maturity in August–September.

RANGE-HABITAT: Confined to the southeastern US; throughout SC (except absent in the maritime strand); sandy or rocky xeric woodlands and thickets, and oak-pine woods.

TAXONOMY: *Crataegus* is a large genus and the subject of considerable controversy among taxonomists as to species definition and number. Some authors, for example, divide *Crataegus flava* to include about a dozen species. Duncan and Duncan (1988) state that there are about 35 species in the southeast. This species is included so the reader will be aware of this large and important genus.

COMMENTS: The fruits of species of *Crataegus* are an important wildlife food, especially for birds. All species have an edible fruit that can be used to make jam or jelly. Duke (1997) recommends all species of *Crataegus* as a herbal remedy for angina.

294. Puccoon

Lithospermum caroliniense (Walter
  ex J. F. Gmelin) MacMillan
  Li-tho-spér-mum ca-ro-li-ni-én-se
Boraginaceae (Borage Family)

DESCRIPTION: Herb 12–40″ tall, from a strong-
staining taproot; leaves alternate; stems very
leafy, rough; flowers in dense cymes, leafy-
bracted; flowers April–June.
RANGE-HABITAT: From se. SC, south to FL, and
west to TX (absent in NC and disjunct in se.
VA); in SC in the sandhills and southeast
coastal plain; xeric sandhills, sandy roadsides,
and fields; common.
COMMENTS: Puccoon is a Native American name for a number of plants that
yield dyes.

295. Barbara's-buttons

Marshallia obovata var. *scaposa* Channell
  Mar-sháll-i-a o-bo-và-ta var. sca-pò-sa
Asteraceae (Aster or Sunflower Family)

DESCRIPTION: Cespitose, perennial herb, 4–24″ tall; stems with
0–3 leaves, restricted to basal region; leaves 3-nerved, entire;
heads with only disk flowers; flowers late April–March.
RANGE-HABITAT: Coastal plain and sandhills species, from e. NC to
se. AL; in SC primarily a plant of the sandhills and inner coastal
plain; xeric communities and pine flatwoods; common.
COMMENTS: The genus honors Dr. Moses Marshall, 1758–1813.
TAXONOMY: This variety is similar to *M. obovata* (Walter) Beadle &
Boynton var. *obovata,* which occurs in the piedmont in old fields,
meadows, clay flats, and woodland borders. Variety *obovata* has
4–7 stem leaves extending ¼ or more up the stem.

296. Hairy phlox

Phlox amoena Sims
  Phlóx a-moè-na
Polemoniaceae (Phlox Family)

DESCRIPTION: Decumbent, perennial herb with
erect sterile and fertile shoots, the latter to 12″
tall; leaves simple, elliptic to linear, opposite
in 5–9 pairs; corolla pink to lavender; stamens
shorter than the corolla tube; flowers
April–June.
RANGE-HABITAT: FL to MS, north to NC; in SC
chiefly in the mountains, piedmont, and sandhills in the mid-central and western counties;
sandhills, dry woodlands, and open banks;
common.

297. Wild garlic

Allium canadense var. *mobilense* (Regel)
  Ownbey
  Ál-li-um ca-na-dén-se var.
  mo-bi-lén-se
Liliaceae (Lily Family)

DESCRIPTION: Perennial, bulbous, scapose, smooth herb; 8–24″ tall; leaves 6–18″ long, linear, flat; umbel entirely of normal flowers; flowers mid-April–May.

RANGE-HABITAT: From s. SC south to FL, and west to TX; in SC occasional, but often locally abundant in the west central counties of the coastal plain, piedmont, and sandhills; longleaf pine-scrub oak sandhills, pastures, moist and dry woodlands, and along roadsides.

COMMENTS: Wild garlic has a brown, fibrous skin on an edible bulb that tastes like onion. Before flowering and after removing wilted leaves, the whole plant can be boiled in salted water and eaten as a delicious vegetable. The water is the base for a delicate cream-of-onion soup.

TAXONOMY: Some authors divide this species into two varieties. *A. canadense* L. var. *canadense* has an inflorescence partly or entirely of bulblets; *A. canadense* var. *mobilense* (Regel) Ownbey has an inflorescence entirely of normal flowers.

298. Eastern green-eyes

Berlandiera pumila (Michaux) Nuttall
  Ber-lan-di-èr-a pù-mi-la
Asteraceae (Aster or Sunflower Family)

DESCRIPTION: Perennial herb to 3.5′ tall, from a large root; leaves alternate, hairy on both surfaces; disk flowers green in bud—hence, the common name; bracts below flower heads wide (easily visible in photograph); flowers late May–frost.

RANGE-HABITAT: Primarily a coastal plain plant from nc. SC to n. FL, then west to e. TX; in SC found in the lower piedmont, sandhills, and inner coastal plain; common; longleaf pine-scrub oak sandhills, sandy fields, longleaf pine-turkey oak sandhills, and sand ridges.

COMMENTS: The genus honors Jean Louis Berlandier, 1805–1855, a Swiss botanist who collected in TX and Mexico.

299. Narrowleaf rose-pink

Sabatia brachiata Elliott
Sa-bà-ti-a bra-chi-à-ta
Gentianaceae (Gentian Family)

DESCRIPTION: Annual herb, with a single stem (rarely 2 or 3) arising from a rosette; 6–20″ tall; branches opposite; stem round below, sometimes lined or finely ridged; stem leaves nearly oblong, 3x or more longer than wide, not clasping; corolla lobes 5, pale pink to darkly roseate, with a greenish yellow "eye" bordered by a reddish line at the base; flowers late May–July.

RANGE-HABITAT: VA south to GA, west to LA, and north in the interior to se. MO; in SC in the sandhills and inner coastal plain; sandhills, longleaf pine flatwoods, and longleaf pine savannas; occasional.

SIMILAR SPECIES: *S. brachiata* is similar to *S. angularis* (L.) Pursh (plate 260), which occurs throughout SC in old fields, pastures, pine flatwoods, ditches, and meadows. *S. angularis* (bitter-bloom) has ovate stem leaves, their bases clasping the stem; stem angled, with membranous wings on the angles.

300. Whorled milkweed

Asclepias verticillata L.
As-clè-pi-as ver-ti-cil-là-ta
Asclepiadaceae (Milkweed Family)

DESCRIPTION: Perennial herb with milky sap; stem erect, simple, or branching in upper third; 12–32″ tall; leaves numerous, whorled or subwhorled, linear; flowers in 2–8 umbels, from upper nodes; flowers June–September.

RANGE-HABITAT: From e. MA west to ND and Manitoba, south to FL, TX, NM, and AZ; occasional but throughout SC; sandhills communities, xeric hardpan forests, sandy, dry, open woods, rocky slopes, and roadsides.

301. Jointweed

Polygonella americana (Fisher & Meyer) Small
Po-ly-go-nél-la a-me-ri-cà-na
Polygonaceae (Buckwheat Family)

DESCRIPTION: Perennial semishrub with numerous, short, leafy branches, 24–32″ tall; appearing as a depressed, matted shrub early in the growing season; petals absent; sepals white; flowers June–September.

RANGE-HABITAT: From sc. NC to s. GA, west to TX and NM, and north to the interior to MO and AR; in SC primarily found in the sandhills, where it is frequent in longleaf pine-scrub oak sandhills and longleaf pine-turkey oak sandhills.

302. Rose purslane

Portulaca pilosa L.
Por-tu-là-ca pi-lò-sa
Portulacaceae (Purslane Family)

DESCRIPTION: Prostrate or erect, many-branched annual, 2–8″ tall; leaves fleshy, with tufts of whitish hairs in the axils; flowers June–October; capsule with a "lid" that opens near the middle to expose the smooth, red seeds.

RANGE-HABITAT: NC to FL, west to NM, and north to TN, AR, and OK; in SC primarily in the sandhills but also in the lower piedmont and inner coastal plain; occasional; disturbed, sandy soils, longleaf pine-scrub oak sandhills, yards, and waste places.

303. Carphephorus

Carphephorus bellidifolius (Michaux) Torrey & Gray
Car-phé-pho-rus bel-li-di-fò-li-us
Asteraceae (Aster or Sunflower Family)

DESCRIPTION: Perennial herb, with ascending stems 6–20″ tall; basal leaves numerous, 2–8″ long, somewhat spoon-shaped; stem leaves few; flowers in heads, pink to lavender; flowers July–October.

RANGE-HABITAT: Southeastern coastal plain endemic, from se. VA to e. GA; in SC common throughout the sandhills and coastal plain; sandy, dry, open woods, and other xeric communities.

COMMENTS: The only other *Carphephorus* likely to be found with *C. bellidifolius* is *C. tomentosus*. The lower stems of *C. bellidifolius* are smooth or with short appressed hairs; *C. tomentosus* has lower stems with obvious, long spreading hairs.

304. Blazing star

Liatris secunda Elliott
Li-à-tris se-cún-da
Asteraceae (Aster or Sunflower Family)

DESCRIPTION: Perennial herb from a globose rootstock; stems arching to reclining; lower leaves linear to narrowly elliptic; heads all disk flowers, usually 5-flowered, 1-sided, with corolla lobes widely spreading; corolla lobes pink to whitish; flowers late July–September.

RANGE-HABITAT: NC to FL, and west to LA; in SC in the sandhills and inner coastal plain, plus Horry and Georgetown Counties; xeric communities, old fields, and woodlands in sandy soil; occasional.

COMMENTS: This is the only species of *Liatris* in SC with heads on one side of the stem.

305. Grass-leaved golden-aster

Pityopsis pinifolia (Elliott) Nuttall
Pi-ty-óp-sis pi-ni-fó-li-a
Asteraceae (Aster or Sunflower Family)

DESCRIPTION: Smooth perennial herb with short stolons, to 20″ tall; leaves grasslike, entire, ascending; heads few to many; flowers late August–September.

RANGE-HABITAT: Limited to scattered counties in the sandhills of s. NC, SC, GA, and c. AL; in SC in Lexington, Calhoun, Richland, and Georgetown Counties; sandhills communities and along sandy roadsides; locally common.

COMMENTS: This plant is locally common and often weedy. It is common at the Peachtree Rock Nature Preserve. Recently, it has been found on Sandy Island Heritage Preserve in Georgetown County, the only known site outside the sandhills.

SYNONYM: *Heterotheca pinifolia* (Elliott) Ahles—RAB

306. Senna seymeria

Seymeria cassioides (J. F. Gmelin) Blake
Sey-mèr-i-a cas-si-oì-des
Scrophulariaceae (Figwort Family)

DESCRIPTION: Erect, profusely branched annual herb, 20–40″ tall; presumably parasitic (on pines?); glandular-hairy; fresh plants green, drying dark; leaves opposite, less than 0.5″ long, with filiform segments; corolla lemon yellow, sometimes marked with purple within; flowers August–October.

RANGE-HABITAT: Essentially a southeastern coastal plain endemic, from se. VA, south to c. peninsular FL, and west to LA; in SC in the sandhills and coastal plain in savannas, sandhills, pocosin margins, and along roadsides; common.

COMMENTS: The genus honors Henry Seymer, 1745–1800, an English naturalist.

307. Turkey oak

Quercus laevis Walter
Quér-cus laè-vis
Fagaceae (Beech Family)

DESCRIPTION: Small tree; bark thick with deep, irregular furrows and scaly, rough ridges; inner bark reddish; leaves alternate, deciduous, generally with 3 wide-spreading, main lobes (like a turkey's foot) that are pointed and bristle-tipped; fruits mature September–October.

RANGE-HABITAT: Southeastern endemic from se. VA south to FL, west to e. LA; common in SC in the coastal plain and sandhills; longleaf pine-turkey oak sandhills, longleaf pine-scrub oak sandhills, Carolina bay rims, sand ridges, sandy, longleaf pine flatwoods, and other sites with dry, sandy soil.

COMMENTS: This is one of the few oaks that will grow in sandy, sterile soil.

Unlike many oaks, turkey oak is adapted to periodic fires. After a fire it spreads rapidly by growth of underground runners. Leaves of young seedlings are orientated at right angles to the ground; this reduces heat absorption that is reflected from bare, white sand and heat absorption from direct sunlight. The tree is not large enough for lumber, but the seasoned wood is excellent as firewood. It is often used as the fuel in hog barbecue pits. The acorns are an important food source for deer, turkey, and small rodents.

308. Whiteleaf greenbrier

Smilax glauca Walter
Smì-lax glaù-ca
Liliaceae (Lily Family)

DESCRIPTION: Woody, slender-stemmed vine, with long underground runners with knotty, jointed, tuberous thickenings; climbing fairly high, but mostly forming thickets closer to the ground; stems green or brown, whitish, round, with green spines; leaves partially evergreen, variegated with lighter green above, whitish beneath, turning reddish to purple in the fall; umbels many fruited; berry bluish black, whitish, usually persistent, mature September–November.

RANGE-HABITAT: Widespread and common in the southeastern US; throughout SC in swamp forests, pocosins, sandhills, upland and alluvial woods, old fields, and fencerows.

COMMENTS: F. P. Porcher (1869) and Fernald and Kinsey (1958) expound on the many uses of *Smilax* species as food, including the making of jelly from the cordlike rootstocks. The young, spring shoots of whiteleaf greenbrier may be cooked like a vegetable; however, they are bitter, unlike some of the other tasty *Smilax* species. This is South Carolina's only species of *Smilax* with leaves whitish beneath.

309. Longleaf pine

Pinus palustris Miller
Pì-nus pa-lús-tris
Pinaceae (Pine Family)

DESCRIPTION: Large, evergreen tree; needles 10–16″ long, in fascicles of 3; female cones at maturity 6–10″ long.

RANGE-HABITAT: Coastal plain and sandhills endemic, from se. VA to FL, west to se. TX, and slightly into the piedmont in most states; in SC common in the coastal plain and sandhills in sandy soils of longleaf pine flatwoods and savannas, longleaf pine-scrub oak sandhills, bay rims, sandy ridges, fluvial ridges, pine-mixed hardwood forests, and disturbed sites.

COMMENTS: Longleaf pine was the dominant pine in the original southern forests of the coastal area. Its thick bark makes it resistant to fires, and, unlike other southern pines, it is naturally resistant to fusiform rust. Growing tall and slender to a height of over 120′ and living from 200–300 years, the original longleaf forests quickly fell to the ax of lumbermen. Lack of natural fires that swept over the cutover areas, fire suppression, feral hogs that consumed the young seedlings, competition from loblolly pine (a more prolific seeder), and the lack of replanting all contributed to longleaf's current occupation of less than 10% of its original acreage.

Longleaf once was the basis of the naval stores industry; its trunks were used for sailing ship masts, and it was used for beams, floors, and general construction. Many of the Carolina lowcountry mansions and plantations are made of "heart pine." The high resinous content makes the wood indestructible by insects and fungi. It is still an important lumber tree.

Longleaf pine-turkey oak sandhills

310. Sandhills pyxie-moss

Pyxidanthera barbulata var. *brevifolia*
(B. W. Wells) Ahles
Pyx-i-dan-thè-ra bar-bu-là-ta
var. bre-vi-fò-li-a
Diapensiaceae (Diapensia Family)

DESCRIPTION: Creeping, perennial subshrub; leaves evergreen, lanceolate, about 0.06–0.19" long, hairy on the entire surface; flowers sessile, about 0.25" across; stamens conspicuous, arising between the petals; flowers December–March.

RANGE-HABITAT: Endemic to a 6-county area of the Carolina sandhills (Chesterfield and Darlington Counties in SC); xeric sandhills; rare, but locally abundant.

COMMENTS: The name of the genus refers not to some relationship with pyxies (fairies) but to the type of opening of the anther from which pollen is released. The Greek *pyxie* means "small box," and *anthera* means "anther." A good site to view this species is at Sugarloaf Mountain in the Carolina Sandhills National Wildlife Refuge in Chesterfield County.

TAXONOMY: Two varieties of *Pyxidanthera* are recognized: var. *brevifolia* (pictured in this book), and var. *barbulata* (common pyxie-moss, *P. barbulata* Michaux var. *barbulata*, plate 318 in *WCL*). The taxonomic status of var. *brevifolia* has been controversial; some authors consider it a species, some a variety, and others consider it an ecotype not worthy of taxonomic status. Variety *brevifolia* has leaves 0.06–0.19" long and is hairy on the entire surface; var. *barbulata* has leaves 0.19–0.31" long and is hairy only toward the base, at least on sterile shoots. Variety *barbulata* occurs in the northern sandhills and Horry County in SC.

PROTECTION STATUS: Federal Species of Concern

311. Tread-softly; spurge nettle

Cnidoscolus stimulosus (Michaux)
Engelmann & Gray
Cni-dós-co-lus sti-mu-lò-sus
Euphorbiaceae (Spurge Family)

DESCRIPTION: Erect or reclining, perennial herb, 6–36" tall; entire plant covered with stinging hairs; petals absent; sepals white; leaves alternate, palmately lobed or dissected; flowers late March–August.

RANGE-HABITAT: From se. VA south to FL, and west to TX, mainly on the coastal plain; common throughout the coastal plain, sandhills, and piedmont of SC; longleaf pine-turkey oak and longleaf pine-scrub oak sandhills, Carolina bay rims, fluvial ridges, sandy, dry, open woods, sandy, fallow fields, and stable coastal dunes.

COMMENTS: Morton (1974) reports that the root is used as an aphrodisiac in rural SC; locally it is called the "courage" plant. The hairs can inflict a painful sting on contact and cause a severe reaction in some people.

312. Southern dwarf huckleberry

Gaylussacia dumosa (Andrzejowski) T. & G. var. *dumosa*
Gay-lus-sàc-i-a du-mò-sa var. du-mò-sa
Ericaceae (Heath Family)

DESCRIPTION: Deciduous or semi-evergreen shrub 4–16″ tall with deep, water-holding taproot; leaves alternate with thick cuticle on upper leaf surface; distinctive, small resinous glands on lower leaf surface; flowers March–June; ripe berry black, mature June–October.

RANGE-HABITAT: NJ south to FL, and west to LA; in SC one of the most common shrubs of the coastal plain and sandhills; sandy or xeric habitats; also in the piedmont and mountains, but uncommon.

COMMENTS: All species of *Gaylussacia* have small, golden, resinous glands on the lower leaf surface. This species is readily distinguished by its small size.

313. Carolina sandwort

Arenaria caroliniana Walter
A-re-nà-ri-a ca-ro-li-ni-à-na
Caryophyllaceae (Pink Family)

DESCRIPTION: Perennial herb from a large basal cushion of decumbent to prostrate stems; flowering stems erect, to 12″ tall (usually much less), with many small glands; leaves opposite, linear-subulate, rigid, overlapping the ones above; flowers April–June.

RANGE HABITAT: Primarily a coastal plain species from RI to FL; in SC in the sandhills and inner coastal plain; dry, sandy communities such as longleaf pine-turkey oak and longleaf pine scrub-oak sandhills; common.

314. Gopherweed

Baptisia perfoliata (L.) R. Brown
Bap-tí-si-a per-fo-li-à-ta
Fabaceae (Pea or Bean Family)

DESCRIPTION: Rhizomatous, smooth, perennial herb, 20–36″ tall; leaves simple and perfoliate; flowers April–May; legume matures May–July.

RANGE-HABITAT: Southeastern coastal plain endemic from SC to peninsular FL; in SC restricted to the coastal plain and sandhills in Aiken, Allendale, Barnwell, Hampton, Jasper, and Lexington Counties; occasional; longleaf pine-turkey oak and longleaf pine-scrub oak sandhills, and sandy, dry, open woods.

COMMENTS: Gopherweed can be found in the Tillman Sand Ridge Heritage Preserve and environs in Jasper County. The whole, dried plants are used in dried arrangements.

315. Woolly-white

Hymenopappus scabiosaeus L'Heritier
de Brutelle
Hy-me-no-páp-pus sca-bri-o-saè-us
Asteraceae (Aster or Sunflower Family)

DESCRIPTION: Perennial herb from a thick taproot, 1–2' tall; leaves more or less clothed with whitish hairs on the underside; basal rosette of leaves present; stem leaves alternate, finely twice-dissected; ray flowers absent, but the subtending bracts have a petal-like, whitish tip; disk flowers white; flowers late April–June.

RANGE-HABITAT: From sc. SC to n. peninsular FL, west to AR and OK, and north to the interior to IN, IL, and MO; in SC locally abundant in the sandhills region in Aiken and Lexington Counties; longleaf pine-turkey oak and longleaf pine-scrub oak sandhills, sandy fields, and along sandy roadsides.

316. Squarehead

Tetragonotheca helianthoides L.
Tet-ra-go-no-thè-ca he-li-an-thoì-des
Asteraceae (Aster or Sunflower Family)

DESCRIPTION: Perennial, cespitose, erect herb with 1–several stems, to 3' tall; leaves opposite, elliptic to ovate, coarsely dentate to serrate; flower heads subtended by 4 ovate bracts; flowers April–July.

RANGE-HABITAT: From se. VA and e. TN, south to c. peninsular FL and s. MS; in SC scattered throughout; longleaf pine-scrub oak sandhills, sandy woods, roadsides, and thickets; occasional.

COMMENTS: The common name and generic name *Tetragonotheca* (meaning "4-angled case") refers to the 4 large bracts that subtend the flower head.

317. Hairy false foxglove

Aureolaria pectinata (Nuttall) Pennell
Au-re-o-lá-ri-a pec-ti-nà-ta
Scrophulariaceae (Figwort Family)

DESCRIPTION: Annual herb, densely covered with glandular hairs; to 3' tall; leaves deeply dissected; flowers May–September.

RANGE-HABITAT: From se. TX to FL, north to VA, KY, and MO; throughout SC, but primarily in the piedmont, sandhills, and inner coastal plain; common; longleaf pine-turkey oak and longleaf pine-scrub oak sandhills, sandy, dry, open woods, and Carolina bay ridges.

COMMENTS: This foxglove is a hemiparasite on the roots of turkey oak or other members of the black oak group.

318. Roseling

Tradescantia rosea var. *graminea* (Small) Anderson and
Woodson
Tra-des-cánt-i-a rò-se-a var. gra-mí-ne-a
Commelinaceae (Spiderwort Family)

DESCRIPTION: Smooth perennial herb, 8–20″ tall; narrow basal
leaves tufted, less than 0.13″ wide; flowers subtended by minute
bracts; petals 3; fertile stamens 6, bearded; flowers May–July.

RANGE-HABITAT: From se. VA through the Carolinas to GA and
peninsular FL; in SC in the inner coastal plain and sandhills;
common; longleaf pine-scrub oak sandhills, sandy, dry, open
woods, Carolina bay ridges, and sand ridges.

TAXONOMY: A similar variety is *T. rosea* Ventenat var. *rosea.* It
occurs more in the piedmont and outer coastal plain, but the
ranges of the two varieties overlap and they share similar habitats.
The leaves of var. *rosea* are more than 0.13″ wide versus less than
0.13″ wide for var. *graminea.*

SYNONYM: *Cuthbertea graminea* Small—W

319. Northern golden-heather

Hudsonia ericoides L.
Hud-sòn-i-a er-i-coì-des
Cistaceae Rockrose Family

DESCRIPTION: Low, spreading, freely branched
shrub, rarely more than 12–16″ tall; leaves
evergreen, alternate, crowded, needlelike,
about 0.25″ long; flowers numerous, on short
stalks, solitary, at the ends of short spur
shoots, or terminating normal branches; flowers in May.

RANGE-HABITAT: Newfoundland south to MA,
NH, and DE; disjunct in SC in Chesterfield
County; longleaf pine-turkey oak and longleaf pine-scrub oak sandhills; rare.

COMMENTS: Golden-heather was originally known in SC from only Cheraw State
Park at the Hudsonia Flats along SC-20. Being disjunct so far from the closest
site in DE prompted some field botanists to consider whether it might have
been introduced into SC. However, the first author and Patrick D. McMillan
found a second site in Chesterfield County, adding support that it is a rare
native disjunct. The genus honors William Hudson, 1730–1793, an English
botanist.

PROTECTION STATUS: State Endangered

320. Wire-plant

Stipulicida setacea Michaux var. *setacea*
Sti-pu-lí-ci-da se-tà-ce-a
Caryophyllaceae (Pink Family)

DESCRIPTION: Dichotomously branched, smooth, wiry annual or short-lived perennial, with taproot and overwintering basal rosette; stem 2–8″ tall; stem leaves reduced to scales; flowers white, very small, in clusters of 1–6; flowers May–August.

RANGE-HABITAT: From se. VA, south to FL, and west to LA; in SC in the sandhills, coastal plain, and maritime strand; common in all xeric communities in its range, including dry pine flatwoods and maritime forests.

COMMENTS: Wire-plant times its life cycle to miss the hot, dry summer days. During spring and early summer, it grows and flowers. During the hot summer months it survives in the seed stage. Its seeds germinate in the fall and it over-winters as a rosette. The minute size of its stem leaves also helps to reduce water loss from transpiration.

321. Narrowleaf dawnflower

Stylisma patens subsp. *angustifolia*
(Nash) Myint
Sty-lís-ma pà-tens subsp.
an-gus-ti-fò-li-a
Convolvulaceae (Morning-glory Family)

DESCRIPTION: Herbaceous, vinelike perennial, prostrate or spreading with no tendency to twine; larger leaves 0.06–0.38″ wide, 7–15x as long as wide; peduncles usually 1-flowered; flowers May–August.

RANGE-HABITAT: Widespread in n. and c. peninsular FL, and FL panhandle, with relatively sparse occurrences north to se. NC; in SC widely scattered locations in the sandhills and coastal plain; xeric sandhills and other relatively dry, sandy areas, including roadsides.

TAXONOMY: Two subspecies of *S. patens* are recognized: subsp. *angustifolia* with leaves 7–15x as long as wide, and *S. patens* (Desrousseaux) Myint subsp. *patens* with leaves 4–6x as long as wide.

SYNONYM: *Bonamia patens* var. *angustifolia* (Nash) Shinners—RAB

322. Sandhills St. John's-wort

Hypericum lloydii (Svenson) P. Adams
        Hy-pé-ri-cum llóyd-i-i
Hypericaceae (St. John's-wort Family)

DESCRIPTION: Decumbent, usually matted shrub, 4–20″ tall; stems angled; leaves linear-subulate; flowers June–September.

RANGE-HABITAT: NC to AL; in SC found in the sandhills and lower piedmont; longleaf pine-turkey oak and longleaf pine-scrub oak sandhills, and margins of rock outcrops; common.

COMMENTS: Good populations of this plant occur in Lexington County in the vicinity of Shealy's Pond Heritage Preserve and at Peachtree Rock Nature Preserve. The specific epithet honors Francis E. Lloyd, 1868–1947.

323. Pickering's dawnflower

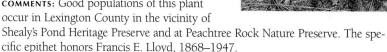

Stylisma pickeringii (Torrey ex Curtis)
        Gray var. *pickeringii*
        Sty-lís-ma pick-er-íng-i-i var.
        pick-er-íng-i-i
Convolvulaceae (Morning-glory Family)

DESCRIPTION: Herbaceous perennial vine; stems numerous, arching from a central point, then trailing radially away, sometimes forming a mound 3–6′ in diameter; leaves linear, held vertically; flowers 1–3, on axillary peduncles; flowers June–August (–September).

RANGE-HABITAT: From s. NC through SC, GA, and AL, and disjunct into the NJ pine barrens; in SC in the sandhills in the driest, most barren, deepest sands; rare.

COMMENTS: This species is easily distinguished from other species of *Stylisma* by its narrow, linear leaves borne vertically and by its numerous stems arching from a central point, then trailing radially away. Fire is necessary for seed germination. Bob McCartney of Woodlander's, Inc, in Aiken, SC, has induced germination by placing the seeds in sub-boiling water for a few minutes. The specific epithet honors Charles Pickering, 1805–1878, an American botanist.

SYNONYM: *Bonamia pickeringii* (Torrey) Gray—RAB

PROTECTION STATUS: Federal Species of Concern

324. Georgia beargrass

Nolina georgiana Michaux
        No-lì-na geor-gi-à-na
Liliaceae (Lily Family)

DESCRIPTION: Perennial herb to 5′ tall; leaves in a basal rosette, linear, 12–18″ long, reduced upward, gracefully arching away from the stem; inflorescence a large panicle; flowers white; flowers late May–June; fruits a 3-lobed, bladderlike capsule, with thin "wings" on each angle; mature late June–August.

RANGE-HABITAT: From nc. SC south to sc. GA;

in SC in the sandhills and inner coastal plain north to Kershaw County; rare; longleaf pine-turkey oak and longleaf pine-scrub oak sandhills.

COMMENTS: A population of beargrass occurs in the Aiken Gopher Tortoise Heritage Preserve. The authors did not discover this plant in the Gopher Tortoise Heritage Preserve until late June, too late to photograph it in flower. However, even in fruit, it is unlikely to be mistaken for any other species of the lily family in the sandhills habitat.

325. Woody goldenrod

Chrysoma pauciflosculosa (Michaux) Greene
Chry-sò-ma pau-ci-flos-cu-lò-sa
Asteraceae (Aster or Sunflower Family)

DESCRIPTION: The following description is taken from Weakley (2001): "*Chrysoma* has a growth habit unlike any other shrub in SC flora. From a trunklike base, numerous branches ascend, forming a flat-topped shrub 12–20″ tall. Each branch has a cluster of evergreen leaves restricted to its terminal few cm, the internodes very short (a few mm at most). In summer, some of the woody branches produce terminal, deciduous, flowering branches, which elongate rapidly, the leaves widely spaced, reaching a height of a meter or more. Following flowering and fruiting, the deciduous branch dies back to the summit of the woody branch. The leaves are gray-green, rather thick-textured, and finely reticulate. . ."; flowers late July–October.

RANGE-HABITAT: From s. NC to n. FL, and west to s. MS; in SC found only in the sandhills of Lexington and Chesterfield Counties; longleaf pine-turkey oak and longleaf pine-scrub oak sandhills; rare in SC, occasional in GA and FL, and locally abundant in the Florida scrub community.

COMMENTS: Woody goldenrod can be seen in Peachtree Rock Nature Preserve and the Hudsonia Flat in Cheraw State Park.

SYNONYM: *Solidago pauciflosculosa* Michaux—RAB

PROTECTION STATUS: State Endangered

326. Sandhill wild-buckwheat

Eriogonum tomentosum Michaux
E-ri-ó-go-num to-men-tò-sum
Polygonaceae (Buckwheat Family)

DESCRIPTION: Perennial herb to 3′ tall; stem erect or often leaning, hairy, freely branched, usually from a basal rosette; basal leaves often numerous, evergreen, sometimes dying with age or because of drought; stem leaves with dense white or tan hairs beneath, in whorls of 3 or 4; flowers July–September.

RANGE-HABITAT: From s. NC to FL, and west to AL; fairly common in the sandhills of SC; longleaf pine-turkey oak and longleaf pine-scrub oak sandhills.

327. Rosemary

Ceratiola ericoides Michaux
Ce-ra-ti-ò-la e-ri-coì-des
Empetraceae (Crowberry Family)

DESCRIPTION: Many-branched, dense shrub, 2–5′ tall; branches with 4 rows of short, slender, needlelike leaves; male and female flowers on separate plants, sessile in leaf axils; flowers October–November.

RANGE-HABITAT: SC south to FL, and west to MS; in SC chiefly in the sandhills, but scattered in the coastal plain; longleaf pine-turkey oak sandhills, Carolina bay ridges, and sand ridges.

COMMENTS: This is not the herb, rosemary. It is highly flammable because of its aromatic compounds. Populations on some bay ridges have disappeared due to vehicular traffic.

TAXONOMY: Some authors place *Ceratiola,* a monotypic genus, in the heath family (Ericaceae).

Streamhead pocosins

328. Dwarf milkwort

Polygala nana (Michaux) Augustin
de Candolle
Po-lý-ga-la nà-na
Polygalaceae (Milkwort Family)

DESCRIPTION: Biennial herb to 6″ tall; leaves mostly confined to a basal rosette; leaves fleshy; flowers lemon yellow, turning a dark bluish green on drying; flowers March–October, and sporadically through the winter.

RANGE-HABITAT: Primarily a sandhills and coastal plain plant of the deeper South; SC to FL, west to TX; in SC in the sandhills and inner coastal plain (and Jasper County); streamhead pocosins, wet longleaf pine flatwoods, and open, wet sands; rare in SC.

PROTECTION STATUS: State Endangered

329. White wicky

Kalmia cuneata Michaux
Kálm-i-a cu-ne-à-ta
Ericaceae (Heath Family)

DESCRIPTION: Deciduous, colonial shrub to 6′ tall; leaves alternate, oblanceolate to narrowly elliptic; flowers in short racemes or axillary fascicles near the tip of branches of the previous season; corolla greenish white with a red band within; flowers May–June.

RANGE-HABITAT: Narrow endemic of the coastal plain and sandhills of se. NC and adjacent SC; in SC known from Darlington, Chesterfield, and Kershaw Counties; pocosins and pocosin-savanna or pocosin-sandhill ecotones; rare.

COMMENTS: White wicky is similar to other species of *Kalmia* but can be separated by the following characteristics unique to white wicky: deciduous leaves; a solid, red band on the inside of the petals; and a curved, fruiting stalk. The only site available to the public with populations of white wicky is in the Carolina Sandhills National Wildlife Refuge.

PROTECTION STATUS: Federal Species of Concern

330. *Herbaceous seepages*

331. Frog's breeches; hunter's cup

Sarracenia purpurea var. *venosa* (Rafinesque) Fernald
Sar-ra-cèn-i-a pur-pú-re-a var. ve-nò-sa
Family Sarraceniaceae (Pitcher-plant Family)

DESCRIPTION: Rhizomatous, perennial, evergreen, carnivorous herb with hollow leaves modified as trapping structures; flowering stalks 8–16″ tall; flowers April–May.

RANGE-HABITAT: Mostly restricted to the Atlantic Coastal Plain Province of the southeastern US; in SC in the mountains, sandhills, and coastal plain counties of the eastern part of SC; rare; favors sphagnum openings in pocosins where it grows more robust; also found in moist, longleaf pine savannas, sandhill seepage bogs, and cataract bogs in the mountains.

COMMENTS: Frog's breeches differs from other pitcher-plants by having leaves that lie horizontally but curve upward, an erect hood that does not cover the mouth, and the inner surface of the hood bears many stiff hairs that point downward toward the mouth. The open mouth permits the pitcher to fill with rainwater where insects that fall in are drowned. It is believed that glands

secrete a wetting agent into the water that denies the insect buoyancy, so it can not fly off the water's surface.

332. Bogmoss

Mayaca fluviatilis Aublet
May-à-ca flu-vi-á-ti-lis
Mayacaceae (Bogmoss Family)

DESCRIPTION: Perennial herb along shores or
truly aquatic; small, mosslike, to 8″ tall; plants
on shores in wet soil or shallow water forming
dense tufts; plants in deeper water with stems
longer, lax, and leaves more distant, thinner,
and more flexuous; leaves numerous, spirally
arranged, linear; flowers with 3 sepals and 3
petals; petals pinkish to violet to white; flowers May–June.

RANGE-HABITAT: From se. NC to FL, west to se. TX; also tropical America; in SC
in the sandhills and coastal plain; common; marshes, streams, seepage areas,
ponds or lakes, ditches, spring runs, and swamp forests.

TAXONOMY: Some authors recognize two species of *Mayaca: M. fluviatilis* and *M.
aubletii* Michaux. However, more recently, Weakley (2001) and Godfrey and
Wooten (1979) recognize only *M. fluviatilis,* stating that different hydrological
conditions induce the differences in growth form between the two.

333. Water sundew

Drosera intermedia Hayne
Dró-se-ra in-ter-mè-di-a
Droseraceae (Sundew Family)

DESCRIPTION: Perennial herb; leaves in basal
rosettes; flowering stalks with or without erect
leaves; leaves narrowly spoon-shaped; leaf
stalks and blades with tentacle-like, glandular
hairs, the secretion of each gland contributing
to the insect-catching function of the leaf;
flower stalk smooth, 2–4″ tall, strongly curved
at base and standing away from the rosette;
flowers white or tinged with pink; flowers
July–September.

RANGE-HABITAT: Newfoundland and MN south to FL and TX; also into tropical
America; in SC in the piedmont, sandhills, and coastal plain; infrequent; bogs,
savannas, edges of pond cypress ponds, seepage areas, pocosins, and margins of
pools or streams, often in standing water.

COMMENTS: This sundew and the following sundew species are photographed in
vegetative form because leaf shapes are their distinguishing characteristic. The
flowers of all sundews are similar and the reader may refer to the photograph of
D. brevifolia, plate 374, for a flower representative of the genus.

334. Round-leaf sundew

Drosera rotundifolia L.
Dró-se-ra ro-tun-di-fò-li-a
Droseraceae (Sundew Family)

DESCRIPTION: Perennial, rosette-forming, scapose herb; leaves with glandular hairs, the secretion of each gland contributing to the insect-catching function of the leaf; leaf blades round to weakly kidney-shaped, about 0.25″ across, tapering abruptly to a distinct leaf stalk; flowering stem 2–6″ tall; flowers with a white corolla often tinged with pink; flowers July–September.

RANGE-HABITAT: Round-leaf sundew is the most widely distributed sundew in the cooler temperate regions; throughout North America, Europe, Russia, and Asia; in SC rare and primarily found in the mountains; disjunct in the sandhills in habitats where cool seepage water provides suitable habitat; sphagnum and cataract bogs, seepage slopes, and vertical seepages on rock or clay.

COMMENTS: Round-leaf sundew can be seen in Shealy's Pond Heritage Preserve in Lexington County and the Chandler Heritage Preserve in Greenville County. It usually occurs rooting in sphagnum moss (seen in the photograph). In fact, the presence of this moss in suitable habitats often indicates that the sundew is not far away.

330. *Atlantic white-cedar forests*

335. Rayner's blueberry

Vaccinium sempervirens Rayner & Henderson
Vac-cí-ni-um sem-pér-vi-rens
Ericaceae (Heath Family)

DESCRIPTION: Evergreen perennial; stems to 16″ tall, erect to ascending in shade and tending to creep in full sun; rooting at nodes where in contact with the ground; leaves with fine, glandular, rounded to pointed teeth most obvious toward the tip; flowers white, urn-shaped, late April–early May; fruit mature fall.

RANGE-HABITAT: Endemic to the sandhills of Lexington County, SC, and known from only a few sites; boggy openings in Atlantic white-cedar forests, especially along the headwaters of Scouter Creek.

COMMENTS: South Carolina botanist Douglas A. Rayner, the second author of this book, and J. Henderson were the first to describe this species of blueberry (Rayner and Henderson, 1980). A population of Rayner's blueberry occurs at Shealy's Pond Heritage Preserve.

TAXONOMY: This species is clearly related to *Vaccinium crassifolium* Andrews (plate 485) and one source reduces it to a subspecies of *crassifolium: V. crassifolium* Andrews subsp. *sempervirens* (Rayner & Henderson) Kirkman & Ballington (Kirkman & Ballington, 1990). Weakley (2001) retains it as a species because it is allopatric (the two do not inhabit the same area) and relatively discrete morphologically. No sites are known where the two species occur together, although a population that seems intermediate in vegetative characters occurs at Peachtree Rock Nature Preserve.

PROTECTION STATUS: Federal Species of Concern

336. Atlantic white-cedar

Chamaecyparis thyoides (L.) Britton,
    Sterns, & Poggenberg
    Cha-mae-cý-pa-ris thy-oì-des
Cupressaceae (Cypress Family)

DESCRIPTION: Moderate to slow-growing tree that may live for more than a 1000 years; to 92′ tall; leaves small, evergreen, opposite, scalelike; male and female cones on same tree, produced in the spring; seed cones green with a bluish white bloom, turning bluish purple at maturity; seeds winged, shed in the fall.

RANGE-HABITAT: Southern ME to n. FL, and west to s. MS; in SC in the sandhills and inner coastal plain; uncommon; when white cedar dominates a community, the community is named for it; also in acid swamps, hillside seepages, wet sands, and streamhead pocosins.

COMMENTS: The light brown wood is unmatched in its resistance to decay. In the 1700s the wood was used for log cabins, roof shingles, barrels, and boats. Today, it is much reduced in abundance and is not a major commercial tree. It is a hardy tree and is still planted as an ornamental on moist sites. Atlantic white-cedar can be seen in Shealy's Pond Heritage Preserve in Lexington County. In local usage and on topographic maps, cedar refers to *Chamaecyparis thyoides* (i.e., Cedar Creek), while juniper refers to red cedar (*Juniperus virginiana* L.).

THE COASTAL PLAIN

337. *Longleaf pine flatwoods*

338. Cleft-leaved violet

Viola septemloba Le Conte
Vi-o-la sep-tem-lò-ba
Violaceae (Violet Family)

DESCRIPTION: Perennial, smooth herb, with a short, erect rhizome; leaf blades variable, some unlobed, others lobed, appearing 3- 5- 7- or 9-lobed; stalks of early spring flowers very variable in length, up to 8″ tall; flowers late March–early May.

RANGE-HABITAT: Coastal plain from se. VA to peninsular FL, west to TX; common in seasonally wet to well-drained longleaf pine flatwoods.

SIMILAR SPECIES: Cleft-leaved violet is similar to *Viola esculenta* Elliott. The spurred petal of the former is bearded, while the spurred petal of the latter is hairless.

339. Southern blueberry

Vaccinium tenellum Aiton
Vac-cì-ni-um te-nél-lum
Ericaceae (Heath Family)

DESCRIPTION: Low-growing, rhizomatous, colonial shrub, 4–12″ tall; leaves deciduous, usually green with glandular hairs below; flowers in 5–15-flowered clusters, before or at expansion of leaves; corolla slenderly sub-cylindrical, pink to milk-white; flowers late March–early May; berries small, black, rather dry, mature June–July.

RANGE-HABITAT: From se. VA to GA, and south and west to n. FL, AL, and MS; common from se. VA to GA; scattered and rare in the rest of its range; in SC it occurs in the lower piedmont, sandhills, and coastal plain; longleaf pine flatwoods, sandhills, dry oak-hickory forests, and xeric woodland borders.

340. Carolina rockrose

Helianthemum carolinianum (Walter) Michaux
He-li-án-the-mum ca-ro-li-ni-à-num
Cistaceae (Rockrose Family)

DESCRIPTION: Erect, herbaceous perennial, 4–12″ tall, from roots with tuberous thickenings; stems hairy, arising from a basal rosette of broad leaves; leaves with starlike hairs on both surfaces; petals lasting a day or less; flowers April–May.

RANGE-HABITAT: From e. NC south to s. FL, and west to AR and e. TX; in SC primarily in the sandhills and coastal plain; longleaf pine savannas, old fields, and dry longleaf pine flatwoods.

COMMENTS: This species is easily separated from the other rock-roses found in SC (including two others pictured in this book, *H. canadense,* plate 418, and *H. rosmarinnifolium,* plate 423). The stem with 2–4 leaves below the flower, a basal rosette of broad leaves, and large flowers (almost 2″ wide) are distinctive for this species. The common name, rockrose, does not apply to SC species, which do not grow among rocks.

341. Stagger-bush

Lyonia mariana (L.) D. Don
Ly-òn-i-a ma-ri-à-na
Ericaceae (Heath Family)

DESCRIPTION: Rhizomatous shrub to 5′ tall; leaves deciduous to semi-evergreen; flowers April–May.

RANGE-HABITAT: RI south to FL; then from LA to TX, AR, MO, and OK; in SC it occurs in the coastal plain (common), sandhills (common), and adjacent piedmont (rare); longleaf pine flatwoods and savannas, pocosin-sandhill ecotones, sandy, dry, open woods, and dry, rocky woodlands in the lower piedmont.

COMMENTS: The genus honors John Lyon, 17?–1818, an early American botanist and explorer of the southern Allegheny Mountains.

342. Dwarf azalea

Rhododendron atlanticum (Ashe) Rehder
Rho-do-dén-dron at-lán-ti-cum
Ericaceae (Heath Family)

DESCRIPTION: Deciduous, low, erect shrub,
3–5′ tall; often forming large colonies from
rhizomes; flowers appearing before the leaves;
corolla white, lavender to deep pink, sticky
from glandular hairs; flowers April–May.
RANGE-HABITAT: Common southeastern coastal
plain endemic; NJ and PA to s. GA; in SC in
the sandhills and coastal plain; pocosins,
longleaf pine flatwoods and savannas, and
sandhill-pocosin ecotones.
SIMILAR SPECIES: Dwarf azalea is similar to *Rhododendron canescens* (Michaux)
Sweet (plate 458), which also occurs in the coastal plain. The reader may refer
to the key to species of *Rhododendron* in the appendix to distinguish between
these two.

343. Yellow false-indigo; horse-fly Weed

Baptisia tinctoria (L.) R. Brown
Bap-tí-si-a tinc-tò-ri-a
Fabaceae (Pea or Bean Family)

DESCRIPTION: Bushy-branched, rhizomatous
perennial up to 3′ tall; usually blackening
upon drying; leaves alternate, palmately compound with 3 leaflets; flowers April–August.
RANGE-HABITAT: Common and widespread in
eastern US; common throughout SC; sandhills, longleaf pine flatwoods, open woods
and clearings, ridges, dry oak-hickory forests,
and along road banks.

COMMENTS: False-indigo was cultivated in colonial times as a source of a blue
dye. It was not a quality dye and could not replace true indigo obtained from
Asian and tropical members of *Indigofera*. The specific epithet *tinctoria* refers to
"tincture," meaning "a dyeing substance." F. P. Porcher (1869) gives a long discourse on the use of this plant as a medicine. He also relates how the fresh plant
was attached to the harness of horses to keep flies off—hence, one of its common names. He further states: "I have noticed that they [flies] will not remain
upon the plant."

344. Lead plant

Amorpha herbacea Walter
    A-mór-pha her-bá-ce-a
Fabaceae (Pea or Bean Family)

DESCRIPTION: Herb 1–4.5′ tall; leaves odd-pinnately compound; flowers with a single petal; flowers May–July.

RANGE-HABITAT: Endemic to FL, GA, SC, and NC; piedmont, sandhills, and coastal plain; common; longleaf pine flatwoods and savannas, open fields, sandhills, and dry oak-hickory forests in the piedmont.

COMMENTS: The genus name is from the Greek *amphoros,* meaning "without form," in reference to the flowers having only one petal.

345. Southern sneezeweed

Helenium flexuosum Rafinesque
    He-lé-ni-um flex-u-ò-sum
Asteraceae (Aster or Sunflower Family)

DESCRIPTION: Perennial herb, 16–36″ tall; leaves alternate, with the base of the blades extending down the stems making them winged; flowers May–August.

RANGE-HABITAT: Common throughout much of eastern US; common and essentially throughout SC; longleaf flatwoods and savannas, ditches and alluvial pastures, wet meadows, and riverbanks.

COMMENTS: The common name comes from the use of its dried leaves in making snuff, which was inhaled to cause sneezing in the belief it would rid the body of evil spirits.

346. Black-root

Pterocaulon pycnostachyum (Michaux) Elliott
    Pte-ro-caù-lon pyc-nos-tà-chy-um
Asteraceae (Aster or Sunflower Family)

DESCRIPTION: Perennial herb from a black, tuberous, and thickened root; stems erect, 16–32" tall, with dense, matted hairs; stem winged by the base of the leaf stalks extending down the stem; vegetative parts often remain through the winter; flowers May–June.

RANGE-HABITAT: Coastal plain from se. NC south to s. FL, and west to AL; common throughout its range; longleaf pine flatwoods, sandhills, and sandy fields.

COMMENTS: The root was used in a variety of folk remedies according to F. P. Porcher (1869) and Morton (1974). The latter states that even today a decoction of the root is taken for colds and menstrual cramps, or the whole root is boiled and the tea taken for backache.

347. American chaff-seed

Schwalbea americana L.
Schwál-be-a a-me-ri-cà-na
Scrophulariaceae (Figwort Family)

DESCRIPTION: Erect, hairy, unbranched, perennial herb, 1–2′ tall; corolla yellow or purplish; leaves alternate, the largest at the base and gradually diminishing in size upwards; flowers May–June.

RANGE-HABITAT: *Schwalbea* is primarily a coastal plain species of the Atlantic and Gulf coasts with extant populations in NJ, NC, SC, GA, and FL; historically rather widespread in eastern North America; in SC in longleaf pine flatwoods and savannas, ecotonal areas between peaty wetlands and xeric sandy soils, and other open, grass-sedge systems.

COMMENTS: The historical record indicates that *Schwalbea* was always relatively rare and local in distribution. Recent field studies in SC, however, have documented over 50 populations in nine coastal counties. *Schwalbea* requires a high frequency of fire, especially in the growing season (perhaps this relates to its establishment ecology). Because of its fire-dependant nature, its populations must be carefully monitored. Any significant increase in fire suppression throughout its range could jeopardize its continued survival. Chaff-seed is a root-parasite, the host species representing components of its habitat. The genus name is dedicated to Christian G. Schwalbe, who wrote on botany.

PROTECTION STATUS: Federal Endangered

348. Goat's rue; devil's shoestrings; hoary-pea

Tephrosia virginiana (L.) Persoon
Te-phrò-si-a vir-gi-ni-à-na
Fabaceae (Pea or Bean Family)

DESCRIPTION: Perennial herb, 8–28″ tall; with dense grayish hairs; leaves odd-pinnately compound, covered with grayish hairs; flowers May–June.

RANGE-HABITAT: NH to MN, and south to FL and TX; common throughout SC; pine-oak heaths in the mountains, dry oak-hickory forests in the piedmont, longleaf pine flatwoods, dry, sandy, open woods, clearings, outcrops, woodlands, and along roadsides in the coastal plain.

COMMENTS: F. P. Porcher (1869) states that North American Indians used goat's rue. He further adds that it was later used as a vermifuge. The common name, devil's shoestrings, comes from its long, stringy roots; the common name, hoary-pea, refers to its grayish hairs. It was once fed to goats to increase milk production. When it was discovered that the roots contain rotenone, the practice was discontinued. Rotenone is used as an insecticide and fish poison; it is not poisonous to mammals.

349. St. Peter's-wort

Hypericum stans (Michaux) P. Adams &
    Robson
    Hy-pé-ri-cum stáns
    Hypericaceae (St. John's-wort Family)

DESCRIPTION: Erect shrub, 1–3′ tall; stems
with shredded, old bark; sepals 4 and
unequal, the two outer, larger ones enclosing
the two much narrower, inner ones; flowers
June–October.

RANGE-HABITAT: NY south to FL, west to TX,
and north to KS and KY; in SC chiefly coastal
plain, sandhills, and lower piedmont; common;
longleaf pine flatwoods and savannas, ditches, and sandy, dry, open woods.

SYNONYM: *Hypericum crux-andreae* (L.) Crantz—W

350. Spiked medusa

Pteroglossaspis ecristata (Fernald) Rolfe
    Pte-ro-glos-sás-pis e-cris-tà-ta
    Orchidaceae (Orchid Family)

DESCRIPTION: Perennial herb from a thickened corm; leaves several, arising from the corm, linear-lanceolate, 6–28″ long, two of
which dominate; single flowering stem grows from the corm near
the leaves, 20″ to 4.5′ tall; flowers June–September; by November the capsules have matured and spread their seeds.

RANGE-HABITAT: Along the coastal plain from e. NC to FL, and
west to s. LA; dry, grassy areas, and longleaf pine flatwoods and
savannas, especially where blackjack oak occurs; rare.

COMMENTS: Little is known about this species in SC. It may be
present in a site one year, then disappear for several years (as do
many orchids). It is easily overlooked because it grows among tall
grasses such as species of *Andropogon* and *Paspalum*. The fieldwork
of Patrick D. McMillan, John F. Townsend, and Eric J. Kiellmark
has expanded its range in SC. The range includes most of the
outer coastal plain, and it may be more abundant than previously
thought. The plant grows in extremely low densities at any one site and requires
large areas of fire-maintained longleaf woodlands for its continued survival.

SYNONYM: *Eulophia ecristata* (Fernald) Ames—RAB

PROTECTION STATUS: Federal Species of Concern

351. Zornia

Zornia bracteata Walter ex J. F. Gmelin
    Zórn-i-a brac-te-à-ta
    Fabaceae (Pea or Bean Family)

DESCRIPTION: Prostrate herb; stems numerous;
leaves palmately 4-foliolate; flowers enclosed
by 2 conspicuous bracts; flowers
June–August; legume mature July–October,
disarticulating into bristly segments.

RANGE-HABITAT: Coastal plain from se. VA
south to FL, and west to TX; common; longleaf pine flatwoods, sandy, dry, open woods,
sandhills, and along sandy roadsides.

COMMENTS: Zornia is a monotypic genus endemic to the southeastern coastal plain. The palmately 4-foliolate leaves are unique. The specific epithet *bracteata* refers to the two bracts that enclose the flower. The genus honors Johannes Zorn, 1739–1799, a German apothecary.

352. Huckleberry; dangleberry

Gaylussacia frondosa (L.) Torrey & Gray ex Torrey
    Gay-lus-sàc-i-a fron-dò-sa
Ericaceae (Heath Family)

DESCRIPTION: Rhizomatous, deciduous shrub, to 6′ tall; leaves and twigs smooth, or essentially so; leaves with sessile, resinous dots on lower surface; corolla greenish white, urn-shaped; flowers late March–April; fruit a berry, with ten seeds, glaucous-blue, matures June–August.

RANGE-HABITAT: Primarily southeastern coastal plain; from NH to SC, less commonly inward to w. NY, w. PA, and w. VA; in SC common on the coastal plain and sandhills, common in the piedmont and mountains; in the piedmont and mountains in pine-oak heaths and dry oak-hickory forests; in the coastal plain and sandhills in longleaf pine flatwoods, pocosins, sandy or rocky woods, sandhill-pocosin and savanna-pocosin ecotones.

SIMILAR SPECIES: A similar species is *G. tomentosa* (A. Gray) Pursh ex Small (hairy dangleberry). This species has twigs and the lower surface of the leaves is hairy. Some authors treat it as a variety of *G. frondosa*. It grows in longleaf pine flatwoods and sandhills from Jasper and Beaufort Counties, south to FL, and west to AL. It is rare in SC, although locally abundant in southern longleaf pine flatwoods.

COMMENTS: Huckleberry makes one of the most luscious of desserts, being juicy with a rich, spicy, sweet flavor.

353. Vanilla plant; deer's-tongue

Carphephorus odoratissimus (J. F. Gmelin) Herbert
    Car-phé-pho-rus o-do-ra-tís-si-mus
Asteraceae (Aster or Sunflower Family)

DESCRIPTION: Smooth perennial to 3′ tall; leaves alternate, the basal ones to 4″ long and 3″ wide; stem leaves reduced upward; leaves usually purple toward the base and white towards the tip; heads in corymbs, the lateral branches usually overtopping the terminal; flowers late July–October.

RANGE-HABITAT: Southeastern coastal plain species; from se. NC to s. FL, and west to e. LA; common; moist to mesic longleaf pine flatwoods and savannas; in SC it is absent from the northeast coastal counties.

COMMENTS: The leaves contain coumarin, giving them a distinct odor of vanilla. They are collected from the wild and sold for flavoring smoking tobacco.

SYNONYM: *Trilisa odoratissima* (Walter ex J. F. Gmelin) Cassini— RAB

354. Barbara's-buttons

Marshallia graminifolia (Walter) Small
Mar-sháll-i-a gra-mi-ni-fò-li-a
Asteraceae (Aster or Sunflower Family)

DESCRIPTION: Fibrous-rooted, perennial herb; stems 16–32″ tall; basal leaves firm and ascending, linear to narrowly elliptic, 2–8″ long; stem leaves not strongly different from basal leaves except in size, usually less than 1.2″ long; fibrous base of old basal leaves persistent; flowers late July–September.
RANGE-HABITAT: Nearly endemic to the coastal plain and sandhills of NC and SC; there is one site in GA; common; longleaf pine savannas and flatwoods, and adjacent ditches, pocosins, and bogs.

355. Eastern silvery Aster

Aster concolor L.
Ás-ter cón-co-lor
Asteraceae (Aster or Sunflower Family)

DESCRIPTION: Perennial herb with 1–several, erect stems; stems 1–2′ tall; leaves about 2″ long, elliptic; bracts subtending flower head whitish with green apices; plant covered with a fine, silvery down; flowers September–October.
RANGE-HABITAT: From VA to FL, west to LA and north to TN and KY; common and essentially throughout SC (rare in the mountains); longleaf pine flatwoods, woodlands, old fields, thickets, and openings in dry oak-hickory forests.

356. Pine-barren gentian

Gentiana autumnalis L.
Gen-ti-à-na au-tum-nà-lis
Gentianaceae (Gentian Family)

DESCRIPTION: Perennial herb 8–24″ tall; stems single (usually) or few, erect or arching; leaves sessile, opposite, dark green, glossy, linear to narrowly oblanceolate, twisted and curved; petals usually indigo blue, but on individual plants may be greenish white, white and blue, or purple; corolla tube brown-spotted within, plaited between the lobes (clearly seen in the photograph); flowers late September–early December.
RANGE-HABITAT: Two widely separated areas: the pine barrens of NJ and adjacent DE, and se. VA south through e. NC to nc. SC; longleaf pine savannas and flatwoods and sandhills; according to Weakley (2001), it is nearly always associated with *Pinus palustris* and *Aristida stricta;* in SC rare and found in the coastal plain and sandhills of the eastern counties.
COMMENTS: Pine-barren gentian's rarity in SC is mainly the result

of it being at the edge of its range. It may be under-reported due, in part, to its late fall bloom, when field studies are usually at a minimum, and because it is inconspicuous except when in flower. Duke (1997) recommends all species of *Gentiana* as an herbal remedy for ulcers.

PROTECTION STATUS: State Threatened

357. Inkberry; bitter gallberry

Ilex glabra (L.) Gray
Ì-lex glà-bra
Aquifoliaceae (Holly Family)

DESCRIPTION: Evergreen, rhizomatous shrub to 9′ tall; leaves with widely spaced teeth towards the tip, smooth, shiny above; flowers May–June; drupe black, bitter, mature September–November, persistent through the winter.

RANGE-HABITAT: Nova Scotia to s. FL, west to ne. TX; in SC chiefly a coastal plain species; common; also extends upslope in the sandhills; longleaf pine flatwoods and savannas, pocosins, and seepage areas in woodlands.

SIMILAR SPECIES: *Ilex coriacea* (Pursh) Chapman (sweet gallberry) is similar but often taller (to 15′) and mostly found in pocosins and related habitats. The leaves of sweet gallberry are 1.5–3x as long as wide, with a few, tiny, irregularly spaced, marginal teeth. The leaves of inkberry are 3–4x as long as wide, with teeth in the apical ½ to ⅓ of the blade.

COMMENTS: Inkberry is an important honey plant in the southeast.

358. Running oak

Quercus pumila Walter
Quér-cus pù-mi-la
Fagaceae (Beech Family)

DESCRIPTION: Suckering shrub from roots or underground stems, often forming large colonies; rarely exceeding 3′ tall; leaves densely white and hairy beneath; flowers March–April; acorns mature in September.

RANGE-HABITAT: Southeastern coastal plain endemic; se. NC to s. FL, and west to s. MS; in SC in the coastal plain and sandhills in sandy longleaf pine flatwoods; common.

COMMENTS: Running oak is readily identifiable in the longleaf pine flatwoods since it is the only narrow-leaf, low-growing oak that produces acorns. It tolerates fire. It can burn to the ground, but it quickly produces new growth. It will produce a crop of acorns the year following a fire. Wildlife readily eat the acorns.

359. Pine/saw palmetto flatwoods

360. Pineland dyschoriste

Dyschoriste oblongifolia (Michaux)
    Kuntze
    Dys-cho-rís-te ob-lon-gi-fò-li-a
Acanthaceae (Acanthus Family)

DESCRIPTION: A dull green, perennial herb to 2′ tall; stems soft and hairy; flowers axillary, bluish purple with dark spots; leaves opposite; flowers April–May.

RANGE-HABITAT: Coastal plain from se. SC to s. FL, and west to FL panhandle; in SC locally abundant in pine/saw palmetto flatwoods and longleaf pine flatwoods.

361. Rusty lyonia; tree lyonia

Lyonia ferruginea (Walter) Nuttall
    Ly-òn-i-a fer-ru-gí-ne-a
Ericaceae (Heath Family)

DESCRIPTION: Normally a deciduous shrub, 3–6′ tall; stems crooked and contorted, forming a small, irregular, open crown; occasionally reaches tree size under favorable conditions in the southern part of its range becoming 20–25′ tall; leaves evergreen, simple, alternate, with lower surface rusty and scaly; flowers April–May.

RANGE-HABITAT: Coastal plain from se. SC to sc. FL, west to FL panhandle; in SC rare and known only from Jasper and Beaufort Counties; common in the center of its range; pocosins and pine/saw palmetto flatwoods.

COMMENTS: The specific epithet *ferruginea* refers to the rusty color of the lower leaf surface due to the presence of rusty-colored scales.

PROTECTION STATUS: State Endangered Peripheral

362. Saw palmetto

Serenoa repens (Bartram) Small
Se-re-nò-a rè-pens
Arecaceae (Palm Family)

DESCRIPTION: Perennial shrub with branched, trailing stems; occasionally a small, branched tree; leaves evergreen, to 3′ across, palmately divided into nonfilamentose segments; leaf stalks armed with spines; flowers produced on elongated branches to 3′ long; flowers May–July; fruit a bluish black drupe, ripe in October–November.

RANGE-HABITAT: Common coastal plain plant from SC to FL, and west to e. LA; in SC reported from the coastal counties of Jasper, Beaufort, and Colleton; pine/saw palmetto flatwoods, longleaf pine-scrub oak sand ridges, maritime forests, and coastal dunes.

COMMENTS: Saw palmetto often forms dense, almost impenetrable stands in flatwoods. It is highly resistant to fire. Prescribed fire in winter promotes its growth. The drupes were an important food for Native Americans and are an important food for whitetail deer. It can be seen in Victoria Bluff Heritage Preserve in Beaufort County.

Saw palmetto is one of the current medicinal herbs that Americans are using to supplement or replace prescription medicines. Saw palmetto is used to treat enlarged prostate glands. Although it appears to significantly improve urine flow in men with enlarged prostates, reviewers of the drug cautioned that studies showed that the effects of saw palmetto lasted only a few weeks, too short a time to determine long-term effects.

363. Southern evergreen blueberry

Vaccinium myrsinites Lamarck
Vac-cì-ni-um myr-si-nì-tes
Ericaceae (Heath Family)

DESCRIPTION: Low, evergreen, colonial shrub, usually less than 2′ tall; leaves evergreen, with stalked glandular hairs beneath; flowers 2–8 in short, axillary racemes before the season's growth; corolla white to deep pink, urn-shaped; flowers March–April; berry black, mature May–June.

RANGE-HABITAT: Coastal plain from se. SC south to peninsular FL, and west to s. AL; in SC reported from Jasper, Hampton, and Beaufort Counties; occasional; pine/saw palmetto flatwoods and longleaf pine flatwoods.

COMMENTS: The berries are edible. Duke (1997) recommends all *Vaccinium* species as an herbal remedy for bladder infections, macular degeneration, and multiple sclerosis.

364. Walter's milkweed

Asclepias cinerea Walter
As-clè-pi-as ci-né-re-a
Asclepiadaceae (Milkweed Family)

DESCRIPTION: Perennial herb 1–2′ tall; stem simple, usually solitary; leaves opposite, linear; corolla lavender; flowers June–July; follicles mature August–September.
RANGE-HABITAT: Coastal plain from se. SC south to n. FL; rare throughout its range; in SC it occurs only in Jasper and Hampton Counties; longleaf pine savannas and pine/saw palmetto flatwoods, often where wet or boggy.

365. Hairy wicky

Kalmia hirsuta Walter
Kálm-i-a hir-sú-ta
Ericaceae (Heath Family)

DESCRIPTION: Low, evergreen shrub, 6–20″ tall; twigs and leaves with stiff hairs; leaves alternate; flowers June–July.
RANGE-HABITAT: From SC to nc. FL, and west to MS; in SC chiefly in the se. counties of the coastal plain; occasional; pine/saw palmetto flatwoods and longleaf pine flatwoods and savannas.
COMMENTS: In newly opened flowers, the 10 stamens are seated in small pockets of the corolla. An insect visiting the mature flowers may cause the stamens to pop out of the pockets, spraying the pollen onto the insect's back, which in turn is deposited on the next flower the insect visits, thus effecting cross-pollination.

366. Savanna honeycomb-head

Balduina uniflora Nuttall
Báld-uin-a u-ni-flò-ra
Asteraceae (Aster or Sunflower Family)

DESCRIPTION: Perennial herb; stem ribbed, stiffly erect, or with 2–20 stiffly erect branches, each bearing a single terminal head; plant 16–32″ tall; basal leaves in a rosette; stem leaves reduced upward; receptacle honeycomb-like; flowers late July–September.
RANGE-HABITAT: Southeastern coastal plain endemic; se. NC to n. FL, west to se. LA; rare throughout most of its range; in SC it only occurs in the extreme southeast portion; wet longleaf pine flatwoods, pine/saw palmetto flatwoods, and longleaf pine savannas.
COMMENTS: The common name refers to the honeycomb-like appearance of the receptacle. The genus name honors William Baldwin, M.D., an American botanist, 1779–1819. Kelly (1914) gives an interesting account for the unusual spelling of the genus name.
PROTECTION STATUS: State Threatened

367. Galactia; Elliott's milk pea

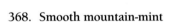

Galactia elliottii Nuttall
Ga-lác-ti-a el-li-ótt-i-i
Fabaceae (Pea or Bean Family)

DESCRIPTION: Twinging, climbing, herbaceous vine, sometimes somewhat woody at the base; leaves pinnately compound with 7 to 9 leaflets; leaves evergreen or nearly so; petals white or tinged with red; flowers July–September.

RANGE-HABITAT: Coastal plain from se. SC south into GA and FL; in SC reported from only Jasper, Charleston, and Beaufort Counties; longleaf pine flatwoods, pine/saw palmetto flatwoods, thickets, and low woods; occasional.

COMMENTS: This is the only species of *Galactia* in SC that has compound leaves with more than 3 leaflets. The specific epithet honors the SC botanist Stephen Elliott, 1771–1830.

368. Smooth mountain-mint

Pycnanthemum nudum Nuttall
Pyc-nán-the-mum nù-dum
Lamiaceae (Mint Family)

DESCRIPTION: Erect, perennial herb 12–28″ tall; leaves sessile, opposite, ovate or elliptic, not over 0.75″ long; corolla lips whitish, purple-punctate on both surfaces; flowers July–September.

RANGE-HABITAT: Coastal plain from se. SC south to n. FL and se. AL; in SC rare and known from only a few locations in Jasper, Beaufort, and Hampton Counties; wet longleaf pine flatwoods, pine/saw palmetto flatwoods, and hillside bogs in pinelands.

PROTECTION STATUS: State Endangered

369. Longleaf pine savannas

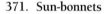

370. Spring bartonia; white bartonia

Bartonia verna (Michaux) Rafinesque
ex Barton
Bar-tòn-i-a vér-na
Gentianaceae (Gentian Family)

DESCRIPTION: Stiffly erect, inconspicuous annual or biennial herb, 2–8″ tall; usually in colonies; stem wiry, purplish (rarely yellow-ish); leaves essentially opposite, minute and scalelike, erect or appressed; flowers mostly solitary, in racemes or panicles in very robust plants; flowers February–April.

RANGE-HABITAT: From se. NC south to s. FL, and west to TX; in SC confined to the coastal plain; wet longleaf pine savannas, shores of depression ponds, and pocosin ecotones; rare?

COMMENTS: Weakley (2001) states that this genus has coral-like mycorrhizae and lacks root hairs and is thus presumably partially mycotrophic. Most references list spring bartonia as either rare or uncommon, but it is probably more common than reported because of its diminutive nature and early flowering period; there is no problem finding it in the coastal area when hunting specifically for it. The genus is named for Benjamin S. Barton, 1766–1815, a Philadelphia botanist.

371. Sun-bonnets

Chaptalia tomentosa Ventenat
Chap-tàl-i-a to-men-tò-sa
Asteraceae (Aster or Sunflower Family)

DESCRIPTION: Fibrous-rooted, perennial herb with a basal cluster of leaves; leaves with dense cover of white hairs beneath, glossy green above; flowering stems 1–several, 3–16″ tall; heads solitary, nodding at first, then erect, but again nodding after flowering; flowers February–April.

RANGE-HABITAT: Southeastern coastal plain endemic from e. NC to s. FL, and west to e. TX; common in longleaf pine savannas and flatwoods, sandhill ecotones, and along roadsides.

372. Leopard's-bane

Arnica acaulis (Walter) Britton, Sterns & Poggenburg
Ár-ni-ca a-caù-lis
Asteraceae (Aster or Sunflower Family)

DESCRIPTION: Perennial herb; stems erect, 6–32″ tall, usually one from a crown; principal leaves basal, forming a cluster; stem leaves few and reduced; both types of leaves glandular-hairy; flowers late March–early June.

RANGE-HABITAT: DE and s. PA, south to FL panhandle; in SC common throughout the coastal plain, sandhills, and lower piedmont; longleaf pine savannas and flatwoods, moist areas within sandhills, open woodlands, and along wet roadsides.

COMMENTS: According to Duke (1997), the European species, *Arnica montana,* has pain-relieving, antiseptic, and anti-inflammatory properties and has been approved by the German Commission E for external treatment of bruises, sprains, and muscle and joint complaints, and for disinfecting cuts. *Arnica acaulis* may have similar properties and uses.

373. Bearded grass-pink

Calopogon barbatus (Walter) Ames
Ca-lo-pò-gon bar-bà-tus
Orchidaceae (Orchid Family)

DESCRIPTION: Erect perennial, arising from a corm; leafless, flowering stalk 6–18″ tall; leaves (when present) 1 or 2, narrowly linear and grasslike, sheathing the flowering stalk at the base; flowers rose-pink, rarely white, mostly opening simultaneously; flowers March–May.

RANGE-HABITAT: Southeastern coastal plain endemic, from se. NC to c. FL, and west to e. LA; widely scattered and occasional; longleaf pine savannas and flatwoods, and sandhill seepages.

COMMENTS: Although the flowering period is given as March–May, its actual flowering period in any one given year is probably 2–4 weeks. In addition, it is sensitive to changes in environmental parameters; one year it may be scarce, the next year more common.

A most unusual feature of the grass-pinks is the inverted perianth where the lip is uppermost. (In almost all other orchid genera, the lip is lowermost.) The upper lip acts like an elevator: The weight of an insect that lands on the lip causes it to bend downward, bringing the insect in contact with the reproductive structure below the column. Cross-pollination is thus effected.

The grass-pinks have no nectar to entice insects. Instead, they mimic flowers that have nectaries. Coastal grass-pinks grow in association with smooth meadow-beauty (*Rhexia alifanus,* plate 383), which has pink petals and long, yellow stamens that provide nectar and food for visiting insects. The pink petals and yellow hairs (the beard) of the lip, mimicking the pink petals and yellow stamens of the meadow-beauty, probably fool insects into mistaking the orchid flower for the meadow-beauty.

374. Dwarf sundew

Drosera brevifolia Prush
Dró-se-ra bre-vi-fò-li-a
Droseraceae (Sundew Family)

DESCRIPTION: Carnivorous herb with leaves in a basal cluster; leaf blades covered with stalked glands that exude a clear, sticky material that aids in catching insects; flowering stalk glandular-hairy, 0.8–2.5″ tall; flowers April–May.

RANGE-HABITAT: From se. VA south to FL, and west to AR, OK, and TX; disjunct in sc. TN; in SC in the sandhills and coastal plain; common; longleaf pine savannas, moist longleaf pine flatwoods, sandy roadside ditches, and seepages.

COMMENTS: The common name of the sundews comes from the sticky, dew-covered tentacles on the leaves that in the early morning shine and glitter with the color of the sun's spectrum.

SYNONYM: *Drosera leucantha* Shinners—RAB

375. Violet butterwort

Pinguicula caerulea Walter
Pin-guí-cu-la cae-rù-le-a
Lentibulariaceae (Bladderwort Family)

DESCRIPTION: Perennial, carnivorous plant to 18″ tall; upper leaf surface covered with short, glandular hairs in which insects become mired; leaves in a basal cluster and retained over the winter; flowers April–May

RANGE-HABITAT: Chiefly outer coastal plain from se. NC to s. FL, west to FL panhandle; common in longleaf pine savannas and moist, longleaf pine flatwoods; it does occur in the sandhills of the eastcentral counties in seepages and sandhill-pocosin ecotones, but it is rare there.

SIMILAR SPECIES: *P. lutea* Walter (plate 321 in *WCL*), with yellow flowers, also occurs in the outer coastal plain of SC.

COMMENTS: The genus name derives from the Latin *pinguis,* meaning "somewhat fat," and refers to the greasy texture of the leaf. The butterworts were used as crude bandages during the Civil War; the upper leaf surface was placed on the wound.

376. Orange milkwort

Polygala lutea L.
Po-lý-ga-la lù-te-a
Polygalaceae (Milkwort Family)

DESCRIPTION: Biennial or short-lived perennial to 16″ tall; stems usually unbranched, smooth, 1 to several from base; flowers April–October, with peak blooming in spring.

RANGE-HABITAT: Long Island, NY, and NJ to peninsular FL, then west to LA; in SC in the sandhills and coastal plain; longleaf pine savannas and flatwoods and adjacent ditches, along roadsides, in pocosins, seepages, and along boggy borders of pond cypress savannas and gum ponds.

COMMENTS: The specific epithet *lutea* is Latin for "yellow" and refers to the flower's color when dried; when fresh, the flowers are bright orange.

377. Hooded pitcher-plant

Sarracenia minor Walter
Sar-ra-cèn-i-a mì-nor
Sarraceniaceae (Pitcher-plant Family)

DESCRIPTION: Carnivorous, flowering herb; perennial, evergreen, rhizomatous; leaves 6–24″ tall, modified into hollow, tubular structures to catch insects; leaves winged; hood arching closely over the opening of the pitcher; upper portion of hood spotted with white or translucent blotches (the windows); flowering stalk usually shorter than the leaves; flowers April–May.

RANGE-HABITAT: From se. NC to n. FL; occasional throughout most of its range, but common in SC; sandhills and coastal plain; longleaf pine savannas, pond cypress savannas, and wet ditches; less frequent in longleaf pine flatwoods.

COMMENTS: Hooded pitcher-plant gets it common name from the hood arching over the opening into the pitcher. The arching hood acts to keep flying insects from exiting the pitcher. After an insect has entered the pitcher and drunk its fill of nectar, it attempts to exit. The hood blocks most of the light entering the pitcher. The insect, seeking escape, flies toward the brightest light, which comes from the back of the pitcher. Here, pigment-free areas (the windows) allow light to enter. As the insect tries to fly through the windows, it repeatedly bumps into the back of the hood, becomes stunned, and ultimately falls down the pitcher and drowns in the water and enzyme mixture at the base.

Morton (1974) reports an unusual folk remedy using hooded pitcher-plant that is still practiced in the coastal plain: "Rootstock is boiled and the decoction kept in a jar, applied warm on skin rashes or eruptions. People say the spots on the leaves are a sign the plant is a remedy for skin troubles, a belief which harks back to the old 'Doctrine of Signatures.'"

378. Venus' fly trap

Dionaea muscipula Ellis
Di-o-naè-a mus-cí-pu-la
Dionaeaceae (Venus' Fly Trap Family)

DESCRIPTION: Perennial, carnivorous herb from a short rhizome; leaves in basal clusters, modified into trapping structures consisting of 2 hingelike, touch-sensitive lobes, each with stout, marginal bristles; each lobe contains 3 trigger hairs by which the trap can be sprung; almost the entire upper surface of lobes covered with glands of two kinds: nectar producing and enzyme producing; flowering stalk 4–12″ tall; flowers white; flowers May–June.

RANGE-HABITAT: Endemic to the coastal plain and sandhills of the Carolinas; in SC it occurs only in Horry and Georgetown Counties; occasional; wet, sandy ditches, longleaf pine savannas, pocosin ecotones, and sphagnum openings in pocosins; historically reported from Charleston County, but no populations are known today.

COMMENTS: Good populations of Venus' fly trap occur in Lewis Ocean Bay Heritage Preserve and Cartwheel Bay Heritage Preserve in Horry County. Habitat destruction, fire suppression, and collection from the wild over the years have reduced considerably the populations of this carnivorous plant. State law in SC protects it from harvest on public lands.

William Bartrum reported the Native American name for this plant was "tippitiwitchet" (Reveal, 1996).

PROTECTION STATUS: Federal Species of Concern

379. Colicroot

Aletris aurea Walter
  Á-le-tris àu-re-a
Liliaceae (Lily Family)

DESCRIPTION: Perennial herb with thick, short rhizomes; leaves mostly basal, rather narrowly lanceolate; stem leaves greatly reduced; flower stalk 16″–4′ tall; perianth covered with small, sticky projections, giving a mealy appearance; flowers mid-May–July.

RANGE-HABITAT: From s. MD south to peninsular FL, and west to e. TX and se. OK; in SC in the coastal plain and sandhills; common; longleaf pine flatwoods and savannas, and pocosin borders.

SIMILAR SPECIES: Occurring in the same habitats and area is *Aletris farinosa* L. (plate 329 in *WCL*) with white flowers. *A. farinosa* flowers several weeks earlier.

COMMENTS: This plant and *A. farinosa* were used medicinally to treat colic in colonial times. Historically an infusion of the roots in vinegar was used as a purgative. Morton's (1974) research indicates rural people still chew the rootstock of both species to stop toothache. The generic name *Aletris* is Greek for "a female slave who grinds corn," in reference to the mealy texture of the flowers.

380. Spreading pogonia

Cleistes divaricata (L.) Ames
  Cleìs-tes di-va-ri-cà-ta
Orchidaceae (Orchid Family)

DESCRIPTION: Perennial herb, 1–2′ tall; leaf solitary, inserted above the middle of the stem; sepals widely spreading; entire plant has a bluish green color with a fine, frosty-white coating; flowers May–July.

RANGE-HABITAT: Coastal plain orchid from s. NJ to sw. GA and ne. FL; in SC in the sandhills and coastal plain; occasional; longleaf pine savannas and flatwoods, swamps, seepages, and openings in pocosins.

TAXONOMY: Some authors recognize another species of *Cleistes*, *C. bifaria* (Fernald) Catling & Gregg, small spreading pogonia, which is common in the mountains in pine-oak heaths. It is smaller in all morphological aspects than *C. divaricata*. Most authors, however, include *C. bifaria* under *C. divaricata* and consider it a smaller form of *C. divaricata*. This book treats the two as separate species.

381. Snowy orchid

Platanthera nivea (Nuttall) Luer
Pla-tán-the-ra ní-ve-a
Orchidaceae (Orchid Family)

DESCRIPTION: Herbaceous, erect perennial, to 1′ tall; leaves 2–3, near the base, rigidly suberect, linear-lanecolate, reduced upward to as many as 10 slender, erect bracts; lip uppermost, with long spur extending sideways, but curved upward; flowers May–September.

RANGE-HABITAT: Essentially a southeastern coastal plain endemic, ranging from s. NJ to FL, and west to TX; disjunct in TN; rare over most of its range, including SC; longleaf pine savannas and moist sites in longleaf pine flatwoods.

COMMENTS: Like many orchids, snowy orchid may cover a site one year, then be absent for several years before again making an appearance. For best development, this orchid depends on a more or less constant supply of acid waters. Many populations have been eliminated because of alteration of drainage patterns near savannas. The common name is derived from the Latin *niveus* meaning "white as snow" in reference to the intense whiteness of the flowers.

SYNONYM: *Habenaria nivea* (Nuttall) Sprengel—RAB

382. Carolina loosestrife

Lysimachia loomisii Torrey
Ly-si-má-chi-a loo-mís-i-i
Primulaceae (Primrose Family)

DESCRIPTION: Perennial herb with stiffly, erect stems 12–48″ tall, freely branched; leaves opposite, or in whorls of 3–4, sessile, linear and tapered to both ends; corolla yellow, with several maroon streaks and a ring of purplish color at the throat; flowers May–June.

RANGE-HABITAT: Endemic to the outer and middle coastal plain of SC and NC; occasional; moist to wet longleaf savannas and pocosin ecotones.

COMMENTS: Two groups of plants are called loosestrife: *Lysimachia* of the primrose family (Primulaceae) and *Lythrum* of the loosestrife family (Lythraceae). The specific epithet honors Dr. H. Loomis.

383. Smooth meadow-beauty

Rhexia alifanus Walter
   Rhéx-i-a a-li-fà-nus
Melastomataceae (Meadow-beauty
Family)

DESCRIPTION: Perennial herb to 40″ tall; stem hairless; leaves bluish green, prominently 3-nerved; the 8 anthers prominently curved; fruiting urn with gland-tipped hairs; flowers May–September.

RANGE-HABITAT: Common coastal plain species from e. NC to nc. FL, and west to se. TX; in SC in the sandhills and coastal plain; longleaf pine savannas and low, longleaf pine flatwoods, pocosin borders, and ditches.

COMMENTS: *Alifana* means an earthenware cup, which the capsule resembles. This is South Carolina's most spectacular species of meadow-beauty. The tall, smooth, unbranched stems with ascending, bluish green leaves set this species apart from all other meadow-beauties.

384. Red milkweed

Asclepias lanceolata Walter
   As-clè-pi-as lan-ce-o-là-ta
Asclepiadaceae (Milkweed Family)

DESCRIPTION: Perennial, smooth herb, 3–5′ tall; stem erect, rarely branched; leaves opposite, linear to narrowly lanceolate and in 3–6 pairs; corolla red, crown usually orange; flowers June–August; follicles mature August–September.

RANGE-HABITAT: Coastal plain from NJ south to peninsular FL, and west to e. TX; wet longleaf savannas, fresh to brackish marshes, cypress depressions, and swamps; rare to occasional over most of its range.

COMMENTS: Several species of milkweed are known to be poisonous when eaten raw; it is likely that most, if not all, raw milkweeds are toxic. Duke (1997) recommends *Asclepias* species as an herbal remedy for warts.

385. Crested fringed orchid

> *Platanthera cristata* (Michaux) Lindley
> Pla-tán-the-ra cris-tà-ta
> Orchidaceae (Orchid Family)

DESCRIPTION: Perennial, stout herb, 7–35″ tall; leafy below, bracteate above; roots numerous, fleshy, tuberous; lip fringed; flowers June–September.

RANGE-HABITAT: Primarily limited to the coastal plain from s. MA south to FL and west to TX; also inland in KY, TN, AR, SC, and NC; in SC throughout the coastal plain and common; rare in the mountains; longleaf pine savannas and flatwoods, pocosins and roadsides, and bogs in the mountains.

COMMENTS: The "crested" in the common name comes from the Latin term *cristata* in reference to the fringed lip. This orchid exemplifies the diversity in orchid distribution. It occurs in the mountains and coastal plain but is absent in the piedmont This is because the mountains and coastal plain have similar habitats, which are absent in the piedmont

SYNONYM: *Habenaria cristata* (Michaux) R. Brown—RAB

386. Toothache grass; orange-grass

> *Ctenium aromaticum* (Walter) Wood
> Cté-ni-um a-ro-má-ti-cum
> Poaceae (Grass Family)

DESCRIPTION: Tufted, erect perennial from short rhizomes; stems 2–4′ tall; the flowering head is distinctive to *Ctenium;* leaves mostly near the base; flowers June–August.

RANGE-HABITAT: Southeastern coastal plain from se. VA to FL, and west to LA; in SC in the sandhills and coastal plain; longleaf pine savannas, wet areas in longleaf pine flatwoods, pocosin-savanna ecotones, and seepages.

COMMENTS: The fresh herbage, inflorescence, and rhizome, when bruised or crushed, produces a strong citrus aroma. The common name, toothache grass, refers to the numbing sensation felt on the mouth, tongue, and lips when the plant is chewed.

387. Buttonweed

> *Diodia virginiana* L.
> Di-ó-di-a vir-gi-ni-à-na
> Rubiaceae (Madder Family)

DESCRIPTION: Perennial herb, erect or spread-ing; stems branched; leaves sessile, opposite; flowers 1 (rarely 2) per leaf axil; stipules with 3–5 projections; calyx segments 2; flowers June–frost.

RANGE-HABITAT: From s. NJ to s. IL and MO, generally south to s. FL, OK, and TX.; com-mon throughout SC; in a variety of natural and ruderal communities, including wet longleaf pine savannas and flatwoods, borders of pond cypress-swamp gum ponds and depressions, shallow ponds, marshy shores, streamsides, rocky shoals, and wet ditches.

388. Redroot

Lachnanthes caroliniana (Lamarck)
    Dandy
    Lach-nán-thes ca-ro-li-ni-à-na
    Haemodoraceae (Bloodwort Family)

DESCRIPTION: Perennial herb with prominent red rhizomes and fibrous roots, both with red juice; flowering plants to 4′ tall; leaves mostly basal, linear, rapidly reduced upward; flowers June–early September.

RANGE-HABITAT: Coastal plain species; s. Nova Scotia; MD to DE; se. VA to FL, and west to LA; disjunct inland to w. VA and c. TN; in SC common in sandy, longleaf pine savannas, ditches, pocosin borders, and in managed freshwater impoundments along rivers.

COMMENTS: Some sources list redroot as poisonous. Kingsbury (1964), however, disputes this with good evidence. Redroot is a prized food for waterfowl along the coastal rivers; both the seeds and rhizomes are used as food. Freshwater impoundments are often managed to encourage the growth of redroot to attract ducks.

389. Pine lily; Catesby's lily

Lilium catesbaei Walter
    Lí-li-um càtes-bae-i
    Liliaceae (Lily Family)

DESCRIPTION: Perennial herb with unbranched, erect stems from scaly bulbs; stems 20–28″ tall; flower solitary, erect; leaves alternate, ascending or appressed to the stem, the lower about 3.5″ long, reduced upward; flowers mid-June–mid-September.

RANGE-HABITAT: From se. VA to FL, and west to LA; in SC in the sandhills and coastal plain; occasional; longleaf pine savannas and flatwoods, and sandhill seepages.

COMMENTS: This lily grows in a delicate balance with its environment and has been declining in coastal SC for unknown reasons. It is best not to remove any specimens from the wild.

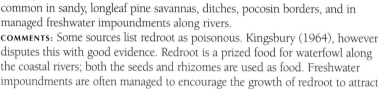

390. Savanna mountain-mint

Pycnanthemum flexuosum (Walter) Britton, Sterns &
    Poggenburg
    Pyc-nán-the-mum flex-u-ò-sum
Lamiaceae (Mint Family)

DESCRIPTION: Erect, perennial herb 16–44″ tall; stems 4-angled,
the angles sharp to rounded; leaves opposite, elliptic to elliptic-
lanceolate; flowers in flat-topped clusters; corolla white to lavender, lip with purple dots; flowers June–August.

RANGE-HABITAT: From se. VA to n. FL, TN, and AL; disjunct
inland in bogs in sw. NC; in SC primarily in the sandhills and
coastal plain; moist to wet longleaf pine savannas, pocosins, and
sandhill seepages; common.

COMMENTS: The English common name is not appropriate. A few
species grow in the mountains, but most are common in the lowlands. Most species of *Pycnanthemum* occur in the eastern US.
They are not easy to distinguish and probably hybridize in
nature.

391. Ciliate meadow-beauty

Rhexia petiolata Walter
    Rhéx-i-a pe-ti-o-là-ta
Melastomataceae (Meadow-beauty
    Family)

DESCRIPTION: Perennial herb with unbranched
or basally branched stems 4–20″ tall; stems 4-
angled, narrowly winged; leaves opposite, sessile or subsessile, 3-nerved with ciliate
margins; flowers June–September.

RANGE-HABITAT: From se. VA south into peninsular FL, and west to se. TX; in SC rare in the
lower piedmont, common in the sandhills and
coastal plain; wet pine flatwoods and savannas, pocosin borders, and ditches.

392. False asphodel

Tofieldia racemosa (Walter) Britton, Sterns &
    Poggenburg
    To-fièld-i-a ra-ce-mò-sa
Liliaceae (Lily Family)

DESCRIPTION: Perennial herb from a short rhizome; flowering
stalk 12–28″ tall; basal leaves erect, linear, variable, to 16″ long;
usually 1 bract-like leaf inserted somewhere below the middle of
the flowering stalk; flowering stalk rough to the touch; flowers
June–early August.

RANGE-HABITAT: Common coastal plain species (except found in
the mountains in VA) from NJ south to n. FL, and west to se. TX;
in SC in the sandhills and coastal plain; longleaf pine savannas
and flatwoods, seepage slopes, and pocosins.

COMMENTS: The genus honors Thomas Tofield, 1730–1779, an
English botanist.

393. Yellow fringeless orchid; frog-arrow

> *Platanthera integra* (Nuttall) Gray ex Beck
>   Pla-tán-the-ra ín-te-gra
> Orchidaceae (Orchid Family)

DESCRIPTION: Perennial herb to 2′ tall, with smooth stems; roots fleshy, tuberous, swollen near base of stem; lip entire; leaves several below, reduced to bracts above; raceme initially conical but soon becomes cylindrical; flowers July–September.

RANGE-HABITAT: Essentially a southeastern coastal plain endemic; from s. NJ to FL, west to se. TX, and disjunct in the mountains to NC and e. and c. TN; rare in SC; longleaf pine savannas and longleaf pine flatwoods.

COMMENTS: Frog-arrow is often mistaken for crested fringed orchid (*P. cristata*, plate 385). Frog-arrow can be identified readily by its entire lip and saffron color; the lip of *P. cristata* is fringed, and the flowers are orange. This orchid is present one year at a site, then absent the next year (or next few years?). No explanation is known for this periodicity. Fieldwork in the coastal plain recently has documented a precipitous decline in frog-arrow. Whether this decline is permanent or a natural population fluctuation is not known. The name *integra* is Latin for "entire," in reference to the nearly entire, fringeless lip.

SYNONYM: *Habenaria integra* (Nuttall) Sprengel—RAB

PROTECTION STATUS: State Endangered

394. Narrowleaf sunflower

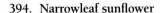

> *Helianthus angustifolius* L.
>   He-li-án-thus an-gus-ti-fò-li-us
> Asteraceae (Aster or Sunflower Family)

DESCRIPTION: Perennial herb to 3–7′ tall; single stem, often many branched in upper half; stems rough and hairy; leaves occurring all along the stem, 10–30x as long as wide, up to 6″ long, dark green and rough above, margins rolled downward; flowers July–frost.

RANGE-HABITAT: Primarily a coastal plain species; Long Island, NY, south to FL, west to TX, and irregularly inland to OH, IN, and MO; in SC common throughout the coastal plain, sandhills, and lower piedmont, scattered in the upper piedmont and mountains; longleaf pine savannas and flatwoods, ditches, bogs, open woodlands, swales and thickets, and along roadsides.

395. Foxtail clubmoss

Lycopodium alopecuroides L.
Ly-co-pó-di-um a-lo-pe-cu-roì-des
Lycopodiaceae (Clubmoss Family)

DESCRIPTION: Stems arching and rooting at the tips, or procumbent and rooting throughout; leaves many-ranked, narrow, awl-shaped, with sharp, distinct, divergent teeth; strobili (cones) bushlike, on upright stalks arising from the upper surface of the stems; spores mature July–September.

RANGE-HABITAT: TX east to FL, and north to MA; throughout SC; rare in the mountains and piedmont; common in the sandhills and coastal plain; acidic sites such as longleaf pine savannas, ditches, wet, sandy meadows, seepages, and sphagnum bogs.

COMMENTS: Clubmosses are primitive vascular plants that reproduce by spores. The spores of clubmosses were involved in a number of fields of early commerce. Their small and uniform size made them ideal for microscopic measurements. Because they are water-repellent and dustlike, they were used as soothing powders for chafes and wounds. They were also used for fireworks and for photographic flashes, because they give off a flash when ignited.

Clubmoss stems are all "annual" in that the current year's growth dies back (or really dies forward) toward a perennial stem tip that roots into the ground and resumes growth with the next growing season.

SYNONYM: *Lycopodiella alopecuroides* (L.) Cranfill—W

396. Marsh fleabane; stinking fleabane

Pluchea foetida (L.) Augustin de Candolle
Plù-che-a foè-ti-da
Asteraceae (Aster or Sunflower Family)

DESCRIPTION: Perennial herb emitting a strong, offensive odor; plant 20–40″ tall; stems densely short-hairy, often spongy and thickened basally; leaves alternate, sessile and clasping; corolla creamy white; flowers late July–October.

RANGE-HABITAT: Common coastal plain species from s. NJ to peninsular FL, west to e. and se. TX; longleaf pine savannas, ditches, marshes, and pocosins.

COMMENTS: This plant was once used as a flea repellant. The genus is dedicated to Abbé Pluche, an eighteenth-century French naturalist.

397. Rose-gentian

Sabatia gentianoides Elliott
 Sa-bà-ti-a gen-ti-a-noì-des
Gentianaceae (Gentian Family)

DESCRIPTION: Perennial herb without rhizomes; stems strict or branched above, 6–36″ tall; basal leaves, when present, much broader and shorter than the stem leaves; leaves opposite, 20–60x as long as wide; flowers sessile or subsessile, in groups of 1–5; calyx subtended by linear bracts that usually exceed the corolla lobes; flowers July–August.

RANGE-HABITAT: NC south to n. FL, and west to se. TX; in SC reported from the coastal plain counties of Charleston, Georgetown, Jasper, Horry, and Williamsburg; occasional; wet longleaf pine savannas and flatwoods, and boggy seepage slopes of pinelands.

COMMENTS: Easily seen in the photograph is a linear bract that projects beyond the corolla, a feature that distinguishes this gentian from other coastal plain species.

398. Scale-leaf gerardia

Agalinis aphylla (Nuttall) Rafinesque
 A-ga-lì-nis a-phýl-la
Scrophulariaceae (Figwort Family)

DESCRIPTION: Annual herb 12–48″ tall; stems smooth, with few branches; leaves absent or inconspicuous scalelike; flowers September–November.

RANGE-HABITAT: Coastal plain from se. NC to n. FL, and west to s. LA; in SC in wet longleaf pine savannas and flatwoods, and edges of pond cypress-gum ponds and depressions; rare.

COMMENTS: The scalelike leaves distinguish this species from all other species of *Agalinis* in SC; all other species of *Agalinis* have conspicuous leaves. The specific epithet *aphylla* comes from the Greek *a* meaning "without" and *phylla* meaning "leaves."

PROTECTION STATUS: State Endangered

399. Coastal plain gentian; Catesby's gentian

Gentiana catesbaei Walter
Gen-ti-à-na càtes-bae-i
Gentianaceae (Gentian Family)

DESCRIPTION: Perennial herb with thick, fleshy roots; stems rough, 12–32″ tall; leaves opposite; flowers sessile, 1–9, in compact cymes; corolla blue to violet, or whitish, with plaits in the sinuses, narrower and shorter than the lobes; flowers late September–November.

RANGE-HABITAT: From s. NJ, south to n. FL; in SC occasional and throughout the coastal plain and sandhills; longleaf pine savannas, pocosins, and edges of moist hardwood forests.

SIMILAR SPECIES: Catesby's gentian is similar to soapwort gentian (*Gentiana saponaria* L.), which is found scattered throughout SC. Catesby's gentian has bright green, ovate leaves widest near the base, and calyx lobes longer than the calyx tube. Soapwort gentian has dark green, linear to elliptic leaves widest near the middle, and calyx lobes shorter than or about equal to the calyx tube.

400. Slender rattlesnake-root

Prenanthes autumnalis Walter
Pre-nán-thes au-tum-nà-lis
Asteraceae (Aster or Sunflower Family)

DESCRIPTION: Slightly whitish, smooth, perennial herb with milky sap; plants 12–48″ tall; leaves alternate, principal ones on the lower part of the stem, abruptly reduced upward; heads borne on a narrow, terminal spike-like panicle; heads nodding; rays pink, 5-lobed; flowers late September–frost.

RANGE-HABITAT: Common coastal plain species from s. NJ to s. GA; seasonally wet longleaf pine savannas and flatwoods, open bogs, and pocosins.

COMMENTS: All species of *Prenanthes* are recognizable by the nodding flower heads. The arrangement of flower heads in a narrow, spike-like panicle is distinctive to this species.

*401. Longleaf pine-turkey oak
xeric ridges*

402. Sandhills milkweed

Asclepias humistrata Walter
As-clè-pi-as hu-mis-trá-ta
Asclepiadaceae (Milkweed Family)

DESCRIPTION: Stems stiff and spreading upward, up to 2′ tall, 1–several from a deep, narrow, tapering root; juice milky; leaves opposite, broad, sessile, clasping, usually 5–8 pairs; flowers May–June; fruits erect, maturing June–July.

RANGE-HABITAT: From e. NC south to FL, and west to LA; primarily a sandhills and coastal plain species; common; also in the piedmont where it is rare; sandy, dry, open woodlands, and all xeric sites.

COMMENTS: This milkweed and *A. tuberosa* subsp. *rolfsii* (Vail) Woodson have the habit of lying nearly flat on the ground, which is unique among SC milkweeds.

403. Sandhills baptisia

Baptisia cinerea (Rafinesque) Fernald & Schubert
Bap-tí-si-a ci-né-re-a
Fabaceae (Pea or Bean Family)

DESCRIPTION: Rhizomatous, perennial herb, 1–2′ tall, with appressed hairs; leaves compound with 3 leaflets; flowers May–June; legume matures June–August.

RANGE-HABITAT: Narrow endemic from se. VA to SC; common in the coastal plain and sandhills of the Carolinas; in SC most common in the eastern counties; longleaf pine flatwoods, longleaf pine-turkey oak sandhills, and sandy, dry, open woodlands.

COMMENTS: The genus name comes from the Greek *baptizien,* which means "to dip in or under water," in reference to a former use of some species as sources of dyes.

404. Sandhills thistle

Cirsium repandum Michaux
    Cír-si-um re-pán-dum
Asteraceae (Aster or Sunflower Family)

DESCRIPTION: Deep-rooted, perennial herb, 8–24″ tall; stems with cobweb-like hairs, leafy to the summit; leaves alternate, margins spiny, with small spines in addition to the scattered, larger spines; heads solitary, or more often terminating short branches from near the summit; bracts below the flower heads spine-tipped; flowers May–July.

RANGE-HABITAT: From se. VA south to e. GA; common; coastal plain and sandhills, nearly endemic to the Carolinas; xeric sandhills and other dry, sandy habitats.

SYNONYM: *Carduus repandus* (Michaux) Persoon—RAB

405. Southern bog buttons

Lachnocaulon beyrichianum Sporleder
    ex Korn
    Lach-no-caù-lon bey-rich-i-à-num
Eriocaulaceae (Pipewort Family)

DESCRIPTION: Clump-forming herb, with tufts of leaves aggregated into dense mats of rosettes; leaves narrowly linear and tapering; separate male and female flowers in same head; heads seldom broader than 0.19″; seeds dark brown, very lustrous, the longitudinal ribs obscure; flowers May–September.

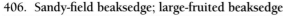

RANGE-HABITAT: Coastal plain of se. NC to c. peninsular FL; in SC on white barren sands of ecotones between pocosins and Carolina bay ridges, and in similar situations on xeric sand ridges.

SIMILAR SPECIES: Identification of the three species of *Lachnocaulon* that occur in coastal SC is difficult. The reader may refer to Radford et al. (1968) or Godfrey and Wooten (1979) for a taxonomic treatment.

COMMENTS: Recent fieldwork by Patrick D. McMillan has documented this species as more common than reported, especially on Carolina bay ridges.

PROTECTION STATUS: Federal Species of Concern

406. Sandy-field beaksedge; large-fruited beaksedge

Rhynchospora megalocarpa Gray
    Rhyn-chós-po-ra me-ga-lo-cár-pa
Cyperaceae (Sedge Family)

DESCRIPTION: Coarse, rhizomatous perennial 12–40″ tall; blades mostly basal; flowers June–August.

RANGE-HABITAT: Coastal plain from se. NC south to FL, and west to MS; in SC in longleaf pine-turkey oak sandhills on Carolina bay ridges and blackwater sand ridges; occasional.

COMMENTS: This is the most conspicuous

species of *Rhynchospora* in the xeric sandhill communities. Although some manuals list it as rare, it appears to be more abundant than once thought and is locally abundant in its preferred habitat.

407. Summer-farewell

Dalea pinnata (J. F. Gmelin) Barneby var. *pinnata*
Dàl-e-a pin-nà-ta var. pin-nà-ta
Fabaceae (Pea or Bean Family)

DESCRIPTION: Perennial, aromatic herb, 12–24″ tall from a taproot; stems smooth, branched above; leaves odd-pinnately compound, glandular-dotted, with 3–11 leaflets; flowers August–frost.
RANGE-HABITAT: From se. NC to c. FL, and west to FL panhandle; a coastal plain species, common through most of its range, but occasional in SC; longleaf pine-turkey oak sandhills and sandy, dry, open woodlands.
COMMENTS: Summer-farewell is very unlike most members of the pea family in appearance. Good populations in SC exist in the Tillman Sand Ridge Heritage Preserve and environs. The genus honors Samuel Dale, 1659–1739, an English botanist.
SYNONYM: *Petalostemum pinnatum* (Walter ex J. F. Gmelin) Blake—RAB

408. Soft-haired coneflower

Rudbeckia mollis Elliott
Rud-béck-i-a mól-lis
Asteraceae (Aster or Sunflower Family)

DESCRIPTION: Annual, biennial, or occasionally short-lived perennial; 1–3′ tall, with deep taproot; stems freely branched with dense, spreading hairs; stem leaves alternate, sessile, with dense hairs; flowers late August–October.
RANGE-HABITAT: Coastal plain of SC, GA, and FL; longleaf pine-turkey oak sandhills on brownwater ridges; rare.
COMMENTS: Soft-haired coneflower is found in SC only in Jasper County in the Tillman Sand Ridge Heritage Preserve and environs.
PROTECTION STATUS: State Endangered

409. Warea

Warea cuneifolia (Muhlenberg ex Nuttall) Nuttall
Wà-re-a cu-nei-fò-li-a
Brassicaceae (Mustard Family)

DESCRIPTION: Annual herb with erect stems to 4′ tall, branched above; leaves alternate, oblanceolate; flowers July–September; fruit sickle-shaped, long-stalked, matures in August–September.
RANGE-HABITAT: From sc. NC south to FL panhandle, west to se. AL; in SC primarily the inner coastal plain; occasional; longleaf pine-turkey oak sandhills and on brownwater ridges.

COMMENTS: In SC, it can be seen at the Tillman Sand Ridge Heritage Preserve and environs in Jasper County.

410. Sandhills gerardia

Agalinis setacea (J. F. Gmelin)
    Rafinesque
    A-ga-lì-nis se-tà-ce-a
    Scrophulariaceae (Figwort Family)

DESCRIPTION: Dark green or reddish annual, 8–24″ tall; leaves long and very slender; corolla throat with yellow lines; flowers September–October.

RANGE-HABITAT: NY south to FL, and west to AL; chiefly coastal plain and sandhills; in SC listed as occasional, but this may reflect it being undercollected; xeric sandhills, longleaf pine-turkey oak sandhills, and sandy, dry, open woodlands.

COMMENTS: All species of *Agalinis* are thought to be parasitic (to various degrees) on roots of grasses or other herbs. Seven other species of *Agalinis* occur in the coastal plain. The reader may refer to the standard floras for descriptions of the various species. Sandhills gerardia is the only species growing in the extreme xeric sandhills.

411. Rose dicerandra

Dicerandra odoratissima Harper
    Di-ce-rán-dra o-do-ra-tís-si-ma
    Lamiaceae (Mint Family)

DESCRIPTION: Freely branched, aromatic herb with appressed hairs; stems erect, 4-angled, 8–20″ tall; leaves opposite, linear to narrowly elliptic; flowers pink to lavender; flowers September–October.

RANGE-HABITAT: Extreme se. SC to se. GA; rare; coastal plain; brownwater sand ridges, and sandy, dry, open woodlands.

COMMENTS: In SC, rose dicerandra is known only from the Tillman Sand Ridge Heritage Preserve and environs in Jasper County.

PROTECTION STATUS: State Endangered

412. Woolly golden-aster

Chrysopsis gossypina (Michaux) Elliott
Chry-sóp-sis gos-sý-pi-na
Asteraceae (Aster or Sunflower Family)

DESCRIPTION: Biennial or short-lived perennial, 12–28″ tall; reclining, ascending or erect; more or less dense, woolly hairs throughout, except sometimes not on the bracts below the flower heads; flowers September–October.

RANGE-HABITAT: From se. VA south to FL, and west through GA into AL; occasional; throughout the coastal plain and sandhills; xeric sandhills, brownwater sand ridges, sandy, dry, open woodlands, and sometimes on beaches.

SYNONYM: *Heterotheca gossypina* (Michaux) Shinners—RAB

413. Gopher-apple

Licania michauxii Prance
Li-cà-ni-a mi-chaùx-i-i
Chrysobalanaceae (Coco-plum Family)

DESCRIPTION: Low colonial shrub to 16″ tall; fire adapted, with an extensive underground stem system; leaves simple, evergreen, alternate and oblanceolate; flowers May–June; fruit matures September–October.

RANGE-HABITAT: From se. SC to s. FL, west to LA; abundant in dry sandy habitats in the southern part of its range; in SC on brownwater sand ridges dominated by turkey oak and longleaf pine.

COMMENTS: In SC, gopher-apple is reported only from the Tillman Sand Ridge Heritage Preserve and environs in Jasper County.

SYNONYM: *Chrysobalanus oblongifolius* Michaux—RAB

414. Sandy, dry, open woodlands

415. Carolina violet; southern woolly violet

Viola villosa Walter
Vî-o-la vil-lò-sa
Violaceae (Violet Family)

DESCRIPTION: Plant without leafy stem, with an elongate, stocky rhizome; very small; low; leaves often flattened on the ground, ever-green, densely hairy on both surfaces, heart-shaped; both chasmogamous and cleistogamous flowers present; chasmogamous flower solitary, often hidden by leaves, appear-ing late February–early April, followed throughout the season by cleistogamous flow-ers that produce abundant seeds.

RANGE-HABITAT: FL to TX, north to s. VA, AR, and OK; in SC in the sandhills, inner coastal plain, and piedmont; habitats with dry, open, sandy or rocky soils, and along roadsides.

COMMENTS: Carolina violet is the earliest flowering of the blue- or violet-flow-ered native violets. It is often overlooked because of its small size. Its heart-shaped, densely hairy leaves separate it from other blue violets.

416. Sky-blue lupine

Lupinus diffusus Nuttall
Lu-pì-nus dif-fù-sus
Fabaceae (Pea or Bean Family)

DESCRIPTION: Clump-forming herb with decumbent stems, 8–16″ tall; more or less dense, short hairs throughout; leaves 1-foliolate, evergreen; petals light to deep blue, with a conspicuous white to cream spot on the standard; flowers March–May.

RANGE-HABITAT: Sandhills and coastal plain from se. NC to FL, and west to MS; common in SC; xeric sandhills and sandy, dry, open woodlands.

SIMILAR SPECIES: The range of sky-blue lupine overlaps with lady lupine, *L. villosus* Willdenow (plate 246 in *WCL*). The standard of sky-blue lupine has a conspicuous white to cream spot, while the standard of lady lupine has a deep reddish purple spot.

COMMENTS: American lupines are complex taxonomically and poorly differentiated into acceptable taxa. In the southeast, how-ever, the species are few and not hard to identify. Some of the western species are known to be poisonous to livestock. The cul-tivated lupines are mostly hybrids.

417. Blue star

Amsonia ciliata Walter
Am-sòn-i-a ci-li-à-ta
Apocynaceae (Dogbane Family)

DESCRIPTION: Perennial herb with hairy stems; 12–28″ tall; leaves alternate, filiform to linear; the star-shaped corolla is distinctive; flowers in April.

RANGE-HABITAT: From central NC to FL, west to TX, and north to s. MO; common in SC in the sandhills and inner coastal plain; sandy, dry, open woodlands, dry pinelands, and xeric sandhills.

COMMENTS: The genus is named for Dr. Amson, a physician of Gloucester, VA.

418. Canada frostweed; Canada sunrose

Helianthemum canadense (L.) Michaux
He-li-án-the-mum ca-na-dén-se
Cistaceae (Rockrose Family)

DESCRIPTION: Erect, herbaceous perennial 4–14″ tall; roots with tuberous thickenings; basal leaves absent; stem leaves alternate; cleistogamous flowers solitary or in 3-flowered cymes, terminating the stem; chasmogamous flowers produced later in the season in the axils of branch leaves; flowers April–May.

RANGE-HABITAT: From s. Ontario to Nova Scotia, south to GA, and west to KY, MS, MO, and WI; in SC chiefly sandhills and coastal plain; common; woodland borders, fields, sandy, dry, open woodlands, and along roadsides.

COMMENTS: Each flower lasts only a day and opens only in the sunlight. The common name, frostweed, refers to the ice crystals that form from sap that exudes from cracks at the base of the stem in late fall.

419. Sundial lupine

Lupinus perennis L.
    Lu-pì-nus pe-rén-nis
Fabaceae (Pea or Bean Family)

DESCRIPTION: Perennial, erect herb 8–24″ tall; from a creeping underground rhizome; leaves palmately compound with 7–11 leaflets; flowers April–May.

RANGE-HABITAT: ME south to FL, and west to LA and MN; most widely distributed eastern lupine; in SC common in the sandhills and coastal plain; sandy, dry, open woodlands, sandhills, and clearings.

COMMENTS: The genus name *Lupinus* comes from the Latin *lupus* (wolf) because they were once thought to deplete or "wolf" the soil of minerals. This is unfounded; members of the pea family actually enrich the soil by harboring bacteria in their roots that fix atmospheric nitrogen.

420. Wild pink; Carolina pink

Silene caroliniana Walter var. *caroliniana*
    Si-lè-ne ca-ro-li-ni-à-na var.
    ca-ro-li-ni-à-na
Caryophyllaceae (Pink Family)

DESCRIPTION: Tufted perennial up to 8″ tall from a thin, deep taproot; leaves oblong, well separated, up to 2″ long; leaves hairy over the surface with appressed, white hairs; petals vary from pink to white, about 0.5″ long; flowers April–July.

RANGE-HABITAT: Lower piedmont, sandhills, and coastal plain from NC south through SC just into e. GA; in the sandhills and coastal plain of SC in sandy, dry, open woods and xeric habitats; in the piedmont in sandy, open woodlands, especially around granitic flatrocks; common.

421. Queen's-delight

Stillingia sylvatica Garden
    Stil-líng-i-a syl-vá-ti-ca
Euphorbiaceae (Spurge Family)

DESCRIPTION: Perennial herb, usually with several stems from a rootstock; to 32″ tall; leaves alternate, simple; male and female flowers on the same plant, in a terminal spike, male uppermost, female at base; spike rachis with numerous, large glands; capsule 3-locular, 1 seed per locule; flowers May–July.

RANGE-HABITAT: Common coastal plain species from se. VA south to FL, west to TX and NM, and north in the interior to KS; sandy, oak-hickory woods, longleaf pine flatwoods, open pine-mixed hardwood forests, and sandy, dry, open woodlands.

COMMENTS: Queen's-delight is a component in S.S.S. Tonic, still sold today. It has been used in a variety of home remedies. In the Old South, it was used to treat constipation and to induce vomiting. The genus honors Dr. Benjamin Stillingfleet, 1702–1771, an English naturalist.

422. Vase-vine

Clematis reticulata Walter
  Clé-ma-tis re-ti-cu-là-ta
Ranunculaceae (Buttercup Family)

DESCRIPTION: Perennial herbaceous vine, ascending or sprawling; leaves opposite, pinnately compound, with 3–9 leaflets; flowers in May–August.

RANGE-HABITAT: SC to FL, west to TX, and north to the interior of TN and AR; in SC primarily in the sandhills and inner coastal plain; occasional; sandy, dry, open woodlands.

COMMENTS: All species of *Clematis* are reported to be poisonous.

423. Rosemary sunrose

Helianthemum rosmarinifolium Pursh
  He-li-án-the-mum ros-ma-ri-ni-
  fò-li-um
Cistaceae (Rockrose Family)

DESCRIPTION: Small perennial herb up to 16″ tall; leaves very narrow, 0.13″ wide or less; chasmogamous and cleistogamous flowers present, the former with showy, yellow petals, the latter without petals; the two types of flowers mature at the same time; both types of flowers produce fertile fruits, but fruits from the chasmogamous flowers generally have more and larger seeds; flowers May–June.

RANGE-HABITAT: From sc. NC to FL panhandle, and west to TX; in SC primarily the sandhills and coastal plain; common; sandy, dry, open woodlands, along sandy roadsides, and in fields.

COMMENTS: In this species of *Helianthemum*, the chasmogamous flowers open for a day and are followed by (or mingled with) the cleistogamous flowers (without petals), which do not open but still fruit.

424. Piriqueta

Piriqueta caroliniana (Walter) Urban
  Pi-ri-què-ta ca-ro-li-ni-à-na
Turneraceae (Turnera Family)

DESCRIPTION: Perennial herb to 20″ tall; spreading and forming colonies from root sprouts; flowers remain open only on sunny days, and the petals fall off easily; flowers May–September.

RANGE-HABITAT: Coastal plain species from the western coastal counties of SC to FL; occasional; sandy, dry, open woodlands.

425. Melanthera

Melanthera hastata Michaux
Me-lán-the-ra has-tà-ta
Asteraceae (Aster or Sunflower Family)

DESCRIPTION: Coarse, erect, rough-haired perennial, 3–6′ tall; stems 4-angled, heavily mottled with purple; leaves opposite; ray flowers absent, disk flowers white; flowers June–October.

RANGE-HABITAT: SC south to FL, west to LA; in SC a coastal plain species found in the southeastern coastal counties; occasional; sandy, dry, open woodlands, moist to dry live oak woods, calcareous sites, and maritime dunes.

SYNONYM: *Melanthera nivea* (L.) Small—W

426. Snoutbean

Rhynchosia difformis (Elliott) Augustin de Candolle
Rhyn-chò-si-a dif-fór-mis
Fabaceae (Pea or Bean Family)

DESCRIPTION: Prostrate or twining herbaceous vine; stem angled, tawny, and hairy; earliest leaves with a single kidney-shaped leaflet; later leaves with 3 rounded-to-ovate or elliptic leaflets; flowers June–August.

RANGE-HABITAT: From se. VA south to FL, west to TX; in SC primarily coastal plain and sandhills; common; sandy, dry, open woodlands, and clearings.

SIMILAR SPECIES: *Rhynchosia reniformis* de Candolle (plate 307 in *WCL*) has 1-foliolate leaves and grows in similar habitats; *R. tomentosa* (L.) Hooker & Arnott grows throughout SC but is an erect plant.

427. Southern dawnflower

Stylisma humistrata (Walter) Chapman
Sty-lís-ma hu-mis-trà-ta
Convolvulaceae (Morning-glory Family)

DESCRIPTION: Prostrate, herbaceous, perennial vine; stems with a tendency to twine, at least near the growing tip; larger leaves 1–2″ long and 0.5–1″ wide, reduced upward; flowers usually in 3-flowered cymes (rarely solitary); flowers June–August.

RANGE-HABITAT: From se. VA to n. FL, and west to AR and e. TX; in SC in the coastal plain, sandhills, and piedmont; common; xeric sandhills, sandy, dry, open woodlands, waste places, and along roadsides.

SYNONYM: *Bonamia humistrata* (Walter) Gray—RAB

428. Horse mint

Monarda punctata L.
Mo-nár-da punc-tà-ta
Lamiaceae (Mint Family)

DESCRIPTION: Aromatic, perennial herb with 4-angled stems 16–40″ tall; leaves opposite; flowers in tight clusters subtended by several wholly or partially pink to lavender bracts; corolla yellow, spotted with purple; flowers July–September.

RANGE-HABITAT: VT to MN, and south to FL, TX, and AZ; in SC primarily a sandhills and coastal plain species; common; sandy, dry, open woodlands, and fields; occasional in the piedmont, growing in sandy or rocky woodlands.

COMMENTS: F. P. Porcher (1869) gives numerous home remedies and medicinal uses of horse mint. There appears to be no medicinal folk use of this plant today. The term "horse" when used in a common name signifies "coarse." The genus honors Nicolás Monardes, a late sixteenth-century author of many tracts on the medicinal application and other uses of plants, especially of the New World.

429. Hog plum; flatwoods plum

Prunus umbellata Elliott
Prù-nus um-bel-là-ta
Rosaceae (Rose Family)

DESCRIPTION: Small, often crooked tree to 20′ tall; usually occurs as single, scattered trees; leaves alternate, deciduous; flowers white; flowers March–April, before leaves appear; fruits very dark purple, sometimes varying to red or yellow, with a whitish sheen, maturing August–September.

RANGE-HABITAT: Piedmont and coastal plain species from s. NC south to FL, and west to c. TX and s. AR; common throughout its range; usually sandy or rocky upland woods, thickets, and riverbanks.

SIMILAR SPECIES: Chickasaw plum (*P. angustifolia* Marshall, plate 623) is similar to hog plum. The teeth on the leaves of chickasaw plum have a small red gland on the tip; the leaves of hog plum lack small red glands.

COMMENTS: The fruits are very tart but are excellent in pies, jams, or jellies. The wood has little commercial value.

430. Poison oak

Rhus toxicodendron L.
Rhùs tox-i-co-dén-dron
Anacardiaceae (Cashew Family)

DESCRIPTION: Erect shrub to 6′ tall; leaves alternate, thick, compound with 3 leaflets; leaflets hairy on both surfaces, shallowly lobed, coarsely serrate, or rarely entire; flowers April–May; drupes densely hairy, mature August–October.

RANGE-HABITAT: Southeastern US; throughout SC; xeric habitats such as the sandhills, dry rock outcrops in the mountains and piedmont, and dry habitats in the coastal plain.

SIMILAR SPECIES: Although poison oak is sometimes confused with poison ivy (*Rhus radicans* L., plate 159 in *WCL*), the distinction between the two is well determined. Poison ivy is either a high-climbing vine with numerous aerial roots, a trailing plant, or is reduced to a subshrub in shady, forested habitats. The leaves of poison ivy are thin and its fruits hairless; the fruits of poison oak are hairy and its leaves are thick and velvety. Poison ivy is equally as allergenic as poison oak.

COMMENTS: All parts of poison oak contain an oleoresin (urushiol) that can cause severe skin inflammation, itching, and blistering on contact. Poison oak is toxic all year, and the oleoresin can also be contracted when it is borne on smoke or dust particles, clothes, and animal hair. Washing thoroughly with soap and hot water or swabbing with alcohol within a few hours after contact prevents the allergic reaction.

SYNONYM: *Toxicodendron pubescens* P. Miller—W

431. Blazing star

Liatris elegans (Walter) Michaux
Li-à-tris é-le-gans
Asteraceae (Aster or Sunflower Family)

DESCRIPTION: Perennial, erect herb to 5′ tall, from a globose, tapered rootstock; stem leaves alternate, linear to narrowly elliptic; bracts below the flower heads dilated, pink; flowers September–October.

RANGE-HABITAT: From c. SC to FL, west to TX and se. OK; chiefly a coastal plain plant in SC; common; sandy, dry, open woodlands, and sandy fields.

Calcareous bluff forests and wet, flat, calcareous forests

432. Mottled trillium

Trillium maculatum Rafinesque
Tríl-li-um ma-cu-là-tum
Liliaceae (Lily Family)

DESCRIPTION: Perennial herb from a rhizome; stems 4–12″ tall; leaves simple, 3, in a whorl, mottled with lighter green and purple; single, stalkless, ill-scented flower; petals narrowly spoon-shaped, mostly 4.5x or more as long as wide; petals maroon or yellow; sepals green; flowers March–mid-April.

RANGE-HABITAT: From s. SC south to n. FL, and west to sc. AL; in SC found in the piedmont, coastal plain, and maritime strand in rich forests and floodplains over calcareous material, basic-mesic forests, and on shell mounds; common.

COMMENTS: In *Wildflowers of the Carolina Lowcountry and Lower Pee Dee,* this species was erroneously identified as *Trillium cuneatum* Rafinesque (plate 190), which is actually a piedmont and mountain species. The difference between the two is slight, and the reader may refer to the photographs and to the key on trilliums in the appendix to separate the two. Separation is necessary because their ranges overlap in the piedmont, although the two are never found together.

433. Prickly-ash

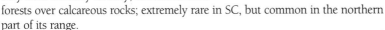
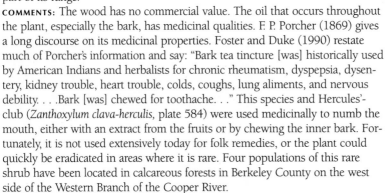

Zanthoxylum americanum P. Miller
Zan-thóx-y-lum a-me-ri-cà-num
Rutaceae (Rue Family)

DESCRIPTION: Deciduous, aromatic shrub or small tree with short paired spines; grows to 9′ tall, but much shorter in SC; leaves odd-pinnately compound with spiny rachis; leaves bitter-aromatic; flowers in small axillary clusters; flowers March–April, before the leaves.
RANGE-HABITAT: From s. Quebec west to e. ND, south to SC, GA, and OK; in SC reported only from Berkeley County; woodlands and forests over calcareous rocks; extremely rare in SC, but common in the northern part of its range.

COMMENTS: The wood has no commercial value. The oil that occurs throughout the plant, especially the bark, has medicinal qualities. F. P. Porcher (1869) gives a long discourse on its medicinal properties. Foster and Duke (1990) restate much of Porcher's information and say: "Bark tea tincture [was] historically used by American Indians and herbalists for chronic rheumatism, dyspepsia, dysentery, kidney trouble, heart trouble, colds, coughs, lung aliments, and nervous debility. . . .Bark [was] chewed for toothache. . ." This species and Hercules'-club (*Zanthoxylum clava-herculis,* plate 584) were used medicinally to numb the mouth, either with an extract from the fruits or by chewing the inner bark. Fortunately, it is not used extensively today for folk remedies, or the plant could quickly be eradicated in areas where it is rare. Four populations of this rare shrub have been located in calcareous forests in Berkeley County on the west side of the Western Branch of the Cooper River.

434. May white

Rhododendron eastmanii Kron & Creel
Rho-do-dén-dron east-mán-i-i
Ericaceae (Heath Family)

DESCRIPTION: Shrub or small tree to 16′ tall, nonrhizomatous; corolla white with a yellow blotch on the upper lobe and pink-tinged lobes on newly opened flowers; outer surface of corolla covered with nonglandular and glandular hairs; corolla tube narrow; flower fragrance strong and sweet; stamens 5, bending downwards, strongly exerted; flowers in May, after the leaves have expanded.
RANGE-HABITAT: Endemic to the piedmont and inner coastal plain of SC; known from Richland, Orangeburg, Union, and Newberry Counties; rare; deciduous forests on north-facing slopes with well-drained, nearly neutral soils, but often near calcium-rich soils.

COMMENTS: Kathleen A. Kron and SC native Michael A. Creel described May white in 1999 (Kron and Creel, 1999). The specific epithet honors Charles Eastman of Columbia, SC, who the authors give credit for discovering the species while bird-watching in Santee State Park.

Presently May white is known from only four sites. Urban development threatens the site in Richland County. Kron and Creel report that approximately 500 individuals occur in Santee State Park in the area of the limestone bluffs.

Herbarium specimens from Beidler Forest in Berkeley County and the Savannah River site possibly are may white, but they have not been confirmed at the time of publication.

TAXONOMY: *Rhododendron eastmanii* can be separated from the other white-flowered species in SC by the following: from *R. alabamense* Rehder by the flowers opening after the leaves have expanded; and from *R. arborescens, R. atlanticum,* and *R. viscosum* by the blotch on the upper corolla lobe, which the other three lack. The report of *R. alabamense* from SC (Radford et al., 1968) probably refers to *R. eastmanii.*

435. Southern sugar maple; Florida maple

Acer barbatum Michaux
À-cer bar-bà-tum
Aceraceae (Maple Family)

DESCRIPTION: Small to medium size, deciduous tree, usually 40–60′ tall; leaves simple, opposite, almost circular in outline, lower surface whitish; lobes 3–5, the terminal lobes of some leaves broader toward the apex than toward the base; sinuses rounded; flowers April–May; fruits June–October.

RANGE-HABITAT: VA to FL, west to TX and OK; in SC in the coastal plain and piedmont; occasional; throughout its range in moist, rich soils along rivers, and in low, wet woodlands; in the coastal plain appears to be confined to calcium-rich soils such as coastal shell mounds, limestone bluffs, and wet marl flats; in the piedmont best developed in basic-mesic forests, beech forests, and rich oak-hickory forests.

SIMILAR SPECIES: *A. barbatum* is similar to chalk maple (*A. leucoderme* Small), which occurs in the piedmont and upper coastal plain. *A. barbatum* has a single trunk, leaves whitish beneath, and the terminal lobes of some leaves broader toward the apex than toward the base with lobe tips acute to rounded. *A. leucoderme* usually has multiple trunks, leaves greenish yellow beneath, and the terminal lobe is narrower toward the apex than the base with lobe tips pointed.

COMMENTS: Southern sugar maple is not tapped commercially for sap. The wood is of good quality but is not much used because of the limited supply. It is occasionally planted as a small shade or lawn tree because of its bright yellow-to-red autumn leaves. It is also resistant to wind and ice damage. The state champion southern sugar maple was 135′ tall and 31″ in diameter in 1991.

SYNONYM: *Acer saccharum* subsp. *floridanum* (Chapman) Desmarais—RAB

436. Crested coral-root

Hexalectris spicata (Walter) Barnhart
Hex-a-léc-tris spi-cà-ta
Orchidaceae (Orchid Family)

DESCRIPTION: Nonphotosynthetic, mycotrophic, perennial herb, 6–30″ tall; stem flesh-colored; leaves reduced to sheathing, scale-like bracts; flowers July–August.

RANGE-HABITAT: Widespread in se. North America; widely scattered locations throughout SC; infrequent; calcareous or circumneutral soils such as Native American shell mounds and marl forests, and dry forests and rocky woodlands on calcium-rich soils.

COMMENTS: This is the most attractive of the saprophytic orchids in SC because the stem supports a spike of richly colored flowers. Like most saprophytes, it is almost impossible to successfully transplant.

437. Shadow-witch; Ponthieu's orchid

Ponthieva racemosa (Walter) Mohr
Pon-thiè-va ra-ce-mò-sa
Orchidaceae (Orchid Family)

DESCRIPTION: Perennial, scapose herb, usually about 1′ tall; leaves in a basal cluster; flowers whitish green, in a lax, terminal raceme; flowering September–October.

RANGE-HABITAT: Coastal plain from se. VA to FL, west to TX; in SC on limestone bluffs and marl flats, bottomlands, floodplains, and moist ravines, nearly always on calcium-rich soils.

COMMENTS: Most sources (e.g., Radford et al., 1968) list this orchid as rare; however, recent fieldwork in the coastal plain indicates that it is more abundant and a listing of occasional is justified. The basal cluster of leaves, white fall flowers suffused with green, and its habitat are distinctive. The genus honors Henri de Ponthieu, who collected Caribbean plants.

438. Black walnut

Juglans nigra L.
Jùg-lans nì-gra
Juglandaceae (Walnut Family)

DESCRIPTION: Large tree, to 100–130′ tall; distinguished in winter by twigs with a light-brown, chambered pith; leaves deciduous, alternate, pinnately compound, with 15–23 leaflets; nut husks thick, green to yellow-green, dark brown at maturity; nuts and shells deeply furrowed; nut kernel oily, sweet; fruits mature in October.

RANGE-HABITAT: Virtually throughout eastern North America, and in states west and adjacent to the Mississippi River; common throughout SC; primarily a tree of moist, nutrient-rich forests, including bottomlands and floodplains.

COMMENTS: The beautifully grained, brownish colored wood makes black walnut one of the finest lumber trees in North America, being used for paneling, furniture, and gun stocks. Today, because the supply of mature trees is limited, it is mostly used for veneer. The wood's ability to absorb the recoil of a gun discharging without damage, and the fact that the wood does not shrink or warp with age, makes it ideal for custom-crafted gunstocks.

Black walnut fruits are used in candies, confections, and ice creams. The fruits are an important wildlife food. Historically, the inner bark was used as a mild laxative, especially during the American Revolution. The peel and juice of the fruit was used as a vermifuge for intestinal worms. Duke (1997) recommends walnut as an herbal remedy for athlete's foot.

Black walnut seldom occurs in pure stands in the wild because they produce juglone in their leaves and roots, which inhibits germination and growth of new walnut trees (and some other plants) and thus limits competition for soil nutrients. Black walnut was often planted around homes, where it often persists after abandonment.

439. Venus'-hair fern; southern maidenhair

Adiantum capillus-veneris L.
  A-di-án-tum ca-píl-lus-vé-ne-ris
Pteridaceae (Maidenhair Fern Family)

DESCRIPTION: Fronds hang vertically from ledges and rocks from short, creeping rhizome; pinnae shining, resistant to wetting, partially evergreen in SC, deciduous in more northern areas; frond stalks lustrous purple.

RANGE-HABITAT: Widespread on several continents; in eastern North America largely southern in distribution, from VA to FL, then to TX and AZ, north to MO, SD, and British Columbia; south to the tropics and in warmer parts of the Old World; in the ne. states it occurs as an escape from cultivation; in SC it is uncommon because of a lack of suitable environments and occurs mostly in the coastal area, but also in Greenwood County; probably common in SC on limestone masonry of old cemeteries and buildings; especially prominent in Charleston; in native habitats found on moist, calcareous slopes, rocks, and limestone sink walls.

COMMENTS: Montpellier, France, was the origin of Syrup of Capillaire, a cough medicine made by using fresh maidenhair fronds, orange-flower water, and honey. This and other interesting folklore about Venus'-hair fern and about ferns in general appear in *Ferns of the Coastal Plain* (Dunbar, 1989).

440. Wagner's spleenwort

Asplenium heteroresiliens Wagner
    As-plè-ni-um he-te-ro-re-sí-li-ens
Aspleniaceae (Spleenwort Family)

DESCRIPTION: Evergreen fern; fronds 3–6″ long, erect to spreading, somewhat leathery, pinnately divided, the pinnae opposite on a black to purplish black rachis.

RANGE-HABITAT: Coastal plain from NC to n. FL, and west to AL; rare throughout its range; moist, shady sites on marl or limestone outcrops, and on masonry composed of tabby (a mixture of sand, lime, and oyster shells).

SIMILAR SPECIES: Wagner's spleenwort is similar to *A. resiliens* Kunze (plate 175 in *WCL*). They can be separated by the following: *A. heteroresiliens* has pinnae with minutely scalloped margins, and A. *resiliens* has entire pinnae.

PROTECTION STATUS: Federal Species of Concern

441. *Bald cypress-tupelo gum swamp forests*

441. Bald cypress

Taxodium distichum (L.) Richard
    Tax-ò-di-um dís-ti-chum
Taxodiaceae (Taxodium Family)

DESCRIPTION: Deciduous conifer with 2-ranked leaves (needles); large tree, 70–130′ tall; bark sloughing in thin, flaky scales; separate male and female cones on the same tree; female cones green, turning brown at maturity in the fall.

RANGE-HABITAT: Bald cypress is a wide-ranging tree, from DE and e. MD to FL, and west to e. TX and se. OK; then north along the Mississippi River and its tributaries to IN and IL; in SC primarily found on the coastal plain, but it does extend into the piedmont along the Savannah and other rivers; common in alluvial swamp forests and hardwood bottoms.

SIMILAR SPECIES: Bald cypress is distinguished from pond cypress (*T. ascendens*) by having flat, linear leaves mostly spreading in one plane; pond cypress has slender, needle-shaped to awl-shaped leaves spirally arranged and appressed to the branchlets.

COMMENTS: Bald cypress historically was one of the most important lumber trees of the South. Its wood is very durable due to essential oils and was used for shingles, barrels, caskets, and beams. Native Americans and early settlers carved cypress logs into boats, troughs, and washtubs. Cypress was also used to make rice field trunks in the 1700s and 1800s, many of which persist today. Much fine, Charleston-made furniture has cypress as the secondary wood. The use of cypress as a major commercial timber source has decreased over the years because it does not reproduce well after clear-cutting. Large stands of bald cypress exist on protected state and federal lands.

The trunk of the majestic bald cypress, when growing in saturated or seasonally submerged soil, produces an enlarged base, the buttress, which has important survival value. The wide buttress gives the tree a base of support in the soft, swamp soil. Indeed, it is seldom that a bald cypress is blown down. Other swamp trees, such as tupelo gum, swamp gum, sweet gum, and pond cypress, also form buttresses.

When growing in sites with fluctuating water, the roots of bald cypress also produce knees projecting above water. Knees were once thought to be pneumatophores (for gas exchange); however, evidence today suggests that the wood does not conduct gasses. A more likely function is that the mass of interlocking roots and knees give a stronger base of support for the tree. One thing is certain: the knees do not grow into new trees.

Bald cypress is also planted as an ornamental because it grows well on a variety of upland soils, where it does not produce a buttress or knees. The SC state record bald cypress, in the Congaree Swamp National Monument, is 131' tall and 8.3' in diameter.

TAXONOMY: Because of hybridization and intergradation between bald cypress and pond cypress, some authors treat pond cypress as a variety of bald cypress: *T. distichum* var. *nutans* (Aiton) Sweet.

442. Leucothoë; coastal fetterbush

Leucothoë racemosa (L.) Gray
Leu-cóth-o-ë ra-ce-mò-sa
Ericaceae (Heath Family)

DESCRIPTION: Deciduous shrub to 13' tall; leaves alternate, simple, toothed, 1–3" long, scarlet in fall; racemes usually curved; corolla white, sometimes pink-tinged; flowers March–early June.

RANGE-HABITAT: MA south to FL, and west to LA; in SC found in the coastal plain and lower piedmont; swamp forests, streamsides, pocosins, cypress-gum swamps, and longleaf pine savannas.

443. American storax; snowbell

Styrax americana Lamarck var.
　americana
　Stỳ-rax a-me-ri-cà-na var. a-me-ri-
　cà-na
　Styracaceae (Storax Family)

DESCRIPTION: Commonly a shrub, rarely a tree; leaves deciduous, alternate, obovate; buds naked; axillary bud adjacent to each end bud; flowers fragrant, semidrooping; petals recurved; flowers April–June.

RANGE-HABITAT: From se. VA to s. peninsular FL, west to e. TX, and northward in the interior to se. OK, se. MO, and s. OH; in SC found in the coastal plain, upper piedmont, and mountains, mainly below 600′; occasional in the coastal plain and piedmont, rare in the mountains; montane bogs, piedmont seepage forests, alluvial and nonalluvial swamp forests, floodplain forests, streamsides, cypress-gum depressions, and pocosins.

COMMENTS: Storax is an excellent landscape species, doing best in full sun or very light shade.

444. Cypress-knee sedge

Carex decomposita Muhlenberg
　Cà-rex de-com-pó-si-ta
　Cyperaceae (Sedge Family)

DESCRIPTION: Cespitose, perennial herb; culms 20–40″ long; inflorescence elongate, twice-compound; flowers May–June.

RANGE-HABITAT: NY west to MI, and generally southward to n. FL and e. TX; in SC confined to the coastal plain; rare; backwater swamps and ox-bow lakes, frequently as an epiphyte on cypress knees and buttresses, and on fallen logs; often forms tussocks in waters of swamps and pond margins; it rarely is found as an epiphyte in deep, frequently flooded swamps since moving water would dislodge it.

COMMENTS: The specific epithet, *decomposita,* refers to the branched or decompound (twice-compound) inflorescence, one of the key characteristics of this rare sedge.

PROTECTION STATUS: State Threatened

445. Lizard's tail

Saururus cernuus L.
　Sau-rù-rus cér-nu-us
　Saururaceae (Lizard's Tail Family)

DESCRIPTION: Perennial herb, often forming extensive colonies by rhizomes; aquatic or terrestrial; spike drooping in flower, but becoming erect in fruit; flowers May–July.

RANGE-HABITAT: New England and sw. Quebec to MN, and south to FL and TX; in SC common throughout the coastal plain and piedmont in a variety of aquatic habitats including alluvial and nonalluvial swamp forests, streams, lake and pond margins, low woodlands, and ditches.

COMMENTS: The common name comes from the drooping spike. There are no sepals and petals; the white color of the spike is due to the stamen stalks.

446. Silky camellia; Virginia stewartia

Stewartia malacodendron L.
   Ste-wàrt-i-a ma-la-co-dén-dron
Theaceae (Tea Family)

DESCRIPTION: Deciduous shrub or small tree, seldom over 20′ tall; leaves thin, alternate, deciduous, with fine, sharp-pointed teeth and fine hairs along the margin; stamen filaments purple; flowers May–June.

RANGE-HABITAT: From se. VA south to FL, and west to se. TX; in SC chiefly on the coastal plain, occasional; rare in the piedmont; most often in hummocks in swamps, or on beech-dominated bluffs.

COMMENTS: The flower of silky camellia resembles the cultivated camellias, and it is often cultivated. The trees are too small for lumber and of little or no value for wildlife. The genus honors John Stuart, 1713–1792, or as often was written formally, Stewart, third Earl of Bute.

447. Ladies'-eardrops

Brunnichia ovata (Walter) Shinners
   Brun-ních-i-a o-và-ta
Polygonaceae (Buckwheat Family)

DESCRIPTION: Partly woody vine climbing by tendrils; leaves alternate, ovate; calyx modified into winglike structures, enclosing fruits; flowers June–July; fruits mature August–September.

RANGE-HABITAT: From northeast SC to FL, west to e. TX, and north in the interior to se. MO, w. KY, and s. IL; in SC a rare coastal plain species found in alluvial swamps and along alluvial riverbanks.

COMMENTS: Ladies'-eardrops is a little-known vine to botanists and laymen. The common name comes from the shape of the winged fruit. The genus honors M. T. Brünnich, an eighteenth-century Norwegian naturalist.

SYNONYM: *Brunnichia cirrhosa* Banks ex Gaertner—RAB

448. Riverbank sundrops

Oenothera riparia Nuttall
    Oe-no-thè-ra ri-pà-ri-a
Onagraceae (Evening-primrose Family)

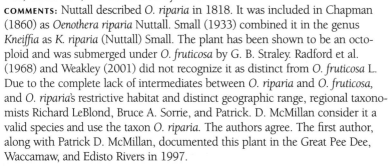

DESCRIPTION: Perennial herb, to 3′ tall; lower stem usually winged, spongy, and thickened; leaves alternate, nearly smooth, linear-lanceolate, rather thick; flowers June–late August; capsule angular and long-stalked; capsules mature in the fall.

RANGE-HABITAT: NC to n. FL; growing on cypress knees and with driftwood just above the tidal drawdown zone in major tidal blackwater rivers; in the Carolinas reported from the ne. Cape Fear, Lower Pee Dee, Waccamaw, and Edisto river systems.

COMMENTS: Nuttall described *O. riparia* in 1818. It was included in Chapman (1860) as *Oenothera riparia* Nuttall. Small (1933) combined it in the genus *Kneiffia* as *K. riparia* (Nuttall) Small. The plant has been shown to be an octoploid and was submerged under *O. fruticosa* by G. B. Straley. Radford et al. (1968) and Weakley (2001) did not recognize it as distinct from *O. fruticosa* L. Due to the complete lack of intermediates between *O. riparia* and *O. fruticosa,* and *O. riparia*'s restrictive habitat and distinct geographic range, regional taxonomists Richard LeBlond, Bruce A. Sorrie, and Patrick. D. McMillan consider it a valid species and use the taxon *O. riparia.* The authors agree. The first author, along with Patrick D. McMillan, documented this plant in the Great Pee Dee, Waccamaw, and Edisto Rivers in 1997.

449. Powdery-thalia

Thalia dealbata Roscoe
    Thàl-i-a de-al-bà-ta
Marantaceae (Arrowroot Family)

DESCRIPTION: Robust, scapose, erect perennial to 7′ tall; frequently whitish throughout; leaves large, 12–20″ long, 6–8″ wide; leaf stalks to 32″ long; sepals 3, pale purple; petals 3, longer and darker purple than the sepals; flowers June–October.

RANGE-HABITAT: MO, TX, and OK, and east to FL; and in SC; in SC rare and confined to the coastal plain; waters of ditches, margins of swamps, pond edges, and freshwater marshes.

COMMENTS: The specific epithet *dealbata* means "whitewashed," in reference to the whitish cast to the plant. The genus honors Johann Thal, a German physician and naturalist who died in 1583.

PROTECTION STATUS: State Threatened

450. Rose coreopsis

Coreopsis rosea Nuttall
Co-re-óp-sis rò-se-a
Asteraceae (Aster or Sunflower Family)

DESCRIPTION: Smooth perennial with creeping, subterranean, stoloniferous base; stem ascending, to 32″ tall; leaves linear, opposite; disk flowers yellow, ray flowers purplish pink to light-rose, or white; flowers July–September.
RANGE-HABITAT: From s. Nova Scotia to GA and TN; unreported from NC; rare in SC and known from two well-determined habitats: upland depression ponds in the inner coastal plain, and drawdown zones of blackwater rivers in the outer coastal plain.
COMMENTS: Rose coreopsis can be found in the Janet Harrison Highpond Heritage Preserve in Aiken County. Weakley (1999) states that it has been reported from the Waccamaw River in Horry County. It does well in cultivation. No other species of coreopsis in SC has purplish pink to light-rose or white flowers.
PROTECTION STATUS: State Threatened

451. Green-fly orchid

Epidendrum conopseum R. Brown
E-pi-dén-drum co-nóp-se-um
Orchidaceae (Orchid Family)

DESCRIPTION: Epiphytic herb; stems erect or ascending, smooth, to 16″ tall; leaves evergreen, leathery; roots with well-developed, whitish velamen; flowers fragrant, blooming July–October (but into December if winter is late).
RANGE-HABITAT: From se. NC to FL, and west to LA; primarily an outer coastal plain species; common; alluvial swamp forests and hardwood bottoms; occasionally found growing on live oak trees in various sites throughout the coastal plain.
COMMENTS: Green-fly orchid is the only epiphytic orchid in the continental US found outside of FL. Based on the first author's field observations, it is common rather than rare, as is reported in most manuals. It is often overlooked because it grows high up in trees where it is sometimes hidden in resurrection fern and/or Spanish moss. Populations have been found in almost every river system in the coastal plain. It generally grows on horizontal limbs of live oak, bald cypress, or tupelo gum.

452. Macbridea; Carolina birds-in-a-nest

Macbridea caroliniana (Walter) Blake
Mac-brìd-e-a ca-ro-li-ni-à-na
Lamiaceae (Mint Family)

DESCRIPTION: Perennial herb to 3′ tall; stems square; flowers in 1 to 3 tight, bracted, separated clusters; leaves opposite, in 7–11 pairs; flowers July–August.

RANGE-HABITAT: Rare coastal plain species from se. NC to n. FL, and west to LA; openings in swamp forests, freshwater marshes, ditches, savanna edges, and bogs.

COMMENTS: The common name, birds-in-a-nest, comes from the birds (flowers) that arise out of the nest (the subtending bracts). The genus honors Dr. James MacBride, 1784–1817, a SC botanist of St. John's Parish, Berkeley County.

PROTECTION STATUS: Federal Species of Concern

453. Ogeechee lime; Ogeechee plum

Nyssa ogeche Marshall
Nýs-sa o-gè-che
Nyssaceae (Sourgum Family)

DESCRIPTION: Small to medium size tree, usually less than 40′ tall; typically with swollen buttresses and multiple, crooked stems; leaves alternate, simple, deciduous, variable in shape but usually broadest at or above the middle; male and female flowers on same tree, flowering in April; drupes red, maturing August–October.

RANGE-HABITAT: Restricted to the coastal plain of se. SC, GA, n. FL, and west to s. AL; in SC rare and known from only Beaufort and Jasper Counties, where it occurs in pond cypress-swamp gum depressions; in the rest of its range it grows along riverbanks and in river swamps.

COMMENTS: The common name, Ogeechee lime, is derived from the Ogeechee River in GA and from the use of the acid juice of its ripe fruits as a substitute for lime. The pulp of the juice makes a good preserve. As a result of its small size, it has never been economically important. Birds and small animals eat the fruits.

PROTECTION STATUS: State Endangered Peripheral

454. Coral greenbrier

Smilax walteri Pursh
Smì-lax wál-ter-i
Liliaceae (Lily Family)

DESCRIPTION: High-climbing, deciduous, woody vine; spines lacking; berries bright red, maturing in September, persisting through the winter.

RANGE-HABITAT: NJ south to c. FL, and west to TN, AR, and TX; in SC common throughout the coastal plain, and rare in the lower piedmont; alluvial and nonalluvial swamp forests and hardwood bottoms, often where the roots are submersed for at least part of the year.

COMMENTS: This is the only totally deciduous greenbrier in SC. In leaf it is difficult to separate from other greenbriers. The leafless vines with berries are often used for Christmas decorations. The specific epithet honors Thomas Walter, 1740–1789, a SC botanist from Berkeley County.

455. Mistletoe

Phoradendron serotinum (Rafinesque)
M. C. Johnston
Pho-ra-dén-dron se-rò-ti-num
Loranthaceae (Mistletoe Family)

DESCRIPTION: Evergreen shrub; obligate hemiparasite on a variety of broadleaf, deciduous trees; flowers small; male and female flowers on separate plants, maturing September–November, and sporadically through the winter; berries white, maturing November–January, persisting into spring.

RANGE-HABITAT: WV and s. NJ, south to FL, and west to e. TX and OK; in SC common in the coastal plain and piedmont, less frequent in the mountains; branches of broadleaf, deciduous trees exposed to sun in swamp forests and other forested areas.

COMMENTS: There are numerous species of *Phoradendron* in North America; however, this is the only species in SC. This is the common mistletoe used in Christmas holiday decorations.

Mistletoes cause enormous economic loss in many parts of the world. In North America it is a pest in walnut, pear, and pecan plantations. In these plantations, injury results from broken branches that allow invasion of insects and fungi; tree growth is slowed due to loss of water and minerals. In SC, little economic loss results from mistletoe since it affects trees that are of little commercial value. (It does not attack pines.)

The berries are covered with a sticky material poisonous to humans. Poisoning often occurs during Christmas when the plant is used for decorations and children eat the berries. Its one-seeded berries, however, can be eaten by a wide variety of birds that use the pulp for food. The birds spread the seeds through droppings and from wiping their beaks on branches. In both cases, germination occurs on the branch, the haustorium penetrates the host tissue, and a xylem bridge forms between the host and mistletoe.

456. Hardwood bottom forests

456. Dwarf palmetto

Sabal minor (Jacquin) Persoon
Sà-bal mì-nor
Arecaceae (Palm Family)

DESCRIPTION: In its eastern range, a shrub with no trunk above ground; in its western range, sometimes a small tree; leaves fan-shaped, almost round in outline, without a midrib, bluish green; flowers May–July; fruits, black at maturity, mature in September–November.

RANGE-HABITAT: Common throughout its range and native to the coastal plain from SC to se. TX, and north along the Mississippi Valley to se. AK; it extends into the piedmont along rivers, especially in the Savannah River drainage system; floodplain forests, commonly where flooded seasonally, swamps, and occasionally on sandy soils, including pinelands.

SIMILAR SPECIES: Where it grows with cabbage palmetto (*S. palmetto,* plate 593), dwarf palmetto may be confused with a immature cabbage palmetto that has not produced an aboveground stem. They can be separated as follows: dwarf palmetto has no filaments on the leaf segments and is without a midrib on the blade except at the very base; cabbage palmetto has filaments on the leaf blades and has a prominent midrib curving downward at the leaf tip.

COMMENTS: The flowers are a source of honey, and Native Americans used the fruits for food. Although the dried leaves are used occasionally for thatch roofs, dwarf palmetto has no economic value and is of limited use to wildlife. It is a good natural-landscaping plant for homes located on coastal barrier islands.

457. Jack-in-the-pulpit; Indian turnip

Arisaema triphyllum (L.) Schott
A-ri-saè-ma tri-phýl-lum
Araceae (Arum Family)

DESCRIPTION: Erect, perennial herb 8–30″ tall from a corm; leaves 1 or 2, palmately divided; flowers on a fleshy spadix, male above, female below; spathe (the pulpit) with a tube and a hood that arches over the spadix (jack); flowers mature March–April; fruit a red berry in clusters, maturing in July.

RANGE-HABITAT: Common and widespread in eastern North America; common throughout SC in rich woods, low woods, and bogs.

COMMENTS: All parts of the plant, but especially the corm, contain crystals of calcium oxalate that can irritate the mucous membranes of the mouth and throat, causing a burning sensation. Death can result by asphyxiation if the air passages swell. Fernald and Kinsey (1958) report, however, that the crystals can be broken up by heat and drying (but not by boiling). Once done, the corm becomes mild and pleasant tasting. Native Americans used it as flour.

TAXONOMY: Weakley (2001) gives four subspecies of *A. triphyllum*. The authors prefer to use the conservative taxonomic treatment.

458. Wild azalea

Rhododendron canescens (Michaux) Sweet
Rho-do-dén-dron ca-nés-cens
Ericaceae (Heath Family)

DESCRIPTION: Deciduous shrub to 16′ tall; flowers fragrant, appearing before the leaves, or with the leafy shoots of the season; corolla pale to deep pink, without yellow markings; flowers March–early May.

RANGE-HABITAT: DE and MD, south to FL, and west to TX and OK; in SC throughout the coastal plain and into the southwest piedmont; primarily a plant of moist, wooded slopes along edges of swamps and hardwood bottoms, low woods and thickets, riverbanks and streambanks, rocky open woodlands, and borders of pocosins and bogs.

COMMENTS: Foote and Jones (1989) state that wild azalea is a superior azalea to plant along streams (and presumably in the other habitats listed above). All parts are poisonous.

459. Carolina least trillium

Trillium pusillum Michaux var. *pusillum*
Tríl-li-um pu-síl-lum var. pu-síl-lum
Liliaceae (Lily Family)

DESCRIPTION: Perennial, rhizomatous herb; stem 2–8″ tall; flower solitary, on short stalk; petals at first white, changing to pink or purple; flowers March–May.

RANGE-HABITAT: From the coastal plain of e. NC to SC, west to the Blue Ridge of NC, and west into AL and TN; rare throughout its range; pocosin borders, bottomland forests among small streams in the inner coastal plain, ecotones of calcareous savannas and swamp forests in the outer coastal plain, and moist slopes in the mountains.

COMMENTS: The most significant population of Carolina least trillium in SC occurs in Francis Beidler Forest in Dorchester County. Hurricane Hugo (1989) removed most of the canopy from the hardwood bottom where it grows. The population has been monitored since the canopy removal, but no significant decrease has occurred in its numbers since the hurricane despite growing in almost full sunlight.

TAXONOMY: The *Trillium pusillum* complex is under active review and is too complex to discuss in this book. Weakley (2001) states a new variety is under study that would include all material from the Blue Ridge of NC and south and west of it, leaving the type variety, described above, as endemic to the coastal plain of NC and SC.

PROTECTION STATUS: Federal Species of Concern

460. Easter lily; naked lady; atamasco lily

Zephyranthes atamasco (L.) Herbert
Ze-phy-rán-thes a-ta-más-co
Amaryllidaceae (Amaryllis Family)

DESCRIPTION: Perennial herb from a bulb; flowering stalk to 1′ tall, generally solitary, terminated by a single flower; leaves basal, linear; perianth usually white, rarely pink; flowers late March–April.

RANGE-HABITAT: VA to n. FL, and west to MS; common in the coastal plain and lower piedmont of SC; bottomland forests and adjacent road shoulders and wet meadows.

COMMENTS: Leaves, and especially the bulb, are highly poisonous to horses, cattle, and fowl (also to people?). The common name, naked lady, comes from the leafless stalk terminated by the beautiful flower.

461. Coastal doghobble

Leucothoë axillaris (Lamarck) D. Don
Leu-cóth-o-ë ax-il-là-ris
Ericaceae (Heath Family)

DESCRIPTION: Evergreen shrub to 5′ tall, with clustered, arching stems, usually forming dense colonies; flowers late March–May.

RANGE-HABITAT: Common coastal plain species from se. VA to FL panhandle, west to LA; pocosins, hardwood bottoms, blackwater swamps, moist and acid slopes, and along streams.

COMMENTS: The common name comes from the dense colonies that are almost impenetrable to walk through, even for a hunting dog.

462. Carolina buttercup

Ranunculus carolinianus Augustin de Candolle
Ra-nùn-cu-lus ca-ro-li-ni-à-nus
Ranunculaceae (Buttercup Family)

DESCRIPTION: Weakly spreading, perennial herb with cordlike roots; plants usually colonial; leaves ternately divided; sepals reflexed; petals bright to pale yellow; flowers April–July.

RANGE-HABITAT: NY west to s. Ontario, to WI and MN, south to n. peninsular FL, LA, and e. TX; in SC scattered in the coastal plain and piedmont; swamps, low woods, banks of wooded streams, floodplain forests, marshy shores, wet thickets, and swales.

463. Fever tree; Georgia bark

Pinckneya pubens Michaux
    Pínck-ney-a pù-bens
Rubiaceae (Madder Family)

DESCRIPTION: Small tree or shrub; leaves deciduous, opposite and simple; flowers borne in clusters; petals greenish yellow with bright-red spots on the inside; flower made conspicuous by enlargement of 1 (often two) calyx lobe(s) that is/are bright rose pink with greenish veins; flowers May.

RANGE-HABITAT: Restricted to SC, GA, and FL; rare in SC and known only from Beaufort, Jasper, and Darlington Counties; coastal plain along the edges of hardwood bottoms or swamp forests.

COMMENTS: Early botanists, such as Mellichamp, reported fever tree from sites in Beaufort County, especially near Bluffton. Recently, it was found in Jasper and Darlington Counties. It is certainly one of the more interesting plants in SC from a historical and biological perspective. It is only conspicuous for a short time when it blooms in May. The common name, fever tree, comes from the use of the bark as a substitute for quinine in treating malaria. André Michaux named this tree in honor of his friend, General Charles Cotesworth Pinckney.

PROTECTION STATUS: State Endangered

464. False nettle

Boehmeria cylindrica (L.) Swartz
    Boeh-mèr-i-a cy-lín-dri-ca
Urticaceae (Nettle Family)

DESCRIPTION: Perennial herb without stinging hairs; stems 1.5–3′ tall; leaves opposite, long-stalked; flowers tiny, in small, headlike clusters, arranged in continuous (female) or interrupted (male) spikes in the axils of opposite leaves; spikes often terminated by small leaves; flowers July–August.

RANGE-HABITAT: Quebec and Ontario to MN, generally southward to s. FL and TX; common throughout its range; throughout SC on fallen logs, stumps, cypress knees and buttresses in alluvial and nonalluvial swamp forests; also in hardwood bottoms, freshwater marshes, wet thickets, canals, and drainage or irrigation ditches.

COMMENTS: The genus honors Georg Boehmer, 1723–1803, a professor at Wittenberg.

465. Virginia dayflower

Commelina virginica L.
   Com-me-lìn-a vir-gí-ni-ca
Commelinaceae (Spiderwort Family)

DESCRIPTION: Coarse, herbaceous perennial with erect stems 10–36″ tall; leaves lanceolate, with conspicuous basal sheaths; flowers from greenish spathes; all 3 petals blue, ephemeral, one slightly smaller; flowers July–October.

RANGE-HABITAT: NJ west to KS and OK, and south to FL and TX; throughout SC, but rare in the upper piedmont and mountains; bottomlands, swamp forests, and other moist to wet forests and forest edges.

COMMENTS: The dayflowers are known for the flowers that open for only one morning. Linnaeus named the genus, with his usual humor, for the brothers Commelin. The two larger petals represent the two brothers, who became well-known botanists, and the smaller petal represents the third brother who died without any botanical achievements.

466. Ironwood; blue-beech; American hornbeam

Carpinus caroliniana Walter
   Car-pì-nus ca-ro-li-ni-à-na
Betulaceae (Birch Family)

DESCRIPTION: Usually a shade-tolerant, understory tree up to 35′ tall and 8–10″ in diameter; trunk irregularly fluted and twisted; leaves deciduous, simple, symmetrical at base, alternate and 2-ranked; male and female flowers on the same tree; male flowers in drooping catkins; female catkins appearing in early spring with emergence of leaves; nutlets subtended by a 3-lobed, leaflike bract.

RANGE-HABITAT: Throughout southern Canada, and eastern and Midwestern US; common throughout SC; low and wet woodlands and floodplain forests, and extending upslope in rich soils.

COMMENTS: The common name, hornbeam, which comes from "horn" (meaning tough) and "beam" (similar to the German "baum" for tree), accurately describes its wood: close-grained, hard, and heavy. Early Americans used the wood for mallets, tool handles, wooden ware, dishes, and bowls. The tree is too small to be commercially used for lumber. Small mammals and song birds eat the nutlets.

467. Possum-haw

Ilex decidua Walter
Ì-lex de-cí-du-a
Aquifoliaceae (Holly Family)

DESCRIPTION: Deciduous shrub or small understory tree, to 33′ tall; male and female flowers on separate plants; fruits maturing in late fall and persisting on the branchlets into late winter.

RANGE-HABITAT: MD to FL, and west to MO and TX; in SC throughout the coastal plain and piedmont; floodplain forests, alluvial swamps, low woodlands along creeks, and wet thickets.

COMMENTS: Winter branches bearing the orange to red berries are gathered for use in Christmas decorations. A variety of wildlife eat the fruits. The wood is hard and dense, but the trees are too small to be of commercial value. The tree is valued as a landscape plant because of its conspicuous fruits and drought tolerance.

468. Sweet gum

Liquidambar styraciflua L.
Li-quid-ám-bar sty-ra-cí-flu-a
Hamamelidaceae (Witch-hazel Family)

DESCRIPTION: Large, deciduous tree; young branches usually with irregularly cork-like wings; leaves alternate, palmately 5-lobed; male and female flowers in separate clusters on the same plant; fruits mature fall-winter; seed capsules in hard, rounded ball-like structures that persist throughout the winter.

RANGE-HABITAT: Native to the southeastern US and extends north along the MS and OH Valleys and along the Atlantic Coast to s. NY; common throughout SC except at higher elevations; variety of wooded mesic sites, wet or swampy woodlands, and occasionally on sites where water stands almost continually.

COMMENTS: Sweet gum is one of South Carolina's most versatile trees. Although it is not strong enough for structural timber, its pink or ruddy heartwood shows handsome figures on the quarter-sawed cut and is used for veneer, furniture, and plywood panels. Today, sweet gum shows a higher commercial harvest than any other deciduous hardwood.

During pioneer times in the South, this gum was used for treatment of sores and skin troubles, for a chewing gum, and the Confederate armies used it to treat dysentery. During World War I and II, its gum was the base of soaps, drugs, and adhesives.

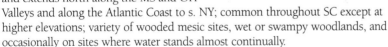

Levee forests

469. Butterweed

Senecio glabellus Poiret
Se-nè-ci-o gla-bél-lus
Asteraceae (Aster or Sunflower Family)

DESCRIPTION: Annual, erect herb with smooth, hollow stems to 3′ tall; often forming dense stands; leaves alternate, deeply divided into narrow segments; flowers March–June.

RANGE-HABITAT: From east NC to s. FL, west to e. TX, and in the interior to OH, MO, and SD; in SC common throughout the piedmont, sandhills, and coastal plain; alluvial and non-alluvial swamp forests, hardwood bottoms, and wet pastures.

COMMENTS: Worldwide there are 1200 species of the genus *Senecio,* and so far at least 25 have proven poisonous to livestock and humans. *S. glabellus* has been suspected of poisoning cattle in FL. The reader may refer to Kingsbury (1964) for an historical account of the genus *Senecio.*

470. Cross-vine

Bignonia capreolata L.
Big-nòn-i-a cap-re-o-là-ta
Bignoniaceae (Trumpet-creeper Family)

DESCRIPTION: Perennial, high-climbing, woody vine; leaves opposite, pinnately compound, with terminal leaflet modified into a tendril; flowers April–May.

RANGE-HABITAT: From e. MD to s. OH and s. MO, and generally southward to s. FL and e. TX; common throughout SC (except in the mountains); alluvial swamp forests, all upland wooded habitats, fencerows, thickets, and disturbed areas.

COMMENTS: The terminal leaflet that is modified into a tendril is highly branched. At the ends of the branches are small adhesive disks that are used for attachment, which allow cross-vine to climb the sides of buildings. The common name comes from the anatomy of the stem, an easy aid to identification. A thin layer of barklike tissue separates the stem longitudinally into four equal segments, which can be seen in cross section.

Cross-vine is a native vine that has spread widely into disturbed habitats. The genus honors the Abbé Jean-Paul Bignon, 1662–1743, a court librarian at Paris.
SYNONYM: *Anisostichus capreolata* (L.) Bureau—RAB

471. Switch-cane

Arundinaria gigantea (Walter) Walter ex Muhlenberg
   A-run-di-nà-ri-a gi-gán-te-a
Poaceae (Grass Family)

DESCRIPTION: Rhizomatous, woody perennial forming extensive colonies (canebrakes); stems 2–30′ tall; plants flower sporadically April–May and presumably die after flowering.

RANGE-HABITAT: Native to the eastern US, ranging from s. DE and s. OH, south to FL and TX; common throughout SC; habitats include, but not exclusively, low lying, moist to wet places such as low woodlands, riverbanks and streambanks, hardwood bottoms, levees, shrub bogs, sloughs, bayous, and longleaf pine savannas; in the mountains and piedmont it also occurs on dry uplands.

COMMENTS: *Arundinaria* is the only member of the bamboo tribe of the grass family (Poaceae) native to the US. Numerous other species of the bamboo tribe are cultivated. Stock browse on the young leaves and seeds. In coastal SC in colonial times, lands were burned to produce a quantity of young plants for grazing.

Stems of large canes are used for fishing poles, mats, and baskets. The stems are split and made into chair bottoms. The tender shoots are edible, and the large grains can also be used for food. Foster and Duke (1990), however, warn that ergot, a highly toxic fungus, occasionally replaces the large seeds of giant cane, making them poisonous.

The term "canebrakes" comes from this plant. Canebrakes are large areas dominated by dense stands of cane. In colonial times, these canebrakes were common in the levees and hardwood bottoms along large rivers. Today these brakes are virtually gone.

TAXONOMY: There is much confusion over the taxonomic status of *Arundinaria* in the US. Some authors, such as Weakley (2001), separate it into two species: *Arundinaria gigantea* (giant cane) and *A. tecta* Walter (small cane); others (i.e., Radford at al., 1968) include both taxa under *A. gigantea*. The morphological characters used to separate the two taxa are not always clear.

Giant cane occurs throughout SC, while small cane is mostly a piedmont and coastal plain species. Giant cane reaches heights of 30′ and is supposed to flower only once every 50–60 years, while small cane is normally 3–6′ tall (unless fire-suppressed where it may reach 12′) and is reported to flower every 3–4 years.

472. River oats; fish-on-a-pole

Chasmanthium latifolium (Michaux)
   Yates
   Chas-mán-thi-um la-ti-fò-li-um
Poaceae (Grass Family)

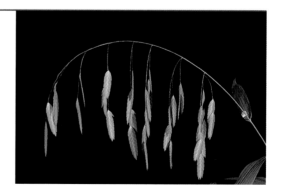

DESCRIPTION: Rhizomatous, perennial herb; stems 2–5′ tall; stem leaves lanceolate, to 8″ long; flowers June–October.

RANGE-HABITAT: Widespread in eastern North America; throughout SC except for the maritime strand; along riverbanks and streambanks, along ditches, in hardwood bottoms, and in seepages and glades over mafic or calcareous rock.

COMMENTS: River oats is sometimes planted as an ornamental; it is also dried and used for bouquets and floral arrangements.

SYNONYM: *Uniola latifolia* Michaux—RAB

473. Spilanthes

Spilanthes americana var. *repens*
(Walter) A. H. Moore
Spi-lán-thes a-me-ri-cà-na
var. rè-pens
Asteraceae (Aster or Sunflower Family)

DESCRIPTION: Colonial, perennial herb with
decumbent stems rooting at the nodes; stem
usually purple, 12–40″ long; leaves simple,
opposite; receptacle conic (high-conic in
fruit); flowers late August–October.

RANGE-HABITAT: NC to MO, south to FL and
TX; in SC a coastal plain plant growing in wet
pastures, swamp forests, seepage areas in woodlands, tidal freshwater marshes,
and riverbanks.

474. American holly

Ilex opaca Aiton
Ì-lex o-pà-ca
Aquifoliaceae (Holly Family)

DESCRIPTION: Small to medium tree; leaves
evergreen, simple, alternate, with sharp marginal spines; male and female flowers on separate trees; flowers April–June; fruits bright red
or orange, containing 4 irregularly grooved
pits (with enclosed seeds); fruits mature September–October, often persisting until flowering the following year.

RANGE-HABITAT: Native to the eastern,
southeastern, and southcentral sections of the US; common throughout SC in a
wide variety of forests, ranging from xeric to wetland.

COMMENTS: This is the most often planted holly because of the red berries and
evergreen, spiny leaves. There are over 300 varieties or cultivated forms. Songbirds eat the fruits but they are poisonous to humans. The trees are too small to
yield commercial quantities of lumber. The tough, white wood (which turns
brown with age) has been used to make small wooden wares.

475. American sycamore

Platanus occidentalis L.
Plà-ta-nus oc-ci-den-tà-lis
Platanaceae (Sycamore Family)

DESCRIPTION: Large, deciduous tree to 115′
tall; outer bark separating into large, thin
scales that fall away and expose the lighter,
inner bark; male and female flowers produced
on the same plant in separate, dense heads in
April–May; female cluster develops into a
hard fruit ball (that breaks apart in early
spring of the following year) composed of
numerous packed, narrow fruits; fruits mature
October.

RANGE-HABITAT: Common throughout eastern North America; lowland tree, from
sea level to about 2800′; rocky streamsides, along streams and rivers, and in

bottomlands and floodplains; may also become established in abandoned fields and spoil banks; common throughout SC.

COMMENTS: Sycamore is often cultivated as an ornamental for its drought resistance and peeling outer bark that exposes the lighter, inner bark. The tree is of little value for wildlife and birds and has never been an important lumber tree. The seeds were, however, a favorite food of the extinct Carolina Parakeet.

476. River birch

Betula nigra L.
Bé-tu-la nì-gra
Betulaceae (Birch Family)

DESCRIPTION: Small to medium size, deciduous tree, often 60–80' tall; bark of trunk peels off in thin, paperlike layers; male and female flowers in separate catkins on the same plant; female catkins mature in the fall, shedding winged seeds.

RANGE-HABITAT: Throughout the eastern US; throughout SC, but chiefly in the piedmont and coastal plain; common; generally associated with periodically wet areas such as streamsides, floodplains, and sandbars.

COMMENTS: River birch is often cultivated because of its attractive peeling bark and high drought tolerance. The inner bark is edible and makes a good emergency trail food. Native Americans made use of the inner bark by drying it, then grinding it into flour. A refreshing sap can be drunk from the tree in the spring or boiled down into a sweet syrup. A tea can be made from the inner bark by simply boiling it in water. The dry, outer bark makes a good fire-starter. The wood is too knotty for lumber. The bark is the most identifiable feature.

477. *Pocosins*

478. Leather-leaf

Cassandra calyculata (L.) D. Don
Cas-sán-dra ca-ly-cu-là-ta
Ericaceae (Heath Family)

DESCRIPTION: Low, rhizomatous shrub, 1–3' tall; leaves evergreen, both surfaces tawny and scurfy, the lower more so; flowers on an arching stem, solitary in axils of previous year's leaves; flowers March–April.

RANGE-HABITAT: Circumpolar in distribution; occasional in SC; bogs in the mountains of NC (but nearly extirpated), and in Carolina bay pocosins in the coastal plain of SC and NC; in SC reported from Berkeley, Horry, Sumter, and Marion Counties.

COMMENTS: A good site to see leather-leaf is Lewis Ocean Bay Heritage Preserve in Horry County.

SYNONYM: *C. calyculata* var. *angustifolia* (Aiton) Rehder—W

PROTECTION STATUS: State Threatened

479. Coastal plain serviceberry

Amelanchier obovalis (Michaux) Ashe
A-me-lán-chi-er o-bo-và-lis
Rosaceae (Rose Family)

DESCRIPTION: Rhizomatous, colonial shrub, to 5′ tall; deciduous, with leaves scarcely evident at flowering; leaves simple, alternate; flowers March–April; pome purple, soft, and sweet, mature May–June.

RANGE-HABITAT: Coastal plain from NJ to GA and AL; in SC throughout the sandhills and coastal plain in pocosins, bays, low woods, and longleaf pine flatwoods and savannas; common.

COMMENTS: This species and other species of *Amelanchier* make excellent landscape plants when used in natural situations. They bloom early, announcing the arrival of spring. The orange fall foliage is outstanding, and the fruits are excellent food for birds. The common name, serviceberry, comes from the mountain species because their flowering branches were used in churches for Easter service. Native Americans used the fruits in making bread and pemmican; the fruits can be cooked as sauces or in pies, or dried for winter use.

480. Coastal witch-alder

Fothergilla gardenii Murray
Fo-ther-gíll-a gar-dèn-i-i
Hamamelidaceae (Witch-hazel Family)

DESCRIPTION: Colonial shrub 1–3′ tall; leaves with starlike hairs; flowers appearing in April–May, before the leaves.

RANGE-HABITAT: Primarily a coastal plain species from se. NC south to FL panhandle, and west to AL; in SC in the sandhills and coastal plain; occasional; pocosins and pocosin margins, wet longleaf pine savannas, and sandhill seepages.

COMMENTS: Coastal witch-alder is planted as an ornamental because of its small size, showy white spikes in the spring, and brilliant yellow-orange to scarlet foliage in the fall.

The genus honors John Fothergill, 1712–1780, a London physician and botanist. The specific epithet honors Alexander Garden, M.D., 1730–1792, a Charleston physician and botanist.

481. Carolina wicky; southern sheep-kill

Kalmia carolina Small
  Kálm-i-a ca-ro-lì-na
Ericaceae (Heath Family)

DESCRIPTION: Evergreen, rhizomatous shrub, 1–3′ tall, forming sizable colonies; leaves in whorls of 3, or occasionally opposite or alternate on some branches; flowers April–early July.

RANGE-HABITAT: Two disjunct areas: se. VA through NC to c. SC; and the southern Appalachians from VA south through NC, SC, and TN to GA; in SC a rare mountain, coastal plain, and sandhills plant; moist, peaty streamsides and montane bogs, wet to moist pinelands, and the ecotones between pocosins and Carolina bay ridges and xeric sand ridges.

COMMENTS: The common name comes from the fact that it is poisonous to livestock. The flowers are miniatures of the larger mountain laurel (*Kalmia latifolia*). The 10 anthers are tucked into pockets of the corolla and pop out when touched by insects, causing pollen to spray the insect, an adaptation that assists in cross-pollination.

Good populations occur in Cartwheel Bay Heritage Preserve, the Vaughn Tract of the Little Pee Dee River Heritage Preserve, Bennett's Bay, and the headwaters of Mathews Creek in the mountains of Greenville County.

SYNONYM: *Kalmia angustifolia* var. *caroliniana* (Small) Fernald—RAB

482. Fetterbush

Lyonia lucida (Lamarck) K. Koch
  Ly-òn-i-a lù-ci-da
Ericaceae (Heath Family)

DESCRIPTION: Rhizomatous, evergreen shrub to 8′ tall; usually forming dense colonies, especially in pocosins; first-year twigs strongly angled; leaves glossy, with a distinct marginal vein; flowers April–early June.

RANGE-HABITAT: From se. VA to s. FL, and west to LA; in SC in the coastal plain and sandhills; common; pocosins, longleaf pine and pond cypress savannas, blackwater swamps, and wet woodlands.

COMMENTS: Fetterbush is often the dominant shrub in pocosins, forming dense colonies that make walking difficult. It sprouts vigorously from rhizomes after a fire, quickly becoming reestablished.

483. Sweet bay

Magnolia virginica L.
  Mag-nòl-i-a vir-gí-ni-ca
Magnoliaceae (Magnolia Family)

DESCRIPTION: Small shrub or tree 30–80′ tall; often a bushy stump-sprout in burned or cutover areas; leaves entire, evergreen or semi-evergreen, persisting into winter with a few remaining until spring; leaves white beneath, easily noticeable from a distance; flowers April–July; fruits (an aggregate of follicles) mature July–October, with stalks keeping the bright red seeds attached to the open follicles.

RANGE-HABITAT: From e. MA and s. PA south to s. FL, west to e. TX, and north in the Mississippi Valley to e. TN and AR; in SC primarily common in the sand-hills and coastal plain, but found in the piedmont and mountains where it is rare; pocosins, longleaf pine and pond cypress savannas, swamp and bay forests, and low wet woodlands.

COMMENTS: The tree form of sweet bay is often cultivated because of its showy, fragrant flowers. It is of little economic importance because of its small size.

484. Sweet pitcher-plant

Sarracenia rubra Walter
  Sar-ra-cèn-i-a rù-bra
Sarraceniaceae (Pitcher-plant Family)

DESCRIPTION: Carnivorous, flowering herb; perennial from rhizomes; leaves modified into hollow tubes (pitchers), 4–20″ tall, as passive traps to catch insects; flowering stalk usually exceeding the leaves; petals maroon on outer surface, greenish on inner; flowers April–May.

RANGE-HABITAT: Primarily limited to the Atlantic Coastal Plain Province, from NC south through SC and GA to n. FL; in SC in the sandhills and coastal plain; occasional, but locally abundant; edge of pocosins, sandhill seepage areas, and in wet longleaf pine savannas.

COMMENTS: Sweet pitcher-plant catches ants; the opening is too small to admit larger insects. It appears to grow more robust in seepage areas along the edge of pocosins and in sphagnum openings in pocosins. In the pine savannas, where it is also found, it is often diminutive.

TAXONOMY: Once a variety of *S. rubra* that occurred in the mountains was recognized, *S. rubra* var. *jonesii* (Wherry) Wherry. This variety is now recognized as a species, *S. jonesii* Wherry (plate 29). *S. rubra* is now considered confined to the coastal plain and sandhills.

485. Creeping blueberry

Vaccinium crassifolium Andrews
Vac-cì-ni-um cras-si-fò-li-um
Ericaceae (Heath Family)

DESCRIPTION: Trailing shrub, with upright branches, usually rooting at the nodes; leaves evergreen; flowers April–May; berry black, matures June–July.

RANGE-HABITAT: Nearly endemic to the Carolinas, barely extending into adjacent GA and VA; primarily a coastal plain species; pocosin-sandhills ecotones and adjacent longleaf pine flatwoods and savannas; common, but often overlooked because it grows close to the ground, hidden in vegetation.

COMMENTS: The berry is edible.

486. Honey-cups

Zenobia pulverulenta (Bartram) Pollard
Ze-nò-bi-a pul-ve-ru-lén-ta
Ericaceae (Heath Family)

DESCRIPTION: Rhizomatous, deciduous shrub to 6′ tall; leaves of two forms: either green on both surfaces, or green above and bluish white beneath; both forms occur together; flowers in corymbs from axillary buds on the upper part of twigs of the preceding season; flowers April–June.

RANGE-HABITAT: Narrow endemic of the coastal plain of se. VA, NC, SC, and e. GA; common; in SC found only in the northeast half of the coastal plain and sandhills; pocosins and margins of pineland ponds.

COMMENTS: This is one South Carolina's most spectacular ericaceous shrubs when in full flower; its flowers are extremely fragrant. Named for Zenobia, queen of Palmyra, in the third century of our era.

487. Rose pogonia

Pogonia ophioglossoides (L.) Ker-Gawl
Po-gò-ni-a o-phi-o-glos-soì-des
Orchidaceae (Orchid Family)

DESCRIPTION: Slender orchid, 3–24″ tall with a single, green leaf about halfway up the stem; stem supports a single flower subtended by a leaflike bract; lip bears 3 rows of fleshy hairs tipped with yellow or brown; flowers May–June.

RANGE-HABITAT: Widespread in eastern North America; in SC primarily in the coastal plain; uncommon; rare in the sandhills, piedmont and mountains; seepage bogs, boggy pocosin margins, openings in pocosins, poorly drained roadside ditches, and longleaf pine savannas.

COMMENTS: *Pogon* means "beard," referring to the hairs on the lip.

488. Clammy azalea; swamp honeysuckle

Rhododendron viscosum (L.) Torrey
Rho-do-dén-dron vis-cò-sum
Ericaceae (Heath Family)

DESCRIPTION: Deciduous shrub with hairy twigs, to 15′ tall; corolla white or rarely pink and covered with reddish, sticky hairs; calyx and leaf stalks densely covered with stipitate glands; flowers fragrant, appearing after the leaves; flowers May–July.

RANGE-HABITAT: Widespread in the eastern US; common throughout SC; bogs, pocosins, moist streamsides, rocky streamsides, shrub balds, and other moist habitats.

COMMENTS: Clammy azalea is South Carolina's latest flowering azalea. Foote and Jones (1989) indicate that with careful selection, a range in flowering time can be obtained from this late bloomer, adding fragrance to a garden for a month or more.

COMMENTS: All parts of all rhododendrons are poisonous.

489. Titi; leatherwood

Cyrilla racemiflora L.
Cy-ríl-la ra-ce-mi-flò-ra
Cyrillaceae (Titi Family)

DESCRIPTION: Small shrub or medium tree to 25′ tall; commonly reproducing vegetatively by sprouts from shallow roots and forming dense thickets; flowers in racemes clustered near the end of the previous year's twig; leaves semievergreen, some falling throughout the winter, but a few remaining until new ones appear in the spring; flowers May–July.

RANGE-HABITAT: Common coastal plain species from se. VA to c. peninsular FL, and west to se. TX; in SC in the sandhills and coastal plain; pocosins, swamp edges, longleaf pine flatwoods and savannas, bogs, and streamsides.

COMMENTS: Titi is a good ornamental because of its attractive flowers and leaves, which turn orange and scarlet in the fall. The trees are good honey plants because the flowers produce large quantities of nectar. Under various ecological conditions, titi can range from a small shrub to a medium tree. The genus honors Domenico Cirillo, 1734–1799, a professor of medicine at Naples.

490. Red milkweed

Asclepias rubra L.
As-clè-pi-as rù-bra
Asclepiadaceae (Milkweed Family)

DESCRIPTION: Perennial herb with simple stem, 16–40″ tall; leaves opposite, simple, sessile, ovate to lanceolate, in 3–5 pairs; corolla dull red to lavender; flowers June–July; follicles mature July–September.

RANGE-HABITAT: Coastal plain from s. NJ and se. PA, south to FL panhandle, and west to e. TX; in SC in the coastal plain and sandhills; uncommon; pocosin ecotones, wet longleaf pine savannas and flatwoods, swamps, and wet meadows.

491. Loblolly bay

Gordonia lasianthus (L.) Ellis
Gor-dòn-i-a la-si-án-thus
Theaceae (Tea Family)

DESCRIPTION: Evergreen shrub on deep peats, small tree up to 75′ tall in rich sites; leaves simple, alternate, shallowly toothed and smooth beneath; generally a few orange-red leaves visible at any season; flowers July–September; fruit a capsule that matures in September–October.

RANGE-HABITAT: Common southeastern coastal plain endemic from ne. NC to s. peninsular

FL, and west to s. MS; pocosins, organic-rich swamp forests, wet longleaf pine savannas, Atlantic white-cedar forests, and bay forests.

COMMENTS: Loblolly bay is sometimes used as an ornamental because of its showy flowers; however, it does not grow well under cultivation except in moist sites. It has little food value for wildlife and little or no commercial use. The leaves often have a ragged appearance because of insect damage. The genus honors George Gordon, 1806–1879.

Loblolly bay often grows in association with two other bay trees, sweet bay (*Magnolia virginica,* plate 483) and swamp red bay (*Persea palustris* [Rafinesque] Sargent). The leaves of loblolly bay are odorless when crushed, while the leaves of red bay are aromatic. The leaves of sweet bay are strongly whitish beneath, while the leaves of loblolly bay are olive-green beneath.

492. Creeping St. John's-wort

Hypericum adpressum Barton
Hy-pé-ri-cum ad-prés-sum
Hypericaceae (St. John's-wort Family)

DESCRIPTION: Erect, rhizomatous, colonial, perennial herb, 16–32″ tall; submerged stems spongy; leaves with depressed midrib on upper surface, strongly elevated beneath, margins revolute; lower leaf surface pale green, upper surface glossy green; flowers July–August.

RANGE-HABITAT: Rare coastal plain species from MA to GA; also WV, IL, and c. TN; in SC known only from Clarendon, Hampton, and Jasper Counties; pocosins, depression meadows, pond cypress savannas, marshy shores, swales, and ditches.

PROTECTION STATUS: Federal Species of Concern

493. White arum; spoonflower

Peltandra sagittaefolia (Michaux)
Morong
Pel-tán-dra sa-git-tae-fò-li-a
Araceae (Arum Family)

DESCRIPTION: Perennial herb from a short, stout rootstock; inflorescence a spadix subtended by a flared, open, white spathe; flowers of two sexes, with the male flowers on the upper part of the spadix and the female flowers on the lower part; flowers July–August.

RANGE-HABITAT: Endemic to the southeastern coastal plain, from e. NC, south to FL and west to MS; rare throughout its range; sphagnum-dominated openings in pocosins.

COMMENTS: All parts of the plant contain crystals of calcium oxalate, which cause irritation of the mucus membranes of the mouth and throat, possibly leading to asphyxiation if a great quantity is eaten.

PROTECTION STATUS: State Threatened

494. Pond pine; pocosin pine

Pinus serotina Michaux
Pì-nus se-rò-ti-na
Pinaceae (Pine Family)

DESCRIPTION: Medium size, evergreen tree; cones top-shaped or almost globe-shaped; needles mostly in 3s, 6–8″ long, persistent for 3–4 years; young cones develop March–April.

RANGE-HABITAT: From s. NJ south to n. FL and se. AL; in SC common in the coastal plain, occasional in the sandhills, rare in the lower piedmont; pocosins, pond cypress savannas, swamps of small blackwater streams, and less common in longleaf pine savannas.

COMMENTS: Pond pine is a "serotinous" species that depends on fire for regeneration. Serotinus means "late to open." Some of its cones remain closed with viable seeds for years, until fire softens the resinous seal, which allows the cone to open. Fire also removes the underbrush, presenting open, sunny conditions, ideal for germination and establishment of the seedlings. Pond pine also has another adaptation to lands frequented by fire: It sprouts new branches along the trunk from latent axillary buds. Although fire may have destroyed the crown, the new shoots are tied to an old, healthy root system and quickly develop into new branches. Pond pine also sprouts from roots or stumps after serious fire injury. Unlike most pines, pond pine thrives in soils with a high water table and can tolerate wide fluctuations in water level. For this reason it is common in Carolina bays.

Pond pine is not an important lumber species because it has poor growth form and grows in wet areas not easily accessible for timbering.

495. Pond cypress savannas

496. Yellow trumpet pitcher-plant

Sarracenia flava L.
    Sar-ra-cèn-i-a flà-va
Sarraceniaceae (Pitcher-plant Family)

DESCRIPTION: Perennial, carnivorous herb from rhizomes; 1.5–3.5′ tall; leaves modified to trap insects; flowers develop in March–April before or with the new leaves; leaves die back during the fall and winter.

RANGE-HABITAT: In the coastal plain and isolated piedmont locations from se. VA to n. FL, west to s. AL and se. MS; in SC in the sandhills and coastal plain; longleaf pine flatwoods and savannas, openings in pocosins and pond cypress savannas, and pineland seepage slopes; in wetter habitats it grows more robust, the leaves reaching over 3′ tall.

COMMENTS: This pitcher-plant is becoming less common due to habitat destruction; good populations still exist, however, in the Francis Marion National Forest (FMNF) and other protected lands such as the Santee Coastal Reserve and Shealy's Pond Heritage Preserve.

The leaves (pitchers) occur in four color forms: (1) pale green to bright yellow in full sun, with a large maroon splotch on the inside of the column from which red veins radiate; (2) bright to deep red color on the external surface of the lid and column, with a weak maroon spot; (3) uniformly golden-yellow in full sunlight, with coarse and prominent veins all over, with the interior column spot weak; and (4) no red pigment at all, the mature pitchers being pale green to yellow. The different forms often grow mixed in the same site.

497. Sneezeweed; bitterweed

Helenium pinnatifidum (Nuttall) Rydberg
He-lén-i-um pin-na-tí-fi-dum
Asteraceae (Aster or Sunflower Family)

DESCRIPTION: Fibrous-rooted, erect perennial herb, 8–40″ tall; commonly only 1 flowering head; basal leaves tufted and persistent; stem leaves few and reduced upward; flowers April–May.

RANGE-HABITAT: Rare southeastern coastal plain endemic from se. NC south to s. FL, and west to FL panhandle and sw. GA; long-leaf pine pine savannas and flatwoods and adjacent ditches, pond cypress savannas, borrow pits, and borders of swamps.

PROTECTION STATUS: State Threatened

498. Pool coreopsis

Coreopsis falcata Boynton
Co-re-óp-sis fal-cà-ta
Asteraceae (Aster or Sunflower Family)

DESCRIPTION: Smooth, perennial herb 25–80″ tall; leaves all alternate, entire, up to 8″ long, the lower sometimes with a pair of narrow lobes at the base of the blade; disk corollas dark purplish red or blackish red distally; flowers May–July.

RANGE-HABITAT: Endemic to the coastal plain and sandhills from se. VA to GA; common; marshes, pocosins, very wet pine and pond cypress savannas, ditches, and borrow pits.

SIMILAR SPECIES: Pool coreopsis is similar to two other species of *Coreopsis* that share the same range and habitats: *C. gladiata* Walter (plate 381 in *WCL*), and *C. linifolia* Nuttall. Pool coreopsis can be separated by phenology from these species since it blooms in May–July and the other two bloom in the fall.

499. Giant white-topped sedge

Dichromena latifolia Baldwin ex Elliott
   Di-chrò-me-na la-ti-fò-li-a
Cyperaceae (Sedge Family)

DESCRIPTION: Perennial herb; stems solitary, usually 2–3′ tall, from elongate rhizomes; leaves appearing mostly basal; inflorescence of crowded clusters of spikes subtended by 7 or more widely linear to lanceolate bracts; bracts conspicuously white at base and green at apex; flowers May–September.
RANGE-HABITAT: Common coastal plain species from VA to FL, and west to se. TX; pond cypress and longleaf pine savannas, ditches, depressions, pocosin borders, and wet sandy-peaty open places.
SIMILAR SPECIES: *Dichromena colorata* (L.) Hitchcock has 5–6 shorter bracts and is 20–24″ tall; it has a similar habitat, range, and flowering period.
SYNONYM: *Rhynchospora latifolia* (Baldwin ex Elliott) Thomas—W

500. Savanna obedient-plant

Physostegia purpurea (Walter) Blake
   Phy-sos-té-gi-a pur-pú-re-a
Lamiaceae (Mint Family)

DESCRIPTION: Perennial herb with erect stem 16–40″ tall; leaves reduced upward; corolla pink to purple; flowers April–July.
RANGE-HABITAT: Coastal plain from ec. NC south to s. FL, west to sw. GA and FL panhandle; occasional; wet longleaf pine savannas, pond cypress savannas, savanna-swamp ecotones, and ditches adjacent to former pinelands.
COMMENTS: The common name, obedient-plant, comes from the fact that the flowers tend to stay in a new position for a while after they are twisted to one side.
SYNONYM: *Dracocephalum purpureum* (Walter) McClintock—RAB

501. Tall milkwort

Polygala cymosa Walter
Po-lý-ga-la cy-mò-sa
Polygalaceae (Milkwort Family)

DESCRIPTION: Biennial herb with a solitary, smooth, flowering stem, 16″–4′ tall; leaves mostly basal, linear to lanceolate, rapidly reduced upward; flowers May–July.

RANGE-HABITAT: Common coastal plain species; DE south to about Lake Okeechobee, FL, and west to LA; wet longleaf pine savannas and pond cypress savannas, shallow waters of pond cypress and gum swamps, borrow pits, wet ditches, and bogs.

COMMENTS: This is the only orange- or yellow-flowered mikwort that grows more than 2′ tall.

502. Lace-lip ladies'-tresses

Spiranthes laciniata (Small) Ames
Spi-rán-thes la-ci-ni-à-ta
Orchidaceae (Orchid Family)

DESCRIPTION: Coarse, perennial plant, 28–40″ tall; leaves basal and on stem; flowers in a single spike, strongly spiraled to one side; hairs on spike glandular; flowers May–August.

RANGE-HABITAT: Southeastern coastal plain endemic from se. NC to s. FL, west to se. TX; in SC restricted to the coastal plain; rare throughout its range; pond cypress savannas, marshes, pools, and boggy depressions.

TAXONOMY: Godfrey and Wooten (1979) consider *S. laciniata* a hybrid between *S. praecox* (Walter) Watson and *S. vernalis* Engelmann & Gray (both of which occur in the coastal plain) and list it as *S. x laciniata* (Small) Ames.

PROTECTION STATUS: State Endangered

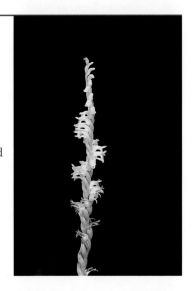

503. Peelbark St. John's-wort

Hypericum fasciculatum Lamarck
Hy-pé-ri-cum fas-ci-cu-là-tum
Hypericaceae (St. John's-wort Family)

DESCRIPTION: Erect shrub, 2.5–5′ tall, many-branched above and spongy and thickened below, with bark peeling in thin sheets; flowers May–September.

RANGE-HABITAT: Uncommon coastal plain species from e. NC south to s. FL, and west to s. MS; pond cypress savannas, cypress-gum ponds and depressions, ditches, and borrow pits.

504. Bay blue-flag iris

Iris tridentata Pursh
Ì-ris tri-den-tà-ta
Iridaceae (Iris Family)

DESCRIPTION: Rhizomatous perennial; flowering stalks 12–28″ tall, usually unbranched, bearing a single flower; flowers late May–June.

RANGE-HABITAT: Common coastal plain species from se. NC to n. FL; seasonally wet longleaf pine savannas and flatwoods, pond cypress savannas, borders of cypress-gum ponds, and ditches.

COMMENTS: This species is readily distinguished from other tall, blue-flowered irises by its petals, which are barely as long as the claws (stalks) of the sepals.

505. Pipewort; hatpins

Eriocaulon decangulare L.
E-ri-o-caù-lon de-can-gu-là-re
Eriocaulaceae (Pipewort Family)

DESCRIPTION: Perennial herb with flowering stalks 12–32″ tall, finely 8–12 ridged; flowers white, in dense, hard heads (buttons) on the tip of leafless stalks; leaves mostly basal, linear, with air chambers visible to the naked eye; flowers June–October.

RANGE-HABITAT: Chiefly on the coastal plain, from NJ to FL, and west to e. TX; in SC common on the coastal plain and sandhills; sandy or peaty lakeshores, longleaf pine flatwoods, pond cypress savannas, margins of cypress ponds, ditches, and sometimes around ponds or lakes.

SIMILAR SPECIES: *Eriocaulon compressum* Lamarck is similar in appearance, but it has heads easily compressed between the fingers; it is occasional in the coastal plain in even wetter habitats, growing with its base submerged.

COMMENTS: The specific epithet *decangulare* means "10-angled," referencing the angled stem.

506. Blue sedge

Carex glaucescens Elliott
Cà-rex glau-cés-cens
Cyperaceae (Sedge Family)

DESCRIPTION: Rhizome-forming, perennial herb, about 28–44″
tall; flowers and fruits July–September.

RANGE-HABITAT: Coastal plain from e. MD to c. peninsular FL, and
west to e. TX; disjunct in TN; in SC common throughout the
coastal plain and sandhills; backwater swamps, pocosins, wet
pine savannas, seepage bogs, and pond cypress savannas.

COMMENTS: *Carex glaucescens* is one of a 100+ species of *Carex* in
the Carolinas, and is one of the very few that are rather strongly
glaucous throughout. This species and *Carex decomposita* (plate
444) represent this large and complex genus of sedges.

507. Tall hydrolea; sky-flower

Hydrolea corymbosa Macbride ex Elliott
Hy-drò-le-a co-rym-bò-sa
Hydrophyllaceae (Waterleaf Family)

DESCRIPTION: Erect, slender perennial herb
24–32″ tall; leaves elliptic to elliptic-lanceolate, alternate, entire; petals light-violet to purplish pink; flowers July–September.

RANGE-HABITAT: Coastal plain from s. SC south
to FL; occasional in FL, rare in GA and SC;
pond cypress savannas, swampy woodlands,
depression meadows, marshes, and ditches.

PROTECTION STATUS: State Endangered

508. Gerardia

Agalinis linifolia (Nuttall) Britton
A-ga-lì-nis li-ni-fò-li-a
Scrophulariaceae (Figwort Family)

DESCRIPTION: Perennial herb with slender rhizomes; stems smooth, round, 28–48″ tall;
leaves opposite, linear; flowers relatively dis-
tantly positioned in about 8–20-flowered
racemes, 1 or 2 flowers per node; corolla light
violet-purple to pink, with the tube lacking
yellow lines; flowers August–September.

RANGE-HABITAT: DE; then from se. NC to s.
FL, and west to s. LA; in SC on the coastal
plain; pond cypress communities, depressions in pinelands, acid marshy shores,
and pine savannas; occasional.

COMMENTS: This is the only species of *Agalinis* in SC that lacks yellow lines
within the corolla.

509. Giant yellow-eyed grass

Xyris fimbriata Elliott
  Xỳ-ris fim-bri-à-ta
Xyridaceae (Yellow-eyed Grass Family)

DESCRIPTION: Perennial herb with only basal leaves; flowering stalk 20–48″ tall; leaves dull, straight, 12–20″ long; flowers in a compact, terminal, round spike, with each flower subtended by a woody scale that hides the flower bud and fruit; flowers ephemeral, projecting from behind the woody scale; flowers August–October.

RANGE-HABITAT: From se. VA to c. FL, and west to se. TX; disjunct in s. NJ, DE, and c. TN; in SC in the sandhills and coastal plain; occasional; mucky or sandy soils of upland depression ponds, pond cypress savannas, bogs, pond margins, and wet sandy ditches.

COMMENTS: This species is used as an example of a large genus in which the various species, occurring throughout SC, are difficult to distinguish, especially using photographs.

Xyris fimbriata has one characteristic that distinguishes it in the genus. Its lateral sepals are exerted beyond the subtending bract, and its keel has a long fringe above the middle. This feature is readily seen with the naked eye and is faintly visible in the photograph. Giant yellow-eyed grass blooms on sunny days from mid-morning to early afternoon, after which the flowers quickly fade.

510. Carolina grass-of-Parnassus; eyebright

Parnassia caroliniana Michaux
  Par-nás-si-a ca-ro-li-ni-à-na
Parnassiaceae (Grass-of-Parnassus Family)

DESCRIPTION: Smooth, perennial herb with rhizomes; leaves primarily basal, usually ovate, with long leaf stalks; stem leaves similar to basal, but smaller and heart-shaped; flowers solitary on elongated stalks, 8–20″ tall; petals 5, with conspicuous veins; stamens 5, shorter than the 5 staminodia, which bear glands; flowers September–November.

RANGE-HABITAT: Coastal plain from se. and sc. NC, south to FL panhandle; in SC known only from Georgetown and Horry Counties; wet longleaf pine, pond pine, or pond cypress savannas, often over calcareous substrates.

COMMENTS: Grass-of-Parnassus is one of the most striking flowers of the wet savannas of the coastal area and is rare in SC. Throughout its range, its distribution is fragmented and disjunct. Much of its habitat has been altered by agriculture, conversion to tree farms, fire suppression, and ditching.

PROTECTION STATUS: Federal Species of Concern

511. Pond cypress

Taxodium ascendens Brongniart
Tax-ò-di-um as-cén-dens
Taxodiaceae (Taxodium Family)

DESCRIPTION: Medium size, deciduous tree; leaves needlelike, pressed against the twig, except on seedlings and fast growing shoots where they are 2-ranked; male and female cones on the same tree.

RANGE-HABITAT: Coastal plain from e. NC south to s. FL, and west to LA; in SC in the sandhills and coastal plain; common; pond cypress savannas, nonalluvial swamps, clay-based Carolina bays, and shores of natural blackwater lakes.

COMMENTS: When pond cypress grows in conditions of fluctuating water levels, the base tends to grow larger, forming a buttress of lighter and more porous wood, and the roots send up shoots called knees. The knees of pond cypress are rounded on top; the knees of bald cypress (*Taxodium distichum*, plate 441) are pointed on top.

Pond cypress wood contains an essential oil that gives it natural durability and makes it valuable for fence posts, shingles, and panelling. Few merchantable stands exist today because it is very slow-growing, and reproduction has not kept up with lumbering. It is often used as an ornamental since it grows well in upland habitats under cultivation.

TAXONOMY: Some sources list pond cypress a variety of bald cypress, *Taxodium distichum* var. *nutans* (Aiton) Sweet.

512. *Pond cypress-swamp gum upland swamps*

513. Climbing fetterbush

Pieris phillyreifolia (Hooker)
Augustin de Candolle
Pì-e-ris phil-ly-rei-fò-li-a
Ericaceae (Heath Family)

DESCRIPTION: Evergreen shrub or woody vine; as a vine, unique in climbing in bark crevices or beneath outer bark of *Taxodium ascendens;* as a shrub, it grows on cypress knees or stumps; leaves alternate, leathery; lateral branches that project from under the bark produce flowers that bloom in April–May.

RANGE-HABITAT: Coastal plain of GA to c. peninsular FL, and west to s. AL; disjunct in SC in the FMNF in Charleston County, several hundred miles from the nearest GA population; in SC found only in pond cypress-swamp gum depressions.

COMMENTS: Climbing fetterbush grows as a creeping woody vine under the bark of pond cypress with its branches exerted through the cypress bark. Fire will kill the stem under the bark; however, it will regrow upward under the bark from the main stem at the base of the tree. The stem under the bark assumes a flattened condition. In SC, climbing fetterbush has been observed only growing on pond cypress. In FL, it also climbs under the bark of Atlantic white-cedar (*Chamaecyparis thyoides*).

PROTECTION STATUS: State Endangered Peripheral

514. Pondspice

Litsea aestivalis (L.) Fernald
Lít-se-a aes-ti-và-lis
Lauraceae (Laurel Family)

DESCRIPTION: Many-branched shrub to 15′ tall; the branchlets zigzag; leaves deciduous; male and female flowers on separate plants; flowers March–April, appearing before the leaves from overwintering buds; drupe red, mature May–June.

RANGE-HABITAT: Southeastern coastal plain endemic, from se. VA (formerly) south to n. FL, and west to LA; rare throughout much of its range, but is often locally abundant; margins of limestone sinks and Carolina bays, pineland depressions, and pond cypress-swamp gum swamp forests.

COMMENTS: Pondspice is locally abundant in the FMNF.

PROTECTION STATUS: Federal Species of Concern

515. Violet burmannia

Burmannia biflora L.
Bur-mánn-i-a bi-flò-ra
Burmanniaceae (Burmannia Family)

DESCRIPTION: Diminutive herb with erect, filiform stems, and threadlike roots; to about 6″ tall; leaves scalelike, remote; 1 flower terminal, the remainder in 2 lateral racemes or spikes; floral tube 3-winged; flowers August–November.

RANGE-HABITAT: From se. VA to FL, and west to e. TX; in SC in the coastal plain on the edges of pond cypress-swamp gum ponds, and in bogs and wet savannas; occasional-common but easily overlooked because of its small size and because it blooms in late fall after many floristic studies are completed.

COMMENTS: Burmannia is closely related to the orchids, and it shares one characteristic with orchids that may have contributed to its being listed as rare: they may flower in a site one year, then may be absent for the next few years. The genus honors Johannes Burmann, 1706–1779, a Dutch botanist.

516. Pondberry; Jove's fruit

Lindera melissifolia (Walter) Blume
Lín-der-a me-lis-si-fò-li-a
Lauraceae (Laurel Family)

DESCRIPTION: Deciduous, aromatic shrub, 3–4' tall; colonial from rhizomes; leaves entire, alternate; male and female flowers on separate plants; flowers March–April, developing before leaves; drupes mature August–September.

RANGE-HABITAT: Coastal plain from NC to FL panhandle, west to LA; disjunct in se. MO; rare throughout its range; in SC known only from Berkeley and Beaufort Counties; along the margins of lime sinks, in wet depressions in pine flatwoods, along the margins of pond cypress-swamp gum swamp forests, open bogs, and sandy sinks.

COMMENTS: The largest concentration of pondberry throughout its range occurs in the Honey Hill region of the FMNF in Berkeley County. The numerous lime sinks in this area provide critical habitat for this rare shrub.

PROTECTION STATUS: Federal Endangered

517. Swamp gum; swamp tupelo

Nyssa biflora Walter
Nýs-sa bi-flò-ra
Nyssaceae (Sourgum Family)

DESCRIPTION: Small to large gregarious wetland tree, commonly where water stands much of the time; bases of trunks swollen; leaves elliptic to lance-elliptic, widest at the middle with long-tapering tips; drupes blueblack, mature August–October.

RANGE-HABITAT: Chiefly coastal plain from NJ to sc. FL, west to e. TX; common in the coastal plain, but scattered inland in several states including SC; blackwater and brownwater river swamps, depressions in pinelands (where it grows alone or in association with pond cypress), pocosins, pond and lake margins, and wet longleaf pine savannas or flatwoods; also in piedmont seepage swamps.

SIMILAR SPECIES: Swamp gum is similar to black gum (*N. sylvatica* Marshall). Swamp gum has leaves widest beyond the middle with obtuse apices and fruits usually 1–2 per stalk; black gum has most leaves widest at the middle with long-tapering apices and fruits 1–5 per stalk. Black gum is mostly an upland tree in well-drained soils, but it does occur in wet sites.

COMMENTS: The SC state record tree was measured in 1995 at 113' tall and 4.6' in diameter; it is in the Congaree National Monument.

TAXONOMY: Some authors (e.g., Godfrey and Wooten, 1981, and Radford et al., 1968) treat swamp gum as a variety of black gum (*N. sylvatica* var. *biflora* (Walter) Sargent).

518. Cassena; dahoon holly

Ilex cassine L.
Ì-lex cas-sì-ne
Aquifoliaceae (Holly Family)

DESCRIPTION: Small to medium size evergreen tree, rarely exceeding 25′ tall; leaves simple, obovate, oblanceolate, or narrowly lanceolate, 1.5–4″ long and over 0.25″ wide; male and female flowers on separate trees; fruit berry-like, red or sometimes yellow, mature October–November, persisting until spring.

RANGE-HABITAT: Primarily a southeastern coastal plain endemic; se. NC to FL, and west to se. TX; occasional in upland pond cypress-swamp gum forests, pocosins, blackwater swamps, depressions in flatwoods, wet hummocks, and edges of spring-fed rivers and streams.

COMMENTS: Cassena is often grown as an ornamental for its attractive red berries and leaves.

519. Myrtle-leaved holly

Ilex myrtifolia (Walter) Sargent
Ì-lex myr-ti-fò-li-a
Aquifoliaceae (Holly Family)

DESCRIPTION: Small tree or more often a shrub; evergreen, with narrow, stiff leaves, less than 1.5″ long and less than 0.25″ wide; male and female flowers on separate plants; fruit berrylike, red, mature October–November, persisting until spring.

RANGE-HABITAT: Southeastern coastal plain endemic; se. NC south to FL, and west to e. LA; common; upland pond cypress-swamp gum swamps, margins of sandy ponds, and wet savannas.

COMMENTS: Wildlife eat the fruits, and the plant is occasionally used as an ornamental.

TAXONOMY: Some manuals treat cassena and myrtle-leaved holly as varieties of *I. cassine* and list them as *Ilex cassine* L. var. *cassine* and *Ilex cassine* var. *myrtifolia* (Walter) Sargent. The differences between the two are based on leaf shape, as described above.

THE COASTAL PLAIN

520. Tidal freshwater marshes

521. Water-spider orchid

Habenaria repens Nuttall
Ha-be-nà-ri-a rè-pens
Orchidaceae (Orchid Family)

DESCRIPTION: Terrestrial or aquatic herb; slender or stout, leafy; 0.5–3' tall; lower stem often producing elongate stolons with plantlets forming at the tips, especially when in floating mats or in soft substrates; flowers April–frost.

RANGE-HABITAT: Coastal plain species from NC to s. FL, and west to TX; common in SC; tidal freshwater marshes, ditches and canals, muddy shores of lakes, ponds, and streams, often in floating mats of vegetation.

COMMENTS: Water-spider orchid is often found unexpectedly while looking for some other plants. Since all parts are green, it is quite inconspicuous. In the tidal freshwater marshes, it is very difficult to spot because of the dense growth of emergent species. In the reservoirs created for the inland rice culture or similar impoundments, water-spider orchid often grows on large floating mats of vegetation in association with other aquatic plants.

522. Pickerelweed

Pontederia cordata L. var. *cordata*
Pon-te-dè-ri-a cor-dà-ta var. cor-dà-ta
Pontederiaceae (Pickerelweed Family)

DESCRIPTION: Emergent, soft-stemmed perennial from a thick, short rhizome; to 3' tall; one leaf not far below the inflorescence, the others basal; leaf bases deeply heart-shaped to truncate; flowers May–October; seeds mature late summer to early fall.

RANGE-HABITAT: Nova Scotia west to MN, and south to FL and TX; common throughout SC in a variety of aquatic habitats, including tidal freshwater marshes, lakes, ponds, roadside ditches, and swamp forests.

COMMENTS: The seeds of pickerelweed are a pleasant and hearty food. The young leaf stalks can be cooked as greens. The roots are inedible, producing a burning sensation if ingested. It can be a serious problem weed in ditches by blocking drainage and can be a problem in small, shallow ponds since it can cover the surface.

The common name comes from a fish called the pickerel, which often occupies the same habitat as pickerelweed. The genus honors Guilio Pontedera, 1688–1756.

TAXONOMY: Two varieties of pickerelweed are recognized based on leaf shape. The leaf blades of variety *cordata* are deltoid (delta-shaped)-ovate to triangular-lanceolate with bases deeply heart-shaped to truncate; the leaf blades of *P. cordata* var. *lancifolia* (Muhlenberg) Torrey are narrowly to broadly lanceolate, with typically unlobed bases. Variety *lancifolia* is found mainly in the coastal plain of SC.

523. Swamp rose

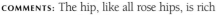

Rosa palustris Marshall
Rò-sa pa-lús-tris
Rosaceae (Rose Family)

DESCRIPTION: Upright, rhizomatous shrub to 10′ tall; prickles curved; flowers May–July; fruit (a hip) red, matures September–October.

RANGE-HABITAT: Nova Scotia to MN, south to FL, MS, and AR; throughout SC, but chiefly in the coastal plain; common; tidal freshwater marshes, along streams, ponds, lakes, wet thickets, and swamp forests.

COMMENTS: The hip, like all rose hips, is rich in vitamin C and can be eaten raw, made into jams, or steeped to make rose hip tea. Swamp rose is easily cultivated and does well in moderate shade, especially in wet sites.

524. Water hemlock

Cicuta maculata L.
Ci-cù-ta ma-cu-là-ta
Apiaceae (Parsley Family)

DESCRIPTION: Erect, branching perennial to 9′ tall; leaves pinnately, bipinnately, or tripinnately compound; the plant can be readily identified by cutting lengthwise through the stem base and root to reveal its diaphragmed nature; stem is magenta-streaked, hollow above; flowers May–August.

RANGE-HABITAT: Widespread throughout North America, ranging from s. Ontario to Nova Scotia, south through New England to FL, west to TX, and north through MO to Canada; common throughout SC in freshwater tidal marshes, swamps, streamsides, low roadside ditches, and seepages.

COMMENTS: All parts of the plant contain cicutoxin, a poisonous compound. The roots are particularly potent, as a mouthful is sufficient to kill an adult. Children making peashooters from the hollow stems have been poisoned. The plant is not related to true hemlocks (*Tsuga* spp., tree species) but to poison hemlock (*Conium maculatum* L.), the plant that was used to kill Socrates.

525. Spiderlily

Hymenocallis floridana (Rafinesque)
Morton
Hy-me-no-cál-lis flo-ri-dà-na
Amaryllidaceae (Amaryllis Family)

DESCRIPTION: Bulbous, smooth, perennial herb to 2′ tall; leaves linear, all basal; unusual arrangement of stamens, where the lower portion of the filament is united into a thin, membranous crown with the upper filament that extends beyond the crown; flowers mid-May–June.

RANGE-HABITAT: From se. NC into FL, and west into LA and AL; confined to the outer coastal plain; in SC common in tidal freshwater marshes and wet riverbanks and occasional in brackish marshes and swamp forests.

COMMENTS: Spiderlily is one of the most spectacular of the river marsh plants; often it hangs over the water from the bulbs that are embedded in the riverbank. Spiderlily occurs in every freshwater river system in the coastal area of SC.

SYNONYM: *Hymenocallis crassifolia* Herbert—RAB

526. Marsh lilaeopsis

Lilaeopsis chinensis (L.) Kuntze
Li-lae-óp-sis chi-nén-sis
Apiaceae (Parsley Family)

DESCRIPTION: Smooth, aquatic, perennial herb, rooting at the nodes; leaves hollow, septate, linear, spoon-shaped, mostly 0.4–2″ tall; petals 5, white; flowers in umbels, with stalks longer than or equaling the leaves; flowers May–June.

RANGE-HABITAT: Nova Scotia south to FL, and west to LA; in SC in the outer coastal plain and maritime strand; rare; tidal freshwater and brackish marshes, generally in open mudflats in the intertidal zone and usually inundated at high tides.

COMMENTS: According to Weakley (2001), the specific epithet *chinensis* is a misnomer. The species is native to eastern North America, and has nothing to do with China. Linnaeus apparently applied this specific epithet under the impression it grew in China.

527. Wild rice; Indian rice

Zizania aquatica L.
   Zi-zà-ni-a a-quá-ti-ca
Poaceae (Grass Family)

DESCRIPTION: Coarse and robust perennial to 10′ tall; often creeping and rooting at the nodes; flower spikes in panicles; lower branches of panicle widely spreading, upper branches ascending; male flowers hang from the lower branches and the female flowers are erect on the upper branches; flowers May–October.

RANGE-HABITAT: MA west to WI, and south to FL and LA; in SC primarily outer coastal plain; brackish and tidal freshwater marshes; occurs in almost every river system along the coast, often locally abundant.

COMMENTS: Wild rice is an important food source for animals and people. Native Americans used the grain to thicken soup, make flour for bread, and to cook game. Today it is marketed as wild rice. Its main distribution is the Great Lakes and upper Mississippi region. The fruits are ready for harvest in mid-summer and fall. The yield is insufficient to make wild rice harvest feasible in SC. Wild rice plants are not abandoned rice plants from the rice growing era in SC. The commercial plant was *Oryza sativa* of Far Eastern origin; it does not persist after cultivation.

528. Groundnut

Apios americana Medicus
   Á-pi-os a-me-ri-cà-na
Fabaceae (Pea or Bean Family)

DESCRIPTION: Perennial, twining, herbaceous vine, 3–10′ long; roots with tuberous enlargements; leaves alternate, pinnately compound with 5–7 leaflets; flowers June–August; legumes mature July–September.

RANGE-HABITAT: Quebec to MN and SD, and southward to FL and TX; common throughout SC; tidal freshwater marshes, swamp forests, bottomland forests, wet thickets, wet meadows, wet pinelands, and streamsides.

COMMENTS: The root tubers are edible. Native Americans used them as a staple food source, and the Pilgrims relied on them during their first year in MA. Very quickly they became a food source of early European settlers. Eaten raw, they leave an unpleasant rubberlike coating in the mouth, which cooking removes. The tubers can be used in soups and stews or fried like potatoes, or they can be ground into flour and used for bread. The seeds are generally too scarce to supply much food, although they are edible.

529. Swamp rose mallow; wild cotton

Hibiscus moscheutos L. subsp.
　　moscheutos
　　Hi-bís-cus mos-cheù-tos subsp.
　　mos-cheù-tos
　　Malvaceae (Mallow Family)

DESCRIPTION: Robust, herbaceous perennial to 6′ tall; petals white, less often pink, but always with a purple-reddish center; flowers June–September.

RANGE-HABITAT: MD west to s. IN, south to n. FL and se. TX; throughout SC; occasional in the mountains, common in the piedmont and coastal plain; tidal freshwater marshes, edges of swamp forests, roadside ditches, and brackish marshes.

COMMENTS: The leaves and roots contain copious mucilage and historically were used as a soothing agent in dysentery and lung and urinary ailments (Foster and Duke, 1990).

TAXONOMY: Radford et al. (1968) and Godfrey and Wooten (1981) recognize three subspecies.

530. Large marsh-pink

Sabatia dodecandra (L.) Britton, Sterns
　　& Poggenburg
　　Sa-bà-ti-a do-de-cán-dra
　　Gentianaceae (Gentian Family)

DESCRIPTION: Perennial herb to 3′ tall, with slender, coarse rhizomes; leaves opposite, entire, sessile; petals 9–12, deep rose-purple, rose-pink, pink (or rarely white), with a mostly 3-lobed, yellow, red marginate patch at base; flowers June–August.

RANGE-HABITAT: CT to FL, and west to LA; chiefly outer coastal plain; in SC common in tidal freshwater marshes, ponds, brackish marshes, roadside ditches, riverbanks, and streamsides.

COMMENTS: This is a variable species; some authors divide it into as many as four varieties.

531. Eryngo

Eryngium aquaticum L. var. *aquaticum*
　　E-rýn-gi-um a-quá-ti-cum var.
　　a-quá-ti-cum
　　Apiaceae (Parsley Family)

DESCRIPTION: Slender to robust biennial (perennial?) herb, 1–6′ tall; flowers in heads, subglobose to hemispherical; bractlets subtending the flowers with middle cusp clearly longer than the lateral cusps; flowers July–September.

RANGE-HABITAT: NJ to ne. FL; primarily an outer coastal plain species; common in SC in tidal freshwater marshes, riverbanks, ditches, ponds, brackish marshes, wet pine flatwoods, swamps, and depressions.

COMMENTS: This is the only genus in the Apiaceae in which the flowers are not in umbels.

TAXONOMY: A second variety exists, *E. aquaticum* var. *ravenelii* (A. Gray) Mathias & Constance. It was named to honor Henry William Ravenel, a SC botanist. It differs from the typical variety by having globose heads, and the middle cusp of bractlets is about equal in length to the lateral cusps. It ranges from southeast NC to north FL and is rare throughout its range. No extant populations are known in SC. It grows in wet savannas, mostly or entirely over calcareous substrate.

532. Seashore mallow

Kosteletzkya virginica (L.) Presl ex Gray
Kos-te-létz-ky-a vir-gí-ni-ca
Malvaceae (Mallow Family)

DESCRIPTION: Perennial herb to 5′ tall; star-shaped hairs on all parts, varying from sparse to very dense, and from harsh to soft-velvety; petals range from pink to lavender to white; each flower lasts only a day; flowers July–October.

RANGE-HABITAT: Long Island, NY, to s. FL, west to e. TX; common in SC in the outer coastal plain and maritime strand; freshwater tidal marshes, brackish marshes, sloughs, ditches, borders of swamps, and wet clearings.

COMMENTS: Plants of this species are highly variable in leaf shape, hair, and flower size, so much so that several varieties have been recognized. Intergrading forms are so common that it is difficult to make varietal determinations. The genus honors Vincenz Franz Kosteletzky, 1801–1887, a Bohemian botanist.

533. Cardinal flower

Lobelia cardinalis L.
Lo-bèl-i-a car-di-nà-lis
Campanulaceae (Bellwort Family)

DESCRIPTION: Erect, usually unbranched perennial from basal offshoots; 2–6′ tall; flowers July–October.

RANGE-HABITAT: Widely distributed, from New Brunswick and Ontario to MN, and south to n. FL and e. TX; common throughout SC; freshwater tidal marshes, swamp forests, riverbanks and streambanks, wet meadows, bogs, and low woods.

COMMENTS: Indigenous species of *Lobelia* were employed in medicines for various purposes; however, cases of death from overdoses of medicinal preparations were frequent. They are now best considered poisonous.

The common name alludes to the bright red robes worn by Roman Catholic cardinals. Hummingbirds pollinate cardinal flower; most insects cannot reach the nectar at the bottom of the long, tubular flowers. Cardinal flower is adaptable to cultivation and can be used in a variety of locations. It can even survive in a pot with frequent watering.

534. Tear-thumb

Polygonum arifolium L.
Po-lý-go-num a-ri-fò-li-um
Polygonaceae (Buckwheat Family)

DESCRIPTION: Freely branched perennial herb; stems slender, weak, to 6′ or more long, erect at first, then reclining; stems rib-angled, with backward-pointing barbs; leaves with hastate basal lobes; flowers few, pink, purplish, or white; flowers July–frost.

RANGE-HABITAT: New Brunswick to MN, generally southward to GA and s. MO; in SC common in the outer coastal plain, rare in the inner coastal plain and piedmont; tidal freshwater marshes and wet open places.

SIMILAR SPECIES: Growing in the same habitats (but throughout SC) is *P. sagittatum* L., which has sagittate leaf bases rather than hastate leaf bases; otherwise similar.

COMMENTS: The common name, tear-thumb, owes its origin to the stiff hooked barbs on the edges of the stem; they can easily tear one's thumb.

535. Climbing aster

Aster carolinianus Walter
Ás-ter ca-ro-li-ni-à-nus
Asteraceae (Aster or Sunflower Family)

DESCRIPTION: Robust, branching, somewhat woody, sprawling perennial; often forming a tangle; stems 3–6′ long; flowers late September–October.

RANGE-HABITAT: From se. NC to s. peninsular FL, and near coastal portions of e. FL panhandle; in SC in the outer coastal plain; occasional; tidal freshwater marshes, river swamps, marshy shores, streamsides, often in water.

COMMENTS: Climbing aster often forms robust growth in abandoned tidal rice fields on weathered posts and docks.

536. Bur-marigold; Beggar ticks

Bidens laevis (L.) Britton, Sterns & Poggenburg
Bì-dens laè-vis
Asteraceae (Aster or Sunflower Family)

DESCRIPTION: Perennial (or annual?) herb from rhizomes; stems ascending, to 3′ tall, often creeping at the base, and rooting at the nodes, often forming dense colonies; rays are lighter yellow at the tips; flowers late September–November.

RANGE-HABITAT: NH to s. FL, and west to CA; in SC chiefly, but not exclusively, a coastal plain species; common; tidal freshwater marshes, shallow ponds, ditches, sluggish streams, and wet meadows.

Inland freshwater marshes

537. Golden-club; never-wet

Orontium aquaticum L.
  O-rón-ti-um a-quá-ti-cum
  Araceae (Arum Family)

DESCRIPTION: Emergent, perennial herb from a thick rhizome; 8″ to 2′ tall; flowers in a spadix; leaves in a basal cluster, either extending above or floating on water; flowers March–April.

RANGE-HABITAT: Primarily on the coastal plain from MA to FL, and west to LA, but local in central NY, WV, and KY; scattered throughout SC, but most abundant in the sandhills and coastal plain; muddy sites in alluvial and nonalluvial swamp forests, edges of ponds, tidal freshwater marshes, and ditches.

COMMENTS: The common name, never-wet, alludes to the fact that when the submerged leaves come out of the water, they are dry. Water drops quickly roll off the leaf surface. Golden-club is a monotypic genus. All parts of the plant contain crystals of calcium oxalate which, when ingested, may irritate the lining of the throat, causing it to swell, resulting in asphyxiation. Native Americans used the roots and seeds for food by heating and drying them extensively, which dissolves the crystals.

538. Carolina water-hyssop

Bacopa caroliniana (Walter) B. L.
  Robinson
  Ba-cò-pa ca-ro-li-ni-à-na
  Scrophulariaceae (Figwort Family)

DESCRIPTION: Aromatic, rhizomatous, perennial herb, forming extensive mats; erect portion of stem 4–12″ tall; leaves opposite, with 3–7 palmate veins; corolla pale to bright blue or violet-blue; flowers May–September.

RANGE-HABITAT: From se. VA to s. FL, and west to e. TX; disjunct in KY; in SC in the coastal plain and sandhills; common; sandy, shallow ponds, marsh or stream margins, cypress-gum ponds, depressions, ditches, and canals.

COMMENTS: The strongly minty fragrance of its stems and leaves is distinctive among aquatic plants.

539. Golden canna; Indian shot

Canna flaccida Salisbury
   Cán-na flác-ci-da
Cannaceae (Canna Family)

DESCRIPTION: Perennial herb to 4′ tall; leaves large, to 2′ long, sheathing at the base; upper leaves smaller; sepals 3, greenish; petals 3, yellowish green, bases united into a tube; showy part of the flower consists of 3 yellow, petal-like false stamens, 2 larger, 1 smaller; a single stamen is attached to one of the largest staminodes; flowers May–early July; fruit covered with small, elongated warts, mature July–August.

RANGE-HABITAT: Along the coast from SC to FL, and west to MS; rare in SC; pine savannas, inland freshwater marshes, swamp margins, and wet ditches.

COMMENTS: Fernald and Kinsey (1958) state that golden canna "presumably has edible young corms."

540. Arrowhead; duck-potato

Sagittaria graminea Michaux var.
   graminea
   Sa-git-tà-ri-a gra-mí-ne-a var.
   gra-mí-ne-a
Alismataceae (Water-plantain Family)

DESCRIPTION: Variable perennial herb to 24″ tall; above-water leaves with blades linear to ovate; below-water leaves phyllodial (bladeless), flat; flowers in 2–12 whorls; flowers May–November.

RANGE-HABITAT: Newfoundland and Labrador, west to MN and SD, south to s. FL and c. TX; in SC restricted to the coastal plain in cypress-gum depressions, wet meadows, swamps, small streams, drainage ditches and canals, and borrow pits; common.

541. Bur-reed

Sparganium americanum Nuttall
   Spar-gà-ni-um a-me-ri-cà-num
Sparganiaceae (Bur-weed Family)

DESCRIPTION: Perennial herb; stems zigzag, erect, 1–3′ tall; leaves alternate, 2-ranked, sheathing at the base; male and female flowers in separate heads; smaller male heads above, female heads below; male flowers wither and die as soon as pollen is shed; flowers May–September.

RANGE-HABITAT: Newfoundland west to MN, south to c. peninsular FL and c. TX; in SC chiefly in the coastal plain, sandhills, and mountains; common; open, muddy areas of swamp forests, streams, roadside ditches, and shallow ponds.

COMMENTS: Bur-weed is an emergent plant that sometimes forms dense stands. Waterfowl and marsh birds eat the seeds.

542. Creeping burhead

Echinodorus cordifolius (L.) Grisebach
E-chi-nó-do-rus cor-di-fò-li-us
Alismataceae (Water-plantain Family)

DESCRIPTION: Short-lived perennial herb; leaves with long-grooved stalks up to 2′ long; blades widely ovate with 5–9 prominent palmate veins; flowers in clusters of 5–15 on a long scape that is erect when young, but becomes decumbent with age; flowers June–November.

RANGE-HABITAT: MD south to FL, west to TX, and north in the interior to s. IL; in SC common in the lower piedmont, sandhills, and coastal plain; swamps, streamsides, ditches, inland marshes, and wet thickets.

COMMENTS: The common name "burhead" refers to the headlike cluster of fruits. Decumbent stems often root where they contact the ground, thus "creeping" along the ground.

543. Long beach seedbox

Ludwigia brevipes (Long) Eames
Lud-wíg-i-a bré-vi-pes
Onagraceae (Evening-primrose Family)

DESCRIPTION: Prostrate, matted perennial with opposite leaves; stems mostly smooth, to 20″ long; petals 4, yellow, spoon-shaped, usually equaling the sepals; flowers June–September; fruit a curved capsule.

RANGE-HABITAT: Coastal plain from NJ to SC; in SC rare and scattered in the coastal plain and sandhills; depression meadows, on pond shores, low wet places, gravel pits, ditches, and inland marshes.

SIMILAR SPECIES: This taxon represents the five species of opposite leaf, prostrate members of the genus *Ludwigia* that occur in SC. They are separated as follows: *L. arcuata* Walter and *L. brevipes* have flowers or capsules distinctly stalked, with stalks over 0.19″ long; the petals of *arcuata* are longer than the sepals, while the petals of *brevipes* have petals equaling or shorter than the sepals. *L. repens* Forster, *L. spathulata* Torrey & Gray, and *L. palustris* (L.) Elliott have sessile flowers and fruits or stalks shorter than 0.13″. *L. repens* has petals; *L. spathulata* and *L. palustris* have no petals. *L. spathulata* is hairy, while *L. palustris* is smooth.

COMMENTS: The genus name honors Christian Ludwig, 1709–1773, a professor of botany at Leipsic.

544. Winged monkey-flower

Mimulus alatus Aiton
Mí-mu-lus a-là-tus
Scrophulariaceae (Figwort Family)

DESCRIPTION: Perennial, rhizomatous herb; stems 16–48″ tall, with narrow wings on the angles; leaves opposite, serrate; flowers solitary in the axils of leaves or bracts; calyx with a relatively long, angled, prismatic tube somewhat oblique at the opening; flowers July–frost.

RANGE-HABITAT: CT to MI and NB, and south to FL and TX; in SC in the lower piedmont and coastal plain; common; floodplain forests, swamps, creek banks, marshy shores, stream margins, and wet ditches.

SIMILAR SPECIES: *M. alatus* is similar to *M. ringens* L., which occurs in the mountains and upper piedmont. Their ranges overlap in the piedmont and their habitats are similar. *M. alatus* has stalked leaves and winged stems; *M. ringens* has sessile leaves and wingless or obscurely winged stems.

Freshwater floating aquatics

545. Mosquito fern

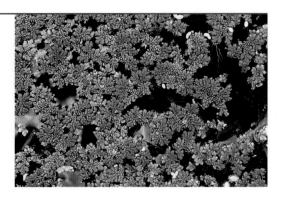

Azolla caroliniana Willdenow
A-zól-la ca-ro-li-ni-à-na
Azollaceae (Mosquito Fern Family)

DESCRIPTION: Free-floating, aquatic fern, about 0.3″ wide.

RANGE-HABITAT: Widespread in the southeastern US, irregularly north into s. New England and MN, and south into the tropics; in SC throughout the coastal plain and maritime strand, sporadically in the piedmont; ponds and sluggish streams, swamps, lakes, and ditches.

COMMENTS: Mosquito fern harbors a symbiotic nitrogen-fixing cyanobacterium (*Anabaena azollae* Strasburger) in its fronds. This nitrogen-fixing ability has resulted in mosquito fern being used historically and presently as a green manure plant in Asian rice paddies.

The common name comes from the belief that its dense growth on a body of water prevents mosquitos from laying eggs and the larvae from obtaining oxygen above the surface.

The mosquito fern fronds change from red in full sun to bright green in shade. It is spread by waterfowl, particularly wading birds. Accordingly, it may appear one year in a pond where it has never been seen before.

546. Cow-lily; spatterdock

Nuphar sagittifolia (Walter) Pursh
Nù-phar sa-git-ti-fò-li-a
Nymphaeaceae (Water-lily Family)

DESCRIPTION: Perennial, aquatic herb from a large rhizome; leaves either floating or submerged; floating and submerged leaf blades typically 3–6x as long as wide, up to 12″ long and 2–4″ wide; flowers April–October.

RANGE-HABITAT: Endemic from e. VA south to ne. SC; in SC it occurs in the Pee Dee River basin; locally abundant on shallow bars in the Waccamaw River; rivers, bayous, sloughs, and blackwater streams, extending down rivers into freshwater tidal areas.

SIMILAR SPECIES: A similar cow-lily, *N. advena* (Aiton) R. Brown ex Aiton (plate 106 in *WCL*), is widespread throughout eastern North America and common in the coastal plain of SC. It differs from *N. sagittifolia* in having leaves floating, erect, and emergent, with blades 1–2x as long as wide.

COMMENTS: Native Americans used the seeds and rhizomes as food. The rhizomes were roasted or boiled, after which they could be easily peeled; the sweet interiors were then cut up for soups and stews.

SYNONYM: *Nuphar luteum* subsp. *sagittifolium* (Walter) E. O. Beal—RAB

547. Big floating-heart

Nymphoides aquatica (Walter ex J. F. Gmelin) Kuntze
Nym-phoì-des a-quá-ti-ca
Gentianaceae (Gentian Family)

DESCRIPTION: Perennial herb; free-floating and anchored from a thick rhizome; stems reddish purple-punctate; leaves green above, usually purple below; stem terminates in an umbel of flowers and one leaf with a short stalk; late in the season the inflorescence is mixed with or subtended by tuber-like roots; flowers late April–September.

RANGE-HABITAT: Coastal plain from s. NJ to FL, then to e. TX; in SC it is frequent in freshwater lakes and ponds, sluggish streams, swamps, and beaver ponds.

SIMILAR SPECIES: Two species of floating heart occur in SC: big floating-heart and little floating-heart (*N. cordata* (Elliott) Fernald). Little floating-heart is restricted to the sandhills and inner coastal plain. Little floating-heart also differs from big floating-heart in having stems not red-punctate, and its smaller leaves are purple and green mottled on the upper surface and purple and smooth on the under surface.

548. Floating bladderwort

Utricularia inflata Walter
U-tri-cu-là-ri-a in-flà-ta
Lentibulariaceae (Bladderwort Family)

DESCRIPTION: Free-floating, carnivorous herb; upper leaves whorled, consisting of an inflated stalk and rachis, forming a flotation device that supports the flowering stalk; submerged "leaves" bear the bladders that trap and digest aquatic animals, providing minerals; flowers May–November.

RANGE-HABITAT: Common coastal plain species that ranges from NJ to s. FL, and west to e. TX; swamps, lakes, ponds, roadside ditches, and pools.

SIMILAR SPECIES: A smaller plant is *U. radiata* Small, which also occurs in the coastal plain in similar habitats, but is rare. In *U. radiata* the inflated leaf stalk and rachis are less than 2″ long, and the racemes are mostly 3–4-flowered. In *U. inflata* the inflated leaf stalk and rachis are more than 2″ long, and the racemes are usually 9–14-flowered.

COMMENTS: An interesting feature of this bladderwort is the springtime development of the stalk and flotation device from the submerged part of the plant. The flotation structures develop at the end of the immature stalk while under water. As both grow, their buoyancy causes them to rise to the surface, by which time the upper part of the stalk is well developed. The flowers (on the end of the stalk) are elevated above the water so cross-pollination can occur. Beholding a pond covered with a mass of floating bladderworts where none existed the previous day is one of the wonders of nature. This plant survives drought by producing drought-resistant tubers; when the pond fills with water, the tubers generate a new plant.

TAXONOMY: Some authors consider these two taxa as one species with two varieties: *U. inflata* Walter var. *inflata* and *U. inflata* var. *minor* (L.) Chapman.

549. Water-shield

Brasenia schreberi J. F. Gmelin
Bra-sèn-i-a schré-ber-i
Cabombaceae (Water-shield Family)

DESCRIPTION: Perennial, anchored herb with floating leaves; leaves and flowers arise from a slender, creeping rootstock with considerable branching of the stem; stems, leaf stalks and underside of the leaves coated with a gelatinous material; leaf underside is purple, the upper side bright green; flowers June–October.

RANGE-HABITAT: Nova Scotia west to MN, and south to FL and TX; also from British Columbia to CA, and in tropical America and the Old World; in SC it is a common coastal plain species in freshwater ponds, swamps, lake edges, and sluggish streams.

COMMENTS: Water-shield often grows in extensive stands that exclude other vegetation in small ponds. The rootstock is a favorite food of ring-necked ducks. The genus name honors Christopher Brasen, and the specific epithet honors Johann Christian Schreber, 1739–1810.

550. Frog's-bit

Limnobium spongia (Bosc) Steudel
Lim-nó-bi-um spón-gi-a
Hydrocharitaceae (Frog's-bit Family)

DESCRIPTION: Perennial herb, generally free-floating in dense mats, or becoming rooted in mud as a pond or marsh dries up; plantlets develop at the ends of runners; flowers June–September.

RANGE-HABITAT: NJ to n. FL, west to e. TX, and in the interior to MO and s. IL; in SC a common coastal plain species occurring in a variety of shallow, quiet-water habitats such as swamps, ponds, drainage ditches, lakes, and marshes.

COMMENTS: Two leaf forms occur during frog's-bit's life cycle: floating leaves and erect leaves. Vegetative, floating, basal clusters of nearly kidney-shaped leaves give rise to more robust plants. These plants consist of clusters of ascending and stalked, erect leaves on which flowers and fruits develop. Extensive growth usually creates problems in management of small ponds.

551. Sacred bean; water chinquapin

Nelumbo lutea (Willdenow) Persoon
Ne-lúm-bo lù-te-a
Nelumbonaceae (Lotus-lily Family)

DESCRIPTION: Rhizomatous, perennial herb; leaves produced early in the season lie on the water surface, and as the leaf stalk grows during the summer, the leaves extend above the surface; flowers solitary on the flowering stalk; leaves and flowers often 3–4′ above water surface; flowers June–September.

RANGE-HABITAT: NY and s. Ontario to MN and IA, south to s. FL, and west to e. OK and e. TX; in SC infrequent and scattered throughout the coastal plain in muddy areas of ponds, sluggish streams, and margins of natural and human-made lakes.

COMMENTS: Water chinquapin was a favorite Native American food. The tender, immature seeds were eaten raw or cooked. The ripe seeds were parched to loosen the shell, then husked and eaten dry, baked, boiled, or ground to make bread. The tuberous enlargements of the rootstocks become filled with starch in the fall and make a tasty food when baked or boiled and seasoned.

The pistil develops into a funnel-shaped fruit about 4″ in diameter, the apex of which contains several cavities, each containing a single seed that shakes out when ripe. Wildlife, especially ducks, prize the seeds.

552. Fragrant water-lily; sweet water-lily

Nymphaea odorata Aiton
   Nym-phaè-a o-do-rà-ta
Nymphaeaceae (Water-lily Family)

DESCRIPTION: Perennial herb; free-floating and anchored from a thick rhizome; distinctive for its showy, sweet-scented, white (rarely pinkish) flowers; leaves purple beneath; flowers June–September.

RANGE-HABITAT: Newfoundland west to Manitoba, south to FL and TX; in SC chiefly a coastal plain species, where it is common; scattered in the piedmont and mountains, where it is rare; pools, ponds, and sluggish stream margins.

COMMENTS: Morton (1974) indicates that rural people of the lowcountry used a root infusion of water-lily as a treatment for diarrhea. For itch of private parts, they bathed with and/or drank a decoction of the root. Water-lily is used as an ornamental in small ponds where it often develops dense stands that may interfere with boating and fishing.

TAXONOMY: The taxonomy of *N. odorata* is too complex to discuss here. It is highly polymorphic, leading to the naming of numerous species, subspecies, and varieties. The conservative treatment of a single taxon is used in this book.

553. Bog-mat

Wolffiella floridana (J. D. Smith)
   Thompson
   Wolf-fi-él-la flo-ri-dà-na
Lemnaceae (Duckweed Family)

DESCRIPTION: Fronds floating near the surface of the water, submerged; fronds rarely solitary, usually 2 or more attached by short, basal stalks forming a starlike colony; fronds 0.3–0.6″ long; no roots; reproduction is mostly vegetative by budding, but occasionally a frond produces one male and one female flower.

RANGE-HABITAT: From MA and n. IL, south to FL and TX; in SC common throughout the sandhills, coastal plain, and maritime strand; slightly acidic and highly organic waters of ponds, roadside ditches, streams, swamps, and marshes.

COMMENTS: Bog-mat most often occurs intermixed with the other three genera of Lemnaceae.

SYNONYM: *Wolffiella gladiata* (Hegelmann) Hegelmann—W

553. Duckmeat; duckweed

Spirodela polyrhiza (L.) Schleiden
   Spi-ro-dè-la po-ly-rhì-za
Lemnaceae (Duckweed Family)

DESCRIPTION: Free-floating aquatic herb; fronds about 0.2″ long and bear 2–4 roots; fronds usually in groups of 2–5, rarely solitary; flowers not seen.

RANGE-HABITAT: Widespread worldwide; in SC in the sandhills, coastal plain, and maritime strand; common; pools, ponds, swamps, ditches, and margins of sluggish streams.

COMMENTS: *Spirodela* can cause problems in small ponds when it covers the surface and interferes with livestock drinking and clogs irrigation pumps. *S. polyrhiza* produces starch-filled turions during adverse temperature and drought conditions. The turion sinks to the bottom until favorable conditions return, at which time the turion expels a small bubble of gas that carries it to the surface where it germinates.

554. *Depression meadows*

555. Boykin's lobelia

Lobelia boykinii Torrey & Gray
   Lo-bèl-i-a boy-kín-i-i
Campanulaceae (Bellwort Family)

DESCRIPTION: Aquatic perennial from rhizomes (the only rhizomatous lobelia in SC); stem 20–32″ tall; leaves very narrow; corolla blue to white; flower stalk without basal bractlets; raceme lax, one-sided; flowers May–July.

RANGE-HABITAT: Coastal plain endemic; s. DE, then from SC to n. FL; in SC in pond cypress savannas, cypress-gum depressions, depression meadows, wet longleaf pine savannas, and wet longleaf pine flatwoods and adjacent ditches; listed as rare in most manuals.

SIMILAR SPECIES: The three species of *Lobelia* that occur in the coastal plain in similar and overlapping habitats are difficult to separate. Godfrey and Wooten (1981) separate the three as follows: *L. boykinii* has narrowly linear leaves and rhizomes; *L. canbyi* Gray and *L. nuttallii* Roemer & Schultes have leaves 0.06″ wide or more and have no rhizomes; *L. canbyi* has a blue corolla without a white eye at the throat, while *L. nuttallii* has a blue corolla with a white eye at the throat. In addition, blooming times differ. *L. boykinii* flowers May–July, *L. nuttallii* May–frost, and *L. canbyi* July–frost.

COMMENTS: Most botanists in SC do not consider it rare; it is overlooked because of the similarity with two other species. A good site to see this lobelia is in Craig Pond in Barnwell County. The specific epithet honors its discoverer Samuel Boykin, 1786–1848, an early GA botanist.

PROTECTION STATUS: Federal Species of Concern

556. Sclerolepis

Sclerolepis uniflora (Walter) Britton,
    Sterns & Poggenburg
    Scle-ró-le-pis u-ni-flò-ra
    Asteraceae (Aster or Sunflower Family)

DESCRIPTION: Mat-forming perennial herb
with slender rhizomes; flowering stems erect,
4–12″ tall (in water to 24″ tall); leaves in
whorls of 3–5, linear; flowers in heads, one
per stem, disk flowers only; flowers pink or
lavender, rarely white; flowers mid-
May–August.

RANGE-HABITAT: Coastal plain from NH south
to c. FL, and west to sw. AL; scattered throughout the coastal plain of SC in
depression meadows and shallow water of clay-based Carolina bays, natural lake
shores, blackwater streambanks, swamps, and seepage wetlands; occasional.

COMMENTS: There is only one species in the genus *Sclerolepis*.

557. Shrubby seedbox

Ludwigia suffruticosa Walter
    Lud-wíg-i-a suf-fru-ti-cò-sa
    Onagraceae (Evening-primrose Family)

DESCRIPTION: Rhizomatous perennial forming
leafy stolons in the fall; flowering stems erect,
12–32″ tall; leaves alternate; flowers in a terminal, headlike cluster; sepals 4, widely ovate;
petals absent; flowers June–October.

RANGE-HABITAT: Coastal plain from se. NC
south to s. peninsular FL, and west to FL panhandle and se. AL; common throughout its
range; periodically to seasonally flooded
portions of lime sinks, depression meadows in clay-based Carolina bays, shallow
pools, wet pineland depressions, and ditches.

558. Awned meadow-beauty

Rhexia aristosa Britton
    Rhéx-i-a a-ris-tò-sa
    Melastomataceae (Meadow-beauty
    Family)

DESCRIPTION: Usually branched, perennial
herb, to 28″ tall; stems 4-angled; nodes with
stiff hairs; leaves opposite, mostly broadly
lanceolate, 3-nerved; petals sharp pointed;
capsules (urns) with coarse, yellow bristles on
the rim (diagnostic for this species); flowers
June–September.

RANGE-HABITAT: Coastal plain from NJ to GA,
west to se. AL; depression meadows in clay-based Carolina bays, pond cypress
savannas, and limestone ponds.

COMMENTS: Although listed as rare in most manuals, SC botanists consider it
common, and suggest it be removed from the federal list.

PROTECTION STATUS: Federal Species of Concern

559. Tracy's beaksedge

Rhynchospora tracyi Britton
Rhyn-chós-po-ra trà-cy-i
Cyperaceae (Sedge Family)

DESCRIPTION: Slender perennial with slender, scaly stolons, commonly forming extensive colonies, especially when growing in shallow water; stems to about 32″ tall; spikelets in 1–2 globose clusters; flowers June–September.
RANGE-HABITAT: Coastal plain endemic from s. NC to FL, west to MS; disjunct in sw. LA and in the West Indies; grass-sedge-dominated depression meadows in clay-based Carolina bays, pond cypress savannas, and shallow lime sinks; occasional throughout its range.
COMMENTS: Tracy's beaksedge can be found in Craig Pond in Barnwell County. Previously listed as rare in most manuals, it has recently been found in numerous sites in the coastal plain and should be listed as occasional. An extensive survey of pond cypress savannas and depression meadows will undoubtedly produce numerous additional sites for this sedge.

560. Depression meadow arrowhead

Sagittaria isoetiformis J. G. Smith
Sa-git-tà-ri-a i-soe-ti-fór-mis
Alismataceae (Water-plantain Family)

DESCRIPTION: Aquatic perennial with very slender rhizomes; leaves bladeless, narrowly straplike, occasionally somewhat dilated at the tips, but not really bladed; flowers June–September.
RANGE-HABITAT: From se. NC south to c. peninsular FL, west to s. AL; in SC in the inner coastal plain; rare; depression meadows in clay-based Carolina bays, lime sinks, marshy shores of impoundments, and pond cypress-swamp gum depression swamps.
COMMENTS: Botanists believe that this plant is more abundant than previously thought; however, one of its prime habitats is clay-based Carolina bays, which are threatened. A good site to view this rare arrowhead is Craig Pond in Barnwell County.
TAXONOMY: The taxonomy of this species is highly controversial. Wooten (1973) did not consider it distinct from *Sagittaria graminea* Michaux var. *graminea* (plate 540). Radford et al. (1968) evidently misapplied it to *Sagittaria teres* Watson. Godfrey and Wooten (1979) and Weakley (2001), however, both recognize it as a species. The morphology of the leaves is the best field characteristic to separate *S. isoetiformis* from the similar *S. graminea* Michaux var. *graminea*. In *isoetiformis* the leaves are all bladeless, narrowly straplike, flattened dorsally to almost round; *graminea* has bladed leaves, and the bladeless leaves, if present, are broadly straplike.
PROTECTION STATUS: State Species of Concern

561. Canby's cowbane; Canby's dropwort

Oxypolis canbyi (Coulter and Rose)
   Fernald
   Ox-ý-po-lis cán-by-i
Apiaceae (Parsley Family)

DESCRIPTION: Perennial, rhizomatous herb with hollow stem, to 4' tall; leaves reduced to phyllodes; flowers August–October.

RANGE-HABITAT: Coastal plain from sw. GA through SC to se. NC, and from e. MD (formerly) to DE; depression meadows in clay-based Carolina bays and natural depression wetlands such as pond cypress savannas; rare throughout its range.

SIMILAR SPECIES: *Oxypolis filiformis* (Walter) Britton is similar to Canby's cowbane. The following features are diagnostic for separation: *O. canbyi* has mature fruits with corky, thickened ribs or wings, rhizomes, and lower nodes that lose their leaves by flowering time; *O. filiformis* has fruits with thin peripheral ribs or wings, no rhizomes, and lower nodes retaining leaves until flowering. The corky, thickened, winged fruit of *O. canbyi* is clearly evident in the photograph.

COMMENTS: Canby's cowbane has been found in 26 sites in SC; many of these are now protected SC Heritage Preserves or Nature Conservancy preserves. South Carolina harbors the largest concentrations of cowbane. One site for viewing of this species is the Crosby Oxypolis Heritage Preserve in Colleton County. The specific epithet honors William M. Canby, 1831–1904, its discoverer.

PROTECTION STATUS: Federal Endangered

THE MARITIME STRAND

562. *Coastal beaches*

563. Sea rocket

Cakile harperi Small
   Ca-kì-le hár-per-i
Brassicaceae (Mustard Family)

DESCRIPTION: Smooth, fleshy, freely branched annual, rarely woody at base; up to 30″ tall; flowers March–October.

RANGE-HABITAT: Common maritime plant from NC to St. Lucie County, FL; coastal beach and adjacent coastal dune communities.

COMMENTS: Young cooked plants are of good quality but without a distinctive taste. The fleshy young foliage and young fruits are palatable when mixed with milder leaves in a salad; eaten raw they have the flavor of mild horseradish.

   The fruit of sea rocket is indehiscent and divided into two segments. The terminal segment becomes dry and corky at maturity, breaking off from the basal segment and able to float great distances. The basal noncorky segment usually falls later and does not travel far.

TAXONOMY: Godfrey and Wooten (1981) and Duncan and Duncan (1987) list this plant as a subspecies, *C. edentula* subsp. *harperi* (Small) Rodman.

564. Carolina saltwort

Salsola caroliniana Walter
Sàl-so-la ca-ro-li-ni-à-na
Chenopodiaceae (Goosefoot Family)

DESCRIPTION: Herbaceous, freely branching annual, 10–25″ tall; leaves fleshy, awn-shaped and sharp-pointed; the flowers vary in color, changing from whitish or gray to yellowish gray or pink in the fall; flowers June–frost.

RANGE-HABITAT: Newfoundland south to FL; common along the SC coast on the upper beach.

COMMENTS: Fragments of the plant that fall on the sand can be hazardous to exposed skin. The stems turn from green to red or pinkish purple in the fall. The dead plants are often blown loose and tumble down the beach, in the process disseminating the seeds.

TAXONOMY: Weakley (2001) recognizes two species of *Salsola*: *S. caroliniana* and *S. tragus* L. *S. caroliniana* has stiff sepals with the midrib projecting as a sharp point and occurs on sea beaches. *S. tragus* has soft sepals with the midrib obscure and not excurrent and occurs on inland areas. He further states that *S. caroliniana* is a native species, while *S. tragus* is a native of Eurasia and occurs in the mountains of VA and the piedmont of NC and VA. Most references on the southeastern flora use the taxon *Salsola kali* L. to include both the above taxa, stating it is native to Eurasia.

565. Seabeach amaranth

Amaranthus pumilus Rafinesque
A-ma-rán-thus pù-mi-lus
Amaranthaceae (Amaranth Family)

DESCRIPTION: Annual herb from a taproot; stems prostrate, erect, or somewhat reclining at their tips, 4–24″ long, numerous, branched from the base, forming mats; leaves fleshy, clustered near tips of the branches, broadly rounded, emarginate, 0.5–1.0″ in diameter; flowers in short axillary clusters; both male and females flowers on the same plant; fruit an utricle; flowers and fruits mature June–frost.

RANGE-HABITAT: Historically from se. MA south to upper Charleston County, SC; presently extant only in NC and SC, and Long Island, NY; its usual habitat is nearly pure silica sand substrate in front of the foredunes on coastal barrier islands.

COMMENTS: Coastal erosion during the 1990s has significantly reduced the populations of seabeach amaranth along the coast of SC. One of the best sites to see this species is Huntington Beach State Park on the barrier beach north to Murrell's Inlet.

Seeds of seabeach amaranth germinate in May; first forming a small, unbranched sprig, but soon branching profusely. The plant then acts as a dune builder, causing sand to form a mound around it as the season progresses. As the mound gets higher, the plant continues to grow, and earlier leaves are buried. Seeds are spread by wind or water in the fall.

PROTECTION STATUS: Federal Threatened

562. Coastal dunes

566. Gaillardia; fire-wheel

Gaillardia pulchella Fougeroux
Gail-lárd-i-a pul-chél-la
Asteraceae (Aster or Sunflower Family)

DESCRIPTION: Short-lived, hairy, perennial herb, 6–28″ tall; creeping to erect; ray and disk flowers reddish, tipped with yellow, or occasionally all yellow; flowers April–frost.
RANGE-HABITAT: From se. VA south to FL, and west to TX and beyond; in SC on the outer coastal plain and maritime strand; beach dunes, along roadsides, and in sandy habitats; common.

COMMENTS: Gaillardia is apparently a southwestern species escaped from cultivation and naturalized in the above habitats (Justice and Bell, 1968; Rickett, 1967). Many color variants and combinations of flowers occur in the red-pink-yellow range. The genus honors Gaillard de Charentonneau, a French botanical amateur.

567. Seaside pennywort

Hydrocotyle bonariensis Lamarck
Hy-dro-có-ty-le bo-na-ri-én-sis
Apiaceae (Parsley Family)

DESCRIPTION: Smooth, fleshy perennial rooting from the nodes of slender, creeping stems; leaves simple and peltate; flowers April–November.
RANGE-HABITAT: VA to s. FL, and west to TX; common along the coast on stable coastal dunes, swales, and moist, open, sandy areas.
COMMENTS: The flowers and fruits of seaside pennywort are often present at the same time, and the compound umbel continues to produce new sections with new flowers.

568. Beach evening-primrose

Oenothera drummondii Hooker
Oe-no-thè-ra drum-mónd-i-i
Onagraceae (Evening-primrose Family)

DESCRIPTION: Spreading to creeping, densely hairy perennial, sometimes appearing shrubby in mild winters; flowers about 3″ wide, turning toward the sun; flowers April–October.
RANGE-HABITAT: Coastal SC to FL and TX; occasional inland, but common on barrier islands; sandy beaches, coastal dunes on the barrier islands, and sandy barrens and grasslands inland.

SIMILAR SPECIES: Dunes evening-primrose (*Oenothera humifusa* Nuttall) is common on the dunes and has flowers about 1″ wide, yellow tinged with pink; flowers May–October.
COMMENTS: According to three sources, this species is not native to SC. Bailey

(1949) indicates that it only occurs along the TX coast. Small (1933) states that it is only native to TX. Rickett (1967) states that it is a western plant sometimes found in the eastern states. Apparently, then, beach evening-primrose was introduced to SC from the west. The specific epithet honors Thomas Drummond, 1780–1835, an American botanist.

569. Dune spurge; seaside spurge

Chamaesyce polygonifolia (L.) Small
Cha-mae-sỳ-ce po-ly-go-ni-fò-li-a
Euphorbiaceae (Spurge Family)

DESCRIPTION: Smooth, creeping to ascending annual with stems radiating from a taproot; rare individuals may overwinter as a weak perennial; flowers are inconspicuous; flowers May–frost.

RANGE-HABITAT: Atlantic Coast from Quebec to ne. FL; in SC in the maritime strand in the open sands of coastal dunes, dune blowouts, and overwashes; common.

SIMILAR SPECIES: *C. polygonifolia* is similar to *C. bombensis* (Jacquin) Dugand (=*Euphorbia ammannioides* Kunth), which is rare. The two sometimes grow mixed. The two species may be separated by seed shape and size. Also, the inflorescence of *polygonifolia* is terminal on the stems, while the inflorescence of *bombensis* is terminal and axillary on the stems. *C. polygonifolia* tends to be a pioneer species on the upper beach and foredune front. *C. bombensis* prefers areas behind the foredune.

COMMENTS: Milky juice may cause skin irritation; plants, when eaten, may cause severe poisoning.

SYNONYM: *Euphorbia polygonifolia* L.—RAB

570. Silver-leaf croton

Croton punctatus Jacquin
Crò-ton punc-tà-tus
Euphorbiaceae (Spurge Family)

DESCRIPTION: Annual or short-lived perennial, to 3′ tall; entire plant, except upper leaf surface, covered with a dense layer of small scales and glands that give the plant a brownish gray appearance; inconspicuous male and female flowers separate on the same plant; fruit a 3-lobed capsule about 0.5″ wide; flowers late May–November.

RANGE-HABITAT: NC south to s. FL, and west to TX; restricted to the maritime strand; common on coastal dunes and the upper strand of beaches.

COMMENTS: No other plant on the dunes even closely resembles this plant. Perennial plants can overwinter and produce new shoots from the old stems.

571. Dune devil-joint; dune prickly-pear

Opuntia pusilla (Haworth) Nuttall
  O-pún-ti-a pu-síl-la
  Cactaceae (Cactus Family)

DESCRIPTION: Perennial, fleshy, leafless plant, creeping, often mat-forming; stems photosynthetic and segmented into loosely attached joints that separate readily; scattered over the stem are clusters of hairlike spines with or without 2–4″ long, sharp spines; flowers May–June.

RANGE-HABITAT: Southeastern maritime strand from NC south to FL, and west to se. TX; common in SC; coastal dunes, sandy maritime forests, and shell deposits.

COMMENTS: The plant is often inconspicuous and hidden in the dune vegetation, where if stepped on with bare feet, its spines inflicting a painful wound. Due to the readiness with which the joints become detached, the spines may become embedded in shoes, after which they can work their way to skin (if the shoes are thin). The spines are barbed, making them difficult to remove.

SYNONYM: *Opuntia drummondii* Graham—RAB

572. Sea purslane

Sesuvium portulacastrum L.
  Se-sù-vi-um por-tu-la-cás-trum
  Aizoaceae (Carpetweed Family)

DESCRIPTION: Fleshy, smooth, perennial herb with elongate, creeping branches rooting at the nodes and forming mats; leaves opposite; flowers and fruits on distinct stalks; flowers May–frost.

RANGE-HABITAT: NC to s. FL, and west to TX; common maritime plant; dune swales, coastal dunes, high salt marshes, dredged spoil disposal sites, and beaches.

SIMILAR SPECIES: *S. maritimum* (Walter) Britton, Sterns, & Poggenburg grows in similar habitats. It differs in having flowers and fruits sessile and being an erect to spreading annual, not rooting at the nodes.

COMMENTS: When growing in sandy sites, it forms mounds where sand builds up around the plant.

573. Sea oats

Uniola paniculata L.
  U-nì-o-la pa-ni-cu-là-ta
  Poaceae (Grass Family)

DESCRIPTION: Coarse, rhizomatous perennial with stems 3–6′ tall; stems readily root at the nodes as the stem becomes covered with sand; reproduction is mainly by rhizomes; flowers June–November.

RANGE-HABITAT: From se. VA south to FL, and west to TX and Mexico; common along the Carolina coast; coastal dunes and adjacent beaches, and interdune swales.

COMMENTS: Sea oats is tolerant of strong winds, sand abrasion, and salt spray, and is one of the most important maritime plants in dune formation and stabilization. On public property, a state law protects any and all parts of the plant from being removed or damaged.

574. Common marsh-pink

Sabatia stellaris Pursh
Sa-bà-ti-a stel-là-ris
Gentianaceae (Gentian Family)

DESCRIPTION: Annual herb to 25″ tall; stems freely branched with opposite leaves; flowers pink with yellowish, star-shaped center edged with red; flowers July–October.

RANGE-HABITAT: From s. MA south along the coast to coastal FL, and west into LA; common; brackish swales within dune systems, brackish and salt marshes, and marl spoil banks or flats.

575. Dune sandbur

Cenchrus tribuloides L.
Cén-chrus tri-bu-loì-des
Poaceae (Grass Family)

DESCRIPTION: Sprawling perennial or annual rooting at the nodes; stem branches 4–28″ long; the small flowers are enclosed within a spiny bur; fruit mature August–October, persisting much of the fall and winter.

RANGE-HABITAT: NY south to FL, and west to TX; common on coastal dunes along the coast and adjacent beaches; also common in sandy fields and woodlands.

COMMENTS: The spines can inflict painful puncture wounds on exposed skin and are equally painful to remove because of the backward-pointing barbs. The spines protect the plant from disturbance and provide an effective mechanism for seed dispersal. The burs turn from green to reddish with age and may remain on the dead stems throughout the winter.

576. Beach morning-glory; fiddle-leaf morning-glory

Ipomoea stolonifera (Cyrillo) Poiret
I-po-moè-a sto-lo-ní-fe-ra
Convolvulaceae (Morning-glory Family)

DESCRIPTION: Smooth, fleshy, trailing perennial, rooting at the nodes; most leaf blades lobed at the base, often deeply so; flowers August–October.

RANGE-HABITAT: From se. NC to s. FL, and west to TX; occasional maritime species; upper strand of the beach and on front dunes.

COMMENTS: Its fleshy leaves and low-growth form (making it less exposed to wind and salt spray) are adaptations that allow it to grow in the hostile beach and dune environments.

PROTECTION STATUS: State Species of Concern

577. Mound-lily yucca

Yucca gloriosa L.
Yúc-ca glo-ri-ò-sa
Liliaceae (Lily Family)

DESCRIPTION: Evergreen shrub or small tree, to about 15′ tall; trunk usually without branches; leaves bayonet-like, crowded, with entire margins that have a very narrow, thin, brownish edge, tapering to a sharp point; flowers white, bell-shaped, hanging, in a large terminal panicle; flowers August–October; fruits, when mature, hang down, not splitting open, mature November–December.

RANGE-HABITAT: From e. NC south to ne. FL; occasional along the SC coast; dunes, other open sandy areas, and along the edges of brackish marshes.

SIMILAR SPECIES: *Yucca gloriosa* is similar to two other yuccas that grow in the coastal area. They can be separated as follows: *Y. gloriosa* has leaves with entire margins and flowers in August–October; *Y. aloifolia* L. (Spanish bayonet, plate 14 in *WCL*) has sharp spiny serrations on the leaf margins and flowers in June–July; *Y. filamentosa* L. (bear-grass) has leaf edges that fray into twisted fibers.

COMMENTS: Mound-lily yucca is one of two yucca species of coastal regions of the southeastern US that often grows large enough to be considered a tree. Only in its southern range limit, however, does mound-lily reach tree size. In SC, it grows about 3–4′ high. The other tree species is Spanish bayonet.

The petals are used in salads, or the entire flowers fried as fritters. The fruits can be cooked and eaten after the seeds are removed. Since mound-lily yucca can withstand salt spray, it is often planted along the coast as an evergreen landscaping choice.

578. Seashore-elder

Iva imbricata Walter
Ì-va im-bri-cà-ta
Asteraceae (Aster or Sunflower Family)

DESCRIPTION: Bushy-branched, perennial shrub to 3′ tall; somewhat fleshy, smooth; lower leaves opposite, midstem and upper alternate; commonly creeping at the base; branches often reclining; tips of branches often dying during the winter; fruit a large achene, yellow-brown when mature; flowers and fruits late August–November.

RANGE-HABITAT: From se. VA to FL, and west to LA and e. TX; restricted to the maritime strand; coastal dunes, the upper beach, and overwash areas; common.

COMMENTS: Seashore-elder is often the most ocean-ward perennial plant, colonizing the upper beach or incipient dunes where it grows mixed with seabeach amaranth, sea rocket, and Carolina saltwort.

579. Seaside panicum

Panicum amarum Elliott
Pá-ni-cum a-mà-rum
Poaceae (Grass Family)

DESCRIPTION: Rhizomatous perennial, usually rooting at lower nodes; stems usually solitary, 15–40″ tall; flowers September–October.
RANGE-HABITAT: Restricted to the maritime strand from CT to FL, and west to TX; common in SC; coastal dunes and swales behind foredunes.
COMMENTS: Seaside panicum contributes to dune building; however, since it becomes buried or uprooted when sand shifts, it is not as effective as other dune grasses in binding soil.

580. Sweet grass

Muhlenbergia filipes M. A. Curtis
Muh-len-bérg-i-a fí-li-pes
Poaceae (Grass Family)

DESCRIPTION: Tufted perennial to 40″ tall; inflorescence a loose, limber panicle that turns pinkish when mature in October–November.
RANGE-HABITAT: NC to FL, and west to e. TX; primarily on barrier islands along the coast; occasional, but often locally abundant; flats between coastal dunes, salt shrub thickets, stable dunes, and edges of freshwater or brackish marshes.
COMMENTS: This is the locally famous "sweet grass" used by the basket makers in Mt. Pleasant, SC. Sweet grass is used in combination with longleaf pine needles, black needle rush, and cabbage palmetto leaves. There is concern that in the future there will not be an adequate supply of sweet grass. Transplanting experiments are being done to test the feasibility of establishing a cultivated source. The genus name honors Henry Ernest Muhlenberg, 1753–1815, a distinguished American botanist.

581. Dune greenbrier

Smilax auriculata Walter
Smì-lax au-ri-cu-là-ta
Liliaceae (Lily Family)

DESCRIPTION: Coarse-stemmed, evergreen vine; usually forming dense, low thickets; stems green, usually spineless; leaves leathery, smooth, green on both sides; fruits mature October–November.
RANGE-HABITAT: Common maritime species from e. NC to s. FL, and west to LA and AR; maritime dunes, maritime shrub thickets, and sandy openings in maritime forests; farther south it grows on inland dunes.
COMMENTS: Its extensive rootstock helps it survive disturbance on the dunes.

582. Maritime forests

583. Trailing bluet

Houstonia procumbens (J. F. Gmelin)
    Standley
    Hous-tòn-i-a pro-cúm-bens
    Rubiaceae (Madder Family)

DESCRIPTION: Prostrate or creeping, perennial herb; flowers solitary on erect stalks; leaves opposite; flowers March–April; then again October–frost.

RANGE-HABITAT: SC to FL, and west to LA; outer coastal plain and maritime strand; common (at least in SC, although listed as rare in manuals); open, sandy sites in maritime forests, beach dunes, and inland in sandy pinelands and along sandy roadsides.

584. Hercules'-club; toothache-tree; pilentary tree

Zanthoxylum clava-herculis L.
    Zan-thóx-y-lum clà-va-hér-cu-lis
    Rutaceae (Rue Family)

DESCRIPTION: Shrub or small tree 20–30′ tall; leaves alternate, odd-pinnately compound with spiny rachis; trunk of tree covered with pyramid-shaped, corky, spine-tipped outgrowths (see plate 31 in *WCL* for a photograph of the spine-covered trunk); flowers April–May, after the new leaves appear; fruit bears one black seed that hangs outside at maturity.

RANGE-HABITAT: From se. VA to FL, and west to TX, AR, and OK; mainly the maritime strand in SC; occasional; maritime forests, shell deposits, dunes, and sandy, thin woods.

COMMENTS: The tree has a prominent place in American folklore. F. P. Porcher (1869) lists numerous medicinal uses of this tree. Another source states that an oil derived from leaves and bark was used as drug to treat toothaches. At first, chewing the leaves gives a pleasant sensation, but later, it causes a numbing sensation. The wood has no commercial value.

585. Spanish moss

Tillandsia usneoides L.
Til-lánds-i-a us-ne-oì-des
Bromeliaceae (Pineapple Family)

DESCRIPTION: Rootless epiphyte on trees; stems usually curled, wiry; leaves filiform; leaves and stems bear gray scales that absorb atmospheric moisture and minerals; reproduction mainly vegetative when animals break and distribute strands of the plant; flowers April–June; reproduction by seeds does occur; spent capsules remain throughout the winter.

RANGE-HABITAT: From se. VA south to s. FL, and west to TX and Mexico; in SC confined to the coastal plain and maritime strand where relative humidity is high; maritime forests, swamp forests, and upland forests.

COMMENTS: The cultural and economic uses of Spanish moss are legend (Martinez, 1959). Its durable fiber is resistant to insects and is highly resilient. These characteristics made it highly sought after as stuffing for mattresses and upholstery. It was also used as a binder in construction of mud and clay chimneys.

The common name Spanish moss probably came from the French who settled in LA. It may have reminded them of the long, gray beards of the Spanish explorers who had come before them and called it "Spanish beard." It was later changed to Spanish moss. The specific epithet *usneoides* refers to its resemblance to the lichen *Usnea*, also common in SC. This note on the genus name comes from Fernald (1950): "The genus honors Elias Tillands, 1640–1693, professor at Abo, who, as a student crossing directly from Stockholm, was so seasick that he returned to Stockholm by walking more than 1000 miles around the head of the Gulf of Bothnia and hence assumed his surname (by land); the genus erroneously supposed by Linnaeus to dislike water."

Spanish moss is the most conspicuous epiphyte in the Carolina lowcountry, and much of the aesthetic appeal of the lowcountry comes from the moss-draped live oaks. It is the only member of the genus to occur north of south GA. Approximately 15 additional species of *Tillandsia* occur in FL.

586. Southern magnolia; bull bay

Magnolia grandiflora L.
Mag-nòl-i-a gran-di-flò-ra
Magnoliaceae (Magnolia Family)

DESCRIPTION: Large, fast-growing tree that produces flowers as early as 10 years old; leaves evergreen, persisting 2 years, shiny green above, often covered with reddish rust-colored hairs on the lower surface; flowers large, fragrant; flowers May–June.

RANGE-HABITAT: From se. NC to FL, and west to TX and AR; chiefly a coastal plain and maritime species; common; maritime forests, alluvial swamp forests, low woods, ravine slopes, and beech forests; generally not above 540′ altitude.

COMMENTS: The leaves of southern magnolia are used in wreaths, and its flowers were used for ornamental purposes. It is not abundant in any one site. The wood turns brown after exposure to air, so it has never been a commercially important lumber tree. Southern magnolia rarely grows in pure stands; it usually grows in association with other hardwoods.

Southern magnolia is one of the trees that has come to "personify" the South. It is planted extensively as an ornamental tree, both within and beyond its natural range. It has become naturalized in many areas where it is not native.

587. Coral bean; Cherokee bean

Erythrina herbacea L.
E-ry-thrì-na her-bà-ce-a
Fabaceae (Pea or Bean Family)

DESCRIPTION: Perennial herb, 2–5' tall; branchlets usually prickly; leaves alternate, trifoliolate; flowers appear before the leaves; fruit pod constricted between the seeds, and upon breaking open, brilliant scarlet seeds often hang from the pod; flowers May–July; fruits mature July–September.

RANGE-HABITAT: From se. NC to FL, and west to se. TX; in SC it occurs in the maritime strand and outer coastal plain; common; maritime forests, open coastal dunes, sandy, dry, open woods, and clearings, often persisting around abandoned house sites.

COMMENTS: Coral bean is often cultivated in gardens. The seeds and bark possess alkaloids that have a curare-like action and may cause death if taken internally. The crushed stems are sometimes employed as fish poisons. In Mexico, the seeds are used for poisoning rats and dogs. Coral bean is a woody shrub in FL, but an herb in the rest of its mainly coastal range. Photographs of its flowers appear in plate 38 in *WCL*.

588. Wax myrtle

Myrica cerifera L. var. *cerifera*
My-rì-ca ce-rí-fe-ra var. ce-rí-fe-ra
Myricaceae (Bayberry Family)

DESCRIPTION: Aromatic shrub or small tree to 25' tall; male and female flowers on separate plants; leaves evergreen, although dropping in severe winters; leaves coated with orange, resinous glands on both surfaces; flowers April; fruits August–October.

RANGE-HABITAT: NJ south to FL, and west to TX; in SC in the sandhills, coastal plain, and maritime strand; common throughout in a wide variety of habitats, including maritime shrub thickets, maritime forests, salt shrub thickets, shell deposits, pine-mixed hardwood forests, loblolly pine plantations, and pocosins.

COMMENTS: Myrtle Beach, SC, gets its name from this plant. The berries are covered with wax that was/is used to make fragrant candles. The wax may be irritating to some people. Wax myrtle is planted as an ornamental. The powdered root bark was an ingredient in "composition powder" once used as a folk remedy for chills and colds; the root bark was used to make an astringent tea and emetic.

TAXONOMY: Some authors recognize two varieties of wax myrtle: *M. cerifera* L. var. *cerifera* and *M. cerifera* var. *pumila* (L.) Michaux. Variety *cerifera* is a medium shrub to small tree and not stoloniferous; var. *pumila* is a small shrub and is strongly stoloniferous. Variety *pumila* grows in the coastal plain pine savannas and flatwoods and in the sandhills.

SYNONYM: *Cerothamnus ceriferus* (L.) Small—W

589. Red bay

Persea borbonia (L.) Sprengel
Pér-se-a bor-bò-ni-a
Lauraceae (Laurel Family)

DESCRIPTION: Aromatic shrub or small tree to 60–70′ tall; leaves evergreen, simple, alternate, dark green and smooth above; lower leaf surface with minute, silvery to shinning, golden hairs appressed to the surface; leaf margins often with swollen knots due to a fungal growth; fruit a dark blue or black drupe, mature September–October.

RANGE-HABITAT: From e. NC south to FL, and west to TX; in SC common in the maritime strand; dunes, maritime forests, and dry, sandy soils on barrier islands.

SIMILAR SPECIES: Red bay is similar to swamp red bay, *P. palustris* (Rafinesque) Sargent, which is common in swamps, pocosins, bay forests, and maritime forests and rarely in dry sites. The lower surface of the leaves of red bay have minute, silvery to shinning, golden hairs appressed to the surface; the under surface of the leaves of swamp red bay has longer, rusty, often crooked hairs that are not appressed.

COMMENTS: The aromatic, spicy leaves of red bay and swamp red bay have been used as a substitute for bay laurel leaves (*Laurus nobilis,* native to Asia Minor and the laurel of history). Fresh or dried leaves can be used as a spice to flavor meats, soups, and other dishes. Because of its attractive evergreen leaves, red bay is often cultivated in the South. The trees are too small to be of commercial importance as lumber. The fruits are of limited importance to wildlife.

590. Yaupon

Ilex vomitoria Aiton
Ì-lex vo-mi-tò-ri-a
Aquifoliaceae (Holly Family)

DESCRIPTION: Evergreen shrub or small tree to 25′ tall; male and female flowers on separate plants; leaves leathery, shiny above; fruit often persisting throughout the winter; fruits October–November.

RANGE-HABITAT: From e. VA south to FL, and west to TX; chiefly an outer coastal plain and maritime strand species; common; in SC it also occurs in the sandhills region where it is rare; salt shrub thickets, maritime forests, shell deposits, maritime shrub thickets, fencerows, pond margins, and swamps.

COMMENTS: The specific epithet, *vomitoria,* refers to the supposed emetic effect. Native Americans used a decoction of the dried old leaves (which were boiled down until the tea was very black and strong) to induce vomiting in purification rites. Hudson (1979), however, indicates that the emetic effect may have been the result of other herbs added to the drink. The young dried leaves have been and are still used today for a tea. The leaves are known to contain considerable caffeine, providing the lift people expect from tea. There were two attempts to grow yaupon commercially in Mt. Pleasant, Charleston County, SC, in the early 1900s; both failed due to competition from oriental teas.

Duncan and Duncan (1988) report that the Native Americans transplanted the species to new campsites; consequently, some inland populations are probably a result of these transplants. Yaupon does well in cultivation and is popular as an ornamental shrub for its evergreen leaves and red berries. Often the plants are trimmed into hedges.

591. Southern red cedar

Juniperus silicicola (Small) Bailey
Ju-ní-pe-rus si-li-cí-co-la
Cupressaceae (Cypress Family)

DESCRIPTION: Aromatic, evergreen tree, 40–60′ tall; leaves on seedlings linear and spreading from the twigs, giving the seedling a prickly feeling; leaves of mature tree are short scales in close, overlapping pairs; often both juvenile and mature leaves occur on the same plant; male and female cones on separate trees; mature female cones bluish black, berrylike, resinous, sweet, mature October–November.

RANGE-HABITAT: From e. NC to s. FL, and west to MS; also se. TX; outer coastal plain and maritime strand; common; shell deposits, maritime forests, dunes, salt shrub thickets, and brackish marshes.

COMMENTS: The following comments refer to both eastern red cedar and southern red cedar. The cedar wood has an essential oil that makes it durable—that is, not readily attacked by fungi or insects—hence, cedar has been used for shingles, fence posts, and cedar chests. Until the larger trees with straight trunks were exhausted, its wood was used extensively for making lead pencils. Early Charleston furniture makers used cedar until mahogany became available. Today, it is more of a specialty wood, being used for cedar chests and interior trim. Many mammals and birds, including the cedar waxwing, eat the mature fleshy cones. Cedar is now grown on plantations for Christmas trees.

TAXONOMY: The taxonomy of *Juniperus* is unsettled. Radford et al. (1968) recognize two species, *J. silicicola* and *J. virginiana* L. (eastern red cedar). Weakley (2001) recognizes two varieties, *J. virginiana* L. var. *virginiana* (eastern red cedar) and *J. virginiana* var. *silicicola* (Small) J. Silba (southern red cedar). Duncan and Duncan (1988) do not recognize the varieties and include both under *J. virginiana*. This book recognizes two species. It is difficult to distinguish between the two taxa in the field.

Eastern red cedar ranges throughout the eastern US. In SC, it occurs more on the inner coastal plain, sandhills, piedmont and mountains. In SC, southern red cedar is confined to the maritime strand and outer coastal plain.

592. Live oak

Quercus virginiana Miller
Quér-cus vir-gi-ni-à-na
Fagaceae (Beech Family)

DESCRIPTION: Large to medium size tree with wide, low-spreading branches and evergreen leaves; acorns mature September–November.
RANGE-HABITAT: Southeastern coastal plain and maritime endemic from se. VA south to FL, and west to TX; common in SC; maritime forests, oak-hickory forests, along streamsides, and in open, sandy woods.
COMMENTS: The deep-grooved bark makes live

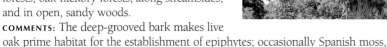

oak prime habitat for the establishment of epiphytes; occasionally Spanish moss, green-fly orchid, and resurrection fern grow on the same branch. The acorns, which ripen in the fall, are the sweetest of all the oaks and contain so little tannin that they can be eaten off the tree. The acorns are a major food source for wildlife.

Live oak was an important lumber tree in colonial times. Curved pieces cut from the junction of the limb and trunk were used for ribs in wooden ships. Expeditions were sent from the ship-building ports of the northeastern US to the barrier islands of the Atlantic and Gulf Coast states to harvest live oak.

Contrary to popular belief, live oak is a fast-growing tree in rich soils and has a normal life span of around 350 years. One only need observe the live oaks that were planted in the 1700s and 1800s along plantation avenues to appreciate how fast live oak grows. Widely planted as an ornamental, it withstands high winds, generally suffering only pruning. It also tolerates inundation of salt water during hurricanes.

593. Cabbage palmetto

Sabal palmetto (Walter) Loddiges
ex J. A. & J. H. Schultes
Sà-bal pal-mét-to
Arecaceae (Palm Family)

DESCRIPTION: Branchless palm tree to 65′ tall; evergreen leaves fanlike at the top of the thick stems; leaf scars persist as shallow, incomplete rings on the trunk; flowers July; drupes mature October–November.

RANGE-HABITAT: Along the coast from NC to s. FL and FL panhandle; common (except in NC where it is rare) in the outer coastal plain and maritime strand; maritime forests on barrier islands, edges of ponds, salt and brackish marshes, and flatwoods; does not occur naturally more than 75 miles from the coast.

COMMENTS: Cabbage palmetto is a wind-adapted species. Its leaves offer little wind resistance, and its soft "wood" allows it to bend with hurricane-force winds without being uprooted or broken. The trunks are used in wharf construction because it is not subject to injury from sea worms. The inner portion of the apical meristem is very tender and palatable, tasting like artichoke and cabbage—hence, its common name. Unfortunately, removing the meristem kills the tree. Cabbage palmetto can tolerate of a variety of soils and can grow in either sun or shade.

Cabbage palmetto is the state tree of SC. During the Revolutionary War, coastal forts were made of palmetto logs. The soft stems absorbed the force of cannon balls without shattering. It is prized today as an ornamental. Cabbage palmetto was once common along the NC coast, but was virtually extirpated for "heart-of-palm." Now it grows only on Bald Head Island in Brunswick County, NC.

594. Resurrection fern

Polypodium polypodioides (L.) Watt
        Po-ly-pó-di-um po-ly-po-di-oì-des
Polypodiaceae (Polypody Family)

DESCRIPTION: Evergreen, epiphytic fern; leafstalks and underside of leaves covered with copious scales; rhizome creeping, scaly.
RANGE-HABITAT: From se. MD, IL, MO, and se. KS, south to FL and TX; common throughout SC; limbs and crotches of large trees in any habitat with large, hardwood trees having a deep-grooved bark; grows on rocks in the mountains and piedmont.
COMMENTS: The common name comes from the curling of its leaves during prolonged drought. The lower side curls outward, giving it a dead appearance. After a few hours of rain, the leaf absorbs water, uncurls, and it is as alive and as green as ever. Evidence suggests that the scales on the underside of the leaf act as channels for supplementary water absorption and hasten the recovery process. Resurrection fern spreads from tree to tree by wind-borne spores; once established on a limb, it spreads by its creeping rhizome.

595. Salt marshes

595. Smooth cordgrass

Spartina alterniflora Loiseleur
        Spar-tì-na al-ter-ni-flò-ra
Poaceae (Grass Family)

DESCRIPTION: Facultative halophyte; rhizomatous perennial; reproduction primarily by spreading rhizomes; flowers August–October.
RANGE-HABITAT: Newfoundland south to FL, and west to TX; dominant plant (often essentially a monoculture) of intertidal salt marshes along the coast.
COMMENTS: Smooth cordgrass is a dominant salt marsh plant, covering vast areas and often excluding other species. Plants in the high salt marshes, especially along the edges of salt flats, may grow only 1′ tall (the short form), while in deep water along the edges of tidal creeks it may grow 8′ tall (the tall form). Smooth cordgrass is a facultative halophyte that can grow in brackish or freshwater systems, but it rarely does because it cannot compete with other species. It dominates the intertidal area because it is the only species that survives daily inundation of salt water.

Five major ecological roles have been assigned to salt marshes, in which smooth cordgrass plays the dominant role: formation of detritus, habitat for animals, stabilization of coastal substratum through spreading rhizomes, filtration of coastal runoff, and removal of organic waste.

596. Sea ox-eye

Borrichia frutescens (L.) Augustin de
    Candolle
    Bor-rích-i-a fru-tés-cens
    Asteraceae (Aster or Sunflower Family)

DESCRIPTION: Rhizomatous shrub, forming extensive colonies; little branched, 6″ to 4′ tall; leaves grayish, opposite, thick, somewhat fleshy; receptacle bracts hard and rigid, with sharp spine tips, remaining on plant throughout the winter; flowers May–September.

RANGE-HABITAT: Maritime strand from VA to the Florida Keys, west to TX; common throughout its range; brackish marshes, salt shrub thickets, salt marshes, salt flats, and often in vacant lots or along roadsides near the sea.

COMMENTS: The genus name honors Ole Borrich, 1626–1690, a Danish botanist.

597. Orach

Atriplex prostrata Boucher ex de Candolle
    Á-tri-plex pros-trà-ta
    Chenopodiaceae (Goosefoot Family)

DESCRIPTION: Annual herb with slightly angular, usually grooved stems; plant dark green, often purple-tinged throughout; lower leaves opposite, upper and medium leaves alternate; principal lower leaves ovate to triangular, mostly truncate at the base; separate male and female flowers on same plant; fruits enclosed by 2 spongy and thickened small bracts; flowers July–frost.

RANGE-HABITAT: Widespread in eastern North America, but also in western North America and Eurasia; common in SC; maritime strand in the upper edge of salt marshes and in brackish flats.

SIMILAR SPECIES: Occurring in the same habitats in the maritime strand is *A. arenaria* Nuttall. This species has principal lower leaves linear to lanceolate or elliptic, with wedge-shaped leaf bases.

COMMENTS: Throughout the summer the young leaves of *Atriplex* species are tender and pleasant to taste, either raw or cooked. Orach is high in vitamins and minerals.

SYNONYM: *Atriplex patula* L., in part—RAB

598. Saltmarsh aster

Aster tenuifolius L.
    Ás-ter te-nu-i-fò-li-us
    Asteraceae (Aster or Sunflower Family)

DESCRIPTION: Perennial herb, 1–4′ tall (commonly 1–2′) from slender, creeping rhizomes; few to many curved, slightly zigzag, spreading branches; flowers late August–November.

RANGE-HABITAT: NH to the FL Keys, and west along the Gulf Coast to se. TX; common in SC in the maritime strand; salt and brackish marshes, sand mud flats, salt shrub thickets, and dredged soil disposal sites.

COMMENTS: Saltmarsh aster is never a major ecological component of the salt marsh. It is generally found in a high marsh dominated by smooth cordgrass and becomes conspicuous only when it blooms. In dredged soil disposal sites along the Carolina coast, it grows more robustly and forms extensive stands.

599. Sea lavender

Limonium carolinianum (Walter) Britton
Li-mò-ni-um ca-ro-li-ni-à-num
Plumbaginaceae (Leadwort Family)

DESCRIPTION: Perennial herb, 6″ to 2′ tall, with basal rosette of leaves 2–10″ long; flowers about 0.13″ wide with white sepals and lavender to purple petals; flowers August–October.

RANGE-HABITAT: Newfoundland and Quebec south to FL, and west to MS and TX; common in the maritime strand; short salt marsh, edges of salt flats, edges of salt marsh thickets, interdune swales, and saline ditches.

COMMENTS: Salt glands on leaves and stems allow sea lavender to excrete excess salt water. It varies in size and vigor, depending on the habitat. It grows about 6–8″ high in salt flats and to 2′ high on the edge of salt shrub thickets.

TAXONOMY: *Limonium* is treated as a single, polymorphic species after Godfrey and Wooten (1981).

600. Sea myrtle; groundsel-tree; consumption weed

Baccharis halimifolia L.
Bác-cha-ris ha-li-mi-fò-li-a
Asteraceae (Aster or Sunflower Family)

DESCRIPTION: Freely branched shrub 3–9′ tall; leaves alternate, fleshy; larger leaves with few to several teeth, glandular-punctate; leaves tardily deciduous, with some hanging on throughout the winter; female plants have a satiny, white look in the fall from the mass of bristle-tipped achenes; male plants have a dull, yellow appearance; flowers and fruits September–October.

RANGE-HABITAT: From se. MA to s. FL, and west to TX, AR, and OK; in SC common throughout except in the mountains; salt shrub thickets, high salt marshes, brackish marshes, freshwater marshes, dune swales, fencerows, old fields, dredged disposal sites, pond margins, and other disturbed sites.

SIMILAR SPECIES: *B. glomeruliflora* Persoon is similar to *B. halimifolia*. *B. glomeruliflora* is strictly a coastal species and has not spread inland. The leaves of *glomeruliflora* are scarcely or not glandular-punctate, and the flowers are scattered along the leafy branches. In *B. halimifolia,* the flowers are at the end of the branches and the leaves are glandular-punctate. Their habitats overlap in the maritime strand and outer coastal plain.

COMMENTS: F. P. Porcher (1869) gives numerous medicinal uses of sea myrtle and states: "This plant is of undoubted value, and of very general use in popular practice in South Carolina, as a palliative and demulcent in consumption and cough." One of its common names is based on this use.

In the fall, during windy days in the maritime strand, it is not unusual for the air to be filled with the whitish achenes of sea myrtle. It is thought that sea myrtle was originally a coastal plant that spread throughout SC as a weed as disturbed areas increased.

601. Salt flats

602. Perennial glasswort

Salicornia virginica L.
Sa-li-cór-ni-a vir-gí-ni-ca
Chenopodiaceae (Goosefoot Family)

DESCRIPTION: Fleshy, smooth halophyte; perennial, somewhat woody; stems trailing or weakly arching to erect, rooting at the nodes and forming mats; this year's stem green, last year's stem tan; leaf blades reduced to scales; flowers inconspicuous, sunken in pits in the axils of a fleshy spike; flowers July–October.

RANGE-HABITAT: Common maritime plant from NH south to FL, west along the Gulf Coast to TX and the Yucatan and s. CA; salt flats, high salt marshes, and brackish marshes.

COMMENTS: Glasswort stems are filled with brine and make a pleasant salty salad. It also has been popular as a pickle, by first boiling the stems in their own salted-water then adding spiced oil or vinegar.

Along with saltwort, perennial glasswort is one of the few plants that can tolerate the high salinity of salt flats. The glasswort has fleshy tissue that is an adaptation that helps it cope with the high salinity of salt flats. Certain internal tissue cells increase in size or abundance, allowing for the additional storage of low-salinity water.

SYNONYM: *Sarcocornia perennis* (P. Miller) A.J. Scott—W

603. Saltwort

Batis maritima L.
Bá-tis ma-rí-ti-ma
Bataceae (Saltwort Family)

DESCRIPTION: Fleshy halophyte; perennial shrub; stems trailing and rooting at the nodes, forming dense patches from which arise erect, flowering branches; leaves opposite; flowers unisexual, on separate plants, small and obscure, crowded in fleshy spikes and solitary in the leaf axils; flowers June–July.

RANGE-HABITAT: SC to s. FL, west to TX; maritime strand; occasional; salt flats and high salt marshes.

COMMENTS: Along with glasswort, saltwort is one of the few species that can tolerate the high salinity of salt flats. Most manuals list saltwort as rare in SC; how-

ever, it is widespread along the coast, and a classification of occasional is justified.

604. Maritime shell forests

605. Godfrey's forestiera

Forestiera godfreyi L. C. Anderson
Fo-res-ti-èr-a gód-frey-i
Oleaceae (Olive Family)

DESCRIPTION: Deciduous shrub or small tree
3–6′ tall; main stem arching or leaning; occasionally a few branchlets develop enlarged
bases to become spinelike; leaves opposite,
simple; male and female flowers on separate
plants; flowers without petals in tight axillary
clusters; flowers mid-January–mid-February;
drupes dark blue, whitish, mature late
April–early May.

RANGE-HABITAT: Known from only three sites in coastal SC, one in GA, and from
n. FL; rare; mesic calcareous bluffs and shell deposits.

COMMENTS: Loran C. Anderson described this species in 1985, separating it from
F. acuminata and *F. pubescens* (Anderson, 1985). It honors Robert K. Godfrey
(1911–2000), a distinguished botanist at Tall Timbers Research, Inc. and Florida
State University. In his paper, Anderson cites J. H. Mellichamp's collections of
Forestiera from near Bluffton in Beaufort County in the 1800s, which Anderson
used in describing this species. The location of Mellichamp's population of *F.
godfreyi* near Bluffton is unknown. It seems likely, however, from Patrick D.
McMillan's research, that the original collection was made along the May River
on shell associated with Buzzard Island.

    In May of 1975, the first author collected a plant on a Native American shell
mound at the intersection of Townsend Creek and the North Edisto River in
Charleston County, but failed to recognize the specimen as a species of
Forestiera. In April of 1996, John F. Townsend and Patrick D. McMillan accompanied the author to the shell mound. The plant noted above was identified as *F.
godfreyi*. Two additional locations of this rare shrub have been located since
1996: a shell hummock along Two Sisters Creek in Colleton County and a shell
mound on Daws Island in Beaufort County, a Heritage Preserve.

    The genus honors Forestier, a physician of Saint-Quentin, deceased about 1820.

PROTECTION STATUS: State Endangered

606. Rough-leaved dogwood

Cornus asperifolia Michaux
Cór-nus as-pe-ri-fò-li-a
Cornaceae (Dogwood Family)

DESCRIPTION: Deciduous shrub to 16′ tall; pith white; leaves opposite, finely roughened above and below with forked, curling, appressed to spreading hairs; flowers May–June.

RANGE-HABITAT: From s. NC to e. FL; in SC in the coastal plain and maritime strand; most often associated with calcareous habitats such as natural or Native American shell deposits along the coast, limestone bluffs, and wet marl flats; common anywhere calcium-rich soils exist.

SIMILAR SPECIES: Rough-leaved dogwood is similar to swamp dogwood (*C. stricta* Lamarck, plate 145 in *WCL*), and their habitats overlap. The leaves of swamp dogwood are smooth above and hairless beneath, or with a few fine, short, straight, appressed hairs. The leaves of rough-leaved dogwood are finely roughened above, and the undersides have forked, curling, appressed to spreading hairs.

607. Indian-midden morning-glory

Ipomoea macrorhiza Michaux
I-po-moè-a ma-cro-rhì-za
Convolvulaceae (Morning-glory Family)

DESCRIPTION: Robust perennial vine with hairy, crinkled leaves, the lower leaves often 3-lobed; calyx hairy; flowers 3″ in diameter; corolla tubular, pale blue to white, throat purplish inside.

RANGE-HABITAT: From se. NC south to FL, and west to s. AL; in SC presently known from one location, a shell hummock in Beaufort County along Mackay Creek south of Buckingham Landing.

SIMILAR SPECIES: Indian-midden morning-glory is separated from *I. pandurata* (plate 662) by its hairy, crinkled leaves and hairy calyx. The leaves and calyx of *I. pandurata* are hairless.

COMMENTS: It only blooms at night and early in the morning.

According to Small (1927), Native Americans, who cultivated the plant for its hugh, starchy tubers, may have introduced it into the Carolinas from further south.

PROTECTION STATUS: State Endangered

608. Tough bumelia

Bumelia tenax (L.) Willdenow
Bu-mè-li-a tè-nax
Sapotaceae (Sapodilla Family)

DESCRIPTION: Small scrubby tree or shrub growing to 30′ tall; bark thick, fissured, reddish brown; branches armed with stout thorns; twigs tough, flexible; leaves oblanceolate, with rounded tips; underside of leaves covered with appressed silky-rust to coppery-gold hairs; fruit a drupe-like berry, mature September–October.

RANGE-HABITAT: From se. NC to c. peninsular FL; confined to the outer coastal plain and maritime strand; maritime forests, dunes, sandy pinelands, and shell deposits; common in SC.

COMMENTS: Some birds and mammals eat the fruits and seeds. The wood has no commercial value because of the plant's small size.

SYNONYM: *Sideroxylon tenax* L.—W

609. Carolina buckthorn

Rhamnus caroliniana Walter
Rhám-nus ca-ro-li-ni-à-na
Rhamnaceae (Buckthorn Family)

DESCRIPTION: Slow-growing, short-lived shrub or small tree, to 30–40′ tall; leaves deciduous, but some often remaining through the winter; parallel veins from the midrib of the lower leaf surface are prominent, evenly spaced; leaves with skunklike odor when crushed; fruits turning red, then black, mature September–October.

RANGE-HABITAT: From sw. VA, west to OH and s. MO, south to FL and TX; common in SC in the piedmont associated with basic rock in moist deciduous woods; rare in the coastal plain on limestone bluffs and in the maritime strand on shell deposits.

COMMENTS: Many birds eat the sweet fruits. The wood has no commercial value.

SYNONYM: *Frangula caroliniana* (Walter) Gray—W

610. Shell-mound buckthorn

Sageretia minutiflora (Michaux) Mohr
Sa-ge-rè-ti-a mi-nu-ti-flò-ra
Rhamnaceae (Buckthorn Family)

DESCRIPTION: Sprawling, weak-stemmed shrub to 10′ tall, with many short, thornlike branches; leaves opposite or nearly so; flowers very fragrant, flowering in August–October; fruit drupe-like, purplish black when mature, persistent over winter and maturing in the spring.

RANGE-HABITAT: From se. NC to s. FL, and west to MS; in SC in the maritime strand; shell deposits; in FL inland on high-calcium hardwood hummocks and limestone.

SIMILAR SPECIES: Shell-mound buckthorn can be easily mistaken for *Ilex vomito-ria* (plate 590), with which it typically grows. The leaves of buckthorn are oppo-site or nearly so; the leaves of Ilex are alternate.

COMMENTS: Shell-mound buckthorn is probably more abundant than is indi-cated by manuals but is certainly not common. Botanists have observed it on numerous sites along the coast, especially on shell deposits. It has the habit of draping over other vegetation, but it is not a woody vine. Its weak stems appar-ently give buckthorn the flexibility to survive the wind and water surge of coastal hurricanes.

The photograph shows the fruits just prior to maturity. A photograph of the mature fruit is not available.

THE RUDERAL COMMUNITIES

611. Common chickweed

Stellaria media (L.) Cyrillo
Stel-là-ri-a mè-di-a
Caryophyllaceae (Pink Family)

DESCRIPTION: Herbaceous, prostrate or creep-ing annual, 3–8″ tall; usually dying com-pletely by June; weak-stemmed and many-branched; stems with hairs in lines; leaves opposite; 5 petals, each deeply cleft; flowers January–May, but occasionally throughout the year.
RANGE-HABITAT: Greenland to e. TX; common throughout SC; lawns, fields, gardens, meadows, and along roadsides; it often invades natural communities but not to the exclusion of native vegetation.
COMMENTS: Chickweed is naturalized from Eurasia. It has long been used as a potherb, with only the young, tender, growing tips being eaten. It is a favorite food of chickens and wild birds. Duke (1997) recommends chickweed as an herbal remedy for the treatment of obesity.

612. Henbit

Lamium amplexicaule L.
Là-mi-um am-plex-i-caù-le
Lamiaceae (Mint Family)

DESCRIPTION: Winter annual to 14″ tall; stems soft, 4-angled, with freely branched ends; flowering stem ends erect; leaves roundish to ovate, opposite, often shallowly 3-lobed; flower clusters subtended by a pair of sessile, leaflike bracts, ascending or horizontal; flow-ers mid-winter-May.
RANGE-HABITAT: Common weed of eastern North America and the Pacific Coast; throughout SC; pastures, abandoned fields, lawns, gardens, and almost any other disturbed site.
COMMENTS: Henbit is naturalized from Europe. The young plants have been used as a potherb in the US and Japan. Kingsbury (1964) reports that it caused "staggers" in sheep, cattle, and horses. Eating large quantities is not recom-mended.

613. Common shepherd's purse

Capsella bursa-pastoris (L.) Medicus
    Cap-sél-la búr-sa-pas-tò-ris
Brassicaceae (Mustard Family)

DESCRIPTION: Winter annual with one main stem and ascending branches; flowers white, in a raceme to 12″ long in fruit; leaves basal and on the stem, reduced upwards; fruits the shape of a shepherd's purse; seeds reddish brown; flowers February–June, or all year if weather permits.

RANGE-HABITAT: Introduced from Europe and now a cosmopolitan and ubiquitous weed; throughout SC; fields, lawns, along roadsides, and in many other disturbed habitats.

COMMENTS: James and Patricia Pietrepaolo (1986) describe shepherd's purse seeds as carnivorous. The seeds produce chemicals that attract protozoans, nematodes, and motile bacteria in its environment. The seeds produce toxins that kill the organisms, and enzymes are secreted that digest the animal protein.

    Numerous sources refer to the plant's ability to stop bleeding. F. P. Porcher (1869) reports the juice of the plant, when placed on a cotton ball, was used to plug nostrils to stop nosebleeds. Dried or fresh herb tea, made from the seeds and leaves, was used to allay profuse menstrual bleeding. The dried plant was also a useful styptic against hemorrhage. The dried, ground seeds can be used as a substitute for pepper, and the young leaves can be cooked like spinach.

614. Mock strawberry; Indian strawberry

Duchesnea indica (Andrzejowski) Focke
    Du-chès-ne-a ín-di-ca
Rosaceae (Rose Family)

DESCRIPTION: Low, trailing, perennial herb with stolons; leaves trifoliolate; flowers and fruits February–frost; fruit an aggregate of achenes embedded in a red, fleshy receptacle.

RANGE-HABITAT: CT south to northern FL, and west to OK; naturalized and common throughout SC; lawns, pastures, open woods, and along roadsides.

COMMENTS: According to some sources (e.g., Strausbaugh and Core, 1977), this species was introduced from India. Although the fruits appear edible, they are flat and tasteless. It is not a true strawberry, which belongs to the genus *Fragaria*. The genus name honors Antoine Duchesne, 1747–1827, an early monographer of *Fragaria*.

615. Common dandelion

Taraxacum officinale Wiggers
Ta-ráx-a-cum of-fi-ci-nà-le
Asteraceae (Aster or Sunflower Family)

DESCRIPTION: Perennial herb; root thick, deep, bitter; milky juice present; leaves basal, deeply and irregularly lobed and toothed; flowering stalks hollow, erect, 2–18″ tall; flowers late February–June.

RANGE-HABITAT: Naturalized nearly throughout the US and s. Canada; throughout SC; lawns, pastures, vacant lots, fallow fields, and along roadsides.

COMMENTS: Common dandelion is a native of Eurasia. In the Old and New World, the leaves have been/are used as a potherb, and the ground roots can be used to make a palatable, bitter drink. The roots can be cooked for food, and a strong wine can be made from the flowers and leaves.

The specific epithet *officinale,* meaning "of the shops," indicates the medicinal uses of this versatile plant. For examples, it is used as a laxative and to alleviate symptoms of arthritis.

616. Creamy wild indigo

Baptisia bracteata Elliott
Bap-tí-si-a brac-te-à-ta
Fabaceae (Pea or Bean Family)

DESCRIPTION: Rhizomatous, perennial herb, 12–24″ tall; plant softly hairy; leaves 3-foliolate; flowers in drooping, one-sided racemes; corolla pale yellow or cream; flowers March–April.

RANGE-HABITAT: From ne. AL through n. GA and n. SC, to w. NC; in SC in the piedmont, sandhills, and inner coastal plain; sandy, dry woods, sandhills, and along roadsides that pass through these habitats; occasional.

617. Early winter-cress; creasy

Barbarea verna (Miller) Ascherson
Bar-ba-rè-a vér-na
Brassicaceae (Mustard Family)

DESCRIPTION: Erect herb to 32″ tall; leaves pinnately dissected, each with 4–10 pairs of lateral lobes; leaf stalks ciliate; flowers March–June.

RANGE-HABITAT: Naturalized practically throughout the US; common throughout SC; along roadsides and in fields and disturbed areas.

SIMILAR SPECIES: *B. verna* is similar to *B. vulgaris* R. Brown. *B. verna* has basal leaves with 4–10 pairs of lateral lobes. *B. vulgaris* has basal leaves with 1–4 pairs of lateral lobes.

COMMENTS: Winter-cress is naturalized from Eurasia. The young foliage and new young stems, while still tender, are a good potherb. They should be cooked twice, or more, in water. The first water removes the strongest bitters. To the people of the mountains and upper piedmont who eat the plant, it is known as "creasy."

618. Yellow thistle

Cirsium horridulum Michaux
Cír-si-um hor-rí-du-lum
Asteraceae (Aster or Sunflower Family)

DESCRIPTION: Biennial herb to 5′ tall; stems covered with cobweb-like hairs; leaves spiny on the margin, pinnately lobed, stalkless, and clasping the stem; flowering heads subtended by a series of narrow, spiny-toothed bracts; corolla light yellow to purple; flowers late March–early June.

RANGE-HABITAT: ME south to FL, and west to TX; common throughout SC (except the mountains); longleaf pine savannas, along roadsides, in fields, meadows, and other waste places.

COMMENTS: This is a native species that has successfully exploited disturbed sites.

TAXONOMY: Two forms occur, yellow flowered and purple flowered; the former is restricted to the coastal plain, the latter grows throughout SC.

SYNONYM: *Carduus spinosissimus* Walter—RAB

619. Fumitory; earth-smoke

Fumaria officinalis L.
Fu-mà-ri-a of-fi-ci-nà-lis
Fumariaceae (Fumitory Family)

DESCRIPTION: Erect, branching, annual herb; stem and branches 8–40″ long; leaves finely dissected; flowers in racemes; corolla purplish and crimson at the tip; one petal with a spur at base; flowers March–May.

RANGE-HABITAT: Naturalized from Europe and widespread in the eastern US; in SC in the maritime strand and coastal plain; fields and waste places, and along roadsides; somewhat local and not common.

COMMENTS: The specific epithet *officinalis* means "of the shops," in reference to its early repute in medicine. The genus name comes from the Latin words *fumus*, "smoke," and *terrae,* "of the earth." The smoke names apparently have many explanations. One alludes to the gray-green color of the plant that from a distance has a smoky appearance. Another explanation is in reference to the nitrous odor of the roots when they are first pulled from the ground.

620. False-garlic

Nothoscordum bivalve (L.) Britton
No-thos-cór-dum bi-vál-ve
Liliaceae (Lily Family)

DESCRIPTION: Perennial herb from a small, onionlike bulb; bulb without onionlike odor; flowering stalks 6–18″ tall; leaves basal, linear, flat; flowers March–May.

RANGE-HABITAT: From se. VA west to south OH and KS, and south to FL, TX and South America; common throughout SC (except in the mountains); around granite flatrocks, in glades and barrens, open woodlands, fields, lawns, pastures, and along roadsides.

SYNONYM: *Allium bivalve* (L.) Kuntze—RAB

621. Common toadflax

Nuttallanthus canadensis (L.) D. A. Sutton
Nut-tall-án-thus ca-na-dén-sis
Scrophulariaceae (Figwort Family)

DESCRIPTION: Winter annual or biennial herb; erect, flowering stems to 30″ tall; stems slender, with linear, alternate leaves; numerous prostrate stems, with opposite leaves, radiate from the base of a upright stem; conspicuous spur projects down from the corolla; flowers March–May.

RANGE-HABITAT: Common throughout the US; throughout SC; in a wide variety of natural and disturbed habitats such as fallow fields, roadsides, lawns, pastures, and vacant lots.

COMMENTS: Weakley (2001) states that it is probably native in thin soils of rock outcrops. Toadflax and sourgrass (*Rumex hastatalis,* plate 626) often grow together in fallow fields where they form a colorful mix of red and blue. Both species are native but weedy. The genus honors Thomas Nuttall, 1786–1859, an English naturalist who collected North American plants.

SYNONYM: *Linaria canadensis* (L.) Dumont—RAB

622. Running five-fingers

Potentilla canadensis L.
 Po-ten-tíl-la ca-na-dén-sis
 Rosaceae (Rose Family)

DESCRIPTION: Low, stoloniferous perennial with short, usually erect, rhizomes; stolons elongating to 20″ or more; leaves palmately compound with 5 leaflets; flowers solitary on axillary stalks from the stolons; first flower is in the axil of first fully developed leaf or of an undeveloped leaf below it; flowers March–May.

RANGE-HABITAT: Nova Scotia to Ontario, south to GA, west to TN, MO, and OH; throughout SC; upland woodland borders, pastures, lawns, disturbed sites, and along roadsides.

SIMILAR SPECIES: Similar is *P. simplex* Michaux, which has the first flower in the axil of the second fully developed leaf. It occurs through SC in similar habitats and flowers April–June.

COMMENTS: Native Americans used a tea of the pounded roots as an astringent to treat diarrhea.

623. Chickasaw plum

Prunus angustifolia Marshall
 Prù-nus an-gus-ti-fò-li-a
 Rosaceae (Rose Family)

DESCRIPTION: Shrub or small tree to 15′ tall; forming thickets by means of root suckers; stems slightly zigzag, with short lateral twigs often ending as a thorn; leaves deciduous, developing after the flowers, with marginal teeth tipped with red glands that may fall with age, leaving a scar; flowers white, solitary, or in clusters from twigs of previous year; flowers (February) March–April; drupes red or yellow, mature in May–early July.

RANGE-HABITAT: Throughout the southeastern and midsouthern US; common throughout SC (except absent from the mountains); fencerows, roadsides, pastures, old fields, woodland borders, and around abandoned house sites.

SIMILAR SPECIES: Chickasaw plum can be separated from hog plum (*P. umbellata*, plate 429) by its gland-tipped teeth on the margin of the leaves; hog plum has glands at the base of the leaf blade, but no glands on the leaf margins.

COMMENTS: Chickasaw plum is a weedy native shrub. The ripe fruits are used for sauces, pies, preserves, jams, and jellies. The fruits are an important food source for wildlife, including deer, bears, raccoons, squirrels, other mammals, and birds. The wood is too soft to be of commercial value. The thicket-forming habit of this plum makes it useful for erosion control and wildlife cover.

624. Wild radish; jointed charlock

Raphanus raphanistrum L.
Rá-pha-nus ra-pha-nís-trum
Brassicaceae (Mustard Family)

DESCRIPTION: Coarse winter annual from a taproot, to 2' tall; stems erect, freely branched, with bristle-like hairs; leaves reduced upward, with basal ones deeply dissected; petals sulfur yellow, distinctly veined, fading white (rarely purple); flowers March–June, and sporadically throughout rest of the year; fruit (a silique) constricted between seeds.

RANGE-HABITAT: Newfoundland to British Columbia, south to GA and KY, and west to TX and CA; common nearly throughout SC but less so in the mountains; cultivated fields, roadsides, and most other disturbed areas.

COMMENTS: Wild radish is naturalized from Mediterranean Europe. Kingsbury (1964) states that wild radish has been considered dangerous to livestock in Europe and the US.

625. Cherokee rose

Rosa laevigata Michaux
Rò-sa lae-vi-gà-ta
Rosaceae (Rose Family)

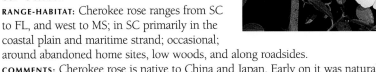

DESCRIPTION: Robust, high-climbing, evergreen vine; leaves trifoliolate; leaflets with prickles on larger veins; prickles on stems curved, flattened, with a broad base; flowers late March–April; hip red, maturing September–October.

RANGE-HABITAT: Cherokee rose ranges from SC to FL, and west to MS; in SC primarily in the coastal plain and maritime strand; occasional; around abandoned home sites, low woods, and along roadsides.

COMMENTS: Cherokee rose is native to China and Japan. Early on it was naturalized in the South. It was first described from plants collected in America, and it is the state flower of·GA.

626. Sourgrass; wild sorrel

Rumex hastatulus Baldwin ex Elliott
Rù-mex has-tá-tu-lus
Polygonaceae (Buckwheat Family)

DESCRIPTION: Annual or short-lived perennial to 4' tall; leaves arrow-shaped with spreading, basal lobes; stems single or in large clumps; male and female flowers on separate plants; flowers March–May.

RANGE-HABITAT: FL to TX, and north to MA and KS; a native species that has become weedy and is common throughout SC; sandy fields, roadsides, vacant lots, lawns, and sandy, open woods.

SIMILAR SPECIES: A similar species is sheep-sorrel (*R. acetosella* L.), which occurs throughout SC in similar habitats. Sheep-sorrel is a perennial with rhizomes, while sourgrass lacks rhizomes.

COMMENTS: A native of the southeast, sourgrass often grows in association with common toadflax (plate 621) in fallow fields, where these two species form a colorful mix of red and blue. The stem of sourgrass has an acid taste and is often chewed as a trail nibble. Eating large amounts, however, can result in poisoning because of the oxalates present.

627. Prickly sow-thistle

Sonchus asper (L.) Hill
   Són-chus ás-per
Asteraceae (Aster or Sunflower Family)

DESCRIPTION: Herbaceous, winter annual, 1–6′ tall; stems smooth, erect; leaves alternate, lobed or undivided, prickly edged, bases rounded with an ear-shaped lobe; milky juice present; flowers March–July.

RANGE-HABITAT: Throughout the US; common throughout SC; along roadsides, and in fields, vacant lots, lawns, and meadows.

SIMILAR SPECIES: *S. oleraceus* L., common sow-thistle, is similar but has leaf bases shaped like an arrowhead. It is common in the coastal plain, maritime strand, and piedmont in the same habitats.

COMMENTS: Prickly sow-thistle is naturalized from the Old World. The fleshy leaves can be used as a potherb.

628. Stiff verbena

Verbena rigida Sprengel
   Ver-bè-na rí-gi-da
Verbenaceae (Vervain Family)

DESCRIPTION: Erect perennial 4–28″ tall, with elongate, underground stolons; often forming large patches; stems and leaves rough-hairy; leaves opposite, simple; spikes stiffly erect; flowers late March–July.

RANGE-HABITAT: VA to FL, and west to TX; in SC from the lower piedmont to the maritime strand; along roadsides, and in fields, pastures, and other waste places.

COMMENTS: Stiff verbena was introduced from South America. It is drought resistant and makes an attractive ornamental.

629. Narrow-leaved vetch; common vetch

Vicia angustifolia Richard
Ví-ci-a an-gus-ti-fò-li-a
Fabaceae (Pea or Bean Family)

DESCRIPTION: Annual herb with decumbent to ascending stems, more or less climbing; leaves pinnately compound with the terminal leaflet usually modified into a branched tendril (clearly seen in the photograph); flowers March–June.

RANGE-HABITAT: Nearly throughout the eastern US; common throughout SC; along roadsides and fencerows, and in lawns, fields, and other waste places.

COMMENTS: Narrow-leaved vetch was introduced from Europe. The seeds of vetches, like many members of the legume family, are an important source of food for animals. It is occasionally used for forage. Species of vetches, many cultivated, have occasionally been reported as producing disease or loss of life in livestock and humans (Kingsbury, 1964).

630. Wild-pansy; Johnny-jump-up

Viola rafinesquii Greene
Ví-o-la ra-fi-nés-qui-i
Violaceae (Violet Family)

DESCRIPTION: Winter annual, about 4–6″ tall; stems simple or branched above; leaves taper gradually into the stem, with large stipules cleft into narrow lobes (like a cock's-comb); lower 3 petals with purple veins; flowers March–April.

RANGE-HABITAT: Widely distributed over the southeast; common throughout SC; along roads, and in lawns, pastures, and other disturbed sites.

COMMENTS: Strausbaugh and Core (1977) consider wild-pansy native to America. Fernald (1950), and others, believe it is naturalized from Eurasia. It often forms dense but ephemeral populations, especially along roadsides. The specific epithet honors Constantine Samuel Rafinesque-Schmaltz, 1757–1817, a self-taught naturalist from Italy who collected in the US. The root contains methyl salicylate, which imparts a wintergreen smell and taste.

631. Mimosa; silk tree

Albizzia julibrissin Durazzini
Al-bíz-zi-a ju-li-brís-sin
Fabaceae (Pea or Bean Family)

DESCRIPTION: Small, flat-topped tree with large, bipinnately compound and feather-like leaves; to about 40′ tall; leaves and leaflets droop as light diminishes; flowers are clustered in fluffy, pink heads; flowers April–May.

RANGE-HABITAT: Essentially throughout the southeastern states; common throughout SC; in a variety of disturbed sites such as roadsides and woodland borders, and around abandoned house sites; generally absent above about 3000′.

COMMENTS: Mimosa is cultivated for its wide-spreading crown, showy flowers, and graceful leaves. It is native to Asia and was introduced by André Michaux. It has become a serious weed in the southeast. The genus honors Filippo degli Albizzi, who, two centuries ago, introduced this genus into European cultivation. Fernald (1950) states the correct spelling should be *Albizzia*.

632. Alligator-weed

Alternanthera philoxeroides (Martius) Grisebach
Al-ter-nán-the-ra phi-lox-e-roì-des
Amaranthaceae (Amaranth Family)

DESCRIPTION: Emersed, perennial, aquatic herb with creeping stems, rooting at the nodes or free floating in mats; stems to 3′ long and forming dense mats; flowers April–October.

RANGE-HABITAT: From VA to TX; in SC chiefly a coastal plain and maritime strand species; common; various freshwater habitats such as tidal freshwater marshes, ditches, ponds, and swamps.

COMMENTS: Alligator-weed is native to South America and was introduced into the US in the early 1950s. One source states that viable seeds have not been found in the US and that reproduction is only by vegetative means. It grows in a wide range of water and soil conditions. Mats of the plant can quickly block canals and ditches, reducing water flow and boat movement. Wildlife do not feed on alligator-weed.

633. Corn chamomille

Anthemis arvensis L.
Án-the-mis ar-vén-sis
Asteraceae (Aster or Sunflower Family)

DESCRIPTION: Hairy annual or biennial; plant about 1′ tall; stems often decumbent at base; leaves alternate, finely 1–2 bipinnately or tripinnately dissected; ray and disk flowers fertile; flowers late April–July.

RANGE-HABITAT: Naturalized over most of the US and native to Europe; essentially throughout SC in fields, pastures, waste places, and along roadsides.

634. Bachelor's button; cornflower

Centaurea cyanus L.
Cen-tau-rè-a cy-à-nus
Asteraceae (Aster or Sunflower Family)

DESCRIPTION: Erect, freely branched winter annual, 12–32″ tall; heads usually numerous; upper leaves linear, unlobed, entire to dentate; flowers blue, less frequently pink, purple, or white; flowers April–June.

RANGE-HABITAT: From VA south to GA; in SC along roadsides, and in fields and waste places throughout the piedmont, sandhills, and inner coastal plain; rare in the mountains and unreported from the maritime strand and extreme outer coastal plain.

COMMENTS: Cornflower is naturalized from Mediterranean Europe.

635. Ox-eye daisy

Chrysanthemum leucanthemum L.
Chry-sán-the-mum leu-cán-the-mum
Asteraceae (Aster or Sunflower Family)

DESCRIPTION: Perennial herb to 3′ tall, with short rhizomes; leaves alternate, the numerous basal leaves usually pinnately lobed or cleft; flower heads one or a few per stalk; flowers April–August.

RANGE-HABITAT: Throughout the US; throughout SC, although less frequent in the southern part of SC; along roadsides, around buildings, in waste places, lawns, old fields, pastures, and meadows.

COMMENTS: Ox-eye daisy was introduced from Europe and has become widely naturalized. It is used as an ornamental but can become a serious invasive pest. This species often dominates fields and, if eaten by cattle, can impart an unwanted flavor to milk.

636. Heliotrope

Heliotropium amplexicaule M. Vahl
He-li-o-trò-pi-um am-plex-i-caù-le
Boraginaceae (Borage Family)

DESCRIPTION: Perennial herb from a strong root; stems several, spreading, creeping or ascending to 20″ tall; plant glandular-hairy; leaves alternate; flowers April–September.

RANGE-HABITAT: NC to FL, west to TX; in SC in the piedmont, coastal plain, and maritime strand; occasional; along city roadsides, in cultivated fields, abandoned lots, and other disturbed areas.

COMMENTS: Small (1933) states that it is naturalized from South America. The genus name comes from the Greek *helios,* "the sun," and *trope,* "a turn." Ancient writers believed the flowers turn to follow the sun.

637. Spotted cat's-ear

Hypochoeris radicata L.
    Hy-po-choè-ris ra-di-cà-ta
    Asteraceae (Aster or Sunflower Family)

DESCRIPTION: Perennial herb without a leafy stem; flowering stems 12–24″ tall; leaves basal, pinnately lobed or dissected; flowering heads 2–7, rarely more; flowers April–July and sporadically later.

RANGE-HABITAT: Newfoundland to Ontario, and south to NC and IL; also in the Pacific states; in SC common in the northern counties; along roadsides, in fields, lawns, and waste places.

SIMILAR SPECIES: *H. glabra* L. is similar to *H. radicata*. *H. glabra* is naturalized throughout the piedmont, sandhills, coastal plain, and maritime strand in similar disturbed places. *H. radicata* is conspicuously hairy, while *H. glabra* is glabrous or apparently so.

COMMENTS: Spotted cat's-ear is naturalized from Eurasia.

638. Japanese honeysuckle

Lonicera japonica Thunberg
    Lo-níc-er-a ja-pó-ni-ca
    Caprifoliaceae (Honeysuckle Family)

DESCRIPTION: Left to right twining, woody vine with opposite, evergreen leaves; often climbing to 30′ or more; flowers April–June, and sporadically into September; berry black, maturing in August–October.

RANGE-HABITAT: MA, NY, and OH, south to FL, and west to TX and KS; common throughout SC; in almost any disturbed habitat including woodlands, fields, fencerows, thickets, abandoned buildings, and along railroad banks.

COMMENTS: Honeysuckle is naturalized from Japan and quickly invades any disturbed opening in native woodlands, sometimes replacing native flora. Birds carry the seeds, which allows it to spread rapidly. When pulled free of the flower, a sweet nectar can be sucked from the base of the stigma/style.

639. China-berry; pride-of-India

Melia azedarach L.
    Mé-li-a a-zé-da-rach
    Meliaceae (Mahogany Family)

DESCRIPTION: Small to medium size tree, fast growing but short lived; stems aromatic; leaves alternate, bipinnately compound; inflorescence a panicle; flowers April–May; fruits yellow, ripe September–October.

RANGE-HABITAT: Throughout the southeast and HI; common throughout SC, except at high altitudes; woodland borders and fencerows, around abandoned homes, and in vacant lots and old fields.

COMMENTS: A native of southwest Asia, André Michaux introduced China-berry into America, planting it in his Charleston garden. From this and other gardens, it escaped and became naturalized. China-berry quickly came to have many uses for plantation slaves and colonists. It was used as a vermifuge to expel worms from the body, and broken branches were placed in a house to keep out fleas. Its use as a fleabane is based on chemicals in the wood that repulse insects. Both the green and ripe fruits of China-berry are poisonous, although poisoning is rare because of the bitter taste of the fruits. Birds eat the fruits, causing a mild intoxication and temporary paralysis if too many are consumed. The fruits and wood have been used medicinally for their narcotic and vermin-killing properties. A complete account of the poisonous nature of China-berry can be found in Kingsbury (1964).

640. Princess tree

Paulownia tomentosa (Thunberg) Steudel & Zuccarini ex Steudel
Pau-lòw-ni-a to-men-tò-sa
Scrophulariaceae (Figwort Family)

DESCRIPTION: Fast-growing, small to medium size tree; leaves deciduous, opposite, ovate, entire or slightly lobed, 6–12″ long; flowers appear before the leaves, in April–May; capsules mature September–October.

RANGE-HABITAT: Throughout the eastern US as far north as Boston, MA, and west to TX; widely scattered throughout SC; along roadsides and fencerows and in waste places and open woodlands.

COMMENTS: Princess tree is native to central China and was introduced into North America in 1834 as an ornamental tree because of its large, upright clusters of purple flowers. It has spread readily from cultivation along roadsides and streamsides because its tiny, winged seeds are blown a considerable distance. Its ability to invade native woodlands is a serious concern. It has been cultivated in Japan for several hundred years for use in making wooden shoes and expensive dower chests. The genus honors Anna Paulowna, 1795–1865, a princess of the Netherlands.

641. Annual phlox

Phlox drummondii Hooker
Phlóx drum-mónd-i-i
Polemoniaceae (Phlox Family)

DESCRIPTION: Erect, herbaceous annual, 4–28″ tall; stems glandular-hairy; lowermost leaves opposite, others alternate; flowers rose-red, pink, white or variegated depending on the cultivar; flowers April–July.

RANGE-HABITAT: Native of TX that has escaped eastward into FL and se. VA, and north at least into se. MO; in SC chiefly the coastal plain and maritime strand; common around abandoned house sites, in lawns, stable dune areas, meadows, and along sandy roadsides.

COMMENTS: There are numerous cultivated forms of annual phlox. The different forms are often found growing together, especially around abandoned house sites. Plants in SC are the progeny of various cultivars derived from hybrids and selections of the wild taxa (Weakley, 2001).

642. English plantain

Plantago lanceolata L.
    Plan-tà-go lan-ce-o-là-ta
Plantaginaceae (Plantain Family)

DESCRIPTION: Stemless, perennial herb with a basal cluster of long, narrow, strongly ribbed leaves; flowering stalks solid, 5-angled, 4–20″ tall; flowers in dense, cylindrical heads; flowers April–frost.

RANGE-HABITAT: Throughout the US; common throughout SC; waste areas, including lawns, vacant lots, pastures, fields, and along roadsides and railroads.

COMMENTS: English plantain is naturalized from Europe. It is often a troublesome weed in lawns. Birds eat the seeds, and the leaves are food for rabbits. Duke (1997) recommends all plantago species as an herbal remedy for obesity and hemorrhoids.

643. American heal-all

Prunella vulgaris var. *lanceolata*
    (W. Barton) Fernald
    Pru-nél-la vul-gà-ris var. lan-ce-o-là-ta
Lamiaceae (Mint Family)

DESCRIPTION: Perennial herb to 6–12″ tall, with short branches anywhere below the central inflorescence; stems 4-angled, leaves opposite; flowers in globose spikes, but spikes becoming cylindrical as fruits mature; flowers April–frost.

RANGE-HABITAT: Newfoundland west to AR, and south to NC, SC, TN, MO, KS, NM, AZ, and CA; common throughout SC; along roadsides, and in lawns, fields, yards, pastures, and gardens.

COMMENTS: As the common names suggest, this plant has been used for a variety of folk remedies in the belief it could cure all ailments. For example, an infusion of the flowers and leaves has been used as a gargle for sore throat. Duke (1997) recommends its use as an herbal remedy for hyperthyroidism. With repeated mowing or grazing, the plants become stunted and matted, flowering when only 2″ tall.

TAXONOMY: The typical form of heal-all, *P. vulgaris* L. var. *vulgaris*, Eurasian heal-all, was naturalized early on from Europe. American heal-all, var. *lanceolata*, is listed as growing in the same area as the typical variety. They differ as follows: var. *lanceolata* has main or median stem leaves lanceolate to oblong and wedge-shaped at the base; var. *vulgaris* has principal or median stem leaves ovate to ovate-oblong, and broadly rounded at the base.

644. False-dandelion

Pyrrhopappus carolinianus (Walter) Augustin de Candolle
  Pyr-rho-páp-pus ca-ro-li-ni-à-nus
Asteraceae (Aster or Sunflower Family)

DESCRIPTION: Annual or short-lived perennial, with milky juice, from well-developed taproot; to 4′ tall; basal leaves pinnately lobed or dissected to merely toothed; upper leaves reduced; heads often solitary; flowers April–June.

RANGE-HABITAT: DE to KS, and south to FL and TX; common throughout its range and throughout SC (but less common in the mountains); along roadsides, and in pastures, fallow and cultivated fields, lawns and meadows.

645. Bulbous buttercup

Ranunculus bulbosus L.
  Ra-nùn-cu-lus bul-bò-sus
Ranunculaceae (Buttercup Family)

DESCRIPTION: Erect perennial, 1–2′ tall, from a corm-like base; basal leaves 1–4″ wide, stalked, cut into 3-lobed or cleft parts; stem leaves smaller, fewer; flowers April–June.

RANGE-HABITAT: Naturalized throughout North America; in SC chiefly in the mountains and piedmont; along roadsides, and in fields, gardens, lawns, and meadows; common.

COMMENTS: Bulbous buttercup is naturalized from Europe. Kingsbury (1964) reports that when eaten fresh several species of buttercups, including *R. bulbosus,* are poisonous to animals such as hogs or cattle.

646. Salt cedar; tamarisk

Tamarix gallica L.
  Tá-ma-rix gál-li-ca
Tamaricaceae (Tamarisk Family)

DESCRIPTION: Shrub with evergreen, scalelike, green leaves; branches flexible; flowers April–July.

RANGE-HABITAT: Throughout much of the eastern US and to a lesser extent into the western states; in SC generally confined to the maritime strand; occasional and locally abundant; sandy roadsides, dredged soil disposal sites, old fields, and brackish areas.

COMMENTS: Salt cedar is naturalized from Europe. The common name, salt cedar, refers to its coastal distribution and its small, leafy twigs resembling forms of southern red cedar. Salt cedar is a flowering plant (angiosperm) not a conifer (gymnosperm) like southern red cedar. Salt cedar is cultivated as an ornamental and is used for windscreens and erosion control.

647. Rabbit foot clover

Trifolium arvense L.
    Tri-fò-li-um ar-vén-se
    Fabaceae (Pea or Bean Family)

DESCRIPTION: Annual herb, 6–18″ tall; stems silky-hairy; leaves palmately 3-foliolate; flowers in heads; sepals covered with soft, long hairs that obscure the small petals; flowers April–August.

RANGE-HABITAT: Widely naturalized and common from Quebec to the Pacific Coast, and south to FL; common throughout SC; along roadsides, and in dry fields and other waste places.

COMMENTS: The common name refers to the clusters of soft, cylindrical, flower heads, simulating a rabbit's foot. Intestinal irritation may result in animals that eat the mature heads; "hair balls" form and cause irritation. This clover was introduced from Europe (Strausbaugh and Core, 1977). The flowers are often used to make a dried bouquet.

648. Crimson clover

Trifolium incarnatum L.
    Tri-fò-li-um in-car-nà-tum
    Fabaceae (Pea or Bean Family)

DESCRIPTION: Erect, annual herb, 8–16″ tall; plant softly downy; leaves palmately 3-foliolate; petals scarlet, deep red, or rarely white; flowers April–June.

RANGE-HABITAT: Widely naturalized in the southeastern US; common throughout SC; along roadsides and in fields.

COMMENTS: Crimson clover is naturalized from Eurasia. It is planted as fodder or green manure, along roads as a soil binder, and for its attractive flowers. The fibrous calyx from overripe flowers may be dangerous to horses because it may become impacted in their digestive tract.

649. Red clover

Trifolium pratense L.
    Tri-fò-li-um pra-tén-se
    Fabaceae (Pea or Bean Family)

DESCRIPTION: Biennial or short-lived perennial herb; 6–24″ tall; stems ascending, somewhat hairy; leaves 3-foliolate; leaflets marked on the upper side with a pale "V" spot; flowers in globose heads; flowers April–September.

RANGE-HABITAT: Naturalized nearly throughout temperate North America; common throughout SC (less so in the outer coastal plain); along roadsides, and in fields, lawns, and other open places.

COMMENTS: Red clover was introduced from Europe and cultivated as a hay and pasture crop. It is now widely naturalized. In past times red clover has been used for a variety of folk remedies. For example, a wash has been used as a cancer remedy, including the once-famous Hoxsey treatment. Science has not confirmed traditional uses although the plant contains many biologically active compounds. Fall or late-cut hay in large doses can cause frothing, diarrhea, dermatitis, and decreased milk production in cattle.

650. Venus' looking-glass

Triodanis perfoliata (L.) Nieuwland
Tri-o-dà-nis per-fo-li-à-ta
Campanulaceae (Bellwort Family)

DESCRIPTION: Herbaceous, winter annual, 8–40″ tall; stems erect, freely branched at base, unbranched above; leaves alternate, sessile and clasping; flowers sessile in leaf axils; lower flowers do not open and are self-pollinating; flowers April–June.

RANGE-HABITAT: From southern Ontario and Quebec, south to FL, and west to TX and to the Dakotas; common throughout SC; in dry fields and gardens, along roadsides, and in abandoned lots and lawns.

SIMILAR SPECIES: *T. biflora* (R. & P.) Greene is similar to and usually occurs mixed with *T. perfoliata*. Both species are unusual in dispersing their seeds through holes (pores) in the sides of the fruit (capsule). In *T. perfoliata* the pores of the capsule are at or below the middle, while in *T. biflora* the pores are near the top.

SYNONYM: *Specularia perfoliata* (L.) Alphonse de Candolle—RAB

651. Bigflower vetch

Vicia grandiflora Scopoli
Ví-ci-a gran-di-flò-ra
Fabaceae (Pea or Bean Family)

DESCRIPTION: Weakly climbing annual to 2′ tall; leaves alternate, pinnately compound with 6–14 leaflets and a weak, branched, terminal tendril; petals pale yellow or often suffused with purple; flowers April–June.

RANGE-HABITAT: DE to FL, and west to MS; throughout SC; occasional; along roadsides, and in fields, abandoned city lots, and other open, disturbed sites.

COMMENTS: Bigflower vetch is naturalized from Europe.

652. Florida betony; hedge-nettle

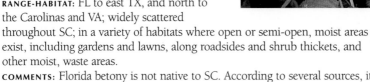

Stachys floridana Shuttleworth ex
    Bentham
    Stá-chys flo-ri-dà-na
    Lamiaceae (Mint Family)

DESCRIPTION: Rhizomatous perennial, 8–20″ tall; extensively colonial; rhizomes slender, becoming tuberous and thickened at intervals; stems square; leaves opposite, with long stalks; corolla whitish to pale pink, with purple spots and lines; flowers April–July.

RANGE-HABITAT: FL to east TX, and north to the Carolinas and VA; widely scattered throughout SC; in a variety of habitats where open or semi-open, moist areas exist, including gardens and lawns, along roadsides and shrub thickets, and other moist, waste areas.

COMMENTS: Florida betony is not native to SC. According to several sources, it was introduced from FL, apparently with nursery stock. It is a noxious weed in moist lawns and gardens and is very difficult to eradicate.

653. Wild leek

Allium ampeloprasum L.
    Ál-li-um am-pe-ló-pra-sum
    Liliaceae (Lily Family)

DESCRIPTION: Perennial, bulbous, scapose, herb; plant with odor of garlic; stems 3–4′ tall; leaves whitish, flat, free portion 12–24″ long, sheathing portion 0.5–2.5″ long, creating a leafy stem; umbel large, many flowered; perianth lavender; flowers May–early July.

RANGE-HABITAT: Naturalized from VA to FL; established widely throughout SC; abandoned home sites, roadsides, and other waste places; uncommon.

COMMENTS: Wild leek is naturalized from Eurasia. Fernald and Kinsey (1958) state that "it is a perfectly possible food for man." This is the only reference to its edibility.

654. Tree-of-heaven

Ailanthus altissima (Miller) Swingle
  Ai-lán-thus al-tís-si-ma
Simaroubaceae (Quassia Family)

DESCRIPTION: Fast-growing tree (up to 10′ in a season), but short-lived, growing to a maximum of 80′; often colonizing by root sprouts; leaves alternate, odd-pinnately compound, with 15–27 leaflets; leaflets entire except for 1–5 rounded, basal teeth, each with a prominent dark green gland beneath near the apex; male and female flowers on separate trees, on the same tree, or flowers perfect; flowers late May–early June; fruits mature July–October.

RANGE-HABITAT: Naturalized from MA and Ontario, south through the eastern US, and to a lesser degree from the southern Rocky Mountains to CA; common throughout SC; along railroad embankments and woodland borders, and in a variety of other waste areas.

COMMENTS: Tree-of-heaven was introduced from East Asia as an urban tree because of its rapid growth and ability to withstand the stresses of cities. However, it is difficult to eradicate because it spreads by winged seeds and root sprouts. It is a serious pest because it often colonizes wind-throw gaps in forests, where it replaces the native vegetation. Another unpopular feature is the unpleasant odor produced by the male flowers and crushed foliage. The tree is of little value to wildlife and has no commercial value. It is easily downed by snow and heavy winds.

655. Indian-hemp; Marion's weed

Apocynum cannabinum L.
  A-pó-cy-num can-ná-bi-num
Apocynaceae (Dogbane Family)

DESCRIPTION: Perennial herb to 4′ tall, branched only at the top; juice milky; leaves opposite, entire, spreading or ascending; corolla white to greenish; flowers May–July; follicles paired, hanging down, mature September–October.

RANGE-HABITAT: Widely distributed in the US and Canada; common native weed throughout SC; woodland margins, along roadsides, and in dry, waste places.

COMMENTS: The name "Indian hemp" comes from Native Americans' use of the stem fiber for cordage, fishing nets, and coarse cloth. In St. John's Parish, Berkeley County it was called "Marion's weed" because it was a favorite remedial agent in General Francis Marion's camp during the Revolutionary War. F. P. Porcher (1869) describes the many and varied historical uses of the plant such as a "substitute for quinine, purgative, cure for dropsy, diuretic, and as an agent to remove ascarides." The milky sap was a folk remedy for venereal warts. The plant contains toxic cardioactive glycosides.

656. Butterfly-weed; pleurisy-root; wind root

Asclepias tuberosa L. subsp. *tuberosa*
As-clè-pi-as tu-be-rò-sa subsp.
tu-be-rò-sa
Asclepiadaceae (Milkweed Family)

DESCRIPTION: Perennial herb from a thick root; stems 1–2.5′ tall, one to several, erect, ascending or creeping; juice not milky; plants rough-hairy throughout; leaves abundant, alternate, obovate to oblanceolate, the margins flat; flowers May–August.

RANGE-HABITAT: Native wide-ranging species, from NH west to OH, south to FL panhandle and e. TX; common throughout SC; sandy oak-hickory forests, sandy, dry, open woods, dry fields, along roadsides, and in woodland margins.

TAXONOMY: Another subspecies of *A. tuberosa* is *A. tuberosa* subsp. *rolfsii* (Britton ex Vail) Woodson. The leaves of subsp. *rolfsii* are hastate, and the margins usually revolute. It is found in the inner coastal plain and sandhills of SC and is uncommon.

COMMENTS: The common name, butterfly-weed, comes from the attraction of its brilliant flowers to butterflies. Pleurisy-root comes from Native Americans chewing the root as a cure for pleurisy and other pulmonary ailments. Wind root refers to its use in relieving flatulence. A tea made of fresh leaves has been used in Appalachia to induce vomiting. The roots of butterfly-weed are poisonous.

657. Hedge bindweed

Calystegia sepium (L.) R. Brown
Ca-lys-tè-gi-a sè-pi-um
Convolvulaceae (Morning-glory Family)

DESCRIPTION: Herbaceous, perennial, trailing or twining vine; leaves mostly hastate or sagittate basally; corolla white to rose-purple; calyx (and later capsule) subtended by and essentially loosely surrounded by a pair of bracts; flowers May–August.

RANGE-HABITAT: More or less throughout temperate North America; common and scattered throughout SC; along roadsides, and in edges of marshes, moist to wet thickets, and other waste places.

COMMENTS: In many areas it is a noxious weed; the roots are reported to be poisonous.

TAXONOMY: *C. sepium* has been separated into several specific or infraspecific taxa based on leaf and bract variation and flower color. This book follows Godfrey and Wooten (1981) and Radford et al. (1968) in using the above taxon to include all variation.

658. Northern catalpa

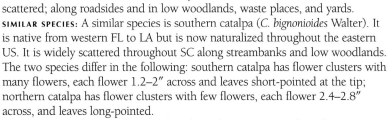

Catalpa speciosa (Warder) Warder
 ex Engelmann
 Ca-tál-pa spe-ci-ò-sa
 Bignoniaceae (Trumpet-creeper Family)

DESCRIPTION: Tree to 120' tall; leaves deciduous, opposite, simple, very broad, widest at the base, long-pointed at the tip; corolla 1.5" long, the lower lip notched; flowers May–June; capsule cylindrical, 12" or more long, mature July–August.

RANGE-HABITAT: Naturalized throughout the eastern US; in SC occasional and widely scattered; along roadsides and in low woodlands, waste places, and yards.

SIMILAR SPECIES: A similar species is southern catalpa (*C. bignonioides* Walter). It is native from western FL to LA but is now naturalized throughout the eastern US. It is widely scattered throughout SC along streambanks and low woodlands. The two species differ in the following: southern catalpa has flower clusters with many flowers, each flower 1.2–2" across and leaves short-pointed at the tip; northern catalpa has flower clusters with few flowers, each flower 2.4–2.8" across, and leaves long-pointed.

COMMENTS: Northern catalpa is native to southwestern IN and southern IL to TN and AR. It was widely planted, especially in the eastern US, where it escaped and became established along roads, in fields, and along the margins of woodlands. Catalpa is a fast-growing tree, but its wood is weak, and it is not a major commercial tree.

The big black caterpillars (catalpa worms) that eat the leaves are a nuisance on cultivated trees. In the South, however, fisherman prized them as bream bait.

659. Queen Anne's lace; wild carrot

Daucus carota L.
 Daù-cus ca-rò-ta
 Apiaceae (Parsley Family)

DESCRIPTION: Freely branched biennial herb, 1–3' tall, with long, slender taproot; leaves bipinnately compound; flowers in umbels with the central flower often maroon; fruits with bristles; flowers May–September.

RANGE-HABITAT: Throughout North America; common throughout SC, although only occasional in the outer coastal plain and maritime strand; most often found along roadsides, but also in fallow fields, fencerows, abandoned lots, and other waste places.

SIMILAR SPECIES: Wild carrot is similar to the native Queen Anne's lace, *D. pusillus* Michaux. This native species is widespread in the southeastern states and occurs in the piedmont, coastal plain, and maritime strand of SC. It differs from wild carrot in being unbranched (or rarely few-branched), and the central flower of each umbel is white.

COMMENTS: Wild carrot is naturalized from Europe and is widely spread as a weed in North America. For centuries the root was eaten in Europe and early America; however, the root is bitter and stringy and needed long cooking. As is often the case, a wild plant is recognized as having important qualities (here vitamin A), and a cultivar is developed from it. In this case the commercial carrot, *D. carota* var. *sativa*.

660. Common Peruvian daisy

Galinsoga quadriradiata Ruiz & Pávon
Ga-lin-sò-ga qua-dri-ra-di-à-ta
Asteraceae (Aster or Sunflower Family)

DESCRIPTION: Annual, freely branched, spreading-hairy, erect herb; 4–24″ tall; leaves opposite; rays 5, white, 3-toothed at apex; disc flowers yellow; flowers May–frost.
RANGE-HABITAT: Throughout the US and s. Canada; in SC common throughout the mountains, but scattered elsewhere; gardens, fields, barnyards, pastures, and waste places.
COMMENTS: Peruvian daisy is native to South America. Small (1933) states: "A particularly pestiferous weed of such rapid growth and seeding as to make eradication difficult." It does not readily invade natural areas. Named for Mariano Martinez de Galinsoga, an early Spanish botanist.
SYNONYM: *G. ciliata* (Rafinesque) Blake—RAB

661. Bitterweed

Helenium amarum (Rafinesque) H. Rock
He-lén-i-um a-mà-rum
Asteraceae (Aster or Sunflower Family)

DESCRIPTION: Annual herb to 40″ tall with taproot; entire plant odoriferous and bitter; freely branched above; leaves linear, often with smaller, axillary clusters of leaves; basal leaves soon deciduous; flowers May–frost.
RANGE-HABITAT: Widespread in eastern North America, apparently spreading from its native western range; throughout SC; in a variety of disturbed areas with poor soils, including pastures, roadsides, abandoned lots, fields, and open woods.
COMMENTS: Bitterweed can be a serious weed in pastures where cattle graze. When other forage is scarce, cattle will graze on bitterweed, giving their milk a bitter taste. Bitterweed is suspected of poisoning humans.

662. Man-of-the-earth; man-root

Ipomoea pandurata (L.) G. F. W. Meyer
I-po-moè-a pan-du-rà-ta
Convolvulaceae (Morning-glory Family)

DESCRIPTION: Perennial, trailing vine from a deep, vertical, enlarged root growing to 30 pounds; corolla white, always with a purple center; flowers May–July.
RANGE-HABITAT: From CT, NY, and s. Ontario, west to OH, MO, and KS, south to peninsular FL and e. TX; common throughout SC; along roadsides and fencerows, in lawns, sandy, open woods, and fallow fields.
COMMENTS: Several sources state that Native Americans used the root for food, but only after long roasting. Caution should be taken since the fresh root is reported to be purgative. A great quantity of starch can be extracted from the

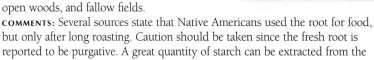

roots, which is probably safe. It is interesting to note that man-of-the-earth is related to sweet potato (*Ipomoea batatas* Lamarck).

663. Everlasting pea

Lathyrus latifolius L.
    Lá-thy-rus la-ti-fò-li-us
    Fabaceae (Pea or Bean Family)

DESCRIPTION: Perennial, long-lived herb with decumbent to high-climbing, broadly winged stems; leaves with a pair of leaflets and a branched, terminal tendril; flowers purple, red, pink, or white; flowers May–September.
RANGE-HABITAT: WV and VA south to GA, and west to TX, AR, and MO; common throughout SC; along roadsides and in open, waste places.
COMMENTS: Everlasting pea is a native of Europe. It is much cultivated because of its profuse blooms and has escaped and become widely naturalized. The seeds are highly toxic.

664. White mulberry

Morus alba L.
    Mò-rus ál-ba
    Moraceae (Mulberry Family)

DESCRIPTION: Shrubby, small, deciduous tree that may reach 50′; leaves variously lobed, or unlobed, smooth and shiny above, hairless below; flowers unisexual, in spikes on the same tree, or on different trees; flowers March–May; fruits mature May–June, and may be white, pink, or dark purple.
RANGE-HABITAT: Widely naturalized in eastern and southern North America; widely scattered throughout SC; along streams and fencerows, around dwellings, in pastures and vacant lots, and forming dense stands in the maritime strand in dredged soil disposal sites.
SIMILAR SPECIES: White mulberry is similar to the native red mulberry (*Morus rubra* L.), which occurs throughout the eastern US. The leaves of red mulberry are dull green and usually rough above. In white mulberry, the leaves are shiny green and smooth above and hairless beneath except on the main veins.
COMMENTS: White mulberry was introduced into the US from China in the 1600s in an attempt to establish a silk industry. The leaves are the chief food of the silkworm. The industry failed, but the trees survived and spread widely because birds carry the seeds. The wood has little commercial value. Although not as sweet and tasty as the fruits of red mulberry, the ripe fruits of white mulberry can be used in a variety of ways.

665. White evening-primrose

Oenothera speciosa Nuttall
Oe-no-thè-ra spe-ci-ò-sa
Onagraceae (Evening-primrose Family)

DESCRIPTION: Erect, usually branched perennial herb 8–24″ tall; leaves linear to oblong-lanceolate, the wider ones irregularly dentate or narrowly lobed; flower buds nodding, opening into pink or white flowers; flowers May–August.

RANGE-HABITAT: Widespread throughout the US; common throughout SC except in the mountains; along roadsides and in meadows, lawns, fields, and various dry, waste places.

COMMENTS: According to several sources, this primrose is native to the west but spread widely when plants escaped from cultivation. It is drought resistant, making it ideal for cultivation in dry sites. The specific epithet, *speciosa,* means beautiful.

666. Maypops; passion-flower

Passiflora incarnata L.
Pas-si-flò-ra in-car-nà-ta
Passifloraceae (Passion-flower Family)

DESCRIPTION: Tendril-bearing, perennial, herbaceous vine, to 6′ long; either creeping and rooting at the nodes, or climbing; leaves deeply 3-lobed; flowers May–September; fruit fleshy, yellow when ripe in July–October.

RANGE-HABITAT: FL to TX, and north to MD, MO, and OK; very common throughout SC; along roadsides and fences and in fallow fields, hedge rows, vacant lots, thickets, and open places.

SIMILAR SPECIES: *P. lutea* L. has similar shaped flowers, but they are much smaller and greenish yellow. It flowers in June–September and is common throughout SC in mixed deciduous woodlands and thickets.

COMMENTS: Passion-flower is a native vine that is weedy and often cultivated. The common name, passion-flower, comes from the resemblance of the floral parts to the story of Christ's Passion: the styles resemble nails; the 5 stamens, the wounds Jesus received; the purplish corona, the bloody crown; the 10 perianth parts, the 10 disciples (Peter and Judas being absent); the coiled tendrils, the whips for scourging; the pistil, the column where Christ was scourged; and the flower in the background of dull, green leaves represents Christ in the hands of His enemies. Interestingly, the flower's life is generally three days.

The fruit is edible raw but is more esteemed when made into jelly.

667. Beard-tongue

Penstemon australis Small
　　Pen-stè-mon aus-trà-lis
　　Scrophulariaceae (Figwort Family)

DESCRIPTION: Opposite-leaved, perennial herb; stems one to several, 8–28″ tall; basal leaves shaped differently from the stem leaves; inflorescence hairy, the hairs simple or glandular; flowers May–July.

RANGE-HABITAT: VA to FL, and west to AL; in SC common throughout the coastal plain, sandhills, and piedmont; a native species more common as a weed than in native communities; sandhills, sandy, dry, open woods, dry, fallow fields, burned-over thickets, and along roadsides.

COMMENTS: The common name comes from the bearded nature of the sterile stamens in some species.

668. Pokeweed

Phytolacca americana L.
　　Phy-to-lác-ca a-me-ri-cà-na
　　Phytolaccaceae (Pokeweed Family)

DESCRIPTION: Robust, perennial herb, 3–10′ tall, from a thick root; leaves alternate, entire, smooth; plant unpleasantly scented; flowers May–frost; berries in long racemes, dark purple when ripe in the fall.

RANGE-HABITAT: "Native weed" widespread in eastern North America and southeastern Canada; common throughout SC; wide variety of natural and disturbed sites, including fields, pastures, vacant lots, railroad embankments, abandoned house sites, newly created openings in forests and pastures, and barnyards.

COMMENTS: All parts or the plant are poisonous except the young shoots, which are eaten as a potherb before the red color appears. Pigs are often poisoned because they consume the roots, the most poisonous part. Native Americans and early colonists used the juice of the berry as a dye. Birds allow for the rapid spread of the seeds, and it quickly colonizes bare soil in natural communities, especially mounds created by windthrows.

669. Japanese knotweed

Polygonum cuspidatum Siebold &
  Zuccarini
  Po-lý-go-num cus-pi-dà-tum
Polygonaceae (Buckwheat Family)

DESCRIPTION: Stout, erect, rhizomatous perennial, usually forming dense colonies; 4–10′
tall; stems hollow; leaves heart-shaped or
truncate at the base; calyx white, tinged with
pink; flowers May–September.
RANGE-HABITAT: Naturalized in the eastern US;
widely scattered throughout SC; along roadsides and in various waste places, often
forming large colonies from the widely branched rootstocks.
COMMENTS: Japanese knotweed is naturalized from East Asia.
SYNONYM: *Reynoutria japonica* Houttuyn—W

670. Sulphur five-fingers

Potentilla recta L.
    Po-ten-tíl-la réc-ta
  Rosaceae (Rose Family)

DESCRIPTION: Perennial, hairy herb with
palmately compound leaves, with 7–9
coarsely serrate leaflets; stems several, 1–2′
tall; inflorescence terminal, flat-topped with
pale yellow flowers with notched petals; flowers in May–August.
RANGE-HABITAT: Newfoundland to MN, and
south to FL and TX; naturalized throughout
SC; common; pastures and meadows and
along roadsides and railroads.
COMMENTS: Five-fingers is naturalized from Europe. It is rapidly spreading. It is
seldom eaten by livestock.

671. Smooth sumac

Rhus glabra L.
    Rhùs glà-bra
  Anacardiaceae (Cashew Family)

DESCRIPTION: Rhizomatous shrub or small tree
to 20′ tall; stems smooth; leaves deciduous,
pinnately compound, with 15–19 sessile
leaflets; rachis not winged; flowers greenish
white, in dense terminal panicles, flowering
late May–July; drupes red, mature June–October.
RANGE-HABITAT: Widespread in eastern North
America; in SC in the mountains, piedmont,
sandhills, and inner coastal plain; common; along roadsides and in pastures,
meadows, thickets, woodland borders, and waste ground.
COMMENTS: Because smooth sumac forms dense colonies, it is well suited as a
landscape plant to halt erosion on sloping road cuts and fills. It is used as a fall
ornamental because of its bright red leaves. Smooth sumac has had countless
uses as folk remedies, both to Native Americans and early colonists. Native

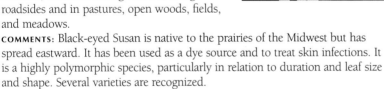

Americans used the berries to stop bed-wetting, and in Appalachia the leaves are rolled and smoked as a treatment for asthma. The fruits have been used to prepare a refreshing drink or a gargle for sore throats.

672. Multiflora rose

Rosa multiflora Thurnberg
Rò-sa mul-ti-flò-ra
Rosaceae (Rose Family)

DESCRIPTION: Erect shrub growing to 6–15′ tall; branches vigorous, 10′ or so long, recurving or climbing; prickles curved, flattened; leaves pinnately compound; leaflets usually 7–9; flowers May–June; hip red, ripe September–October.

RANGE-HABITAT: NY to FL, west to TX; scattered nearly throughout SC; along fencerows and roadsides and in pastures and thin woods.

COMMENTS: Multiflora rose is naturalized from Japan and China. It was once planted as a living hedge and provides excellent wildlife cover. It is, however, a pest in many areas, spreading into fields and pastures.

673. Black-eyed Susan

Rudbeckia hirta L.
Rud-béck-i-a hír-ta
Asteraceae (Aster or Sunflower Family)

DESCRIPTION: Tap-rooted annual to more often biennial or fibrous-rooted perennial; 12–40″ tall; leaves and stems very rough and bristly-hairy; as a biennial it forms a rosette of leaves the first year, followed by flowers the second year; leaves alternate; flowers May–June.

RANGE-HABITAT: Nearly throughout North America; common throughout SC; along roadsides and in pastures, open woods, fields, and meadows.

COMMENTS: Black-eyed Susan is native to the prairies of the Midwest but has spread eastward. It has been used as a dye source and to treat skin infections. It is a highly polymorphic species, particularly in relation to duration and leaf size and shape. Several varieties are recognized.

674. Soapwort; bouncing bet

Saponaria officinalis L.
Sa-po-nà-ri-a of-fi-ci-nà-lis
Caryophyllaceae (Pink Family)

DESCRIPTION: Smooth, perennial herb, spreading from seeds and rhizomes to form sizable colonies; stems 20–60″ tall, erect or decumbent; leaves opposite; petals white to light pink; flowers May–October.

RANGE-HABITAT: Naturalized essentially throughout the US; common throughout SC; in fields, around abandoned home sites, and other waste places.

COMMENTS: Soapwort has had a long history of folk use. When mixed with water, the crushed leaves and roots make lather—hence, the common name. Native Americans used the poulticed leaves for boils. The second common name, bouncing bet, is an old-fashioned nickname for a washerwoman, again in reference to its use as soap. It is naturalized from Europe. The seeds contain saponin and have a generally accepted reputation for potential toxicity.

675. Small's ragwort

Senecio smallii Britton
Se-nè-ci-o smáll-i-i
Asteraceae (Aster or Sunflower Family)

DESCRIPTION: Clump-forming annual, 12–28″ tall; stem densely woolly at base; basal leaves wedge-shaped, lanceolate, serrate, and pinnately dissected; flowers May–early June.

RANGE-HABITAT: NJ to IN, south to FL and MS; common throughout SC; along dry roadsides, and in meadows, fallow fields, pastures, and open woodlands; in the piedmont and mountains on the margins of granitic flatrocks and granitic domes.

SYNONYM: *Packera anonyma* (Wood) W. A. Weber & Á. Löve—W

676. Bull nettle; horse nettle

Solanum carolinense L.
So-là-num ca-ro-li-nén-se
Solanaceae (Nightshade Family)

DESCRIPTION: Erect, weakly branched, perennial herb, 1–3′ tall; stems and underside of leaves with sharp prickles; leaves coarsely lobed, both surfaces with star-shaped hairs; corolla light purple to white, with yellow center; flowers May–July; berry yellow when ripe.

RANGE-HABITAT: From southern Ontario to New England and NY, south to FL, west to TX, and north to NE; common throughout SC; along roadsides, in fallow and cultivated fields, and around farm lots, abandoned house sites, and lawns.

COMMENTS: The berries are poisonous. Kingsbury (1964) reports one case of a child's dying from eating the berries. Poisoning in cattle and deer have been reported. This is another native weedy species that became more abundant as disturbed habitats increased.

677. Hairy vetch

Vicia villosa Roth
  Ví-ci-a vil-lò-sa
Fabaceae (Pea or Bean Family)

DESCRIPTION: Annual or rarely perennial herb, trailing or climbing by tendrils; stems, flower stalks, and leaves with spreading hairs; leaves alternate, pinnately compound with 10–20 leaflets; terminal leaflet modified into a branched tendril; racemes with flowers borne on one side; calyx bulging at base, the flower stalk appearing lateral; flowers May–September.

RANGE-HABITAT: Naturalized throughout the US; common throughout SC; fallow fields, along roadsides and fencerows, and in other open, disturbed sites.

SIMILAR SPECIES: A similar vetch is smooth vetch (*V. dasycarpa* Tenore plate 436 in *WCL*), which also occurs naturalized throughout SC in similar habitats. The stem of smooth vetch is sparsely appressed, short hairs to hairless; otherwise similar.

COMMENTS: Hairy vetch is naturalized from Europe and is cultivated for fodder.

678. Cow-itch; trumpet vine

Campsis radicans (L.) Seemann
    ex Bureau
  Cámp-sis ra-dì-cans
Bignoniaceae (Trumpet-creeper Family)

DESCRIPTION: Deciduous, woody vine, trailing or high-climbing by means of 2, short rows of aerial roots from the nodes; sometimes climbing over 100′; stem with yellowish and shreddy bark; leaves opposite, pinnately compound with 7–15 leaflets; flowers June–July.

RANGE-HABITAT: NJ west to OH, and south to FL and c. TX; common throughout SC; swamps, bottomlands, and woodlands, along fencerows and roadsides, and in vacant lots and yards.

COMMENTS: Cow-itch is a native vine that has exploited disturbed habitats throughout its range. It is often cultivated for its attractive flowers. Contact with cow-itch may cause skin inflammation and blisters in sensitive people.

679. Crown-vetch

Coronilla varia L.
    Co-ro-níl-la và-ri-a
Fabaceae (Pea or Bean Family)

DESCRIPTION: Perennial herb with trailing to ascending stems, 1–2′ tall; leaves pinnately compound, 9–25-foliolate; flowers in headlike clusters that arise from the leaf axils; stalks of heads 2–6″ long; standard pink, the wings white or purple; flowers June–September.
RANGE-HABITAT: New England south to SC, west to MO, and north to SD; becoming widely established in the mountains and piedmont of SC; along roadsides and woodland borders and in fields.
COMMENTS: Crown-vetch was introduced from Europe and is often planted along road-cuts as a stabilizing perennial. The seeds are reported to be poisonous.

680. Water hyacinth

Eichhornia crassipes (Martius) Solms
    Ei-chhórn-i-a crás-si-pes
Pontederiaceae (Pickerelweed Family)

DESCRIPTION: Free-floating, freshwater aquatic herb with a basal cluster of leaves; often rooted in mud as the water recedes and may persist for several months; flowers June–September.
RANGE-HABITAT: VA south to FL, and west to TX and MO; throughout the coastal plain of SC; ponds, ditches, canals, and abandoned rice fields along coastal freshwater rivers.
COMMENTS: Water hyacinth was introduced into FL in 1884, and through prolific growth, has rapidly become a serious weed, clogging waterways in the warmer, frost-free coastal areas of the southeast. The inflated leaf stalks consist of aerenchyma tissue that gives the plant great buoyancy. Reproduction is mainly by vegetative means, with sections breaking off then carried by currents or driven by wind. The genus name honors Johann Eichhorn of Berlin, 1779–1856.

681. Sand blackberry

Rubus cuneifolius Pursh
    Rù-bus cu-nei-fò-li-us
Rosaceae (Rose Family)

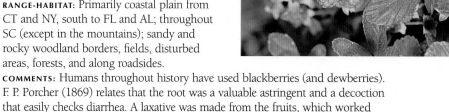

DESCRIPTION: Woody plant with erect to arching stems, to 5′ tall; thorns broad-based, flat and curved; leaves palmately compound; berry black when ripe June–July.
RANGE-HABITAT: Primarily coastal plain from CT and NY, south to FL and AL; throughout SC (except in the mountains); sandy and rocky woodland borders, fields, disturbed areas, forests, and along roadsides.
COMMENTS: Humans throughout history have used blackberries (and dewberries). F. P. Porcher (1869) relates that the root was a valuable astringent and a decoction that easily checks diarrhea. A laxative was made from the fruits, which worked

because of the mechanical irritation of the seeds. Wine, syrup, cordials, jelly, and jam are made from the fruits. Blackberries and related dewberries are among the most important summer foods for songbirds and many mammals.

682. Standing-cypress

Ipomopsis rubra (L.) Wherry
I-po-móp-sis rù-bra
Polemoniaceae (Phlox Family)

DESCRIPTION: Erect, hairy, herbaceous biennial, to 3′ tall (exceptionally 5′) the second year; first-year leaves in a large, basal rosette; stem leaves alternate, divided into numerous, narrow segments; flowers in racemes, often ¼ to ⅓ the total plant height; flowers bright red, or sometimes pale yellow; flowers June–August.

RANGE-HABITAT: Ranging as a native from sc. NC south to FL, west to TX and OK; scattered and rare in SC and recorded from only seven sites; piedmont, fall-line sandhills, and coastal plain; sandhills, waste places, riverbanks, roadsides, sand ridges of Carolina bays, and openings in dry woodlands.

COMMENTS: Standing-cypress is a native that has adapted to ruderal sites as fire-suppression has reduced woodland openings. In gardens, it is found sometimes under the synonym *Gilia coronopifolia* Persoon. It is closely related to the large western genus *Gilia,* and thus represents another example of the affinity between the sandhills flora and the flora of the dry southwestern US. It is often cultivated. It escaped from New England to MI and MO and southward. It grows in FL orange groves, where it is often called "Spanish-larkspur." The long, tubular flowers are adapted to cross-pollination by hummingbirds.

Standing-cypress can be found at Glassy Mountain Heritage Preserve in Pickens County.

PROTECTION STATUS: State Threatened

683. Perennial wild bean

Strophostyles umbellata (Muhlenberg ex Willdenow) Britton
Stro-pho-stỳ-les um-bel-là-ta
Fabaceae (Pea or Bean Family)

DESCRIPTION: Trailing or climbing, twining, herbaceous vine from a perennial root; stems to about 5′ long; leaf blades pinnately 3-foliolate; petals pink or pale purple, often fading yellowish; flowers few to several in headlike clusters on stalks to 12″ long; flowers mature in June–September; legumes mature in August–October.

RANGE-HABITAT: From s. NY west to OH, s. IL, and KS, south to FL and TX; common throughout SC; fields, thickets, dry, sandy woods, and clearings.

COMMENTS: Wild bean is a native species that is more adapted to disturbed sites than to wooded habitats. There is no reference to this species having any food valve for humans. A variety of birds eat the seeds, including bobwhite quail and wild turkey.

684. Woolly mullein

Verbascum thapsus L.
    Ver-bás-cum tháp-sus
Scrophulariaceae (Figwort Family)

DESCRIPTION: Densely woolly biennial, 2–6′ tall; basal cluster of thick, velvety leaves present only in first year; stem develops the second year, with leaves gradually reduced upward; flowers fragrant, appearing the second year; flowers June–September.

RANGE-HABITAT: Throughout the US; common throughout SC; along roads, and in pastures, fallow fields, sandy, open woods, vacant lots, and coastal shell deposits.

COMMENTS: Woolly mullein is a native of Eurasia and naturalized in North America. It is perhaps one of the most widely distributed introduced plants. Few plants have had as many former uses as woolly mullein, both in the Old and New World. Roman soldiers dipped the stalks into grease for torches. Native Americans, plantation slaves, and colonists lined their shoes with the velvety leaves as cushions and to keep out the cold. Quaker women, not allowed to use cosmetics, rubbed their cheeks with the leaves to achieve a rosy look. A tea from the plant was used to treat colds. Native Americans smoked the dried leaves, flowers, or roots for pulmonary ailments, and slaves on southern plantations used a decoction of the plant to relieve the pain of hemorrhoids or to induce sleep. Mullein does contain a narcotic principle, and Duke (1997) recommends it as an herbal remedy for bronchitis and laryngitis.

685. Sicklepod

Cassia obtusifolia L.
    Cás-si-a ob-tu-si-fò-li-a
Fabaceae (Bean or Pea Family)

DESCRIPTION: Erect annual herb to 5′ tall; leaves evenly once-pinnately compound; leaflets 4–6, obovate, terminal pair largest; elongate gland just above the stalks of the lowest pair of leaflets; flowers July–September.

RANGE-HABITAT: Common weedy species from FL to TX, and northward to PA and KS; throughout SC; variety of weedy habitats such as abandoned agricultural fields, waste places, and pastures.

COMMENTS: Sicklepod is a tropical species that has invaded the southern US (Rickett, 1967). It is reported to be poisonous when eaten in large quantities.

686. Mexican-tea; worm-seed

Chenopodium ambrosioides L.
   Che-no-pò-di-um am-bro-si-oì-des
Chenopodiaceae (Goosefoot Family)

DESCRIPTION: Typically an annual plant, but in the South mostly a perennial from a stout root; erect herb, 2–4′ tall, covered with glandular-resin dots; strongly pungent; leaves alternate; flowers in dense clusters on short to long spikes; flowers July–frost.
RANGE-HABITAT: Throughout much of eastern North America; common throughout SC; cultivated and fallow fields, pastures, vacant lots, fencerows, and along railroads and roadsides.
COMMENTS: Mexican-tea is naturalized from tropical America. In earlier times, rural people in the coastal area used it as a vermifuge. Today, it is the source of chenopodium oil, which is used to treat domestic stock for intestinal worms and humans for hookworm infections.

687. Jimson-weed; Jamestown-weed

Datura stramonium L.
   Da-tù-ra stra-mò-ni-um
Solanaceae (Nightshade Family)

DESCRIPTION: Rank-smelling, coarse, annual weed, 1–5′ tall; leaves alternate, irregularly lobed; flowers July–September; fruit an erect, spiny, many-seeded capsule, matures August–October.
RANGE-HABITAT: Common throughout the US; common in SC; along roadsides and in barnyards, fields, vacant lots, over-grazed pastures, and other disturbed areas.
COMMENTS: Jimson-weed is a corruption of Jamestown-weed, the latter name derived from its growing around Jamestown, VA, where it was reported that soldiers who were sent there in 1676 to quell the Bacon Rebellion became intoxicated from smoking the plant. Inadvertently, leaves of *Datura* were included in their meal, and, as reported in Robert Beverly's *History of VA*, ". . .the effect of which was a very pleasant Comedy; for they turn'd natural Fools upon it for several days. . .and after Eleven Days, returned to themselves again, not remembering any thing that pass'd." Jimson-weed is the only hallucinogenic flowering plant in SC. All parts of the plant are poisonous. Cattle and sheep died from grazing on it, and children have been poisoned after eating the fruit. Touching the leaves or flowers may cause a dermatitis in sensitive people.

There seems to be a question in the literature about where jimson-weed is native. One source says it comes from tropical America, another source says Europe. Yet another source questions both of these by pointing out that it was reported growing around Jamestown in 1676, suggesting it is native to North America.

688. Honey locust

Gleditsia triacanthos L.
   Gle-díts-i-a tri-a-cán-thos
Fabaceae (Pea or Bean Family)

DESCRIPTION: Medium to large size tree, living over 120 years; stems and trunk with strong thorns that are frequently branched; leaves deciduous, either pinnate with 18–28 leaflets, or bipinnate with 8–14 pinnae; flowers inconspicuous, odorless, and greenish; flowers April–May; legume broadly linear, 12–15″ long, with seeds embedded in sugary pulp, mature July–November.

RANGE-HABITAT: NY west to SD, south to FL panhandle and TX; throughout SC; woodlands and woodland borders, bottomland forests, fencerows, abandoned home sites, and as a planted shade tree.

COMMENTS: Several references indicate that the native range of honey locust is not known because it is adventive and has been extensively planted. No reference was found to indicate whether it is native to SC.

   The pulp of the pod, which remains sweet for some time after ripening, is a pleasant trail nibble. F. P. Porcher (1869) stated that a beer was made in the South by fermenting the fresh sugary pods. A wide variety of animals eat the fruits. The wood is hard and durable, but has never been commercially important. Its main use has been for fence posts and railway ties. A thornless form has been used more often as an ornamental. The genus name was simplified and latinized for Johann Gottlieb Gleditsch, 1714–1786, a botanist contemporary with Linnaeus.

689. Beaked hawkweed

Hieracium gronovii L.
   Hi-e-rà-ci-um gro-nòv-i-i
Asteraceae (Aster or Sunflower Family)

DESCRIPTION: Perennial herb with milky juice; stems pubescent, to 3′ tall; leaves mostly basal, or on the lower part of the stem and reduced above; inflorescence a panicle with numerous heads; ray flowers only, yellow; flowers July–frost.

RANGE-HABITAT: MA to KS, and south to FL and TX; throughout SC; common; old fields, roadsides, meadows, pastures, and woodlands.

COMMENTS: The term "beaked" in the common name refers to the plants' achenes (fruits), which are distinctly narrowed toward the apex. All other hawkweeds in our area have achenes that are truncate at the apex.

690. Common morning-glory

Ipomoea purpurea (L.) Roth
    I-po-moè-a pur-pú-re-a
Convolvulaceae (Morning-glory Family)

DESCRIPTION: Twining, annual, herbaceous
vine with one main stem from a taproot;
leaves simple, heart-shaped; corolla purple,
red, bluish, white or variegated; flowers
July–September.

RANGE-HABITAT: Throughout the southeastern
US; common throughout SC; in fallow and
cultivated fields, along roadsides and
fencerows, and in abandoned lots.

COMMENTS: Common morning-glory is native to tropical America and was introduced into North America as an ornamental. It escaped from gardens and is
now widely naturalized. Its broad, heart-shaped leaves are distinctive.

691. Sericea

Lespedeza cuneata (Dumont de
    Courset) D. Don
    Les-pe-dèz-a cu-ne-à-ta
Fabaceae (Bean Family or Pea)

DESCRIPTION: Perennial with erect or strongly
ascendent, strigose stems to 5′ tall; leaves narrowly oblong, wedge-shaped to linear-
oblanceolate; petals creamy-white, with
violet-purple along the veins of the standard;
flowers July–September; legume matures
October–November.

RANGE-HABITAT: Naturalized and common
throughout the southeast; common throughout SC; along roadsides, in fields,
and in waste areas.

COMMENTS: Sericea was introduced into the southeast from east Asia as a hay
plant and as a soil-binder along roads. The genus honors Vincente Manuel de
Céspedes, governor of FL in 1790. A note from *Gray's Manual of Botany* (Fernald, 1950) explains the difference in the spelling of the genus and de Céspedes:
"Dedicated to Vincente Manuel de Céspedes, Spanish Governor of East Florida
during the explorations there of Michaux late in the 18th Century; the name
later misspelled, probably by Michaux's editor, as de Lespedez."

692. Common reed

Phragmites australis (Cavanilles) Trinius ex Steudel
   Phrag-mì-tes aus-trà-lis
Poaceae (Grass Family)

DESCRIPTION: Coarse, rhizomatous perennial, 5–15′ tall; often forming large colonies; some plants rarely produce seeds, and instead spread by rhizomes and long, leafy stolons; inflorescence a dense, tawny to purple panicle; flowers July–October.

RANGE-HABITAT: Throughout the US and in South America, Europe, Asia, Africa, and Australia; common along the coastal area of SC; dredged soil disposal sites, fresh and brackish marshes, pond margins, ditches, sloughs behind coastal dunes, and other disturbed habitats.

COMMENTS: Common reed began to appear along the SC coast in the 1970s, apparently spreading as dredging barges moved up and down the Intracoastal Waterway carrying rhizomes in the mud that adhered to the barges.

Common reed is a serious weed in wetland areas managed for wildlife because it can dominate the site at the exclusion of native food plants. Common reed itself is not a valuable food source. Common reed grows so fast and on such a variety of soils that it is being explored as a potential energy crop. Some of the uses worldwide are thatched homes, pulp for paper, making alcohol, biological filter for waste water, cemented reed blocks, synthetic fibers, and insulation material.

SYNONYM: *Phragmites communis* (L.) Trinius—RAB

693. Northern obedient-plant

Physostegia virginiana (L.) Bentham
   subsp. *virginiana*
   Phy-sos-té-gi-a vir-gi-ni-à-na
   subsp. vir-gi-ni-à-na
Lamiaceae (Mint Family)

DESCRIPTION: Upright, nearly glabrous perennial herb with rhizomes; stems with 15–22 nodes, up to 5′ tall; leaves opposite, simple, sessile, elliptic to lanceolate, long-tapering, with toothed margins; corolla white to deep pink, spotted with reddish purple; flowers July–October.

RANGE-HABITAT: As a native plant, from Quebec west to Manitoba, south to e. VA, nc. TN, and ne. KS; in SC escaped from cultivation; common; streamsides, seepages, marshes, roadsides, abandoned home sites, and other disturbed sites.

COMMENTS: Several references state that it is probably not native in the eastern part of its range but escaped from cultivation. The common name obedient-plant relates to the flowers' tendancy to stay in a new position for a while after they are twisted to one side.

SYNONYM: *Dracocephalum virginianum* L.—RAB

694. Bladderpod; bagpod

Glottidium vesicarium (Jacquin) Harper
Glot-tí-di-um ve-si-cá-ri-um
Fabaceae (Pea or Bean Family)

DESCRIPTION: Annual, but rather woody; to 12′ tall; leaves even pinnate, with 12–40 leaflets; petals yellow, tinged with red; legume 2-seeded, at maturity the firm outer layer separating from a thin, soft layer enclosing the seeds; flowers July–September; fruits mature August–November.

RANGE-HABITAT: Coastal plain from NC to FL, west to TX; in SC common in the coastal plain and maritime strand; a weedy plant, found in a variety of disturbed habitats such as ditches, freshwater marshes, low fields, and disturbed, wet areas.

COMMENTS: Weakley (2001) states that bladderpod was probably introduced from the deeper South. Small (1933) states that bladder pod was evidently introduced but does not say from where. One source reports that it is probably native to the West Indies.

Bladderpod is a vigorous annual, and the firm, woody stems, with the dangling pods, may persist throughout the winter. Kingsbury (1964) reports that the seeds and fruits of bladderpod are poisonous to a wide variety of animals, including sheep, cattle, and fowl. Hundreds of cattle from a single herd have been killed. Cattle poisoning occurs in the fall and winter when the pods (still carried by the erect, dead stems) are available to cattle after other forage has become scarce.

695. Winged sumac

Rhus copallina L.
Rhùs co-pal-lì-na
Anacardiaceae (Cashew Family)

DESCRIPTION: Rhizomatous shrub or small tree, 20–25′ tall; stems densely short-hairy; leaves deciduous, alternate, pinnately compound; midrib of leaf winged; leaves turn bright red in fall; male and female flowers in clusters on different plants; flowers July–September; drupes in clusters, dark red when ripe in the fall.

RANGE-HABITAT: NY south to FL, west to TX, and north to KS and WI; common throughout SC; natural communities such as oak-hickory and pine-mixed hardwood forests, longleaf pine flatwoods, and disturbed sites such as fencerows and roadsides, thickets, pastures, and old fields.

COMMENTS: The hairs on the surface of the drupes contain malic acid, a pleasant tasting acid. Native Americans, then European settlers, used the fruit as the source of a cool, summer drink. It is prepared by bruising the fruits in water to free the acid, then straining the water to remove the hairs. Sugar can be added. The resulting drink is similar to pink lemonade. The fruits are rich in vitamin A and are a valuable food source in winter when other fruits are scarce. It is a native species that exploits disturbed habitats throughout its range.

TAXONOMY: Weakley (2001) gives two varieties of winged sumac based on differences in leaflet morphology. He further states that the two varieties of winged sumac are not clearly delineated. This book uses the conservative treatment, recognizing one taxon.

696. Kudzu

Pueraria lobata (Willdenow) Ohwi
Pu-e-rà-ri-a lo-bà-ta
Fabaceae (Bean or Pea Family)

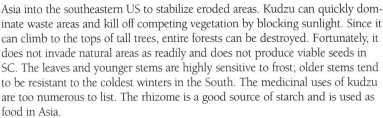

DESCRIPTION: Trailing or climbing, robust, semiwoody vine up to 90′ long; leaves pinnately 3-foliolate; flowers reddish purple, grape scented; flowers July–October.

RANGE-HABITAT: PA to FL, and west to TX and AR; common throughout SC; along roadsides, around abandoned home sites, and in woods, fields, and other waste areas.

COMMENTS: Kudzu was introduced from east Asia into the southeastern US to stabilize eroded areas. Kudzu can quickly dominate waste areas and kill off competing vegetation by blocking sunlight. Since it can climb to the tops of tall trees, entire forests can be destroyed. Fortunately, it does not invade natural areas as readily and does not produce viable seeds in SC. The leaves and younger stems are highly sensitive to frost; older stems tend to be resistant to the coldest winters in the South. The medicinal uses of kudzu are too numerous to list. The rhizome is a good source of starch and is used as food in Asia.

Named for M. W. Puerari, 1765–1845, a Swiss botanist.

697. New York ironweed

Vernonia noveboracensis (L.) Michaux
Ver-nòn-i-a no-ve-bo-ra-cén-sis
Asteraceae (Aster or Sunflower Family)

DESCRIPTION: Robust, perennial herb, 3–7′ tall; stem leafy, green to dark purple; without basal leaves; leaves alternate, numerous; disk flowers purple; flowers July–September.

RANGE-HABITAT: MA and NY, south to GA and FL panhandle, and west to MS; then inland to WV and OH; common throughout SC; wet meadows, streamsides, low, open woodlands, thickets, and swales.

COMMENTS: The genus honors William Vernon, 16?-1711, an English botanist who traveled in North America.

698. Cocklebur

Xanthium strumarium L.
Xán-thi-um stru-mà-ri-um
Asteraceae (Aster or Sunflower Family)

DESCRIPTION: Annual herb, to 6′ tall; leaves alternate, triangular-ovate; male and female flowers in separate heads; female flowers two each in burs beset with strong, hooked bristles; flowering and fruiting July–frost.

RANGE-HABITAT: Throughout North America; common throughout SC; in a wide variety of weedy habitats, including cultivated and fallow fields, pastures, floodplain forests and their clearings, ditches, pond shores, and along roadsides.

COMMENTS: Cocklebur poisoning has occurred in all classes of domestic live-stock. Kingsbury (1964) states: "It is always associated with ingestion of seedlings in the cotyledonary stage of growth. Cocklebur seeds sprout readily when present in soil that has been under water but is drying out. Such conditions are found along streams, or about the shores of shallow ponds as summer progresses. Frequently, as the shore area is extended by a receding water margin, there is continual germination and sprouting of cocklebur seedlings which, as the water withdraws, provide potentially toxic forage over an extended period of time. Although cocklebur is an annual, its seeds may persist for several years before germinating. This must be taken into consideration when planning control measures for its eradication." The burs of cocklebur can cause puncture wounds to animals if they become tangled in their fur.

699. Common ragweed

Ambrosia artemisiifolia L.
  Am-brò-si-a ar-te-mi-si-i-fò-li-a
Asteraceae (Aster or Sunflower Family)

DESCRIPTION: Annual herb to 6' tall, with taproot; stems freely branched; leaves deeply bipinnately dissected, lower opposite, upper alternate; flowers inconspicuous; male and female flowers on same plant; male flowers in clusters near top; female flowers in small clusters in upper leaf axils; flowers and fruits August–frost.

RANGE-HABITAT: Native species growing virtually throughout the US; throughout SC and weedy, invading almost any open, disturbed site, including fields, roadsides, pastures, and vacant lots.

SIMILAR SPECIES: Giant ragweed, *A. trifida* L., grows in the mountains and piedmont in waste places and alluvial fields. Its pollen, spread by wind, is also a significant cause of hay fever. It differs from common ragweed because it is about twice as tall and has leaves 3–5-lobed.

COMMENTS: Wind-borne pollen from the genus *Ambrosia* is the cause of approximately 90% of pollen-induced allergies in the US. Today's way of life creates abundant disturbed sites, so there is little relief for hay fever sufferers. The best control is to allow perennials to crowd out this annual.

700. Rattlebox

Crotalaria spectabilis Roth
  Cro-ta-là-ri-a spec-tá-bi-lis
Fabaceae (Pea or Bean Family)

DESCRIPTION: Annual herb, 2–4' tall, from a woody taproot; leaves simple, alternate, markedly obovate; stems commonly dark purple; flowers July–September; legume inflated, many seeded, becoming black at maturity in August–October.

RANGE-HABITAT: From se. VA to FL, and west to the east half of TX and c. MO; naturalized and common in the piedmont, sandhills, coastal plain and maritime strand; roadsides, cultivated and fallow fields, and other disturbed areas.

COMMENTS: A native of India, it was introduced as a soil-building green manure. It quickly was naturalized and became a serious pest in agricultural crops. It is poisonous and has caused severe losses in fowl, cattle, horses and swine. It is also poisonous to humans. The common name comes from the legume; when mature, the seeds break loose inside and rattle.

THE RUDERAL COMMUNITIES

701. Dodder; love vine

Cuscuta gronovii Willdenow ex J. A.
   Shultes
   Cus-cù-ta gro-nòv-i-i
   Convolvulaceae (Morning-glory Family)

DESCRIPTION: Hemiparasite; annual, twining, herbaceous vine; leaves reduced to a few minute scales; haustoria develop all along the stem where it is in contact with the host plant; flowers August–October.

RANGE-HABITAT: Quebec to Manitoba, generally southward to FL and NM; scattered localities throughout SC; parasitic on a variety of woody or herbaceous hosts in tidal freshwater marshes, wet roadside ditches, brackish marshes, swamps, and pond margins.

COMMENTS: The seeds of dodder germinate in the soil; later the seedling tip undergoes a spiraling movement that often brings it into contact with a suitable host. As soon as it wraps itself around the host and the haustoria develop, the roots die and soil contact is lost. Water and minerals and a limited amount of organic material are transferred through the haustorium from the host.

Five species of dodder occur in SC, and they are difficult to distinguish from one another. All five species can readily be identified as dodders because of the orange to yellowish twining stems and clusters of small, white flowers.

The specific epithet honors Jan Fredick Gronovius, 1690–1762, professor at Leyden, teacher of Linnaeus, and author of *Flora Virginica*.

702. Boneset

Eupatorium perfoliatum L.
   Eu-pa-tò-ri-um per-fo-li-à-tum
   Asteraceae (Aster or Sunflower Family)

DESCRIPTION: Perennial herb with erect, solid stems, 2–4′ tall; often growing in clumps; leaves opposite, perfoliate; plant conspicuously hairy; flowers August–October.

RANGE-HABITAT: Widespread in eastern North America; common throughout SC; damp, moist areas such as wet meadows, alluvial woods, marshes, ditches, thickets, clearings, and pastures.

COMMENTS: Boneset is a native species that has become weedy as disturbed habitats increased.

Boneset has been used in a number of folk remedies in SC and elsewhere. It was a common home remedy of nineteenth-century America, extensively used by Native Americans and early settlers. The common name comes from the belief that the plant could cause rapid union of broken bones, as suggested by the basal union of each pair of opposite leaves. F. P. Porcher (1869) reported that slaves on coastal plantations employed it as a febrifuge in fevers and typhoid pneumonia. Also, a tea from the leaves was a substitute for quinine to treat malaria. In Appalachia, a tea from the leaves is used as a laxative and as a treatment for coughs and chest illnesses.

703. Rabbit tobacco; life everlasting

Gnaphalium obtusifolium L.
Gna-phá-li-um ob-tu-si-fò-li-um
Asteraceae (Aster or Sunflower Family)

DESCRIPTION: Erect, fragrant, winter or summer annual herb; stems erect, 1–3′ tall, densely whitish woolly; dead stems tend to remain throughout the winter; stem leaves alternate, green above, whitish woolly beneath; flowers August–October.

RANGE-HABITAT: Quebec to Manitoba, and south to FL and TX; common native plant found throughout SC; along roadsides, in fallow fields, pastures, open, sandy woodlands, and other disturbed sites.

COMMENTS: Rabbit tobacco was once the most popular native cold remedy in coastal SC (Morton, 1974). "Flower ladies" in the Market Place in Charleston still sell it. The tea is drunk as a febrifuge. The tea is bitter and lemon juice is added to make it palatable for children. Rural people smoke the plant for asthma. F. P. Porcher (1869) said that the plant was an astringent, and the leaves and flowers were chewed and the juice swallowed to relieve ulcerations in the mouth and throat. Foster and Duke (1990) give a long list of the past medicinal uses of rabbit tobacco.

704. Popcorn tree; Chinese tallow tree

Sapium sebiferum (L.) Roxburgh
Sà-pi-um se-bí-fe-rum
Euphorbiaceae (Spurge Family)

DESCRIPTION: Small to medium size tree, to 50′ or taller, easily spreading; sap milky; leaves alternate, with a pair of glands near base of blade; flowers produced in long, slender spikes, with male flowers above and female flowers near the base; flowers May–June; fruits mature August–November; capsule walls fall away, exposing the white seeds.

RANGE-HABITAT: Naturalized from NC to FL, and west to TX and OK; in SC primarily in the outer coastal plain; common; moist areas in maritime forests, edge of fields, disturbed areas in coastal cities, barnyards, impoundments, and ditch banks.

COMMENTS: Popcorn tree is native to China and Japan and was introduced into the colonies as an ornamental or shade tree as early as the 1700s. It quickly became naturalized and is a serious weed in many areas because it has adapted to a wide range of soil types. It is still highly prized as a cultivated tree because of the brilliant yellow to red leaves in the fall. The Chinese used the waxy coating on the seeds to make soap and candles. All parts contain a poisonous milky juice. The common name, popcorn tree, alludes to the cluster of white seeds that look like popcorn. In the Carolina lowcountry, the seeds are used in Christmas decorations.

705. Rattle-bush; purple sesban

Sesbania punicea (Cavanilles) Bentham
Ses-bàn-i-a pu-ní-ce-a
Fabaceae (Pea or Bean Family)

DESCRIPTION: Shrub 3–10′ tall; leaves even-pinnately compound with 12–40 entire leaflets; flowers June–September; legume 4-winged, matures August–November.

RANGE-HABITAT: NC south to FL, and west to TX; common weed in the coastal plain and maritime strand of SC; along roadsides and in ditches and sandy wet places.

COMMENTS: Rattle-bush was introduced into FL as an ornamental. It escaped and spread throughout the southeast. Kingsbury (1964) reports that rattle-bush is highly poisonous to fowl and sheep (and presumably to humans).

SYNONYM: *Daubentonia punicea* (Cavanilles) Augustin de Candolle—RAB

706. Elliott's aster

Aster elliottii Torrey & Gray
Ás-ter el-li-ótt-i-i
Asteraceae (Aster or Sunflower Family)

DESCRIPTION: Perennial, colonial herb with slender, often elongate rhizomes; stems to 6′ tall; leaves gradually reduced upward, acute to slightly acuminate, with tapering base, non-clasping, sessile, smooth; flowers late September–November.

RANGE-HABITAT: Coastal plain species from se. VA to se. GA, throughout peninsular FL to the coastal FL panhandle; in SC in the outer coastal plain; most common in roadside ditches, but also in swamps and their borders, wet thickets, fresh to brackish shores, and marshes.

SIMILAR SPECIES: A similar species is *A. puniceus* L. Radford et al. (1968) state that *A. elliottii* is probably not distinct from *A. puniceus*. The leaf bases of *A. puniceus* are auriculate, while the leaf bases of *A. elliottii* are not auriculate. *A. puniceus* occupies similar habitats but occurs in the mountain and piedmont.

707. Small-flowered morning-glory

Ipomoea lacunosa L.
I-po-moè-a la-cu-nò-sa
Convolvulaceae (Morning-glory Family)

DESCRIPTION: Twining, annual, herbaceous vine; stems sparsely hairy; leaves ovate, entire, or with two basal lobes, heart-shaped, and usually with maroon margins; corolla white, bell-shaped, 0.25–0.75″ long; flowers September–frost.

RANGE-HABITAT: Native weedy species from NJ west to OH, IL, and KS, south to FL and e. TX; common throughout SC; moist fields and thickets, along roadsides, and in waste places.

708. Cypress-vine

Ipomoea quamoclit L.
I-po-moè-a quá-mo-clit
Convolvulaceae (Morning-glory Family)

DESCRIPTION: Twining, herbaceous, annual vine; leaves pinnately divided into narrow, linear segments; corolla crimson, with a long tube; flowers September–frost:

RANGE-HABITAT: FL to TX, and north to VA and KS; in SC chiefly in the coastal plain and maritime strand; occasional; roadsides and fences, and in cultivated fields and other waste areas.

COMMENTS: Cypress-vine is naturalized from tropical America. The common name refers to its leaves, which resemble the terminal, needle-bearing twigs of cypress trees.

709. Chinese privet

Ligustrum sinense Loureiro
Li-gús-trum si-nén-se
Oleaceae (Olive Family)

DESCRIPTION: Shrub or small tree; leaves evergreen, or somewhat deciduous in severe winters or in colder parts of its range; leaves opposite, simple, short-stalked; blades mostly elliptic; flowers white, with a disagreeable odor; flowers May–June; drupes dark blue or bluish black, mature September–November.

RANGE-HABITAT: Widely naturalized throughout the southeast; common throughout SC; moist forests, especially alluvial bottomlands, fencerows, wet thickets, well-drained and poorly drained places, and around abandoned house sites.

COMMENTS: Chinese privet is a native of China and has presumably spread due to birds feeding on the fruits of ornamental plantings and dispersing the seeds in their droppings. It is one of South Carolina's most noxious weeds, choking out native species in hundreds of square miles. How quickly it has spread can be determined from Small (1933), who stated that it "occurs as an escape in S La." Once established in a site, it is difficult to eradicate by mechanical or biological methods; chemical treatment is the only effective method.

710. Common goldenrod; field goldenrod

Solidago altissima L.
   So-li-dà-go al-tís-si-ma
Asteraceae (Aster or Sunflower Family)

DESCRIPTION: Perennial herb 2–7′ tall, with long and slender rhizomes; stems with appressed hairs; lower leaves narrowly lanceolate, 3-nerved; flowers September–October.

RANGE-HABITAT: Native to the eastern US and essentially throughout SC; dry soils in old fields, pastures, meadows, and along roadsides.

COMMENTS: Common goldenrod is one of the most abundant and widely distributed species of *Solidago*. Some authors consider it a variety of the northern *S. canadensis* L.

SYNONYM: *Solidago canadensis* var. *scabra* Torrey & Gray—W

711. Huguenot fern; spider brake fern

Pteris multifida Poiret
   Pté-ris mul-tí-fi-da
Pteridaceae (Maidenhair Fern Family)

DESCRIPTION: Rootstock short, scaly, sending out close-set spreading fronds; blade divided pedately below and pinnately above into 5–7 well-spaced, long, narrow segments; rachis winged; sori marginal.

RANGE-HABITAT: New Hanover County, NC, south to peninsular FL, and west to c. TX; in SC chiefly in the coastal plain; occasional; circumneutral soils of wooded slopes and ravines and in damp crevices of masonry around towns and cemeteries.

SIMILAR SPECIES: Huguenot fern is similar to ladder brake fern (*P. vittata* L.), an escapee from cultivation and native of China. Both species occur in similar habitats in the coastal area. The rachis of *P. multifida* is winged; the rachis of *P. vittata* is not winged.

COMMENTS: Huguenot fern is an escapee from cultivation and is native to east Asia. Its presence in the crevices of masonry is due to the calcium content from the limestone that was used to make the masonry. Over the years, as the masonry weathers, crevices are created that allow for the establishment of new plants by spores. Repointing of brick foundations with modern cement is reducing the habitat for Huguenot fern, and its numbers are decreasing.

   The common name, Huguenot fern, refers to its 1868 discovery on the masonry in the cemetery of the Huguenot Church on Church Street in Charleston. It still grows there and at the adjacent St. Philip's Episcopal Church. Huguenot fern is readily grown in gardens.

Field Guide to Natural Plant Communities

THE MOUNTAINS

Greenville County

Caesar's Head State Park (Raven Cliff Falls Trail to Raven Cliff Falls Overlook)

The trail begins in a montane oak-hickory forest and passes through Canada hemlock forests in the ravines, pine-oak heaths, more montane oak-hickory forests, and chestnut oak forests. The montane oak-hickory forests are by far the most diverse community. In the fall, areas on the slopes are covered with wildflowers, including several species of eupatorium and Joe-pye-weed, at least two asters, three goldenrods, wild lettuce, gall-of-the-earth, and bear's-foot. Additional species in bloom include hog peanut, jewelweed, horsebalm, American heal-all, and Indian-tobacco.

Because the diversity of fall wildflowers corresponds with the migration of hawks, songbirds, and butterflies (especially the monarch), this trail should be hiked in late September or October. The view of Raven Cliff Falls from the overlook is spectacular any time of year.

Eva Russell Chandler Heritage Preserve

The South Carolina Department of Natural Resources (SCDNR) owns and manages this 251-acre property. The cataract bogs and the granitic domes are the most spectacular wildflower communities. The loop trail, which begins at the parking area, goes through a pine-oak heath community, over a small knoll, and down through a chestnut oak forest to a steep granitic dome, with a small stream running along its eastern border. Water slides, rather than falls, over the smooth granitic exposure (hence the name cataract bog). The water and seepage produce a bog along the water slide that has abundant moisture and high light intensity. Many species characteristic of more common bogs in the piedmont and mountains are present, such as tag alder, red chokeberry (*Aronia arbutifolia*), yellowroot, small green wood-orchid, and cinnamon fern (*Osmunda cinnamomea*). These bogs also provide habitat for some distinctive species, including limeseep grass-of-Parnassus, Indian paint brush, and mountain sweet pitcher-plant.

Although the granitic dome here is quite steep, the visitor can explore the dome as long as care is taken. Most species typical of acidic granitic domes are found here, except for species associated with higher elevation domes like mountain dwarf-dandelion and prolific St. John's-wort (*Hypericum prolificum*). Showy species include Appalachian fameflower, pineweed, and rattlesnake-master.

For those willing to make their own trail, there are several more water

slides and granitic exposures, as well as some distinctive seepage islands farther downstream. Cross the stream at the head of the water slide, being careful not to slip on the algae, and proceed downslope. About 100 yards
downstream are some small seepage islands with a variety of interesting plants
including horned bladderwort, round-leaf sundew, Joe-pye-weed, and Virginia
meadow-beauty (*Rhexia virginica*). Water slides and granitic domes intermittently bound the stream for another 0.5 mile, nearly to US 276.

Back at the top of the first water slide, the loop trail continues northward and to the west of the stream (Slickum Creek) and takes the visitor back
to Persimmon Ridge Road, about 0.25 mile east of the parking area. During a
visit in early October, look for autumn coral-root in the pine woods just before
the trail intersects with Persimmon Ridge Road.

Note: In order to see the full array of wildflowers in bloom, visit in mid-
April, mid-June, mid-July, and early October.

Watson Heritage Preserve (Mathews Creek Bog)

Mathews Creek Bog is within the 1600-acre Watson Heritage Preserve, which
the South Carolina Department of Parks, Recreation, and Tourism (SCDPRT)
designated as the Mountain Bridge Wilderness and Recreation Area. Go east to
west on the Gum Gap Trail (Mountain Bridge Trails; Naturaland Trust, 1994)
to the confluence of Mathews Creek and Julian Creek. From there the Gum
Gap Trail proceeds west across Mathews Creek and follows Julian Creek. From
the east side of Mathews Creek, proceed north on an old logging road that parallels Mathews Creek. Follow this road up and down hills for about 0.5 mile
until it junctions with Mathews Creek at a boggy area dominated by sphagnum
mosses. Mathews Creek Bog is on the other side of Mathews Creek. The best
part of the bog is about 100 yards upstream on the west side. The logging road
that once accessed this site is becoming quite overgrown. If you resist the
temptation to take better trails that veer to the east or northeast, you should
not have any trouble finding this site.

This is South Carolina's only montane bog community. It occupies a
gently sloping area between the base of a southeast-facing slope and Mathews
Creek. The sphagnum-dominated areas occupy bands of varying width along
a number of seepage channels that originate at the base of the slope. Between
the sphagnum-dominated areas are thick zones of shrubs, formerly harboring
acid-loving bog species, but now dominated by great laurel. Tree cover in the
bog is sparse, with scattered small stems of red maple and pitch pine (*Pinus
rigida*). A dense thicket of great laurel surrounds the bog, with white pine
(*Pinus strobus*) dominating the canopy. Typical shrubs in the bog include tag
alder, mountain white-alder, hardhack, mountain laurel, clammy azalea, sweet
azalea, and common winterberry (*Ilex verticillata*). Typical herbs include cinnamon fern (*Osmunda cinamomea*), royal fern (*Osmunda regalis* var. *spectabilis*),
red turtlehead (*Chelone obliqua*), American climbing fern, and a variety of
sedges and rushes. This is the only known location in South Carolina for
swamp pink. Galax and fly poison (*Amianthium muscaetoxicum*) appear to be
invading the bog.

Although this was once a good example of the montane bog community, natural succession has significantly degraded the site. Since 1979, the

invasion of shrubs, mostly great laurel, has reduced the extent of the sphag-num-dominated areas by more than half. The population of swamp pink has drastically declined. Two rare orchids, Appalachian twayblade and bog-rose orchid, have completely disappeared. Shrub diversity has declined, while species such as male-berry (*Lyonia ligustrina*) and clammy azalea have increased. The herb layer has less diversity, while climbing fern and galax appear to have increased. Although the absence of fire as a periodic natural dis-turbance is the likely culprit, the exact cause of this rapid natural succession is unknown. If appropriate active management is not initiated soon, this site may not be recoverable.

Mountain Bridge trails

Mountain Bridge is a series of contiguous lands in protective public or private ownership that connects two undeveloped watersheds of Greenville: a water-shed associated with the Table Rock Reservoir to the east and the Poinsett Reservoir to the west. The North Carolina border forms the northern bound-ary, and only a 3.0-mile-long segment is needed to complete the "bridge." Included in the Mountain Bridge are Jones Gap State Park (3,346 acres), Cae-sar's Head State Park, the Watson Heritage Preserve (1600 acres), Naturaland Trust property (nearly a 1000 acres), Camp Greenville (1600 acres protected in perpetuity by a conservation trust), and a private 500-acre tract protected by a conservation easement.

Thirty-five miles of well-maintained trails provide direct access and/or scenic vistas of four waterfalls with drops of several hundred feet, smaller waterfalls or water slides, granitic domes and sheer cliffs, boulder outcrops, and miles of pristine rocky streams. The Mountain Bridge is in the heart of the Blue Ridge Escarpment where the mountains drop abruptly from 1500 to 2000 feet to the piedmont.

Most of the wildflower communities typical of the mountains are pres-ent in the Mountain Bridge, with the exception of the rocky streamside and the bottomland hardwood. Seventeen well-maintained trails (13 main trails and 4 connectors) allow the visitor direct access to all communities except the state's only montane bog. Trails were built for day hikes, with numerous and varied possibilities.

From streamside to ridge crests, the typical plant communities encoun-tered in the Mountain Bridge are Canada hemlock forests, cove forests (rich and acidic variants), chestnut oak forests, and pine-oak heaths. At high eleva-tions, or sometimes at ridge crests or at low elevations, oak-hickory forests are present. Additional and more uncommon communities include granitic domes (both true granitic dome and acidic cliff communities), spray cliffs, and cataract bogs.

The *Guide to the Mountain Bridge Trails* contains trail descriptions, topo-graphic and perspective maps, advice, and detailed rules and regulations. Copies may be obtained by contacting:

Naturaland Trust
Box 728
Greenville, SC 29602

Trail (1)—Jones Gap Trail

Jones Gap Trail follows old Jones Gap Road. It is an easy trail with a constant, gentle grade. Its western sections go through the acidic variant of cove forests and to a lesser extent Canada hemlock forests. Along its eastern extent, near the Jones Gap parking lot, it goes through oak-hickory forests as well as the above community types. Scattered pockets of rich cove forests are present. The Canada hemlock forest that is near the junction with the Tom Miller Trail is at a high elevation and includes several unusual species, including yellow birch (*Betula lutea*) in the canopy and painted trillium and long-spur violet (*Viola rostrata*) in the herb layer. Jones Gap harbors one of the two known populations of yellow birch in the state, as well as the only known location for painted trillium in South Carolina. Much of the trail upstream from the junction with the Tom Miller Trail goes through the acidic cove forest. The trail has many gravelly seepages that harbor plants more typical of spray cliffs, including the rare American water-pennywort. The rare Dutchman's pipe is common downstream from Dargan's Cascade.

Trail (2)—Tom Miller Trail

Because of the high elevation (> 3000 feet) at the trailhead at Raven Cliffs parking lot, the oak-hickory forests here are sometimes described as a montane variant. Red oak, sweet birch, and tulip tree dominate the canopy, and the herb layer is moderately rich. Farther along the trail in this community, look for yellow lady's slipper. The pine-oak heath community is typical, with no unusual components. The oak-hickory forest about 100 yards down the trail from the interpretive sign has a population of three-birds orchid (*Triphora trianthophora*). The acidic cove forest near the junction of the trail with the Middle Saluda River includes a nice population of Vasey's trillium. Painted trillium is abundant along the trail as it enters the Canada hemlock forest along the Middle Saluda River. South Carolina's only population of French Broad heartleaf is found with this attractive trillium.

Trail (5)—Bill Kimball Trail

The eastern portions of this trail contain examples of rich cove forests, acidic cove forests, and Canada hemlock forests that sometimes blend together. Beech is an important component of the cove forests canopy, and Fraser magnolia and cucumber magnolia (*Magnolia acuminata*) are important understory components. Unusual plants include puttyroot, yellow lady's slipper, striped maple (*Acer pensylvanica*), and Dutchman's pipe. One of the highlights of this trail is the acidic cliff called "El Lieutenant," which is more than 300 feet high. The trail follows the base of this granite massif, but the massif is so steep that there are few footholds for vascular plants, and those that are present are difficult to observe. The trail traverses chestnut oak forests that have a thick zone of great laurel and a poor herb layer. At one of the switchbacks that bypasses and climbs above El Lieutenant, there are several small populations of mountain spleenwort (*Asplenium montanum*). The trail next follows a narrow ridge crest through a pine-oak heath community, which is typical except for occasional Carolina hemlock saplings.

Trail (20)—Pinnacle Pass Trail

This trail is described as the longest, most strenuous, and one of the most diverse of the Mountain Bridge trails. The diversity of plant communities, scenic vistas, and other attributes make this trail a "must see" in its entirety. To see all the plants of interest and this trail's most outstanding features, a granitic dome community and its associated cataract bog, visit this site in the spring, summer, and fall. For a shortcut that takes you quickly to the middle of the trail, turn onto River Falls Road (SC-97) from US 276/SC-11. After about 3.0 miles turn left onto Oil Camp Creek Road. Go about 3.0 miles (the last several hundred yards are unpaved) to a pipe gate that bars further vehicle access. Park and walk about 0.5 mile to where the road intersects with Pinnacle Pass Trail on your right. The trail junction is easy to miss. You will cross two bridges before you reach the trail junction, and a third bridge is just past the junction.

It is a cool and pleasant walk along Oil Camp Creek Road through beech forests and Canada hemlock forests. Many of the characteristic species of these communities are present. Once Pinnacle Pass Trail has been reached, it is 1.8 miles to the granitic dome and cataract bog. The elevation changes from 1320 to 2520 feet. The trail mostly goes through chestnut oak forests and pine-oak heaths. The chestnut oak forest along the first one-third of the trail is young and has a significant pine component, but larger trees and fewer pines are present along the last two-thirds. Rock exposures, small water slides, and a jumble of large boulders at the base of a steep rock exposure provide an opportunity to examine distinctive features of granitic domes. Look up at the top of the rock exposure and note the exfoliation.

The highlights of this trail are reached when you cross a large granitic dome that has good scenic vistas. The dome has pockets of vegetation as well as large steep expanses with little vegetation. The larger vegetated islands are occupied by Virginia pines (*Pinus virginiana*), which exhibit varying degrees of stunting, or in some places by Carolina hemlock. The upper margins of the dome have an abundance of fringe-tree, which makes a flowering display in late April. Most of the species characteristic of acidic granitic domes are present. Mountain dwarf-dandelion is abundant and in flower all summer. Appalachian fameflower also blooms most of the summer, but remember that its flowers don't open until about four o'clock in the afternoon.

The trail goes across the upper part of the granitic dome and crosses Eastern Stream before it reenters the forest and turns upslope. Excellent cataract bogs are found both upstream and downstream. The upstream portion is easily accessible and poses few hazards. The downstream portion can be dangerous when approached from the open granitic dome. The stream spreads widely over the dome following heavy rains, promoting algal growth that makes the rocks slick.

The cataract bog upstream is small and somewhat shaded but still has excellent populations of most cataract bog species. Of special note is the large population of frog's breeches pitcher-plant. Along with Indian paint brush, this makes a spectacular flowering display in May. Other distinctive spring-blooming species include common grass-pink (*Calopogon tuberosus,* plate 331 in WCL) and northern wild raisin (*Viburnum cassinoides*). Summer blooming species in or adjacent to the cataract bog include northern sundrops, Carolina tassel-rue, galax, and round-leaf sundew. In the fall, the contrast of the large white flowers of limeseep grass-of-Parnassus to the dense heads of tiny white flowers of cowbane and the yellow flowers of several species of coreopsis is spectacular.

Table Rock State Park

This 3000+ acre property is a registered National Natural Landmark and is one of the most outstanding natural areas in South Carolina. Table Rock State Park is the trailhead for the Foothills Trail and includes 11.4 miles of well-maintained trails. Although most of the trails are demanding, the Carrick Creek Loop is suitable for all but the most infirm; its beginning segment is wheelchair accessible. The park trails go to or through at least six wildflower communities, and the granitic dome community here is the best of this type. The spray cliffs community is the only major wildflower community in the park that is not accessible by trail. Trails take the visitor to numerous scenic overlooks, hugh boulder outcrops, overhanging rock ledges, many waterfalls and slides, and the tallest mountain in South Carolina. The most spectacular natural communities here are the granitic domes at the terminus of the Table Rock Trail and the montane oak-hickory forests at the top of Pinnacle Mountain.

Table Rock Trail

This trail begins at the Nature Center at an elevation of 1160 feet and ends at a scenic granitic dome community, 0.4 mile beyond the top of Table Rock Mountain (3124 feet). From beginning to end, the following plant communities are traversed: Canada hemlock forests, cove forests (acidic variant), oak-hickory forests (mesic to dry), chestnut oak forests, pine-oak heaths, montane oak-hickory forests, and granitic domes. A dramatic example of the influence of soils on plant community composition is evident in the transition of communities leading up to and including Panther Gap (the junction of the Pinnacle Mountain Trail with the Table Rock Trail). From the Nature Center until just below Panther Gap, the plant communities become drier as elevation increases. The driest of these, the pine-oak heath, merges into a mesic oak-hickory forest just below and including Panther Gap. What would allow a high elevation community to be more mesic than a low elevation community? In two words—soil characteristics. The soils at Panther Gap are deeper and richer than any of the soils at the lower elevations along the Table Rock Trail, so it can support a more abundant and diverse herbaceous flora. Note that Small's dwarf iris (*Iris verna* var. *smalliana*) of the dry pine-oak heaths is abruptly replaced by dwarf crested iris of the montane oak-hickory forests.

The Canada hemlock forests here are typical, with the canopy dominated by Canada hemlock (*Tsuga canadensis*), white pine, and sweet birch. Great laurel forms dense thickets immediately adjacent to streams. Be sure to break the bark on a small sweet birch twig and smell the strong wintergreen odor. Interesting species to look for in different seasons include round-leaf violet and Indian cucumber-root.

The cove forests are an acidic variant and are not as diverse as the typical community. Interesting species to look for include pagoda dogwood (*Cornus alternifolia*) and pale Indian-plantain. The legume that covers the ground in much of this community is hog peanut.

The oak-hickory forests and pine-oak heaths communities are typical.

Common herbaceous species in the oak-hickory forests include halberd-leaved violet, Biltmore carrion-flower (*Smilax biltmoreana*), and spotted wintergreen. Typical herbs in the pine-oak heaths include pale yellow bellwort and galax. Horse sugar is a common shrub. To verify horse sugar identification, chew the leaf for its sweet taste. Mountain laurel and Carolina rhododendron (*Rhododendron carolinianum*) are the common tall heaths, and both form attractive displays when in full bloom.

As mentioned previously, a montane variant of oak-hickory forests dominates the ridge at Panther Gap. White oak and tulip tree dominate the canopy. The herbaceous cover is dense and diverse.

Table Rock Trail traverses sections of three excellent domes. The first, Governor's Rock, a few tenths of a mile beyond the wooded top of Table Rock Mountain, provides a beautiful scenic overlook, and most of the typical granitic dome species are here, including the rare divided-leaf ragwort (*Senecio millefolium*), cliff saxifrage, and Appalachian fameflower. A spectacular plant here, and on the other granitic domes along the trail, is the prolific St. John's-wort (*Hypericum prolificum*). These sites are among the few South Carolina locations where prolific St. John's-wort is found.

Additional species of interest that can be seen at the next granitic dome (one that provides a scenic overlook to the south, including the two lakes in the park) are hop-tree and white mountain-mint, which has a delightful smell. The trail next turns to the north and onto the property of Greenville Watershed. The granitic dome here provides habitat for many unusual plants, including horned bladderwort and the mountain variety of sand myrtle (*Leiophyllum buxifolium* var. *prostratum*). This is also one of the best places to see Table Mountain pine, which is easily recognized by its short, thick leaves and female cones with sharp curved spines.

Pinnacle Ridge Trail (Panther Gap to the top of Pinnacle Mountain)
This trail traverses a variety of mesic to dry oak-hickory forests. Plants of special note between Panther Gap and the junction with the Mill Creek Pass Trail include three-parted violet (*Viola tripartita*) and Dutchman's pipe. Between Mill Creek Pass and Pinnacle Mountain are some large silverbells, pink lady's slipper, and large-flowered trillium.

The most spectacular part of this trail is the top and sides of Pinnacle Mountain, which harbor a montane oak-hickory forest and a large number of herbs that are unusual for South Carolina. The top is somewhat weedy as a result of some past disturbance (natural?) as indicated by (1) the abundance of bear's-foot, ox-eye (*Heliopsis helianthoides*), and a species of blackberry (*Rubus* sp.), and (2) the abundance of black locust (*Robinia pseudo-acacia*) in the canopy. Unusual herbs include monkshood, Walter's crownbeard (*Verbesina walteri*), and poke milkweed.

Pinnacle Mountain Trail
All of the wildflower communities that occur along Table Rock Trail are present on Pinnacle Mountain Trail. This trail goes through vegetation that often has a different look. The trail is steep in places and follows streams or ridges for a significant portion of its length. Mill Creek Falls and Bald Rock Overlook are two of the more scenic portions, but the trail also goes near a sheer cliff,

some large boulder outcrops, and under a large rock overhang, which is the typical habitat for cave alumroot (*Heuchera parviflora*). Unusual plants along this trail include piedmont horsebalm (*Collinsonia tuberosa*), which is found along the south loop of the Carrick Creek loop trail, gaywings, which is found in several places below Mill Creek Falls, and autumn coral-root, which is found just east of the large, cavelike rock overhang.

The Bald Rock Overlook provides a panoramic view and is less dry, and hence more weedy, than the other granitic domes in the park. Typical granitic dome species are present, including a large population of Appalachian fame-flower. Attractive weedy species include leather-flower (*Clematis crispa*) and Carolina spinypod.

Oconee County

Buzzard Roost Heritage Preserve

This 285-acre heritage preserve includes most of Buzzard Roost Mountain and parts of adjacent Poor and Hurricane Mountains. The SCDNR owns and manages it. Hiking and nature trails are accessible off of USFS 744-I. Follow the directions in the preserve guide that is available from the SCDNR.

This site has seen considerable past disturbance, especially heavy logging, as evidenced by old roads, eroded slopes, and relatively young forests. Nonetheless, significant major features abound at this foothills site. Outcrops of marble and other rocks high in calcium and magnesium provide habitat for rare rock-dwelling ferns; in addition, these rocks weather to produce high calcium and magnesium soils, which promote the growth of other rare plants. Pine-oak heath forests, which are rare in the piedmont, are dominated by Table Mountain pine. Most of the site was prescribe-burned by helicopter in the spring of 1998 in an effort to regenerate Table Mountain pine and to improve the growing conditions for several rare plants. The burn was designed to be very hot in order to reduce significantly the tree and shrub cover and to promote the opening and release of seeds from cones of Table Mountain pine (plate 155).

The trail forks at the base of the slope, which is a short distance from the trailhead. The left fork climbs to the top of Buzzard Roost Mountain. The fire apparently got hotter as it approached the top, evidenced by the number of trees and shrubs that were killed. The pine-oak heath forests are now open. Even the dense growth of mountain laurel on the north-facing slopes has been reduced. More species are in flower in this community than would be expected. Butterflies are abundant, as are some bird species in the early successional habitats. The upper, south-facing slopes below the ridge top are occupied by a chestnut oak forest, which is not diverse and seems to have been minimally affected by the fire.

The trail loops around the top of Buzzard Roost Mountain and returns the same way. On the way back, when the trail turns sharply to the north, the adventurous hiker may go off the trail and follow the south edge of the ridge downslope. Some large boulders and open hardwood slopes with Blue Ridge bindweed are encountered. A small population of Virginia marbleseed is found here. This is a species that is common to barrens and glades on calcium-rich soils. Continue southward on the ridgeline to the gap between Poor Mountain and Buzzard Roost Mountain. An old logging road splits the gap. Go 300 feet due southeast to a steep slope with marble boulders; here you can find two of South Carolina's rarest rock-dwelling ferns, purple cliff-brake and blackstem spleenwort (*Asplenium resiliens,* plate 175 in *WCL*). In the rich forests straight downslope is whorled horsebalm.

Back at the trail junction, take the right fork downhill to the southwestern property boundary near road USFS 744-A. After about 0.25 mile, rocks and small boulders are visible on both sides. The best outcrop of marble rocks is on the right in an oak-hickory forest. Of particular interest are blackstem spleenwort, Georgia hackberry (*Celtis tenuifolia*), and supplejack (*Berchemia scandens,* plate 142 in *WCL*), which is rare vine in the piedmont and usually associated with coastal plain bottomlands. Near the property boundary, as the trail becomes severely eroded, smooth purple coneflower grows in a successional pine-oak-hickory forest. The surveyor's flags that mark most plants indicate that these plants are part of a monitoring effort. Please no not disturb the flags. The trail does not loop back to the trailhead. When you come to the intersection of another logging road, turn around and walk back.

Sumter National Forest: Andrew Pickens District

Station Cove

This site is a "must visit" because of the spectacular display of wildflowers, especially the two different color forms (maroon and yellow) of little sweet Betsy in mid-March, almost two weeks before any other site in the mountains has wildflowers in bloom. The trail leading to Station Cove Falls is short, and the hike is easy. Access to this site is off SC-11, a few miles east of Walhalla. From SC-11 take a left on Oconee Station Road (SC-95). Proceed for several miles and park in a turnout to the left, 0.25 mile after the entrance to Oconee Station. A well-used trail is unmarked, but obvious.

The trail begins in a pine-mixed hardwood stand that is an old field reverting to forest. It passes through a more mature oak-hickory forest, goes by an old beaver pond, crosses a few small creeks, passes a broad streamside flat, and leads to a steeper ravine and Station Cove Falls.

Along the way you may see Robin's-plantain, pink lady's slipper, and several species of violets and blueberries. The oak-hickory forest is mature and has some interesting trail-side wildflowers, including green-and-gold, the two color forms of little sweet Betsy, and bloodroot. The streamside flat is probably best described as a beech forest and harbors little sweet Betsy, may-apple, windflower, and black cohosh.

As the trail approaches Station Cove Falls, the slopes steepen, and the beech forest gradually changes into a rich cove forest. The dominance of tulip tree in the canopy suggests past disturbance; otherwise, this is a typical cove forest with diverse tree and shrub strata and a dense and diverse herb layer. Silverbell is the dominant understory species. Shrubs include painted buckeye, pawpaw, wild allspice, strawberry-bush, and sweet-shrub. The herb layer includes unusual species such as blue cohosh, doll's-eyes, sharp-lobed liverleaf, and sweet white trillium, as well as more common species such as bloodroot and maidenhair fern.

Station Cove Falls is two-tiered and harbors the spray cliff community.

Bull's Sluice

The rocky streamside wildflower community is the main community of interest at Bull's Sluice. From the end of the paved path that leads from the parking area to just below Bull's Sluice, the community contains a mix of wet, mesic and dry species, as well as weedy species. The streamside consists of deep, dry sands and rocks interspersed with lower lying moist to mesic areas. Dry-loving species include sensitive briar (*Schrankia microphylla*), whorled-leaf coreopsis, stiff-leaved aster (*Aster linarifolius*), and the rare ash-leaf golden-banner. Moisure-loving to mesic species that are more typical of this community include bush-honeysuckle, Virginia willow (*Itea virginica*), sweet azalea, clammy azalea, greenhead coneflower, and bushy St. John's-wort (*Hypericum densiflorum*).

The rocky streamside community upstream from Bull's Sluice is much more mesic and includes such typical species as brookfoam, Carolina tasselrue, and hollow-stem Joe-pye-weed. Here, dry rock crevices harbor mountain dwarf-dandelion.

Tamassee Falls

This is one of the most spectacular wildflower sites in the Andrew Pickens District. It contains excellent examples of the rich cove forests and spray cliff communities, as well as examples of oak-hickory forests and cove forests that are transitional between the rich cove forests and acidic cove forests. The following directions are provided because the roads in the area are confusing. From the junction of SC-183 and SC-11, just west of Walhalla, proceed east on SC-11 for about 4.0 miles. Take a left on SC-95, also called Oconee Station Road. Past Oconee Station, SC-95 becomes USFS Road 108 or Tamassee Knob Road. At an unmarked fork in the road, bear left. After a few miles, take a left on C37CH9, which is still USFS Road 108, also called Jumping Branch Road. In about 1.5 miles, you will pass USFS Road 715 on your left; in a short distance, take a left on USFS Road 715A. Follow this road for about 0.6 mile to the crossing of Tamassee Creek. Park and follow the gated road/trail to the northeast.

A sense of adventure is needed to make the 1.5-mile trek from the parking area to the falls. A primitive trail leads to the falls. As you proceed upstream to the falls, keep in mind that you always want to follow the main left branch. The access road/trail in the lower half crosses three long broad bottoms (coves) that were once farmed, but as of July 1997, were planted as wildlife openings. Go through each wildlife opening, and at the upper end of each, find the road or trail that proceeds upstream. After you pass the third wildlife opening, the trail becomes obvious until you get to within 300 to 400 yards of the falls. When you come to a junction of two main creek branches, be sure to take the left fork. When you get to within about 200 yards of the falls, it is best to follow the creekbed. Be careful! The rocks can be slippery.

Just beyond the first wildlife opening and at the first trail crossing of Tamassee Creek, there is a population of Canada enchanter's-nightshade in the cobble next to the creek. The wildlife openings are planted with a variety of crop plants to attract deer and other wildlife. The trail traverses a variety of communities, mostly an acidic variant of cove forests and oak-hickory forests. The acidic cove forest is a transitional community because it is richer in herbs than the typical acidic cove forests but not as rich as the typical rich cove forests. Keep an eye out for small trees of butternut (*Juglans cinerea*), a species that is in serious decline because it is being attacked by the same fungus that devastated American chestnut. The oak-hickory forests along the trail have a typical assemblage of species, except that it has some large populations of lousewort.

Rich cove forests occupy the jumbled rocks and rich soil in the amp- itheater-like area surrounding Tamassee Falls. Tree and shrub layers have the typical assemblage of species, but the herb layer is atypical in its diversity of unusual ferns. Fern species include walking fern, Goldie's wood fern, fancy fern (*Dryopteris intermedia*), silvery spleenwort (*Athyrium asplenoides*), as well as the common maidenhair fern and marginal woodfern (*Dryopteris margin- alis*). Many typical rich cove species are present. Sweet white trillium and spikenard are found in small numbers.

Tamassee Falls drops vertically about 60 feet over the middle of a 100- yard-wide rock ledge. A broad zone of spray cliff surrounds the falls, but this area becomes drier with increased distance from the waterfall. The spray cliff community occupies the jumbled rocks in and adjacent to the stream for per- haps 200 feet downstream. Mosses and liverworts cover the cliffs and rocks, with vascular plants occupying small crevices and ledges. Almost all species typical of the spray cliff community are present.

Foothills Trail—Burrells Ford to SC-28
This 10.4-mile segment of the Foothills Trails begins at Burrells Ford and ends at SC-28. The trail traverses Canada hemlock forests, chestnut oak forests, pine-oak heaths, and rocky streamsides. All except the streamside community, which by definition is without a canopy, are dominated by white pine. Good examples of all these communities are present. On a 10-mile trail that takes the visitor from riverbank to ridge top several times, you would expect to go through at least some rich cove forests. None are present. This is probably due to the higher than usual soil acidity that results from an abundance of white pine (*Pinus strobus*). Botanists argue about the existence of a natural white pine- dominated community in the southern Appalachian Mountains. Natural or not, white pine is abundant, especially along the upper reaches of the Chat- tooga River.

The highlights of this segment are the scenic vistas of the Chattooga River, the rocky streamside community, two small waterfalls, several rare plants, and the abundance of large white pines. Scenic views of the Chattooga are numerous all year, but a hike in the winter or early spring, before decidu- ous species leaf out, is an especially good time. About 0.6 mile along the trail from Burrells Ford, shortly after crossing King's Creek, a population of sweet pinesap may be seen (smelled!) on the north side of the trail. In mid-June the streamside community is delightfully scented by sweet azalea. Other stream- side blooming species include brookfoam, galax, mountain laurel, mountain dwarf-dandelion, and Appalachian bluet. Carolina tassel-rue blooms in July and many other species in August-October.

Waterfalls are visible from short spur trails that extend off the main trail, including Big Bend Falls at mile 3.9 and Lick Log Falls at mile 8.1. Neither falls is spectacular, but each is worth a short visit. If interested in a shorter hike, consider walking as far as Big Bend Falls, backtracking less than 1.0 mile to a trail junction, and taking the 2.7-mile-long trail to Cherry Hill Campground on SC-107.

Turkey Ridge Road

Turkey Ridge Road is 2.5 miles west-southwest of Longcreek on US 76. To reach the site, drive to a ridge top that is about 0.4 mile along Turkey Creek Road (USFS Road 755) after its junction with Battle Creek Road (SC-102).

The authors recommend visiting this site on a sunny, still day in mid-March. These conditions provide the greatest chance for viewing the very rare sweet pinesap (plate 139). The purplish-brown sweet pinesap is only a few inches tall, and most plants are hidden under leaf litter. Since this plant is a nonphotosynthetic root parasite, it requires no sunlight. The best way to find this illusive plant is to search by smelling. Its fragrance resembles cinnamon, nutmeg, or cloves. Zigzag slowly through the oak-pine heath on either side of Turkey Ridge Road in a 200-foot-wide band. Use smell to find the vicinity of the plant, then carefully turn over leaf litter to expose the plants.

The community here is a pine-oak heath dominated by scarlet oak, black oak, black gum, and scattered pines, mostly shortleaf pine. The subcanopy is dominated by sourwood and sassafras. Herbaceous vegetation is sparse but includes most species typical of pine-oak heaths or dry oak-hickory forests.

Pickens County

Foothills Trail (Laurel Valley-Laurel Fork Falls)

This 8-mile trail segment is difficult to reach since the western access is by boat via Lake Jocassee. The eastern access is SC-178 via a logging road that is often severely eroded but still passable. A one-way hike is of moderate difficulty. A roundtrip hike may be considered strenuous. The "Guide to the Foothills Trail" (Morris, 1983) provides information about access, topographic maps, trail descriptions, and other information.

Except for a section of virgin Canada hemlock forest along Laurel Fork Creek near the end of the western trail, the plant communities are generally not spectacular in maturity or species diversity, but they do contain species typical of each community. Other communities include chestnut oak forests, cove forests (both the acid and rich cove variants), oak-hickory forests, hardwood bottoms (montane variant), and spray cliffs. Overall, more than 100 species whose photos are included in this book can be seen along the trail.

The trail begins at about an 1800-foot elevation in a reasonably good example of a chestnut oak forest. The canopy is nearly closed and dry oaks dominate, especially chestnut oak and species more typical of cove forests. Red maples are abundant, which is probably an indication of past disturbance. Mountain laurel, great laurel, and gorge rhododendron form a thick, tall shrub layer, and bear huckleberry and buffalo-nut are important shrubs. Galax dominates the herb layer. Additional herbs include large-flower heartleaf, trailing arbutus, dwarf crested iris, devil's-bit, pale yellow bellwort, and plantain pussytoes.

The first one-third of the trail climbs about 2400 feet before gradually descending to the headwaters of the western fork of Laurel Fork Creek. The trail passes in and out of chestnut oak forests. At different elevations, exposures, and soils chestnut oak forest is replaced by cove forests (acid variant), oak-hickory forests, and in small creek drains, by Canada hemlock forests. The acid variant is recognizable by the dominance of tulip tree, red oak, and beech in the canopy; Fraser magnolia and common silverbell in the understory; and characteristic herbs such as dwarf crested iris, halberd-leaved violet, Indian cucumber-root, and sessile-leaf bellwort. The oak-hickory forests are dominated by white oak in the canopy; sourwood, sassafras, and flowering dogwood in the understory; and false solomon's-seal, Indian pipe, spotted wintergreen, and downy rattlesnake plantain in the herb layer.

At mile 4.0 the trail descends to Laurel Fork Creek. From this point to the end, the dominant communities are Canada hemlock forests. Excellent examples are present, including a small segment of virgin forest at mile 6.9. Characteristic species include Canada hemlock (*Tsuga canadensis*), great laurel, and mountain doghobble. Herbs include partridge berry, Indian cucumber-root, common foamflower, round-leaf yellow violet, spikenard, sweet white violet, and Vasey's trillium.

At mile 4.7 the trail descends a slope and, as it levels off, passes through a rich cove forest to a true cove, a level area sheltered by mountains. A dense and diverse herb layer, which is typical of rich cove forests, is present. The canopy is unusual because tulip tree is the overwhelming dominant (an indication of past disturbance) and butternut (*Juglans cinerea*) forms a conspicuous part of the canopy. Northern spicebush dominates the sparse shrub layer. Typical herbs include doll's-eyes, maidenhair fern, Dutchman's pipe, Canada enchanter's-nightshade, Canada violet, wood-nettle, false Solomon's-seal, southern nodding trillium, and Catesby's trillium. This is the preferred habitat for ginseng in South Carolina. Hog peanut dominates the herb layer, which is probably due to a past disturbance.

A spur trail leads to the base of Laurel Fork Falls, which consist of tiers over two ledges, and falls about 45 feet. The spray cliff community is poorly developed, but characteristic species such as branch-lettuce and jewelweed are present. Rocks are slippery, so use great care when investigating this site.

The trail follows Laurel Fork Creek and eventually comes to a weedy opening next to a major logging road. Just beyond this point the trail traverses a montane variant of the hardwood bottom community. Characteristic species include switch-cane, false nettle, coneflower, Canada enchanter's-nightshade, pawpaw, northern spicebush, and painted buckeye.

From mile 6.3 through mile 7.0, numerous colonies of Oconee bells dominate the acid cove forests and adjacent Canada hemlock forests. Although locally abundant, this spectacular wildflower is restricted to a few counties in the mountains of the Carolinas and Georgia. According to one researcher, nearly one-half of the population was lost with the development of Lake Jocassee.

At mile 7.5, a short spur trail leads to the head of Laurel Fork Falls, which in two tiers falls about 160 feet. The last 80 feet falls directly into Lake Jocassee. Care should be taken when viewing of the waterfall from the top. Better views are available farther along the trail or by boat.

Jocassee Gorges (Lower Eastatoe Creek Bluffs)

Access to this site is off Roy Jones Highway (SC-143), which junctions with SC-11 between the Oconee-Pickens county border to the west and US 178 to the east. After the junction of Roy Jones Highway and SC-11, proceed 0.7 mile north on Roy Jones Highway to a turnout and a gate on the right side. Walk 0.3 mile through a recent clear-cut. Enter the uncut woods and take the left fork. Where the road forks sharply to the left and down to Eastatoe Creek, continue walking straight. From this point northward and adjacent to Peach Orchard Branch, the best part of this site occupies only a few acres on either side of the old woods road. The walk through the clear-cut is not without its interesting aspects. Many weedy species bloom at different times, including the fall bloom of the rare Blue Ridge bindweed and a variety of composites. You might also hear birds calling, such as the yellow-breasted chat and the prairie warbler.

This site is one of only two locations for Allegheny spurge (plate 207) in South Carolina and is the only site in protective ownership. It is part of the 30,000+-acre Jocassee Gorges property acquired by the SCDNR from Duke Power Company in 1998. This site is on calcium-rich soils and is in the piedmont, 0.25 mile from the Blue Ridge. It is not surprising that the main plant community here does not fit into any well-defined category. Beech dominates the canopy. Chalk maple (*Acer leucoderme*) dominates the subcanopy, which is suggestive of a typical beech forest of the upper piedmont. However, there is a greater diversity of shrub and herb species than is usually found in beech forests, and these species are of mixed affinities. Allegheny spurge, wild geranium, partridge berry, and bloodroot are suggestive of beech forests. Doll's-eyes, whorled horsebalm, and northern spicebush, when they occur on mid-slopes, are suggestive of basic-mesic forests, which occur on adjacent private property. Most of the remaining unusual species are typical of cove forests, including maidenhair fern, sharp-lobed liverleaf, Canada violet, lily-leaved twayblade, yellow mandarin, pale yellow trillium, puttyroot, common foam-flower, yellow buckeye (*Aesculus flava*), moonseed, wood-nettle, and spike-nard. There are additional spring wildflowers, so careful exploring is in order.

THE PIEDMONT

Abbeville County

Sumter National Forest: Long Cane-Edgefield District

John's Creek Rich Woods

John's Creek Rich Woods, owned and managed by the US Forest Service (USFS), is on an east-northeast-facing slope along an unnamed tributary of John's Creek. On SC-72, between Greenwood and Abbeville, take a right onto SC-133 just before Ebenezer Church. After 0.45 mile take a right on SC-159 and follow it for 1.2 miles until you reach the bridge over John's Creek. Park here. Since the creek junction is private property, walk back along the gravel road until you come to a National Forest boundary sign on the left. Enter the woods' trail at this point. Follow this trail until it ends. Go down the adjacent slope and follow the base of the bluffs eastward. In about 0.75 mile the presence of huge beech and tulip trees indicates that you have reached the site.

The rich beech forest includes a mix of species that are associated with beech forests and basic-mesic forests. The abundance of hop hornbeam, doll's-eyes, southern sugar maple, slippery elm (*Ulmus rubra*), and umbrella magnolia (*Magnolia tripetala*) suggest the presence of the calcium-rich soils that are associated with basic-mesic forests, as does the presence of wild allspice and Shumard's oak (*Quercus shumardii*) on the bluffs and floodplain. However, most of the other species are more typical of beech forests. Additional species to look for include lopseed (*Phryma leptostachya*), pale yellow trillium, perfoliate bellwort (*Uvularia perfoliata*), and violet wood sorrel (*Oxalis violacea*).

The adjacent floodplain is an extension of the uplands, except sweet gum is the dominant tree. The weedy Japanese grass (*Microstegium vimineum*) is abundant here, as is Japanese honeysuckle.

Parson's Mountain Recreation Area
The USFS owns and manages this recreation area. It includes Parson's Mountain Lake, the site of a variety of recreational activities, and Parson's Mountain, a monadnock with a fire tower.

Parson's Mountain hiking trail (1.2 miles one way) begins at the boat ramp parking area. It parallels the south margin of the lake on lower to mid-slopes and turns southwest and climbs to the top of Parson's Mountain. Parson's Mountain is a nearly undisturbed and completely forested monadnock with a maximum elevation of 832 feet; it rises about 400 feet from trailhead to the top.

The plant community at the beginning of the trail is rich but difficult to characterize. The canopy is dominated by northern red oak (*Quercus rubra*), white oak, and beech. Hop hornbeam, redbud, and southern sugar maple dominate the subcanopy. Shrubs include pawpaw, painted buckeye, and bigleaf snowbell (*Styrax grandifolia*). Except for white oak, these are the expected species in a basic-mesic forest. However, the herbaceous species are characteristic of a beech forest, including bloodroot, wild geranium, round-lobed liverleaf, and American alumroot. This community is replaced by a less-rich oak-hickory forest. After this point, the trail goes through oak-hickory forests that become increasingly drier, with shorter trees and more lichen covering the trunks and branches.

This trail is a wonderful place to see the full array of piedmont oak-hickory forests variants in a fairly small area, from the most mesic to the very driest. Ten different oak species are present and at least five hickory species. The mesic oak-hickory forest is dominated by white oak, black oak (*Q. velutina*), and tulip tree, with some bitternut hickory (*Carya cordiformis*). Look for Solomon's-seal, pale Indian-plantain, Carolina moonseed, bear's-foot, as well as many species of beech forests. Dry oak-hickory forests are dominated by white oak, southern red oak (*Q. falcata*), scarlet oak (*Q. coccinea*), mockernut hickory (*C. tomentosa*), and pignut hickory (*C. glabra*), while the driest oak-hickory forests are dominated by post oak, (*Q. stellata*), blackjack oak (*Q.

marilandica), and sand hickory (*C. pallida*). In both of these dry forest types, the ground is nearly covered with low-growing heaths, especially dryland blueberry and southern deerberry. Interesting species include creamy wild indigo, lead plant, goat's rue, several species of *Polygala,* and at least two species of oak-leach (*Aureolaria*).

The trail passes an old gold mine with several open pits 0.2 mile from the top. The fire tower is open. Climb to the top for good views. The scattered distribution of shortleaf pine (*Pinus echinata*) on Parson's Mountain is obvious from the fire tower. Unfortunately there is no loop to this trail.

An "unofficial" trail leads from the southeastern part of the parking lot and provides access to the slopes and bottomlands along one of the upper branches of Cane Creek that drains Parson's Mountain Lake. Go off the trail immediately and walk southward along the base of the bluffs to see interesting species not seen on the "official" hiking trail, including umbrella magnolia (*Magnolia tripetala*) and green violet. Green violet is a typical indicator of basic-mesic forests. On an east-facing bluff, 0.2 mile south of the Parson's Mountain Lake dam and 300 feet west of the junction of Cane Creek with USFS Road 515, green violet occurs with doll's-eyes and pale yellow trillium.

Aiken County

Savannah River Bluffs Heritage Preserve

The SCDNR owns and manages this 83.8-acre site. It is a diverse site with many rare plants. The uniqueness of the site is not immediately obvious, and without specific directions many features would be overlooked. Access is difficult, so be sure to carefully follow the directions provided in the preserve guide available from the SCDNR. The foot trail through the property follows an old dirt road through successional pine-oak woods, a power-line right-of-way, and oak-hickory forests before coming out through bluffs to a floodplain of the Savannah River. From there the trail follows the bluff-floodplain ecotone southward, loops across the floodplain, and parallels a stream back to the original trail near the power line.

The floodplain forest is essentially a finger of coastal plain swamp forests that extends into the piedmont. Bald cypress, sycamore, and river birch dominate the floodplain. All are draped with Spanish moss. Dwarf palmetto is an abundant shrub. Hop-tree is found at the base of the rocky bluffs near the southern trail end. Herbaceous species of interest include trepocarpus (*Trepocarpus aethusae*), a rare member of the carrot family, short-spurred corydalis (*Corydalis flavula*), nemophila (*Nemophila microcalyx*), false rue-anemone, Easter lily, and the only South Carolina population of dwarf larkspur (*Delphinium tricorne*)

Before the trail loops back through the floodplain, look down the Savannah River beyond the heritage preserve boundary to an extensive rocky shoals community. In late May to early June, these shoals have a spectacular display of rocky-shoals spiderlily. During periods of low water, piles of rock form a low dam, with scattered small openings, across the Savannah River. These rock piles are probably remnants of ancient Indian fishing weirs.

The mid to upper slopes of these bluffs have a relatively open canopy, including an abundance of red cedar, which is an indicator of high-calcium soils. An interesting species on these dry slopes is the rare southern privet (*Forestiera ligustrina*), which looks similar to Chinese privet.

Where the trail parallels a small stream that divides the bluffs along the Savannah River, leave it. Cross the stream and follow the base of the bluffs northward into the next small drainage. Here one fines bottlebrush buckeye and yellowwood (*Cladrastic kentukea*).

Return to the main trail and follow it as it parallels a small stream to the northeast. Most of the trail goes through a basic-mesic forest with a diverse herb layer and several unusual wildflowers. Shooting star may be seen at the first bridge crossing. Also look for early saxifrage on the steep banks above the stream. There are two trilliums here, relict trillium and mottled trillium. Dimpled trout lily is abundant in early March. Other species typical of basic-mesic forests include painted buckeye, wild ginger, roundleaf ragwort, and hairy spiderwort. Many of the species typical of beech forests and rich oak-hickory forests are also present.

As you leave the basic-mesic forest and enter a successional pine-oak forest, be sure to look for a low, freely branched woody mint with its delightful fragrance. Georgia savory is a common component of dry woods in the Savannah River drainage, and its crushed leaves are indeed something to savor.

To see all of the species in bloom here, visit in mid-March, mid-April, and mid-May.

Chester County

Landsford Canal State Park

Landsford Canal, a 2.0-mile-long canal with lifting locks, was completed in 1830. It allowed boat traffic to bypass the extensive rocky shoals of the Catawba River. Although interpretation of this nineteenth-century river canal is the focus of this 222-acre state park, viewing a spectacular display of the world's largest population of rocky-shoals spiderlily (*Hymenocallis coronaria*, plate 167) is a major attraction. Well-marked signs along the Canal Trail direct the visitor to a scenic overlook. Spiderlily blooms mid-May to mid-June, and peak bloom is often around 1 June. Other distinctive rocky shoals plants can be seen by exploring the shoals. The first trail off to the left of the Canal Trail, south of its junction with the Nature Trail, provides easy access to the shoals. Distinctive species include riverweed (*Podostemum ceratophyllum*), water willow (*Decodon verticillatus*), as well as a host of weedy species.

The Nature Trail skirts the Catawba River and traverses a mix of levee, bottomland, upland, and ruderal communities. The trees are large, and the trail is a shady, pleasant walk. Common silverbell is abundant and produces a spectacular display in early spring. Numerous showy herbs that are typical of mesic oak-hickory forests also are present. Interesting species flowering in June include smooth spiderwort (*Tradescantia ohiensis*), a sage (*Salvia urticifolia*), a dayflower (*Commelina* sp.), fire pink, tall scouring rush, and several species of bedstraw (*Galium* spp.).

The Canal Trail is on the old tow path that was used to pull boats. Since most of the area on either side of the tow path was completely cleared when the canal was functioning, the Canal Trail goes through secondary growth forests. The forest is mostly a mix of bottomland hardwood, oak-hickory, and beech forest species. The vegetation is somewhat weedy, but a variety of species that are typical of these communities is still present. Common silverbell is abundant and reaches tree height. Interesting species include Carolina phlox (*Phlox carolina*), lopseed (*Phryma leptostachya*), diabase woodmint, Canada columbine, wild allspice, red buckeye, pawpaw, horsebalm, cucumber magnolia (*Magnolia acuminata*), and green violet.

There is standing water in many places in the canal, providing habitat for a variety of wetland and aquatic species. At the Guard Lock you can observe water hemlock, creeping primrose (*Ludwigia palustris*), lizard's tail, elderberry, smartweed (*Polygonum setaceum*), and pickerelweed, as well as a variety of sedges and rushes.

Greenville County

Bunched Arrowhead Heritage Preserve

The SCDNR, with the assistance of the Greenville Audubon Society and volunteers, owns and manages this 133-acre area. The area was acquired to protect one of the few remaining populations of bunched arrowhead (plate 279) and its unusual piedmont springhead seepage forest. The preserve is northeast of Traveler's Rest. Follow the Wildlife Viewing Area signs. Enter at the far (east) end of a fenced parking area and follow the loop trail that begins near the sign.

Bunched arrowhead grows in springhead seepage forests. Unfortunately, the preserve contains little of this community. Most of the area, especially in the vicinity of the parking lot, is in old fields. The other areas are young mixed pine-hardwoods or bottomland forests. The extensive uplands were acquired to preserve the recharge area for seepage, which is a required habitat component for bunched arrowhead. The uplands are managed for wildlife and consist of a mix of low grass-herbs, clusters of shrubs, tangles of briars, blackberries, roses, and islands of forest remnants at old home sites. The trail is well maintained. It snakes in and out of the managed fields and mixed pine-hardwoods and passes near or crosses the springhead forest. It then proceeds to the dam of an old farm pond, crosses the dam, and heads back to the west end of the parking area.

Since bunched arrowhead depends on a continuous flow of shallow seepage water, its habitat is delicate. Any activity that increases sediment, such as regular foot traffic, degrades the quality of the habitat and hastens its demise. For this reason, the visitor is not specifically directed to areas where bunched arrowhead occurs, and the trail does not cross drainages that harbor bunched arrowhead downslope. Most of the species that are characteristic of springhead seepage forests can be seen from the short boardwalks that cross small stream channels. In one springhead adjacent to the trail, there is a large population of bunched arrowhead and a good example of seepage forests. Bunched arrowhead occurs just beyond the first short boardwalk downslope from the only area of the trail that goes through undisturbed oak-hickory forests (without a strong component of pines). Be careful not to alter the seepage with foot traffic.

Springhead seepage forests are probably the only habitat in the piedmont where poison sumac can be found. It is abundant here and at several stream crossings. Look for the bright red petioles that are associated with large compound leaves. Bunched arrowhead blooms over a long period in spring and early summer. Small green wood-orchid blooms for much of the summer. Other typical species found here or at stream crossings include American storax, Virginia willow (*Itea virginica*), tag alder, netted chain fern (*Woodwardia areolata*), blue flag iris (*Iris virginica*), water hemlock, false nettle, and murdannia, a weedy species that is taking over some populations of bunched arrowhead.

Ruderal species can be seen along the trail, especially Queen Anne's lace in the spring and early summer, and various composites in the fall. Probably the most interesting species in the pine-mixed hardwoods are pink lady's slipper, common running pine, and southern agrimony (*Agrimonia parviflora*); all are abundant in places.

Lancaster County

Flat Creek Heritage Preserve (Forty Acre Rock)

The SCDNR owns and manages this 598-acre property. A registered National Natural Landmark, it provides habitat for numerous rare and/or endangered plants. It is unquestionably the most diverse protected area in the piedmont. Natural communities include granitic flatrocks, basic-mesic forests, chestnut oak forests (varying from very dry to mesic), a semipermanent impoundment, as well as examples of xeric sandhills, hardwood bottoms, successional pine, pine-mixed hardwoods, and ruderal environments. This habitat diversity is due to extensive amounts of flatrock and boulder rock outcrops, acidic (granitic) and circumneutral (diabase) rocks, an extensive floodplain that has been transformed into a beaver pond, and because the site straddles the boundary between the fall-line sandhills and the piedmont.

The granitic flatrock known as Forty Acre Rock (actually only 14 acres) is the best known and most significant wildflower community. It contains all of the distinctive habitats that are associated with granitic flatrocks, including solution depressions (sometimes called vernal pools) with widely varying amounts of soil. These depressions provide habitat for many of the most unusual flatrock species; many are endemic to granitic flatrock outcrops. In spring, the wet depression species to look for include pool sprite, elf orpine, piedmont sandwort, and Appalachian fameflower, and two species of quillwort (*Isoëtes* sp.). Outcrop margins and pools with deep soil harbor such showy species as woolly ragwort, erect dayflower (*Commelina erecta*), false garlic, as well as the weedy Small's ragwort. In the spring, look for Puck's orpine in shallow soils under red cedar. Sandhills St. John's wort forms an attractive display of yellow in midsummer. In late summer, look for pineweed and a variety of weedy sunflowers, goldenrods, and other composites.

At least five additional granitic flatrocks are on this property. They are notable for their lack of human disturbance and striking display of mosses and lichens. A long, narrow flatrock to the east-northeast of Forty Acre Rock is worth visiting in early June because near its extreme northeast end a large seepage that overlays shallow soil harbors horned bladderwort and flatrock pimpernel (*Lindernia monticola*).

The main access to Forty Acre Rock is a trail that originates from a parking lot on SC-27, about 0.5 mile north of its junction with US 601. The trail forms a figure eight, with the southern loop circling a large beaver pond and the northern loop circling Forty Acre Rock. Follow the western portions of each loop first since the trail markings are easy to follow. The loop around Forty Acre Rock goes through a variety of dry to mesic oak-hickory forests. Noteworthy species along the western loop, mostly dominated by chestnut oak forests, include an unusual coreopsis (*C. verticillata*), sandhills gerardia, nestronia, trailing phlox, and Virginia marbleseed. The northern Forty Acre Rock loop has many of species that are typical of oak-hickory forests, including arrowleaf, Catesby's trillium, dwarf crested iris, Solomon's-seal, false Solomon's-seal, and diabase woodmint.

The beaver pond loop traverses some oak-hickory forests, but the main communities of interest are the hardwood bottoms, the beaver pond, and ruderal habitats. The hardwood bottoms are dominated by sweet gum, hackberry (*Celtis laevigata*), black walnut, and box elder (*Acer negundo*). Noteworthy species include moonseed, green dragon (*Arisaema dracontium*), common white snakeroot, buckthorn (*Bumelia lycioides*), and microstegium (*Microstegium vimineum*), which forms a dense cover. The semipermanent impoundment formed by a beaver dam includes a diversity of wetland trees, shrubs, and herbs. Breaks in the vegetation along the trail allow a glimpse of the beaver pond, but without a canoe, exploration is difficult. Red maple, tag alder, buttonbush (*Cephalanthus occidentalis),* and black willow dominate. Wetland herbs include water-shield, fragrant water-lily, lizard's tail, *Sagittaria* spp., burreed, and water hemlock. A well-developed stump and floating log community is present. The western portion of the beaver dam loop contains an interesting assemblage of species in an open successional pine stand, including New Jersey tea and aromatic sumac (*Rhus aromatica*). Ruderals blooming in June include Indian pink, Venus' looking-glass, and *Coreopsis lanceolata*.

No official trail leads to Flat Creek Heritage Preserve's basic-mesic forest community. The community occupies a northeast-facing slope above Flat Creek. To reach it, follow the old route of US 601, which is evident on SC-27 a few hundred yards north of its junction with US 601. Follow the old road bed to the west. The site lies just northeast of the abandoned bridge over Flat Creek. This site was cutover 30 to 40 years ago, so the canopy is not impressive, but the herb layer is dense and diverse, which is the most distinctive aspect of basic-mesic forest communities. Noteworthy herbs include southern nodding trillium, green violet, wahoo (*Euonymous atropurpureus*), blue cohosh, creeping phlox (*Phlox stolonifera*), eastern slender toothwort, moonseed, and wild ginger. Green dragon (*Arisaema dracontium*) is abundant in the adjacent floodplain.

Laurens County

Sumter National Forest: Tyger and Enoree Districts

Enoree River Rich Woods

The USFS owns and manages this site. A trail leads to the site from the end of USFS Road 334 in Laurens County. Proceed east on Ridge Road (SC-554) from its junction with SC-26. After 1.7 miles, SC-554 turns from pavement to gravel and becomes USFS Road 333. Continue for 0.5 mile on USFS Road 333 and then turn left onto USFS Road 334. The trail leads over the top of a steep, north-facing bluff and then downslope to the floodplain, where it ends.

This site provides excellent examples of three communities: hardwood bottoms, beech forests, and basic-mesic forests. All are as remarkable for the size and height of many canopy trees as for the diversity of the associated flora. The hardwood bottoms are dominated by trees that are generally in excess of 3 feet in diameter and are so tall that it is often difficult to see the leaves. Canopy dominants include sweet gum, green ash (*Fraxinus pennsylvanica*), and hackberry (*Celtis laevigata*), with occasional large individuals of swamp chestnut oak (*Quercus michauxii*) and Shumard's oak (*Quercus shumardii*). Bladdernut and wild allspice are two interesting shrubs. Herb cover is typical and includes honewort (*Cryptotaenia canadensis*), river oats, butterweed, Pennsylvania smartweed (*Polygonum pensylvanica*), and clearweed (*Pilea pumila*). At the edge of the richest north-facing slope is a small population of wild ginger.

Large trees do not uniformly dominate the beech forest, but large individuals of a variety of species are scattered on bluffs both east and west of the end of the entrance trail. East (downstream) of the trail end, you may find tulip tree, black oak (*Quercus velutina*), bitternut hickory (*Carya cordiformis*), and cucumber magnolia (*Magnolia acuminata*). West (upstream) of the trail end, you may find beech, white oak, shagbark hickory (*Carya ovata*), northern red oak (*Quercus rubra*), and common silverbell.

The visitor is rewarded when exploring bluffs (both east and west of the trail end) for the herbaceous flora and large trees. The steepest, most extensive bluff is just west of the trail end. As is typical of beech forests, the herbaceous flora here is diverse but does not blanket the slopes. All the typical species are present, from the early spring ephemerals such as spring beauty and round-lobed liverleaf, to spring-flowering perennials such as Solomon's-seal and Catesby's trillium, to early summer species such as Canada avens (*Geum canadense*) and skullcap (*Scutellaria elliptica*), and ending with attractive fall bloomers such as horsebalm and lion's foot (*Prenanthes serpentaria*). Storax (*Styrax grandifolia*) is one of the most unusual shrubs.

The next bluff west of the first steep bluff is the richest, especially where the base of the bluff is adjacent to a well-developed slough of the Enoree River. This bluff is not steep or wide, but the herbaceous flora here is both dense and diverse. The presence of such species as southern nodding trillium and wild ginger suggests calcium-rich soil. Other unusual herbs include bunchflower (*Melanthium hybridum*), yellow lady's slipper, tripartate violet (*Viola tripartita*), and cancer-root.

Several northward-facing bluffs south of the trail end are worth exploring. Pawpaw and red buckeye are especially abundant in places. Wildflowers that are present in greater abundance here than east of the trail end include diabase woodmint, hairy spiderwort, starry campion (*Silene stellata*), and common white snakeroot.

In mid-May through June, go up the ravines east of the trail end to see the spectacular columbo (plate193) in bloom. Since columbo is a biennial or triennial that requires considerable light for flowering, most of the plants will consist of rosettes of large basal leaves. Some plants with flowering stalks 4 to 10 feet tall will probably be present, however.

There is a narrow, steep bluff adjacent to the Enoree River just west (after crossing a small stream) of the trail end. This bluff has a thick cover of mountain laurel. A steep northward-facing slope along a major stream or river is the typical habitat for mountain laurel in the piedmont. A beech forest with chalk maple (*Acer leucoderme*) is at the top of this narrow bluff.

McCormick County

Stevens Creek Heritage Preserve

This preserve harbors the most spectacular basic-mesic forest in South Carolina and perhaps in the entire piedmont of the eastern United States. Most of the typical piedmont species are present, including many that are very rare or unusual. Other communities present are mesic and dry-mesic oak-hickory forests, a narrow strip of floodplain dominated by large bottomland hardwoods, and successional pine forests. All are accessible by a loop trail.

The head of the loop trail is on SC-88. It is recognized by a small, unmarked parking area and large sign that describes the significance of this heritage preserve. The first section of the trail is on a gentle slope and passes through a forest of shortleaf and loblolly pine. As the trail steepens, oak-hickory forests replace the pine forests. At the junction of two intermittent streams, one stream is at the upper edge of the basic-mesic forest, which is obvious by a profusion of wildflowers.

The basic-mesic forest dominates the steep, north-facing bluffs that are adjacent to Stevens Creek and extends into the ravines that dissect the bluffs. From mid-March through early June, a profusion of wildflowers is obvious. In mid-March, the base of the bluffs and upper portions of the adjacent floodplain are covered with spring beauty and false rue anemone. Dimpled trout lily should be in full bloom, as well as Dutchman's breeches and at least two species of toothwort. A mid-April visit should provide the greatest number of species in bloom, including wild ginger, red buckeye, lanceleaf trillium, southern nodding trillium, Miccosukee gooseberry (a federally threatened species), green violet, bladdernut, hairy spiderwort, lanceleaf anemone, shooting star, roundleaf ragwort, southern stoneseed, cucumber magnolia, and cancer-root. The largest southern sugar maple in South Carolina is also here.

The trail turns to the east (right), crosses the second stream, and parallels another small stream, which in April is lined with shooting star and roundleaf ragwort. The trail soon crosses this stream and climbs to the top of a steep, north-facing bluff overlooking Stevens Creek. Green-and-gold, several species of meadow parsnip, and hairy spiderwort are noteworthy. Look for a low shrub that has leaves comprised of three leaflets and resembles a small variety of poison ivy. This is aromatic sumac (*Rhus aromatica*), a nonpoisonous relative of poison ivy. Also look for the broomlike clusters of tiny branches in the tops of hop hornbeam. These are called witches broom and are caused by bacterial (or fungal) infections that induce excessive branching via excess production of the plant hormone cytokinin.

The trail follows a series of ridges, mostly through pine or pine-hardwood forests. Noteworthy is southern deerberry with its hairy fruits. The trail eventually turns to the north and passes through an oak-hickory forest, which increases in wildflower density and diversity as it approaches the floodplain and the basic-mesic forest at the base of the north-facing bluffs. Many of the wildflowers typical of mesic oak-hickory forests are found here, including common foamflower, false rue-anemone, wild geranium, Solomon's-seal, false Solomon's-seal, bloodroot, bellwort, and may-apple. The narrow floodplain between the basic-mesic forest and Stevens Creek is an unusual hardwood bottom. It is unusual because some of the species of the basic-mesic forest extend into it, and it includes such coastal plain species as bald cypress and dwarf palmetto. The ground cover is dominated by switch-cane and typical wildflowers such as jack-in-the-pulpit, wild ginger, wood-nettle, and species of violet and buttercup.

Sumter National Forest: Long Cane-Edgefield District

Turkey-Stevens Creek Canoe Trail

This 12-mile canoe trail is in the Long Cane District of the Sumter National Forest. Paved areas provide parking at the put-in point on SC-283 and at the take-out point on SC-23. Well-maintained foot trails, with wooden steps at steep areas, provide easy access to the canoe trail from the parking areas. The canoe trail is described in the Forest Service brochure as "managed," but this is an overstatement. In July of 1999, there were two huge logjams, one a few miles above Key Bridge and another a few miles below. Logjams make travel dangerous during periods of high water. During low water, canoe travel is not recommended.

During periods of intermediate water levels, this is an outstanding canoe trail. Bedrock is exposed along almost the entire canoe trail, producing rock ledges and small rapids. Regularly flooded bedrock is clothed in riverweed (*Podostemon ceratophyllum*). Intermittently flooded bedrock is clothed in moss (*Porella* sp.). Steep slopes with relatively mature forests and large trees occur throughout. Wildflower diversity is high, and bird life is abundant. Communities along the trail include beech forests, mesic oak-hickory forests, hardwood bottoms, and gravel bars.

Riverbanks along most of the trail corridor are steep and vary from 8 feet or less to over 20 feet. The floodplain is all but nonexistent but may be a few hundred feet wide near the take-out point at SC-23. Without a floodplain to spread into, water funnels down the narrow stream channel. During high waters, the effects of the steep riverbanks and funneled stream channel impact one of the dominant trees, bald cypress. The bark on the upstream bases of bald cypress is gnarled. The bark has been worn smooth by the abrasive action of high waters and debris. In addition, the knees grow out in line on either side of the mother tree rather than is a circle. The steep riverbank precludes any other positioning.

The riverbanks and floodplains are dominated by a mix of swamp forests, levee forests, and hardwood bottom trees, including bald cypress, sycamore, river birch, box elder (*Acer negundo*), sugarberry (*Celtis tenuifolia*), and occasionally Shumard's oak (*Quercus shumardii*). Ironwood and pawpaw

are important subcanopy and shrub species, respectively. Two of South Carolina's most aggressive weeds, Chinese privet and Japanese grass (*Microstegium
viminium*), dominate the shrub and herb layers. The abundance of these weeds
suggests significant past disturbance in or adjacent to the floodplain. Nonetheless, a full suite of herbaceous species that are typical of levees or hardwood
bottoms is present, including butterweed, wood-nettle, honewort (*Cryptotaenia canadensis*), avens (*Geum canadense*), river oats, switch-cane, and dicliptera
(*Dicliptera brachiata*). Partridge berry is present in the adjacent upland forests.
Wild ginger and moonseed here and in the adjacent beech forests suggest the
presence of calcium-rich soils.

Steep bluffs tower above the riverbanks along the canoe trail. Beech
forests, often with an abundance of mountain laurel, dominate the north-facing bluffs. Beech forests or moist oak-hickory forests occupy bluffs that face
south, east, or west. Because of the steep riverbanks, these forests often are not
accessible. Riverbanks tend to be lowest where small streams enter the main
stream, so these are the recommended access points. Canopy trees in these
upland forests include beech, white oak, shagbark hickory (*Carya ovata*), black
oak (*Quercus velutina*), swamp chestnut oak (*Q. michauxii*), and American ash
(*Fraxinus americana*). Subcanopy trees include chalk maple (*Acer leucoderme*),
hop hornbeam, ironwood, flowering dogwood, and slippery elm (*Ulmus
rubra*). Appalachian mock-orange, red buckeye, pinxterflower, and American
storax are abundant. A variety of herbs are found on the hardwood slopes,
including many common spring wildflowers like pale yellow trillium, hog
peanut, lousewort, and Carolina spinypod.

Gravel bars are present and may be occupied by an interesting array of
species. Waterpepper (*Polygonum hydropiperoides*) was the dominant herb during a recent visit.

Before organizing a trip on this canoe trail, determine the water level by
contacting both the local office of the SCDNR (1-803-637-3397) and the local
office of the USFS (1-803-637-5396).

Pickens County

Glassy Mountain Heritage Preserve

The term "glassy" refers to the extensive exposure of bare rock on the north
face of this monadnock (figure 10), which, when the sun bounces off it at just
the right angle, appears "glassy." The granitic dome is the primary community
of interest. Additional plant communities include oak-hickory forests and the
ruderal communities that are associated with the paved access road and some
areas adjacent to the granitic dome community.

This 65-acre property is owned and managed by the SCDNR, which has
constructed a short nature trail and provides a descriptive brochure. Access is
via the end of South Glassy Mountain Road off SC-183. Look for the Wildlife
Viewing Area signs along SC-183, about 2.0 miles east of Pickens. The nature
trail begins about 0.25 mile below the end of the access road, but the authors
suggest beginning at the top of the mountain, at the end of the road, just north
of a fire tower.

The trail proceeds down the north-facing slope, curves to the northwest

FIGURE 10. Piedmont Monadnock, Glassy Mountain Heritage Preserve, Pickens County.

(going through oak-hickory forests), and down to the extensive granitic dome community on the north slope. After exploring the granitic dome community, backtrack and take the fork to the left, which continues on a level grade around to the eastern slope and back to the access road. Walk up the access road to the fire tower.

The forest here is a piedmont monadnock variant of the oak-hickory forests. Chestnut oak dominates the canopy, and sprouts of American chestnut are present. Most of the shrubs and herbs are more characteristic of oak-hickory forests rather than chestnut oak forests. Typical oak-hickory forests species include climbing butterfly-pea, Indian pink, white milkweed, fringe-tree, thimbleweed, and painted buckeye. Notice the occurrence of dwarf pawpaw (*Asimina parviflora*), the dry-woods relative of the well-known pawpaw of hardwood bottoms and rich woods. Robin's-plantain is abundant and provides showy displays in the spring. Common white snakeroot is abundant in the fall.

The granitic dome community is on a classic dome with no flat areas. Most of the species typical of granitic domes are present. The areas of exposed rock are bounded by an oak-hickory community that has a stunted canopy, somewhat spaced trees, and a thick, grass-dominated herb layer. On small islands of vegetation and on outcrop margins with shallow soil, eastern red cedar (*Juniperus virginiana*) shares dominance with pitch pine (*Pinus rigida*). The abundance of red cedar and the rare yellow honeysuckle suggests sites with calcium-rich soil. St. John's-wort (*Hypericum denticulatum*) and a tickseed (*Coreopsis lanceolata*) add a touch of yellow to the dome and adjacent forest. The rare standing-cypress occurs in gladelike openings in the forest.

The return trail around to the eastern slope goes through less-developed examples of the same communities. In June, keep an eye out for flower clusters of eastern bergamot (*Monarda fistulosa*). Small rock faces are common along this trail segment, and various composites are abundant.

Union County

Sumter National Forest: Tyger and Enoree Districts

Tyger River Canoe Trail

The Tyger River Canoe Trail is the easiest and most enjoyable way to see the best wildflower communities in the Tyger and Enoree Districts of the Sumter National Forest. The trail begins where SC-49 crosses the Tyger River, and it ends at Gordon's Bridge. The trail is 24 miles long and can be completed in two days. Primitive camping is allowed on Forest Service land, but a permit must be obtained from the Enoree USFS District Office. Five bridges and the end of USFS Road 323 provide access and opportunity for day trips. The river has no rapids in this section, although fast-moving water is present. The only potential danger is getting though or around fallen trees. Following heavy rains when the water is high, canoes can be pushed against fallen trees and can roll and fill with water.

From the riverbank to upslope, the typical plant communities encountered are levee forests, bottomland hardwoods, and oak-hickory forests. Typical levee species occur along the entire length of this river except where the levee is very narrow. A narrow levee often includes species that are typical of bottomland hardwood communities. The entire array of trees and shrubs that are typically associated with both levee forests and bottomland hardwood forests can be seen from a canoe.

Interesting or unusual species to look for include bald cypress, a species mostly confined to the coastal plain but which invades the piedmont along the larger rivers; red mulberry (*Morus rubra*), a species that requires the high light intensities of riverbanks or clearings to produce fruit; northern catalpa, which is known for the caterpillar that commonly feeds on the leaves and is prized by fishermen as a bream bait; cow-itch, whose attractive, trumpet-shaped flowers strongly attract hummingbirds; and Virgin's-bower, whose mass of white flowers smell as sweet as they look.

The river trail is punctuated with sand bars and bluffs of varying size. The sand bars shift so dramatically and frequently that they are not botanically interesting, but they provide places to stop for a picnic or a swim. Some of the sandbars and bluffs are on private property and are posted. Please respect the wishes of the landowner by not trespassing.

The plants found on the occasional bluffs vary with the steepness and aspect. West-facing bluffs are drier than north-facing bluffs, and this is reflected in the plants. White oak and mockernut hickory generally dominate the west-facing bluffs. Red cedar is common, and a variety of dry-site oaks may be present, including post oak, southern red oak, and black oak. Sparkleberry is the most common shrub. The herb layer is sparse and low in diversity, but you are certain to see partridge berry, spotted wintergreen, and arrowleaf.

Mesic oak-hickory forest or beech forests occupy north-facing bluffs. The mesic oak-hickory forests are dominated by white oak, shagbark hickory

(*Carya ovata*), pignut hickory (*C. glabra*), and black walnut, which may climb from the floodplain, a typical phenomenon on rich soils. Hop hornbeam and chalk maple (*Acer leucoderme*), both species more typical of calcium-rich soils, dominate the subcanopy. Painted buckeye and witch-hazel (*Hamamelis virginiana*) are abundant shrubs. The herb layer, although not dense, is diverse and includes many of the species that are typical of mesic oak-hickory forests.

The most spectacular bluffs are two north-facing bluffs that are 1 to 1.5 miles above Gordon's Bridge. The first of these two is long and steep, dropping almost vertically 100 feet in one place. Rock or clay faces, 8 to 10 feet tall, line the river margin, making access difficult but also presenting an attractive assemblage of mosses and liverworts in multiple shades of green. The steeper bluffs are covered in mountain laurel and mountain doghobble. Scattered beech dominates the canopy. The more gentle bluffs include oaks and hickories in the canopy, hop hornbeam and chalk maple in the understory, and a diverse herb layer. Showy herbs include Catesby's trillium, dwarf crested iris, American alumroot, perfoliate bellwort (*Uvularia perfoliata*), common black cohosh, and horsebalm. This bluff is unusual, having pawpaw on the richer lower slopes and dwarf pawpaw (*Asimina parviflora*) on the upper drier slopes.

The Tyger River Canoe Trail is recommended for anyone interested in the outdoors. It is a true wilderness experience. Except for a few cow pastures, there is no obvious development along the entire length.

York County

Rock Hill Blackjacks Heritage Preserve
The SCDNR owns and manages this 263-acre preserve. From the junction of SC-901 and the SC-72 bypass in Rock Hill, go north 0.5 mile on the SC-72 bypass, turn right on Blackmon Road and go 0.25 mile to a parking area on the right. Wildlife Viewing Area signs also leads you to the site. Information about the site can be obtained on-line at frostman@infoave.net or by calling 1-803-366-7024.

This site is part of a 1700-acre area that is the largest single assemblage of piedmont xeric hardpan forests and related communities in South Carolina. These forests and glades are probably second only to granitic flatrocks in the number of rare species. Unfortunately, this heritage preserve has been subjected to significant past disturbance. Much of the area is being restored to a more natural condition, and it is bisected by an underground cable, sewer right-of-ways, and a power line. It contains, nonetheless, good examples of hardpan forests and associated glade communities.

The 1.0-mile-long loop trail begins at the far end of the parking lot. Take the right fork; the left fork is the return trail. The trail first goes through a young hardpan forest that is being restored by removal of weedy shrubs, especially spring silverberry (*Elaeagnus umbellata*). Look for the rare Carolina shagbark hickory (*Carya carolinae-septentrionalis*), with its shaggy bark, in the areas of mafic rock outcrops. From April to May, the distinctive curlyheads bloom. The next opening you come to was created by bulldozing and is part of an effort to restore Schweinitz's sunflower; 290 plants were transplanted here in the mid-1990s. Here you can first see the rare prairie dock (*Silphium tere-binthinaceum*, plate 273), with its huge, basal leaves and 6 to 8 foot tall flowering stem.

The trail system then leads you through several glade openings and into relatively undisturbed hardpan forests. In addition, the power-line and sewer right-of-ways provide gladelike habitat. The hardpan forest can be recognized by the large boulders (plate 268). The authors recorded the following species in the various habitats during visits to this preserve: in May, wild quinine, New Jersey tea, lanceleaf coreopsis (*Coreopsis lanceolata*), Carolina rose, Solomon's-seal, Small's ragwort (*Senecio smallii*), American heal-all, nettle-leaf sage (*Salvia urticifloia*), *Tragia urticifolia,* deceptive spinypod, and butterfly-weed; in September and October, prairie dock, two species of blazing star (*Liatris gramini-folia* and *L. squarrulosa*), eastern false-boneset (*Brickellia eupatorioides*), black-eyed Susan, whorled milkweed, and skullcap (*Scutellaria integrifolia*).

THE FALL-LINE SANDHILLS

Chesterfield County

Cheraw State Park (Hudsonia Flat)

This small but unique site is readily accessed 1.1 miles southeast on SC-20 from its junction with US 1. After crossing Juniper Creek, park in the small turnout on the right. The park is on either side. Visitors must explore to find the unusual plants because no trails exist.

This site consists of a streamside flat dominated by pocosin vegetation, a gently sloping, fall-line sandhills, and more pocosin upslope from the sandhills. The site is pocketed with small depressions created from past sand mining. The pocosins are dominated by pond pine, sweet gum, and pond cypress in the canopy, swamp red bay (*Persea palustris*) and sweet bay in the understory, and typical pocosin shrubs. In mid-April, more than ten pocosin shrubs and trees bloom in a spectacular display. Of particular interest in the lower pocosin-sandhill ecotones are small populations of coastal witch-alder, sweet pitcher-plant, and sandhills pyxie-moss. In a broader zone between the dense pocosins and the xeric sandhills is an unusual community dominated by longleaf pine, pond pine, sweet bay, creeping blueberry, and sand myrtle. It is here, often on the slopes of the depressions, that the namesake species for this site is found: northern golden-heather (*Hudsonia ericoides,* plate 319). This South Carolina rarity is disjunct from the heart of its range in New England and Delaware. Early May is a good time to see this species in bloom. The sandhills are somewhat disturbed, but many typical species are present, including Carolina ipecac, Carolina sandwort, wire-plant, southern dwarf huckleberry, and woody goldenrod.

Sandhills State Forest (Sugarloaf and Horseshoe Mountains)

Sugarloaf and Horseshoe Mountains are the primary features of botanical interest in this state forest, owned and managed by the South Carolina Forestry

Commission. To reach the site, take a left on SC-63 between McBee and Patrick. Proceed 6.0 miles, and at Sugarloaf Mountain Recreation Area, turn right onto an unpaved road. Travel 1.5 miles, bearing right at the only fork. Sugarloaf Mountain is on the left, and Horseshoe Mountain is on the right.

Sugarloaf and Horseshoe Mountains are some of the most dramatic monadnocks in the fall-line sandhills. A cap of iron-cemented sandstone prevents erosion. The resistant cap is underlain by loose, coarse sands that are typical of the sandhills region. Several large sandstone boulders lie at the base of the monadnocks. Sugarloaf Mountain is dome-shaped and abruptly rises more that 160 feet. Horseshoe Mountain is horseshoe-shaped and rises about 50 to 55 feet.

Sugarloaf Mountain is a good example of the heterogeneous nature of plant communities that are associated with sandstone. Vegetation here is a mix of xeric sandhills, heath bluffs, and seepage pocosins. Longleaf pine dominates the sparse canopy throughout, and in the driest areas turkey oak is an important subcanopy species. Other typical dry-adapted oaks dominate the more mesic north slope. The shrub layer is dense throughout and is dominated in xeric areas by sparkleberry, stagger-bush, and southern dwarf huckleberry. The more mesic areas are dominated by a dense layer of mountain laurel, sand myrtle, creeping blueberry, coastal doghobble, horse sugar, and titi. Herbaceous species that are most prevalent in open xeric areas include the very rare and unusual sandhills pyxie-moss, sandhills St. John's-wort, yellow jessamine, wire-plant, and hairy false foxglove, with wiregrass (*Aristida stricta*) abundant in places. Herbaceous species in the more mesic areas include trailing arbutis, spotted wintergreen, and common pyxie-moss (*Pyxidanthera barbulata* var. *barbulata,* plate 318 in *WCL*). The presence of both varieties of pyxie-moss and some hybrids (?) between the two has led some to question whether the varieties are distinct.

Horseshoe Mountain is the best place to find sandhills pyxie-moss, and mid-March is the best time to see it in bloom.

Carolina Sandhills National Wildlife Refuge

The United States Fish and Wildlife Service manages this 46,000-acre property in the fall-line sandhills to provide "habitat and protection for threatened and endangered species, as well as for migratory birds." The 30 man-made lakes and ponds are mostly managed for waterfowl. Two walking trails take the visitor through the main wildflower communities, including sandhills, small depression ponds, and streamhead pocosins. Atlantic white-cedar forests, seepage pocosins, and herbaceous seepages are present in less accessible areas. For brochures with trail routes, write:

US Fish and Wildlife Service
Carolina Sandhills National Wildlife Refuge
Route 2, Box 330
McBee, SC 29101

Tate's Trail

Tate's Trail begins at the Lake Bee Dam and provides an introduction to the variants of the fall-line sandhills communities as well as good examples of streamhead pocosins and small depression ponds. The beginning of the trail traverses the most mesic of the sandhills communities—a longleaf pine-scrub oak community. Longleaf pine and a variety of dry oaks (especially post, *Quercus stellata,* southern red, *Quercus falcata,* and blackjack, *Quercus marilandica*) dominate the canopy. Flowering dogwood and sourwood dominate the understory. Typical herb species include goat's rue, bracken fern (*Pteridium aquilinum*), yellow false-indigo, pineweed, and Nuttall's lobelia (*Lobelia nuttallii*).

Just east of the main trail and south of the junction with the loop trail is a small depression pond. The pond is ringed with sphagnum moss. Downslope it harbors such species as two-flowered bladderwort (*Utricularia biflora*), round-leaf sundew, big floating-heart, meadow-beauty (*Rhexia mariana*), and fragrant water-lily. A variety of pocosin shrubs grow upslope.

Before the trail turns and crosses the dam to Lake 12, it crosses a good example of a streamhead pocosin. All the typical pocosin species are present. Note particularly the bright red leaf stalk of poison sumac. Tate's trail continues through more streamhead pocosins, downslope and away from the trail, but all the xeric communities eventually merge into streamhead pocosins.

At the next junction of the loop trail, you see a longleaf pine-scrub oak community, which is recognizable by scrub oaks, including blackjack (*Quercus marilandica*), turkey oak, bluejack (*Quercus incanna*), and scrubby post oak (*Quercus margaretta*). Species of interest include lady lupine (*Lupinus villosus*), trailing arbutus, horse sugar, stagger-bush, sensitive briar (*Schrankia microphylla*), Adam's-needle (*Yucca filamentosa*), and many species that are associated with xeric sandhills.

Longleaf pine-turkey oak, along with a few other oak species, dominates the driest variant of xeric sandhills. Most of the herbs that are typical of this community are present, including Carolina sandwort, wire-plant, tread-softly, jointweed (*Polygonella polygama*), Carolina ipecac, sand spikemoss (*Selaginella arenicola*), southern dwarf huckleberry, and poison oak. Additional sandhills species include Queen's-delight, hairy false foxglove, sandhills milkweed, carphephorus, roseling, and silver-leaved grass (*Chrysopsis graminifolia*).

Woodland Pond Trail

The sandhills along the Woodland Pond Trail are not in good shape, but the downslope streamhead pocosins are excellent. Pond pine dominates the canopy, with red maple and black gum (*Nyssa sylvatica*) abundant in areas that are protected from fire. The dense and diverse (and impenetrable) shrub layer that is typical of this community is well developed, and all the typical species are present. Most shrubs bloom in mid-April. Especially impressive are sweet bay and the midsummer blooming loblolly bay. Somewhat unusual species to look for include American storax, leucothoë, and the early-summer blooming clammy azalea.

Streamhead pocosin along Roger's Branch

One of the best streamhead pocosins on the refuge is along Roger's Branch just southeast of its junction with Refuge Route 3, which forks off of SC-657 just east of the Ruby Fire Tower. The streamhead pocosin is particularly well developed, and it harbors one of South Carolina's few populations of white wicky (*Kalmia cuneata,* plate 329) as well as coastal witch-alder.

Lexington County

Peachtree Rock Nature Preserve

The Nature Conservancy of South Carolina owns and manages this nature preserve. It is named for an unusual outcrop of sandstone that is shaped like an upside down pyramid (or a peach tree?). The site includes the state's most extensive sandstone outcrops, with abundant marine fossils, and one of the few waterfalls in the fall-line sandhills, as well as a diversity of communities, including variants of the pocosin community.

Although the sandhills are still recovering from the effects of man's past activities, most of the typical species are present and accessible by the established trail system. Interesting species include rosemary, woody goldenrod, tread-softly, sandhills St. John's-wort, hairy false foxglove, Carolina ipecac, wire-plant, sandhill wild-buckwheat, and at least six species of huckleberries and blueberries.

The pocosins are on hillsides downslope from xeric sandhills. An unusual number of pocosin variants are present, including one with a typical evergreen shrub component, another with mountain laurel dominating the tall shrub layer, sand myrtle dominates another, and another has many components of a typical seepage community, including pitcher plants. The sites dominated by mountain laurel or sand myrtle provide spectacular displays when these species are in bloom.

Look for the sandstone outcrops. Since they are small, the canopy is usually open around these outcrops. Trees of the adjacent community also dominate the outcrops, with longleaf pine being typical. Sourwood is usually the understory dominant, and fringe-tree is often present as a tall shrub. Herbaceous species include pineweed as well as a variety of ferns growing on the rock, including resurrection fern and ebony spleenwort (*Asplenium platyneuron*).

The Nature Conservancy is working to restore this preserve to its natural, presettlement condition by using prescribed fires at appropriate intervals in fire-adapted communities. If the evidence of recent fire is obvious and not especially aesthetically pleasing, remember the important role of fire. There is overwhelming evidence that fire is necessary for the long-term maintenance of many plant communities, including xeric sandhills and pocosin communities.

Shealy's Pond Heritage Preserve

This site harbors one of the best stands of Atlantic white-cedar in South Carolina, a herbaceous seepage community, fall-line sandhills, bald cypress-tupelo gum forests, and freshwater aquatics. The heart of the site is the communities surrounding an old mill pond. The pond is on a blackwater stream, Scouter Creek, and it contains a diverse community of freshwater aquatics that merge gradually into a seepage community that is best developed on the lower (downstream), east margin of the mill pond. The herbaceous seepage community merges into an Atlantic white-cedar forest that gradually transitions upslope to xeric sandhills. A bald cypress-tupelo gum forest dominates at the head of the mill pond and at a narrow band along the stream above the mill pond.

Typical freshwater aquatics in the deep, slowly moving areas include fragrant water-lily, cow-lily (*Nuphar advena*), water-shield, bur-reed, and golden-club. Boggy margins without significant seepage harbor such species as bogmoss and several species of bladderwort (*Utricularia* spp.). Margins that receive significant input of seepage harbor diverse grasses, sedges, and rushes. The stream above the mill pond contains numerous circular sinkholes up to 6 feet deep and 4 to 5 feet wide. They are best explored by canoe.

The herbaceous seepage community is interesting because of its carnivorous plants. There are three pitcher-plants (yellow trumpet, sweet, and frog's breeches) and several rare hybrids; three species of sundew, including round-leaf sundew, which is disjunct here from its typical range in the mountains; and three species of bladderwort (*Utricularia*). Other noteworthy species include brown bog buttons (*Lachnocaulon minus*), yellow hatpins (*Syngonanthus flavidulus*), and violet burmannia. The latter two are inconspicuous; look closely for them.

The Atlantic white-cedar forest contains mature trees and most of the species that are typical of white-cedar forests in the sandhills. This community is essentially a pocosin or evergreen shrub bog with Atlantic white-cedar dominating and forming a closed canopy. The most unusual member of this community is Rayner's blueberry, a rare relative of the creeping blueberry. Other noteworthy species include groundpine (*Lycopodium obscurum*), a species usually found in the mountains, a rare variety of the southern dwarf huckleberry, and the rare Collins' sedge (*Carex collinsii*).

The Atlantic white-cedar forest grades into the sandhills. The sandhills community is not extensive or well developed, but it does harbor one of the rarest sandhill species, Pickering's dawnflower, and other unusual sandhills species such as rosemary and woody goldenrod. The best sandhills habitat is on the west side.

Well-worn footpaths run several hundred yards up the east and west sides of the site, taking the visitor through Atlantic white-cedar forests to the best seepage habitats. Since the white-cedar forests and seepages are dependant on water, be prepared to get your feet wet. Please limit your travel in the seepage habitats since the plants can be easily damaged. Exploration off these footpaths is discouraged. Poison sumac is abundant. The long-term management plan for the area includes construction of a boardwalk.

THE COASTAL PLAIN

Aiken County

Aiken Gopher Tortoise Heritage Preserve

This preserve consists of 968 acres purchased primarily to protect the northernmost known population of Gopher Tortoise, a state threatened species. It lies adjacent to the South Edisto River southeast of Aiken State Park. The preserve is reached from SC-4 near Keadle Bridge. Turn off SC-4 onto the secondary road S-2-22 (Veterans Road), cross the South Edisto River, and take Oak Ridge Road (unpaved) for 1.2 miles. The sign to the preserve is on the left. A trail leads into the preserve from the parking area.

The preserve lies below the fall-line sandhills, and its sand ridges are of blackwater origin from the nearby Edisto River. The site harbors an extensive longleaf pine-turkey oak/southern wiregrass (*Aristida beyrichiana*) xeric community. Numerous stages of regeneration and composition of this community are evident. One tract harbors a longleaf plantation. Prior to SCDNR's purchase, one section was clear-cut, site-prepped with herbicides, and planted in longleaf. In another site, the longleaf pine-turkey oak/wiregrass community has been timbered but is recovering. Wiregrass is the dominant ground cover. This is the state's best preserve for viewing this keystone grass of the sandhills and coastal plain. Wiregrass provides the fuel that facilitates the spread of lightning-set fires that maintains the biologically rich sandhills, pine flatwoods, and pine savannas that were once widespread in the South.

Many of the herbaceous wildflowers that are characteristic of the sandhills are present. Among the species that can be seen along the trail leading from the parking area are eastern green-eyes, carphephorus, Carolina ipecac, jointweed, Carolina sandwort, hairy false foxglove, gopherweed, tread-softly, sandhill wild-buckwheat, wire-plant, sandhills milkweed, sandhills thistle, sandy-field beaksedge, butterfly-weed, sensitive briar, pineweed, Queen's-delight, and grass-leaved blazing star. This is the only protected site in South Carolina where the rare Georgia beargrass (plate 324) occurs. Follow the trail from the parking lot until it intersects with a wide fire break. Go left for about 0.25 mile. The population is on the left before an intersection with another fire break. Numerous trees and shrubs that are pictured in this book occur throughout the preserve, including persimmon, sparkleberry, winged sumac, turkey oak, longleaf pine, and whiteleaf greenbrier.

This is a large preserve, and the trail system covers only a small portion. A pocosin occurs on the northern and southern boundaries. More adventurous visitors may leave the trail and wander throughout the preserve.

Bamberg County

Cathedral Bay Heritage Preserve

Cathedral Bay is also known as Chitty Bay or Chitty Pond. To reach Cathedral Bay, turn east off US 321 at Olar onto SC-64, and go 1.67 miles. The bay is adjacent to the highway. Only the bay, with clearly marked boundaries, is public; the adjoining land is private.

The bay harbors a pond cypress savanna. During dry seasons, you can easily walk into the interior. During wet seasons, you can canoe through the bay. Canoes can be put in from SC-64. No motorized boats are allowed. Pond cypress dominates the canopy; also present are swamp gum and sweet gum. This savanna is not rich in wildflowers, but you can see tall milkweed and Virginia meadow-beauty. Walter's sedge (*Carex walteriana*) dominates the herbaceous layer.

Barnwell County

Craig Pond

Craig Pond is a clay-based Carolina bay that harbors a depression meadow. A longleaf pine-turkey oak community occurs on the adjoining sand ridge on the southeast side. Craig Pond is jointly owned by ChemNuclear Systems, Inc. (three-fourths) and the federal government's Savannah River Site (one-fourth). ChemNuclear allows its portion of Craig Pond to be used for education and research; permission must be obtained through the Community Relations and Public Affairs office at 1-803-758-1806. The SCDNR holds a conservation easement on ChemNuclear's portion of Craig Pond.

Presently, final plans for a visitor's center, parking lot, and nature trail have yet to be implemented. The trail will pass through the xeric community and lead to a boardwalk that goes into the depression meadow. Do not leave the boardwalk unless accompanied by someone who has been cleared by ChemNuclear to lead a trek into the depression meadow.

The longleaf pine-turkey oak community harbors a plethora of xeric and sandy woods wildflowers; most can be seen from the trail. Herbaceous species include Carolina ipecac, tread-softly, sandhill wild-buckwheat, wire-plant, carphephorus, eastern green-eyes, woolly golden-aster, sandhills gerardia, and sandhills milkweed. Two rare herbs, narrowleaf blue curls (*Trichostema setaceum*) and Michaux's whitlow-wort (*Paronychia herniarioides*), have been documented near the property line road. Ask the guide to show you these rare plants. Otherwise, do not leave the trail. Flowering shrubs include stagger-bush, southern dwarf huckleberry, and sparkleberry.

The depression meadow harbors many rare herbaceous species. Look for Boykin's lobelia, shrubby seedbox, awned meadow-beauty, Tracy's beaksedge, sclerolepis, purple bladderwort (*Utricularia purpurea*), water-shield, fragrant water-lily, frog's-bit, spike-rush (*Eleocharis equisetoides*), Florida bladderwort (*Utricularia floridana*), *Sagittaria isoetiformis*, giant beard grass (*Erianthus giganteus*), and redroot.

Beaufort County

Victoria Bluff Heritage Preserve

The entrance to the road (SC-744) leading into Victoria Bluff Heritage Preserve is off US 278 west of Hilton Head Island. Signs clearly mark the entrance. To locate the preserve's many trails, a map is necessary.

Victoria Bluff Heritage Preserve consists of approximately 1000 acres, harboring a mix of natural communities. The heart of the preserve is the pine/saw palmetto flatwoods community, which is rare in South Carolina. Longleaf pine and slash pine (*P. elliottii*) are the dominant trees. Controlled burning has maintained this fire-dependent community. Wildflowers to look for are black-root, bracken fern (*Pteridium aquilinum*), stagger-bush, yellow jessamine, hairy wicky, horse sugar, inkberry, species of aster, and vanilla plant. The most open flatwoods occur along US 278 and SC-744, beginning 0.4 mile from US 278.

Other communities to look for are pond pine woodlands with associated pocosin species, including fetterbush, swamp red bay, inkberry, wax myrtle, saw palmetto, and the rare rusty lyonia. In the canopy look for bay forests with pond pine and loblolly. The shrubs include swamp red bay, wax myrtle, fetterbush, and rusty lyonia. The inland maritime forests include live oak and cabbage palmetto. Upland swamp forests harbor red maple and sweet gum, and an upland pond includes scattered button-bush, bog-mat, duckweed, and frog's-bit. Swamp gum savannas include the rare pondspice, swamp red bay, Virginia chain-fern (*Woodwardia virginica*) and fetterbush along the edge. A laurel oak forest harbors loblolly pine, sparkleberry, bull bay, saw palmetto, water oak (*Quercus nigra*), and wax myrtle.

Berkeley County

Francis Marion National Forest

The Francis Marion National Forest (FMNF) consists of approximately 250,000 acres in Berkeley and Charleston Counties. Most of the natural communities described in this book for the coastal plain and maritime strand occur in the FMNF. Visitors may obtain a map of the forest by writing or visiting one of two ranger stations:

> Wambaw Ranger District
> P.O. Box 106
> McClellanville, SC 29458

> Witherbee Ranger District
> HC 69 Box 1532
> Moncks Corner, SC 29461

The Witherbee District covers only Berkeley County, while the Wambaw District includes Berkeley and Charleston Counties. Only a few sites that harbor the most accessible and best examples for each natural community are given below:

Bald cypress-tupelo gum swamp forests

The Santee River is a major brownwater river. Many acres of bottomland bald cypress-tupelo gum swamp forests occur along this river where it passes through the FMNF. A good site to see this community is at Lake Guilliard Scenic Area and Natural Area east of Jamestown. At either end of Lake Guilliard, one can follow a series of sloughs that harbor large bald cypress and tupelo gum trees. Cypress knees, some as high as 6 feet, are evident.

Hardwood bottoms

Significant stands of hardwood bottoms, like the swamp forests, occur along the Santee River. Hardwood bottoms occur at Lake Guilliard Scenic Area and Natural Area at elevations slightly above the swamp forests.

Longleaf pine flatwoods

Several roads provide access to mature stands of longleaf flatwoods. Here are five examples: (1) SC-41 for approximately 5.0 miles north of the Wando River; (2) USFS Road 173; (3) SC-171 northwest of Witherbee; (4) a 5-mile section of SC-98 north of Wando; and (5) SC-654 (Halfway Creek Road) southwest of Honey Hill.

Pocosins

An outstanding example of a Carolina bay with pocosin vegetation is Big Ocean Bay Scenic Area northeast of Bethera. The site actually has two Carolina bays. The smaller, Little Ocean Bay, is adjacent to USFS Road 110 and harbors a low pocosin throughout. Look for honey-cups and coastal witch-alder along the edge, and the rare leather-leaf in the center.

Pond cypress savannas

Many examples of pond cypress savannas occur in the FMNF. Directions to two accessible sites are as follows: (1) take SC-654 southwest of Honey Hill where it intersects with USFS Road 201-B; on the northwest side of SC-654 is a pond cypress savanna with numerous wildflowers, including pine lily, sneezeweed, yellow trumpet pitcher-plant and awned meadow-beauty; and (2) north of Cainhoy, turn east off SC-41 onto USFS Road 183 (Hoover Road), go about a 100 yards, look to the left to see the savanna through a stand of pines. Look for yellow trumpet pitcher-plant, bay blue-flag iris, tickseed, and pipewort.

Pond cypress-swamp gum upland swamps

An example of this community, where swamp gum dominates, is northwest of the intersection of USFS Road 166 and SC-10-98 (Halfway Creek Road). The interior of the swamp opens up and wading is easy. Pondspice is common in the interior. The endangered pondberry occurs on the south margin.

A series of lime sinks around Honey Hill harbor numerous examples of this community. You can find pondspice, pondberry, and a variety of herbaceous wildflowers. Visitors may inquire at the office of the Wambaw Ranger District for directions since the roads leading to the sinks have no signs.

Depression meadow

Red Bluff Creek Carolina Bay harbors one of the two clay-based depression meadows protected in the state. It is a shallow bay dominated by grasses, sedges, and rushes. It is difficult to locate. Directions can be obtained from the Wambaw Ranger District. Look for yellow trumpet pitcher-plant, Boykin's lobelia, awned meadow-beauty, Tracy's beaksedge, tall milkwort, pealbark St. John's-wort, bay blue-flag iris, and pipewort.

Old Santee Canal Park

This 200-acre park is located southeast of the junction between the Tailrace Canal and US 17 near Moncks Corner and encompasses part of Stony Landing Plantation. The Santee Cooper Public Service Authority (SCPSA), headquartered in Moncks Corner, owns the property.

The most significant natural community is the calcareous bluff forest flanking Biggin Creek. The nature trail passes along a short portion of the bluff. Serious botany students can get permission from the park ranger to visit the remainder of the forest. Numerous trees that are characteristic of calcareous forests can be found, including hop hornbeam, Carolina buckthorn, yellow chestnut oak (*Quercus muhlenbergii*), the rare nutmeg hickory (*Carya myristicaeformis*), southern sugar maple, and slippery elm (*Ulmus rubra*). Look for the following calcicoles: American alumroot, thimbleweed, and horsebalm (*Collinsonia tuberosa*, plate 182 in *WCL*). Showy wildflowers and shrubs along the trail include wild ginger, may-apple, pawpaw, sweet-shrub (*Calycanthus floridus* L. var. *floridus),* bloodroot, red buckeye (*Aesculus pavia*), fringe-tree, Indian pink, and coral honeysuckle.

The trail crosses Biggin Creek in several places where a freshwater tidal marsh is present. Herbs include pickerelweed, alligator-weed, water-spider orchid, water hemlock, obedient plant (*Physostegia leptophylla,* plate 74 in *WCL*), swamp rose mallow, lizard's tail, cardinal flower, climbing aster, and indigo-bush (*Amorpha fruticosa,* plate 67 in *WCL*). Showy shrubs and vines include coral greenbrier, swamp rose, and climbing aster. Numerous swamp trees occur along the edge of the marsh, including bald cypress and red maple.

Wadboo Creek calcareous bluff forest

The calcareous bluff forest along Wadboo Creek is one of the most significant botanical sites in the coastal area. It is owned by the SCPSA. The only public access is by boat. The Rembert Dennis Boat Landing on SC-402 east of Moncks Corner provides access to Wadboo Creek. Approximately 0.25 mile north of the landing is a steep, calcareous bluff. Past the bluff, the land slopes to the river. This is where you can land a boat. The calcareous forest occurs on the bluff that runs along the floodplain. There is no maintained trail system.

Numerous uncommon and rare trees and herbs occur here. Look for yellow chestnut oak (*Quercus muhlenbergii*), black walnut, hop hornbeam, white basswood, slippery elm (*Ulmus rubra*), Carolina buckthorn, southern sugar maple, redbud, flowering dogwood, and eastern red cedar. Rare or uncommon herbs include bloodroot, mottled trillium, thimbleweed, autumn coral-root, American alumroot, wild ginger, round-lobed liverleaf, and incised groovebur (*Agrimonia incisa*). The rare blackstem spleenwort (*Asplenium resiliens,* plate 175 in *WCL*) grows in the crevices of the exposed limestone.

Charleston County

Francis Marion National Forest

Longleaf pine flatwoods

Stands of longleaf flatwoods are common in the Wambaw District. One good site is South Tibwan Plantation on US 17 south of McClellanville. Also, FR-211 north of SC-45 passes through stands of mature fire-maintained longleaf pine flatwoods.

Pocosins

Situated on both sides of SC-1032, southeast of the county line, is a vast pocosin and associated bogs. Species of note are yellow trumpet pitcher-plant, loblolly bay, sweet bay, pond pine, honey-cups, rose pogonia, and the rare white arum.

Pond cypress-swamp gum upland swamps

East of McClellanville, northeast of the intersection of US 17 and SC-857, is an upland swamp dominated by swamp gum with pond cypress. Here you can find the rare climbing fetterbush growing under the bark of pond cypress.

Shell deposits

Take USFS Road 243 to reach the Sewee Indian Shell Ring. Next, find the marked trail on the right that leads to the shell ring, which is a protected archeological site. The rare shell-mound buckthorn is conspicuous. Look for crested coral-root orchid, white basswood (*Tilia heterophylla*), tough bumelia, rough-leaved dogwood, and Carolina buckthorn.

Tidal freshwater marshes

The best examples of tidal freshwater marshes occur along Wambaw Creek from Still Landing (at the end of USFS Road 211-B) to the boat ramp on USFS Road 204. Wambaw Creek and the adjoining swamp is a nationally designated wilderness area (Wambaw Creek Wilderness Area). Look for green-fly orchid on cypress branches, and in May, look for spiderlily on the creek bank.

Tidal freshwater swamp forests

The tidal swamp forests along Wambaw Creek from Still Landing to USFS Road 204 are secondary forests growing on abandoned rice fields. The banks and trunks of the former rice fields are evident. Swamp gum is the dominant tree. Other species include bald cypress, red maple, and swamp red bay (*Persea palustris*). Button-bush (*Cephalanthus occidentalis,* plate 100 in *WCL*), swamp rose, and Virginia willow (*Itea virginica,* plate 147 in *WCL*) are common shrubs. The herbaceous flora is a mix of tidal marsh and swamp species. Look for lizard's tail, golden-club, butterweed, water willow (*Decodon verticillatus*), coral greenbrier, pickerelweed, water hemlock, arrow arum (*Peltandra virginica),* and southern rein-orchid (*Habenaria flava*).

Santee Coastal Reserve

The SCDNR owns and operates the Santee Coastal Reserve (SCR), encompassing approximately 24,000 acres. Contained within the reserve is Washo Reserve, a 1040-acre natural area owned by The Nature Conservancy of South Carolina. The SCR is located on the South Santee River. From US 17 take SC-857, which is about 52 miles north of Charleston. For information about the reserve, contact:

Santee Coastal Reserve Manager
P.O. Box 107
McClellanville, SC 29458
1-803-546-8665

Prescribed burning maintains the longleaf pine flatwoods, SCR's dominant upland community. The flatwoods line the main road leading into the SCR and harbor blazing star (*Liatris spicata* var. *resinosa*), black-root, sweet pepperbush (*Clethra alnifolia*), lead plant, deer's-tongue (*Carphephorus paniculatus*), and cinnamon fern (*Osmunda cinnamomea*). Laced throughout the flatwoods are longleaf pine savannas that have a rich display of herbs, including hooded pitcher-plant, yellow meadow-beauty (*Rhexia lutea*), orange milkwort, colicroot, white sabatia (*Sabatia difformis*), false asphodel, toothache grass, red-root, yellow trumpet pitcher-plant, and crested fringed orchid. Three Carolina bays occur on the SCR. Two harbor pond cypress-swamp gum upland swamps, and one harbors a pond cypress savanna.

Washo Reserve is a former rice reserve that was created by damming a creek. It harbors three natural communities: a blackwater bald cypress-tupelo gum swamp forest, the freshwater aquatics, and an inland freshwater marsh. An 800-foot boardwalk traverses these communities. Among the aquatics you can see are species of Lemnaceae, floating bladderwort, and fragrant water-lily. Swamp species include red maple, tupelo gum (*Nyssa aquatica*), bald cypress,

Virginia willow (*Itea virginica*), supplejack (*Berchemia scandens*), blue flag iris (*Iris virginica*), and coral greenbrier. Marsh species include alligator-weed, arrow arum (*Peltandra virginica*), water hemlock, pickerelweed, and water willow (*Decodon verticillatus*).

The Washo Reserve Nature Trail takes the visitor through a transitional maritime forest that includes live oak, Spanish moss, resurrection fern, beautyberry, American holly, and bull bay.

Clarendon County

Bennett's Bay

Directions and permission to enter Bennett's Bay must be obtained through The Nature Conservancy of South Carolina at its Columbia office (1-803-254-9049). Even with a map, locating the bay and adjacent ridge is difficult. Bennett's Bay was formally called Junkyard Bay, and this name appears on maps. It is located 2.0 miles northwest of Foreston between US 521 and SC-211. A sometimes hard-to-find dirt road leads off US 521 to the bay. In wet weather, vehicles should not use this road. There is no trail system within Bennett's Bay. The road leading to the bay from US 521 terminates at a xeric ridge, and the bay is to the right.

Bennett's Bay is a Carolina bay that harbors a pocosin community in the bay and a longleaf pine-turkey oak community on the adjacent sand ridge. Typical pocosin species occur in the bay, including swamp red bay (*Persea palustris*), loblolly bay, sweet bay, honey-cups, titi, pond pine, and fetterbush. Two rare plants, Carolina wicky and southern bog buttons, grow in the ecotone between the pocosin and ridge. Turkey oak and scattered longleaf pine dominate the xeric sandhills community. Xeric herbs include sandhills gerardia, sandhills milkweed, sandy-field beaksedge, and wire-plant.

Dillon County

Little Pee Dee State Park

This park is the treasure of the Pee Dee area for wildflower enthusiasts. Six natural communities occur: xeric sandhills, pocosins, upland swamp forests, freshwater aquatics, inland freshwater marshes, and pine-mixed hardwoods.

The park lies along the east side of the Little Pee Dee River. Adjacent to the river is a series of ridges and swales. They were created as wind-blown sand was deposited during the early formation of the coastal plain. The ridges support typical xeric sandhills species, while the swales support pocosins and upland swamp forests. These communities lie along SC-22. Wildflowers in the pocosins include possum-haw (*Viburnum nudum*), fetterbush, honey-cups, sweet bay, and titi. Red maple, coastal doghobble, and Virginia willow (*Itea virginica*) occur in the swamps.

Beaver Pond Nature Trail begins off the main road and passes through a loblolly pine plantation. Toward the latter half, the trail passes through pine-mixed hardwoods. The trail ends at Beaver Pond, about 1.0 mile beyond the pine-mixed hardwoods. Fragrant water-lily and species of Lemnaceae occur in the pond. The edge of the pond harbors a freshwater marsh with arrow arum (*Peltandra virginica*), common cat-tail (*Typha latifolia*), water willow (*Decodon verticillatus*), lizard's tail, and bur-reed.

Dorchester County

Francis Beidler Forest

The Francis Beidler Forest is a National Audubon Society Sanctuary near Harleyville. The 3600-acre Sanctuary, located in Four Holes Swamp, harbors the largest remaining stand of original growth blackwater bald cypress-tupelo gum swamp forest in the world. It is reached via SC-28 off US 178. From the east take I-26 west to exit 187. Go south (left) on SC-27 to US 78. Go west (right) on US 78 to US 178. From there, follow the Francis Beidler Forest signs to the Sanctuary. From I-95 or the west, take I-26 east to exit 177. Go south (right) on SC-453 to US 178. Go east (left) on US 178, through Harleyville, and follow the signs to the Visitor's Center.

Four Holes Swamp is a flowing blackwater swamp-stream fed by springs and by rain runoff from surrounding higher areas. A 1.5-mile board-walk takes visitors through a portion of the blackwater swamp. In the heart of Four Holes Swamp are ancient groves of bald cypress and tupelo gum towering over clear pools and blackwater sloughs. Many of the cypress trees are believed to be 600 years old. In season, canoe trip reservations can be made with the sanctuary director (1-803-462-2150).

Herbs seen from the boardwalk or from a canoe are golden-club, Spanish moss, green-fly orchid, resurrection fern, cardinal flower, false nettle, butterweed, aquatic milkweed (*Asclepias perennis*), and lizard's tail. The stump and floating log microhabitat is common throughout the swamp, with false nettle, skullcap (*Scutellaria lateriflora*), *Lycopus rubellus,* and *Hypericum virginicum* visible from the boardwalk.

Flowering shrubs, vines, and trees seen along the boardwalk include Virginia willow (*Itea virginica*), poison ivy (*Rhus radicans*), swamp dogwood (*Cornus stricta*), American storax, red maple, leucothoë, cross-vine, supplejack (*Berchemia scandens*), button-bush (*Cephalanthus occidentalis*), and coral green-brier. The rare Carolina least trillium, a federal species of concern, which blooms from late March to April, grows along the boardwalk. The visitor can have the naturalist help locate this inconspicuous trillium. The boardwalk also passes through another natural community, the hardwood bottom (plate 456), which is recognized by the presence of dwarf palmetto.

Georgetown County

Samworth Wildlife Management Area and Great Pee Dee River

The Samworth Wildlife Management Area is reached from SC-52. A boat ramp is availabe for access to the Great Pee Dee River and various creeks, some of which connect to the Waccamaw River. Vast tidal freshwater marshes occur in abandoned rice fields along and between these rivers and creeks. Wildflowers on the former rice field banks and in the fields include groundnut, water hemlock, climbing aster, cardinal flower, eryngo, swamp rose, pickerelweed, elderberry, wild rice, tag alder, indigo-bush, obedient-plant (*Physostegia leptophylla,* plate 74 in *WCL*), leather-flower (*Clematis crispa*), and Virginia willow.

For an additional wildflower adventure, consider crossing over to the Waccamaw River and trek to the area around the border between Georgetown and Horry Counties. Look for three rare species: cow-lily (*Nuphar sagittifolia,* plate 546), riverbank sundrops (*Oenothera riparia,* plate 448), and rose coreopsis (*Coreopsis rosea,* plate 450).

Hampton County

Webb Wildlife Center

The Webb Wildlife Center is one of the premier public wildflower sites in the coastal plain. It is owned and operated by the SCDNR. Over 600 species of vascular plants have been identified on this site. The 5866-acre wildlife center borders the Savannah River and extends 6.0 miles inland. It is open to the public all year; however, during deer season (October to 1 January) and turkey season (April), public access is controlled. Call the SCDNR at Garnett (1-803-625-3569) to make arrangements to visit. Overnight accommodations and boat trips can be arranged. A brochure covering activities and a map detailing roads can be obtained from the SCDNR. All the significant natural communities can be reached by roads. To reach the Webb Wildlife Center, turn west off US 321 in Garnett onto SC-20. Drive for approximately 2.0 miles until you come to the Webb Wildlife Center sign on the left.

Select timbering and prescribed burning of the pine forests have created excellent wildflower conditions. There are many roads that traverse the extensive stands of longleaf pine flatwoods and savannas as well as loblolly pine forests. Oak-hickory forests and pine-mixed hardwoods interlace the pinelands. Two natural lakes, Bluff and Flat, which are remnants of former riverbeds, support bald cypress-tupelo gum swamp forests on their margins. The floating log community occurs in both lakes. Two artificial lakes support freshwater aquatics, including sacred bean. A 2.0-mile trail leads from Bluff Lake to the Savannah River, passing through mature hardwood bottoms that are laced with wetland sloughs supporting bald cypress-tupelo gum swamp forests.

Special plants to look for include ladies'-eardrops along the margin of Bluff Lake, spreading pogonia in the longleaf pine savannas, and hairy wicky, southern evergreen blueberry, and spiked medusa in the longleaf pine flatwoods.

Horry County

Cartwheel Bay Heritage Preserve

Cartwheel Bay Heritage Preserve is difficult to locate. Those visiting the site for the first time should obtain a SCDNR map. From Conway, take US 701 to where it forks with SC-410. Go left on SC-410 and continue to Play Cards Crossroads, where SC-19 intersects SC-410. Tturn left on SC-19 and continue for 8.3 miles. A large, red wood building is on the right. This is the Cartwheel Bay Community Center. Proceed 0.2 mile until you see a red building on the left, a small access road after this building, and another red house. The access road between the two buildings leads to Cartwheel Bay Heritage Preserve.

Cartwheel Bay is a 680-acre Carolina bay complex, with one large 150-acre bay and five smaller ones. Natural communities include pocosins, longleaf pine flatwoods, longleaf pine savannas (both toothache and wiregrass), oak savannas, and xeric sandhills. Regular fires have maintained the open nature of the preserve.

The longleaf pine-toothache grass savannas are especially spectacular because of orchids and carnivorous plants. Look for snowy orchid, crested fringed orchid, white fringed orchid (*Platanthera blephariglottis*), yellow-fringed orchid (*Platanthera ciliaris*), hooded pitcher-plant, sweet pitcher-plant, frog's breeches, and yellow trumpet pitcher-plant. Other flowering herbs occur at different times. In the ecotones between the pocosins and longleaf pine savannas occur two rare species, common pyxie-moss and Venus' fly trap.

Lewis Ocean Bay Heritage Preserve

Lewis Ocean Bay Heritage Preserve consists of approximately 9300 acres. To reach the preserve, take SC-90 off US 501, east of Conway. Travel north approximately 6.0 miles to International Road (formally Burroughs Road) across from the Wild Horse subdivision. Turn east onto International Road, take a left at Kingston Road, and travel until it dead ends into Target Road. The entrance to the Lewis Ocean Bay Heritage Preserve is on the right.

Lewis Ocean Bay Heritage Preserve is too large to cover in one trip. Visits should be made at different growing seasons to fully appreciated the plant diversity. The following natural communities can be seen: pocosins, longleaf pine-turkey oak xeric sandhills, longleaf pine flatwoods, and longleaf pine savannas (both types, one dominated by wiregrass and one dominated by toothache grass). Many of the savannas and flatwoods were timbered and planted in loblolly pine before the preserve was established.

The rare Carolina ipecac and xeric species such as sandhills milkweed, tread-softly, reindeer moss, and sandhills baptisia grow on the xeric ridges of the Carolina bays. The pocosins harbor the rare leather-leaf and frog's breeches and ericads such as fetterbush and the spectacular honey-cups. Between the pocosins and sand ridges are ecotones that harbor creeping blueberry, Venus' fly trap, and Carolina wicky. The pine savannas harbor native orchids, including bearded grass-pink and spreading pogonia, and the carnivorous plants hooded pitcher-plant, violet butterwort, and sundews (*Drosera* spp.).

Little Pee Dee River Heritage Preserve (Vaughn Tract)

The Vaughn Tract of the Little Pee Dee River Heritage Preserve can be reached from SC-917, which runs between Mullins in Marion County and Loris in Horry County. The tract lies along the east side of the Little Pee Dee River. A dirt road leads off the northeast side of SC-917 through an iron gate and runs parallel to the river through the 3771-acre tract.

The heart of the Vaughn Tract is a series of fluvial sand ridges interspaced between pocosins and bay forests. The ridges support the xeric sandhills communities. Species of note include reindeer moss, prickly-pear, longleaf pine, turkey oak, Pickering's dawnflower, wire-plant, jointweed (*Polygonella polygama*), wiregrass, gerardia, and sandy-field beaksedge

The ecotones between the sand ridges and pocosins support creeping blueberry, common pyxie-moss, and Carolina wicky. Good populations of these rare species can be found along the first sand ridges encounter after you turn off of SC-917. Extensive pocosins occur throughout the tract. Look for loblolly bay, sweet bay, fetterbush, bamboo-vine, and titi.

Jasper County

Tillman Sand Ridge Heritage Preserve

Tillman Sand Ridge Heritage Preserve is located 5.0 miles west of Tillman on SC-19. The 953-acre preserve harbors three natural communities: an alluvial bald cypress-tupelo gum swamp forest, a hardwood bottom along the brownwater Savannah River, and a longleaf pine-turkey oak community on the fluvial sand ridges. The longleaf pine-turkey oak community is the heart of the preserve. Xeric herbs include wiregrass (*Aristida stricta*), gopherweed, gopherapple, sandhills milkweed, sandhills baptisia, warea, soft-haired coneflower, summer-farewell, woolly golden-aster, wire-plant, wild pink, blue star, and rose dicerandra.

There is no trail system on the preserve. Several abandoned roads give access to the interior, but the visitor can observe most of the plants from the road or by walking a short distance from the road.

Kershaw County

Savage Bay Heritage Preserve

Savage Bay Heritage Preserve was named to honor the late Henry Savage, Jr., Camden lawyer and author of *The Santee: River of the Carolinas* and *The Mysterious Carolina Bays,* and other publications. It is reached from SC-835 (Drakeford Road), which cuts off US 1 northeast of Camden. A sign directs visitors to an unpaved road that ends at a fork where narrow off-terrain trails go in two directions. The parking area is in the middle of a bay ridge that is dominated by longleaf pine and turkey oak. You can see numerous xeric species, including Carolina ipecac, senna seymeria, hairy false foxglove, tread-softly, sandhill wild-buckwheat, roseling, sandhills milkweed, sandhills thistle, carphephorus, and wire-plant.

The heart of the preserve is a large Carolina bay that is dominated by a pond cypress upland swamp forest. The large cypresses were cut years ago. A poorly defined trail leads from the parking area into the bay. If you cannot discern the trail, look straight ahead to see the pond cypress trees (about a 100 yards). You can easily traverse the open woods to the edge of the bay.

The edge of the bay consists of a dense zone of ericaceous shrubs and bay trees, including titi, swamp red bay, sweet bay, red maple, fetterbush, honey-cups, and swamp gum. The trail through the shrub zone is poorly defined and is not maintained. It was created as visitors pushed their way through the shrubs. You then enter the pond cypress community. The bay is flooded in wet years, and you must either wade or use a canoe. During dry seasons, you can easily move through the bay. A significant portion of the middle of the bay harbors a pond cypress savanna, with *Carex walteriana* the dominant herb. Small swamp gum saplings are present. The remainder of the bay harbors a pond cypress upland swamp with a moderate to dense understory of shrubs. The shrubs primarily occur in patches, so exiting through the bay is easy. Shrubs of note include titi, fetterbush, honey-cups, Virginia willow (*Itea virginica*), sweet bay, and the rare pondspice.

Lee County

Longleaf Pine Heritage Preserve

Longleaf Pine Heritage Preserve is located in Lee County southwest of Lynchburg off SC-101, 0.5 mile southwest of the intersection of SC-101 and SC-53. A sign marks the entrance to the parking lot. This 843-acre preserve was purchased primarily to protect seasonally wet longleaf pine flatwoods and savanna communities. The preserve harbors the federally endangered, fire-dependant red-cockaded woodpecker, American chaff-seed, and Canby's dropwort. The preserve also harbors several excellent pond cypress depressions.

From the parking lot, follow the gravel road 0.5 mile to the power-line crossing. Here you can find a restored longleaf pine flatwoods community that harbors a colony of red-cockaded woodpeckers (den trees are marked with white paint). A small pond cypress depression is in the middle. Next, follow the gravel road as it turns left, then right, and at 0.8 mile, you enter a spacious longleaf stand with red-cockaded woodpecker den trees. Mechanical treatment and burning have restored the longleaf stand to an open condition. Wildflowers that can be observed in mid-April include cleft-leaved violet, yellow stargrass (*Hypoxis micrantha*), leopard's-bane, daisy fleabane (*Erigeron strigosus*), lance-leaved violet (*Viola lanceolata*), sundew, dwarf iris, and blue-eyed grass. In mid-June the visitor may see galactia, huckleberry, savanna mountain-mint, smooth meadow-beauty, broad-leaved eupatorium (*Eupatorium rotundifolium*), pale meadow-beauty (*Rhexia mariana*), sundrops (*Oenothera fruticosa*), narrow-leaved skullcap (*Scutellaria integrifolia*), Samson's snakeroot (*Psoralea psoralioides* var. *psoralioides*), whorled-leaf coreopsis, blue-hearts (*Buchnera floridana*), and coastal plain rattlebox (*Crotalaria purshii*).

The pond cypress swamp forests and savannas harbor numerous wildflowers throughout the year, starting with fetterbush and honey-cups in April.

Orangeburg County

Santee State Park

Santee State Park consists of 2496 acres and is located on the edge of Lake Marion in Santee. The park is open all year. Most of the park is covered in upland pine-mixed hardwoods; however, one site harbors deciduous forest communities that are a must for wildflower observing. The deciduous forests occur around limestone caverns. Because of the presence of a rare bat in the caverns, the southeastern myotis (*Myotis austroriparius*), visitors must get permission from park officials to visit.

The deciduous communities present are a calcareous bluff forest, oak-hickory forest, and beech forest. The key to locating the three communities is the limestone cave, which park officials will show visitors. To locate the oak-hickory forest, follow the east fork of the stream that comes out of the limestone cave. This forms Chapel Branch. Chapel Branch (a small lake) runs east, and the oak-hickory forest occurs on the sloping bluff adjacent to the branch. Species of note are white oak, southern red oak (*Quercus falcata*), mockernut hickory (*Carya tomentosa*), redbud, horse sugar, coral honeysuckle, flowering dogwood, squaw-root, sparkleberry, red buckeye (*Aesculus pavia*), sassafras, green-and-gold, yellow jessamine, black cherry, fringe-tree, Indian pink, crab-apple, lyre-leaved sage (*Salvia lyrata*), and needle grass (*Stipa avenacea*).

The west fork of the stream that leads from the cave eventually heads into a ravine with an exposed limestone bluff on the south side. Species of the calcareous bluff forest and beech forest merge, making it difficult to separate the two communities. Typical calcareous species are southern sugar maple, meadow-parsnip (*Thaspium barbinode*), and American alumroot. Round-lobed liverleaf, which is rare in the coastal plain, occurs on the bluff. Species more characteristic of the beech forest are bloodroot, may-apple, mottled trillium, arrowleaf, green-and-gold, sweet-shrub, tulip tree, spotted wintergreen, wind-flower, strawberry-bush, and cranefly orchid. Along the stream edge are species such as jack-in-the-pulpit, pawpaw, Easter lily, golden-club, and wild allspice.

The rare May white azalea (*Rhododendron eastmanii*, plate 434) flowers in May and can be seen along the edge of Chapel Branch and along the ravine bluff.

Sumter County

Woods Bay State Park

Woods Bay State Park is located in Sumter and Clarendon Counties. To reach the bay from US 301, take SC-152 west of Olanta until it turns into SC-48. Follow SC-48 to the park sign. From I-95 in Sumter County, take exit 146 and follow the signs to SC-48, then follow the signs to the park.

The southeastern side of the bay harbors a relatively undisturbed xeric ridge and an ecotone between the ridge and the bay. Arrangements to visit this site must be made with park officials. The ridge harbors a longleaf pine-turkey oak xeric community with the following herbs: Carolina sandwort, senna seymeria, wire-plant, prickly-pear, Carolina ipecac, and hairy false foxglove. The adjacent ecotone is rich in ericaceous shrubs, including honey-cups, fetterbush, titi, highbush blueberry, Carolina wicky, and huckleberry.

THE MARITIME STRAND

Charleston County

Accreted Beach at Sullivan's Island

Accreted Beach is a section of beach and dunes that is owned by the town of Sullivan's Island. The Lowcountry Open Land Trust holds a protective easement. It is open to the public all year and is reached from either Station 18 or Station 16. Limited parking is available at the end of each road. Trails lead to the beach.

Sea rocket and Carolina saltwort are found in the beach community. The dunes harbor dune devil-joint, beach evening-primrose, gaillardia, silver-leaf croton, sea purslane, dune spurge, beach pea (*Strophostyles helvola*), sea oats, dune sandbur, seaside panicum, seashore-elder, and beach morning-glory. The maritime shrub thickets harbor wax myrtle and dune greenbrier; however, numerous weedy species, such as rattle-bush and giant foxtail (*Setaria magna*), have invaded the shrub thickets.

Beachwalker County Park

Beachwalker County Park is located on Kiawah Island and is leased and operated for the public by the Charleston County Parks and Recreation Commission. Information about the park can be obtained by calling 1-843-762-2172. The park is closed from November to March.

Beachwalker Park is located on the southwestern end of the island on an accreting beach ridge approximately 1.0 mile long. The coastal beaches and coastal dunes harbor seaside panicum, dune sandbur, beach evening-primrose, sea oats, sea rocket, Carolina saltwort, seashore-elder, silver-leaf croton, beach morning-glory, dune spurge, and beach pea. Sweet grass occurs in the flats between the dunes. Common marsh-pink grows in the wet swales behind the dunes. The stabilized dunes on the ridge support typical maritime shrub thickets that are dominated by wax myrtle.

You can walk down the beach to the end of the ridge, then turn back east along the back of the ridge that is bordered by the Kiawah River. Along the river you can see salt marshes, salt flats, and salt shrub thickets. In the fall, sea lavender blooms on the edge of the salt flats and in the higher salt marsh.

Colleton County

Edisto Beach State Park

Edisto Beach State Park offers typical coastal dune and beach communities. Severe erosion has eliminated most of the dunes; however, sand dunes extend north of the island to Jeremy Inlet, where you can view species of the dune and beach communities. The maritime forest has mostly been developed for park facilities.

The nature trail passes through a modified maritime forest, ending at a Native American shell mound at the edge of the salt marsh. The mound has eroded greatly because of the nearby creek. The only true calcicole on this mound is shell-mound buckthorn; the rest of the plants are typical maritime species. Numerous wildflowers occur along the trail including elephant's foot and coral bean.

St. Helena Sound Heritage Preserve (Otter Island)

St. Helena Sound Heritage Preserve consists of five islands: Big Warren Island, Little Warren Island, Ashe Island, Beet Island, and Otter Island. Of the five, Otter Island and its associated hummocks harbor the greatest diversity of natural communities. Otter is a barrier island and can easily be reached from three boat landings: (1) Edisto Marina at the south end of Edisto Island (a commercial landing that requires a fee); (2) Live Oak Landing on Big Bay Creek (take SC-1461 off SC-174); and (3) the public landing at the end of State SC-26 (Bennetts Point Road) on the Ashepoo River. You can come down either the Ashepoo or Combahee rivers into St. Helena Sound to Otter Island. Otter Island and its associated hummocks are bounded by the ocean on the south,

Fish and Jefford creeks on the east and north, and the Ashepoo River and St. Helena Sound on the west.

Landing on the front beach may be difficult because of the ocean waves. The front beach is best reached by going down the Ashepoo River and landing on the sheltered west side. The Ashepoo River is reached from Edisto Marina or Live Oak Landing by going up the Edisto River to Fenwick Cut and then into the Ashepoo River.

The dunes on Otter Island harbor a rich mix of plants, including dune devil-joint, silver-leaf croton, sea oats, camphorweed (*Heterotheca subaxillaris*), dune sandbur, dunes evening-primrose (*Oenothera humifusa*), seaside panicum, and trailing bluet. Maritime shrub thickets lace the dunes. The front beach is eroding, so the beach community is absent. Well-developed maritime forests are on the eastern end.

Landward to the barrier island are numerous smaller islands and hummocks. These can best be reached from Fish and Jefford Creeks and from two smaller creeks on the west side of Otter Island. Salt marshes, salt flats, salt shrub thickets, and shell deposits are present. Sweet grass grows on the edge of the hummocks. Look for shell-mound buckthorn along the edge of hummocks on shell deposits.

The hummocks and smaller islands offer exceptional opportunities to view maritime forest species because the underbrush is thin and entering them is easy. Good stands of wild olive (*Osmanthus americana*) occur on several hummocks. Also look for saw palmetto, which reaches its northern range on these hummocks. The pines are slash pine (*P. elliottii*).

Glossary

The terms marked with an asterisk (*) are illustrated in figure 11 in the appendix.

ACE Basin. Lower part of the watershed of the Ashepoo, Combahee, and Edisto Rivers.

Achene. A small, dry, one-loculate, one-seeded, indehiscent fruit; for example, in the Asteraceae (sunflower family).

Acuminate. Tapering to the apex, the sides more or less pinched in before reaching the tip.

Acute. Ending in a point less than 90 degrees (a right angle); applied to tips and bases of structures.

Aerenchyma. Aerating tissue in aquatic plants, characterized by large intercellular spaces filled with gasses; functions in flotation of the plant and storage and diffusion of gasses.

Alkaloid. Organic compound that is alkaline and produces a marked physiological effect in animals, including man; examples are nicotine, morphine, and cocaine.

Alluvial soil. Soil developing from recent alluvium (material deposited by running water); exhibits no horizon development; typical of floodplains.

Alternate leaves. Only one leaf at a node.

Amphibolite. Rock, usually metamorphic, with large amounts of amphibole, complex silicate minerals that weather to produce soils high in calcium, magnesium, and iron.

Apical. At the tip or summit.

Angiosperm. A flowering plant.

Annual. Plant growing from seed to fruit in one year, then dying.

**Anther.* The pollen producing part of the stamen.

Aphrodisiac. Stimulator of sexual desire.

Appressed. Lying flat against something.

Aromatic. Having a fragrant, sweet-smelling, or spicy aroma.

Artesian. Water capable of rising to the surface by internal hydrostatic pressure.

Ascending. Growing obliquely upward at about a 40 to 60 degree angle from the horizontal.

Asexual reproduction. Reproduction that does not involve fusion of gametes; for example, fragmentation of a rhizome, each fragment growing into a new plant.

Asphyxia. Unconsciousness or death resulting from lack of oxygen.

Astringent. Agent that causes contraction of tissues, thereby lessening secretion.

Auricle. Any earlike lobe or appendage.

Axil. The angle formed by the upper side of a leaf and the stem from which it grows.

Axillary. In an axil.

Barrier island. Narrow islands of sand that run parallel to the shoreline; a river, marsh, or lagoon separates them from the mainland; Otter Island and Capers Island are examples.

Basal leaves. Leaves at the base of the stem.

Basic soil. Soil with an alkaline pH, i.e., a pH greater than 7.0.

Berry. A simple, fleshy, usually indehiscent fruit with one or more seeds; for example, a tomato or grape.

Biennial. Living for two years, then dying naturally.

Bipinnately compound leaf. Twice pinnate, the primary leaflets once again pinnate. (*See* pinnate)

Bisexual. Having both stamens and pistils, usually used in reference to a flower.

Blade. Flattened and expanded part of a leaf.

Blackwater river. River that originates in the coastal plain, receiving its water from local rain, with a narrow floodplain, its black color due to organic acids from decaying leaves; examples are the Black and Edisto Rivers.

Bract. Modified leaf, usually smaller than a foliage leaf, often situated at the base of a flower or inflorescence.

Bracteate. Having bracts.

Bractlet. A very small bract.

Branchlet. A small branch.

Brownwater river. River that originates in the mountains or piedmont, has a wide, alluvial floodplain, with brown water colored by suspended silt and clay that originates from erosion of the piedmont and mountains; examples are the Santee and Savannah Rivers.

Bryophyte. Terrestrial, nonflowering, nonvascular plant; comprising mosses, liverworts, and hornworts.

Bulb. An underground, fleshy enlargement of stem and leaves, as in the onion.

Buttress. Additional, often flattened, supporting tissue at the base of the trunk, as in bald cypress.

Calcareous. Consisting, having, or typical of calcium carbonate, calcium, or limestone; for example, calcareous soil.

Calcicole. A plant that thrives in soil abundantly supplied with calcium ions.

Calyx (pl. *calyces*).The collective term used to describe all the sepals of a flower.

Canopy. The top layer of leaf growth within most woody communities.

Capsule. A dry dehiscent fruit with more than one chamber; it may open by pores, by splitting vertically, or by the top coming off like a lid.

Catkin. A spikelike inflorescence bearing either male or female flowers, as in willows and oaks.

Cespitose. Tufted, growing in clumps.

Chasmogamy. Having flowers that open to expose reproductive organs, allowing cross-pollination.

Chlorophyll. The green pigment of plants that traps light energy and makes photosynthesis possible.

Ciliate. Beset with a marginal fringe of hairs.

Circumboreal. Around northern regions.

Circumneutral soils. Soils that are only slightly acidic or slightly alkaline; such soils are usually relatively high in calcium and magnesium.

Clasping. For example, a leaf whose base wholly or partly wraps around or surrounds the stem.

Cleistogamy. Self-pollination within a perfect flower that does not open.

Climax community. That stable community culminating succession that is capable of self-perpetuation under prevailing environmental conditions.

Coadaptation. The adaptive response of two organisms to each other; e.g., flower structure and pollinator.

Colonial. Adjective of colony.

Colony. Growing in clumps produced asexually from underground structures such as rhizomes, rootstocks, stolons, or roots.

Column. In orchids, a structure formed by the union of stamens, style and stigma; the supporting structure of the hood in pitcher-plants.

Community. Group of interacting plants and animals inhabiting a given area.

Composite. Any member of the Asteraceae (sunflower family).

*Compound leaf. Leaf in which the blade is subdivided into two or more leaflets or pinnae.

Cone-bearing plants. Technically the gymnosperms, plants that produce seeds not enclosed by an ovary, as in pine trees.

Conifer. Any of the cone-bearing gymnosperms, such as Carolina hemlock (*Tsuga caroliniana*).

Connective. Filament extension between thecae.

Consumption. Colloquial term for tuberculosis.

Cordate. With a sinus and rounded lobes at the base of the leaf.

Corm. A thickened, vertical, underground stem with thin, scalelike leaves.

*Corolla. All the petals of a flower, separate or united; the inner whorl of the perianth.

Corymb. A flat-topped or rounded inflorescence with the outer flowers on longest stalks and opening first.

Cross-pollination. Pollination between two different plants of the same species.

Culm. The flowering stems of grasses and sedges.

Cultivated plant. A purposely grown plant; it may be a native plant moved from local woodlands into a garden or yard, or a plant introduced from another country.

Cusp. A strong sharp point.

Cuticle. Waxy, noncellular layer on outer surface of epidermal wall of plant organs (mostly leaves) that prevents water loss.

Cyme. A broad, flattish inflorescence, the central flowers maturing first.

Deciduous. Falling away, not persistent or evergreen; for example, leaves falling from oak trees in the autumn.

Decoction. An extraction of a plant made by boiling a plant part in water.

Decomposition. Breakdown of complex organic substances from dead organisms into simpler, inorganic substances.

Decumbent. Prostrate at or near the base, the upper parts erect or ascending.

Decurrent. Fused to the stem or leaf stalk and extending beyond the point of attachment, as in the leaf base of blackroot.

Dehiscent. Opening by pores or slits to discharge the contents.

Demulcent. A soothing usually mucilaginous or oily substance used for relieving pain in irritated mucous surfaces.

Dentate. Toothed with the teeth directed outward.

Dermatitis. Inflammation of the skin.

Detritus. Accumulated mass of partially decomposed remains of animals and plants that form in aquatic systems.

Diabase. Dark-colored, igneous rocks that are granitic and fine-grained in texture and weather to produce soils high in calcium and magnesium; diabase rocks are fine-textured variants of gabbro rocks.

Dichotomous. Two-forked, the branches equal or nearly so.

Dioecious. Having male and female flowers on different plants of the same species.

Disjunct. A population of plants growing far from its main range.

*Disk flower. The small tubular flowers in the central part of a floral head, as in most members of the Asteraceae (sunflower family).

*Dissected leaf. The blade cut into more or less fine divisions.

*Divided leaf. Any blade cut into divisions that reaches three-fourths or more of the distance from the margin to the midvein or to the base.

Doctrine of Signatures. Medieval belief that the key to man's use of plants was hidden in the form of the plant itself; for example, the red juice of bloodroot to treat blood disorders.

Dredged soil disposal site. Site used to dispose of soil dredged to maintain harbor or river depths; in the coastal area most often a section of banked marsh.

Drupe. A stone fruit; fleshy fruit with the single seed covered by a hard covering (stone).

Ecosystem. The biotic community and its abiotic environment functioning as a system.

Ecotone. Transitional area between two different communities, having characteristics of both, yet having a unique character of its own.

*Elliptic. Widest in the center and narrowed to two equal ends.

Emarginate. Having a shallow notch at the tip.

Emergent. Aquatic plant with its lower part submerged and its upper part extended above water.

Emergent, nonpersistent. Emergent marsh species that fall to the surface of the water at the end of the growing season.

Emergent, persistent. Emergent marsh species that usually remain standing at least until the beginning of the next growing season.

Emersed. Rising above the surface of the water; applies to leaves.

Emetic. An agent that induces vomiting.

Endemic. Restricted to a small area or region.

Endosperm. The nutritive tissue of most seeds.

*Entire leaf. Leaf margin without teeth, lobes, or divisions.

Ephemeral. Lasting only a short time.

Epiphyte. A plant growing on another plant but obtaining no nutrition from it; often referred to as an air plant; for example, Spanish moss.

Ericaceous. Having characteristics similar to those of the heath family (Ericaceae).

Ericad. A member of the Ericaceae (heath family).

Escarpment. A long cliff or steep slope separating two comparatively level or more gently sloping surfaces and resulting from erosion or faulting.

Essential oil. Volatile oils with characteristic odor, composed of various constituents and contained in plant organs.

Estuary. An area where freshwater and sea water meet and mix.

*Even-pinnately compound. Refers to compound leaves having an even number of leaflets; this is easily determined because there is a pair of leaflets terminally.

Evergreen. Bearing green leaves throughout the year; holding live leaves over one or more winters until new ones appear.

Exfoliating. To come off or separate as scales, flakes, sheets, or layers.

Facultative. Ability to adjust optionally to different environmental conditions.

Falcate. Sickle-shaped.

Fascicle. A small bundle or tuft, as of leaves.

Febrifuge. Agent which relieves or reduces fever.

Female flower. With pistils and without fertile stamens.

Fibrous roots. Root system composed of a mass of fiberlike roots with no main root predominating.

*Filament. Part of the stamen that bears the anther.

Filiform. Threadlike; long and very slender.

Flatwoods. Poorly drained, low-lying, nearly level timberland.

Fleshy. A plant having tissue that serves to store moisture, such as a cactus.

Floodplain. A level, flat area bordering a river, subject to frequent flooding.

Flora. Collective term to refer to all plants of a area; a book dealing with the plants of an area.

*Flower stalk. The stalk of each single flower.

Flowering plants. Technically the Angiosperms, plants that produce seeds enclosed in an ovary.

Fluvial. Caused by the action of flowing water.

FMNF. Francis Marion National Forest.

Follicle. A dry fruit produced from a single ovary, opening along one suture.

Food. An organic compound from which an organism can derive a source of energy and contributes materially to growth and repair of tissues.

Forb. Herbaceous plant other than a grass, sedge, or rush.

Forest. Vegetation dominated by trees with their crowns overlapping, generally forming 60–100% cover.

Frond. In Lemnaceae (duckweed family), the expanded leaflike stem that functions as a leaf; the leaf of ferns.

Fruit. The seed-bearing structure of the plant; a matured ovary with its contents, often with attached parts.

Fusiform. Cylindrical except thick near the middle and tapering to both ends.

Gabbro. Dark-colored igneous rocks that are granitic in texture, very tough, and weather to produce soils high in calcium and magnesium.

Glade. An open space in a forest or woodland.

Gland. A secreting surface or structure, or an appendage having the general appearance of such an organ.

Glandular. Bearing glands.

Glaucous. Whitened with a bloom.

Globose. Globular or spherical.

Gneiss. A metamorphic rock corresponding in composition to granite.

Granite. A coarse-grained igneous rock.

Gymnosperm. A seed plant in which the seeds are not enclosed in an ovary; pines, firs, spruces, cedars, are examples.

Habitat. Place where a plant or animal lives.

Halophyte. Plant able to survive and complete its life cycle in high salinity.

Hardpan. A cemented or compacted and often clayey layer in soil that is impermeable to water.

Hastate. Like an arrowhead but diverging at the base.

Haustorium. A bridge of xylem (figure 3) between host and parasite in plants through which water, minerals, and limited amounts of food pass from host to parasite.

*Head. A dense inflorescence of sessile or subsessile flowers on a short or broadened axis, as in the Asteraceae (sunflower family).

Hemiparasite. Dependent on the host for water and minerals; contains chlorophyll and can make its own food, but may receive some food from the host, as in chaff-seed (*Schwalbea americana*).

Herb. Having no persistent woody stem above ground; also, a plant used in seasoning.

Herbaceous. Having the characteristic of an herb.

Herbarium. A collection of dried plants; an institution that houses a collection of dried plants.

Heterotrophic. Requiring a supply of organic matter (food) from the environment.

Hip. The fleshy to leathery hollow fruit of roses.

Holoparasite. Parasite completely dependent on the host for water, minerals and food, as in beech- drops (*Epifagus virginiana*).

Hummock. A low mound or ridge of earth; like the small hummocks that rise above the salt marsh along the coast.

Humus. Organic material derived from partial decay of plant and animal matter.

Hydric. Habitats characterized by an abundant water supply.

Hydrophyte. A plant that grows in water.

Hypanthium. A cup-shaped, or tubular organ below, around, or adhering to the side of the ovary.

Hyphae. The threadlike filaments that make up the mycelium, or major part of the body, of a fungus.

Indehiscent. Remaining persistently closed; not opening by definite pores or sutures.

Indigenous. Native to an area.

Inflorescence. A flower cluster on a plant, or, especially, the arrangement of flowers on a plant.

Infusion. An extraction of a plant made by soaking the plant part in water.

Internode. The portion of a stem between two nodes.

Introduced. Plant brought intentionally from another area; such a plant may escape and become naturalized; for example, *Crotalaria spectabilis* was brought as a green manure from India.

*Irregular flower. A flower with petals that are not uniform in shape but are usually grouped to form upper and lower "lips."

Knee. Vertical outgrowth from the lateral roots of trees growing on soil subjected to long periods of inundation; the function is unknown; for example, bald cypress.

*Lanceolate. Lance-shaped, much longer than wide and broadest near the base.

*Leaflet. One of the leaflike parts of a compound leaf.

*Leaf stalk. The basal stalk of a leaf.

Legume. A dry fruit from a single ovary usually dehiscent along two sutures.

Lenticels. Small openings in the bark of roots and stems of flowering plants used for gas exchange.

Levee. Soil deposits along channels of large rivers that form a natural embankment.

Lichen. Unique composite organism formed by a symbiotic relationship between some sac fungi (and, to a lesser extent, club fungi) and a photosynthetic partner, either a blue-green or green algae.

Limestone. Sedimentary rock composed mostly of calcium carbonate.

*Linear. Narrow and elongate with essentially parallel sides.

*Lip. The lower petal of some irregular flowers, often showy, as in the orchids.

Litter. Accumulated mass of partially decomposed remains of plants (and animals) that collects on the forest floor.

*Lobed leaf. Blade divided into parts separated by rounded sinuses extending one-third to one-half the distance between the margin and the midrib.

Locular. Having one or more locules.

Locule. Compartment of an ovary or an anther.

Lowcountry. Physiographically the outer coastal plain; traditionally the tidewater and rice growing area of South Carolina.

Mafic. Dark-colored minerals high in magnesium and iron.

Male flower. Having stamens and no functional pistil.

Malodorous. Having a foul odor.

Manual. Book that provides an inventory of the flora of a specific region, and provides the means of identifying the plants using keys.

Many-ranked. Leaves that are arranged in many rows along the stem.

Maritime. Located on or close to the sea.

Marl. Sedimentary rock formation composed of unconsolidated mixture of 35–65% calcium carbonate and 65–35% clay.

Marsh. Wetland dominated by emergent, herbaceous vegetation.

Marsh, brackish. Marsh flooded regularly or irregularly by water of low salt content.

Marsh, freshwater. Marsh saturated or flooded with freshwater.

Marsh, tidal freshwater. The zone of marsh along a coastal river above the influence of salt water (the salt point), and to the point where the tidal amplitude vanishes.

Mesic. Moist but well-drained soils.

Mesophyte. Plant adapted to a mesic environment.

Monadnock. A hill or mountain of resistant rock surmounting a peneplain (figure 10).

Monoecious. Having both male and female flowers on the same plant.

Monotypic. A genus with only a single species in it.

Montane. Related to mountains.

Mucilage. A substance of varying composition produced in cell walls of plants; hard when dry, swelling and slimy when moist.

Mycelium. A large, entangled network of filaments that forms the body of a fungus.

Mycorrhiza (pl. *mycorrhizae*). A special compound structure formed between a fungal mycelium and certain underground parts of a vascular plant, particularly a root.

Mycotrophy. The nutritiion of most vascular plants (and bryophytes) directly tied up with the nutrition of higher fungi.

Native plant. One that originated in the area where it grows.

Naturalized. Plant from another area that is thoroughly established in a new area because it is able to naturally and successfully reproduce; for example, white clover introduced from Europe is now naturalized throughout the southeastern United States.

Natural selection. Natural process that results in survival of the best-adapted individual of a species and elimination of individuals less well adapted to their environment.

Naval stores. Crude turpentine, and its products (pitch, resin, etc.), from southern yellow pines used chiefly in connection with wooden sailing ships.

Nectar. Sweet substance secreted by special glands (nectaries) in flowers and in certain leaves.

Needle. A stiff, narrow leaf, as in pine trees.

Nitrogen fixation. Conversion of atmospheric nitrogen to forms usable by plants.

Node. Point on a stem where one or more leaves are borne or attached.

Nomenclature. The assignment of scientific names to plants and animals.

Nut. Indehiscent, one-seeded fruit having a hard outer wall, as in oaks and hickories.

Nutlet. A small nut or nutlike fruit.

*Oblanceolate. Lanceolate, and attached at the narrow end.

Obligate. Limited to one mode of life or action, as an obligate parasite.

Oblique. Sides unequal, especially the base of a leaf.

Oblong. Elongate and with parallel, or nearly so, sides.

*Obovate. Ovate and attached at the narrow end.

Obtuse. Blunt or rounded at end, the angle at the end exceeds 90 degrees but is less than 180 degrees.

*Odd-pinnately compound leaf. Refers to compound leaves having an odd number of leaflets, this is usually easily determined because there is a single, terminal leaflet.

Opposite leaves. Two leaves inserted at the node opposite each other on the stem.

Ornamental. A plant cultivated for its beauty.

Outcrop. A stratum or formation, as of limestone or marl or granite, that protrudes above the soil.

Ovary. The basal, enlarged part of the pistil that contains the ovules or seeds.

Ovate. Egg-shaped, and attached at the broad end.

Ovule. The structure that develops into the seed.

Palmate. Having three or more divisions or lobes, looking like the outspread fingers of a hand.

Palmately compound leaf. The leaflets diverge from a common point at the end of the leaf stalk.

Panicle. A compound inflorescence in which the main axis is branched one or more times and supports racemes.

Parasitic. A plant (or animal) deriving food or mineral nutrition, or both, from another living organism.

Peat. The partially decomposed remains of plants and animals.

Peduncle. The main flower stalk, supporting either a cluster of flowers or the only flower.

Peltate. Leaf attached to its stalk inside the margin, as in species of *Hydrocotyle.*

Peneplain. A nearly flat land surface representing an advanced stage of erosion.

Perennial. A plant lasting for three or more years.

Perennating. Surviving from one year to the next.

Perfect flower. A flower having both female (pistil) and male (stamen) parts.

Perfoliate. Describes those stalkless leaves whose base surrounds the stem, the stem thus apparently passing through it.

Perianth. The calyx and corolla collectively; the calyx alone if the corolla is absent.

Persistent. Remaining attached; not falling off.

Petal. One of the individual parts, separate or united, of the corolla.

pH. A measure of the acidity or alkalinity of a solution (e.g., the soil solution).

Pharmacopoeia. Book containing an official list of drugs along with recommended procedures for their preparation and use.

Photodermatitis. Dermatitis in the form of a sunburnlike rash resulting from contact with plants and containing compounds that sensitize the skin to subsequent exposure to ultraviolet light.

Photosynthesis. Synthesis of carbohydrates from carbon dioxide and water by chlorophyll-containing plants using light as energy and releasing molecular oxygen as a by-product.

Pinna (pl. *pinnae*). One of the first or primary divisions of a pinnately compound leaf; applied especially in ferns.

Pinnate. Arranged along the sides of a common axis.

Pinnately compound leaf. Leaf with leaflets placed on either side of the rachis; featherlike.

Pinnatifid. Pinnately lobed, cleft or parted, usually halfway or more to the midrib.

Pistil. The central, seed-bearing organ of a flower, usually composed of stigma, style, and ovary; the female part of a flower.

Pith. The central portion of a dicot stem.

Plantlet. Literally a small or young plant; used in this book to refer to vegetative offshoots produced by some specialized horizontal stems or from buds in the inflorescences of some plants that can develop into new plants.

Pollen. Spores formed in the anthers that produce the sperm.

Pollination. The transfer of pollen from an anther to a stigma.

Pollinium (pl. *pollinia*). An agglutinated pollen mass in orchids and other plants.

Polygamous. Having perfect, male, and female flowers all on the same plant.

Polymorphic. With three or more forms, such as the entire, two-lobed or three-lobed leaves in sassafras.

Pome. A simple, fleshy fruit like an apple in which the fleshy part is derived from nonovary parts.

Poultice. A moist, soft mass (usually heated) of an adhesive substance, such as meal or clay, spread on cloth and applied to warm, moisten, or stimulate a sore or inflamed part of the body.

Prairie. An extensive tract of flat or rolling grassland.

Prescribed burn. An intentionally set fire, usually by professional foresters or land managers, under the right conditions of wind, humidity, and temperature to remove ground litter, reduce wildfire threat, promote growth of desirable plants, and control underbrush buildup.

Prickle. A small, usually slender outgrowth of the epidermis.

Primary succession. Vegetational development starting on a site never before colonized by plant communities.

Propagule. Any of the various structures of plants capable of developing into a new individual.

Prostrate. Lying flat on the ground; if a stem, may or may not root at the nodes.

Pubescent. Covered with short, soft hairs.

Punctate. With translucent or colored dots, depressions or pits scattered over the surface.

Pungent. Affecting the organs of smell or taste with a strong, acrid sensation.

Purgative. Tending to cleanse or purge, especially tending to cause evacuation of the bowels.

Quartzite. Hard and tough rock that consists mostly of quartz; usually recrystallized sandstone.

Quinine. Main drug for treatment of malaria, derived from bark of species of *Cinchona* native to South America.

Raceme. A simple, indeterminate inflorescence of stalked flowers borne on a single, more or less, elongated axis.

Rachis. The central elongated axis of an inflorescence or a compound leaf.

Rank. A vertical row.

Ray flower. The regular flowers around the edge of the head in many members of the Asteraceae (sunflower family); each ray flower resembles a single petal.

Receptacle. The base of the flower, where flower parts are attached.

Recurved. Curved outward, downward, or backward.

Reflexed. Abruptly recurved or bent downward or backward.

Regular flower. With petals and/or sepals arranged around the center, like the spokes of a wheel; always radically symmetrical.

Resin. Any of numerous clear or translucent yellow or brown solid or semisolid viscous substances of plant origin, as amber.

Resinous. With the appearance of resin; glandular-dotted.

Revolute. Rolled backward, with margins rolled toward the lower side.

Rhizome. Underground stem, usually horizontally orientated; sometimes functions in food storage.

Rhizomatous. Bearing rhizomes.

Rhizosphere. The soil immediately surrounding the root system.

Rootstock. An erect, rootlike stem or branch under or sometimes on the ground.

Rosette. Arrangement of leaves radiating from a crown or center, usually at or close to the ground.

Ruderal. Growing in waste places or among rubbish.

Runcinate. Margins that are coarsely serrate to sharply incised with the segments pointing toward the base, as in common dandelion (*Taraxacum officinale*, plate 615).

Sagittate. Like an arrowhead, with the basal lobes pointing downward or inward toward the leaf stalk.

Saline. Of, relating to, or containing salt; salty.

Samara. A dry, indehiscent, winged fruit, as in red maple (plate 27).

Saprophyte. An organism that derives its nourishment from dead or decaying organic matter.

Savanna. A flat area with widely spaced trees, usually dominated by grasses.

Scape. A leafless stem bearing flowers and rising from the ground or near it.

Scapose. Having a scape.

SCDNR. South Carolina Department of Natural Resources.

SCDPRT. South Carolina Department of Parks, Recreation and Tourism.

Schist. Highly metamorphosed, crystalline rocks, usually splitting along parallel planes, and named for their most prominent mineral (e.g., mica schist).

Secondary forest. The forest occupying a site where the original forest was removed.

Secondary succession. Plant succession taking place on sites that previously supported vegetation.

Seed. The matured ovule consisting of an embryo, seed coat, and stored food.

Seepage. Water that has passed slowly through porous soils.

Self-fertilization. Fertilization of an egg by sperm from the same flower, or by sperm from another flower of the same plant.

Self-pollination. The transfer of pollen from an anther to a stigma on the same plant.

Sepals. One of the parts of the calyx, either separate or united.

Serotinous cones. Cones that remain on the tree several years and require the heat of fire to open them to release the seeds, as in pond pine (*Pinus serotina*).

Serrate. Having sharp teeth pointed terminally.

Sessile. Without a stalk of any kind, as a sessile leaf.

Sexual reproduction. Reproduction resulting from the fusion of gametes (sex cells).

Shade tolerance. Capacity of a tree to develop and grow to maturity in the shade.

Sheath. A tubular envelope, usually used for that part of the leaf of a sedge or grass that envelops the stem.

Shoal. A shallow area in a body of water; if covered with rocks, a rocky shoal.

Shrub. A woody plant that remains low to the ground and produces several shoots or trunks from the base.

*Simple leaf. A leaf with a blade in a single part, although it may be variously divided.

Sinus. The depression or recess between two adjoining lobes.

Slate. Metamorphosed shale (clays hardened into rocks by heat and pressure).

Sp. (pl. *spp.*). Species.

*Spadix. A spike with a fleshy axis in which the flowers are embedded, as in jack-in-the-pulpit.

*Spathe. A large bract enclosing an inflorescence.

Sphagnum. A large genus of distinctive mosses that grow in wet, acidic sites; often called peat mosses because of their importance in the formation of peat.

*Spike. An elongated, indeterminate inflorescence of sessile or subsessile flowers.

Spine. A sharp-pointed, rigid, deep-seated outgrowth from the stem, not pulling off with the bark, as in the Cactaceae (cactus family).

Spur. A tubular or saclike projection from a petal or sepal.

*Stamen. The pollen-producing organ of a flower; the male part of a flower.

Staminode. A sterile stamen.

Staminodium (pl. *staminodia*). A sterile stamen or any structure lacking an anther but corresponding to a stamen.

*Standard. Uppermost petal in a pea flower; also called the banner.

*Stigma. The part of the pistil that receives the pollen; usually hairy or sticky.

Stipitate. Provided with a stipe or with a slender stalklike base.

*Stipule. Small appendages, often leaflike, on either side of a leaf stalk at the base.

Stolon. A slender stem that runs along the surface of the ground, or just below, and produces a new plant at the tip.

Stoma (pl. *stomata*). Small opening on the surface of a leaf through which gas exchange takes place with the atmosphere.

Strigose. With sharp, stiff, straight appressed hairs that are often basally swollen.

*Style. The elongated portion of the pistil that connects the stigma and ovary.

Styptic. Agent that stops bleeding.

Subcanopy. The layer of leaves just below the canopy in a forest.

Subclimax community. A long persisting vegetational stage immediately preceding the climax community.

Submerged. Growing entirely under water.

Subsessile. Nearly sessile; with almost no stalk.

Subtending. Situated closely beneath something, often enclosing or embracing it.

Subterranean. Below the surface of the ground.

Subulate. Narrowly triangular and tapering to a sharp point.

Sucker. Lateral underground shoot that breaks from the roots or rhizomes and roots itself, forming an independent, individual plant.

Swamp. Forested, freshwater wetland often with saturated soil or standing water.

Symbiosis. Two or more individuals of different species living together in intimate association, as in the fungal-algal symbiosis in the lichens.

Synonym. An invalid or illegitimate scientific name no longer in currant taxonomic use.

Taproot. A large, elongated root, usually vertical.

Tendril. A slender twining or clasping structure that enables plants to climb.

Ternate. Arranged in threes.

Terrestrial. Growing or living on land.

Theca (pl. *thecae*). One half of an anther containing two pollen sacs.

Topography. Physical structure of the landscape.

Trailing. Prostrate but not rooting.

Transpiration. Loss of water vapor from aerial parts of land plants.

Tree. A perennial woody plant of considerable stature at maturity and with one or few main trunks.

*Trifoliolate leaf. A compound leaf with three leaflets.

Truncate. Base or apex essentially straight across.

Tuber. Fleshy, thickened, short, usually subterranean stem having numerous buds called "eyes," such as the potato.

Tuft. A dense clump, especially of bushes or trees.

Twining. Ascending by coiling around a support.

Two-ranked. Leaves that are in two rows along a stem.

*Umbel. A flat-topped or rounded inflorescence having flowers on stalks of nearly equal length and attached to the summit of the peduncle, the characteristic order of blooming being from the outside toward the center.

Unisexual. Of one sex, either male or female.

USFS. The United States Forest Service.

Utricle. A bladderlike, one-seeded, usually indehiscent fruit.

Valve. One of the parts or segments into which a dehiscent fruit splits, as in a legume.

Vascular plant. Any of various plants typified by a conducting and supporting system of xylem and phloem; includes the ferns, cone-bearing and flowering plants.

Velamen. A specialized moisture-absorbing tissue, especially in roots of epiphytic orchids.

Vermifuge. An agent that expels worms from the intestine.

Vine. A plant that climbs by tendrils or other means, or creeps or trails on the ground.

Water, brackish. Water that has salt concentration greater than fresh water and less than sea water.

WCL. *Wildflowers of the Carolina Lowcountry and Lower Pee Dee* (Porcher, 1995).

Weed. In the broadest sense, a plant growing in a place it is not wanted. Usually weeds are aggressive colonizers of disturbed areas and are frequently nonnative; they are generally noxious and of no economic value and compete with agricultural crops.

*Whorled leaves. Three or more leaves inserted at one node.

*Wing. A thin, flat extension found at the margins of plant parts; the lateral petal in a pea flower.

Witches broom. An abnormal broomlike growth of weak, closely clustered shoots or branches on a woody plant caused by fungi or viruses.

Woodland. Open stands of trees with crowns not usually touching, generally forming 25–60% cover.

Xeric. Dry soils and sites, or adapted to dry conditions.

Xerophyte. Plant adapted to a xeric environment.

APPENDIX 1
South Carolina Herbariums

Charleston Museum (CHAR), Charleston, SC 29403
Curator: Albert E. Sanders
Location: 360 Meeting Street
Telephone: 843-722-2996, ex 247
Email: asanders@charlestonmuseum.com
Founded: 1820
Number of Specimens: 25,000
Primary Collection: South Carolina, especially Charleston area
Status: City museum

Clemson University (CLEMS), Clemson, SC 29634-0326
Curator: Patrick D. McMillan
Location: Campbell Museum of Natural History
Telephone: 864-656-7234
Email: @clemson.edu
Founded: 1926
Number of Specimens: 58,000
Primary Collection: South Carolina and Southeastern States
Status: State university

The Citadel (CITA), Charleston, SC 29409
Curator: Richard D. Porcher
Location: 303 Duckett Hall
Telephone: 843-953-5203
Email: porcherr@citadel.edu
Founded: 1970
Number of Specimens: 7000
Primarily Collection: Vascular plants of the coastal plain of South Carolina
Status: State college

Furman University (FUGR), Greenville, SC 29613
Curator: A. Joseph Pollard
Location: Biology Department
Telephone: 864-294-3244
Email: joe.pollard@furman.edu
Founded: 1930
Number of Specimens: 20,000
Primary Collection: Vascular plants of southeast United States
Status: Private university

Newberry College (NBYC), Newberry, SC 29108
Curator: Charles N. Horn
Location: Room 231 Math and Sciences Building
Telephone: 803-321-5257
Email: chorn@newberry.edu
Founded: 1986
Number of Specimens: 14,000
Primary Collection: Flora of South Carolina, especially the piedmont
Status: Private college

The University of South Carolina at Spartanburg (USCS), Spartanburg, SC 29303
Curator: Gillian Newberry
Location: Corner of I-85 and US 176
Telephone: 864-503-5764
Email: gnewberry@uscs.edu
Founded: 1976
Number of Specimens: 12,000
Primary Collection: Western Carolinas
Status: State university

The University of South Carolina (USCH), Columbia, SC 29208
Curator: John B. Nelson
Location: Coker Life Science Building
Telephone: 803-777-8196
Email: nelson@sc.edu
Founded: 1901
Number of Specimens: 80,000
Primary Collection: All groups, except fungi, of South Carolina
Status: State university

Keys to Heartleafs, Rhododendrons, and Trilliums of South Carolina

The following keys are provided to assist in identification of South Carolina species of heartleafs (*Hexastylis*), rhododendrons (*Rhododendron*), and trilliums (*Trillium*). It is intended to supplement the photographs and species descriptions in the text.

The key (called a dichotomous key) for each genus consist of a series of paired statements about the flowers, leaves, or other aspects of the plant that can be answered either "yes" or "no." Each key is a key to the species of a genus, and ultimately ends with the name of an individual plant.

KEY TO THE HEARTLEAFS (*HEXASTYLIS*)*

1. Style extension split all the way to the stigma; leaves triangular or egg-shaped, with lobes straight, pointed inward or slightly pointed outward; leaf margins straight or concave; mottled leaves with light green areas along the veins .... *H. arifolia*

1. Style extension split only at the apex, if at all; leaves nearly round, base cordate, margins convex; mottled leaves with light-green areas between the veins 2

  2. Calyx tube cylindrical or narrowly urn-shaped 3

    3. Calyx lobes 0.12 to 0.2″ long, erect or slightly spreading .... *H. virginica*

    3. Calyx lobes 0.12 to 0.6″ long; moderately spreading to bent downward 4

      4. Calyx tube longer than wide; distinctly cylindrical 5

        5. Opening of the calyx tube greater than 0.2″ in diameter .... *H. heterophylla*

        5. Opening of the calyx tube less than 0.2″ in diameter .... *H. naniflora*

      4. Calyx tube as wide as long at its widest part, flared, not perfectly cylindrical 6

        6. Calyx tube about as wide as long; mouth of the tube less wide than the calyx lobes are long .... *H. heterophylla*

        6. Calyx tube wider at its widest part than long; mouth of the calyx tube wider than the calyx lobes are long .... *H. minor*

  2. Calyx tube broadly urn- or bell-shaped, or broadest near the middle 7

    7. Calyx tube urn- or bell-shaped; calyx lobes more than 0.33″ wide at base (to 0.9″ wide); flower very large .... *H. shuttleworthii*

7. Calyx tube broadest near the middle; calyx lobes to 0.33″ wide at base **H. rhombiformis**

*Adapted from Weakley (2001)

KEY TO THE RHODODENDRONS (*RHODODENDRON*)*

1. Leaves evergreen, leathery, margins smooth; flowers with 10 stamens **2**
   2. Lower leaf surface with circular brown scales; largest leaves 3–5″ long **R. minus**
   2. Lower leaf surface without circular brown scales; largest leaves 6–12″ long **3**
      3. Leaves rounded at base, obtuse at apex; corolla (petals) purple to dark pink **R. catawbiense**
      3. Leaves wedge-shaped at base, acute at apex; corolla (petals) white or pale pink **R. maximum**
1. Leaves deciduous, thin and flexible, margins with small saw-teeth or smooth with obvious hairs; flowers with 5–7 stamens **4**
   4. Corolla orange, yellow, or red **5**
      5. Scales of flower buds with glands on the margins; outside of corolla tube glandular and hairy **R. calendulaceum**
      5. Scales of flower buds with hairs; outside of corolla tube hairy, or sometimes with just a few glands **R. flammeum**
   4. Corolla white, pink, or white marked with yellow **6**
      6. Sepals to 0.2″ long **7**
         7. Shrub to 5′ tall, forming dense colonies; young stems densely pubescent, usually with a mix of glandular and nonglandular hairs **R. atlanticum**
         7. Shrub or small tree to 20′ tall, not forming dense colonies; young stems without pubescence or only weakly pubescent **R. arborescens**
      6. Sepals very short, less than 0.04″ long **8**
         8. Lower leaf surface smooth except for stiff hairs on the major veins **9**
            9. Flower stalks densely covered with long-stalked glands; calyx and corolla with dense, long-stalked glands; flowers appearing after the leaves **R. viscosum**
            9. Flower stalks pubescent but without long-stalked glands; calyx without stalked glands; corolla tube hairy and rarely with stalked glands; flowers appearing before or with the leaves **R. periclymenoides**
         8. Lower leaf surface moderately to densely soft pubescent **10**
            10. Corolla light to dark pink, without yellow markings; outer surface of winter bud scales pubescent **R. canescens**
            10. Corolla white, with a splotch of yellow in the upper lobe; outer surface of winter bud scales smooth but glandular on the lower margins **R. eastmanii**

*Adapted from Kron and Creel (1999) and Weakley (2001)

KEY TO THE TRILLIUMS (*TRILLIUM*)*

1. Flowers stalkless; petals erect (at least with age); leaves mottled with 2–3 shades of green — **2**
    2. Sepals abruptly bent downward between the leaves; anthers incurved; rootstalk long and slender — *T. lancifolium*
    2. Sepals divergent to spreading; anthers erect, with connective extending 0.04–0.08″ beyond the pollen sac; stigmas spreading; stamens about 2x as tall as pistil — **3**
        3. Stem erect, more than 2x the length of the leaves; petals incurved and spoon-shaped, with stalklike base, pale yellow, with yellow to maroon base — *T. discolor*
        3. Stem forming an open S-shape; less than 2x the length of the leaves; petals erect, narrowly elliptic or lance-shaped, purple or yellow green — *T. reliquum*
    2. Sepals divergent to spreading; anthers erect, with connectives not prolonged beyond the pollen sacs; stigmas erect; stamens less than 1.5x as long as the pistil — **4**
        4. Petals narrowly spoon-shaped, with stalklike base, usually 4.5x or more as long as wide; outer whorl of 3 stamens broader than inner; anthers open toward the inside — *T. maculatum*
        4. Petals narrowly elliptic to oblanceolate; usually less than 4x as long as wide; two whorls of three stamens alike; anthers usually open to the side, sometimes to the inside — *T. cuneatum*
1. Flowers with distinct stalk; petals spreading; leaves solid green, not mottled — **5**
    5. Petals with wavy margins, quite delicate in texture, white to dark pink (white flowers fade to pink with age); stigmas thin, fused into a short style; ovary greenish to white — **6**
        6. Petals white with an inverted red V at the base; pollen sacs lavender to white; fruit a berry (red) — *T. undulatum*
        6. Petals white, light pink, or dark pink; pollen sacs yellow; fruit a greenish white capsule that opens at maturity — **7**
            7. Flower stalk usually positioned below the leaves; sepals recurved (sickle-shaped); anthers twisted outward; pollen sacs dark yellow — *T. catesbaei*
            7. Flower stalks erect or at least held above the leaves; sepals not falcate; pollen sacs light yellow — **8**
                8. Flower stalk erect, flowering-fruiting; sepals as wide as the petals, obtuse; anthers purplish between the anther sacs — *T. pusillum*
                8. Flower stalk not strictly erect; sepals narrower than the petals, acute; anthers white or greenish white between the anther sacs — **9**
                    9. Petals rolled into a tube at the base, obovate; leaves broadly egg-shaped, acuminate; style less than 0.04″ long — *T. grandiflorum*
                    9. Petals elliptic, loose; leaves narrowly elliptic or ovate-lanceolate; style more than 0.06″ long — *T. persistens*

5. Petals with straight margins, relatively thick in texture, maroon or white, less often yellow or green (white flowers turn brown with age); stigmas separate, thicker at the base; ovary dark purple, maroon, pink, or white   **10**

    10. Flower stalk held horizontally or below leaves; petals recurved between the sepals   **11**

        11. Leaves elliptic, longer than wide; stamens extend well beyond the pistil (2x or more) filaments at least as long as the ovary, with some purple   *T. vaseyi*

        11. Leaves broadly elliptic, wider than long; stamens less than 1.5x longer than the pistil; filaments shorter than the ovary and white   *T. rugelii*

    10. Flower stalk erect or held below the vertical, flower held above the leaves; petals usually spreading in the same plane as the sepals or overlapping at the base and forming a cup which conceals the ovary when flower is viewed from the side   **12**

        12. Petals spreading in the same plane as the sepals, sepals weakly boat-shaped at the tip; flower fragrance like that of a wet dog   *T. erectum*

        12. Flowers usually very large; petals producing a funnel-like appearance (gaping); sepals strongly boat-shaped at the tip; flower fragrance pleasant, like green apples   *T. simile*

*Adapted from Weakley (2001) and Case and Case (1997)

Illustrations of Plant Structures

This section presents the shapes and arrangements of basic flower and leaf parts. The illustrations will help understand the terminology in the text. Each term is defined in the glossary.

FIGURE 11: Illustrations of Plant Structures

Leaf Shapes

Linear   Elliptic   Lanceolate   Oblanceolate

Ovate   Obovate   Peltate   Perfoliate

Leaf Parts

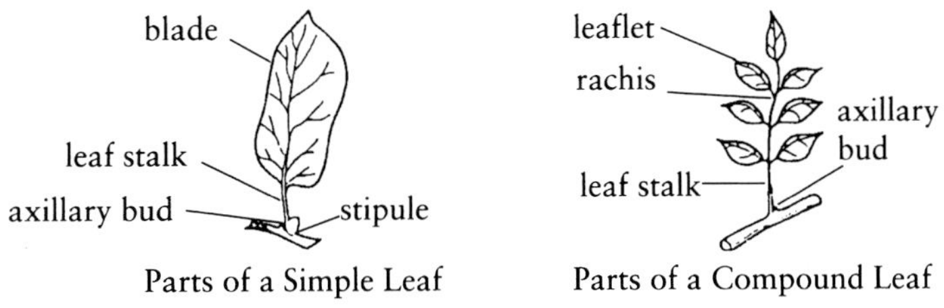

blade

leaf stalk

axillary bud — stipule

Parts of a Simple Leaf

leaflet

rachis

axillary bud

leaf stalk

Parts of a Compound Leaf

Leaf Arrangement

Alternate   Opposite   Whorled

Types of Compound Leaves

Palmately Compound   Trifoliolate   Odd-pinnate

Even-Pinnate   Bipinnate

Leaf Margins

Entire   Divided   Dissected   Lobed

Parts of a Generalized Flower

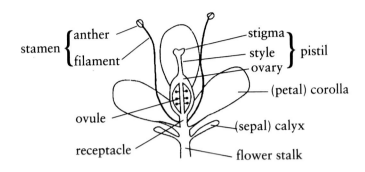

Irregular Flowers

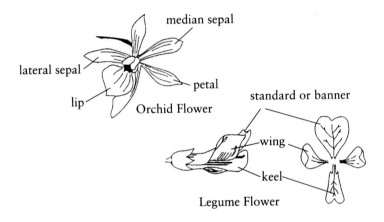

Orchid Flower

Legume Flower

Types of Inflorescences

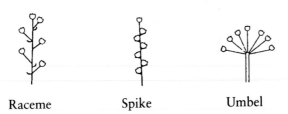

Raceme   Spike   Umbel

Panicle   Catkin

spathe

spadix

Spadix

disk flower

ray flower

receptacle

bract

Head

General References

POPULAR WILDFLOWER BOOKS FOR THE SOUTHEASTERN STATES

Ajilvsgi, Geyata. 1979. *Wild Flowers of the Big Thicket: East Texas, and Western Louisiana.* College Station: Texas A&M University Press.

Batson, Wade T. 1987. *Wild Flowers in the Carolinas.* Columbia: University of South Carolina Press.

Bell, C. Ritchie, and Anne H. Lindsey. 1990. *Fall Color and Woodland Harvests: A Guide to the More Colorful Fall Leaves and Fruits of the Eastern Forests.* Chapel Hill, NC: Laurel Hill Press.

Bell, C. Ritchie, and Bryan J. Taylor. 1982. *Florida Wild Flowers.* Chapel Hill, NC: Laurel Hill Press.

Brown, Clair A. 1972. *Wildflowers of Louisiana and Adjoining States.* Baton Rouge: Louisiana State University Press.

Case, Frederick W., Jr., and Roberta B. Case. 1997. *Trilliums.* Portland, OR: Timber Press.

Coffey, Timothy. 1993. *The History and Folklore of North American Wildflowers.* New York: Houghton Mifflin Company.

Dean, Blanche E., Amy Mason, and Joab L. Thomas. 1973. *Wildflowers of Alabama and Adjoining States.* Tuscaloosa: University of Alabama Press.

Duncan, Wilbur H., and Leonard E. Foote. 1975. *Wildflowers of the Southeastern United States.* Athens: University of Georgia Press.

Duncan, Wilbur H., and Marion B. Duncan. 1999. *Wildflowers of the Eastern United States.* Athens: University of Georgia Press.

Hemmerly, Thomas E. 1990. *Wildflowers of the Central South.* Nashville, TN: Vanderbilt University Press.

Hemmerly, Thomas E. 2000. *Appalachian Wildflowers.* Athens: University of Georgia Press.

Gaddy, L. L. 2000. *A Naturalist's Guide to the Southern Blue Ridge Front.* Columbia: University of South Carolina Press.

Gupton, Oscar W., and Fred C. Swope. 1979. *Wildflowers of the Shenandoah Valley and Blue Ridge Mountains.* Charlottesville: University Press of Virginia.

Gupton, Oscar W., and Fred C. Swope. 1982. *Wildflowers of Tidewater Virginia.* Charlottesville: University Press of Virginia.

Hunter, Carl G. 1984. *Wildflowers of Arkansas.* Little Rock, AR: Ozark Society Foundation.

Justice, William S., and C. Ritchie Bell. 1968. *Wild Flowers of North Carolina.* Chapel Hill: University of North Carolina Press.

Martin, Laura C. 1989. *Southern Wildflowers.* Atlanta, GA: Longstreet Press.

Midgley, Jan W. 1999. *All About Mississippi Wildflowers.* Birmingham, AL: Sweetwater Press.

Murdy, William H., and Eloise Brown Carter. 2000. *Guide to the Plants of Granite Outcrops.* Athens: University of Georgia Press.

Niering, William A., and Nancy C. Olmstead. 1979. *The Audubon Society Field Guide to North American Wildflowers (Eastern Region).* New York: Alfred A. Knopf.

Nourse, Hugh, and Carol Nourse. 2000. *Wildflowers of Georgia.* Athens: University of Georgia Press.

Rickett, Harold W., and the New York Botanical Garden. 1967. *Wild Flowers of the United States.* Volume 2, *The Southeastern States.* New York: New York Botanical Garden and McGraw-Hill.

Smith, Richard M. 1998. *Wildflowers of the Southern Mountains.* Knoxville: University of Tennessee Press.

Taylor, Walter K. 1992. *The Guide to Florida Wildflowers.* Dallas, TX: Taylor Publishing Company.

Timme, S. Lee. 1989. *Wildflowers of Mississippi.* Jackson: University Press of Mississippi.

Wharton, Mary E., and Roger W. Barbour. 1979. *Wildflowers and Ferns of Kentucky.* Lexington: University of Kentucky Press.

CARNIVOROUS PLANTS

Lloyd, Francis E. 1976. *The Carnivorous Plants.* New York: Dover Publications, Inc.

Pietropaolo, James, and Patricia Pietropaolo. 1986. *Carnivorous Plants of the World.* Portland, OR: Timber Press.

Schnell, Donald C. 1976. *Carnivorous Plants of the United States and Canada.* Winston-Salem, NC: John F. Blair.

Slack, Adrian. 1979. *Carnivorous Plants.* Cambridge, MA: MIT Press.

NATIVE ORCHIDS

Correll, Donovan S. 1978. *Native Orchids of North America.* Stanford, CA: Stanford University Press.

Gupton, Oscar W., and Fred C. Swope. 1986. *Wild Orchids of the Middle Atlantic States.* Knoxville: University of Tennessee Press.

Luer, Carlyle A. 1972. *The Native Orchids of Florida.* Brooklyn: New York Botanical Garden.

Luer, Carlyle A. 1975. *The Native Orchids of the United States and Canada Excluding Florida.* Brooklyn: New York Botanical Garden.

POISONOUS PLANTS

Kingsbury, John M. 1964. *Poisonous Plants of the United States and Canada.* Englewood Cliffs, NJ: Prentice-Hall, Inc.

Westbrooks, Randy G., and James W. Preacher. 1986. *Poisonous Plants of Eastern North America.* Columbia: University of South Carolina Press.

WOODY VINES

Duncan, Wilbur H. 1975. *Woody Vines of the Southeastern United States.* Athens: University of Georgia Press.

PARASITIC VASCULAR PLANTS

Kuijt, Job. 1969. *The Biology of Parasitic Flowering Plants.* Berkeley: University of California Press.

CAROLINA BAYS

Bennett, Stephen H., and John B. Nelson. 1991. *Distribution and Status of Carolina Bays in South Carolina.* Columbia: Nongame and Heritage Trust Section, South Carolina Wildlife and Marine Resources Department.

Johnson, Douglas. 1942. *The Origin of the Carolina Bays.* New York: Columbia University Press.

Savage, Henry, Jr. 1982. *The Mysterious Carolina Bays.* Columbia: University of South Carolina Press.

RICE CULTURE

Doar, David. 1970. *Rice and Rice Planting in the South Carolina Low Country.* Charleston, SC: Charleston Museum.

Heyward, Duncan C. 1937. *Seed from Madagascar.* Chapel Hill: University of North Carolina Press.

Littlefield, Daniel C. 1991. *Rice and Slaves.* Chicago: University of Illinois Press.

Wood, Peter H. 1974. *Black Majority: Negroes in Colonial South Carolina from 1670 through the Stono Rebellion.* New York: Alfred A. Knopf.

BIBLIOGRAPHIES OF BOTANISTS AND NATURALISTS

Berkeley, Edmund, and Dorothy S. Berkeley. 1969. *Dr. Alexander Garden of Charles Town.* Chapel Hill: University of North Carolina Press.

Earnest, Ernest. 1940. *John and William Bartrum: Botanists and Explorers.* Philadelphia: University of Pennsylvania Press.

Frick, George, and Raymond Stearns. 1961. *Mark Catesby.* Urbana: University of Illinois Press.

Gee, Wilson. 1918. "South Carolina Botanists: Biography and Bibliography." *Bulletin of the University of South Carolina* 72: 1–52.

Haygood, Tamara M. 1987. *Henry William Ravenel, 1814–1887.* Tuscaloosa: University of Alabama Press.

Herr, J. M., Jr. 1984. "A Brief Sketch of the Life and Botanical Work of A. C. Moore." *Abstracts. Botanical Society of America,* in *American Journal of Botany* 71 (5, pt. 2): 106–7.

Kastner, Joseph. 1977. *A Species of Eternity.* New York: Alfred A. Knopf.

Reveal, James L. 1996. *America's Botanical Beauty.* Golden, CO: Fulcrum Publishing.

Sanders, Albert E., and William D. Anderson, Jr. 1999. *Natural History Investigations in South Carolina from Colonial Times to the Present.* Columbia: University of South Carolina Press.

Savage, Henry Jr. 1970. *Lost Heritage.* New York: William Morrow and Company, Inc.

Savage, Henry, Jr., and Elizabeth J. Savage. 1986. *André and François André Michaux.* Charlottesville: University Press of Virginia.

Shuler, Jay. 1995. *Had the Wings: The Friendship of Bachman and Audubon.* Athens: University of Georgia Press.

Slaughter, Thomas P. 1996. *The Nature of John and William Bartram.* New York: Alfred A. Knopf.

Taylor, David. 1998. *South Carolina Naturalists.* Columbia: University of South Carolina Press.

Waring, Joseph I. 1967. *A History of Medicine in South Carolina, 1825–1900.* Columbia: South Carolina Medical Association.

Wilson, Scofield David. 1978. *In the Presence of Nature.* Amherst: University of Massachusetts Press.

ECONOMIC AND CULTURAL

Butler, Carroll B. 1998. *Treasurers of the Longleaf Pine.* Shalimar, FL: Tarkel Publishing.

Hill, Albert F. 1952. *Economic Botany.* New York: McGraw-Hill.

Rosengarten, Dale. 1986. *Row upon Row: Sea Grass Baskets of the South Carolina Lowcountry.* Columbia: McKissick Museum, University of South Carolina.

Schery, Robert W. 1972. *Plants for Man.* Englewood Cliffs, NJ: Prentice-Hall, Inc.

Simpson, Beryl B., and Molly C. Ogorzaly. 1986. *Economic Botany: Plants in Our World.* New York: McGraw-Hill.

Wood, Virginia S. 1981. *Live Oaking: Southern Timber for Tall Ships.* Boston: Northeastern University Press.

CULTIVATED AND ORNAMENTAL PLANTS

Bailey, L. H. 1949. *Manual of Cultivated Plants.* 2d ed. New York: MacMillan.

Batson, Wade T. 1984. *Landscape Plants for the Southeast.* Columbia: University of South Carolina Press.

Briggs, Loutrel W. 1951. *Charleston Gardens.* Columbia: University of South Carolina Press.

Foote, Leonard E., and Samuel B. Jones, Jr. 1989. *Native Shrubs and Woody Vines of the Southeast.* Portland, OR: Timber Press.

Halfacre, Gordon R., and Anne Shawcroft. 1989. *Landscape Plants of the Southeast.* Raleigh, NC: Sparks Press.

Shaffer, Edward T. H. 1963. *Carolina Gardens*. 3d ed. New York: Devin-Adair Company.

FOLK REMEDIES AND MEDICINAL PLANTS

Duke, James A. 1997. *The Green Pharmacy*. New York: St. Martin's Paperbacks.

Erichsen-Brown, Charlotte. 1979. *Medicinal and Other Uses of North American Plants*. New York: Dover Publications, Inc.

Foster, Steven, and James A. Duke. 1990. *A Field Guide to Medicinal Plants*. Boston: Houghton Mifflin Company.

Hamel, Paul B., and Mary U. Chiltoskey. 1975. *Cherokee Plants: Their Uses—A 400-Year History*. Sylva, NC: Herald Publishing Co.

Hudson, Charles M. ed. 1979. *Black Drink: A Native American Tea*. Athens: University of Georgia Press.

Hutchens, Alma R. 1973. *Indian Herbology of North America*. Boston: Shambala Publications.

Hutchens, Alma R. 1992. *A Handbook of Native American Herbs*. Boston: Shambala Publications.

Krochmal, Arnold, and Connie Krochmal. 1973. *A Guide to the Medicinal Plants of the United States*. New York: Quadrangle/New York Times Book Company.

Lewis, W. H., and M. P. F. Elvin-Lewis. 1977. *Medical Botany: Plants Affecting Man's Health*. New York: John Wiley and Sons.

Moerman, Daniel E. 1998. *Native American Ethnobotany*. Portland, OR: Timber Press.

Morton, Julia F. 1974. *Folk Remedies of the Low Country*. Miami, FL: E. A. Seemann Publishing.

Moss, Kay K. 1999. *Southern Folk Medicine: 1750–1820*. Columbia: University of South Carolina Press.

Porcher, Francis P. 1869. *Resources of the Southern Fields and Forests*. Charleston, SC: Walker, Evans and Cogswell, Printers.

Tyler, Varro E. 1994. *Herbs of Choice: Therapeutic Use of Phytomedicinals*. Binghamton, NY: The Haworth Press.

TREES AND SHRUBS

Brown, Clair A., and Glen N. Montz. 1986. *Baldcypress: The Tree Unique, The Wood Eternal*. Baton Rouge, LA: Claitor's Publishing Division.

Brown, Claud L., and L. Katherine Kirkman. 1990. *Trees of Georgia and Adjacent States*. Portland, OR: Timber Press.

Duncan, Wilbur H., and Marion B. Duncan. 1988. *Trees of the Southeastern United States*. Athens: University of Georgia Press.

Elias, Thomas S. 1980. *The Complete Trees of North America*. New York: Times Mirror Magazines, Inc.

Godfrey, Robert K. 1988. *Trees, Shrubs, and Woody Vines of Northern Florida and Adjacent Georgia and Alabama*. Athens: University of Georgia Press.

Peattie, Donald C. 1966. *A Natural History of Trees of Eastern and Central North America*. New York: Bonanza Books.

Walker, Lawrence C. 1990. *Forests: A Naturalist's Guide to Trees and Forest Ecology*. New York: John Wiley and Sons.

Walker, Lawrence C. 1991. *The Southern Forest: A Chronicle*. Austin: University of Texas Press.

NATURAL HISTORY GUIDES AND REFERENCES

Barry, John M. 1980. *Natural Vegetation of South Carolina*. Columbia: University of South Carolina Press.

Braun, E. Lucy. 1950. *Deciduous Forests of Eastern North America*. Philadelphia: Blakistin Company.

Conner, R. C. 1998. "South Carolina's Forests, 1993." *Resource Bulletin SRS-25*. Asheville, NC: USDA Forest Service, Southern Research Station.

Cowdry, A. E. 1996. *This Land, This South: An Environmental History*. Lexington: University of Kentucky Press.

Dennis, John V. 1988. *The Great Cypress Swamps*. Baton Rouge: Louisiana State University Press.

Duncan, Wilbur H., and Marion B. Duncan. 1987. *Seaside Plants of the Gulf and Atlantic Coasts*. Washington, DC: Smithsonian Institution Press.

Fenneman, N. M. 1938. *Physiography of the Eastern United States*. New York: McGraw-Hill.

Godfrey, Michael A. 1980. *The Piedmont: A Sierra Club Naturalist's Guide*. San Francisco: Sierra Club Books.

Hackney, C. T., S. M. Adams, and W. H. Martin. 1992. *Biodiversity of the Southeastern United States: Aquatic Communities*. New York: John Wiley and Sons.

Horton, J. W., Jr., and V. A. Zullo. 1991. *The Geology of the Carolinas*. Knoxville: University of Tennessee Press.

Jones, S. M. 1988. "Old-growth, Steady-state Forests within the Piedmont of South Carolina." Ph.D. dissertation, Clemson University.

Kovasik, Charles F., and John J. Winberry. 1987. *South Carolina: The Making of a Landscape*. Columbia: University of South Carolina Press.

Lyons, Janet, and Sandra Jordan. 1989. *Walking the Wetlands*. New York: John Wiley and Sons.

Nelson, John B. 1986. *The Natural Communities of South Carolina*. Columbia: Technical Report, South Carolina Wildlife and Marine Resources Department.

Pirkle, E. C., and W. H. Yahi. 1977. *Natural Regions of the United States*. Dubuque, IA: Kendall Hunt Publishing Company.

Porcher, Richard D. 1985. *A Teacher's Field Guide to the Natural History of The Bluff Plantation Wildlife Sanctuary*. New Orleans, LA: Kathleen O'Brien Foundation.

Radford, A. E., D. K. S. Otte, L. J. Otte, J. R. Massey, and P. D. Whitson. 1981. *Natural Heritage Classification, Inventory, and Information*. Chapel Hill: University of North Carolina Press.

Shafale, Michael P., and Alan S. Weakley. 1990. *Classification of the Natural Communities of North Carolina*. Third Approximation. Raleigh: North

Carolina Department of Environment, Health, Natural Resources, Division of Parks and Recreation, Natural Heritage Program.

Smith, Richard M. 1989. *Wild Plants in America*. New York: John Wiley and Sons.

Tansey, J. B. 1986. "Forest Statistics for the Piedmont of South Carolina, 1986." *Resource Bulletin SE-89*. Asheville, NC: USDA Forest Service, Southeastern Forest Experiment Station.

Wells, B. W. 1932. *The Natural Gardens of North Carolina*. Chapel Hill: University of North Carolina Press.

EXHIBIT BOOKS

Blagden, Tom, Jr. 1992. *South Carolina's Wetland Wilderness: The Ace Basin*. Englewood, CO: Westcliffe Publishers, Inc.

Blagden, Tom, Jr., and Barry Beasley. 1999. *The Rivers of South Carolina*. Englewood, CO: Westcliffe Publishers, Inc.

Blagden, Tom, Jr., Jane Lareau, and Richard D. Porcher. 1988. *Lowcountry: The Natural Landscape*. Greensboro, NC: Legacy Publications.

Blagden, Tom, Jr., and Thomas Wyche. 1994. *South Carolina's Mountain Wilderness: The Blue Ridge Escarpment*. Englewood, CO: Westcliffe Publishers, Inc.

TECHNICAL MANUALS AND FLORAS

Aulbach-Smith, C. A., and S. J. deKozlowski. 1996. *Aquatic and Wetland Plants of South Carolina*. 2d ed. Columbia: South Carolina Department of Natural Resources and the South Carolina Aquatic Plant Management Council.

Batson, Wade T. 1984. *Genera of Eastern Plants*. 3d ed. rev. Columbia: University of South Carolina Press.

Conquist, A. J. 1980. *Vascular Flora of the Southeastern United States*. Volume 1, *Asteraceae*. Chapel Hill: University of North Carolina Press.

Godfrey, Robert K., and Jean W. Wooten. 1979. *Aquatic and Wetland Plants of the Southeastern United States: Monocotyledons*. Athens: University of Georgia Press.

Godfrey, Robert K., and Jean W. Wooten. 1981. *Aquatic and Wetland Plants of the Southeastern United States: Dicotyledons*. Athens: University of Georgia Press.

Radford, Albert E., Harry E. Ahles, and C. Ritchie Bell. 1968. *Manual of the Vascular Flora of the Carolinas*. Chapel Hill: University of North Carolina Press.

Small, John K. 1933. *Manual of the Southeastern Flora*. Chapel Hill: University of North Carolina Press.

Strausbaugh, P. D., and Earl L. Core. 1977. *Flora of West Virginia*. Grantsville, WV: Seneca Books, Inc.

Tobe, John D., et al. 1988. *Florida Wetland Plants: An Identification Manual*. Tallahassee: Florida Department of Environmental Protection.

EDIBLE WILD PLANTS

Angier, Bradford. 1974. *Field Guide to Edible Wild Plants.* Harrisburg, PA: Stackpole Books.

Berglund, Berndt, and Clare E. Bolsby. 1971. *The Edible Wild.* New York: Charles Scribner's Sons.

Brown, Tom, Jr. 1985. *Tom Brown's Guide to Wild Edible and Medicinal Plants.* New York: Berkley Publishing Group.

Elias, Thomas S., and Peter A. Dykeman. 1982. *Field Guide to North American Edible Wild Plants.* New York: Outdoor Life Books.

Fernald, Merritt L., and Alfred C. Kinsey. 1958. *Edible Wild Plants of Eastern North America.* New York: Harper and Row.

Gibbons, Euell. 1962. *Stalking the Wild Asparagus.* New York: David McKay Company, Inc.

Gibbons, Euell. 1966. *Stalking the Healthful Herbs.* New York: David McKay Company, Inc.

Hall, Alan. 1976. *The Wild Food Trailguide.* New York: Holt, Rinehart and Winston.

Harris, Ben C. 1968. *Eat the Weeds.* Barre, MA: Barre Publishing.

Peterson, Lee Allen. 1977. *Edible Wild Plants, A Peterson Field Guide.* Boston: Houghton Mifflin.

FERNS

Dunbar, Lin. 1989. *Ferns of the Coastal Plain.* Columbia: University of South Carolina Press.

Wherry, Edgar T. 1964. *The Southern Fern Guide.* New York: Doubleday.

PHOTOGRAPHY OF WILDFLOWERS

Adams, Kevin, and Mary Casstevens. 1996. *Wildflowers of the Southern Appalachians: How to Photograph and Identify Them.* Winston-Salem, NC: John F. Blair.

Shaw, John. 1987. *Closeups in Nature.* New York: AMPHOTO.

HIKING GUIDES IN SOUTH CAROLINA

Dehart, Allen. 1994 *Hiking South Carolina Trails.* 3d ed. Old Saybrook, Conn.: Globe Pequot Press.

Gaddy, L. L. 2000. *A Naturalist's Guide to the Southern Blue Ridge Front.* Columbia: University of South Carolina Press.

Giffen, Morrison. 1997. *South Carolina: A Guide to Backcountry Travel and Adventure.* Asheville, NC: Out There Press.

Manning, Phillip. 1995. *Palmetto Journal: Walks in the Natural Areas of South Carolina.* Winston-Salem, NC: John F. Blair.

HISTORICAL BOOKS

Drayton, John M. 1802. *A View of South Carolina.* Charleston, SC: W. P. Young
   (reprint, Spartanburg, SC: The Reprint Co., 1972).
Ramsey, David. 1858. *History of South Carolina.* Newberry: W. J. Duffie (reprint,
   Spartanburg, SC: The Reprint Co., 1960).

Literature Cited

Anderson, Loran C. 1985. "*Forestiera godfreyi* (Oleaceae), A New Species from Florida and South Carolina." *Sida* 11(1): 1–5.

Bailey, L. H. 1949. *Manual of Cultivated Plants.* 2d ed. New York: MacMillan.

Barden, L. S. 1997. Historic Prairies in the Piedmont of North and South Carolina, USA. *Natural Areas Journal* 17:149–52.

Barry, John M. 1980. *Natural Vegetation of South Carolina.* Columbia: University of South Carolina Press.

Bartram, William. 1791. *Travels through North & South Carolina, Georgia, East & West Florida, the Cherokee Country, the Extensive Territories of the Muscogulges, or Creek Confederacy, and the Country of the Choctaws.* Reprint, 1955, of the 1928 edition, ed. Mark Van Doren (New York: Dover Publications).

Bennett, Stephen H., and John B. Nelson. 1991. *Distribution and Status of Carolina Bays in South Carolina.* Columbia: Nongame and Heritage Trust Section, South Carolina Wildlife and Marine Resources Department.

Berkeley, Edmund, and Dorothy S. Berkeley. 1969. *Dr. Alexander Garden of Charles Town.* Chapel Hill: University of North Carolina Press.

Brown, D. S. 1953. *A City without Cobwebs: Rock Hill, South Carolina.* Columbia: University of South Carolina Press.

Case, Frederick W., Jr, and Roberta B. Case. 1997. *Trilliums.* Portland, OR: Timber Press.

Chapman, A. W. 1860. *Flora of the Southern United States.* New York: Ivison, Phinney, & Co.

Childs, Arney Robinson, ed. 1947. *The Private Journal of Henry William Ravenel, 1859–1887.* Columbia: University of South Carolina Press.

Coker, William C., and Henry R. Totten. 1945. *Trees of the Southeastern States.* Chapel Hill: University of North Carolina Press.

Cross, J. K. 1973. "Tar Burning, Forgotten Art?" *Forests and People* 23(2): 21–23.

Duke, James A. 1997. *The Green Pharmacy.* New York: St. Martin's Paperbacks.

Dunbar, Lin. 1989. *Ferns of the Coastal Plain.* Columbia: University of South Carolina Press.

Duncan, Wilbur H., and Marion B. Duncan. 1987. *Seaside Plants of the Gulf and Atlantic Coasts.* Washington, DC: Smithsonian Institution Press.

Duncan, Wilbur H., and Marion B. Duncan. 1988. *Trees of the Southeastern United States.* Athens: University of Georgia Press.

Fernald, Merritt L. 1950. *Gray's Manual of Botany.* 8th ed. New York: American Book Company.

Fernald, Merritt L., and Alfred C. Kinsey. 1958. *Edible Wild Plants of Eastern North America.* New York: Harper and Row.

Foote, Leonard E., and Samuel B. Jones, Jr. 1989. *Native Shrubs and Woody Vines of the Southeast.* Portland, OR: Timber Press.

Foster, Steven, and James A. Duke. 1990. *A Field Guide to Medicinal Plants.* Boston: Houghton Mifflin Company.

Gaddy, L. L. 1986. "A New Heartleaf (*Hexastylis*) from Transylvania County, North Carolina." *Brittonia* 38: 82–85.

Gee, Wilson. 1918. South Carolina Botanists: Biography and Bibliography. *Bulletin of the University of South Carolina* 72:1–52.

Gibbes, Lewis R. 1859. "Botany of Edings Bay." *Proceedings of the Elliott Society of Natural History* 1(4): 241–48.

Godfrey, Robert K., and Jean W. Wooten. 1979. *Aquatic and Wetland Plants of the Southeastern United States: Monocotyledons.* Athens: University of Georgia Press.

Godfrey, Robert K., and Jean W. Wooten. 1981. *Aquatic and Wetland Plants of the Southeastern United States: Dicotyledons.* Athens: University of Georgia Press.

Hardin, James W., and Committee. 1977. Vascular Plants. In *Endangered and Threatened Plants and Animals of North Carolina,* edited by J. E. Cooper, S. S. Robinson, and J. B. Funderburg. Raleigh: North Carolina State Museum of Natural History.

Haygood, Tamara M. 1987. *Henry William Ravenel, 1814–1887.* Tuscaloosa: University of Alabama Press.

Hill, Steven R., and Charles N. Horn. 1997. "Additions to the Flora of South Carolina." *Castanea* 62(3): 194–208.

Hudson, Charles M., ed. 1979. *Black Drink: A Native American Tea.* Athens: University of Georgia Press.

Hunt, Kenneth W. 1942. "Ferns of the Vicinity of Charleston." *Charleston Museum Leaflet Number* 17.

Hunt, Kenneth W. 1943. "Floating Mats on a Southeastern Coastal Plain Reservoir." *Bulletin of the Torrey Botanical Club* 70(5): 481–488.

Hunt, Kenneth W. 1947. "The Charleston Woody Flora." *American Midland Naturalist* 37: 670–756.

Justice, William S., and C. Ritchie Bell. 1968. *Wild Flowers of North Carolina.* Chapel Hill: University of North Carolina Press.

Kelly, Howard A. 1914. *Some American Medical Botanists.* Troy, NY: Southworth Company.

Kingsbury, John M. 1964. *Poisonous Plants of the United States and Canada.* Englewood Cliffs, NJ: Prentice-Hall, Inc.

Kirkman, W. B., and J. R. Ballington. 1990. Creeping blueberries (Ericaceae: *Vaccinium* sect. *Herpothamnus*)—a new look at. *V. crassifolium* including *V. sempevirens. Systemic Botany* 15(4): 679–99.

Krochmal, Arnold, and Connie Krochmal. 1973. *A Guide to the Medicinal Plants of the United States.* New York: Quadrangle/New York Times Book Company.

Kron, Kathleen A., and Mike Creel. 1999. "A New Species of Deciduous Azalea (*Rhododendron* section *Pentanthera;* Ericaceae) from South Carolina." *Novon* 9: 337–380.

Lawson. John. 1709. *A New Voyage to Carolina.* Reprint edition, Readex Microprint.

Martinez, R. J. 1959. *The Story of Spanish Moss and its Relatives.* New Orleans, LA: Home Publications.

Melton, Frank A., and William Schriever. 1933. The Carolina Bays: Are They Meteorite Scars? *Journal of Geology* 41:52–66.

Mills, Robert. 1826. *Statistics of South Carolina.* Charleston: privately printed.

Morris, Karen, ed. 1983. *Guide to the Foothills Trail.* Greenville, SC: Foothills Trail Conference, Inc.

Morton, Julia F. 1974. *Folk Remedies of the Low Country.* Miami, FL: E. A. Seemann Publishing.

Naturaland Trust. 1994. *Guide to the Mountain Bridge Trails.* Greenville, SC: Naturaland Trust.

Pietropaolo, James, and Patricia Pietropaolo. 1986. *Carnivorous Plants of the World.* Portland, OR: Timber Press.

Porcher, Francis P. 1869. *Resources of the Southern Fields and Forests.* Charleston, SC: Walker, Evans and Cogswell, Printers.

Porcher, Richard D. 1987. "Rice Culture in South Carolina: A Brief History, The Role of the Huguenots, and Preservation of its Legacy." *Transactions of the Huguenot Society* 92: 1–22.

Porcher, Richard D. 1995. *Wildflowers of the Carolina Lowcountry and Lower Pee Dee.* Columbia: University of South Carolina Press.

Radford, Albert E. 1959. "A Relic Plant Community in South Carolina." *Journal of the Elisha Mitchell Scientific Society* 75: 33–34.

Radford, Albert E., Harry E. Ahles, and C. Ritchie Bell. 1968. *Manual of the Vascular Flora of the Carolinas.* Chapel Hill: University of North Carolina Press.

Radford, Albert E., et al. 1974. *Vascular Plant Systematics.* New York: Harper and Row.

Rayner, Douglas A., and J. Henderson. 1980. "*Vaccinium semperevirens* (Ericaceae), a New Species from Atlantic White-Cedar Bogs in the Sandhills of South Carolina." *Rhodora* 82: 503–507.

Rembert, David H. 1979. "The Carolina Plants of André Michaux." *Castanea* 44: 65–80.

Rembert, David H. 1980. *Thomas Walter: Carolina Botanist.* Museum Commission Bulletin, No. 5. Columbia: South Carolina Museum Commission.

Reveal, James L. 1996. *America's Botanical Beauty.* Golden, CO: Fulcrum Publishing.

Rickett, Harold W., and the New York Botanical Garden. 1967. *Wild Flowers of the United States:* Volume 2, *The Southeastern States.* New York: New York Botanical Garden and McGraw-Hill.

Salley, A. S., Jr. 1919. "The Introduction of Rice into South Carolina." *Bulletin of the Historical Commission of South Carolina,* No. 6. Columbia, SC: State Company.

Sanders. Albert E., and William D. Anderson, Jr., 1999. *Natural History Investigations in South Carolina from Colonial Times to the Present.* Columbia: University of South Carolina Press.

Savage, Henry, Jr. 1982. *The Mysterious Carolina Bays.* Columbia: University of South Carolina Press.

Savage, Henry, Jr., and Elizabeth J. Savage. 1986. *André and François André Michaux*. Charlottesville: University Press of Virginia.

Slack, Adrian. 1979. *Carnivorous Plants*. Cambridge, MA: MIT Press.

Small, John K. 1917. "Cactus Hunting on the Coast of South Carolina." *Journal of the New York Botanical Garden* 18: 237–246.

Small, John K. 1927. "Among Floral Aborigines." *Journal of the New York Botanical Garden* 28(325): 1–20.

Small, John K. 1933. *Manual of the Southeastern Flora*. Chapel Hill: University of North Carolina Press.

Sorrow, James A., John F. Townsend, and Richard W. Christie. 1999. *South Carolina Plant and Fish Atlas: Helixatl*. Beta CD-ROM. Columbia: South Carolina Department of Natural Resources, and Clemson, SC: Clemson University.

Stern, William T. 1992. 4th ed. *Botanical Latin*. Brunel House, England: David & Charles Publishers.

Strausbaugh, P. D., and Earl L. Core. 1977. *Flora of West Virginia*. Grantsville, WV: Seneca Books, Inc.

Taylor, David. 1998. *South Carolina Naturalists*. Columbia: University of South Carolina Press.

Trimble, S. W. 1972. *Man-induced Erosion on the Southern Piedmont 1700–1970*. Ankeny, IA: Soil Conservation Society of America.

Tyler, V. E. 1994. *Herbs of Choice: Therapeutic Use of Phytomedicinals*. Binghamton, NY: The Haworth Press.

Weakley, Alan S. 2001. *Flora of the Carolinas and Virginia*. Chapel Hill, NC: Nature Conservancy, Southeast Regional Office.

Wharton, C. H. 1978. *The Natural Environments of Georgia*. Atlanta: Geologic and Water Resources Division and Resource Planning Section, Office of Planning and Resource, Georgia Department of Natural Resources.

Wooten, J. W. 1973. "Taxonomy of Seven Species of *Sagittaria* from Eastern North America." *Brittonia* 25: 64–74.

Index of Scientific Plant Names

Page references in bold indicate the main entry and plate.

Index of Common Plant Names

Page numbers in bold indicate the main entry and plate.

General Index